ATARI® Inc.

Business Is Fun

© 2012 Syzygy Company Press

Authors: Marty Goldberg & Curt Vendel
Editors: *Loni Reeder. Marty Goldberg*
Art Director: *Marty Goldberg & Curt Vendel*
Layout Design: *StockInDesign.com, Marty Goldberg*
Images: *Atari Museum & Donations from Ex-Atari Inc. Employees*

First Published in November, 2012.

REV X2A
Syzygy Company Press, 117 Duke Drive, Carmel, NY, 10512-1598
Printed in United States of America
ISBN 978-0-9855974-0-5
10 9 8 7 6 5 4 3 2 1

Marty: *To my parents, Izzy and Lois Goldberg. Who were always there with another quarter for me to play my favorite arcade game, inspiring my love of video games. And who raised me to have the passion in life to pursue what I love.*

Curt: *For my wife, my love of a lifetime; thank you for your patience, and understanding while my life, my office and half our home had become an Atari Archive. To my daughter, who will always be my baby-girl. You were my 2 year old Asteroids world champion and have always been my helper, as we spent hours in my office programming chips, building electronics and you helping me so many times to 'play test' all of those joysticks that we built together as the dragons chased us we chased the ghosts with Pac-Man, I couldn't have done it without you.*

Acknowledgements

While it would take an entire book just to acknowledge and thank everyone who helped make this book a reality, we do want to give a general thank you to all the ex-Atari employees for your time, and efforts to meet and be interviewed by us. We want to thank everyone for their donations of photos, memos, artwork, equipment and so much more. With the over 10,000 employees who at one time or another worked at Atari, there is just no way to possibly include everyone, but from the hundreds of persons we did speak with and through their stories and through internal documents, court records and permission from Atarians to use their materials we've attempted to give an overall recounting of the culture and feeling of what it was like to have worked at Atari. This is Atari from its good times and triumphs to the bad times and tragedies. This is a time capsule of people, personalities and a culture that will probably never be repeated again, and this book is a tribute to the Atarians, that race of creatures from a company and a culture now far far away...

It should also be noted to the readers of this book: This book was never intended to be a corporate or product book. It does not list every arcade, game console, computer device or software program ever created by Atari. Nor is it a brand book. *Atari Inc: Business Is Fun* is about Atari, the culture and the people who made it such a unique, inspiring and creative place to work. It was not a perfect place, or a storybook romance. Atari had its dark days and tough times, not everything that happened was all perfect and positive, this is the true recounting of Atari from its beginnings as a dream between two men in an office to a massive empire that would implode onto itself. Most Atarians were very eager to contribute to this book, while others were reluctant to want to be involved for fear of contributing to a book that would tell the real truth about them, not wanting to tarnish a carefully constructed history of myth and misconceptions. So if the readers see a noticeable absence of a Forward or other contributions to this book by certain Atarians who they had hoped to read more from, this explains why.

Prepare to begin your journey, now reach into your pocket, pull out a quarter and insert it into the coin slot. Now press Player 1 to start...

Contents

FOREWORD

By Ted Dabney

I grew up in an era before zip codes, area codes, television and vending machines, where my idea of entertainment was listening to "Sky King" on the radio (KGO in San Francisco).

My first engineering job was to design power supplies and video circuits using vacuum tubes, and from there I have watched the development of technology my whole life, and for years, I was part of it.

Nolan Bushnell was my office mate at Ampex and had seen Steve Russell's Spacewar! game at Stanford Artificial Intelligence Laboratory in Palo Alto, CA. He thought it was the best thing ever and had me go back with him so I could see it for myself. After we had seen it together, he told me what he wanted to do.

Digital Equipment Corporation (DEC) of Maynard, Massachusetts had introduced a minicomputer called the PDP-8 in 1965. Nolan wanted to use this computer to time-share several play-stations and have people pay to play this *Spacewar!* game. By this time, advancing technology was old-hat to me so I said, "Let's do it."

We did some preliminary work on this concept to see what we needed to do to make this happen. Finally we did some number crunching and realized that there was no way to make this idea financially viable. The proposed project was dead.

All this silliness began when I designed a rather simple circuit that could replace the computer. We then came up with a novel approach to create a game played on a tv set and were very successful at it.

Unbeknownst to me, there have been many stories and books about what we did and how we did it that were based on rumors and guess-work. In 1994, Leonard Herman wrote a book called "Phoenix, The Fall and Rise of Videogames." Several years later, while doing some follow-up research, he came across my name and contacted me. It really surprised me to find out how much interest there was in all this stuff. I gave him the whole story about how all of this came about, including how I did the design work in my daughter's bedroom. That's how I found out that Nolan Bushnell had been telling everybody that he designed this whole thing in his daughter's bedroom. This had absolutely no basis in fact.

This didn't really bother me much until one day somebody calling themselves Nolan Bushnell posted on a website called AtariAge that "Dabney didn't even have a daughter." Nolan Bushnell knew my daughter Terri very well, and this was so upsetting to me that I answered the post. Nolan called me on the phone and told me that he just forgot. This was pure crap. As I dug in further, it turned out that almost everything he has said publicly about me and the early days of Syzygy/Atari was pure crap.

Enter Martin Goldberg and Curt Vendel. These guys had become video game aficionados and wanted to know everything there was to know about the beginning days of Atari.

Other than my brief involvement with the start-up, I know almost nothing about the video game industry, but Curt and Marty know practically everything. Based on the research that I've been a part of and that I've seen them do, this book is the culmination of over two generations of video-game development.

It was over forty years ago that this adventure began, and until about three years ago, my contribution to it had been obscured. I never thought it was such a big deal actually. In fact, I have been very surprised and grateful to find out that a lot of folks find this whole thing to be a very big deal indeed.

I have always prided myself on the ability to solve almost any electronic problem. Nolan asked me to come up with a circuit to replace a computer. I didn't know anything about computers but I did know what the circuit needed to do, so I did it. The rest, as they say, is history. I must say that I very much appreciate the recognition that I have had for the last few years. Thank you.

Computer Space was the birth of this phenomenon and *PONG* was that which gave it life. A whole lot has happened since then and this book will bring the reader up to date on all the comings and goings of video games and the people involved in making it happen.

- Ted Dabney
  May 28th, 2012

FOREWORD

By Ralph Baer

I'm happy to be writing this forward for Marty and Curt, for a book that promises to recognize all the unsung heroes behind Atari. It's great that they're all finally getting the recognition they deserve, and I should know:

Over the past seven or eight years or so, I too have finally been recognized as the man who invented the home console video games way back when. When my first introduction occurred on a warm Summer evening at an outdoor event G4 was putting on, it was William Shatner, TV's Captain Kirk, who did the honors.

William started his speech with "There was a time when there were no computers or video games..."

Imagine that! While he was obviously referring to personal computers instead of computers in general, the rest of that statement was very insightful. The 1960s, when this book begins, was a time period when people like myself, Ted Dabney and Nolan Bushnell ventured into the unknown world of playing games through a TV set via its video signal - the very way this great entertainment medium got its name.

It was way back in 1966 when I came up with the concept of how to play games on ordinary TV sets. We were barely out of the vacuum tube era and into transistor circuits and the very beginning of integrated circuits. Microprocessors didn't exist, and what computers there were weighed a ton and cost hundreds of thousands, if not millions, of dollars.

Five years later Nolan Bushnell and associates started the arcade video game business with their Computer Space game, taking a pioneering leap into an industry then dominated by gears and blinking lights.

Soon, the semiconductor guys figured out how to put a bunch of transistors on one chip and "wire them up" to make a functioning state machine. A single chip with a few external parts connected to it and Bingo! There was a *PONG*-type home console game. Atari made one first and sold it through Sears... then dozens of off-shore outfits went into the business courtesy of General Instrument's AY-3-8500 chip. During 1976 and 1977, many millions of ping-pong games with those chips and similar ones wound up in home video games and were distributed worldwide.

Then microprocessors got cheap enough so you could actually think about building video games around them.

Imagine that!

My patents and those of the two associates of mine, Bill Harrison and Bill Rusch, were the pioneering patents of the new medium and the ones that were licensed to just about every big name in the business over the next several decades.

But it was Atari, after a headstart by Magnavox, that really breathed life into the home video game business with the Atari Video Computer System (2600) game system... and it was all onwards and upwards in that business after that.

I'll bet that you can't wait to turn the pages and find out how and who made it all happen.

Enjoy the book,

Ralph H. Baer

FOREWORD

By Marty Goldberg

First, let me give thanks to my wonderful co-author Curt Vendel and our editor, Loni Reeder. Both were just a joy to work with, just great people - and they'd have to be to put up with long hours with me. Yes, I'm the kind of person that when I have a vision I go for it full speed ahead with blinders on until it's reached. And in this case, the result of that vision is the book you hold in your hands. And it was quite worth it if I do say so myself!

This book, for me, really started many years ago - in the mind of a five year old. When I was growing up, Sundays were my dad's bowling league day, and in the mid-1970s he did most of his bowling at an alley in Milwaukee called Petroff's. A split level building, the bottom half had a restaurant that I swear to this day looked exactly liked the restaurant in the infamous Honey-Bunny scene in *Pulp Fiction*. The top half was the alley, complete with a small bar/restaurant off to the side. That bar/restaurant is where I'd be found while my dad was enjoying knocking down pins and laughs with his buddies. Parked in front of the TV watching reruns of *Lost In Space* on the bar's black and white TV, I'd eat the breakfast my dad had ordered up for me from the restaurant downstairs. I thought it was the neatest thing when the plate of scrambled eggs came from a square hole in the wall behind the bar, which turned out to be a dolly between the bar and the kitchen.

What filled me with wonderment and changed my life forever though, was the day I wandered out of that safety zone towards the row of arcade games along the walkway by the bowling lanes. The blinking lights and colorful play fields of the pinball machines caught my attention first, and I climbed onto a chair to watch as some guy stood there, hands draped over the sides of the machine as he leaned into it, rapidly clicking the buttons mounted on the side over and over, launching the steel ball which would fly up the angled length of the machine, hitting everything in site before descending back toward the flippers and the player. I went back to ask my dad for money to play, and after getting on top of the chair, quickly found out that as a five year old, I lacked the coordination to make the bumpers hit the damn ball. With my game over, so too was my interest in this game.

So I moved on to the other games in the row, which looked decidedly different: they all had TV screens. Names like *PONG, Tank, Gun Fight* and *Sprint 2*. It was the *Sprint 2* that caught my attention, because it had steering wheels just like in the car my dad drove to get us here. So I shuffled my little five year old feet over to my dad, nudging him for more money and pointing at the machine I wanted to play now. He took out a bigger coin this time, a quarter. Looking at it curiously, I skipped back over to the *Sprint 2* machine, plopped the quarter in its slot, and so began my introduction to video games. Trying to touch the pedal to make my car go while reaching up to the large steering wheel was a complete challenge for someone of my height, and I'm sure looked amusing to any of the other fathers in the bowling alley. And forget about that strange lever on the side which turned out to be for changing gears, I had no idea what it was for. But there I was, looking up at the screen above me and watching something I was actually controlling move around. Granted, my game probably looked more like a jerky destruction derby than a car race, but the experience was much more fun than pinball had been. I was hooked!

Over the years, my interest in these games only intensified as I became part of the generation of kids who grew up during the video game boon of the late 1970s and early 80s. I like to refer to us as the 'Star Wars Generation' because in my opinion, that was really the defining moment for everything high tech in the popular consciousness. After Star Wars debuted in 1977, 'high tech' and 'futuristic' were simply on everyone's minds. There was an explosion of high tech electronics-driven products from the living room to the kitchen. From microwaves to VCRs and even home game consoles.

I was there in 1978 when *Space Invaders* was first unleashed locally at a popular restaurant/pub my parents took me to called Ground Round. I was also there when the multi-colored joy and eerie sounds of *Galaxian* enthralled me the following year, to be replaced by games like *Missile Command, Pac-Man, Donkey Kong, Centipede*, and too many more to list here. I remember my friends and I coming to school and replacing swings and basketballs during recess with LED driven handheld games like Mattel *Electronic Football* or *Racing*. And even more importantly, I remember the joy of getting an Atari 2600 for Hanukkah '77, and upgrading to a ColecoVision for Hanukkah of '82, my parents feeding my addiction for high tech fun and innovative leisure from Day One.

Fast forward to the early 2000's and I found myself running GameSpy's site dedicated to the games of my youth - ClassicGaming.Com. I had also co-founded a show with Dan Loosen and Gary Heil, dedicated to these games and games from every generation's youth, including the current games, which we exhibit every year at the Midwest Gaming Classic. Looking at someone's five year old daughter experience playing a Vectrex game system for the first time in my museum area, I suddenly realized how things had come full circle. Here I was now an adult, introducing a new generation to the same fun I had some two decades before. In that *Cat's in the Cradle* moment I realized I wanted to find some way of thanking all the people who made this possible, Not just my parents, who I had thanked many times over the years, but the people behind all the games and experiences I held dear.

And so, I decided to write a book about the one company and people behind it that were responsible for 90% of those memories: Atari. Now unbeknowst to me, the only other guy with an arguably bigger passion (and certainly greater knowledge) to the subject than me was also working on his own Atari book: Curt Vendel. As we became acquainted and he eventually drew me into work with him on products for the current corporate incarnation wearing the Atari brand name, we quickly decided it'd be a good idea to work on the book together as well. After all, our driven need for digging to the bottom of things and getting as accurate info as possible was the same. And my writing background and Curt's massive Atari archive - he literally has most of what's left of the Atari described in this book - were a perfect fit. Of course it helped we have a similar sense of humor as well and get along great in person.

With Curt in New York, me in Wisconsin, and the Internet between us, we began combining our work to produce this book which has now come to fruition. If you're reading this book and are someone who worked at Atari, I truly hope we did you proud with our efforts. If you're someone who grew up with Atari and are reading this to learn more about the people responsible for your childhood, I hope you walk away with the same sense of wonderment from the behind the scenes stories that we did. And finally, if you're from a Nintendo/Sony/Microsoft generation that grew up long after Atari's heyday, then my only words to you are: Enjoy! I know we did.

Marty Goldberg
On his iPad (with an Atari 400 nearby)
in Bayside, Wisconsin
August 3rd, 2012

FOREWORD

By Curt Vendel

In today's world, we barely give a second thought to the luxury of technology that surrounds us – from smart phones (which we can't seem to put down for a second!), to flat screen TV's, to the latest, greatest and fastest computers, laptops, notebooks, tablets, electronic book readers... cars that can parallel park themselves, navigation systems which can pinpoint our exact location... and so much more.

'Slaves to Technology?' Perhaps – but those of us who embrace the constant evolution willingly jettison to the next greatest thing... AND with our wallets wide open!

Technology oozes from every corner of our lives, including our homes; even things as simplistic as a light switch or even a light bulb all seem to have a built-in microprocessor of some sort to intelligently control and/or communicate with their surroundings.

When you look at today's videogames, they are an abundance of sight, sound and stimulation with graphics so real, sounds so vivid and rich and storylines so complex, that you can almost get lost within them. We take for granted all of the technology we are exposed to and have at our fingertips for prices so low, that if something breaks, it is easier and less expensive to just throw it out and buy a new one than trying to have it repaired.

Now let's take a trip back in time... back to the 1960s and 1970s. The most technologically advanced items in a home in that era could probably be summed up by two items:

1. A rotary dial telephone hanging on the wall in the kitchen, and
2. A black & white (color if you were lucky!) television set.

Rotary dial phones were a prehistoric treat - having to spin the dial around one number at a time to dial your number, wait for the dial to return back to the start and then dial the next number, the subtle 'click-click-click' of the rotation of the dial had a very distinctive sound. We become impatient today standing in front of a microwave – imagine a child of today's technology dealing with a rotary phone! You could probably invest 30 to 45 seconds just dialing a number before your call would start. Sorry… redial buttons, 'no call waiting,' call forwarding and other 'fancy' features had not been invented… yet! The notion of an Answering Machine on your telephone line was still the 'chatter' of a futuristic world yet to be seen as well.

Now onto the even more sophisticated showpiece of technology within the 'modern home'– the Television Set. With its rabbit ear antennae, or… if you had the money to invest in a roof top antenna for better reception, you could be the lucky recipient of a whopping 12 or so channels in total! (Channels 2 through 13 on VHF) Some would come in fuzzy, or have some static or other interference and you were always at the mercy of the weather and broadcast conditions. 24 hour television programming was unheard of. At around 12 a.m. after Johnny Carson, you'd be greeted by a test pattern with an American Indian in the center of it, and the strains of "The Star Spangled Banner," which, upon its conclusion, the network would sign off from its programming for the day and give you white noise static to see and listen to (if you looked close enough at the screen, you'd swear you were watching ants tunneling underground!). No cable TV feeds quite yet except to deliver reception in areas too far from a transmitting tower. Cable TV back then was not the Cable TV we know today with hundreds of channels and content. Why HBO hadn't even been invented yet. No 'video on demand' or even a VCR to watch recorded programs - those were just being introduced into the market in the mid 1970s and that new technology cost a fortune!

No, for the masses in those years, TV was what was on, when it was on – and if you didn't like it, you got up and went and did something else (like maybe play outside with your friends – a lost concept with the kids of the 21st Century…). Oh, and let's not forget…. You got up off your butt to change the channel, raise and lower the volume and turn the darned thing on and off. YOU were the TV remote! (… though Zenith would introduce the first TV remote - it was a 'clicker' - you pressed the buttons on it and it would snap a plastic rod within it and make a particular click sound. One sound would make the channel go up, and another sound would make the channels go down). This was the 'high tech living room' of the 1960s and 1970s. You watched TV and you accepted whatever programming was given to you.

I was a big fan of Sci-Fi and Horror movies when I was a kid…. One show – called, The "Outer Limits" used to start off by saying, "We control the horizontal, the vertical…" and so forth. It was a play on the old fears of people that others could control them and their lives which added to the suspense of the show (always best viewed late at night with the lights off for a more dramatic effect). Well, the time would come in the 1970s that people would become empowered and could actually control their TV's at long last. To customize their TV's display to what THEY wanted. This would happen in 1972 with the Magnavox Odyssey game console; the very first home video game. Atari would join the home game market in 1975 with its *Home PONG…* VCR's were beginning to make their debut so people could record TV shows and watch them whenever they wanted… and Cable TV networks began to bring more channels and higher quality video into the home as well…

These were the beginnings of technology invading our lives, in small, entertaining and very welcomed ways, setting the stage for where we are today 40 years later. TV's as we knew them are actually a dying icon. No longer even a fixed piece of hardware in our living rooms, today's 'TV' requires redefining the very term. We now watch movies, shows, and home-made videos on everything from enormous 100" flat screen displays to our tablets, laptops and even cell phones. Rumors abound of possibly taking smart phone technology and its "APPS" and implementing that technology to stretch out to become a TV on the wall, but equipped to be less 'TV' and more 'Smart Screen' with TV just being one of its myriad of functions.

The concept of what TV's were has changed dramatically, just as vid-eogames themselves have changed dramatically over the last 40 or so years. What happened in the labs of Ampex and in Sanders that started as wistful dreams and wishful conceptualizations would become reality in bars, arcades and in living rooms, shaping, changing and defining the very way we live today.

Growing up, technology changed and defined me on a deep and personal level. I had fanciful dreams of wanting to command a Starship… to fight off evil with a saber of light, all the while dreaming of robots and computers at my command. When video arcades started to show up in local roller rinks, I had my first taste of the future - playing the arcade games that lived in these huge magical cabinets was exciting. It was real - not just something on TV but really there in real life, which I could access for the price of a quarter! Later as the games became available for TV's, I longed for an Atari VCS - it was all anyone ever talked about and I so wanted one more than anything else. But at Christmas (to my huge disappointment) I received a Radio Shack TV game system, and as any disappointed kid feeling screwed over by Santa, family and the 'Christmas Naughty or Nice Wish System,' I was pretty vocal in that disappointment. After receiving a rather harsh scolding from my mother for my selfish complaining about not getting what I wanted, and about being grateful to have gotten such a nice gift from my grandparents, I realized she was right and apologized.

… but my mother never forgot my disappointment, and worked extra long hours during the summer and fall of 1981. Little did I know she was making the extra money to surprise me that Christmas - under the tree was an Atari 2600 with Activision 'Skiing.' I still have that Atari 2600 and still play that skiing game to this very day.

The reason I wanted an Atari VCS more than anything else was because a year or so earlier while going to Intermediate school, I saw it - the game that would change my life. It brought me countless hours of dreams and excitement just thinking about the wonders that existed inside this magical box. I first saw it over at a friend's house one afternoon after school; the game was 'Atari Adventure.' The bat chased you, the dragons chased you, the game seemed to 'think' - it had intelligence and was doing more than just displaying a race track or a skiing course. The game would awake a passion and a devotion in me that to this day burns just as strong. I have always loved Atari, their products, the myth and lore… and all of the stories. I owe so much to Atari for shaping my life and even my career path. But over time, I realized that what was more important than the products was that in each and every one of them, there was a heart, a soul and a story from each and every person who helped bring to life the ideas which turned into those products which became, in more ways than one, 'game changers.'

So with that in mind, get ready to immerse yourself in a time long ago past – but which still burns so brightly in the hearts and minds and spirits of those who were so willing to give of their time to this book. THIS is the story of the people of Atari – the Atarians - their unsung contributions and the Atari products they brought to life. This is also the once-in-a-lifetime story of how a company so great could fall so far from grace in what seems like the blink of an eye.

I honestly don't believe there will ever come another time in history where a group of such diverse and talented people will unite and build a company and culture that will forever change the world as we know it.

Atari was that 'lightening in a bottle…'

Curt Vendel
New York

We would like to thank the following individuals for their generous financial support in helping this project and this book come to fruition. These individuals all "Helped make Atari History."

Thank you,

Curt & Marty

ABBUC
Pauline Acalin
Jason Boyens
Michael Current
Robert DeCrescenzo
Laurent Delsarte
Jon J. Echevarria
Jeffrey J. Ellen
David 'Ozyr' Flemming
Stephane Hilbold
Mark Kohler
Philip Louie
Chris Martin
Greg McLemore
Marc Oberhäuser
Sven Pink
Xavier Uriarte Ramalho
Loni Reeder
Owen Rubin
Kevin Rust
Filippo Santellocco
Sijmen Schouten
Jason Scott
Capt. Spot
Richard Tsukiji
Brian Wiklem
Jon Willig
Cuauhtemoc Yescas

About The Book

You may be pleasantly surprised to find that this book breaks with a number of standard book conventions in an effort to best tell the story of Atari in the manner we felt it needed to be told.

First of all, rather than looking back in the past, we wanted to give you the reader the sense of actually living history alongside the people who created it. As such, this book is written in present tense wherever applicable.

Second, it's written in an informal style. Video games are fun, and so are the people who created them. Stuffiness doesn't have a place here.

Third, each 'chapter' is actually several chapters grouped together. We felt it grouped topics together better. Quite frankly, at over 800 pages, a long rambling list of chapters wasn't needed.

Finally, not wanting to include a small section of images in the center of the book, we came up with a novel concept: at the end of each 'chapter' is a chapter review in images. A visual summation for the MTV generation if you will.

For More Information

Additional information regarding this book and forthcoming titles is available at ataribook.com.

Supplemental material is available at the Atari History Museum -

www.atarimuseum.com

For the latest in Atari related news and information, visit the Atari Gaming Headquarters-

www.atarihq.com

Lastly, to hang out with rabid fans of all things Atari, head on over to:

www.atariage.com/forums

Chapter 1

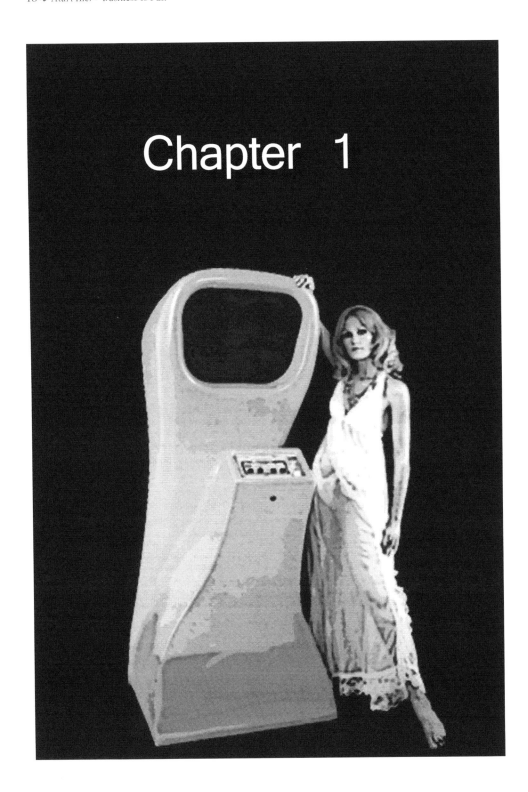

Lights, Camera, Ampex

The average dream job for a Californian in the late 60s probably wouldn't have been an engineering gig. Maybe something more along the lines of a job that allowed you to enjoy the sun and fresh air, take in a little surfing, or make the trek to Southern California to become the "next big Hollywood star." But then, this job was in Silicon Valley - the "Hollywood" of the electronics industry, where the groundwork for the 'next big thing' of consumer electronics, computers, and more for the next 40 years was beginning to grow past its roots and ready to bear its fruit.

Ampex was the company this particular dream job was at, and the location was their new Videofile division in Sunnyvale. Ampex, based north of Silicon Valley in Redwood City, had been a pioneer in the business of magnetic recording thanks to a jumpstart by an actual Hollywood star – Bing Crosby. Bing, co-star of the "Road to..." movies with Bob Hope and singer of such classics as *White Christmas,* preferred to pre-record his radio performances rather than do them live. He felt more freedom in being able to go back and edit out anything that didn't meet his standards, but more importantly it helped him avoid his legendary stage fright. Being fickle and eccentric about what you do is a trait common among Hollywood types (and their later Silicon Valley counterparts).

Initially though, Bing's employer, the American Broadcasting Company (ABC), had other ideas and wanted Bing to stick with the live format, forming a standstill in their relationship. Like a lone gunman in Clint Eastwood spaghetti western, enter Jack Mullen into the fray, with reel-to-reel recording technology based on captured German World War II electronics research. Jack's technology proved to be just what Bing was looking for, and ABC was won over as well, ending the 'High-Noon' like standoff.

In fact, Bing was actually so impressed with the technology that, like the venture capitalists that would become a fixture in the Silicon Valley landscape 30 some years later, he decided to help Jack's device make a foray into the commercial arena. Investing money into Ampex to produce the first commercial reel to reel tape recorder, he launched Ampex into the forefront of magnetic recording technology in the late 40's. Fast forward about 15 years later, and Ampex has now also become a leader in video recording technology – also developed by Jack Mullen. Videofile was their latest research foray, looking to adapt video recording into a searchable document database of sorts. Picture the primordial World Wide Web done by literally recording images of documents on video tape – fully indexed and searchable.

Of course with a new research division comes the need for new research jobs, the 'dream jobs' if you will. Ted Dabney (his full name being Samuel Frederick Dabney Jr.) was the person filling one such dream job. By now you may be asking yourself, "Why are we starting with Ampex?" and "Who is this Ted Dabney, I've never heard of him before?" Well, it's because the company that this book is about, and the technology that would go on to turn the traditional electromechanical (EM) arcade industry on its head, came from the technology developed at Ampex. And the person that would help pioneer the technology that lead to a consumer industry that today is worth more than $21 billion, is this person: Ted Dabney. The irony is that he didn't know it – and had no motivation to do it. If you were to talk to Ted, he'll tell you he'd have been just as happy to stay at Ampex Videofile in his dream job. Just as Steve Wozniak would have been happy to have stayed at Hewlett-Packard and never have pushed his Apple I computer out of the hobby stage. And imagine if the fruits of their labors that so many of us take for granted now, would never have been.

Ted had come to Ampex by way of Hewlett-Packard, among other businesses, following a now legendary Silicon Valley practice of hopping from tech business to tech business. Originally trained in the Navy's electronics and radio relay schools on Treasure Island and in San Diego respectively, he went to work in Bank of America's research lab after being discharged. There, he helped to develop IRMA, an electronic check scanner that introduced all those numbers on the bottom of your check and was a very big deal for the banking industry. Not exactly the sexy device one associates with coming out of today's Silicon Valley, but this was, after all, the primordial version of that tech wonderland.

Wanting to leave the banking industry, a co-worker who was also leaving suggested he apply at both Hewlett-Packard and Ampex, though he felt unqualified as an engineer for the latter position. He applied for both and it was Hewlett Packard that gave him the next rung in the ladder of his career – at least for a little while. Shortly after starting the Hewlett-Packard job as a test technician, Ampex wound up contacting him for a job opening in Redwood City. Ted jumped at the opportunity, and the future of the video game industry came one step closer to becoming a reality on the basis of an off-chance long shot of an application.

Assuming he'd get a few months of experience before they caught on to his lack of experience and fired him, it turned out to be quite the opposite. Six years later Ted found himself transferring to the Videofile division from the Military Products group, with his boss and new head of Videofile, Kurt Wallace. During his time in the Military Products Group, Ted's job had been to design video processing, control circuits and power supplies using vacuum tubes. As you may have probably just figured out, this was where the groundwork for his early video game design work was cultivated – learning to process and manipulate a video signal. At Videofile he moved to learning transistor based circuits on the job, and the skills he'd need to design the circuitry for the first arcade video game – Computer Space – were in place.

Fast forward several years later and Videofile had grown into a project with a projected $1.5 billion in earnings over the next several years. On this one particular sunny California day, Ted pulled into the corporate park where the Videofile building was located. Parking his 1956 Mercedes 180 sedan in the Videofile lot, he began walking up the steps to go to his office as he would any other day. Only this wasn't just any day - it was a day that would soon provide the final and more important catalyst to Ted's brew of technological skill.

As with any good tech story, the catalyst is usually a visionary; a Steve Jobs to the Steve Wozniak if you will. In this case, it arrived in the form of a kid who came up as a 'carnie weight guesser' turned 'amusement park arcade tech' turned 'University of Utah Electrical Engineering graduate,' Nolan Bushnell. After moving to California and failing to get a job at Disneyland as an engineer, 26 year old Bushnell wound up at Ampex and was now moving in to share Ted's office.

The office itself was that era's version of the cubicle: a windowless office in the south east corner with two desks and two workbenches. Isolated and practical, it was all about the work being done. The idea of rock star perks such as gourmet meals and back massages had yet to be considered, and engineers like Ted and Nolan were treated like your average employee. They'd be making the first efforts to change that image problem in several years, but at the moment they were spending time getting to know each other, given they were going to be sharing a compact work area and spending every waking work hour together there.

Although there was a good age difference between the two, they immediately found out they had something in common: beautiful women. Not the type Atari would become known for in the 70s of course. No, at this point, both were family men. Ted and his wife Joan had a 4-year old daughter named Terri, and Nolan and his wife Paula had two daughters – 3-year old Alyssa and 2-year old Britta.

Both men of course also had a love for technology and engineering, with Nolan admiring Ted's solid skills and Ted admiring Nolan's ability to quickly learn... and Nolan did have a lot to learn; even spending time on the job studying books to learn anything he could to increase his own skills and understanding. Their boss at Ampex, Ed De Benedetti, put it in succinct terms: "Ted was conservative in the extreme, incorporating his own ideas but he was a plodder. Nolan was also brilliant but inexperienced enough that he had no idea of what one could not do." Many have said over the years now that the latter probably served Nolan well in his career – he was never known to be one to build a fence around an idea or concept, always exploring boundaries and pushing those, even if he didn't have the skill set to bring them to fruition.

Nolan had graduated from the University of Utah the previous year in 1968 and claimed he was now taking graduate courses at Stanford, though according to Ted, he doesn't see how it was possible. Because of the time involved with the studying Nolan did simply to keep afloat at Ampex, he most likely was just visiting his friend who worked in the SAIL computer lab. Still considered wet behind the years by experience standards, that didn't stop Nolan from feeling like he was destined for more, though at this point, that 'more' consisted of visions of talking bears and pizza. "Nolan's grand idea at that point was a pizza parlor with things like 'singing barrels' and 'talking bears'," explains Ted.

That need to do something bigger and better, even if it included talking bears, probably came from his childhood. Or rather the childhood that was thrust into adulthood when he was 15 and forced to take over the family business. Raised as a Mormon in Utah, Nolan's father had built up a concrete business before suddenly passing on. Nolan, taking over as the man of the house and taking care of his mother and sisters, also stepped in and kept the company going until all contracts were finished and then got a job at one of the few places exciting enough to hold the interest of a teenager in Utah: Lagoon Amusement Park. Lagoon helped Nolan continue to support the family while working his way through college, but it was the 'people education' via this job that helped form his future the most. Carneys are notorious for their barking skills and being able to size people up, making them believe they're having fun parting with their money and getting almost nothing but a cheap stuffed animal in return - skills that would serve Nolan well later in life when he struck out with Ted on their new business ventures. For now, while stuck in the windowless workspace with Ted, those dreams were of stuffed talking bears and cheap pizza.

Talking Ted into possibly joining him in this venture, the two began scoping out local pizza restaurants in the evenings and on weekends. They needed to first understand how things ran before they could even consider adding the singing animatronic animals; an idea borrowed from their popular use at Disneyland.

As the two became friends and budding business partners, they also began developing another shared passion: the Chinese board game of GO. Nolan had learned to play not long before joining Ampex and after teaching Ted what he knew, the two delved even deeper into the psychology of this complex game. GO is a highly competitive game that some would say has an order of magnitude of difficulty over Chess. It served as a perfect bonding experience between the two. Initially playing on a cheap fold-up board Nolan had since college, the meeting of the minds soon took place on a hand carved GO board done by Ted. Made from window cutouts, the board was set up between them on two trashcans when supervisors weren't looking... and when they were looking, the board was inconspicuously hung on the wall displaying a hand carved Videofile logo emblazoned on the back of the board. Today, office workers would be doing the same James Bondesque clandestine activity via the click of a mouse to quickly hide their midday foray into porn or Facebook. But this was 1969 and even the Internet's predecessor, the Arpanet, was just coming on line that year. It would be another few years before ASCII generated breasts (usually Playboy centerfolds scanned into a computer and rendered via text, made to look loosely like the original image) made their appearance on the network. Besides, these were family men and would never think of such diversions. At least not yet.

It was during one of Nolan's visits to Stanford that his 'Eureka' moment struck. Dragging Ted to see it, he posed a question: "Could we do something like this as a coin-operated game?"

The 'this' was a computer game running on the Stanford Artificial Intelligence Laboratory's (SAIL) PDP-6 mini-computer; the now legendary game by the name of *Spacewar!* A game of dueling space ships played on expensive equipment worth hundreds of thousands of dollars, proving that even the most expensive equipment intended to augment human brain power can be used just as equally well to screw around! The game had been created by hackers at M.I.T. in 1962 at a time when hackers meant people who live, sleep, and breathe computers and technology rather than the black hat connotation it would take on in the 80s. When we talk about 'created' though, it's being used in its original sense of the word because true software hackers never actually finish a project. It's not because they're lazy - though their bathing habits at the time lead people to question that on a daily basis. Rather, like a work of art, software is continuously evolved. And by 1969, *Spacewar!* had taken on a life of its own, as hacker upon hacker had added to its source code. New features, evolving game play and more had turned it into a game with as many different variations as there were labs with equipment to run it. By 1969, if you ran or had access to an expensive mainframe with an equally expensive vector monitor display, you had seen or played *Spacewar!* DEC had made sure of that by shipping the game as its test program for their mainframes. When you bought one of DEC's expensive PDP-1 mini-computers, *Spacewar!* was left running when the computer was shut off and packaged up. If you saw the glowing lines of the dueling ships when powering it up for the first time, then your computer came through the shipping A-ok. Stuart Brand would immortalize the game in the pages of the December 7, 1972 issue of Rolling Stone. Standing in the very same SAIL lab, the masses of pop-culture connoisseurs would be exposed to geek-tainment for the first time. But in the Fall of 1969 it was Nolan Bushnell and Ted Dabney standing there looking to thrust computer games into the world.

Years later the two would tell very different stories about that eureka moment. Nolan claims he first saw *Spacewar!* in the mid 1960s at the University of Utah, at a time when he himself was jotting down ideas for computerized games and working in the University's graphics lab. 'Graphics' being used in the loosest sense, as it was the mid 60s after all. That he himself asked his friend Jim Stein at the SAIL laboratory to install *Spacewar!* there so that he could play it again. Ted claims there was zero talk about computerized games between him and Nolan until the time Nolan dragged him to the Stanford lab, just prior talks about pizza and singing bears.

One has to wonder if it's the 'Carney' aspect of Nolan's background surfacing with his version, linked in an attempt to one-up video game inventor Ralph Baer in their long-running feud. Regardless, on that day it was two men standing there looking to parlay one's vision and the other's engineering skill into a new form of arcade game.

While at Lagoon Amusement Park, Nolan had also worked on servicing electromechanical arcade games; the popular format of coin-operated entertainment before video games took over that industry. Consisting of everything from pinball to intricate simulations of western shootouts, space landings, and horse races, their mechanical nature made them prone to breakdowns. So he had some minor previous experience in 'high-tech' amusement.

Now here was Nolan, living up to De Benedetti's "inexperienced enough that he didn't know what one could not do," premise by asking Ted if they could put a coin slot on a $200,000 computer. And put it in arcades. And make a profitable business out of it. And Ted bought it.

If you're doing a double take on that last part, it's because it speaks volumes on Nolan's salesmanship skills. To talk a conservative workhorse engineer into somehow turning expensive computer equipment into a full time game machine and to produce them for sale in an industry neither had any real experience in should have you impressed. In the future, It was the kind of reality distortion field that an Atari employee named Steve Jobs would become famous for taking to the extreme.

Of course in some ways, as it does with most people with a strong vision but not the experience, the reality distortion field seems to influence them just as much as others. Their sense of reality gets warped enough that they often ignore hard facts. Case in point: both Bushnell and Dabney were engineers and not programmers. Granted, Nolan had done some minor programming work at Utah. However, that's a far cry from managing a mini-computer, setting up the *Spacewar!* software on it and modifying the game to interact with a coin slot. Then there was the other problem with said mini-computer. Beyond the $200,000 price tag, the mini part was anything but mini. Remember, this was before the personal computer era of desktop sized computers, so mini was relative to the times - and at that time, 'mini' simply meant it took up one side of a room instead of a complete room.

Blind vision can be a funny thing that way. Driving you to succeed one minute but also providing road blocks the next. Luckily in this case, blind vision turned into a good kind of double-vision for Nolan via the addition of a partner, Ted Dabney. Someone to ground the vision, and set it back a bit into reality. With that balance, the two began looking at the vision at least a little more objectively. First and foremost they both knew; if they forged ahead down this mini-computer route, they were going to need a another partner - someone who knew how to program.

In a move that would be repeated time and again during these formative years, Nolan and Ted turned in-house to a programmer they knew at Ampex - Larry Bryan.

It can't be stressed enough, the cosmic kismet that resulted in Nolan and Ted finding each other at Ampex Videofile. It was the catalyst environment which provided the platform for them to make the leap forward they were about to. Not only was this a place that centered around video technology... a breeding ground for the needed know-how, but it was also a ready-made talent pool of individuals they could tap.

Larry was to provide the actual coding know-how to get a game like *Spacewar!* up and running in a timesharing mainframe environment. In the days before personal computers, this equipment costing hundreds of thousands of dollars was basically limited to one program for one person at a single time. People had to sign up and wait for their allotted time on the computer. That is, unless they weren't lucky enough to have direct access to the computer itself. In the 50s and 60s, most were subject to submitting stacks of cards with little punched holes that in total represented the program they wanted to run. Only they didn't actually see their program run - that was the privilege of the guys in lab coats (often sarcastically referred to as 'the priesthood' by the lowly users). Instead they were given printouts of the results of their program as a consolation. Some colleges and universities were lucky enough to give students access to these computers in off periods of use - which was exactly when *Spacewar!* was ly written. What became known as the traditional 'hacker' hours of midnight to seven. So the idea of giving someone direct access to the system input and display let alone allowing them to monopolize the equipment to play a game on was very rare indeed.

As what usually happens though, some smart people came up with a solution. If the computer is fast enough, it can handle multiple people and their programs at once by a method called 'time-sharing.' Essentially it's like cutting up a piece of pie to give to a room full of hungry people, with the pie representing the computer's total resources - only they have no idea they're only getting a slice. They all share that pie, with the computer rapidly doling out a bit of one individual's piece before moving to the next one and so on; it creates an illusion of that computer being completely for each person even though their time is being shared.

Nolan and Ted wanted to use a mini-computer like one of DEC's PDP series or Data General's Nova, combined with a time-sharing system to allow them to run something like *Spacewar!* on multiple game stations. With Larry handling the programming, Ted's job would be to make these station's displays into video driven terminals instead of the expensive XY or 'vector' monitors currently used to display *Spacewar!* on the computers. Oh, and to also fit a coin-slot mechanism on each one that would somehow register back to the main computer. All together, repurposing costly equipment that was never used or intended to be used this way: a piece of amusement equipment costing thousands upon thousands of dollars!

The first meeting was held at Larry's house in October of 1969, where they set about trying to map out a plan for the project. First and foremost was a $350 startup contribution by each that would be placed into a checking account Ted was going to open up. Subsequent meetings were then held at either Nolan's or Ted's house, and it was during these meetings that they tried to hash out a name for their new venture. Originally Nolan and Ted had been considering B&D or D&B for Bushnell and Dabney, depending on who felt their name should come first. The problem they found with these though, was that both sounded too similar to the initials for Black & Decker or Dunn & Bradstreet. Larry then suggested the name Syzygy; a name used in astronomy to describe three celestial bodies aligned in a single straight line. Larry's inspiration was because of some sort of feeling of the cosmic significance of the new venture. It wasn't even because there were now three people in the group. Rather he picked it simply because he thought it was a 'neat' word that looked good on paper. With that, Syzygy was born.

As with any celestial body however, things are constantly in motion. Alignment is never permanent, and this one smashed apart against the first large wall it hit while chasing Nolan's grand idea. The time-sharing available at the time was great for driving multiple text driven displays. However, it simply wouldn't be fast enough to run several instances of a graphics intensive program like *Spacewar!* Certainly not on any equipment that they could afford, let alone the volume of these computers they'd need to turn this into a business that sells more than one setup.

As the popular tagline from the movie *Alien* goes, "In Space No One Can Hear You Scream." With Larry and the mini-computer attempt there wasn't even a whimper, because with the mini-computer idea now dead there was simply no need for a programmer. Larry's only contribution and lasting role in this whole odyssey would be the name Nolan and Ted would carry on with; Larry never even contributed the $350.

Ted and Nolan continued on with the daily grind of their work at Videofile, and Ted thought the *Spacewar!* idea was pretty much dead in the water. That is, until one day when Ted was busy working and Nolan strolled across their workroom to ask him a question on video technology: "Why did the vertical hold button on a television move the screen up and down?" In today's age of digital televisions, such a question is more likely to get a Scooby Doo "Huh?" look complete with tilted head and goofy eyeballs rather than the intelligent answer Ted responded with. The vertical positioning of the picture on your screen is simply not a factor anymore with the move from analog to digital tuned TV sets, and in fact most of the dials and knobs people over the age of 40 remember using to adjust their television picture are simply not there anymore.

"It works by controlling the difference between the sync and picture timing," Ted stated. In layman's terms, that older television most of us grew up with consisted of a large picture tube or Cathode-Ray Tube (CRT). Inside of it is an electron gun that shoots a beam of light at the screen, making it magically light up at a single spot. A single spot wouldn't be much fun to watch of course, and in fact many of these 'spots' or 'pixels' are drawn across the screen row after row to make up a single picture - or in TV lingo, a 'frame.' With television, frame after frame is transmitted encoded via what's called a video signal, and drawn one after another on the screen creating the illusion of motion. The end result being that episode of the *I Love Lucy* you like to catch... or maybe catching up on the latest episode of *Jersey Shore* if that's more your taste. What Ted explained is that the little dial that controls the vertical hold adjusts where the beam starts to draw the picture at the 'top' of the screen, which in turn affects where its 'bottom' is. It controls the vertical centering of the picture, and is usually accompanied by a horizontal counterpart.

Ted's abbreviated engineering lingo response allowed Nolan to hit on another 'Aha!' moment. Essentially could they control the vertical and horizontal hold circuits to manually draw and 'move' something on the screen. Ted said "Yes they probably could," and started to work on the simple proof of concept that would drastically change both of their lives.

Needing to work during his off hours, Ted started working on it at his house. His daughter Terri's bedroom became the first casualty as it was turned into a study for Ted to work in while he and his wife gave up the master bedroom for Terri. The utter dedication to the shared vision - that a spot on a screen was worth disrupting family life, is staggering. Staggering, but necessary - as future generations of entrepreneurs would demonstrate by turning their office into their home instead of the other way around.

Modifying a television set to bypass the channel tuner and turn it into what's called a 'monitor,' Ted built a nest of circuitry on a breadboard; essentially a board with lots of holes in it to plug electronic components in and wire them together. It allows electrical engineers to build and test designs during a process where frequent adjustments and changes to the design are needed. What's commonly called breadboarding or protoyping.

Ted's circuit, when it was completed, had reversed the magic of television to create a different kind of magic. He had gotten it to draw that single un-fun spot, but now one that they could manually control where it was drawn. Called 'spot motion circuitry,' it was the important breakthrough they needed and the most crucial building block. If they can 'move' that single boring spot on the screen, then they have the bare minimum of what's needed to create an actual game on a television. That single spot was soon to become a whole lot of fun!

Bringing the circuitry to Nolan, he became ecstatic. His vision was now coming to fruition, thanks to Ted. The secrets of interactive television were now in their grasp, and Nolan was becoming flush with expectations on the next stages they needed: a ship and an investor.

As with all Silicon Valley startups, they start with dreams. But those dreams usually have to be paired with economic reality. Money is needed to fund the transition from thoughts and prototypes to full blown product. So while Ted and Nolan continued on with the daily grind at Ampex, Nolan began looking for a source of funding.

The search began in their backyard once again, as Nolan started presenting the concept based on Ted's circuit to his boss Ed De Benedetti. Ed and Ampex weren't interested, so Ted decided they should talk to an ex-Ampex employee by the name of Irving Roth who was a manager when Ted had worked at Ampex's Military Products division. Irv had taught Ted "what engineering was all about," and would be a perfect mentor for a new startup. Ted and Nolan visited him at his lab where he was working on video disc technology and asked him if he would help them set up an engineering company for creating video games. Unfortunately, Irv himself had just come off a startup that didn't work out, so he wasn't keen on getting involved in a new one. Years later, once Nolan and Ted's startup had been renamed Atari and was well on the road to success, Ted ran into Irv and an acquaintance outside a restaurant. Irv started giving Ted a hard time about not giving him a chance to be a part of Atari, to which Ted reminded him they came to him first and he declined. The acquaintance burst into laughter over his friend's decision, which diffused the situation. But it's an all too common tale of lost opportunities and fortunes passed under the guise of 'personal insight' and wisdom.

With internal resources becoming exhausted, it became clear that they were going to need to look outside of their immediate circle for funding. But with just a spot on a screen and a dream, who would be interested from the local electronics firms? They certainly couldn't approach any of the established coin-operated arcade companies; the old guards of the business like Bally, Gottlieb, Williams, or Chicago Coin. That industry was completely based out of Chicago. Or was it?

Something
Nutty Going On

A chance meeting in early 1970 would set Nolan and Ted back on course. It was on a visit to his dentist that February, during the usual dentist/ patient banter, that Nolan set things into motion. "Ima-whorking-on-a-wideo-spash-awcade-gayme" is how it most likely came out of his utensil filed mouth. Regardless, by the end of the visit the message came through loud and clear to his dentist, who suggested he contact another patient: Dave Ralstin, the sales manager for a young California based coin-operated company called Nutting Associates.

Nutting Associates' nearby location in Mountain View was borne more out of coincidence than any grand plan to break away from the Chicago stranglehold on the coin industry. It was founded by Bill Nutting, then a resident of Menlo Park. The son of the executive vice president of Marshall Fields, he was one of four brothers that would leave their River Forest, Illinois home to blaze their own paths in life.

Bill wound up in California, working at the legendary White House Department Store in San Francisco during the mid 60s, apparently following in his father's footsteps by starting at the bottom in the gloves department. Unlike his father however, Bill had a bit of an entrepreneurial spirit and had also invested in a teaching machine company that was developing programs for the Navy. To test students they would use a film strip projected onto a screen to ask multiple choice questions, which the students would then answer by pushing A, B, C, D, or E buttons. An entertaining way of presenting a multiple choice test compared to the usual exam format that even today is the bane of many student's scholastic existence. During one of their meetings, one of the other investors jokingly suggested, "Why not put a coin slot on the quiz machine and make it an entertainment device?"

Realizing the idea might have legs, Bill began to interview local distributors of coin operated devices to see if there was a market. Their response was positive enough that Bill decided to form a startup based around the quiz entertainment machine concept. "I want you to help repackage my group's multiple choice teaching machine into a coin operated quiz game" came the call to his brother David in Milwaukee, Wisconsin, setting up the same successful startup formula mirrored later by Bushnell/Dabney and Jobs/Wozniak; The visionary and the doer.

Unlike brother Bill, David's path had taken him towards becoming an engineer after getting the inventor bug early on. "I wanted to be an inventor, creating and designing new products for the consumers of the world" he would later state in his intro to quantum physics book *Language of Nature*. The irony is, Dave fit the profile for the typical engineer at a startup in Silicon Valley instead of Milwaukee where he currently found himself. However, at the time his brother called him, David had a successful career as head designer at Brooks Stevens Associates where he had created the world's first SUV in 1961 - the Jeep Grand Wagoneer.

A national corporation based in California and Wisconsin was Bill's plan, and the details that they hashed out when Bill flew to Milwaukee were based around that idea. David would design and engineer the new machine as well as set up manufacturing, and Bill would handle all marketing and sales. As David started on the new machine with his electrical engineer friend Harold, Bill went on to Chicago, Detroit, and New York to learn more about the coin-op industry and distributors.

The arrangement worked fine as the prototype was developed and tested successfully, that is until another relationship - one that usually takes a toll in any startup - took precedence. Bill's wife Claire decided she didn't like the arrangement and played the divorce card, threatening to become another notch in a staggering statistic. Silicon Valley has the highest divorce rate in California, and California itself is 20% above the rest of the nation. Bill didn't want to become part of the statistic so he called David and said he was going to manufacture the game in California and that David should shut down his operation. Describing Claire as a control person who was threatened by her husband's relationship with his brother, David decided she could control his brother but not him. He had already sunk way too much money into the operation to stop.

So the brothers went their own ways and started their own companies to market the same game. Bill, under Nutting Associates, would be marketing it as *Computer Quiz* and Dave, under Nutting Industries, would be marketing it as *I.Q. Computer*. Both became an instant success, though for a reason neither of them initially knew about.

The coin-operated industry was in the midst of a long battle against the stigmatism of gambling and organized crime; something it would not shed until the 70s when video games took over the industry. New York State even had a ban on pinball games that lasted for over 30 years, treating them no different than slot machines or other gambling devices.

By the late 1960s, the industry had organized under the Music Operators of America (MOA). The MOA's existence owes itself to the age old battle against the music industry that ex-Atarian Steve Jobs more recently fought in the format of Digital Rights Management and 'renting' of digital music. That being the music industry has consistently tried to squeeze every nickel and dime out of people's enjoyment of music that they could. The MOA was started in 1948 by a group of influential Jukebox distributors and operators to fight against the repeal of the jukebox royalty exemption - the fact that jukebox owners shouldn't have to pay royalties on songs played on a jukebox. It eventually grew to become a powerful organization representing the entire spectrum of coin-operated devices, including electromechanical, pinball, pool tables, jukeboxes, and vending machines.

At the time of the release of *Computer Quiz* and *I.Q. Computer*, the MOA had been working hard to fight the typecasting of coin-operated machines, specifically pinball. A stigma that had severely limited the amount of locations operators could place machines. For instance in Los Angeles, California, about six hours south of where Bill was living, pinball machines were banned until the mid 1970s. The Nutting brothers' games proved to be the right tool at the right time as operators used the machines to work their way into new locations. *Computer Quiz* could go everywhere because of its perceived value as an edutainment game. Operators would get into a location with the game, establish a relationship, and then slowly bring in pinballs, pool tables and vending.

In a lesson learned by both Nuttings and later leveraged by Nolan with his creation of the fake competitor Kee Games, the fact that there were two manufacturers of 'Quiz' games also awoke the market place and opened up more operators and locations. In the amusement industry at that time, a great manufacturing run for a machine like a pinball was somewhere around 1,000 to 1,500. *Computer Quiz* had a run of 4,200 units and *I.Q. Computer* had a run of 3,600.

As is the way of the Valley, big hits mean fast expansion. Bill moved his operation to a 4,500 sq. ft. building at 500 Logue Avenue in Mountain View in early December of 1968, housing over 50 employees. Plans were made to begin pushing *Computer Quiz* overseas and into the home, while he had some of his new engineers work on a followup. 1969 brought more changes in the form of David Ralstin replacing Lance Hailstone as Bill's Sales and Marketing Manager.

When Ralstin got the call from Nolan, Nutting Associates already had several more games on the market and ones that were to be introduced at the MOA show in Chicago that October. These included *Astro Computer* - a horoscope machine, a two player *Computer Quiz*, *Sports World*, and a novel game of guess the blinking lights called *ESP*. However, with the amusement industry going through a game renaissance of sorts led by SEGA and Bally under their newly acquired subsidiary Midway Mfg., Nutting just didn't have that 'oomph' in the market place anymore. They were still looking for their 'next big thing;' something to ignite the same spike in sales and profits that *Computer Quiz* had. That's why when Nolan called Dave Ralstin out of the blue, both he and Bill were interested in this new game technology Nolan claimed to be able to build.

The leaves were brown and the sky was gray and rainy, and though Nolan wasn't walking into a church that Winter's day in February, he was walking into the next best thing; the place he and Ted would come to cut their coin-op industry teeth over the next two years. Nolan was at Nutting to sell them on the idea of a game played on a television screen that you could plug quarters into. A decade later, Bill Gates would be standing in front of IBM doing the same thing Nolan was doing now: selling something he had no experience in; an operating system to run their new computer. Something which he didn't actually have - though in Nolan's case he at least had a little something. Technically a very little something. All Nolan and Ted had at the moment was the ability to move spots on the screen, but here was Nolan presenting himself as a far more experienced engineer than he was while selling them on his vision of a full game of fighting space ships. Simply called 'the rocket ship game,' he also made it clear that he and Ted had no intention of giving up own-ership of the special technology. They wanted to license it to Nutting.

Nolan came into the office at Videofile he shared with Ted the next day and discussed the happenings of his meeting with Bill. Ted, being more experienced, had prepped Nolan on the sorts of questions he thought would be thrown out. Simply put, Nolan thought it "went well." No agreement, no money, but he had his foot in the door.

It just so happened that Bill had the habit of creating a revolving door. Em-ployees regularly got into arguments on the way he ran the business and would quit. The last exodus had left him lacking a 'chief engineer' or any real sort of technical troubleshooter for their games. In fact, his industrial engineer, Richard Ball, had been summarily fired when he criticized Bill about spending too much money from the company on his personal passion: airplanes.

Bill did a callback to Nolan, offering for him to come on as Chief of Engi-neerg at Nutting while working on the game. Over several additional meetings, No-lan countered that he'd be happy to come on, but didn't want to give them ownership of the technology. He offered to work on it during off hours so it wouldn't be done on their dime, only having them pay for things when it was ready to go into production. When it was time for production and manufacturing, Nutting would pay for that and secure that right by paying Nolan and Ted, as Syzygy, a 5% royalty on all sales. This smart move cut Nutting's claim on any of the technology, since none of it was done on the job except for the licensed manufacturing part. The deal was perfect for Bill, because he'd get the possibility of a new game technology at no cost. If it didn't work out, he still came out of it with a new engineer.

It was settled, and Nolan gave two weeks notice to his boss Ed De Benedetti. Charlie Steinberg, the head of the whole Videofile division, had a talk with Nolan as sort of a pre-exit talk. "Son, you're making a big mistake here quitting Ampex to do this thing" he said. "You know, you really ought to reconsider. You're giving up a career here." But Nolan had conviction that it'd be worth it, and while finishing out his time he and Ted planned out how they'd proceed.

Ted didn't want to leave his job. He had worked too long and hard to get where he was and took comfort in the regular paycheck and security for his family. No small feat considering he didn't have a degree - just his experience from the Navy's electronics school. Putting it in jeopardy on the off chance they would be able to build a full game just wasn't in the cards, especially with a family to support. Ironically, he was willing instead to burn the candle at both ends again and work evenings with Nolan on the complicated circuitry that would make up the full game.

So in March of 1970, Nolan became the backbone of Nutting while leading himself and Ted in a project that would change their lives. By that time, the project had taken so long to get this far that Ted had expanded the workroom at his house by building an addition. It would serve them well as Nolan came over in the evenings to work out circuits with Ted. Since they now had someone to license their technology to, the dynamic duo decided to change the name of their partnership to Syzygy Engineering. The plan was to continue to make new games (even though they hadn't actually done one yet) and to keep licensing them. But they had already been marketed and sold; now was the time to actually do the important part - build the games.

Ships were the first order of business, but imagine being in their position for a second. You have a way to control a dot on the screen. How do you draw a ship? Remember, this is at the very beginning: no 2-D graphic sprites, no 3-D polygonal immersive worlds or Hollywood style graphics and no overclocked graphics processor. There wasn't even a microprocessor, that was in the final stages of invention over in Santa Clara at Intel. Everything had to be done in hardware - no programming. Now to the reader, that's an extremely important distinction to make - video games needed to be engineered at this point in time. Built from circuits and components rather than coded. What Nolan and Ted were doing was engineering a game, and that's exactly why for most of the early years of the video arcade and home industries, game 'designers' were engineers rather than coders.

In a move that would hearken to the Pointillism days of art, they decided the best way to make the ships was with what they had: dots. At a distance, each object would look like a ship or saucer. But up close the illusion would be shattered. No different than Cameron Frye's spaced out deconstruction of Pointillism artist Georges Seurat's painting "Sunday Afternoon on the Island of Le Grande Jatte" in *Ferris Bueller's Day Off*.

Ted modified the spot motion circuit to allow continual motion on the screen, and then began the process of creating the shapes of the ships. He used diodes, finding a friend that had a couple of boxes of them. An electronic component that works sort of like a valve to control the flow of energy, each diode would represent a dot in the ship. By forming a matrix of these diodes, he was then able to rotate the pre-planned network of dots on the screen, allowing the ship to appear to rotate. Nolan was then able to take these circuits and begin refining them for the actual game, including fixing a bug in the rotation.

The rotation matrix, for example, was very complicated and still buggy. Nolan was able to refine and fix the bug by coming up with a unique mirroring approach. Nolan knew they needed a good 16 different pre-rendered rotations to make it look as if the rocket was rotating smoothly. Now for those of you that skipped or fell asleep during basic coordinate mathematics and plotting in high school, it's really simple. If you take that full set of images that make a rocket, they form a complete circle. If you take that circle and divide it into four even sections, you'll basically see each section can mirror another section. So a rocket ship pointing straight up mirrors a rocket ship pointing straight down, and a rocket ship pointed right mirrors a rocket ship pointed left. Likewise for all the ones in between. What this boiled down to is the complicated rotation matrix could be cut down to produce just four rocket images that would then be flipped to various orientations to produce all the other angles.

The process would continue like this for some time, with Ted designing circuits and helping Nolan with any circuit design work he was stuck on, then Nolan going and building each circuit towards the final game. Ted's daughter Terri warmly remembers this time period just like she was still that little girl peering into her dad's work area, recalling the oscilloscope that had "waves going up and down like an EKG machine" and Ted and Nolan using "chips that looked like bugs and were flat with legs." When they weren't working at Ted's place under Terri's inquisitive eye, they were working at Nutting through the evening.

At this point, Nolan and Ted were about as close as the two would ever be, spending as much time together socially as they did working. As Ted built the expansion to the house, including a deck, Nolan was there to help. When one of Terri's friends fell from their tree and hurt her head, Nolan was there to put pressure on the wound. When they were there working together through dinner and beyond, Ted's wife would make sure Nolan and Ted ate. When they weren't working on their rocket ship game together, they still found time to play GO on a second board Ted made for them to use, substituting white and black stones for game pieces.

Unbeknownst to Ted however, Nolan had also brought an 'unofficial third party' into their project that he was offloading some of his own work to. Ampex valued cheap college labor as much as the next company, and they routinely brought in engineering interns from Stanford and other local universities on a six month rotation. Ampex, as much as any other company, gets cheap labor and the interns get 'valuable work experience.' Two such interns did a rotation in Nolan and Ted's Videofile division: Al Alcorn and Steve Bristow. Besides working on the normal small intern jobs for Ed De Benedetti, Nolan also enlisted Steve to wire up portions of the circuits that Ted designed, including the special diode matrix.

About three months into their routine, Ted decided to put both feet in the pond of their partnership. Things were moving along now, and he was blown away by the progress that Nolan had made constructing the game. Everything was promising enough that he decided to take a leap of faith and leave his dream job at Ampex Videofile for their entrepreneurial future at Nutting. Joining Nolan as an engineer, the two would continue to work on projects for Bill while completing their rocket ship game prototype. The conditions for them at Nutting as they started working together more and more on the game were spartan at best. Unlike Ampex where they had their own office and abundant resources, all they had at Nutting were benches to work on.

Ted remembers it being a scary time for him because he had just left a company he'd been with for ten years where he had been making good money. Nolan was still young enough and fresh out of college that he could afford this kind of latitude and risk, even if he was gambling his family's future with it - which is probably why his wife Paula wasn't happy about any of it. Ted's family had a harder time adjusting though, having lived on a far more established level of income. Money became tight enough that Ted's wife had to go back to work for a while, working part time at Santa Clara County doing data processing and getting babysitters from a babysitting co-op. Her father had been in an unfortunate accident at a missile silo and was killed - leaving a small inheritance that helped considerably during this time as well. It seemed everyone was pitching in, in some way, to make this game come to fruition. But it was Nolan who kept their eyes on the prize as they soldiered forward.

This Is The Dawning Of The Age Of....Syzygy

Dotted ships began moving and dueling on the screen, illuminating the small child's face in the dark workroom. Terri was playing the latest version of the game, which by now had come a long way under Nolan's direction. It seems fitting that the first arcade video game tester, and the first tester for Nolan and Ted, was a small child - the symbol of a new generation. It was now the Summer of 1971 and their game was in the home stretch. Ted had designed additional circuitry, at Nolan's request, to create a noise that sounded like an explosion, and more circuits to trigger the sound and other game mechanics at the right time. This pioneering effort to add sound to the game cannot be understated. The computer games that were influencing Nolan and Ted ran on big mainframes and minis, where sound for a game was an unheard of luxury in a time when a graphical vector display was also still hard to come by for personal use. In the EM driven coin-op business however, sound was a necessity. The clicks, whirs and buzzes of pinball and other novelty machines were common sounds to arcade and pub dwellers. So Nolan knew the game had to have sound - there was just no question. Ted delivered it by using a Zener diode and adding more circuitry to cause a decay effect so the sounds would roll off into the distance.

Nolan had also been busy, basically living at the drafting table at Nutting, putting together the full schematics and laying out the printed circuit board (PCB) that would be used in production. He had made some pretty hefty contributions to gaming's future as well, inventing a primitive artificial intelligence (AI) for the enemy saucers that's part of Game AI 101 nowadays. Using the same quadrant mathematics trick described earlier, he divided the screen into quadrants that the ships would fire towards. Done completely in discrete electronics again, he would track what quadrant the player was in and have them fire away in that direction.

The illusion to little Terri right now, dueling the saucers in her father's work-room, was that the ships were smart and able to track her around the screen. There were neat explosions and firing sounds everytime she got one of them or they got her. There weren't actually little aliens in there, of course, and ships weren't really exploding, but that was all part of the 'magic.' While she was enjoying the magic that generations would come to know, Ted was out in his garage building a wooden cabinet to put the prototype game into, using materials he purchased from his por-tion of the money contributed to start Syzygy.

Nolan came to Ted to deliver a possible bombshell - he heard about someone else, at Stanford no less, was also working on a coin-operated game influenced by *Spacewar!* A man by the name of Bill Pitts, who had been a student at Stanford - had the exact same vision as Nolan: bring computer games (to date only available to a selective crowd with access to big expensive computers!) to the masses by throwing a coin slot on it.

Bill Pitts also had a partner; Hugh Tuck - a hardware engineer to compli-ment Bill's software engineering skills. The two were busy installing their first proto-type at the Tresidder Memorial Union when Nolan and Ted showed up. The location for Pitts and Tuck's test was perfect - Stanford's student union. Named after a former President of the university, it also was symbolic for the meeting of the minds that was to occur - the 'sit down' of two groups of potential business adversaries. Like Bushnell, Dabney, Pitts and Tuck, Donald Tresidder had started his career wanting to go in one direction - medicine - and found himself answering a higher calling. He was asked to become President of Stanford and ushered in an era of high level orga-nization, infrastructure and business growth. Now as the fates decided, here were two groups of men, both from completely different backgrounds from the field they now found themselves in, seeking to do the same thing within the coin-op industry.

Drinking coffee and discussing their individual ideas, Bill Pitts gave Nolan and Ted a look behind the curtain of his version of Oz, which he named *Galaxy Game.* Much to Nolan and Ted's glee, Pitts and Tuck had gone the exact route the duo had abandoned back in '69 when they were still a trio. There was a full DEC mini-computer running an actual version of *Spacewar!* on a dedicated vector display. Compared to Nolan and Ted's much cheaper custom hardware and television display, the potential difference in market dominance was obvious. There was no way *Galaxy Game* was targeted towards mass production. It suffered from the same overly expensive drawback that caused Nolan and Ted to go the route they did. A reciprocated visit to Nutting to view Nolan and Ted's rocket ship game had Pits and Tuck feeling their version was vastly superior because of its closer accuracy to *Spacewar!* In Nolan's mind, that couldn't have been farther from the truth. The most important issue was... was it cost effective and could you mass produce it? Nolan was proven right when Pitts and Tuck put out a newer multi-station model the following year, and they too realized that a single location was as far as they could take their vision.

The one thing *Galaxy Game* did prove however was that there was indeed a demand, if not a craving for a new type of game different from the standard EM ones. When it debuted fully functional in September of 1971, *Galaxy Game* had people waiting for hours to play at $.10 cents a pop - though at that rate it would take years to recoup the over $20,000 investment.

Nolan and Ted had a similar experience though when they tested their prototype unit the month before, surrounded by beer swilling college kids. The Dutch Goose had only been open for five years, but was already a popular Menlo Park hangout for kids going to Stanford and Menlo College. Bill Nutting chose the location, which was on salesman Dave Ralstin's coin-op route that he had started up on the side for extra income. Bill also chose the name for the new game: *Computer Space*. The name was uninspired, a play on Nutting's previous 'Computer' tagged games, but the location was an obvious choice. College kids have lots of money to burn, and drunken college kids are willing to spend it on just about anything for a good time.

Hauling the game to the Dutch Goose in Ted's Datsun pickup, the duo watched happily as the college kids swarmed the game, quickly figuring it out and forming lines to play it. Patting each other on the back, they realized they had a winner on their hands. That feeling was short lived though when they tried it out at other locations on Ralstin's route, including a pizza place. Confusion was the order of the day, but the answer became obvious: The Dutch Goose was full of college students pursuing high level degrees in engineering, physics and computers. At the pizza joint, as with other similar locations, the 'average Joe' were the regular clientele. Middle and lower class people unwinding after a hard day on the job that, like most in their professions, weren't there to think. They were there to get drunk and unwind from the stress of the day with their buddies. Their dream wasn't flying rocket ships; it was a beer in one hand and a babe or pool cue in the other. Nolan and Ted's accurate rocket mechanics and control scheme was just plain confusing to them. It became clear that they were going to need to make some changes to garner a broader base appeal when it hit the market.

September came, and Nolan and Ted were racing to try and get that tweaked version fully produced in time for the October 1971 MOA show where Nutting was finally going to show off their new game technology they had first publicly talked about releasing that past January. Plagued by the reputation of showing 'more of the same' at the previous year's show, they had a lot riding on this product. Nolan once again surprised Ted with two contributions; one, clever marketing and the other, from out in left field.

First, the final production layout of the game's PCBs was stunning, convincing Ted that Nolan must have had help. Besides being clear and concise, he had also added the gimmick of laying out the diodes of the ship matrix in actual patterns of ships. Claiming it would make it easier for site operators to track a display problem and repair whatever diode was on the fritz, it showed a glimpse into the marketing Nolan would employ years later at Atari with terms like 'dura-stress.' Completely made up, it was meant to draw the operator into a sense of quality - and the notion that this product was designed with them in mind as much as the player.

What Nolan knew from his coin-op repair days at Lagoon Amusement Park and his time at Nutting, is that the operators and distributors are the actual target audience; the people who purchase the product from the manufacturer and keep them in business. Getting them to buy your game and for them to know it was going to be easy to operate (and repair, if needed to keep it running) was just as important as convincing them the game would be a hit with the players they were renting time to. That's really all the player of an arcade game is: a renter. They're renting time on the machine at $.10 cents to a quarter a play, and if the game is good enough, you'll have people lining up for their chance to rent it - no different from a timeshare in Florida.

The other thing that came out of left field with Nolan was when he showed up one day with a handmade clay model that he fashioned. Looking like an art class project composed of Plasticene, plastic and wood, he had fashioned his vision of how the cabinet for a space-age game should look. Nolan found a fiberglass pool and hot tub manufacturer up the street from Nutting and talked them into manufacturing the unique cabinet. When the full size smooth fiberglass cabinet was completed, at first glance the 'rounded edge/dual pedestal' looking shape of the proposed cabinet would remind someone of a Sid and Marty Krofft designed set piece. Something H.R. Pufnstuf would be seen frolicking around while Jimmy played his magic flute.

Ted was back in the garage after the first delivery, trying hard to make *Computer Space*'s internals fit into the awkward custom shape, but in the end, they had a stellar space battle experience ready to go. They also had one more surprise in store too. Like Neil Armstrong planting the U.S. flag on the moon to let any future visitors know who had been there first, printed right there on the control panel of the game was a statement to let everyone know who had actually built it: 'Syzygy Engineered.'

Testing of the new design brought strange looks and similar reactions from patrons as previously exhibited. There was confusion with the controls and the game play, enough that some even attributed ridiculous imaginative traits to the game. Like not making the game 'angry' with the wrong button. Nolan and Ted briefly tried out a new format with a twisting contoured metal 'joystick,' and this model actually made it on the back of the first advertising flyer. But that's as far as it got representing the futuristic game. When they placed it on location at a Round Table Pizza restaurant in Alameda, California, it didn't even make it through the night. The patrons basically manhandled the stick trying to get their ship to move how they wanted it to move, and destroyed it. So it looked like buttons it was...

Bill Nutting, Dave Ralstin and Nolan flew to Chicago to help *Computer Space* make its official debut at that year's MOA show. In the rows upon rows of jukeboxes, EM game machines, pinball and vending machines, the strangest sight was in Nutting's booth. Walking up the aisle to where the booth was located, show attendees were greeted by a tall, lanky and very hyper man flanking an odd looking curvy fiberglass encased machine with a television in it. The man was hyper because he appeared to be enthusiastically extolling the virtues of this new technology and what he felt was the future of coin-operated games.

The reception at the MOA was anything but enthusiastic though; actually more like downright skeptical. Nutting managed to take a handful of orders, but most of the operators and distributors that visited their booth questioned the viability and reliability of the technology:

'How would your average operator, used to servicing electromechanical technology, be able to service a computerized game?'

'Wasn't this just a novelty?'

'Wasn't it expensive to get the signal broadcast?'

Regardless of all these questions, the trio still felt they had a solid product and came back ready to soldier on. Bill even took Nolan and Ted up in his expensive Waco E Biplane as a sort of bonding celebration.

Dave Ralstin sent off the first five manufactured *Computer Space* games to various distributors around the country to garner interest in the new game as he began to work his marketing magic. Allowing the five well known distributors to place one for free to ascertain their earning potential was a stroke of genius. By Spring 1972, Nutting had sold over 1,000 of the machines, and Bill rewarded Ralstin by... firing him. Ralstin was getting a commission for every unit sold and Bill felt, "Why pay someone all that extra money for something I could do myself?" That blunder meant only another 500 or so machines were sold. As Ted put it, "Your salesman should be the highest paid person at the company. They're the ones making all the sales and bringing the money in."

We'll probably never know how successful *Computer Space* could have been before Bill's interference caused an artificial decline in its sales. Bill would later claim trying to sell Computer Space in the coin-op industry was hard and that some they'd have to sell 'by force.' What do you expect when you fire your marketing talent? After the next exodus of Nutting people through the middle of the year, Bill would eventually hire a new batch, including a return to using a marketing person. The new marketer would manage to get a custom, all white *Computer Space* into the Charlton Heston film *Soylent Green*; the first appearance of a video game in a film and which would start a long-standing tradition of video games used in Hollywood productions.

However, Nolan and Ted were also about to become victims of Bill's strange business sense. Thank God for us it happened, because if not, then there'd never have been an Atari...

Chapter 1 Review In Images

Upper Left: Nolan Bushnell (back row, third from right) in 1960.
Upper Right: Ted Dabney during his time in the Marines.
Bottom: Ampex headquarters.

Top: Ampex Videofile headquarters.

Bottom: Ted's first house, where Ted moved his daughter Terri out of her bedroom to invent *Computer Space*'s spot motion circuitry.

The original GO board hand built by Ted Dabney for Nolan and Ted to play on in their office, now in posession of the Atari Museum.

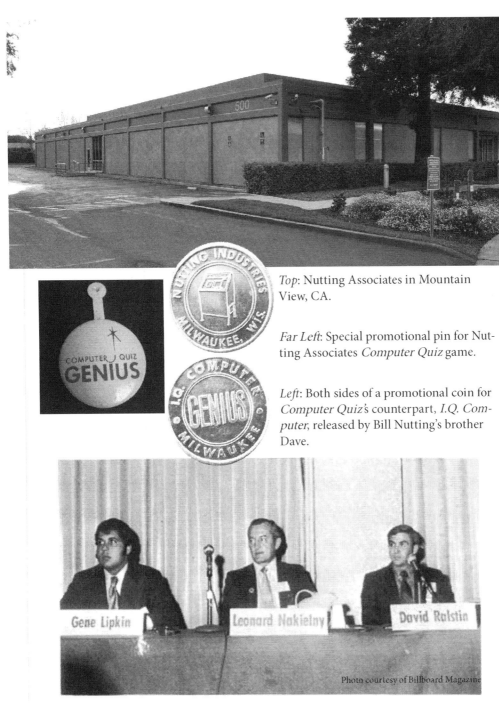

Top: Nutting Associates in Mountain View, CA.

Far Left: Special promotional pin for Nutting Associates *Computer Quiz* game.

Left: Both sides of a promotional coin for *Computer Quiz*'s counterpart, *I.Q. Computer*, released by Bill Nutting's brother Dave.

Photo courtesy of Billboard Magazine

Left to right: Gene Lipkin (Allied Leisure), Leonard Nakielny (Williams), David Ralstin (Nutting Associates) at the October 1970 MOA show.

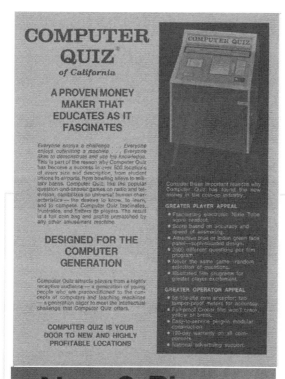

Advertising flyers and a *Two Player Computer Quiz* advertisement from MOA show.

NUTTING ASSOCIATES, INC.

500 LOGUE AVENUE ■ MOUNTAIN VIEW, CALIFORNIA 94040

(415) 961-9373

May 1972

Test and heighten
your extrasensory perception!

Gentlemen:

Nutting Associates, Inc., the manufacturer of Computer Quiz, proudly introduces the all new Psychic, a coin-operated game. Psychic is a step forward, presenting today's generation with the challenge of Extrasensory Perception (ESP). ESP has long been a controversial and much studied topic by individuals and institutions throughout the world. For one dime Psychic indicates that ESP does exist in many persons. To the player Psychic may uncover ESP powers that he never before thought existed.

Psychic is a low priced game selling direct from us the manufacturer to you the operator for a cost of $545.00, f. o. b. Mountain View, California.

Order Psychic today for what promises to be your biggest season ever!

Very truly yours,

David A. Ralstin
Marketing Director

DAR/k
enc.

A letter from David Ralstin promoting Nutting's new EM game *Psychic*, just before he was fired for selling too many *Computer Space* games. *Top inset*: the flyer for *Psychic*.

A   169

```
                    SYZYGY CO.
            STATEMENT OF OWNER'S EQUITY
            Year Ended December 31, 1971
                    (Unaudited)
```

	Dabney	Bushnell	Total
Owners contributions	$350	$350	$700
New loss (note 1)	[194]	[290]	[484]
Balance at end of year	$156	$ 60	$216

See accompanying notes

Page from a financial statement for year end 1971 for Syzygy Company, showing the original $350 both Nolan and Ted put in.

The original *Computer Space* flyer

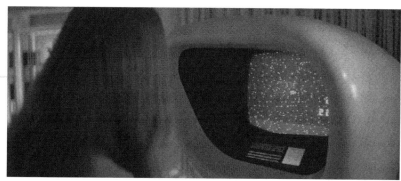

Top: Leigh Taylor-Young plays *Computer Space* in the 1973 film Soylent Green, the first known appearance of a video game in a film. (*Courtesy of Metro-Goldwyn-Mayer*)

Bottom: Promotional postcard for *Computer Space*.

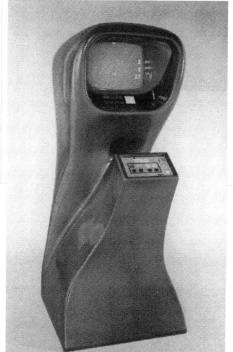

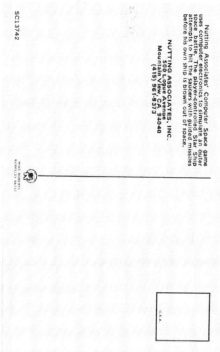

Chapter 2

The Juice Is Worth
The Squeeze

P op quiz: You're working for a man notorious for firing people at the drop of a hat or at the slightest hint that they're cutting into his money. What do you do?

Answer: If you're Nolan Bushnell you tell him you want 33% of his company.

That's exactly what he did in the Spring of '72 after discussing with Bill about doing a simpler version of *Computer Space*. Whether it was a huge pair of balls or genuine youthful naivety is debatable, but Nolan threw the figure out there. Apparently Bill was feeling generous, because he offered him 5% instead of firing him on the spot. He'd still have to stay as Bill's engineer though: meaning, Bill called all the shots on the marketing and sales of any future games.

When Nolan told Ted about his exchange with Bill, it was clear to both they had gone as far as they could go at Nutting Associates. But what do they do now? They'd both left their stable jobs at Ampex for a shot at a future they believed was right around the corner.

Just as when they first discovered Nutting two years prior, Nolan took the reins to find a solution. Around Bill they were business as usual, but on the side, Nolan was busy contacting Nutting's rivals in Chicago - the old guards of the coin industry.

Flying to Chicago in early April 1972, Nolan was supposed to be there as a representative of Nutting. Though 'technically' Nutting's Chief Engineer, Nolan's responsibilities also included flying around to some of the larger distributors carrying Nutting's games and teaching them how to service machines. On this particular trip, Nolan was educating the technicians at Empire Distributing, owned by Joe Robbins and Gil Kitt.

Gil and Nolan had been friends for some time now, first meeting during Nutting's appearance at the MOA show the previous year. Gil was well connected to the old guard coin-op manufacturers in Chicago, many of which he did business with via Empire Distributing. Now Nolan was going to leverage Gil's connections to hopefully get Ted and himself their first client outside of Nutting.

Gil was able to get Nolan a meeting with John Britz at industry leader Bally. The 54 year old Britz was an engineer himself and a 'lifer' in the Chicago coin industry. Starting in the 1930's at Bally and heading their coffee vending machine division before it was bought out by competitor Seeburg in the 50s, he returned to Bally in 1963 to become general manager of all operations at Bally. By the time Nolan met Britz during a typical wet Chicago Spring, Britz was now Executive Vice President of Technology.

Just as with Bill Nutting several years earlier, here was Nolan trying to share his vision for the future. But the major difference between 'then' and 'now' was that NOW Nolan and Ted had fully proven their technology with *Computer Space*, even if the game wasn't lighting up the industry like they'd hoped. Britz was interested in getting into this new medium that was slowly creeping into the industry, and possibly having Syzygy engineer some other, more traditional arcade games. There was just one hitch: they wouldn't work with Nolan and Ted if they were still at Nutting.

It's a decision that none of us would make lightly, cutting the safety rope to jettison yourself into self-employment. For most of us, that kind of decision would be paralyzing, bringing doubt and worry – and for two family men like Nolan and Ted, it was no different. But they weighed the decision and decided to go for it and turn Syzygy Engineering into a fully independent startup called Syzygy Company, with Bally as their first customer. Just like Bill and his brother Dave almost a half decade before, these two young bloods felt they knew better than everyone what the future of coin-operated gaming would be and were ready to prove to the rest of the established industry that THEY were its future. As Roy Ash, co-founder of defense contractor Litton Industries once put it, "An entrepreneur tends to bite off a little more than he can chew hoping he'll quickly learn how to chew it." This challenge of the 'chewing' would help them both define who they really were.

It was early May 1972 and Nolan began looking for a place beyond the old fallback of Ted's home for him and Ted to operate their engineering firm out of. The house was spacious to be sure, purchased while Ted was still at Ampex in an effort to get higher returns on their taxes than what they were getting. However, the 1425 Blackstone Ave. address wasn't exactly zoned for a commercial startup - Ted couldn't displace his entire family again as he had done with his daughter at the previous house.

At least Nolan and Ted would have some money coming in to keep them afloat when they resigned from Nutting, enabling them to pay rent at whatever new location they found. When Ralstin had been fired from Nutting, he sold Nolan and Ted his coin route. Bringing this route under Syzygy, it was making them a decent amount of money; about $300 a week from the pinball machines, pool tables and a few *Computer Space* games. Ted would often enlist his daughter Terri to help collect quarters out of the machines and roll them up. Keeping it a family affair, she enjoyed spending the time with her father and learning about the value of money (though one time she learned about the weight of money literally, after she dropped a huge bag of quarters on her foot and broke her toe - Ted amusingly had to spend time trying to convince the school about why she had to miss classes and that yes, it really was from a bag of quarters).

Besides the money though, they needed to formalize their partnership, at least in the eyes of the State of California. Without telling Ted, Nolan found a law firm that specialized in representing clients in the 'new' tech industry: Hopkins, Jordan, Mitchell and Sullivan. Using attorney David Mitchell as a notary public to file papers of incorporation for Syzygy Company, Nolan also 'questioningly' used Ted's address as the base of operations rather than his own. We say, 'questioningly' because at this point, they were long past the days of working out of Ted's residence. So one has to ask; what benefit would there be in choosing Ted's address instead of Nolan's, other than having Ted's property bearing the weight of liability and risk should they ever be sued? Regardless, Nolan and Ted spent the rest of May getting ready to fly the Nutting coop with Ted unaware of Nolan's dealings.

After they were finally free from Nutting, at the beginning of June, Nolan and Ted still had to prove to Bally they weren't under Nutting anymore before they could move forward. Bally, being a large corporation and used to covering all the legal angles, had taken care of how they'd deliver their burden of proof. Bally took the liberty of drawing up and sending off some affidavits for the two to sign; the gold standard of sworn statements. Dated the 1st of June 1972, the documents attested they "no longer had any obligatory duties to Nutting and Associates." Signing the documents and sending them back to Bally, Nolan and Ted were now able to focus on writing the agreement and setting up shop. Well sort of... what is curious was that Nolan, AFTER signing that document, spent time over June and July designing a 2-player *Computer Space* for Nutting, which Steve Bristow (now working at Nutting Associates as an engineer) and his wife spent time building for Nutting.

Within the week after submitting the document to Bally, Nolan did find the location for their new offices; a rental unit in a small business park on Scott Blvd. in Santa Clara, CA. The late 1960s 'modern architecture' designed buildings housed a network of compartmentalized offices available for rent that are still in use today. Each one is the perfect size for a new, budding business in need of a real office and additional facilities, but not yet big enough for a regular corporate office. Nolan chose the rental space at 2962, set in a building two buildings back from Scott Blvd. Longer in length than in width, the rental spaces in this building were designed for businesses that were regularly shipping out products. Offices in the front and an open work area with a garage door in the back - it was perfect for their needs. Receiving coin-operated manufacturing materials and sending out their finished prototypes to clients would be a breeze with the garage door in the back.

Like new college roommates choosing their section of the dorm room, Nolan and Ted chose their offices. Nolan immediately picked the office predominantly in front, directly to the right as you walked in and the only one with a window looking out - a symbol of his desired importance. Ted got the second office to the right by default, which didn't bother him at all; he just wanted to start digging in on the still-being-negotiated Bally contract. Still fleshing it out based on the verbal agreement between Nolan and John Britz from April, this contract was to be for a more traditional pinball machine and a new video game. The terms of the contract would ensure regular payments from Bally, which in turn would allow Nolan and Ted to hire some engineering staff and pay them a salary. The duo wouldn't take a cent out of the company yet; they'd continue to support themselves from the coin route - a far cry from today's typical Web 2.0 tech startup where founders immediately seek venture capital and start living high on the hog.

As they were moving into the building, an interesting predicament happened. Nolan walked into Ted's office showing him a letter he'd received from David Mitchell and the attempted incorporation as Syzygy Company. "Who is David Mitchell and what are you talking about? What incorporation?" asked Ted. That's when Nolan informed him about the law firm he'd engaged and the filed papers, which had now come back from the California Secretary of State as denied. It appears another law firm had already reserved the name for a client, so they'd have to pick a new name for their engineering firm to do business under.

They had been identifying themselves as "Syzygy" for almost three years now, so there was reluctance to change. It was a good, solid name and it fit their partnership. Not to mention they already had their business cards, stationary, etc. already made up with their first ever logo; their name in a stylized font with a few 'GO' pieces that resembled a star constellation. Should they go back to looking at D&B or B&D, or look through the dictionary again for more inspiration? No - their beloved game of GO still had the answers.

Cycling through some terms from the game for possible names, they came up with three: Hane, which is a move that reaches around another player's piece. Sente, a move that describes the initiative a player has when they have an overwhelming follow-up that forces the opponent to respond... and finally Atari, which is a state in the game when your piece or a group of your pieces are in danger of being taken.

Arriving in David Mitchell's backyard for the first full meeting between the three, David couldn't help but notice how informal Nolan and Ted looked - t-shirts, jeans and tennis shoes. These were the early days of Silicon Valley; when meetings in backyards were common, and the California startup dress code of wearing whatever makes you comfortable was just taking root. Giving David Mitchell the proposed names, David in turn submitted them to the Secretary of State, Edmund G. Brown Jr. Brown's name might seem familiar to some Californians reading this, but certainly not to video game fans. A two term Governor in the 70s, most recently he's returned to that seat to succeed Arnold Schwarzenegger as the Governor of California.

He's also responsible for giving the legal stamp of approval to the name: 'ATARI.' Choosing that name out of the three, Brown sent the response back to David, who in turn, informed Nolan and Ted that would be the name of their new company.

Drawing up new incorporation papers, they were signed on June 9th, naming Nolan, Ted and their wives Paula and Joan as the four founding board members. They had 75,000 shares at $1.00 a share to distribute between themselves and any future employees. There was one detail, however, that still went unnoticed in the paperwork: Ted's address was 'again' copied over as the address for the company instead of the new Scott Blvd. address, with all four listed as doing business out of Ted's home address.

The new business was starting to shape up now that they had cleared the way with Bally, filed their incorporation papers and found a place to work out of. But it was clear that they already needed help keeping things organized, and most importantly someone to serve as their 'buffer' with the outside world. After all, if you're going to be portraying yourself as a well organized engineering firm, you should at least have a receptionist answering the phone and looking pretty for visitors coming through the door. Nolan didn't have to look far to find her, hiring Cynthia Villenueva as their first official employee. Babysitting Nolan's kids for some time, Cynthia was a 17 year old girl just graduating from high school who had been looking for a regular Summer job. So she was hired during the second week of June to be a secretary for Nolan and Ted, and act as Nolan's personal assistant. Much like the role Ted's wife previously played, Cynthia was also there to look out for the men and make sure they ate and took care of themselves during the long nights ahead of them. Her modest salary for the role of playing mother hen/answering service/receptionist was paid for from the same source that was paying the rent: *Computer Space* royalties and money from the coin route (or 'street operations' as Nolan and Ted liked to call it).

When the $4,000 advance from Bally came in, they were finally able to start hiring the first of their engineering staff. The engineer that would begin working on their new video game for Bally and answer the question of, 'who would be employee number two?' - the answer, which would be the go-to answer for engineering staff for Syzygy/Atari for years to come, was Ampex.

Allan 'Al' Alcorn had been another one of the interns at Ampex Videofile during Nolan and Ted's tenure there. A tall bear of a man, if not often described as a jolly bear, Al was a native of the area, growing up in the Haight-Ashbury district of San Francisco during its hippie heyday. However growing up, Al didn't go the hippie route he could have easily fallen into. Maybe it was his merchant marine father, or his longstanding interest in electronics, or possibly even the fact he had been a foot-ball player in high school. Good enough to make the San Francisco All-City team that included future football notables OJ Simpson and Mike Holmgren, Al was able to leverage the experience to go to the higher education route of Berkeley instead of the expected UC-Santa Cruz, because Santa Cruz had no football program. His time playing Berkeley football lasted only a week however, as he soon discovered he couldn't play while pursuing his chosen degree, electrical engineering. At the time, Al had no idea how profound an impact his choice of 'resistors and diodes' over pig-skins would have on his life.

As with much of his early life, Al's path from 'here' to 'there' was compli-cated and full of interesting timing. While he didn't fall into the Haight-Ashbury scene growing up, the turbulent 60s caught up with him at the Berkeley campus, the notorious collegiate center of 60s radical counter culture. Al was involved with Peo-ple's Park; an area around campus that students took over to make into a commune. He was there for the May 15th, 1969 police attack known as 'Bloody Thursday.' An aggressive action only overshadowed by Kent State years later, the University police and county sheriff's department dropped tear gas on crowds of students via helicop-ter and opened fire on students with shotguns, spraying buckshot into their backs as they ran. Al luckily survived unscathed, and while his work path wasn't as full of drama, it was just as tumultuous.

Initially doing workstudy at Ampex in the Videofile division during his studies at Berkeley, when Al was close to graduation in 1971 he wasn't able to be hired back due to financial problems at Ampex. However, the Videofile group's old supervisor, Ed De Benedetti, was able to find him a job at Peripheral Technology, Inc. (PTI), until he could get Al in again at Ampex. But PTI was soon bought out, forcing him to move and leave Berkeley. Working there until he left later that year to take a one unit course at UC-Irvine that he still needed to graduate, by the time he was done, he was able to get back into Ampex - which is where he was working when Nolan walked through the door.

"I'd like to take you to lunch and discuss your future," was how part of the conversation went. Initially under the guise of catching up on things, during lunch, Nolan pulled out all the stops. First, he was pointing out the 'company car' they rode over in; Nolan's Buick station wagon. While in reality it was more his family car than today's standard sign of corporate success and excess, it was paid for by Syzygy Company through the royalties and route earnings. Still, it was a concept unfamiliar to the young Al, who, when he questioned Nolan, was told: "You don't have to pay for it - the company does and you can drive it for free."

Nolan also offered Al a $1000 a month salary and 10% of the new company's stock. Pulling out all the stops to try and lure Al away from Ampex, Nolan had no idea it had zero sway with Al. The stock held little interest, as Al figured the company would probably fold within two years anyway. $1000 a month salary? He was making $1200 a month at Ampex already.

Why did Al ultimately take the offer? Because he thought it would be fun. After everything he went through at Berkeley and what he saw going on in the country, he felt the time to enjoy life was 'now.' And what could be more joyful than making games? Besides, he figured when the whole thing went down in flames after a few years, he could go back to Ampex and use the experience to negotiate a higher rung up the corporate ladder. So in mid-June, Ampex's Videofile division lost yet another young, promising engineer.

The Birth Of A Legend

It was three events at the end of June 1972 that started the real momentum for the new Syzygy Company. First, on June 26th, Nolan and Ted signed the royalty agreement with Bally for the two amusement machines they were to design. Apart from a few addendums, this would finalize Syzygy's first development contract. Second, the very next day, the incorporation papers Nolan and Ted had filed at the beginning of the month came back from the Secretary of the State of California. Although they'd continue to do business as Syzygy Company, as far as the State of California and the U.S. Government were concerned, as of June 27th they were now known as Atari, Inc.

The final event was the beginning of the two projects for the Bally contract. There were no titles at the time, and no official 'president' or 'vice president,' so the doling out of responsibilities between Nolan and Ted just kind of fell into place. While Nolan was acting as the outside face for the company, Ted was making sure things ran well internally. Whether it be 'keeping the books' for their finances, making sure they had the parts they needed, or making sure the coin route was running smoothly, Ted filled in. When the money from Bally started coming in and Ted also took on the pinball part of the contract, it was clear they needed someone dedicated to watching their finances to take over the books. Nolan brought in Fred Marincic, and after an orientation by Ted regarding his bookkeeping methods, Ted was free to concentrate almost fully on the pinball project. To assist, Ted brought in another acquaintance from Ampex, Bob Herbert, placing him under contract to help with the mechanical design of the board.

That left Nolan to get Al started on the video game portion of the contract. Now with Nolan (as you may have guessed by now), nothing is ever as simple as it seems. And by writing standards it would be boring if we only had to state "...and then Nolan gave Al a game, which he then started working on." Luckily the un-simple truth provides for a very entertaining story. Nolan knew he wanted a game that was simpler to control than *Computer Space* had been, but with the same level of complexity of game play. Maybe something in the sports arena like a driving game would work out? Nothing could be simpler than a steering wheel and gas pedal, right? Al needed to get his feet wet first though before jumping right in. Work on something to get him familiar with Ted's spot motion circuitry and the basics of video game engineering design which Nolan had done with *Computer Space*.

A straight enough concept so far, but now comes the part that is pure Nolan: the game he gave Al to start out with... and the reason he told Al it was being done. The first would give the company its greatest legendary success while simultaneously leading to serious legal problems throughout the early to mid-70s for Atari. The latter is pure Nolan mischievousness (or "motivation" as he calls it).

During May, before Nolan and Ted had completely cut ties with Nutting Associates, Nolan had learned that a new home video game product was being released by the consumer electronics company Magnavox that August. Called the Magnavox Odyssey, the system promised to plug directly into any TV through its antenna and allow its owner to play games directly on the screen. The Odyssey was scheduled to be shown at the Airport Marina Hotel in Burlingame, CA during an all product show called the Magnavox Profit Caravan. As with *Galaxy Game* the previous year, Nolan knew he had to check out this possible competition.

Nutting actually had three people coming to the Magnavox Profit Caravan that day: Nolan, Rob Geiman and Charles Fibian. The show was meant to peacock all the latest Magnavox products to dealers and rivals, since at that time Magnavox was at the top of the food chain in consumer electronics. Nutting, along with a lot of the other electronics companies in the area, had received an invitation to the show to check out the Odyssey.

When he came back, Nolan discussed the Odyssey with Ted and separately with Steve Bristow, who had joined Nolan and Ted at Nutting as a service technician just before they left. Nolan's candor was at its usual amped level, and he stated to

Steve, "I think it's shit." What he actually meant was, like *Galaxy Game*, he thought the execution could have been done better and didn't live up to the potential he envisioned for a home experience. At the time though, he had no idea this 'shit game system' was based on video technology in development long before he and Ted developed *Computer Space*, or how it would come back to affect him and Atari. Nor how the one game that stuck in his mind from the system (*Tennis*) would affect Atari, both in good and bad ways.

On a sunny day in late June of 1972, Nolan decided to give Al Alcorn a 'warm-up project' as he called it. A project that would be used to get Al acquainted with the spot motion technology Ted had developed and the overall game technology Nolan had engineered for *Computer Space*. After cutting his teeth on this beginning project, he'd move Al on to the real project he wanted him to do: a driving video game. So what was the beginning project? A 'better' version of the Odyssey's *Tennis*.

Nolan told Al the basics of the 'ping-pong' game he wanted him to do while actually recounting the basics of the *Tennis* game he had seen: two paddles, a ball and a net. Next came Nolan's mischievous method of motivation; by telling Al he had a contract from General Electric to do a home video game, and that this game he was tasking Al with was actually for them. But wait for it... there was a catch. This ping-pong game had to be very, very cheap and inexpensive, costing no more than $15 in materials. The wide-eyed young Al thought for a second that he had stepped into a very tough situation, building an entire game with $15 in parts.

Given the times, the changeover to a ping-pong angle was most likely no accident. President Nixon had just visited China that past February, set in motion the previous year by what was called China's "Ping-Pong Diplomacy" (the opening of diplomatic channels with Communist China by inviting a country's ping-pong team to visit and play their own). In 1972, ping-pong was at an all time high in the public's consciousness. That, combined with telling Al it was for a GE contract would have made it seem very legit in Al's mind.

What Nolan did next however, would become a ritual for all the game engineers that joined Atari in the early 70s; he dumped the schematics for *Computer Space* into Al's lap and said, "Go to it." Al was expected to give himself a crash course in the technology of game engineering by simply looking at these schematics. As Al soon found out, that was going to be next to impossible because, "He drew schematics in such a bizarre way that I couldn't really ever understand them."

So Al instead got Nolan to directly explain everything on their chalkboard, like a coach going over plays with the star quarterback. Then that quarterback set about getting the first thing up on the screen - a spot that would represent a ball. That spot alone took Al fifteen to twenty parts, which instilled a sense of failure in the young engineer before the game had even truly begun. Nolan's motivation factor did kick in though because of it, and Al was forced to do the rest of the design through brute force engineering. A good portion of the parts he was using were parts left over from his time at Ampex, and the rest were parts that had to be ordered. The chips that would have made his life much easier were way too expensive, so he had to fall back on the 7400 series of digital TTL (Transistor-Transistor Logic).

A logic chip is basically a chip that contains a collection of logic gates, which are in turn the building blocks needed to create complex electronic decisions via boolean logic. What's boolean logic? It was developed by a mathematician in the 1850s by the name of George Bool as a way of representing decisions via 0's and 1's. Logic gates generally take two signals coming in and use boolean logic to send one signal or none out. With the advent of integrated circuits, it became possible to put several of these on a single chip, which evolved over time into the millions upon millions of logic gates on today's powerful microprocessors in the computers of today.

Invented in the mid 1960s and used in mainframes, mini-computers and major electronic circuitry, the 7400 logic chip was cheap by the time Al was working on his game - about fifty cents to seventy five cents a chip, mainly because the industry standard chip was second-sourced (available from more than just the inventor) by a good number of companies.

Within time, the objects for the game started to fill the screen, with Al's circuitry driving all of them. One spot for the ball, digits for the score and a segmented line for the net. Next came the paddles (the rectangular blocks that the player would control on screen to hit the ball with). On the original *Tennis* game, the controlling scheme allowed movement of the paddle both forwards and backwards as well as up and down. It also provided a special control for 'english' - the random side spin of the ball. The complicated scheme needed to be dumbed down for the coin-op, which Al decided would only use a simple spinner for paddle motion.

This in turn meant you had to have some way to make an exciting volley; otherwise players would get bored pretty quick. The volley is actually the most important play mechanic of the game, and certainly the most important aspect of an actual tennis or ping-pong match. So Al created a way for the ball to speed-up by adding a counting circuit to count the number of volleys. After the fourth and twelfth volleys, the ball would speed up.

The 'english' was taken care of by a unique paddle segmenting scheme that Al invented. In video games at this time, the drawing of objects was related to the number of scan lines on the TV. Remember, a single frame of a TV screen consists of rows of spots or 'pixels.' These rows are called scan lines, and an object can be spread across several of these lines. The paddle blocks in Al's game were sixteen scan lines high, so he came up with dividing the paddle into eight segments each, two lines high. The two middle segments produced a flat shot straight across, and starting from the outer segments inward, the vertical velocity of the ball would change from greater to less. Combined with the horizontal velocity decided by the number of volleys, the illusion of angles and 'english' were successfully produced in a much more streamlined version than it had been on the Odyssey. In fact, because the horizontal speed could vary, so could the angles produced as the action heated up, creating a very dynamic and fun game play.

Now to move those paddles, he needed some form of circuit that shifts the pixels in those 16 scan lines up and down to create the illusion of motion. That's the magic of these video games; there's no real object in front of you. It's just computer graphics - lit pixels on a screen being shifted around each picture frame, drawing you into interact with them. Because of the cost concerns, the timing chip that Al had to use to control what scan lines the paddle was drawn across couldn't handle the full range of the screen. It actually left a small gap at the top of the screen. However as Nolan and Ted played it during the design process, everyone realized that problem actually enhanced the game play. If two players were that good, the small hole would provide a break in the stalemate if a player could direct the ball through it. Rather than fix it by going a more expensive route, it was decided the bug would stay. The experience led Al to the mantra, "If you can't fix it, call it a feature."

Already well over budget, the final part of the development of Al's game involved the sound. Because of their work on *Computer Space*, Nolan knew Al had to get acquainted with creating sound; so the test game had to have sound. Nolan's suggestion was for the sound of cheering people when the ball was missed by a player. Ted added, "… it'd be nicer to hear boos and hisses." The problem was, Al had no idea how to go about adding sound, already being way over budget. *Computer Space*'s had been an analog buzzing sound, but this had to be digital. So Al came up with the unique idea of probing around some of the display circuitry to see if there were any signals there he could use for sounds… and he found them. The first iconic sounds of the new industry were simple tones being generated by the synch generator of the game. Al then told Nolan and Ted defiantly, "If you don't like the sounds, go do something better. But this is it for me." So the sounds stayed.

It was now mid-August, and Al and Ted knew they had a good game on their hands. Nolan wasn't convinced though. He still saw it as just a warm-up exercise. Ted sat in his office chair thinking this was it - this was the game they should be giving Bally for their contract, no matter how much Nolan didn't want to. Determined, he walked from one doorway to the other, his office to Nolan's, and spoke his mind. Then the door shut and the real screaming match began. Nolan was adamant he didn't want this to be their game, and Ted was just as adamant that it should be. They had, what Ted describes, as a knock down drag out argument. Maybe it was that Nolan really wanted a different game, or maybe it was the fact they all knew the game had been inspired by the Odyssey's *Tennis* game. As Al put it more recently, "It was like the movie *The Producers*, because he figured we'd rip off the idea for a game, but so what? It's no good, we're not going to sell it, we'll throw it away, so what harm is there? So it didn't work out that way…."

Keep in mind, the tech industry has a long history of people and companies copying other people's work and presenting it as their own. It's a strangely accepted practice, only when they do it, it's called 'inspiration' and 'innovation.' Computer clones were borne from competitors making 100% 'compatible' versions of mainframe and mini-computers, and later, personal computers. Both the Macintosh and Windows systems started as copies of the ideas and operating systems done at Xerox; the Altos' graphical and Smalltalk driven system. The Sony Walkman came from the originator of the portable cassette system - Andreas Pavel and his Stereobelt.

As former Atarian Steve Jobs stated in the Cringley produced *Triumph of the Nerds*, "We have always been shameless about stealing." *PONG* was Odyssey's *Tennis*, but done in a format with tweaks that would ultimately make it the more popular version - the version that was remembered, which in the industry is all that's important. How many people remember the SaeHan/Eiger MPMan or Diamond RIO over the iPod now?

Nolan finally relented, and agreed to at least testing the game on their coin route. He then turned around and spoke to Al, saying, "This is kind of a playable game. You know, let's put it at one of our route locations and see if anybody plays it. It might be fun to see if we have a real game." Al agreed to a trial, "...just to see how the public accepts it."

Over the coming weekend, Ted worked to build a cabinet for the game in his garage. What emerged was a tabletop cabinet, with wood grain sides, a front painted orange with a trapezoid cutout for the monitor and a steel control panel with the decided name of the game printed on it: *PONG*, after the sound of the ball hitting a paddle in the game. Steel spinners concealing pots (potentiometers, an electronic component that twists, providing different values that can be interpreted by the hardware to provide motion or interaction in the game) were mounted on the control panel for players to use. The half size cabinet also featured a coin-mechanism appropriated from a laundromat washing machine mounted on the side, with a bread pan for catching the quarters.

The monitor itself was what most of the early 1970s video arcade games would be using inside: An actual black and white television set. In this case, a 13" black and white television set that had been modified by Ted to bypass the tuner just as he had done for *Computer Space*. That Monday, he and Al worked to cram everything inside the cramped cabinet and get it ready for placement. Nolan and Ted decided to use the most popular location on the Syzygy route, a bar by the name of Andy Capp's Tavern in Sunnyvale.

Andy Capp's was owned at the time by Bill Gattis, a man Nolan and Ted had built a good working relationship with. A rustic looking tavern with wine caskets and a game room off to the side, the clientele was more of the everyday people they knew by now to be their target audience. Nolan and Al brought *PONG* over that next day, placing it in the game room that already housed six of their pinball's and a *Computer Space*. Taking one of the wine caskets to put the tabletop sized *PONG* on, the two decided to blend back into the bar and grab a few beers while watching to see if anyone would play.

Several beers and a good half hour later, two of the patrons finally walked over and started playing. There were no instructions on the machine; just the controls and the screen lit with a ball bouncing around and a net up the middle. One of the men noticed it took a quarter. A quarter? Most arcade games cost $.10 cents at the time, with maybe the larger EM games taking a quarter. Maybe it was the lure of the high technology amusement awaiting them, but they decided to put a quarter in. Sliding through the washing machine coin mechanism and clanking into the bread pan inside, two paddles popped on to the screen on either side. Then suddenly a ball appeared in the middle flying towards one side of the screen and off it, followed by the big zero at the top of the screen changing to one. Now it didn't take a rocket scientist - or this time a college science student - to figure out how to play this game. The men put their hands on the spinners, which moved the paddles on screen and then suddenly they found themselves in a game of TV ping-pong.

When they were done with their game, Nolan left Al at the bar and moseyed over to them, asking them what they thought of the game. Briefly mentioning enjoying the game, they immediately went on to bullshit Nolan about knowing the designers. Nolan nodded and smiled, and walked back to Al. Waiting a little longer to drink a few more beers and not seeing anyone else playing it, they left.

The next day, Nolan and Ted got a call from Bill Gattis. No, it wasn't an angry call that their *PONG* had broken down, that's a long told myth. The call was because Bill noticed something pretty peculiar that morning after opening up that day. Besides the usual drunks that come in that early to drink, a couple of guys came in and made a beeline to the *PONG* game - no drinks in hand. After some digging it turned out they were people from a competing engineering firm, Ramtek Corporation. Maybe the two guys Nolan had talked to actually did know someone and tipped them off to the new game, because they were there studying it and would eventually release a clone of their own the next Spring.

In about a week and a half to two weeks though, they did get a friendly call from Bill Gattis about *PONG* breaking down. Al went over to Andy Capp's to take a look at what was causing the problem and found a small group waiting to play the game, upset that they couldn't get their fix. Figuring it could have been any one of many different things because of how cheap it had been made, Al pulled out the barrel and gave the patrons a free play to shut them up while he worked. In fact, about a week after this call Al would be called back again, this time fixing the POTS inside the spinners. Doing the math, Al figured out every player spun the spinners at least 15 or 20 turns every game, which meant that multiplying that by the number of quarters in the laundromat coin box at the time meant the spinners were getting around a 100,000 turns in a month - well past the intended lifetime of these POTS.

They needed to replace them with a higher grade version: Allen Bradley's JAN (Joint Army Navy) POTS, which were military grade spinners.

At this visit though, after opening the laundromat coin mechanism, Al was startled to find about $100 in quarters spill out. There simply wasn't anymore room for coins. That $100 also meant there had been a good 400 plays since the last time they emptied out the coin box the week before. Nolan had flown out to Chicago again to meet with Bally, displaying a portable version that hooked directly into a TV for discussion purposes about the coin-op. Bally wasn't biting; there were still questions on the potential of the game since the game played on the screen was so simple looking compared to the more dazzling looking *Computer Space*. When Nolan got back though, and Al reported to him and Ted what had been going on at Andy Capp's, they realized something really good was going on here. They decided to build 12 more *PONG*'s in full size cabinets; Ten to put out on routes, one to keep at Syzygy/Atari, and one to send to Bally to evaluate for their video game portion of the contract.

Over the next several weeks, the earnings from the 10 *PONG*'s were good... really good, completely blowing *Computer Space* earnings out of the water. Nolan kept in touch with Bally to find out their thoughts, but for some reason they kept stalling. It was making Nolan and Ted a little nervous, because the contract with Bally had been for a specific number of months, and instead of going on to do the driving game Nolan wanted, here they were putting their efforts into this electronic ping-pong game. As an engineering firm, the future of Syzygy/Atari was in Bally's hands, and limbo is not an enviable place for any firm relying on one major contract to be. So... Nolan, Ted and Fred put together an income report from their *PONG* locations to try and give Bally some incentive. There was just one problem though: when they actually put it on paper, Nolan and Ted realized the earnings were way too high for Bally to believe. Almost as if Nolan and Ted had 'cooked the books.'

So they did what anyone in their position would do; they cooked the books. But in this case to make it look like they took in less so it would be more believable. First cutting them down by a half, the numbers still looked too high so they went to one-third. A couple of the machines were much lower in earnings than the others, so Nolan suggested that they not cut those ones so drastically. Ted said though, "If we're going to lie, then we have to be consistent so we remember what the lie was." Nolan agreed, and they submitted the drastically cut earnings to Bally.

It didn't work though, and Bally didn't accept the numbers, considering them too high. They were at a stalemate. The earnings were really good; they obviously had a product with strong potential, because people... average everyday people... wanted to play it. But now since they had already submitted the game to Bally, they couldn't go anywhere else with the game until Bally declined the game... and they still weren't doing that either.

Squeezing More Juice...

N
olan and Ted were in Nolan's office trying to figure out what to do when they decided maybe they could get someone else to manufacture and distribute *PONG*, possibly even Nutting. Nolan had stopped into the Nutting booth at the MOA show in Chicago that past September, attending the show while he had been there to demonstrate the portable *PONG* in the Bally board room. Steve Bristow and his wife had been there for Nutting, showing off the 2-player version of *Computer Space* - only it wasn't Nolan's design. Apparently Bill Nutting had simultaneously contracted an engineer to design and build a competing version to the Nolan designed one that Steve and his wife had prototyped, and decided to go with the former. Steve was looking at leaving Nutting right after the show, so without a lead engineer Nutting might be amicable to another game from Nolan. It was worth a shot, right?

The meeting with Bill didn't go well at all, in fact it went horrible. After the 2-player *Computer Space* experience, Nutting felt he didn't need Nolan or Syzygy/Atari and could easily bring in other engineers to do new games for him, cutting out the need to pay them royalties.

Realizing they couldn't go to any of the other big Chicago names, and the only other local manufacturer was out, they had to do something. Nolan, Ted and Al were in Nolan's office discussing their frustration, when Ted hit on an idea of getting Bally to reject the game and manufacturing it themselves: "Either we build it ourselves or we go home. I don't want to go home!" They went over what the costs would be and Nolan and Al agreed that they couldn't afford to do it, all three haggling back and forth on the pluses and minuses. Ted echoed the demanding statement again and said that they needed to make a decision, saying, "If we decide to build it ourselves then we can work on how to get it done. If not, we go home." Nobody opted for 'going home.'

It was settled. Syzygy/Atari would enter the manufacturing business. There was no 'bottle of champagne' and no toast or celebration to a defining moment in the company's history. The three just went right to work deciding who would do what. Ted said that he would handle the TV's and cabinets and Al and Nolan could work on the PCBs and components.

Next came dealing with Bally and getting them to formally reject *PONG*. Working together, Ted dictated most of the letter that would decide their future, if not that of the video coin-op industry. Picture Obi-Wan Kenobi doing his Jedi mind trick through a letter, because that's what was going on here. "This isn't the game you're looking for... we'll give you another." Nolan sent it off, asking for written refusal of the game and while they waited, Nolan, Ted and Al focused on getting their manufacturing resources together.

The PCBs and components were the easiest to take of. A guy named Marty Carlucci happened to have a PCB manufacturing shop literally right across from their back shipping at 2930, and they already had contacts with IC (integrated circuit) suppliers from their Nutting days.

Ted found a Hitachi TV supplier in San Francisco that would sell him 50 TV's for $60 each. Using money in his savings account, he bought them and had them shipped down, beginning the process he had developed of stripping their tuners and turning them into monitors.

They also had cabinet contacts from Nutting, who had used P.S. Hurlbut Woodworking Inc. for their *Computer Quiz* cabinets. Although Nolan and Ted had used another contractor for the first 12 test *PONG*s, this was different. This was for machines actually being sold. Ted contacted P.S. Hurlburt and gave the manager Frank a drawing of the cabinet they had used for the first twelve *PONG*'s, telling Frank what was going on and saying they needed 50 cabinets, "but I don't know when we would be able to pay for them." Frank's only response was, "You can pick them up in two weeks." Ted countered with the fact they didn't have a truck, and Frank said, "I'll deliver them. What's your address?" Maybe it was blind faith - the fact that not only would Frank NOT take money up front, but that he also offered to deliver them. For whatever reasons he had for his benevolence, it was simply unheard of.

In the meantime, Nolan and Ted's letter had worked. Bally got back to them stating they weren't interested in *PONG*, but that they'd still want another game as part of the contract. That could wait, and when Midway contacted them and said they still were interested in *PONG* even if their parent company Bally wasn't, they had to be put off for a future licensing deal. After all, Syzygy/Atari was going to be manufacturing *PONG* now, and the last thing they wanted was another company releasing one as well right out of the gate.

When the cabinets and PCBs came in that early November, Ted and Al started the process of putting the fifty *PONG*'s together. Not as cramped as the original prototype, but it still was a heck of a lot of work. So they began hiring people to come in and help with the first run.

Picture this scene: A small, cramped shipping area (1700 sq. ft. to be exact) full of fifty *PONG* cabinets in various states of assembly - *PONG*s with no actual customers to buy them, and the man who, up to this point, is the public face and the negotiator of the small engineering firm standing there watching. Ted looked up and saw Nolan standing there, surveying everyone. Ted takes a break, walks through the maze of cabinets over to Nolan and asked him what he's doing. Nolan looks at him like, "What do you mean what am I doing?" Ted continues, "Well you have to sell all these things." As Ted's comment sunk in, Nolan literally turned white. He had zero experience as a sales person, which was a far cry from negotiating engineering contracts. Sure he had some Carny experience from his days at Lagoon as a kid, but would enticing people to step up to have you guess their weight translate to selling fifty PONGs? Nolan disappeared into his office to find out.

An hour and a half later, he came walking out of his office and over to Ted, and Ted asked him how it went. Then Ted noticed a weird look on Nolan's face; one that he had never seen on Nolan before - a look of astonishment. Nolan slowly answered, "I made three phone calls and sold three hundred units." Nolan had found his calling.

Ted just stared at him in amazement for a bit, and then Nolan began breaking down the numbers. Bob Portale Entertainment bought 150 *PONG*'s, 50 were purchased by another guy and 100 were sold to another buyer. First excitement set in, then more terror. They were already maxed at the 50 cabinets they had, so what were they going to do for all the rest? They were going to need more people too!

Credit is of course important when starting a new business, it allows you to do things like buy equipment or pay off suppliers and other expenses when you don't have the up-front cash. Right now they had no credit and were going to be in desperate need of it in order to start ramping things up to fill these orders. Nolan came up with the idea of having their largest customer, Bob Portale, write up a purchase order that he could take to a bank and use as leverage to establish credit.

Ted contacted Gary Teasdale at Wells Fargo Bank in Cupertino, whom he knew from banking there himself, and made an appointment. On the way over, Nolan told Ted to let him do the talking. Ted told him to be careful; he knew Gary and he wasn't going to see any upside, just the downside in giving credit, so he'd be more interested in hearing about that. Nolan cut him off and said, "Oh, I know, I know." So Nolan did all the talking in the meeting, using his newfound confidence to sell Gary, and then spent the ride home raving about how good the meeting had gone. But two days later, Ted got a call from Gary saying he wasn't going to give them credit... and wasn't thrilled about loaning money to a company that basically didn't exist yet. Nolan knew he screwed up, and now Ted had to go in and fix it.

Ted went back to Gary and talked 'uncle' to him as he puts it, and lectured him: "That's what your money is for (helping new companies establish credit) - your money is for that sort of thing." After talking frankly back and forth, Gary finally agreed to give them a $3000 line of credit.

The next hurdle came when they ordered more cabinets, and Fred from P.S. Hurlburt brought them right over without staggering the order. Now they have close to 300 cabinets stacked inside their small space and outside in the parking lot with nowhere to move, let alone continue to put them together. What on earth were they supposed to do?

As fate would have it, the answer would present itself that very night. The office unit next door had been occupied by a candle manufacturer who had recently come under hard times. Under cover of the night, they had simply moved out and took off. In Ted's pragmatic mind, the quickly vacated space, the same size as the space they were now renting, presented a perfectly timed opportunity. Grabbing a saber saw, he walked up to the wall separating their work area and the one next door and simply started cutting - cutting a full doorway through the wall, large enough for people and *PONG* machines to be shuttled through, and that's exactly what they did. The entire overflow of *PONG* cabinets were moved into the extra space. They were now set to move on with the building of the 300 *PONG* machines.

The next day, the manager of the complex came by, screaming at Nolan and Ted, "You can't do that!" Nolan stared him down and said, "We did it. It's done. You just have to figure out how much it's going to cost." Talked down, that's exactly what the manager did. Nolan and Ted literally had doubled their space overnight. Of course, that still wasn't enough - as they soon found out as the new area filled up quickly. Nolan immediately started looking for more space for manufacturing. They also started looking left and right for more people to keep up with the pace of manufacturing, which showed no signs of slowing down.

One of those people who came in looking for a job was a long haired teen named Jeff Bell, who had wanted to do video games after seeing a *Computer Space* earlier that year. Sick and in the hospital, a good friend (Derrick Becker) came to visit and told him about a great job he had landed at this new company working out of a garage; Syzygy. Derrick was servicing pinballs and *Computer Space* machines on the Syzygy route and had told Jeff about a new game coming out from them called *PONG*. So when Jeff got out of the hospital that November, he made a beeline over to the garage with his friend Keith to sign up for a job. It turned out that at that point, most of his high school buddies were working there as well. Cheap labor provided by long haired hippie teens with zero experience was certainly a plus for the cash strapped Nolan and Ted.

Jeff was introduced to Nolan who was the acting HR person at that point as well, and Nolan put him on a *PONG* for a half hour to forty-five minutes. Going back to Nolan's office, Nolan asked him what he thought. Jeff's face burst with glee and he just said, "Yahhh!" Nolan asked him, "Do you want to work here?" and Jeff countered with "Yahhh!" That was then followed with Nolan asking Jeff when he could start, and Jeff said "I can't." He went on to explain about his medical issues and that he couldn't start until his doctor gave him the OK. That actually turned out to be sometime in February when he became the third *PONG* inspector, one of three people responsible for checking over a *PONG* machine at the end of production before it was shipped out. In fact at the completion of the process they'd stamp their own specially numbered personal inspection stamp by the monitor shelf. Those lucky enough to actually own a *PONG* today that was inspected by Jeff can look at his number twelve stamp proudly and recall this young man who would become a lifer at Atari.

As 1972 closed out, Nolan and Ted had no time to look back. If they did, they would have seen how in less than a year they had come from working for someone else… to owning their own engineering firm… to now becoming a coin-op manufacturer and employing over 40 people. No, Nolan and Ted only had time to look to the future. Though if Ted hadn't been so involved in keeping operations going, he might have seen the warning signs that Nolan was already looking toward a future without him…

Chapter 2 Review In Images

The actual address used for Atari's incorporation - Ted Dabney's second home.

The original location of Syzygy Company/Atari Inc. - 2962 Scott Blvd.

654542

FILED
In the office of the Secretary of State
of the State of California

JUN 2 7 1972

EDMUND G BROWN Jr, Secretary of State

By _____
Deputy

ARTICLES OF INCORPORATION

OF

ATARI, INC.

FIRST: The name of the corporation is:

ATARI, INC.

SECOND: The corporation's purposes are as follows:

(a) Primarily to engage in the specific business of manufacturing, distributing and selling of novelty games.

(b) To engage generally in the business of inventing and licensing of games.

(c) To engage in any business related or unrelated to those described in clauses (a) and (b) of this Article SECOND and from time to time authorized or approved by the Board of Directors of this corporation;

(d) To act as partner or joint venturer or in any other legal capacity in any transaction;

(e) To do business anywhere in the world; and

(f) To have and exercise all rights and powers from time to time granted to a corporation by law.

The above purpose clauses shall not be limited by reference to or inference from one another, but each such purpose

HOPKINS, JORDAN, MITCHELL & SULLIVAN
ATTORNEYS AT LAW
SAN JOSE, CALIFORNIA 95112

between the shares of the corporation or the holders thereof.

IN WITNESS WHEREOF, the undersigned and above-named incorporators and first Directors of this corporation have executed these Articles of Incorporation on June 5, 1972.

NOLAN K. BUSHNELL

S. FRED DABNEY

PAULA N. BUSHNELL

JOAN M. DABNEY

-3-

HOPKINS, JORDAN, MITCHELL & SULLIVAN
ATTORNEYS AT LAW
SAN JOSE, CALIFORNIA 95112

The Board of Directors
Atari, Inc., a California corporation

The undersigned, S. Fred Dabney and Nolan K. Bushnell, are the General Partners of a partnership doing business under the name of "Syzygy Company" (herein called the "firm"). For the consideration and upon the terms and conditions hereinafter set forth, the undersigned hereby offer to sell and transfer to you certain of the assets of the firm, which assets are described on the Statement of Assets and Liabilities attached to this offer, in consideration for your agreement to do the following:

1. To assume and pay those certain debts and liabilities of the undersigned as set forth in the said Statement of Assets and Liabilities attached hereto.

2. To issue and deliver fully paid and non-assessable shares of your $1.00 par value capital stock on the condition that you shall have first rendered a Notice of Issuance of Securities to the Commissioner of Corporations of the State of California to the persons and in the amounts as follows:

Nolan K. Bushnell   3,000 shares;
S. Fred Dabney   2,000 shares.

3. To issue and deliver your 6 year 5% note in favor of the undersigned in the following amount:

To Nolan K. Bushnell $3,321.00
To S. Fred Dabney $2,711.00

If you should accept this offer, the undersigned agree to hold and use said assets for your account from and after July 1, 1972 and will transfer, assign and deliver possession of said assets to you when you inform the undersigned that a Notice of Issuance of Securities' receipt has been obtained from the State of California. The undersigned further agree to execute and deliver to you such instruments of transfer and other documents as

Plaintiff's   5
WENDY   6-28-'06
Bushnell Depo.

1 unsigned, entitled "Affidavit" and it states in part "I,

2 Nolan Bushnell, of (   ) hereby state and

3 affirm that as of the 1st of June 1971 I no longer had any

4 obligatory duties to Nutting and Associates" and it goes on.

5 Do you recall having seen that affidavit before?

6 A. Yes, I have.

7 Q. Do you know who prepared it?   A. Bally Corporatic

8 Q. Did you provide them with the information for its prepara-

9 tion?   A. No, I didn't.

10 Q. Do you know, did they ever give you any reason why they

11 prepared it?   A. They felt that there might be

12 some kind of a conflict because I was previously in the employ

13 of Nutting, and there was a document signed with Nutting with

14 regard to certain things, certain tasks, that I would perform

15 there, and they were concerned since they were in competitive

16 areas that there may be some cause for legal action.

17 Q. Do you know if you signed the form Affidavit which com-

18 prises the third page of Bushnell deposition Exhibit 2?

19 A. Yes.

20   MR. HERBERT:. I would like to point out to the witness

21 the third page of Exhibit 2 looks very similar to the fourth

22 page of Britz deposition Exhibit No. 3 and request that the

23 witness look at it more closely rather than upside down as he

24 is doing now.

25   MR. ANDERSON: That is an excellent suggestion. I might

26 say I'm not trying to create an erroneous record, I only want

Court testimony where Nolan testified to signing an affidavit for Bally that he no longer had any obligations to Nutting Associates - Even though he was still overseeing the design & creation of his 2-player *Computer Space* for Nutting.

(408) 247-4825

SYZYGY CO.
ENTERTAINMENT ELECTRONICS DEVELOPMENT

NOLAN K. BUSHNELL
PRESIDENT

2962 SCOTT BLVD.
SANTA CLARA, CA. 95050

(408) 247-4825

SYZYGY CO.
ENTERTAINMENT ELECTRONICS DEVELOPMENT

ALLAN E. ALCORN
SENIOR STAFF ENGINEER

2962 SCOTT BLVD.
SANTA CLARA, CA. 95050

Right: Nolan and Al's original
Syzygy Company business cards

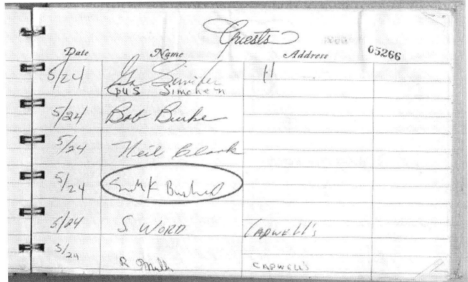

Top: Nolan's signature in the Magnavox Caravan guest book from May 24th, 1972.

Bottom: Signatures from Nutting Associates President Rod Geiman and Charles Fibian.

The original Andy Capp's
PONG prototype.

A look inside. Notice the standard black & white television.

Top: The PCB
manufacturer
across the lot,
2930.

Left (l to r): Ted
Dabney, Nolan
Bushnell, Fred
Marincic, Al
Alcorn.

P.S. Hurlbut would still be producing Atari's cabinets some 15 years later. Seen here are cabinets for Atari's *Asteroids Deluxe*.

Chapter 3

CH..CH..CHANGES
Major changes as Syzygy/Atari becomes just Atari

92

POWER TO THE PEOIPLE
Atari's people shine when some changes don't

101

14600 Winchester Blvd.
Los Gatos, Ca. 95030

Ch..Ch..Changes...

The Doors… Country Joe and the Fish… Janis Joplin… Jimi Hendrix… Psychedelic body painting… *PONG.* What do they have in common, you ask?

Answer: the new manufacturing location Nolan found in January 1973.

Located just up the street from the Syzygy/Atari building, the 1600 Martin Avenue address had an amazing and available 10,000 square feet. During the late 1960s, it had been a local hippie hangout; a concert hall called the Continental Ballroom. Jimi Hendrix was the last rocker to play there before it was converted into a roller rink, which is what it was still set up as when Nolan found it. Looking it over with Ted, Nolan was worried about justifying the cost of such a large place and its farther-than-expected location from their headquarters. Ted responded, "We don't have to justify it to anybody - it's our company." And with that, they went through with the purchase.

Nolan and Ted were also continuing to hire people from anywhere and everywhere to meet their needs for *PONG* production as more orders kept coming in. They raided the high schools, the local colleges; they were even picking up hitchhikers off the streets to come and work for them and build *PONG*'s.

If you could transport back and talk to some of the young hippie women who walked through Syzygy/Atari's doors looking for work at that time, it was clear there was a sexual segregation of sorts going on. Just about all the women coming in were put on the job of stuffing *PONG* PCBs while the men were assigned to build the actual machines. Even Cynthia Villanueva, the secretary at Syzygy/Atari had spent some time helping out stuffing PCBs before moving on to other odd jobs. About the only difference between that PCB stuffing line and a modern day cocaine lab is the fact that the women working on *PONG* PCBs weren't naked. Well for the most part… as it was the sexual 70s in California and some of the women certainly dressed for the times. But it would have been hard for a woman coming in during the *PONG* days to get any other job there.

Christine Maddox (though she was Bush at the time) is representative of one of those women. A free spirited young hippie girl who had come from the East Coast to San Francisco like so many young teens, to live the hippie dream as summed up in a popular 'Mamas & the Papas' song. She had actually worked at the Continental until it closed down in 1969. After drifting around following bands and holding several jobs (including a PCB stuffing job), she was now living with a roommate named Betsy, who herself was working at Syzygy/Atari stuffing *PONG* PCB boards by hand. Betsy talked her into leaving one PCB stuffing job for another, and the difference was stark. At her previous job they had machines to help the women stuff and solder PCBs, but at Syzygy/Atari, everything was done by hand.

In fact, because of how quick Syzygy/Atari was growing, pretty much everything was done in a spartan cost-saving manner fueled by Nolan's wheeling and dealing. At one point when they were looking for more parts for manufacturing *PONG* PCBs Nolan had, in a fit of showmanship and bravado, bragged to Ted and Al he could buy a particular expensive component in bulk below their normal $.08 cent cost. Getting on the phone, an hour later he returned to say he had gotten parts for $.03 1/2 cents from the supplier. Except he wasn't telling the full story, as Ted and Al found out when Al quickly ran out of the needed component. Letting Ted know and wondering aloud how this could be because their suppliers were really good about delivery, Ted contacted the distributor, only to find out Nolan's victory had been at the cost of something more important: shipping. They wouldn't ship the parts to them for that negotiated cost. With no choice (because they couldn't have manufacturing stop), Ted had to run over to a local electronics store and buy the components in bulk - for $.15 each.

There was no denying there was this 'seat of the pants' figurehead manage-ment style growing around Nolan. Ted was so busy overseeing actual operations that the pinball portion of the Bally contract had long been abandoned in favor of *PONG* operations. It also meant Ted was becoming less and less of a grounding force in Nolan's plans, ceasing to become the Id to his Ego; his own personal Jiminy Cricket.

But when news outlets caught on about the groundbreaking happenings with *PONG* and Syzygy and the Associated Press conducted an interview with them in January giving the company its first national coverage, that's when Ted started noticing just how much their relationship had really changed.

Maybe the first signs were when Nolan hired a PR firm for himself instead of for the entire company after their first *PONG* sales. Or maybe it was their conversa-tion after looking at the roller rink they were purchasing, when they returned back to their Scott Blvd. location. Ted passed by Nolan's office to see him staring outside his window as if lost in thought, a look of worry on his face. "What are you looking at?" asked Ted. "All the cars in the lot," responded Nolan briefly before pausing and then stating, "All these people rely on us, don't they?" Ted countered, "Yes, and their landlords and grocery stores do too."

Nolan's next question took Ted by surprise. "What's it going to be like to be very, very rich?" he asked. Dabney, in perfect Jiminy Cricket style told him, "Every-thing would be the same. The only thing that would change is the number of zeros."

But Ted noticed now, when they did interact, it was more of a 'boss to em-ployee' attitude from Nolan than as co-founders. Nolan appeared to be caring less and less about Ted's input. In fact to Ted, it seemed Nolan was treating him like more of a thorn in his side vs. a valuable asset and friend. Nolan's behavior conveyed to Ted that he was living his own dream and vision - a vision that he now demoted Ted to as a follower of, and no longer a participant in a mutually shared, contributing partnership.

Ted always felt that he personally was more geared to that of a creator and a doer than toward being management material. The stock they had assigned for the company was about to be formally issued, now that it looked like the company was actually going to be worth something. With all the stock tied up between just the two of them and their respective spouses, it'd be harder to lure in upper management talent with nothing to offer them.

Perhaps in Nolan's mind, what he was about to do was business and not personal (which he also stated in court documents) – but that isn't how this played out. The following is an accounting of those events as recounted to us by Ted Dabney and via substantiating court records and emails:

On February 5th, 1973, Nolan and Ted had a meeting; their last meeting as equals. It was clear from the onset of the meeting that Nolan now viewed Ted with contempt and as an obstacle in the way of his personal future, his potential fame and fortune. He states in this meeting that he wants to buy Ted out of his share of the company and for Ted to leave the company to go his own way. Suffice it to say, Ted was equal parts shocked and equal parts angry, but he wasn't going to back down without duking this out. At this point, that's when the REAL venom oozed from Nolan, his attempt at trying to play hardball… insensitive statements which included threatening to transfer all the assets from Syzygy/Atari to another company, leaving Ted with nothing.

As the unconscionable threats continued from Nolan, Ted finally had enough and capitulated. It simply wasn't worth this insanity, trying to keep his position as co-founder in the company – especially if this was just a small slice of the future he could expect to have, remaining business partners with Nolan - the very different and polar opposite Nolan… light years different from the one that had spent many nights at his house, and who engaged his daughter Terri to help babysit his youngest.

When it came down to it, Ted simply didn't care about the mass amounts of money that Nolan was sure 'he' was going to make. As Ted puts it, "anything over a full belly is just gravy." What he did care about though was ensuring that full belly and more importantly, being able to make sure his family's bellies were full. By that time, he and Nolan had been drawing regular paychecks, and Ted's $60,000 a year was pretty much all he was looking to keep. So he agreed to sell his shares back to the company but also wanted to stay on doing what he had been doing: keeping things under control for manufacturing, checking out facilities, supplies, etc. – having the ability to keep that regular paycheck.

The two entered into tenuous negotiations during the month of February, bringing in their lawyers to haggle with each other. Initially agreeing on a $246,418 buyout based on Nolan asking Ted what it was going to take to get him out, Nolan and his lawyer eventually came back with the 'claim' that the stock value couldn't support that amount.

But it was their counter offer that both shocked and enraged Ted. Not for monetary reasons, but for the sheer audacity of what Nolan had done behind his back. The offer was to pay Ted $86,500 for his stock and make up the difference by paying him for his share of company assets, including an additional $50,000 to make up the difference for his share in the 'spot motion circuit patent.'

His share in WHAT?!?

Apparently back on November 24th, 1972, Nolan had filed a patent (Serial No. 309,268) for the spot motion circuit Ted had created in Terri's old bedroom those few years before, claiming it as his own – something which Nolan still adamantly claims as solely his to this day. And the $50,000 wasn't for his direct ownership in the patent (as Ted's name had been left off completely from the filing). It was for his 'interest' in it as co-owner of the company.

Sadly there was nothing Ted could do about it at that point; the patent had already been filed and going into expensive lawsuits would have jeopardized the money he was getting, along with his continued employment at the company, which he financially depended on. So he reluctantly bit the bullet, and on March 1st, signed the papers. Nolan spread Ted's payments out over time in small increments to try and cut down on any cash drain to Syzygy/Atari, as well as accommodating Ted's request to break it up for income tax purposes. After the ink dried, Ted returned to doing what he had been doing - but now as head of Manufacturing, instead of Executive VP of the company. Likewise, what the buyout didn't account for was the removal of Ted from Syzygy/Atari's board, where he still held a seat - at least for another year.

Nolan was now officially the sole 'big cheese' - the President of Atari, overseeing a quickly expanding empire... of one game. Granted, it was a popular game - popular enough that companies were starting to come up with their own blatant ripoff's... companies that Nolan would later refer to as 'The Jackals' after the small wolf-like opportunistic predators of the wild. And who he hoped to - according to an interview he gave in Time Magazine and in court testimony that following year – 'collect royalties from, for violation of his patent.' The same patent he would sign over to Atari later that year so the company could go after them. As if to taunt them all however, on May 19th he ran an ad in *Cash Box Magazine* showing the "One and Only Atari Bandwagon" that the competitors were trying to jump onto.

That March, he was able to collect on his first royalty when he finally answered back to Midway's request to still do *PONG*. Licensing them the game and its technology for a $200,000 royalty, Midway would release their version - called 'Winner' - later that year.

By the time Syzygy/Atari completed its first full year in operation on June 3rd, the company had brought in $3,267,451 from *PONG* sales, the coin routes and the royalty payments from Midway. It also owned $1,713,136 in assets (cash, property, cars, inventory, arcade machines from the route, etc.)... and Nolan was sitting atop it all, very conscious of the fact that he could lose it at any minute.

He needed to trust that the people he kept bringing into the company and the decisions he was making to try and keep Syzygy/Atari ahead of the game were the right ones. So the Spring and Summer of '73 would be an important time of development in the early days of Syzygy/Atari's growth.

Probably the most important event during that period, and ultimately very symbolic of the failure of the Bushnell/Dabney partnership, was the push to fully identify the company as Atari Inc. Stripping away the past (so to speak) by also coming up with a logo in time for their new game in the works - *Space Race*.

The task fell on Atari's first product designer, George Faraco and his recent hire, George Opperman. George Faraco was a creative and out of the box thinker whose first exposure to Atari was when he saw a *PONG* arcade machine. Looking around the back and getting the address for Atari, he contacted them and went in for an interview, after which he was hired as a design director. "At the time there were two places, the original Syzygy office over on Scott Boulevard and then the skating rink on Martin. The first time I went to the skating rink, it was a big building, I could barely see across to the other side of the room. That was because the whole place was filled with pot smoke," recalls George Faraco.

There's a lot of legend surrounding this now very famous logo that became registered on November 20th, 1975 - with stories being told that it was intended to resemble two players playing *PONG* with a tennis net down the middle, to it being a stylistic representation of Mt. Fuji. George Faraco sums all that up very succinctly nowadays with a simple "Bullshit. It was just a design."

Here's how the monumental event went down: George Faraco and George Opperman were sitting in their little area at the roller rink facility and started doodling ideas for a logo on a piece of paper. Faraco saw one of Opperman's doodles that he liked, and picked it. It was as simple as that.

It was first revealed on the *Space Race* cabinet and promotional sheet given to dealers, the former of which Faraco had also designed. Faraco's cabinet design was a throwback to *Computer Space*, a tall fiberglass unit with a multi-faceted surface that was unique looking enough that Nolan even tossed around the idea of offering *PONG* in the same cabinet as well. Unfortunately, the cabinet costs ensured that only 50 of the unique *Space Race* cabinets were built before being changed to a more traditional, but definitely less exciting looking cabinet.

Codenamed VP-2, the concept of the game poetically enough came from Ted Dabney in a single swoop, giving Nolan his 'racing' game and providing a game that Ted thought "seemed like an easy thing to do." The concept was simple enough: Two space ships race from the bottom of the screen to the top while dodging asteroids. Al did the engineering and implementation, and after it was released on July 16th, 1973, the team of Faraco and Alcorn moved on to their next project: *Gotcha*.

The idea for *Gotcha* came from Al and a defect he often saw when powering up new *PONG* boards for testing: if you had a bad gate in a circuit that decoded the segments that made up the scores on the screen, you would see the segments all over the screen. Al's idea was to connect part of that circuit to a motion circuit and make the segments move to create a dynamically changing maze. In *Gotcha*, one player chases the other through the maze trying to catch them; one player earning points the longer they evade and the other gaining points for catching.

Faraco unleashed his unique sense of design - or humor - on the controllers for the design (though maybe it was a sign of those 'sexual 70s' and the open atmosphere at Atari). Regardless, the design also inspired the racy advertising flyer which featured a man chasing (and just about to catch) a scantily clad woman while behind them is Faraco's unique cabinet and controls: joysticks encased in boobs - pinkish domes that players were supposed to palm to play the game. As George recently chalked it up, "They didn't have bumps on them or anything, but the way they were the size of grapefruits next to each other, you got the picture of what they were supposed to be."

Once again, not many of George Faraco's unique designs were produced before the too risqué controllers were pulled from the release during October of 1973. But what George did have also was a knack for was finding good design talent, as evidenced by George Opperman and two new hires by the name of Regan Cheng and his college roommate Pete Takaichi.

Both Regan and Pete have a very natural talent for design in fact. Graduating from San Jose State University with Industrial Design degrees, in 1973 Pete took a job at Atari and brought Regan in for an interview with George Faraco. George at the time had just finished the design on the Space Race cabinet when he interviewed Regan. Regan and Pete would work on *PONG in a Barrel* (a brief attempt to put *PONG* in wine caskets for the bar crowd) before moving on to work on *Gotcha* with George and move on to become very important to the developing Atari 'look and feel.'

At the time though, Nolan and his growing workforce were trying to milk as much as they could from *PONG* by continuing to repackage it for different markets… like with their *Barrel PONG* and *Dr. PONG* custom cabinet. In fact Christine Maddox, who by now had worked her way to being a gopher for the company and was shuttling between both facilities and other odd locations, remembers picking up *PONG* cabinets and having them changed to *PING* cabinets for the Australian market. What Nolan hadn't counted on was that *PONG* was slang for 'shit,' both there and in the UK, so the name had to be changed at the distributor's request. *PONG*

Doubles, started around this time as well, upping the ante by allowing four players to compete in a doubles match while hunched over the same compressed cabinet as the main release of *Space Race*.

The most telling of where Nolan's mind was at during this period was a memo he sent to the Engineering Department on August 3rd, laying out his goals. Among them were to have four games total out by the end of the year, have a 20-player *Gotcha* in time for a show that Fall, and have the packing and PCB done for a "color modulated" consumer *PONG*. Yes, that last one meant he was looking to move *PONG* into the home.

That would have to wait though, because his next decisions would almost cost him the company... and that was the move to bring in a full management staff of his choosing that Summer. First was Dr. John Wakefield, Nolan's brother-in-law, by virtue of marriage to Paula's sister. A psychiatrist and industrial consultant, Nolan brought him into take over as President because he thought John's background would give him a unique insight into the minds of players and what they wanted. Nolan would assume the role as Atari's Chairman of the Board, keeping a watchful eye over things.

Next hired were Richard Mobilio and Pat Karns to head up Marketing. Richard had been General Manager of the Intercontinental Sales Region at Hewlett-Packard and was serving as VP of Sales for a time before Pat took over. Pat had come over from Cramer Electronics, where he had been the salesman supplying Atari with IC's.

Rounding it out was H. Leslie Oliver as Vice President of Finance and Administration. Another defector from HP, his job was to oversee the financial health of Atari after Fred had been let go (as a result of skimming from the company). The people at Atari could tell right away something was wrong with this group, who came in not long after Atari moved its offices to new headquarters on Winchester Blvd. in Los Gatos.

Power To The People...

The new workers helping to assemble *PONG* received around minimum wage, $1.75 an hour. When shifts became extraordinarily long as orders increased in 1973 however, Nolan and Ted found some unique ways to help workers let off steam - and the permissible atmosphere allowed workers to find their own ways for release. This could be anything from the innocent flying of .049 toy model airplanes in the open spaced former roller rink plant or playing pool on the pool table set up in the break room, to riding a skateboard through the rows of *PONG*s being manufactured or taking advantage of the many after parties.

In fact the Friday night beer busts and weekend parties were a major part of these early days. When Nolan brought in the new suits however to manage Atari, the worries about how these parties reflected on the professional image they wanted to create forced the major parties to be moved to an outside location. After one such party Atari management even stood outside the location handing out dollar bills for people to BYOB (bring-your-own-beer) for the next party, so Atari wouldn't be held responsible for that either. The change in specifics didn't stop the mood of the festivities though, and even Nolan still showed that spirit when at the October '73 Halloween party he showed up in a cow costume complete with baby bottle nipples.

Smoking some weed was a pretty common occurrence, both on the *PONG* manufacturing line (and out the side door) at the roller rink, or while taking a break on the docks after the move to Winchester. It was California in the 70s after all, and the hastily put together crew of workers were from all walks of life. Young hippie teens just out of high school, bikers, drifters, the recently unemployed and even job hoppers from assembly lines at the more established tech firms. As Jeff Bell described it, a culture sprung up at Atari from this mix of people, "a bunch of free thinking, dope smoking, fun loving people. We sailed boats, flew airplanes, smoked pot and played video games."

Of course, some of the management was known to partake of the ganja as well, helping to release some of the stress of running a company expanding at breakneck pace. While that may sound incredible to read in this day of random drug screenings and 'no tolerance immediate terminations,' it was hardly the first instance of drugs in the workplace. John Markoff has very entertainingly covered the intersection of drugs and the high tech industry in *What the Dormouse Said*, painstakingly recounting the use of LSD amongst engineers in the 1960s to expand their creativity and how the marijuana fueled counter culture of the late 60s lead the first efforts to bring computing to empower the average person.

That counterculture sensibility was certainly present in the new culture at Atari. In fact as a sense of community began to grow among Atari's employees, so came the attempts to organize and make sure their voices were heard; power to the people, a proud legacy of 1960s San Francisco area. Their efforts to unionize the assembly line, which ultimately failed, did result in weekly meetings with management to hear gripes and concerns. At one point these meetings became very intense when Wakefield summarily fired everyone in the TV modification group in an attempt to reorganize and put his stamp on Atari. While he may have understood the way people thought, he didn't have a clue about how manufacturing was supposed to work - a fact pointed out by an angry Christine Maddox whose boyfriend (and future husband) Steve 'monkey' Maddox was one of the many let go in the move. "Who the hell is going change the TV's to monitors now? You got rid of everyone!" exclaimed Christine. Wakefield stumbled for a bit, and finally stated "Well... we'll find someone." Christine quit after the meeting, ironically accusing the man who was supposed to have much insight into the human mind of having no humanity himself. A number of people - including designer George Faraco - would also leave after Wakefield's continuing masterful demonstration of ineptness. In fact, when we asked George why he quit because of Wakefield he responded: "He had no skills to run a company like Atari and it became very apparent very quickly, so I left. When I first started at Atari, they told me I was going to be rich beyond my wildest dreams. When I quit Atari, they actually sent me a bill for $25."

The workers themselves weren't entirely inculpable for the problems at Atari though, as theft also ran rampant during this time. Some of the members of the TV modification group had been taking brand new TV's and throwing them out into the dumpster as bad - then coming back later to pick them out and pawn them. It didn't stop there, as the routine was duplicated by members of other divisions with additional parts. During *Space Race*'s creation, one co-worker of Al Alcorn's walked out with what were called 'blue line' versions of the schematics, thumbing her nose at everyone's worry about corporate espionage in this demonstration of how lax security actually was. The new suits hired Pinkerton, who brought in security people that were placed secretly throughout the company to try and catch theft and corporate espionage.

Atari's first newsletter was a direct result of this rising culture (or counter-culture) at Atari, because what's a movement without its own printed voice or 'zine?' The very first one, entitled *Syzygy/Atari Newsletter* and released on June 20th, 1973, was a mixture of handwritten and typed content including psychedelic artwork. Besides the work commentary, birthdays, want ads and poetry, an introduction letter from Nolan opened the newsletter. The letter pleaded for workers to "show as much sophistication to the outside community as possible," because their neighbors in Los Gatos were uptight and "the thought of a company composed of longhairs is frightening to them." When the next issue came out on July 25th, the look had morphed into a more traditional looking typewritten corporate newsletter complete with logo and a new name: *The Gospel According To St. PONG*, named by Dennis Flynn of the Purchasing Department after a contest.

It was during these turbulent times in the later half of the year that Nolan and Ted had one of their final parting of the ways. In October '73, Nolan came to Ted to find a solution to the ongoing buyout payouts that for some reason, Atari was having problems paying. Nolan wanted to give Ted the Syzygy coin route as a final solution, and thinking about it briefly, he accepted. He'd simply had enough of working there. Maybe it was the people Wakefield hired to evaluate management positions at the company, who, when they got to Ted, asked the co-founder, "So what do YOU do here?" Or maybe it was the way Ted felt he saw his friend Nolan change for the worse when the money started rolling in, becoming more about the trappings of the money, women, self-promotion and success than the old Nolan he knew, respected and co-founded a company with. Other employees had been feeling it as well, along with the possibility that the real reason he had hired Wakefield to take his place was because he was too busy going off and giving interviews to newspapers and magazines like *Playboy*. At that moment, all Ted knew was that he just wanted off the Atari roller coaster.

Taking the route, he still remained a board member of Atari but never came to the meetings. He was just too busy running his new coin route, which he renamed Syzygy Games Company. There had been one catch with the final buyout though: Ted owned the route but had to pay Atari for the machines every month. A final kick in the ass on the way out, he still had to maintain contact with the company and share space at the old roller rink for servicing operations. Meeting with Nolan at one point, he told him just what he thought of the new management team that he had heard was running Atari into the ground. "I advised Nolan to get rid of all these 'bad actors' that he had running the company," said Ted recently. Nolan tried to defend his pics, pointing out that Leslie Oliver had been Bushnell a hot-shot from HP that had really increased HP's profit. "I reminded Nolan that David Packard being Under Secretary of Defence probaly had more to do with it," says Ted.

Nolan did eventually get rid of the bad 'actors' - in less than a year, actually, but the problems in engineering, manufacturing and marketing had already taken their toll. So how was Ted rewarded for this final bit of insight? In March, Nolan 'orchestrated' Ted's removal from the board by purposely telling Ted the wrong info about their 'secret' subsidiary Kee Games and its ties with Atari. Instead of keeping the information off the radar (as it was supposed to be), Ted was telling people they were actually Atari's subsidiary, which according to him is what Nolan told him to say – essentially setting him up for a confidentiality breach. No longer interested in being a part of the team guiding Atari anyway, Ted showed up that one last time – and the only time he had been to a board meeting in over a year – to sign the papers removing him.

Nolan had managed to surround himself with a court of jesters, and by late 1974, also lost Al Alcorn who left as VP of Engineering to take care of his sick mother. There were still a lot of great people at Atari, in fact just about everyone was working their asses off (and still partying their asses off) to make sure it succeeded. But would that be enough?

Chapter 3 Review In Images

1600 Martin Ave.

Top: The roller rink that Nolan found in January, 1973 and that Nolan and Ted converted over to their new *PONG* manufacturing plant.

Bottom: Employee #1, Cynthia Villanueva had moved from receptionist to wire wrapper.

Top left: Christine Maddox (PCB stuffer and gofer) and Steve 'Monkey' Maddox (TV to monitor mod department).

Top right: Jeff Bell, the third *PONG* inspector hired and one of the "free thinking, dope smoking, fun loving people" at Atari.

Above: Syzygy Co. token from Nolan and Ted's coin route.

Right: Atari's first chip tester, hand built by Christine Maddox.

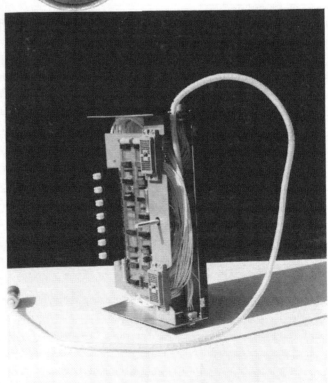

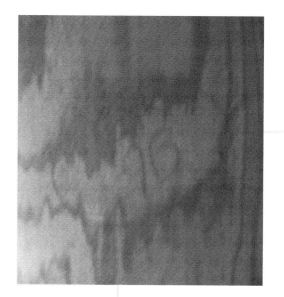

One of Jeff Bell's OK signatures inside a *PONG*.

The first *PONG* ad, from the March 3rd, 1973 issue of Cash Box magazine. Next to it is the original price listing given to dealers.

PONG

The Wraps Are Coming Off.

A TWO PLAYER Video Skill Game

FROM **ATARI** INC.
syzygy engineered

1600 MARTIN AVE • SANTA CLARA, CA 95050

PONG PRICE LIST

PRICE	QUANTITY
$910	1-9
895	10-24
885	25-49
875	50-99
865	100-249
850	250 up

TERMS: 3% 10, net 30

The above prices are available for firm P.O.'s.

Full credit will be given on previous shipments at the lower price for orders if the quantity purchase order is received within three weeks of receipt of your initial order.

SYZYGY CO.

ENTERTAINMENT ELECTRONICS DEVELOPMENT

2962 SCOTT BLVD.
SANTA CLARA,
CALIF. 95050
404-247-4825

ADJUSTMENT PROCEDURE FOR PONG VIDEO GAME

This machine has been fully tested and adjusted prior to leaving
the factory. It has been designed to be as maintenance free as
possible. An effort has been made to reduce the heat generated
by the machine to increase the lifetime of the components. The
following adjustments can be made if the operator feels they are
needed.

    1. The contrast, brightness, volume, horizontal, and vertical
hold controls on the television set still operate as in a normal
T.V.

    2. The end of the game can be set to occur at a score of 11 or
15 by adjusting the slide switch on the printed circuit board. Two
labels are provided to affix to the front of the machine to indicate
where the game will end.

    3. Two (2) potentiometers are provided on the circuit board to
adjust the travel of the paddles. Turn the front panel player
knobs fully counter clockwise, then adjust the potentiometers on the
circuit board until the paddle is as far down as you want it to go.

    4. An anti-slam switch is located next to the coin mechanism.
This can be adjusted to prevent game from starting automatically
when the machine is struck forcefully.

The "PONG" computer is fully guaranteed for a period of one year
after the date of purchase. Should any questions arise, contact
your dealer or ATARI, INC., Los Gatos, California. Telephone (408)
374-2440, Customer Service Department

A statement of quality assurance and adjustment instructions packed in every *PONG*
cabinet. Atari was growing so quickly that this letterhead with the Scott Blvd. address
was still in use even after the move to Winchester Blvd.

Rare *PONG-In-A-Barrel*, made at the Scott Ave. location. Only about 20 were made. Employees took home the unused barrels.

Dr. PONG and Puppy PONG - Atari's attempt at expanding coin-op placement by going in to doctor waiting rooms.

555	FACE OFF	
556	BULL'S EYE (DART GAME)	5/72
557	HOOP-LA (AIR-BALL GAME)	
558	DUCK HUNT	1-29-73
559	DART CHAMP	8/72
560	TABLE TENNIS (PING PONG)	11/72
561	GOLF CHAMP	9/72
562	BOWLING (WALL GAME)	
563	GANGBUSTERS (MACHINE GUN)	
564	PADDLE CHAMP	
565		
566	GOAL TENDER (AIR HOCKEY GAME)	2/73
567	WINNER (T.V. TENNIS)	3/73
568		
569		
570		
571		
572		
573		
574		

Top: Midway's project book showing their licensed version of *PONG*, *Winner*, starting in March of '73. Paddle Champ may have been the original name.

Bottom: An ad run in the May 19, 1973 Cash Box magazine making fun of clone makers jumping on the Atari band wagon.

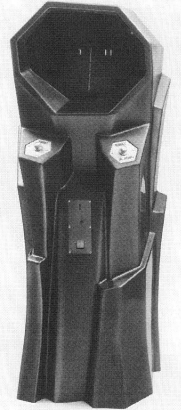

Space Race in its rare fiberglass cabinet.

A previously unseen testing of *PONG* repackaged in a *Space Race* cabinet.

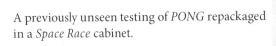

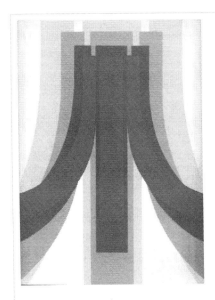

Original Regan Cheng artwork for various
coin-op concepts and a stylized Atari logo.

The 1973 post Dabney partnership lineup

Clockwise starting upper right: Dr. John Wakefield (President), Lloyd Warman (VP of Engineering), Al Alcorn (VP of Research), Nolan Bushnell (Chairman of the Board).

The loading dock at the 14600 Winchester Blvd. headquarters.

Clockwise from top: The lobby at Winchester Blvd., *Quadra PONG* manufacturing, PCB soldering.

2982 SCOTT BLVD.
SANTA CLARA,
CALIF. 95030
404-247-4825

August 3, 1973

TO: ENGINEERING

FROM: NOLAN BUSHNELL

In accordance with a concise business plan, the following is the charter for Engineering.

1) Have a minimum of 4 acceptable production ready machines by December 31, 1973, in excess of the production needs.

2) Have a design and manufacturing set up for a Chicago type coin door A.S.A.P. (Chicago type coin box)

3) Have sufficient staff that at least one engineer can be assigned to "emergency projects" without upsetting major schedules.

4) Have a custom installed 20 player Gotcha for show this fall at I.A.A.P.

5) Packaging for Doctor Pong.

6) Packaging and P.C. for color modulated consumer Pong.

7) Develop staff to provide game documentation and manuals, parts order catalogs, etc. for a more finished type machine.

8) Design a booth for the November M.O.A.

Every effort should be made to develop adequate staffing to handle this work load.

Statements concerning our manufacturing capacity are inapplicable to the above design schedule.

Nolan Bushnell

NB:sa

A potluck party at Atari in 1973 in the coin-op manufacturing area. In the bottom photo, center, is Ron Wayne; the brief third co-founder of Apple Computer later in 1976. (*Photos courtesy of Scott Evans*)

NEWSLETTER

SYZYGY
ATARI

14600 Winchester Blvd.
Los Gatos, Ca. 95030

20 JUNE, 1972

VOL 1   NUMBER 1

The first issue of the employee run newsletter, St. Pong.

Atari's Growing Pains

A Look At Atari's Attempts At Expansion In The U.S. And Abroad During The Early 70s

Nolan began to realize a cold, hard fact during the first half of 1973: there simply weren't enough distributors of Atari coin-operated games out there among the masses. The 'law of the land' had been set up long ago by the arcade amusement industry old guard in Chicago; companies like Gottlieb, Bally and Williams. The law was: manufacturers sold to distributors and then distributors sold the machines to the operators - the people who actually ran the locations where the machines were placed. Most markets (which refers to cities or areas of states where these machines are sold and placed) in the U.S. traditionally had three main distributors, each with one exclusive pinball/amusement manufacturer, one jukebox manufacturer and one vending machine manufacturer that they'd carry. So for instance, one distributor might only carry Bally amusement machines and Seeburg Jukeboxes.

The video game portion of the amusement market in the early 1970s, though growing, was still in its infancy and Atari itself was still a very small company compared to the big names in the traditional amusement industry. With competitors beginning to enter the market selling their own clones of *PONG*, not only was the market becoming more crowded - but the established practice of coin-op distributors only distributing from a certain manufacturer also cut the number of potential customers. Adding to those complications was the fact that international demand for *PONG* and possibly other future Atari games was growing but they had no ability to support that demand.

Nolan, now solely the Chairman of the Board, and new Atari President, John Wakefield set up a series of Atari subsidiaries and partnerships across the US and its territories to boost distribution and placement. They then brought in Ron

Gordon to serve as a consultant to start their international expansion. Ron, in turn, set up Multi-National Corporation (of which he was sole owner) to act as Atari's financial arm and hastily begin setting up operations in other countries. The bulk of these companies and arrangements would be short lived, and more than anything they became proof of the old adage, 'you live and learn.'

International Partnerships

France

Atari was partnered with Socodimex in France until 1975, and considered them the most competent of the overseas distributors who also manufactured. 90% of their business was in game kits (the innards and needed parts to put in a game cabinet) with the rest of their sales in whole games. In 1975, the partnership was transferred to a new company co-founded by Atari and Socodimex: Safari.

Sweden

AB ROULETTEKONSULT was Atari's largest European customer in the early 1970s. Rather than kits, they exclusively bought whole games from Atari, shipping them over from the US.

Germany

Atari had two distributors in Germany in the early 1970s: Seevend who carried the Kee Games line and bought whole games exclusively, and Lowen/Automaten who had the Atari line and bought chiefly whole games from Atari as well. However, in the past, Lowen/Automaten had purchased kits heavily on particular games.

Spain

Segasa was the main carrier of Atari games in Spain, and bought kits exclusively since they owned a pinball machine factory where all assembly was done. Segasa sold under the Atari and Kee brand names in Spain; however they also sold Atari games in Portugal where local distributors used their own brand names, though not under Atari's name.

The International "Atari's" and Subsidiaries

Atari UK

Ron helped set this up with Phillip Smith, who in turn set up Atari UK as an independent company to sell and place Atari games throughout the United Kingdom in 1973. Atari would send over game kits, and Smith would build the finished games and place them. At least that was the plan. Atari UK went bankrupt within a year, and Atari was forced to go through an established UK distributor: Ruffler and Deith. Ruffler and Deith eventually began buying kits and manufacturing Atari games locally as well, and remained the source of Atari games in the UK until Atari opened Atari Ireland in 1978.

Atari Canada

Atari Canada was incorporated in January, 1974 as a wholly owned subsidiary of Atari, with Ted Grunau as the President. The goal was to establish a manufacturing presence in Canada in order to penetrate that market. However, after a year in operation when it became clear that local manufacturing was too costly and unnecessary, Atari Canada was shut down.

Atari Japan Corporation

Atari Japan was formed in August 1973 as part of Ron's push for international distribution of Atari's games in the Pacific. Or rather than a push, it could be called a lob, as Ron's strategy for finding distributors left something to be desired. As Gene Lipkin, who took over for Ron's boss Pat Karns as head of Marketing in 1974 put it, "When Ron first started doing international distribution, he was just giving it to people he met. There were no coin-op people involved." Japanese-American businessman Kenichi "Ken" Takumi had been one such acquaintance - a graduate of the Commerce Department at Waseda University in Tokyo who went on to study modern merchandising methods at NCR Headquarters in Dayton, Ohio and the University of Ohio State. His sales credentials were impressive, but you have to ask what that had to do with running a new coin-op company. Regardless, Ron tapped Takumi to start up what was to be Atari's launching pad for moving its arcade games into the Pacific Rim.

The idea was for Atari to send over game kits, along with other needed parts, and then Takumi would build the full machines in Tokyo, Japan.

From there, he was to sell them to already established distributors across Japan, as well as establish his own coin route to place them on and get more immediate cash flow coming in. After all that was done, then hopefully Atari Japan would start expanding to the rest of the Pacific Rim. Atari would initially start by supplying cash to help jumpstart the company, which would give Atari a 90% stake, followed by sending over the parts on credit.

Takumi, as the President of Atari Japan, was expected to start up the local operations and hire staff on his own. The first position he went looking for was a General Manager, and it was the lawyer that was helping him file the legal papers for the startup that gave him a tip on the right person for the job: his own brother, Hideyuki Nakajima. Nakajima was then a part of Japan Art Paper Company - a long term employee having 17 years tenure. Company hopping was not common to the Japanese culture at that time, where the norm was to give your all to one company for life - a modern day Samurai serving their clan: the Company. Nakajima was becoming disillusioned with his current employer though, seeing an endless number of corporate ladders to climb, even after 17 years. This new company that his brother told him about was looking to bring an exciting entertainment technology pioneered in the U.S. to Japan. It was a chance to get in on the ground level of something that could be big - a clan that he could potentially one day be the head of - so he jumped at the offer.

After Nakajima's hiring, the two started to hire staff to begin manufacturing the coin-ops from the parts being sent over to them. Simultaneously, they looked to create a route to place them in a position to begin earning money or hopefully sell them outright to distributors. To that end, the latter initiative was slow at first, mainly because of Japan's notoriously closed culture and business market; a practice going back centuries. The fact that a U.S. company was trying to open a subsidiary in Japan wasn't exactly endearing to the already established coin market there either – something that became painfully obvious to Takumi as he tried to reach out to the people and companies that ran already established routes or sold to them, to try and jumpstart things. Maybe if it was a Japanese company to begin with like Nakamura Manufacturing, or even a company founded in Japan by transplanted Americans like Sega Enterprises, things would have faired better. Of course there were also the naysayers of the technology, approaching it not much differently than the U.S. arcade industry had when Nolan and Ted first introduced *Computer Space* and *PONG*. It wasn't until Takumi showed up at Nakamura Manufacturing brandishing his 'President of Atari Japan Corporation' business card and an offer that luck began to change - at least for a little while.

Nakamura Manufacturing had been created in 1955 by Masaya Nakamura as an amusement company to manufacture children's rides – giant mechanical rocking horses specifically - and place them on the rooftops of Japanese department stores. Japan had been in a period of recovery from World War II. An intense period of Industrial Capitalism driven by the economic boon provided by the Korean War and its close industrial ties with the U.S. Tokyo, like many other growing metropolis areas in the world, was undergoing a population explosion due to this rapid industrial modernization – and just like any rapidly modernizing area facing massive growth, the transition from 'peasant to employee' starts demanding a large supply of working class basics like clothing and home items. Then there's the demand for entertainment. Nakamura hoped to fill the latter need, and when Takumi arrived, Nakamura was already running a very successful business.

Takumi's offer to Nakamura was, quite simply, that Atari Japan would like to partner with Nakamura for the placement and selling of Atari Japan games throughout Tokyo and Japan for a cut of the sales and earnings. Nakamura took Takumi up on the offer, seeing it as a low risk proposition that would allow Nakamura Manufacturing to get its feet wet in this new technology.

But even when the money from the coin placements and sales started coming in, Takumi and Nakajima found they were still losing money. The culprit wasn't lack of sales - that would have at least been a more honorable way to go out of business. No, the money problems turned out to be via their own employees who were stealing the cash almost as fast as it came in. Atari Japan just couldn't catch a break, and it appeared far more than Takumi could take. By Summer of 1974, he had completely bailed on the company - just literally no longer showing up. That left Nakajima at the head position by default.

Nakajima flew to the U.S. to meet with Nolan and the board to discuss what to do with the company given Takumi's disappearance. He told the Atari board he wanted to soldier on and keep the company going, still feeling it could be saved. He had even started putting in some of his own money to help pay off the company's debt.

The problem was, with Atari's own financial problems gaining momentum throughout 1974 the end of the year was bringing Atari to the realization that their relationship with Atari Japan was coming to an end. "We're losing, not making money from the operations and there just has to be some way to get out and recover something," said Gene Lipkin on the matter. Atari needed to dump Atari Japan while somehow recovering their investment. Hoping to get a million dollars for it, they went to established Japanese coin companies all over Japan, including Taito. Very few wanted the company, and the offers were paltry at best with Sega leading the pack at $50,000.

As a last minute 'Hail Mary," (or as Gene Lipkin calls it, a "boob prize"), they offered the operation to Nakamura. Nakamura was hesitant at first, considering it might be too large of a burden and having no prospects to run the new division if he were to buy it. However, when Nakajima offered to sweeten the deal by staying on for six months after the purchase to help keep operations going, Nakamura saw it as an opportunity to expand his company and the already established partnership with the Atari brand. Negotiations began on July 27th and after an initial offer of $800,000 and some haggling, the price went down to $550,000 by the time a final agreement was reached in August. The sale agreement also called for the return of the 500 game PCBs that payment was never received for, plus a five-year exclusive, technical know-how license to manufacture in Japan only and the rights to exclusively market Atari products in Japan. The license would cost Nakamura an additional $250,000 in royalty payments spread over the next three years.

So while Atari got some of the money back, the sale wound up actually being a far more important investment for Nakamura. His company, which would formally change its name to Namco Ltd. in 1977, would use the former Atari Japan to bootstrap its video game operations - the same operations that would go on to create the iconic *Pac-Man* and other beloved games like *Dig Dug, Pole Position, Galaxians, Galaga, Tekken* and *Soul Calibur.*

As for Nakajima... he wound up staying far past his six month stint, becoming an important part of Namco for the rest of the 1970s and 80s, including starting up their NAMCO America Inc. operations. Ultimately he would return to his beloved Atari brand during the latter half of the 80s, helming Atari Games into the 1990s and creating Tengen before passing away on July 11, 1994. But that's a story for another book.

Atari Pacific Inc.

Atari Pacific was another Ron Gordon initiative that was related to Atari Japan and also presents a lot of unanswered questions in our minds. Like, "What was he thinking having the former President of the Hawaiian beer company Primo Beer, Bill Kaya involved?" and, "How did running a local beer company translate to running a coin-op distribution company?" As Lipkin said about Bill, other than his beer gig, "He didn't know shit." Formed in February 1974 to operate Atari Games in the Pacific Basin area, Atari Pacific Inc. was based out of Hawaii and Guam. Atari owned 80% of Atari Pacific, with Nolan as a board member. While the company was supposed to allow Atari to create coin routes on islands in the Pacific basin for its games, in reality the games were never placed anywhere outside of their Hawaiian and Guam base of operations before the division was shut down and sold around the same time as Atari Japan.

Computer Games LTD.

This company was also started by Ron Gordon in February 1974 to start getting Atari into the Southeast Asian market. Ron had Atari sign a letter of intent to buy 25% ownership in the company to be paid for with $10,000 in product. The agreement required Computer Games to sell a specific quantity of games in the first year or lose exclusivity to the Atari brand. As predicted by the performance of the other international subsidiaries, the company did not meet the minimum sales goal and the relationship was terminated after that year.

Safari, Inc.

Safari, formed in 1975, was located in the southeastern part of France as a partnership between Atari, jukebox manufacturer Seeburg and French manufacturer and distributor Socodimex. Atari held a 35% stake. Safari Inc. was to acquire the assets, personnel and facilities of the French coin-op manufacturer Jupiter; a company being run by Socodimex for the French government after it had been seized for its failure to pay taxes. Atari wanted to use it as a major European manufacturing base. It was eventually superseded in the late 1970s by the creation of a formal entity, Atari France. On a side note, Jupiter's jukebox background and the involvement of Seeburg in the Safari corporation resulted in Atari branded jukeboxes. That's right, Safari did put out jukeboxes in Europe under the Atari name.

U.S. Efforts

Merlin Enterprises

A curious early on effort: Nolan wanted to establish a presence in his old stomping grounds of Salt Lake City, Utah. Merlin Enterprises was created in July of 1973, for the purpose of distributing and placing coin-ops in the Salt Lake City area including his alma mater, Lagoon Amusement Park. Maybe it was out of personal pride in his accomplishments and how far he had come in his career at a relatively young age, or maybe it was out of ego (which had grown into larger than life proportions during Atari's heyday) - or it could have even been just a desire to show the people back home that a former local boy was doing good for himself. But in looking at the bigger picture, Salt Lake City was hardly the next important piece of real estate in the quest for market dominance. Regardless, in the Spring of 1974, the company and its operations were sold directly to Lagoon's owners, Lagoon Corporation.

Kee Games Inc.

To talk about Kee Games we have to go back to the previously introduced Steve Bristow. Steve had done two tours of duty as a co-op Jr. Engineer at Ampex Videofile and was signing up for a third in April, 1972 when Kurt Wallace called him back from Ampex. With Ampex going through financial restructuring and Videofile itself having layoffs, the work study program he assumed he'd be starting after finals at Berkeley closed down. Steve, now in a financial bind because he was (as a lot of college kids would do in these days before loans and grants were absolutely needed) paying for college himself. Thinking quickly, Steve had remembered Nolan was over at Nutting Associates and phoned him up, asking, "Need any help?" So just as Nolan and Ted were getting ready to exit, Steve came on to help debug and fix *Computer Space's* circuitry. Once Nolan and Ted left, Steve suddenly found himself as the lead engineer at Nutting, being the only one that could keep production of *Computer Space* going and possibly design new games. The next several months were busy for Steve: he got married, he and his wife worked on a 2-player version of *Computer Space* that Nolan had mapped out and then he left Nutting after the MOA show in Fall of '72 to concentrate on finishing up at Berkeley.

Still needing a source of income for his last stretch of college, Steve had once again turned to Nolan and Ted, who now put him on the Syzygy Company coin route servicing the machines. Upon graduation in June of 1973 he officially started at Atari and was put under Al Alcorn, working on games like *PONG Doubles, Quad-*

rapong, and *Gotcha*.

Several months into Steve's tenure, Nolan hit upon what he thought would be a solution to the dealer exclusivity issue so they could sell more games to dealers vs. having to front dealerships or routes of their own: set up their own 'competitor.' Borrowing a page from the Nutting brothers playbook, he'd put together another 'Atari' that Atari would secretly own 90% of. This new company would release copies of Atari's games while Atari's manufacturing facilities would secretly manufacture their game PCBs. So with that 'pay no attention to the man behind the curtain' motion, Kee Games was born in September 1973.

Nolan staffed Kee with a motley crew of individuals he handpicked in a style reminiscent of a scene in the movie *Major League* years later. First was the President, who was picked because of his locale to Nolan rather than his background in sales at Applied Logic and IBM. His main qualification was that he was Nolan's neighbor, Joe Keenan. Picture this: one day, Nolan nonchalantly strolled over to Joe's, saying to Joe that he'd basically like to hire him for a company he wanted to start, and that they'd name it Kee Games after his last name and give him the remaining 10% of the company stock. He further explained the whole fake competition and market strategy concept, and that they'd even give him some of the Atari staff and make it look like they left to join his company. Nolan essentially made Joe an offer he couldn't refuse - Joe bit and became the President of Kee Games, which to distributors looked like just another of the many fly by night entries into the new video arcade game market that seemed to be popping up every month.

Next, Nolan went through the ranks of Atari to see who he thought was dispensable or would most likely sign up to go to Kee. Three people wound up moving over to Joe's new company: Bill White, Gil Williams and Steve Bristow. Bill had been an outside contractor that helped Fred Marcincic do an audit for Atari in the Spring of '73. After Fred was fired due to having his hand in the cookie jar in June, Bill was brought into head up Finance. When Nolan asked him to join Kee, he would essentially be doing the same thing he had been doing at Atari.

Gil Williams was another acquaintance of Nolan and Ted's from Ampex, and had come to Atari during its transition to the Winchester Blvd. headquarters, where he began working under Ted helping to oversee manufacturing. When Ted's participation began diminishing, Gil was moved up to his old position just before being moved out to Kee Games as its Director. Steve's move to Kee had bumped him up from a regular engineer to VP of Engineering. The presence of fancy titles didn't mean a thing though, Kee was a small operation where everyone pitched in. Even the sign in the front of their new building was hand-made by Joe, Steve and Steve's wife.

As the Kee startup was set in motion, Nolan's blueprint ensured that the games Steve worked on for Kee as its lead engineer involved tweaking games provided by the Cyan research labs and Atari just enough to be slightly different. Their first game, the October '73 released *Elimination* was the game *Quadrapong* that Steve Bristow had been working on at Atari. *Spike*, released in March '74, was Atari's volleyball game *Rebound* that had just been released that February, albeit with an extra spiking feature on it. *Formula K*, released in April of '74 was Atari's *Gran Track 10*.

Something was in the air though at Kee, because Joe and Steve began having inklings that Kee could be much more than a copycat or "the #2 video game company under Atari" as Nolan wanted. Though Kee had to rely on Atari for game design and any needed game PCB repairs, Kee did have its own cabinet manufacturer. They also had their own equipment and tools that were legally transferred from Atari to Kee. In fact to keep up appearances of a rivalry, instead of transferring product off of the loading dock like a normal pickup, Steve and his wife would come to Atari one weekend in a clandestine move that would make Bluto of Animal House proud. While Steve's wife was distracting the security guard, he snuck inside and threw circuit boards and equipment out a back window to be loaded up in his car. Shenanigans and fake rivalries aside, Joe and Steve wanted to take the perceived competitiveness even further and set up their own engineering department to make original Kee games.

Steve's big opportunity to set Kee apart came in the form of an epiphany he had while thinking about a concept of "what was wrong with *Computer Space*?" In his opinion, it had been hard to control the spacecraft because of the concept of momentum and the need to turn the ship with that in mind. So the next question was "What's easier to control?" Steve remembered back fondly to his youth when he worked on his uncle's farm and ran his tractor. Something that goes forward and back and had no momentum - you could control it. Why not change the rocket ship into a tank and make it a 2-player game? It was that leap from tractor to tank that would provide Kee, and later Atari, with one of its most iconic games: *Tank*.

The code name for the new original Kee game (while Steve built the pro-totype of it) was *K2 Tank*, for Kee Games #2 Tank. Because it was all being done under a compressed time frame with a staff of just Steve, he knew they were going to have to hire someone else to take the game from breadboard and concept to finished product so he could focus on his next vision - an 8-player full color driving game. So he went back to his alma mater Berkeley and interviewed engineers through the campus job office. In the end he settled on a student by the name of Lyle Rains.

Lyle did the heavy lifting on the game, literally cutting his teeth overnight on a technology where he would later be known for birthing such classic arcade games as Atari *Football* and *Asteroids*. His finished game of *Tank* was a sight to behold! Steve's original concept of two players dueling with tanks instead of saucers was now expanded to include a maze of walls to provide cover for the players, plus a minefield no-mans-land in the center of the screen represented by small x's, both of which added a need for strategy and prolonged game play time. The cabinet was a behemoth, more in the style of the EM games someday facing extinction, and hous-ing a (for the time) giant 23" CRT monitor. On the control panel were two pairs of heavy duty dual control sticks; the right one of each with a red fire button on the top. Steve's vision of simple controls were personified in the stick usage: Pushing both forward makes you go forward, pulling both back makes you stop . Pushing forward on the right while pulling back on the left produces a left turn, and the reverse does a right turn.

During this time Nolan was forced to make a choice, because while this was happening, back at Atari the ship was sinking. Due to the poor leadership of his brother-in-law Dr. John Wakefield and the management team Nolan and John had put into place, Atari was now in severe financial trouble. Its rehash of *PONG* themed games was getting tired, and the release of its first driving game, *Gran Trak 10*, had been severely botched. Its international expansion was also a disaster, and it appeared the Kee Games subsidiary was the only positive thing going on. Ironically it was Ron Gordon, the man responsible for the international portion of the financial problems that offered a solution. After Wakefield was let go, Ron was filling in as temporary President of Atari and made a suggestion to Nolan to try and help save the company; close down Atari Pacific and Japan, and merge Kee Games back into Atari.

The popular story is that it was the sales success of *Tank* that caused the merger, but it's not the case - it had yet to be finished when the merger was announced by Nolan in September. Announcing that Atari had 'purchased' Kee and the two were merging, Joe Keenan was installed as President of Atari, Gil Williams came back as VP of Manufacturing and Bill White became VP of Finance. When Al Alcorn was persuaded to come back and fix Gran Trak, shortly after he was moved over to VP of Research & Development and also started overseeing a project Nolan hoped would save Atari and bring in big bucks: a home version of *PONG*. Al's shuffle meant Steve was now instated as VP of Engineering. As Steve would later say about the experience of the merger, "The minnow was swallowed by the whale, but the minnow wound up with all its key people in charge." The new management team (including Gene Lipkin), was referred to at Atari as 'The King (Nolan), the Queen (Joe), and the Five Princes (Gil, Bill, Al, Gene and Steve).' This 'royalty' would form the 'classic' Atari management team.

When *Tank* was released in November of '74, nobody at Kee or Atari had any idea how vindicating Steve's ideas would become. Within a month *Tank* became so successful that the newly merged company started generating the much needed cash for Atari. To this day, Lyle Rains even keeps a reminder of that success: a gold plated *Tank* game PCB set he was given commemorating the 10,000th *Tank* manufactured.

Atari did keep operating Kee's separate brand and facilities, moving it to a new larger location at 1280 Reamwood during the merger and then to fully join up with Atari at the new Martin Avenue location by February. Kee continued operations until Warner Communications shut it down as a brand about a year after their purchase of Atari in 1976. Regardless, games were still being released under the Kee label the entire time before and for several years after. First was Steve's gigantic driving game, *Indy 800*.

Started in 1974 after he turned *Tank* over to Lyle Rains, *Indy 800* was a technological masterpiece, Kee's and ultimately Atari's first full color video game. The common method to add 'color' at the time was to cheat; affixing colored cellophane strips directly to the monitor screen, creating the illusion of a game object in that area being in color. This was commonly referred to as the 'Winky Dink' method, in honor of the 1950s children's TV show where kids would affix a colored strip of vinyl to the TV tube and draw on the screen to create 'interaction' with the broadcasted characters. Steve designed a method to generate actual colored game objects, wanting to clearly distinguish it from the driving games being designed over at Atari. At the time, the cost of a color CRT was extremely expensive, which would have prohibited its use in games expecting a large run. The fact that this was to be an 8-player racing game, large enough to support eight people standing around all sides meant that the unique size and scope of the game moved it to a premium product - significant enough that the additional cost of a color CRT became cost effective. When it debuted in April 1975 at a price of $6,495, it would be the most expensive video game to date.

To anyone walking in to see *Indy 800* during its debut at the MOA show in November 1974, it must have played out much like the early ape men discovering the monolith in Kubrik's *2001: A Space Odyssey*. There in the hotel room suite Kee had rented is a game of gigantic dimensions, supporting 8-players (two per side on the rectangular 16 square foot cabinet) surrounding the horizontally mounted 25 inch display. A four sided canopy hovering above proudly displayed the name of the game and supported a set of suspended mirrors that were meant to allow spectators to see the game play. This was the video game industry's first true multi-player game and the first to encourage spectators. To top it off, it was in full color! *Indy 800* was also provided with bells and whistles like a remote starter for operators to run competitions and Kee provided 'Indy 800 Pit Crew' t-shirts for operators to wear specially for their competitions.

This MOA show appearance also provided a unique challenge for Steve and the guys when they found out the doors leading into their hotel suite where they planned to show *Indy 800* off weren't as large as they had been told. They had requested a room that had double doors; however the hotel's idea of double doors meant a door on one wall and a door on another wall instead of the expected two side by side double doors that would swing open allowing for the large game to be moved in. The game was just not going to fit. Undaunted, the engineers opened up the cabinet and examined the best way to separate sections of the internals and carefully dismantled the cabinet sections so that it could then be moved into the room, reassembled, then fired up to run. This entire process would have to be repeated when the show concluded and they needed to remove the game. It was clear *Indy 800* wasn't going to be your average distributed coin-op because of its sheer size, and that's probably why there are so few left today.

Other games released under the Kee moniker after the merger included *Crossfire* and *Tank II* in May of '75; the 8-player and color *Tank 8* and *Quiz Show* - a quiz game nod to Nutting - in April '76; and the baseball game *Fly Ball* in July '76. After Atari's purchase by Warner Communications however, Kee was shut down entirely and used simply as a brand name. A handful of games were released under the brand; the classic racing game *Sprint 2* in November '76; *Drag Race* in June '77; the multi-directional scrolling *Super Bug* in September '77; and the last Kee branded game and last *Tank* follow-up *Ultra Tank* in February of '78. Short of considering the use of using the Kee brand again in its original vein - to market a Kee branded 2600 to increase the console's market share - the Kee name was retired out and never heard from again.

Review In Images

Top (left to right): William C. Kea Jr. (President of Atari Pacific), Kenichi Takumi (President of Atari Japan).

Bottom: Steve Bristow (bottom center) with NAMCO founder and President Masaya Nakamura to his right and Hideyuki Nakajima to his left in 1976. To Nakamura's right is Bob Skyles (Atari Pinball Division.) Back Row (left to right) Frank Lawson (Atari Manufacturing), Curt Russell and Steve Perrera (Atari Purchasing), unknown, unknown, John Petlansky (Atari PCB manufacturing), Marty Rosenthal (Coin-op Engineering manager).

Top: Kee Games headquarters at 330 Matthew Street.

Right: Kee Games head Joe Keenan.

Bottom: Steve Bristow discussing a plan of action.

Top: The 8-player full color Indy 800 being demonstrated at the '74 MOA show.

Bottom: Indy 800 at the 1975 IAAPA Trade Convention in Atlanta

Top: Nolan playing Tank on the assembly line
Below: The unique control scheme developed for Tank.

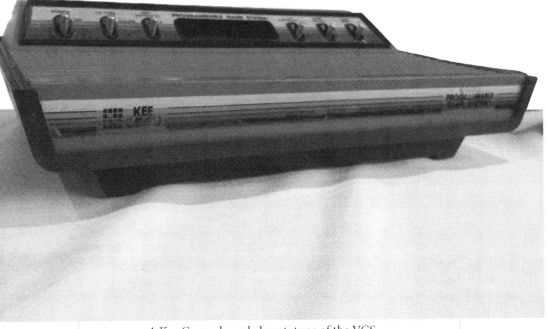

A Kee Games branded prototype of the VCS.

Chapter 4

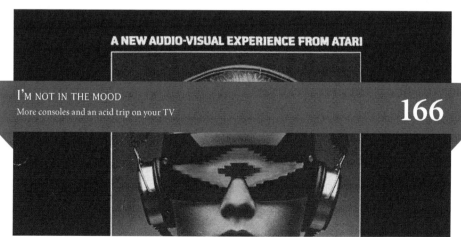

Homeward Bound

Atari was doing very well in the video coin-op industry by mid-1975 and was finally starting to stabilize itself again under the new management team led by Joe Keenan. Coin-op had certainly proved to be Atari's foundation, the technology of arcade video games filling a void in the entertainment field in ways that had never been done before, all thanks to advances in technology, mixed with lots of creative dreaming by individuals who may have been considered outcasts or nonconformists by the rest of the tech industry. For whatever reason, they were drawn into this single gathering place of likeminded folk; this company that was bringing the future within the reach of normal people, enabling them to play high tech challenges which would become the foundation for a whole new era of man-machine interaction.

Their new creations with a mesmerizing mixture of unique cabinet shapes and eye catching artwork, combined with realistic controls and enticing sounds were catching everyone's attention, both young and old. Atari was breaking the stigmatism of the traditional amusement industry being run by organized crime and gamblers, and replacing it with a fully socially accepted form of entertainment. Video games were popping up in bars, bowling alleys, restaurants and of course, in arcades. The machines were becoming the new 'ice-breaker' for opening a conversation; perhaps an innocent challenge of a game or two, some drinks and who knows what else might follow.

Continuing to release a string of popular and profitable video coin-ops, Atari was finding out what could well be called, its 'comfort zone.' Even with things getting better though, they were certainly not easy as there were still many times where bills were due but funds weren't available. Competition was heating up as well and making it through these years while trying to stay ahead of the pack was going to be a struggle.

During this time of growth compounded with trials and tribulations, Nolan's desire to enter the home industry and go after Magnavox finally found its right timing. *PONG* would not only make its way into the home as a consumer product, but it would be in full color too. Having color may not sound like such a big deal today; after all, everything is in color and it's a rare oddity to see a movie or TV show done in black & white for effect. However even though color television was introduced in the early 1950s, by the 1970s not every station was broadcasting in color yet and the bulk of TV shows on color stations - including the staple 1950s and 60s sitcom reruns - were in black and white. This was further reflected in the demand (or lack thereof) of color televisions in the average househould where they were seen as a luxury item, costing considerably more than their black and white counterparts. The Magnavox Odyssey had been in black and white, using screen overlays to add color. Although Ralph Baer's prototype Odyssey – called the 'Brown Box' did have color, producing color was too expensive at the time and would have required additional FCC testing and requirements. So it was both a bold and forward-thinking statement to set forth to have a color video game console system in the home. This was especially true since Atari's own arcade games were all still largely in black and white with the same type of screen overlays as the Odyssey to add color.

It turned out though, that Atari wasn't the first to plan to take on Magnavox in the home market. Although sales of the Odyssey were also slightly hampered by the fact that salespeople were trying to sell the Odyssey as a way to get buyers to buy a Magnavox TV, and Magnavox further compounded the issue by fielding ads that suggested that an Odyssey game console would only work on a Magnavox TV, the sales were still promising. Close to 120,000 Odyssey game consoles were sold over the four months in 1972 alone, and almost 350,000 were sold in total by the end of its U.S. production run in 1974, clearly showing that there were the beginnings of a home market ripe for competition

The Magnavox Odyssey finally saw that competition in 1974, when a few companies sought to scale down the experience of the Odyssey to just a TV-tennis game given the immense popularity of that game in the arcades. Universal Research Labs (URL) was the first to release a home TV tennis type console of its own, called

Video Action. Originally contracted by Allied Leisure to produce its arcade *Paddle Battle* PCB (which rivaled Atari's *PONG* in the arcades), in 1974 URL looked to market the same board for bartop coin-op use and in a home console format as Video Action. Unfortunately its price tag of $499 was well outside the budget for almost any consumer wanting a home game console, virtually assuring sales were dismal and the console would die in obscurity.

Another firm by the name of Executive Games was also looking to put competitive blips and pixels onto home televisions during this time. Started by a group of MIT students in Massachusetts, Executive Games came out with its own home game console called *Electronic TV Tennis*. With an advertised price of just $69.99, their *Electronic TV Tennis* looked perched to take a big bite out of sales of the Magnavox Odyssey until they ran into several issues during design and manufacturing. One serious issue for example was with a necessary low power TTL chip. Just before production they were informed it wasn't available, causing them to try and scramble for a replacement. Unfortunately they weren't successful and only about 2% of their orders were actually fulfilled, causing the operation to fold.

An even worse fate of a would-be competitor to the Magnavox throne was met by yet another tiny flash in the pan company called First Dimension. Founded by Oliver and Hooker with a $500,000 investment, they would try to get their TV tennis game onto the consumer market in late 1975 for a cost of $129.99 a unit. However, with extremely poor quality control, crooked lawyers and just poor overall management putting them $3 million in debt, they would produce only 7,000 units for Christmas 1975. Making a second go of it in 1976 and acquiring a large amount of components to go into a full scale production, their entire business model was thrown into chaos when General Instruments blindsided them with their 'six game-in-one' dedicated game chip that they planned to OEM to any company wanting to build their own home TV-tennis console. With First Dimension's overpriced console quickly losing its value, they were crushed under mounting debt and continued problems with suppliers, production and component inventory. With the company collapsing, the founders would go their separate ways and in their wake was left a pile of debt and a failed attempt at the home video game market.

You would think it wouldn't be that hard to get a product of this type on the market, where two paddles, a ball and a net are thrown up on a screen. It wasn't just about the fun on the screen however, it was what was under the hood. These new entries had tried to unsuccessfully take that arcade *PONG* circuitry and try to reproduce it in a cost effective version for the home. They simply failed. Things were about to be turned on their head once again however when Atari succeded where the rest failed by taking a different route.

Prior to this point, all of the game systems, including video arcade games and most of the nascent home game consoles, were being designed and built around the use of dozens of digital logic chips - the TTL chips we introduced you to earlier in this book. These were wired together and could do just about anything - from making a dot appear on a TV screen, to making a buzzing sound, to displaying who had the highest score in a round of TV tennis. Yet the drawbacks of the technology, in no particular order, were cost, space, power and heat. These issues could be handled by the arcade game manufacturers, but for the companies trying to move it into the home it just wouldn't fly.

Things changed significantly though as Atari embarked into what would be a new territory for them. For their home version of *PONG*, Atari was going to design and build its first custom Integrated Circuit, or as it's commonly known – an IC or 'Chip,' attempting to put their entire *PONG* PCB on a single chip. Now, creating your very own chip was certainly not for the faint of heart; especially back in the 1970s when chip designers and chip design hardware were both few and far between and expensive. Atari's solution came by way of a former Standard Microsystems employee named Harold Lee who had joined Atari in late 1973.

Harold had just finished a 'road trip,' traveling about with a lady friend in a van. She suggested he should come down to the Los Gatos area to apply at Atari where she had been hired as the executive secretary. It may have been the Masters in Electrical Engineering he had, or it could have been that she felt his hippie persona would fit in perfectly, but she persuaded him to come in and apply for a job.

Interviewing with Al Alcorn and Joe Keenan, both Al and Joe were so impressed with Harold's skills that he was hired immediately as a Production Designer. According to Harold, "I fit right in - this was a happening place and my attitude seemed to fit right in - I was just another street hippie. This felt like home. Other places I worked at you felt like desk fodder - at Atari they utilized everyone's talents."

Harold's first assignment was a new arcade game called *World Cup Football* that had just been spec'd out. At that point in time, new concepts for games would be discussed and prototyped up at Atari's Grass Valley research lab. Bushnell, Alcorn, Keenan and others would often take the drive up (or sometimes fly up in Alcorn's small private plane) to throw concepts and ideas around and then the Grass Valley engineers would turn those ideas into reality with circuits in the form of wire wrapped prototypes. Wire wrapping itself is the art of laying out your circuits in a non-committed manner by seating the chips and components into holes in the board and then literally wrapping a wire around one component's post. Stringing the end of that wire to the post of another component, before you know it you're creating circuits along with a rats nest of wires. When they're completed, these wire wrapped prototypes are then delivered down to Atari in Los Gatos, where they get changed into a properly laid out PCB of the type you normally see inside a product.

It was Harold's job to make those production-ready PCBs for the product, with all of the chips laid out, and map the edge connectors for the necessary wiring harnesses to attach a power supply, speakers, video display, coin mechanism and of course, the controls. Many times, the wire wrap prototypes would be delivered late, so it was all too common to work the day shift and the graveyard shift getting the bugs out of the designs and moving them to production level.

Alongside Harold, there were four other production design engineers working on various games to get them debugged and production ready, as well as a pool of technicians that would work with and assist the production design engineers in that process. On a unique side note, in 1974 a young nineteen year old joined this pool of technicians and was assigned to Harold for a time. In fact he should be very familiar to you - Steve Jobs.

Besides *World Cup Football*, Harold also worked on the coin-ops *Touch Me*, *Pin-Pong* and a light gun duck hunting game called *Qwak!* that would years later be copied by Nintendo for the launch of the Nintendo Entertainment System. Harold recalls: "I believe it was on *Touch Me* that Steve Jobs was my tech. We got that arcade out the door and in later years it was stolen by Milton Bradley and sold as Simon." More on Steve and his Atari years later though. *Touch Me* and ultimately Harold are the subjects we're more interested in right now.

The production version of *Touch Me* came in a simple black and yellow pedestal cabinet, but early prototype designs were more 'colorful' in more ways than one! One prototype of the *Touch Me* arcade was done in blue and instead of the flat wide buttons to slam down on when they lit up in the memory sequence, the prototype had big yellow 'boob' buttons, providing for a certainly more subliminally interesting aspect of the game play. The last game to attempt using these "boob" style controllers was Atari's *Gotcha*, but to this day there is still some question as to whether they were really supposed to represent breasts. One definitive answer comes from Don Lange, who had come out of UC Berkeley a year after Al Alcorn and was interviewed by Nolan, Ted and Al at which point he was hired as Atari's second engineer. Don, who helped bring *Gotcha* into production, recalled: "Oh, they were boobs, definitely. You can ask Regan Cheng and Pete Takaichi - they designed the cabinet and controls." Further corroborating the boob lore: "The tops of the *Gotcha*'s controls? Yeah they did look like boobs. Those were done by George Faraco - he had some really far out ideas," recalls Regan Cheng.

After *Touch Me*, Harold was getting burnt out doing just production design work. Working a lot of hard hours and overtime on the various games at Atari had taken its toll. Reaching a breaking point, in the Fall of '74 Harold basically quit. As the popular *Godfather Part III* quote goes though, "Just when I thought I was out... they pull me back in." No sooner had Harold been out the door and looking around for a new job than Al Alcorn called him and asked him if he'd like to do something a little different... at least 'different' than what he had been doing for Atari. Prior to coming to Atari, Harold worked at Standard Microsystems where his job had been to design custom IC chips. During his time there he had designed about twelve different chips, around five of which had gone into production.

Al's question to Harold was: "Do you think *PONG* could be put on a single chip?" Harold said it should be possible, so Al put Harold to task to start laying out a *PONG* on a chip as a contractor. No longer working at Atari anymore (that is to say, he wasn't coming in the door every day), Harold was free to choose where he wanted to design the chip. Harold and a friend of his had just bought a Christmas tree farm up in the hills above Los Gatos which had a cabin, so Harold set himself up with a drafting table in the cabin and in September of 1974. One of Atari's most important steps, its entry into the home market, would rest on the shoulders of one man holed up in a cabin in the woods.

It was under the peacefullness of chirping birds that he began to sketch out the circuits for what would eventually become *PONG*-on-a-chip, codenamed Darlene. This rustic location had become his new company headquarters, which he called 'MOS Sorcery.' Harold broke the design up into different sections, with the initial chip design completed on nine separate sheets of circuit drawings. As he completed each section he would emerge from the woods, bringing that sheet down to Atari and Al Alcorn where Al's wife Katie would then wire wrap that portion. When a section was completed, it would then be wired to the previous sections and Al would debug the design, make corrections and sending them back to Harold who would correct his circuit drawings accordingly. In the end they had what was called a 'Golden Schematic' - the final 'gold standard' schematic that Harold would use to layout the chip.

Once the proof of concept wire wrap was done, it was time to begin laying out the *PONG*-on-a-chip into a single Large Scale Integrated (LSI) circuit chip (a then new technology that allowed an engineer to pack tens of thousands of transistors on a single chip). Applicon Inc., a company founded in 1969 in Massachusetts, provided the needed key to that next stage. It was one of the first companies to provide Computer Aided Design and Manufacturing (CAD/CAM) systems, the computer based systems needed to layout LSI chips. Before CAD systems, chip designers actually would use large sheets of what was called rubylith, which consist of a Mylar sheet with a thin layer of semitransparent, red material that can be cut and peeled off. This 'by hand cutting,' manual process was tedious and prone to mistakes and flaws, usually limiting it to simpler TTL chips. The early Intel 4004, the world's first microprocessor, was originally done in rubylith.

Harold's previous work at Standard Microsystems centered around Applicon CAD systems to design and create chips, so it made sense that Atari's first custom chip would be done on an Applicon CAD system. The problem with the first Applicon systems though was that they stored the designs on a cassette tape. Harold recalls: "The early Applicon's were using regular cassette tapes for storage. They were very unreliable and often didn't store the design files on them. After you've been working on the graveyard shift and working for eight hours, only to find out you lost everything - yeah, you could put the design back together pretty quick the next night, but man you'd be pissed!"

Luckily Harold wasn't working completely alone, and was assisted by fellow Standard Microsystems alumni Bob Brown. Harold recalls: "Once we got to the point where we had *PONG* chips on wafers, we needed to run tests to exercise the chip inputs and outputs to make sure they were working right. That's where Bob came in."

Unfortunately, Applicon systems were also sparse in the Valley. Because of their expense, only a small handful existed. Lucky for Harold and Bob, of the four or so Applicon systems in the Valley, they found one such system set up in an office building in East Palo Alto that could be rented by the hour. It was even better that it was one of the nicer Applicon systems too - with a big, fat 14" wide platter hard disk in it - so working on the *PONG*-on-a-chip design would be a lot easier than the earlier work Harold had done on the cassette storage tape version Applicon systems.

Rental costs were $100 an hour on the day shift and $80 an hour on the night shift, so the choice became obvious and the night shift it was! Harold recalled that working on the *PONG*-on-a-chip design late at night in the Palo Alto office building housing the Applicon system wasn't always uneventful or tedious: "One night I'm working and all I heard were the fans going on the system - it was based around a PDP-11 system. Well I hear someone come into the office behind me and they are stealing the typewriters, the chairs - EVERYTHING. I couldn't do a thing about it. I was only worried that I was going to get blamed for walking out with that stuff."

When Harold had working samples of *Home PONG* chips ready by July of 1975, Atari then needed to ensure it could get them produced and in a high enough quality to minimize failures and returns - the bane of any consumer electronics product producer. Harold brought the chip designs to four different Silicon production houses in the Valley: American Microsystems, MOS Technologies, Synertek and Electronic Arrays.

Surprisingly, Intel was also approached but turned Atari down, being in the middle of their own boom. Intel's 8080 chip was introduced at the end of 1973, saw its speed increased in 1974 – and at the moment Intel was right in the middle of developing its 8085 processor with an expected release in early 1976. So doing 'game chips' was not high on Intel's priorities.

Atari found out that Electronic Arrays could never get a chip done right, so they were quickly eliminated it as a resource. But even with that elimination however, there were various problems with the runs of the *PONG* chips from the other chip production houses. For instance, some had leaky input transistors that made the paddles jiggle, which is not something you want happening during an intense game of *PONG*. Even though Harold got the engineering memos on the status of production, the design was done and Harold was out and off to his next project: the design of Atari's *Home Super Pong* chip as a follow-up release to *Home PONG*, which would incorporate more games into it, including the *Handball* and *Catch* games that he came up with. Any bugs were the Production team's problem now as far as he was concerned, those chirping birds and remote isolation of the cabin were calling him. Luckily the issues were quickly ironed out by Wade Tuma and Niles Strohl, who had recently joined Atari's newly formed Consumer group.

Getting the *PONG*-on-a-chip done was a very important step, but it was only one small piece in a much bigger puzzle of producing a consumer product. Atari was a coin-operated video arcade manufacturer. They knew wooden cabinets, wiring harnesses and big bulky coin-op PCB-based games. Designing a consumer product was a totally different animal and they had no experience whatsoever in this field. However, maybe a major retail outlet like JC Penney, Sears, or maybe even a toy chain…

When the original wire wrap prototype was ready, Gene Lipkin and Al Alcorn flew *Home PONG* to the New York Toy Faire in January of 1975 to begin shopping it around. There was certainly a lot of interest in the new console; especially given it was a product from Atari; a brand that many were very familiar with - in the arcades. But the buyers and the Atari reps weren't quite on the same page on a number of important issues. Issues such as Atari not have any consumer manufacturing experience or capabilities whatsoever, or a set price for the unit. In fact, they weren't even sure how much it was going to cost to actually manufacture the product. Gene Lipkin explains: "We had this meeting with the Radio Shack guys, Tandy, the ones from Texas. Well they are really interested in our product, so they tell us they want an 'Anticipation Discount.' We'd never heard of that before and we asked what that was. The Tandy guy tells us, 'it's in anticipation of us paying you.'" Gene continues: "So we looked at each other and asked, 'does this mean you might not pay us?'" at which point we promptly turn down Tandy's offer to buy." Tandy was in shock. This was when everyone at Atari realized they didn't know how the toy business worked, and that they and their product really weren't ready for the toy market.

However, the appearance did strike an interest in Gene's mind for trying a different market for *Home PONG*. It hooks up to a television, right? Maybe Atari could try Magnavox's route and get affiliated with a major TV outlet? So they tried Sears. As Gene recalls: "It all came down to Tom Quinn (in the end). We built *Home PONG* for your TV. I identified Sears, and we approached their TV department... and were rejected."

The way things work at Sears and other department stores, it's the buyers in the departments who decided on products they want to carry. They themeselves do the research and then go out to fill the need, which makes a buyer the key relationship to getting your foot in the door. "Tom Quinn was in sporting goods: Department 606. He was a rogue - he did all this research on televisions and the market," Gene remembers. Al Alcorn further explains, "Quinn was able to get the Magnavox Odyssey out of the current arrangement of being sold with big console TV sets. He could sell them alone through the Sears catalog. The problem was he couldn't get enough. So here we come along, we've got the real deal and we can provide him what with he wants."

Gene, being the master sales person he is, cold calls Tom Quinn and tells him about Atari and their *Home PONG* product. That Atari can provide Sears with a superior product and in the quantities he'd need, as opposed to the Magnavox consoles Sears was selling. Two days later, bright and early that morning in Los Gatos, Atari has an unexpected visitor: Gene Lipkin's assistant, Jeannie Russell, informs Gene there is someone waiting out in the lobby for him. Gene recalls: "Jeannie says to me, 'We have a guy in the lobby, Tom Quinn.' I said, 'No he's the guy from Sears in Chicago.' She tells me, 'Well he's in the lobby.'" It turned out that Tom Quinn showed up at Atari's doorstep in Los Gatos and he's ready to discuss the *Home PONG* product.

"So, Quinn arranges for us to do a demo of the *Home PONG* at the Sears Tower in Chicago. It's myself and Alcorn, with this wire wrapped prototype on top of this wooden box. We were so worried about it getting stolen that Stevie Kauffman, (later) an executive at Stern in Chicago, kept it locked in his apartment for us overnight," recalls Gene. "We got to present *Home PONG* to Tom Quinn and his guys at the Sears Tower. First of all, I think it was one of the first times Al had on a tie for any kind of meeting. We go inside to show it working for them on a TV they had set up in the room - and it didn't work. Al was sweating bullets when that happened, but he got right under it, changed some things and got it working and we did the demo to Sears."

After the demo, Carl Lind, one of the Sears exec's asked Al Alcorn a question: "Mr. Alcorn, so you're saying you are going to take that rats nest of wires and shrink it down to a piece of silicon the size of your finger nail?" Al responds back, "Yes, sir." So Carl Lind continues with a follow-up question: "So how are you going to solder the wires to it?" It's easy to say Carl Lind was out of his mind, or just out of touch to even conceive of the mental image of taking a bunch of large wires and soldering them to a little chip. But Carl Lind was out of the Appliances division, so his understanding of large and bulky wiring for wire wrapped prototypes versus the complexities of micro-sized integrated circuits for production may have contributed to him asking such a ridiculous question.

As for the prototype of the *Home PONG* console, it worked fine during the rest of the demonstration. There was actually nothing wrong with the unit itself – but given that the demonstration was taking place in the Sears Tower and on top of the building was the largest and most powerful transmitting antenna in the area, this transmitting power completely overwhelmed the TV signal coming out of the prototype *Home PONG* console. Al had quickly realized this was the problem and traced where the channel setting wires were within the 'organized' chaos of wires underneath the *Home PONG* demonstrator. Once the unit was changed to transmit on a different channel, the issue was fixed and the familiar display of *PONG* appeared on the screen of the TV in the meeting room. But the experience compelled them to consider placing channel switches on their consoles to mitigate this problem in the future.

With the demo behind them, Gene and Al returned to Los Gatos to report their mishap and ultimate triumph: they might actually be doing business with Sears now! Nolan, Joe and Gene went into the next meeting with Sears and Tom Quinn, which was to discuss additional issues Sears had. One of the issues brought to the table was the 50 foot ape Atari dragged into the room and in fact had been carrying for over a year: Magnavox, and their April 17, 1974 lawsuit against Atari and several other companies over video game technology patents. Tom questions whether there is going to be any legal issue with Atari releasing a game product similar to Magnavox's. Nolan assured Tom that there was no issue, and they'd be safe to proceed. As Nolan later testified under oath in a March 2, 1976 deposition to Magnavox lawyers, he gives his recounting of what he said to Tom Quinn regarding Magnavox, and their patents: "I think we said that they were suing us and we were suing them, that they had their patents and we had ours and we felt that there was no cause for any alarm." Tom said "Fine" and the deal proceeded.

Next on the agenda was that Sears wanted an exclusive on the product and also wanted it to be a Sears Branded device under a product line called Tele-Games that Sears would create. That was not something Nolan and company had expected to be put on the table, so the Atari contingent stepped into the other room to discuss the terms like a football team discussing their strategy before the next big play. Huddled together, they discussed that giving Sears an exclusive wasn't something they wanted to concede. However this was, after all, Sears they're dealing with. Nolan realized that for once in his short-lived career as a video game maven, Atari (and ultimately he himself) is not in any kind of position of leverage. Finally after some further discussion, the trio returned to the meeting and presented their counter offer.

Atari was not willing to give Sears an exclusive - however, they will commit to shipping the Sears branded product first, with a target of the Christmas sales season of 1975. The counter offer also included that Atari's name had to be on the product somewhere. The presence of a third party name on a Sears-branded product was unheard of at the time - it just wasn't done. As Gene explains: "This is the first time Sears allowed a company to put their own name onto a Sears branded product. The Sears guys thought we were lunatics, we're making all these demands on them, they thought we were nuts." Sears did ultimately agree to the terms however and Atari agreed to sell the *Home PONG* units to Sears for $55 each, which Sears would then bump up to a suggested retail price. On March 17, 1975 Sears signed on the dotted line and the purchase agreement with Atari was completed. Now if you note, for those of you collectors out there who still have one, the Sears Tele-Games *PONG* units actually have the name ATARI on top of the power button of the unit. Not exactly prime real estate, but it was enough to let everyone know who was making these for Sears.

It was after signing that agreement however, that there came a Zen-like moment of clarity... of reality... and once again, of pure terror of the kind Nolan felt when Ted originally told him now he had to go out and sell the coin-op *PONG's* they were building. In this case the terror was in the manufacturing, since they had put the cart before the horse. As Gene recalls: "We had no clue what it was going to cost, but it had to retail for $99 - their first order from us was 75,000 units." Gene continues, "We came from a mindset if we sold 10,000 of these we were going to be rich. The problem was we had no clue how to build them."

If there is one thing that really needs to be understood in all this, it's just how important Sears was to the relationship with Atari. Without the Sears partnership, Atari's move into consumer products would have died right there. Gene Lipkin points out: "We couldn't get money for the purchase order, so Sears walked us over to their own bank. At this point Sears still owned a bank over in Chicago. No one else would give us money, but the Sears bank would." Sears also brought in their quality control guys and their large scale factory manufacturing guys. While Atari knew coin-op, Sears knew mass production and would work with Craig Manning (Atari's Facilities Manager) to get Atari's new consumer assembly building in Moffett Park up to the task. Sears also helped with the RF issues and the FCC compliance submission testing to help make sure something like the Sears Tower demo didn't happen once the product was in the consumer's hands.

The case design and plastics however, the shell of the *Home PONG* - those were Atari's responsibility; more specifically, Al Alcorn's task. Regan Cheng recalls it was a blacksmith and Hollywood prop designer named John Kelso who would design the look of the *Home PONG* 'pedestal' plastic shell. Al Alcorn had found a company to do the machine shop work to have molds built that would stamp out these plastic shells for the *Home PONG* consoles. "I'm figuring, the chip is the hard part - how hard can plastics be? The *Home PONG* plastics were a boondongle. It was done in a little shop in Los Angeles. There was this other vendor and he wanted Atari's business and knew what was going on, so he pays to fly me down with him to do a surprise visit to this tooling shop in Los Angeles. All they had was a drill press and mill in this little garage. There was no mold base - they had nothing," recalls Al Alcorn.

Smartly, Al brought in the other vendor shop, and despite massive complaining from the mechanical engineer (a Welshman who was not too happy with the straightening and corrections that had to be made and not afraid to share that fact), they got it done.

If you're wondering where *Home PONG* got its codename of 'Darlene,' one must also wonder if the console case design was actually inspired by the woman whose name the console was given. After all, the console has a big upper assembly and then curves down to a narrow midsection and then sweeps back out. As Nolan had described Darlene, 'she had big breasts and then the tiniest waist,' so is the console a reflection of this? We'll let you decide.

It was during the design process of the actual PCB for *Home PONG,* that another occurance demonstrating Atari's naivety in consumer electronics design lead to a great story to tell. Generally, a board is designed around the pinouts of the main IC chip, in this case, the *PONG*-on-a-chip. These pinouts are the signals and electrical lines to and from the IC chip to get its power, to send out video and audio signals, monitor switch selections and get input from controllers such as the two paddle knobs on the *Home PONG* console. Only in this case, Atari was doing things a little different, Niles Strohl explains: "The PCBs for the home consoles were being laid out and then we would design the IC chips to best fit into the PC board design, having the lines coming out of the chips match up with where the PC boards had their signal lines brought to the spot where the IC chip would be installed. We were doing things backwards."

After all the electronics and case work were done, next came the formalities and legalities that most of you who enjoy video game consoles in the U.S. probably aren't aware of: dealing with the FCC. For most companies it can be an arduous experience, with many back and forth rounds of revisions and resubmissions to get their product to meet FCC standards. But with Sears' guidance however, it became an almost painless experience for Atari. On July 2, 1975, Al submitted the application for Model 637.25796 TV Game to the Laboratory Division of the FCC along with a $1,500 check for the application fee. Phillip Inglis of the FCC responded on July, 17th that he received the application and Atari was approved to ship the testing sample to the FCC. Atari was now ready to start manufacturing and shipping them off to Sears, getting the company a step closer to their destiny!

When November 1975 came around, Atari was shipping the Sears Tele-Games version of *Home PONG* in bulk, delivering to Sears the initial 75,000 consoles order for the Christmas sales season. *Home PONG* was a huge hit that Christmas season, and along with Magnavox's simultaneous entry into the scaled down TV tennis-only console market with their Odyssey 100 and 200, it seemed the home video game industry was re-invigorated overnight. Unbeknownst to both however, on November 26th, a game changer was taking root that would affect both companies' home efforts drastically the following year.

On that November date, a man by the name of Gene Landrum delivered a 'Business Opportunity Analysis' report to Greg Reyes of Fairchild Semiconductor's consumer products group. Fairchild was interested in getting into the consumer video game market as well, and had begun the research to do their own game console, a project codenamed 'Stratos.' The project would be known as the Fairchild 'Channel F' when it would be released the following year. Instead of a 'game-on-a-chip' design, the Stratos report laid out a game system driven by a microprocessor, with the games as programmed software instead of being engineered. The move would allow games to now be interchangeable, rendering Atari's new home products already obsolete. Luckily at the same time this report was being delivered, the wizards at Cyan Engineering also had their crystal ball engaged on a solution. But that's another story for another part of this book.

Home PONG's success did end Atari's year on a high note, and with things looking up so did the employees (according to the company newsletters). Though mundane in the grand scope of things, Atari's newsletters give a good insight into the family that was Atari at that point. The employee of the month was David West, also known around the company as 'Hurricane West.' December was to be a very special month for David as he planned to get married on Christmas Eve with his Atari cohorts present. Two employees also got promotions, with Jackie Fowler moving from rework to Assistant Lead in Assembly and Rick Gomberg becoming Assistant Parts Manager. On December 14th, the Atari Christmas Party was held in the Sunsweet hall at The Factory. Two hundred employees and friends attended, enjoying a warm fireplace, good spirits, a banquet of goodies and music by The Midnight Flyers. Atari also put together a company Christmas List for the party, with some notable presents being asked for. Ever the jokester, Nolan wanted "An amusement park of my very own to play with," (in reality, he would soon have a mini-version of that Christmas wish in the form of the first Chuck E. Cheese). Elaine Thompson simply wanted "To beat Carl Bishoff at *Crash N Score*." Paul Mancuso asked for that rarely seen California "Snow!!!!!!!!!" and Melissa Fuller wanted "Nolan Bushnell" as her gift.

Atari ended 1975 walking away with invaluable exposure to the disciplines and procedures of producing consumer products from the education Sears gave them. Of course, there were a few serious bumps along the way with plastics design work... They were also getting their feet wet in custom designing their own IC chips... But regardless of what Atari's engineers and designers did in the coming years, they knew they learned from this experience... and would continue to study and improve upon that knowledge. That's not to say there wouldn't be more bumps and humorous stories down the road, but their foundation for dominating the home game market was now set.

Sears would sell the Tele-Games *PONG* through its more than 860 outlets over the following year, giving Atari a nationwide distribution outlet for the sale of its product, and ordering in total 150,000 units to sell. More importantly, Sears picked up the tab for advertising in its catalog and in TV ads as well. "I remember I was home watching a football game and up on the TV comes an ad for Tele-games *PONG*," recalls Al Alcorn. "I remembered back during Christmas of 1972, when I brought home the arcade *PONG* proto we had in a portable steel chassis, hooking it up to a TV in the house and hearing my dad tell me, 'That'll never sell.'"

Atari moved on to produce their own Atari branded *PONG* consoles in late January 1976, which were ready to ship in early February. The home TV-tennis market exploded in 1976, and by the time Atari would release its final single chip console (also known as a 'dedicated console' due to the games being built-in) in 1977, it was joined by over 100 competitors worldwide.

Breaking Out of Myths and Legends

A fter working on *Home PONG*, one day while Harold Lee was working on another game to bring into production, his former technician came into the building. Walking with a defined bounce in his step - as if on air, proud and happy - in his hands was his schematic for a new game called *Breakout*. The technician was Steve Jobs, and for some unknown reason to everyone, he had been assigned the game as a project - just four days before!

Harold recalls: "I was probably one of the first persons to see the *Breakout* schematic. Steve came in so excited one morning. He comes over to me and says, 'you have to see how I did this.' He shows me the breakthrough design. It was absolutely THE most clever piece of architecture I'd seen in my life."

It had started when Atari had this hot new game concept which essentially took *PONG* and turned it on its side. More to the point, it was a digital version of the widely popular game of racquetball that was popular in the 1970s, but with its own unique twist: Instead of just hitting a ball against the opposing walls, the objective was to hit rows of blocks (in this case, bricks) to increase your score. Just as in *PONG*, after a certain number of hits, the speed of the ball increases. Conceived by Nolan Bushnell and Steve Bristow, to try and maximize profits and make the throwback game cost effective they needed to get the total chip count down as low as possible. In a move similar to the one he first tried with Al all those years before, Nolan offered a bonus to anyone that could keep the chip count below 120 IC chips. None of the project managers or engineers at Atari wanted to touch it; they considered 'ball and paddle' games to be passé by that time, preferring to work on the more advanced games being designed.

Seeing an opportunity to earn some more money for another trip he wanted to take, Steve Jobs went to Nolan to volunteer for the project. Amused but impressed by the gumption, and knowing full well he didn't have the actual skills to engineer this game that was dead in the water anyways, Nolan and Steve Bristow assigned Jobs the game. He showed up four days later with a finished, wire wrapped prototype, expecting the bonus in full.

A question that has to be lingering in your mind right now, if not most of the general populace that's by now heard the candy coated version of the story is this: Why would Atari assign a new and complex game design to a 19 year old technician who, at that time, had only assisted Production Developers with their new arcade board designs and modifications? Steve Bristow answers the question: "We assigned the design to Steve Jobs because he kept telling us that he would do it with the help of his talented friend working at HP. We knew he was referring to Steve Wozniak. That's the only reason it got assigned to Jobs."

Al Alcorn recalls: "There was this planning session about *Breakout* with Joe Keenan, Nolan and myself. So we all go off (on our own way) and that's it on that. Apparently Nolan had assigned this to Jobs behind my back. Well, I walk into the lab one day and there is this demo of a prototype of *Breakout* running. I'm like, 'WHAT!?'" Al continues, "I've got normally four to five projects going with about twenty engineers and techs. It usually takes three, four, sometimes five months to get a game developed. To walk in and just see this game running that we had just barely talked about, well that got my attention."

Unfortunately while the design was in fact very clever and did drastically reduce the chip count of the board as requested, it was not something that could be put into production, so a new design had to be made. You see, what was delivered was only what had been specified; a design with a chip count below 120 chips - in fact, down to around 42 to 46 chips. However the requirements didn't say it had to be designed to be producible, i.e., that it could be readily transferred to a production PCB format as all other Atari coin-op games normally go through.

According to Bristow and Alcorn, Steve Jobs still got paid the $700 standard design fee plus his $5,000 bonus for the 'clever' chip count reduction design. Unfortunately he had never told Wozniak about the bonus, simply turning around and splitting the $700 design fee. Wozniak received $350 for a design which was ALL his work save for the wire wrapping of the proto which Jobs did. Nobody knows what Jobs' motivation for doing what he did was. Maybe in his mind he rationalized that because he did the wire wrapping he was owed half the design fee, and because it was 'his' project he should get the bonus.

With this legendary occurrence in mind however, much has also been written about his famous personality, his temper, and why his personality drove him to create some of the less likeable employee interactions he had when he went on to Apple Computer. Some within Atari have said that personality was present and counted for during Jobs' time at Atari; that Steve Jobs was difficult to work with, and often called their work 'crap' or 'garbage.' But according to Harold Lee, there was another side to him as well. Having Steve working as Harold's technician on some of Harold's projects gave Harold a unique perspective into Steve. Harold recalls: "Steve as a 19 year old wasn't pushy, he was like a little sponge and he was always very excited about everything." Harold continued, "I always got along well with him. When Steve got back from India, I was heavily involved in Consumer Engineering and we ran across each other from time to time in the halls. He never called me a shithead or anything."

As for the specifics of Wozniak's unique yet incomplete design, "Wozniak was a Savant; what he did with designs and implementing them, most mere mortals just couldn't understand," Al Alcorn recalls. Steve Wozniak remembers: "I used a 256x1 bit RAM chip for the bricks, as I recall. It was a very inexpensive chip, running only a couple of bucks, I'm sure. This is nothing when all the chips together ran maybe $40-$80 and the machine was thousands of dollars when sold. Steve Jobs told me right at the time that Atari couldn't understand how my design worked."

It had been speculated that the use of RAM (Random Access Memory, normally used with computers and very expensive at the time) might have been the negating factor as to why the Wozniak design was not used as the basis for the production model. This turns out not to be the main issue however. Al Alcorn continues: "Nolan laid out the rules, but none of the rules said that the *Breakout* board had to be manufacturable. Woz also used LED displays for the scoring instead of displaying the score on the video screen. Cute, but he cheated. Fair is fair and Nolan laid out the rules; he just didn't make them tight enough. Woz's board design just wasn't something that we would be able to use in production." Steve Bristow further recalls: "The original design did not have all the features that were needed to make *Breakout* work. My recollection is that it did not have all the coin control, scoring, and sound features. It was treated internally as a working basis but not a finished product. No evil here, just a starting point."

When it came time to redo *Breakout* and turn it into an actual product, Gary Waters at Cyan was given the task. "I believe Gary was given the breadboard and did a new design based on the game play," recalls Steve Mayer. As Gary told us, "I did the new board; I became the engineer on the game. I did it from the wire wrap board and schematic that Steve Jobs gave us. Don Lange handed it to me, and said 'here is your project' and told me how it worked. It had no scoring, no sound and it was only a 1-player game. I found out pretty quickly there was also a glitch in the logic in certain areas." Gary essentially started over with a new board layout using the vertical and horizontal syncing that other Atari boards had been routinely using. This was where a great deal of the chip saving had taken place, so he got permission to go back to the standard way Atari had been doing board design and he finished the game. Scoring was now on the screen; it now had 1 and 2-player capabilities and sound was added. *Breakout*, released in April 1976, wound up becoming just the hit to carry Atari's Coin-op Division into the late half of the 1970s.

I'm Not In The MOOD

A tari's Consumer division started 1976 with a move. Leaving the spartan Division Street location, their new offices and manufacturing were split between 155 Moffett Park Drive, and 1195 Borregas Avenue. Ironically the move was faster than the the FCC's own plodding governmental pace to approve Atari's new and pending submissions; mostly games that were home recreations of their previous *PONG* arcade games: *Super PONG, Super PONG Doubles, Hockey PONG* and more. The home market was *PONG* spam all over again and the public was buying it up because now it was in the privacy of their own home.

An interesting product unlike anything Atari had ever done before though was in development, something that was a step outside the box. Selling it, on the other hand, would prove a bit more difficult than *PONG* spam. Its codename was MOOD, and it was started by yet another former Standard Microsystems employee, Bob Brown, who had joined Atari's Consumer Division to assist Harold Lee on the *Home PONG* chip. A technician by the name of Jim Luby, also formerly from Standard Microsystems, had been busy doing much of the wire wrapping of the *PONG* spam prototypes and was moving on to wire wrap the MOOD prototype.

Jim comments about coming to Atari: "This was such a great place to work at - people really got along great and because a lot of us knew each other from other companies we worked at, it made us really want to work together that much harder to succeed. Atari was the neatest place to work. I was happy with my job and it was a great place."

Super PONG is one of his first projects he is to wire wrap in his new job and throughout the Spring and Summer he would work on several other *PONG* console variants as well. When the Summer of 1976 arrived, his next project came up: wire wrapping MOOD. Bob Brown was the Project Leader of MOOD and Harold Lee had engineered it.

MOOD had started from a series of conversations between Harold and Bob to produce a 'Audio-Video Color Kaleidoscope for Home Television.' A rather unique concept - not a video game in any respect, but still a high tech product that would further enhance people's experience with audio and video in a home setting. Yes, it was the ultimate experience for sitting at home and smoking your dope: turning your TV into a swirling maze of psychedelic patterns, all to the tune of your favorite music. In fact, by the time it was released, MOOD's name had been officially changed to its more familiar product name: Video Music.

The initial circuitry work began as far back as early November 1975 with the TV Sync circuit (a circuit that allows the device to coordinate with the television's display process) and then by April 1976 the remaining major circuit designs were completed. Along the way, Bob and Jim also upheld a by then ongoing tradition at Atari. Engineering and Wire Wrapping used to have a contest with every project: if the engineering circuits had an error, there would be a red-line drawn marking the error and where the correction was made for it. If wire wrapping connected up the lines wrong, each wrong connection was counted. Whoever had the most errors would lose the contest. What would the prize be? The loser would buy beers for the winner and everyone at the end of the project. Jim won on project MOOD.

FCC approval for Video Music was issued in February 1977, and Wade Tuma has to send an additional $500 check to the FCC for the change of type approval for TV 300 for the device, model # C-240. You should be seeing a pattern here. Design - send money to FCC - fix - send money to FCC - update - send money to FCC… Nolan and company began wondering if they were in the wrong business.

The IC design and PCB layout were completed in November 1976 and a wood and metal case design was then crafted to make Video Music at home in any 1970s entertainment center. Thinking they had a good relationship with Sears because of their mutual hit with *Home PONG*, Al Alcorn demonstrated Video Music to a Sears rep to see if he could convince Sears to carry the product. The Sears rep asked Al, "So how many of these have you sold so far?" Al replied back that so far they'd sold none. So the Sears rep came back and said, "Great, well I'll order twice as many." That's when it hit Al that the opportunity and doors opened to Atari during the past year was truly the luck of the draw in connecting them with Tom Quinn.

Sears had very stringent ways of doing business, and Tom Quinn's action of having a vendor with an already designed product coming into Sears and being able to sell that product went against the grain. Luckily for Atari, the Sears branded Tele-Games *PONG* consoles were a big success and Atari would follow with many more Sears-branded video game consoles in the future.

In this case however, Atari once again tried to 'push' a product that Sears didn't have its buyers go out, research and request a supplier to create. Just as when they first approached with *Home PONG,* the result was denial - and in this case Tom Quinn wasn't there to back them up. As highly successful and profitable as the Atari and Sears relationship had been thus far, it was not a two-way street, and to further prove this point, Tom Quinn would become a casualty of his own rogue actions. No matter how highly positive and financially lucrative the end result of Tom's efforts had been, Sears would fire him in the end.

Atari attempted to market and sell Video Music on its own, but it turned out to be an uphill battle. Whether it had to do with not reaching the right buyer channels or just a lack of understanding as to what the device was, the Video Music's just weren't selling. "We couldn't give them away - many Atari employees went home with boxed, unopened Video Music's - we just couldn't sell them," recalls Niles Strohl. Al Alcorn still has his original Video Music sitting in a box in his closet to this day.

There was also a great deal of work going on back in coin-op during this period (besides *Breakout,* of course), but organizationally it was now at odds, management wise, with the newly created Consumer group. After all, Atari was a coin-op manufacturer and there were several key and important new machines being released in 1975, with others being conceptualized and prepared for release in 1976. But now, resources are being used by and income generated from Consumer products.

Gene Lipkin was on the case again, and he now needed to make a decision; one that would impact the company significantly: Atari was now going to have two divisions. There would be the continuing of the Coin-op Division, which was now officially joined by the Consumer Division.

By February of 1976, Gene had done all he could to see to it that Atari's new consumer products and division were moving along full swing. When the action was done, curiously Gene chose to go back to the Coin-op group. In his words, "Consumer games were shit - all they had were the *PONG* games, but in coin-op we had the computing power so we were doing the neat stuff. While I liked all the guys in the consumer side, I'm a coin-op guy."

Gene became General Manager of Coin-op, the place where he had earned his nickname, the "wheelin' dealin' whirlwind." In his place, Joe Keenan brought in three people to help head the Consumer Division: Kerry Crosson would manage Consumer Products, Malcolm Khun would become VP and Director of Sales and finally Michael Shea, who would become VP and Director of Product Marketing. Yes, you're beginning to see why he was referred to as the wheelin' and dealin' whirlwind when you need three people to take over for one!

Of course, the coin-op engineers also had a few other choice words that Gene was known by too! You see, as would be the norm, Gene Lipkin and Frank Ballouz would routinely go from their offices in 1265 Borregas to walk across the street to 1272 Borregas to do 'game review.' This trip was akin to the Grimm Reaper and his accomplice walking over to see which coin-op project might receive 'the kiss of death' by being abruptly canceled. Well, walking across actually wasn't the norm; the long and tenuous commute of roughly 1,000 feet was typically made by Gene and Frank taking one or the other's car. As Frank recalls, "We'd hop in the car, smoke a joint and go over across the street for game review." Game review and the dread of having a game canceled didn't go without retribution by the coin-op engineers on Gene and especially on Frank. In fact a few years later, the coin-op engineers really pushed their luck with Frank Ballouz and a game review when they did a version of *Asteroids* substituting the asteroids with turtles. Instead of button controls, they told Frank to yell at the screen to make the turtles move. With the engineers collapsing in laughter, Gene and Frank realized the whole thing was done behind their back for payback. Yelling at turtles on a screen would now haunt Frank for years to come - the coin-op engineers made sure of that. When it came time for Frank to make a sales presentation some time later, at one point he picked up his glass of water to have a drink, only to find a wind-up plastic turtle swimming in his glass.

Atari's coin-op offerings during this period now had a new quality (or creative) label added to their marketing description: 'Durastress.' The idea was to enhance the company's sales pitch that Atari coin-ops underwent strenuous testing to ensure that Atari's products would be of a higher quality than their competitors.

Among the games released were *Dodgeball* in January, designed by Steve Bristow, as well as *Pursuit* designed by Howard Van Jepmond. This was followed in May by two games; the not so well known *Crossfire* and then a follow-up to the smash 1974 arcade hit game *Tank* which is called (no surprise), *Tank II*. June sees the release of *Anti Aircraft* by Gary Waters, (though in the manual it's referred to as *Anti Aircraft II*). While not a follow-up, the name refers to it being a two player game. Also of note is an undocumented 'feature' or easter egg in the game; by grounding a pin on the PROM chip, you could change the planes into UFO's. In July comes *Goal IV* by Steve Mayer and Steve Bristow, which is a simplified digital version of Foosball. Although there was supposedly an upright version, only a cocktail table version is known of and the only advertising flyer of the product shows the cocktail version.

In September, 1975 a rather interesting game is released called *Shark JAWS*. What makes this particular game very interesting is that it's an Atari game... or is it? A hot new movie called *Jaws* had hit the big screen in 1975, directed by Steven Spielberg, and based on Peter Benchley's novel of the same name. (Interestingly enough, in the movie itself is a scene on the beach where several video arcades can be seen; among them is a yellow *Computer Space*.) With everyone looking to cash in on the unexpected success of the movie, Atari looked to join in on the 'shark fever' sweeping the nation. So, Atari releases a game based on divers avoiding a shark.

The cabinet and the title of the game blatantly puts the word JAWS in huge letters with tiny letters of 'shark' next to it. Essentially, anyone looking at the game would immediately think the game is directly related to the movie *Jaws*, which of course was no accident. Furthermore, the game proudly states it's being released by a licensing company called 'Horror Games' - a completely fake company set up by Nolan to protect Atari from a possible lawsuit. Atari's name is scrubbed from much of the owner/operators manual schematics and wiring drawings, but the address listed in the owner/operators manual (14600 Winchester Ave.) is the same address as Atari, Inc. It doesn't take Universal long to figure out that this game is from Atari directly. Gene Lipkin explains: "It took Universal Studios only three days to figure out the game was Atari's and there was no Horror Games."

As October came, we see the final three arcade games released that year: *Steeplchase* (based on a previous *AstroTurf* project), *Jet Fighter*, which was designed by Lyle Rains... and another coin-op game called *Crash n' Score*. It was *Jet Fighter*, though that provides our next story.

During the development of *Jet Fighter*, Pat Karns from Marketing and Larry Leppert from Engineering will take the designs for *Jet Fighter*, *Tank*, and several other games and leave Atari to form their own coin-op game company called Fun Games. Their first product is *Bi-Plane* which is a direct copy of *Jet Fighter*; however, the planes have been altered to look like bi-planes instead of jet fighters. Holly LeRoy, who had done work on various projects from *Barrel PONG* to *Doctor PONG*, to a unique Atari carnival trailer equipped with 26 built-in coin-op games, would also take part in the creation of Fun Games by removing parts and components out of Atari's stock to supply to Fun Games for their first couple of machines. Soon after, Fun Games announces another game called *Tankers*; screen shots and sell sheets show what appears to be the same playfield and game design as Atari/Kee Games *Tank*.

That's also followed by a multi-game arcade design sell sheetcalled *Take 7* where one of the games shown on the sell sheet appears to be *Breakout*. While the sell sheet flyer is from 1975, and *Breakout* is not known outside of the company until 1976, it is possible that Karns, Leppert and LeRoy may have either gotten information specs on the new game or perhaps got their hands on designs for the new game. But that was the last straw. Atari immediately sued Fun Games, and the company was shut down almost as quickly as it started, moving Fun Games into a footnote, instead of the Kee Games-like competitor they had hoped to become.

Review In Images

Joe Keenan and Nolan Bushnell.

Top: The prototype for *Home PONG* that was demonstrated at Sears. The circuitry is actually inside the wooden box.

Bottom: Inside the prototype for *Home PONG* that was demonstrated at Sears.

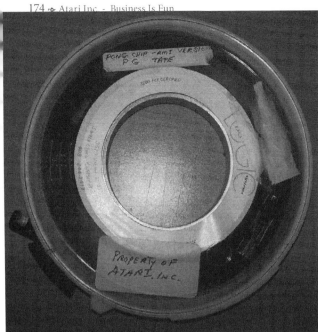

Left: The data tape containing *Home PONG*'s chip layout.

Bottom: The unique Applicon system, the Applicon Design Assistant, used to lay out the PONG-On-A-Chip.

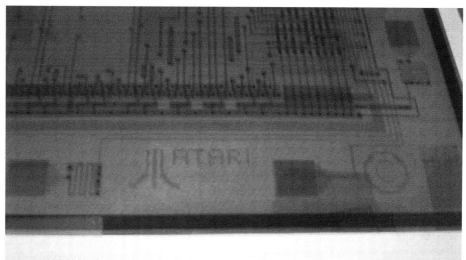

HOME PONG CHIP PLOT 1975
(Atari Museum Archives)

The Home PONG custom chip layout. Note Harold Lee's initials "easter egged" on to the chip below.

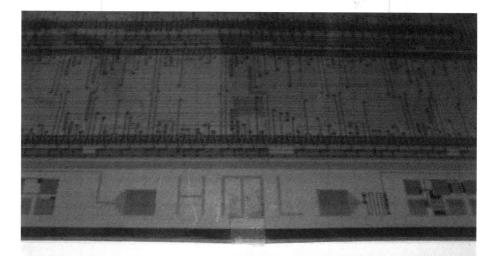

HOME PONG CHIP PLOT 1975
(Atari Museum Archives)

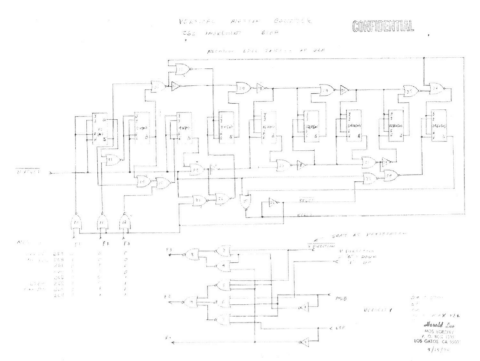

One of nine sheets of Harold Lee's *Home PONG*'s schematics.

Home PONG's PCB film.

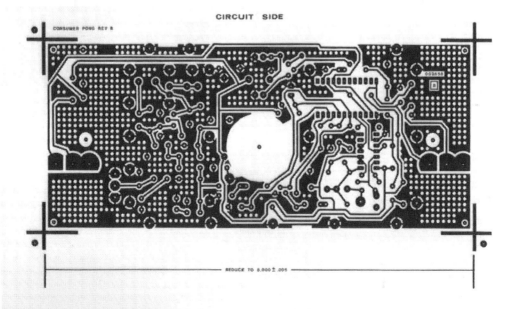

Top From Left to Right: Uknown, Regan Cheng, Betty Dahl, Pete Takaichi. Testing out Regan and Pete's mockup of a *PONG Doubles* console for its ergonomics. *(Courtesy of Scott Evans)*

Right: A *PONG*-on-a-chip tester.

Top and bottom: 155 Moffet street 1195 Borregas where the new Consumer Division offices and manufacturing were located in the mid 1970s.

PONG™

THIS IS THE GENUINE GAME,
MADE BY THE ORIGINATORS OF THE GAME.

We at Atari, the inventors of Pong and many of
your favorite coin-operated electronic video games, are
pleased to present Pong™ for home television.

It has on-screen digital score-keeping, true "Pong"
sounds, variable speed and color. The same features your
customers want and have come to expect from our
original coin-operated game.

We know of no other game on the market made with
this sort of craftsmanship. We feel we can truly say if
you're going to sell any electronic video game, there's
only one way to go. And that's with the originators
of the game.

Features:
- "Pong" sounds
- On-screen digital scoring
- Automatic speed-up
- Color (on color TV sets)
- Plugs in easily to any size home TV
- Operates on four "D" cell batteries (included)
- AC adapter (optional)
- Proven circuitry
- 90 day warranty

PONG,™ INVENTED BY ATARI.

World Cup in console and cocktail cabinet formats. This is the first game Harold Lee, the *PONG*-on-a-chip designer worked on.

It was also one of the early games Steve Jobs worked on as a tech, coming up with ways to mod the circuit board to provide new game play features.

ATARI™
Innovative
leisure

14600 Winchester Boulevard
Los Gatos, California 95030
(408) 374-2440
TELEX 34-5589

Top: The prototype of *Touch-Me* with the 'boob' controllers.

Bottom: The production version.

1974 saw Atari gain its first identity and solid mission: To provide 'innovative leisure.' Under Nolan's vision, Atari would not be limited to just arcade games, and would look to take over people's free time with high tech fun in a variety of platforms and formats.

An organizational chart of the Engineering Department in early '74, pre-Wakfield's departure. Steve Jobs had just talked his way in to Atari as a technician and reported to Don Lang. Future Apple Computer co-founder Ron Wayne was head of Industrial Design/Design Services.

Note: Position in the lower listings under each department head does not denote seniority or job description, this is just a generic listing.

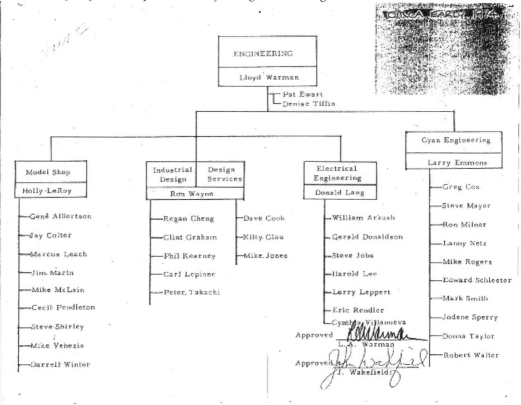

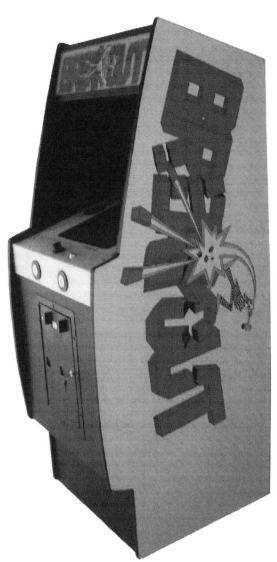

The *Breakout* odyssey

Clockwise starting upper right: Steve Jobs not long before joining Atari. Steven 'Woz' Wozniak, who designed a prototype of *Breakout* for Jobs and was only given half of the design fee and none of the bonus money. The production version of *Breakout*, designed by Gary Waters.

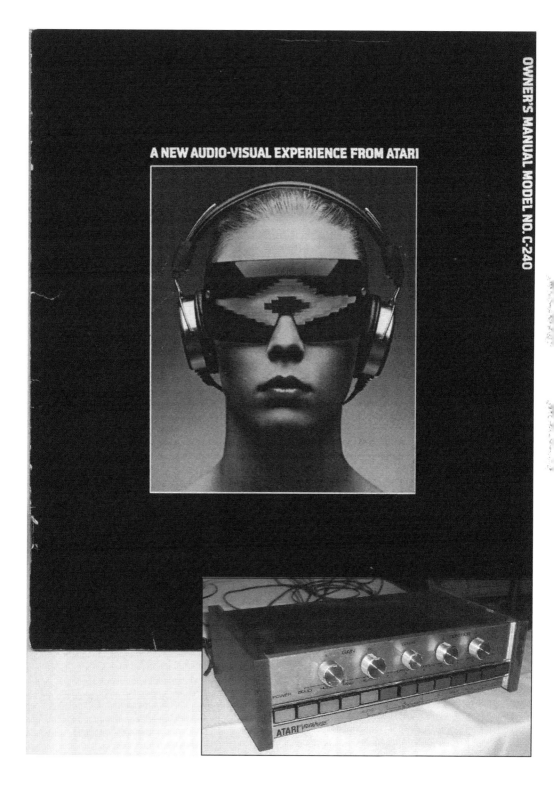

Clockwise from top right: The original *Home PONG* made for Sears and their Tele-Games label. A *Home PONG* promotional photo. Video Music marketing meeting. Stocking *Super PONG* at a department store.A typical Atari style promotional photo of a family playing *Super PONG Ten*.

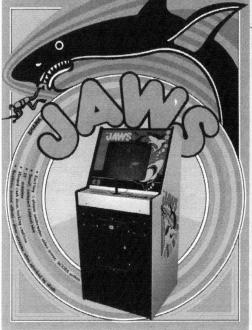

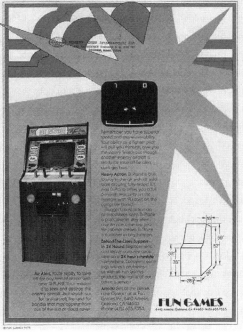

This page and next: The burn-in oven designed and built by Dennis Koble, Craig Manning, and Steve Richie in 1976. Burn-in is a common process of literally baking a PCB to accelerate the breakdown of weak parts before shipping these to customers. After the process, faulty parts are replaced. The original ovens at Atari were made of plywood, and after one caught fire this project was given the go ahead.

Chapter 5

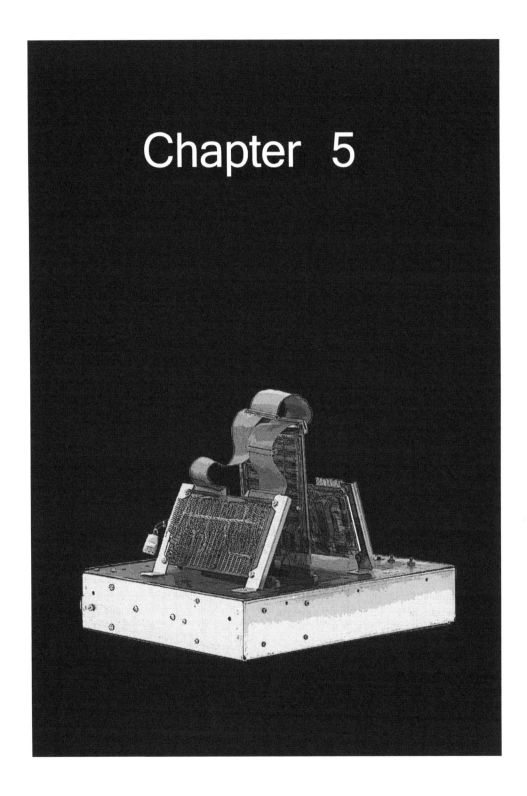

More Games
More Fun

Tthanks to a lot of creative ingenuity surrounding an idea put to paper in a memo back in 1973, the Sears version of *Home PONG* was a big success. However, as the followup consoles were being developed, the inherent limitations of having to develop custom chips for every single new console was becoming apparent as well. *Home PONG, Super PONG, Hockey PONG* and then the later consoles such as *Video Pinball* and *Stunt Cycle* - ALL had a limited shelf life as they only played a small handful of variations of games. Classed as 'dedicated consoles' because all the games were built directly into each console, development time also took several months to almost a year for each and the costs ran up to nearly $100,000 per product. To compound the problems, the home game console field was also suddenly starting to get rather crowded due to the release of the AY-3-8500 '*PONG*-on-a-chip' IC by General Instruments (GI). It was basically a clone, rather than a copy of Atari's chip, with six different games built into it. The kicker was that GI had designed the chip not for their own use, but to be sold to clone manufacturers to build their own TV Tennis consoles. And sell well it did, driving the amount of competitors to Atari and Magnavox up to around a 100 world wide within a year.

GI was soon joined by Texas Instruments and their SN76410N chip, and along with others a saturated home market of the type Atari had already seen happen with the original *PONG* coin-op market was created. Then in the Fall of 1976, Fairchild launched their microprocessor-driven programmable console, the Fairchild Channel F, instantly making the dedicated TV Tennis console market obsolete.

With all this adversity on all fronts, Atari followed the same plan that allowed its Coin-op Division to thrive under the same circumstances: it relied on research to stay one step ahead of the competition. In fact, the researchers at Cyan had already started working on a possible solution to the dilemma back before *Home PONG* even hit the shelves at Sears.

The idea was both simple and brilliant: Take what is normally done in hardware and leave it to programmers to implement in software by basing the console around the relatively new technology of microprocessors. The effect was two-fold: it 'cost reduced' the design, but opened up the system to be more powerful and more flexible than even the engineers could ever envision.

The timing, in fact, couldn't have been any more perfect. Initially putting together a few 'wish lists' of systems based around various microprocessors, Steve Mayer and Ron Milner received a curious letter about a new microprocessor that promised to deliver what others couldn't: an insanely low price.

Called the MOS 6502, the microprocessor was designed by former Motorola microprocessor designer Chuck Peddle, who had parted ways with the former when it was clear they weren't interested in pursuing a second generation of his 6800 chips at the time. Joining a friend's electronic calculator company called MOS Technology, Chuck and his team were able to design an entire series of microprocessor chips - the flagship of which was the 6502. The chip series was set to make its debut at the September Western Electronics Show and Convention (Wescon), the then defacto convention for the computer industry. Sending out letters to what were considered by Chuck to be potential customers, nobody could have had any foresight at just how much the 6502 would become the mainstay of the computer and video game industry; becoming a staple in computers, game consoles and even video arcade games across the 70s and 80s.

Chuck had also placed ads in computer and electronics trade magazines, which lead to a last minute problem for him to navigate. The ads were eye catching, offering to sell a full microprocessor for $25 right there on the Wescon show floor. While the first half of the offer caught the public's eye, it was the latter that infuriated the Wescon organizers when they heard about it. Wescon was an industry trade show, not a flea market; so upon arriving to set up in their area at Wescon, Chuck and the MOS Technology people were promptly reamed and told under no circumstances would they be selling their chips at the show.

Being quick thinking, Chuck came up with another solution: There was nothing prohibiting them from selling off the show floor, nor mentioning where to go to buy them. So Chuck used their booth for the standard information presentation but directed people to their hotel suite to actually purchase the chips. Stationing his wife just outside the suite with a literal barrel full of microprocessors and a stack of manuals to purchase, the plan was for people to buy a chip and accompanying manual from Chuck's wife and then enter the suite to see the full series demonstrated by Chuck and company.

It wasn't long before a large line of hopeful engineers started developing. Notable among them were Steve Mayer and Ron Milner from Cyan, a young Berkeley graduate by the name of Joe Decuir and another young engineer - this one from Hewlett Packard who was looking to build his own personal computer: Steve Wozniak. Explains Wozniak, "I didn't have to fill out any forms or agree to credit. I just forked over the cash (to Chuck Peddle and his wife) and walked away with my first microprocessor." Little did they know the barrel of microprocessors had been a little bit of smoke and mirrors, as only the top half of the barrel contained working microprocessors.

After getting their 6502 with documentation, Mayer and Milner headed into see Chuck and his people demonstrating the chips in use. Meeting for about an hour and a half with Chuck, they negotiated for him to come over to Cyan the next day to discuss plans for using MOS's 6502 and its support chip in their proposed game system.

Chuck and company headed over to Cyan after the show, where they met and discussed the proposed game console proof of concept over the next two days. Mayer and Milner's previous 'dream systems' specs were discussed, as well as possible board designs and financial targets. In the end, Cyan decided to sign on with MOS Technology's chip, but not the 6502. Because it was targeted for a mass produced game system, cost was an issue and even the 6502's low price was still not as cost effective as needed. Chuck's proposed 6507, a scaled down version of the 6502, was more in line to meet that goal. With the 6507 and the 6532 support chip, they'd just need to design a custom chip for graphics and sound support. MOS also had a relationship with another engineering firm by the name of Microcomputer Associates of Los Altos, California, who had developed the debugging software for MOS's training systems. They had also developed their own publicly available development system that was being pushed out the following month, complete with a terminal interface and built in debugging software. Called the 'JOLT Computer,' it was suggested by Chuck to use this as the main board of the game console during development of the custom chip.

The 'JOLT' itself was a breakthrough at the time, allowing anyone from a hobbyist to a development engineer to get experience with the new MOS 6502 microprocessor chips by providing them a low cost bare bones computer. As a $249 kit, it features everything necessary for a basic micro-computer: the MOS 6502 microprocessor, 512 bytes of RAM, a terminal interface connection, onboard debugger/monitor firmware and sixteen programmable input/output lines. Assembly of the full single board computer could take only three or so hours to complete, making it the perfect research tool. Ron Milner built the proof of concept programmable game system around the 'JOLT' board by getting it to display a simple version of Atari/Kee's popular game *Tank*.

That young Berkeley graduate, Joe Decuir, was then hired in Decmber, 1975 to debug the design. Joe had in fact been working with microprocessors since their beginnings, studying them at Berkeley and going out on his own to purchase an Intel 4004, the world's first microprocessor. He had then joined the throngs at Chuck's hotel room who were all there for that same reason simple reason: the need to delve into the powerful microprocessor that promised to deliver a full 8-bit experience at a time when comparable microprocessors cost $100-$300 each. Purchasing a 6502 and one of MOS's KIM-1 development boards, he set about learning the ins and outs of developing for this game changer.

Ed DeWath, a friend of Joe's, also happened to be friends with Milner and Mayer. So when Ed heard they were looking to hire someone familiar with microprocessors to debug their proof of concept, he let Joe know about the position. Joe's marriage of both engineering and programming skills made him uniquely qualified, but it was his recent experience with the 6502 that made him the perfect candidate. The opportunity was actually just as beneficial for Joe - being an engineer's engineer, Joe was always looking for the next big challenge to help improve his skills. In fact, before taking the job with Cyan and Atari, he was actually offered a job with a medical electronics company but turned it down on the advice of his father and a friend. According to Joe, "My dad said 'Pick the job that teaches you more' and my buddy,

Greg Voelm, said 'You can do good for the world with games. Most people are sick by their own hand; smoking, bad eating, etc. They are lonesome and bored, go ahead and entertain them!'"

The yet unnamed programmable game system project needed someone who could wrap their arms around it and champion it at the Atari Consumer offices down on Division Street in Campbell, California and Joe was also the perfect candidate for that. So once the debugging had finished, Joe moved down to Division Street in February, 1976 to begin work bread boarding a gate-level prototype of the graphics chip needed to take the proof of concept to a full fledged game console. With the gate-level prototype, the design would be able to mimic as close as possible what the special graphics chip - eventually called the TIA (Television Interface Adapter) - would be as a final chip design.

The Division Street location turned out to be a newer separate location from their ongoing *Home PONG* operations; it was actually a secret location, set up by Al Alcorn so word of the new console project wouldn't get leaked out by the people in Coin, who Al felt had loose lips. Like a secret MI-5 lab creating James Bond's latest gadget, at Division Street Joe began to apprentice under the newly acquired VLSI (Very Large Scale Integration) chip designer, Jay Miner, that March to build that gate-level prototype.

Jay himself had come over from Standard Microsystems, thanks to his friend and *Home PONG* chip designer, Harold Lee. You see, Harold's chip designing experience was in what's called Static Logic; an older design technology that was slower than the newer Dynamic Logic used in VLSI and which forced him to rely mostly on NOR gates. Harold knew that for a project of this scale and complexity, someone with Jay's skills would be essential, so he had Al negotiate to get Jay over immediately.

Once things were underway in the secret Division Street engineering labs, Jay said to Joe that their project would need a codename, did he have any ideas? Joe thought for a minute, and remembering his password for the mainframe account he had been using to code the original game program for the proof of concept, simply said 'Stella.' Stella had been the nickname of the French built bicycle he had been riding to and from work, which is why he had originally chosen it as the password. So it was as good a name as any for the project name as well. Ironically, given the track record for engineers at Atari using women's names for their projects, marketing had thought that the name was also for a woman and as a result, they began to officially assign female names to projects.

To help spec out this new game console, Nolan and Joe Keenan had hired on a consultant from National Semiconductor's consumer products group around the time Joe Decuir was also being hired. The goal was to do a product spec market recommendation on the proposed new console, and the man doing it was none other than Gene Landrum. Yes, the same Gene Landrum who had just delivered an analysis report to Fairchild regarding their 'Stratos' project, which would become the Fairchild Channel F game console.

A direct report to Nolan who sees him as a strong asset, in May, 1976 he delivers a Market Analysis as well as a Product Planning Strategy for Consumer Video Games; specifically for a programmable cartridge-based system. Likewise, the Production Planning data on this proposed new programmable game system was put together by another former National Semiconductor employee who joined Atari's fledgling Consumer Division: John Ellis. The almost incestual relationship between Atari and other tech firms is classic Silicon Valley behavior, where employees are constantly jumping ship and entire teams of individuals from one company can wind up as a competitor the next. "We essentially gutted National Semiconductor's consumer product group - all of their engineers now worked for me in Consumer Research and Development," recalls Al Alcorn.

Engaged as the Vice President of Consumer Engineering, John builds out what the bill of materials would be for two versions of consoles – models 100 and 101. Initial specifications call for the device to use four batteries in the Model 101 version.

Gene Landrum's Product Planning document calls for the new device to be a "Universal T.V. Interface capable of accepting game cartridges which will interplay with the console electronic logic system." The document further details it to be "designed for living room or den esthetics (wood grain hot stamping) analogous to stereo designs for permanent setting." So if you've ever wondered where the Atari Video Computer System (better known to most as the Atari 2600) got its wood grain look from, it was all detailed by Gene as far back as May, 1976.

One avenue originally suggested in the report but quickly dropped was that the new console should contain three to four dedicated games. The concept suggested that the console would come with some built-in games to default to when no cartridge was installed, a feature also included in Fairchild's console. As far as the 'cartridges' portion of the report were concerned, four vehicles were reviewed: Philips Type Audio Tape Cassette, Philips Type Digital Tape Cassette, MAG Cards, and MOS Cartridge. Out of the four selections, the MOS solution was the most expensive due directly to the high cost of the needed Read Only Memory (ROM) chip. However, it was the preferred choice even with known static electricity damage concerns - at that point in time plugging in and pulling out a cartridge still produced static electricity. Not something you want with a consumer device.

The cartridge design specs were most telling about what companies think of the average consumer when designing a product: 2 inch by 4 inch by 1/2 inch in size and "Must be idiot proof, child proof and effective in resisting potential static problems in a living room environment." In the end, James C. Asher and Douglas A. Hardy would design the cartridges for Atari. Eliminating the static problem thanks to the guidance of their friend Jerry Lawson who actually solved the issue while working on Channel F's design at Fairchild.

Of course the new product also needed some games, and what was already being considered was tapping into Atari's existing arcade titles, clearly showing what this new console was being designed to play. The following is a list of games we found being considered under the non-sports category: *Trak 10, Steeplchase, Tank, Stunt Cycle, Jet Fighter, Outlaw, Space Race, Qwak, Crash 'n' Score, SharkJAWS, Touch Me, Gotcha, Breakout,* and *Quiz Show.*

Al, as the project manager, also did a very novel thing (for game development anyway) during the development of the custom graphics chip. He specifically brought in game programmers during that stage so they could have input into the still-being-developed graphics chip, conveying features they'd need to help them code the games.

During all this development and analysis, Atari was still facing some very real issues however that could effect the project if not Atari itself. In early 1975 they were still reeling from the cash problems of 1974. Wanting to get into the consumer market with their *Home PONG* and any future products, Atari knew it was going to need a substantial injection of capital to bring everything to fruition. But up until that time, Nolan had been very careful not to be beholden to anyone, staying far away from outside money. That just couldn't be the case anymore though. Would Atari go public in the difficult and volatile stock market of the 1970s? Would Atari go out and look for more investors? Or would they look to sell themselves to a larger company that would have the financial resources to take Atari's goals and objectives to the next level?

Nolan and Joe Keenan had Atari's financial team put together an extensive and detailed 'Company Prospectus' in April 1975, so that they could shop Atari around to potential investors to raise the needed capital.

It worked for a time, raising small capital through investors like Don Valentine, but it wasn't anywhere near what they needed for their planned growth - raising needed capital was turning out to be much more difficult than the Atari board originally thought. At that point in May of 1975, Atari was expected to make after-tax profits in excess of $750,000 and employed 347 people. While this was a big turnaround from the $600,000 loss it incurred for fiscal 1974, it wasn't enough to truly snag someone looking to invest the big bucks Nolan thought Atari deserved. Perhaps it was time to consider looking to sell Atari into a larger company with the type of cash resources Atari would need to grow.

Looking at a range of companies to sell Atari to including General Electric, as they entered 1976 no one had been found. Video games were still considered a fad at best by many companies, and the already crowding home market was also appearing to publicly erode Atari's major part in that fad. Nolan turned to one of the investors brought in during '75 for a solution, Gordon Crawford of California Capital Investments. At the same time Jay Miner and Joe Decuir were starting work on TIA in March, 1976, Nolan was asking Gordon to assist in locating potential buyers who would have interest in purchasing Atari. What Nolan didn't know is that Gordon owned a 10% stake of a large entertainment company through a previous investment his firm had made. The company was called Warner Communications and the timing, they soon discovered, couldn't have been better.

Back in New York, Warner Communications' Manny Gerard had conveniently been looking to expand the company into new areas to invest and branch out with. The entertainment and record industry were in a major downturn and Gordon thought bringing high tech entertainment together with a powerhouse like Warner could be a perfect match.

Emanuel "Manny" Gerard initially had started his career as an entertainment research analyst on Wall Street and would join Warner Communications as their Executive Vice President. Also a member of Warner's Office of the President, he was then promoted to Warner's Chief Operating Officer.

Manny gets a call from Gordon one day, stating he's got a line on a hot company out West looking to be bought in order to finance its already skyrocketing growth. Wanting to know more about the possible investment, Manny begins to investigate this Atari company and its products, and his views run contrary to some of the other companies Atari had approached. He sees Atari as smack dab in the middle of an explosive new growth in 'entertainment through technology;' that it has its name out in all of the various arcades and entertainment centers across the country, and it also has several products for use at home on television sets. This is exactly what Manny had been looking for to bring into Warner to get it out of its own slump.

While Manny was doing his research on Atari, Steve Ross (CEO of Warner Communications) and his son Mark had just gotten off the Space Mountain ride at Disneyland in California when they wandered into an arcade adjacent to the ride. Recently added by Disney to add high tech entertainment machines within its Tomorrowland area theme, Steve and his son Mark played several rounds on the Atari/Kee *Tank* video arcade game inside. When Manny came to Steve Ross and presented the idea that Warner Communications should consider negotiating to purchase this California technology-based entertainment company called Atari, Steve Ross immediately asked Manny, "Are they the ones who make the *Tank* game?" With that, Warner's intent was sealed.

Steve Ross himself was a self made millionaire and dynamic entrepreneur the likes of which had rarely been seen in the business world up to that point in time. From his meager beginnings (coming out of the U.S. Army, to working in a funeral home company and an office cleaning company owned by his father in-law), he would move up and then merge these companies together with Kinney Parking Systems. Going public on the stock exchange in 1962 for $12.5 million as Kinney National Services, his accomplishments didn't end there. Ross had a keen interest in the entertainment industry and negotiated for Kinney National Services to buy the then ailing Warner Bros. – Seven Arts film and record studios for $400 million in 1969. Kinney National Services then changed its name in 1971 to become Warner Communications, with Steve Ross becoming its Chairman and CEO in 1972 (around the same time Al Alcorn first began working on *PONG*).

Negotiations were long and tenuous between Atari and Warner, and at one point it was thought that while Warner was negotiating with Atari on its purchase, Nolan had also approached National Semiconductor about possibly buying Atari. This turned out to be far from the truth, as in fact it was National who had approached Nolan and Al about Atari buying National's own consumer group. That meeting with National, like a poorly played round of poker, didn't last long at all. Both Nolan and Al put their cards on the table, telling the National Semiconductor rep that Atari already hired over their entire staff, that National has nothing worth buying and… to toss a little salt on the wound… they point out how National had barred Atari, just as it had previously barred Apple, from buying National's IC components. Now the shoe was on the other foot… and the foot figuratively kicked National Semiconductor to the curb. But the entire instance, even though it was missunderstood, forced Warner to play a higher poker game than expected.

Steve Ross was not a man who was about to lose an opportunity or give up a fight for something he wanted. After all, he'd been dealing with recording artists and the Hollywood crowd for years. This Nolan guy might know how to play video games, but Ross knew how to play people's egos. When Nolan and Don Valentine planned to fly to New York for a negotiating meeting, Steve Ross arranged to not only have the Warner corporate jet pick them up, but to have the flight make a quick stop to pick up actor Clint Eastwood and have him join them on his way to a shoot for his upcoming movie *The Enforcer*. To further sweeten Warner's appearance in the negotiations, Ross arranged that the pair from Atari would also be put up in the ultra lavish Waldorf Towers while in New York. With those carrots dangled in the form of luxury perks, Warner Communications all but fully ensured it would be the only company at the table negotiating to buy Atari.

Apparently Nolan wanted to make sure this deal wasn't a lost opportunity either, by quickly getting rid of the same 300 pound gorilla that Sears had previously been concerned about: Magnavox. Atari, along with several other companies named in the suit, had still been fighting its patent infringement case with Magnavox. Under advisement of Atari's legal counsel, Atari settled. (Years after this event, Nolan has consistently downplayed the facts in interviews, stating this was a 'junk royalty' settled for pennies on the dollar. The actual terms of the agreement were anything but). Entering in to an agreement with Magnavox to license the patents, they've agreed to a global non-exclusive license in exchange for royalty payments totaling $1.5 million over the course of several years. The agreement also includes the stipulation that any technology from Atari that went into production from June 1st, 1976 to June 1st, 1977 would be accessible to Magnavox for their own use. While no longer possibly being a hold up the sale to Warner, the new agreement does delay the public unveiling of the VCS. In a calculated move, it remains hidden to everyone until the June 4th, 1977 Summer Consumer Electronics Show, where the show goers at CES thought the big announcement of the show was only going to be about the US debut of the VHS tape.

On July 26, 1976, Warner Communications incorporates 'Atari Holdings, Inc.' in Delaware and the discussions now move into more meticulous and intense terms for asset assignments and transfers, ownership rights, compensation, stock and other financially heavy areas. After nearly three months of rough and hard fought negotiations, Manny commits Warner Communications to move full speed ahead for the purchase of this California high tech firm.

Troubles during negotiations didn't end there however. Adding to the difficulties, Atari's financial guy William (Bill) White became very ill and was unable to fully participate in negotiations, and likewise Gene Lipkin had to focus his responsibilities on a full schedule of coin-op products both in development and for release that year. But the biggest problem that was thrown into the mix was a difficult personal issue that arose for Nolan; an issue that has haunted many a man and woman in various walks of life for centuries: a disgruntled 'ex.' Nolan had divorced his wife Paula in 1974 and had long before bought her out of her original shares in the company. But one of Nolan's recent self-publicity campaings had caused her to come back with a vengeance.

During the Atari and Warner negotiations, Nolan had given another in one of his long string of self-promotional interviews to a local newspaper. This one had been for the local Bakersfield Californian, and the July 18th, 1976 newspaper's article which appeared in the Business and Finance section detailed how Nolan's company was expected to make $39 million that year, how he'd bought a 41 foot sailboat, a $160,000 house and just acquired adjacent land for a tennis court and a swimming pool. The article goes into detail about Nolan's wall-to-wall waterbed, his obsession with hot dogs and buying mustard by the gallon, his love of popcorn and how he was the only guy he knows who burned out up to two popcorn makers a year. He jokingly commented that his employees call him the 'junk food king.' Then the article makes several mentions about lunches at lavish hotels and talk of 'lady friends' who always accompany him. Lastly, the article is accompanied by a photo of Nolan in a hot tub with one of his aforementioned 'female friends.' Nolan's ex-wife Paula saw the article and became livid, contacting her lawyer who in turn contacts Nolan, informing him that she is going to rescind their 1974 divorce agreement.

Manny Gerard of course now sees a huge problem. If the divorce is rescinded this will mean that Paula becomes a 25% owner in Atari and as such, involved in Atari's sale to Warner. There were already too many complications and issues with this deal as it was, so it needed to be resolved now! Over the next four weeks, Manny has the Warner lawyers work with Nolan to put together a new divorce agreement with Paula and to get this situation cleared up as soon as possible.

It turns out that the issue had more to do with Paula being angry about Nolan and accusations of past philandering than about money, but in the end, a settlement is reached. Paula receives $300,000 in exchange for making no future claims on Atari or on Nolan's earnings.

The path was now clear for Atari to move foreward with its sale to Warner Communications. During much of this drama, it was the stalwart hand of Joe Keenan that kept the negotiations and agreements moving forward over the next several months to bring the company together to sell to Warner. "Joe was the business man, he handled most of the management of the company, Nolan was more of a figure head," recalled Roberta Kendall, Joe Keenan's executive secretary.

The sale of Atari to Warner was one of the most complicated deals Manny Gerard ever had to handle, and he felt that some of the people only added to the complications. William (Bill) White, Atari's financial guy, he felt while a good man, was a real light-weight. But what was unbeknownst to Manny was that Bill has been fighting the sudden onset of Epilepsy. In fact at one point, Bill collapsed and had a seizure just as he stepped into Joe Keenan's office. But to his credit, Bill held on through the negotiations as best he could while fighting his ongoing seizures which would haunt him daily until 1990 when he would finally get a reprieve thanks to medical advancements.

In contrast to his opinion on Bill, Manny also noted that one of the sharper guys at the negotiating table was Al Alcorn, who was there for nearly every meeting and even brought in his own lawyer. Al actually had two lawyers at one point! Steve Bristow too, was also keeping a very keen accounting of the negotiations.

During the past six months of Manny working to get this sale done, he realized something very key about Nolan - something that those who worked with Nolan at the management level had known for years. "Nolan could be a big bullshitter," recalls Manny. This became glaringly obvious at an incident at the law offices the day Atari was about to sell itself to Warner. At the final negotiations meeting before signing the deal, Nolan's antics nearly bring the entire sale to a screeching halt.

Picture this: About thirty people are sitting around the table and the last piece of open discussion had come up: an anti-trust lawsuit Atari was embroiled in over the original spot-motion patent Nolan had filed. The irony here, is that Atari and Nolan had done the very thing they just settled with Magnavox over; going after other video game companies to try and force them to license their patent. In fact as early as 1973, Nolan was giving very public interviews on wanting to do that very thing. One has to wonder if his very public bitterness towards Magnavox and Sanders's Ralph Baer over the years since is simply because they did what he wanted to do first. Regardless, the anti-trust suit against Atari is what all focus is on right now.

This was the final hurdle, and like a crowd watching the last hand at the US Poker Championship, a hush fell upon everyone in the room. After a long pause of silence in the room, Nolan finally looks over at Manny Gerard and says, "That's a deal breaker." All attention turns to Manny. It's like a stage spotlight is glaring in his face, but poker in ANY form was not something you'd ever want to play against Manny Gerard. After all this work, had Manny just wasted six months putting this deal together to see it fall apart because of Nolan? Manny knows he needs to say something, but waits. He must've waited 15 seconds which probably felt more like 15 minutes to everyone sitting there, as if the air was sucked out of the room.

Finally a response comes, in a very low voice so that everyone would have to lean in to listen, Manny says: "You know what Nolan, you're right... it is a deal breaker." Calling Nolan's bluff, now the spotlight has been redirected to Nolan - now HE is the center of attention in the room. At this point an even longer pause occurs.

Nolan sits there for 20 to 25 seconds without saying a word, trying to decide if he should 'hold' or 'fold.' Finally Nolan's lawyer speaks up and asks if he can take his client and step outside for a few moments. They step out of the room and the lawyer asked Nolan flat out if he wants this deal or not; that Warner is not going to give in on this point. Nolan indicates that he really does want the deal; his lawyer says if that's the case, then they need to quit screwing around and accept the terms and sign the contracts. They return to the room and Nolan's lawyer informs Manny Gerard that Nolan agrees to all points of the agreement.

On October 1st, 1976, after several months to allow for board and stock-holder approval of the purchase, the sale contracts are officially signed. The sale totals an unheard of almost $28 million for an entertainment tech firm. In the end, the venture capitalists who invested in Atari got a 100% cashout. Nolan owned 49% before pre-options, and in total he owned 50% of the company and ended up with almost $15 million from the sale. The other principles (including Joe Keenan and Al Alcorn) would be paid out the next largest amounts respectively, and Gene Lipkin, William White, Steven Mayer, Larry Emmons and Steve Bristow would each receive a sizable chunk of the payments from the sale as well. Then you had the 'ESOP' Employee Stock Options that got paid out, rewarding the people who had been with the company in the early days. Nolan and the principles received 10% in cash and the rest in Atari debentures. Warner made sure these debentures were not guaranteed - this way, if Atari failed, then their debentures would be worthless. This also gave all of Atari's original management team incentive to make sure they were involved in the company and would work to see it succeed.

We Take Fun Seriously

C oin-op had also been quite busy preparing to release a new breed of arcade machines for 1976 also based upon Cyan's microprocessor research. While some coin-ops were still being finished and shipped using the older 'engineered game' design methodology, now they were joined by these microprocesoor driven games. Software was the new medium for game design, and programmers would be the new designers. The engineers were now able to concentrate on their craft and design what are essentially custom general purpose computers based around a specific microprocessor and one planned game. *Quiz Show* would be the first, using a Signetics S2650 microprocessor chip, to be followed by others that would be based on the MOS 6502 and Motorola 6800 microprocessor chips.

Speaking of computers, during all of this expansion and development within Atari, an old familiar face returned to Atari's doorstep at the Atari Division Street building: Steve Jobs. But not as the green behind the ears 'Tech' to help Product Development engineers build arcade boards. No, Steve was now the co-founder of a garage startup called Apple Computer and had returned with a proposition for Atari. Just as the last time they saw Steve, in his hands is a board that is strangely familiar in shape and layout to an Atari arcade board. But this is no arcade game; this is a home computer - called the Apple I. Steve was there to take a meeting with Joe Keenan to propose that Atari buy the rights to sell the Apple computer for $50,000.

Yes, Atari had the chance to buy and produce the Apple I computer and ultimately passed on it. But before you slap your forehead in armchair quarterback hindsight, you need to be taken though where the myth meets reality. Myth has it that there was an incident where Steve Jobs puts his dirty feet up onto Joe Keenan's desk, with Joe throwing him out, saying he smells and exclaiming, 'Take your dirty feet and your computer and get out!' Now comes reality; Joe Keenan did not say those things the way they have been portrayed.

According to Joe, who told the facts of this meeting directly to Al Alcorn, this is how the meeting went and was explained to us by Al: "The events that took place are actually in two different meetings. Yes, there was a meeting where Steve Jobs is thrown out of Joe's office. However, it is not related to the Apple Computer pitch. Putting your feet on someone's desk is a sign of disrespect. Maybe not in Steve Jobs point of view, but for others it is." Al Alcorn recalls. "In a later meeting, when Steve Jobs returned to Atari regarding the Apple Computer, yes Joe Keenan did turn down the offer for Atari to buy the rights to sell it. Not because of feet being on his desk." Al Alcorn continues.

"I remember Steve Jobs bringing his prototype computer into a conference room; I saw them bring it in. I wasn't in the meeting though," Don Lange recalls. As to why Atari turned down the opportunity to buy the rights to sell the Apple computer, Don Lange comments: "We were a game company. We figured it wasn't our market." Other curious onlookers peeked into the conference room to see what was being shown. "If there was an official meeting (as opposed to a general look), I wasn't in it. The Apple I was set up in the conference room and several of us checked it out. At the time, I just thought of it as a guy who used to work here showing us his new toy," recalls Mike Albaugh.

So Atari's chance to sell a home computer would not happen in 1976 and would not be an Apple designed product. Atari already had its hands quite full with twelve new video arcade games and its first pinball game coming out in 1976 anyways; a computer was just going to have to wait. But the wait would be short....

Returning to the coin-op front, *Stunt Cycle* kicks off Atari's 1976 arcade lineup in January. Based around jumping over buses, this game is a true homage to the hero of the day, ever popular Evil Knievel, who in the 1970s filled stadiums to the brim with fans watching his daring motorcycle stunts. (this homage was more significant than anyone would actually know - the internal codename for the game was Evel with an "e" Knievel and before that, its earlier codename was Sleezey Shifter) The cabinet, designed by Regan Cheng, is decked out in a red, white and blue color scheme and the game controls actually have real bike grips on the handle bars for an authentic look and feel.

Next up was Atari's answer to Midway's popular gun battle game, which also happened to be the first microprocessor driven coin-op, *Gun Fight*. Released in March, the light gun game *Outlaw* features a very heavy, solid metal realistic light gun and was internally codenamed 'Marshall' during development.

April was one of the busiest months for coin-op, with *Tank 8* and then as mentioned Atari's first microprocessor based game, called *Quiz Show* being released. Designed by Lyle Rains, besides using a Signetics S2650 CPU, another unique feature of *Quiz Show* is that its 1,000 questions were all stored on an 8-track cartridge tape deck connected into the coin-op board.

8-track cartridges, also known as 'Stereo 8' were being widely used for applications in the 1970s; from car radio decks to home audio entertainment systems and now, into arcades. 8-track was the more popular and familiar name, but the real name for the technology is actually 'Stereo 8.' Designed by a consortium consisting of Lear Jet, RCA, General Motors, and an all too familiar name – Ampex, the idea was to create a closed loop magnetic tape package for mobile usage on airplanes, cars and in homes. The closed loop 8-track system was robust and didn't require rewinding, which is why it wound up being used in *Quiz Show* and in other later coin-ops for data storage.

As mentioned in the last chapter, Breakout provided plenty of intrigue inside Atari up until its release in 1976. However the drama didn't end at its release. During a visit out to Atari's Japan offices, Mike Coogan reported some disturbing news back to Gene Lipkin. Apparently Breakout just wasn't selling in Japan. When Gene received a direct phone call from Mike, he soon finds out why: "We have a problem; Masaya Nakamura is stealing from us. Breakout isn't selling because he made nearly 40,000 copies of it and sold them all over Japan."

Nakamura was, of course, the head of NAMCO, Atari's longstanding partner in Japan and the Far East. It turns out the copies were originally being made by the Japanese Yakuza, and when Nakamura confronted them they made him an offer he couldn't refuse. Come into business with us and we'll help make NAMCO the biggest coin-op company in Japan. Their offer worked, and NAMCO was soon selling tons of Breakout's across East Asia, putting the company on the map. Unfortunately, it also severely strained their relationship with Atari, which launched and won a lawsuit against NAMCO.

October 1976 became a pivotal month for Atari. Not just because of Atari being sold to Warner Communications. A big announcement was made and on October 15th, a big party was held to celebrate the official opening of Atari's new Corporate Headquarters, located at 1265 Borregas Avenue in the Moffett Park complex in Sunnyvale, California. The two story building is state of the art, with an incredibly spacious engineering area for coin-op on the first floor. The second floor is houses all of the executive offices and meeting rooms which would soon be nicknamed 'Mahogany Row.' All Atari employees were invited as well as friends and family to take a tour of the new facility, where they're also treated to beer, wine and munchies.

This month also sees an important release of what becomes one of Atari's more popular arcade games (which would also make its debut onto the Atari VCS game console). The arcade game was called *Night Driver*. Based on a license from a German affiliate (but actually programmed by description only of the original), unlike previous driving games, *Night Driver* offers the player a first person perspective. The thrill of being directly behind the steering well and seeing the road ahead. The added element that gives the game its name (but was really just a creative way of explaining the spartan black screen with white blocks whizzing by to represent the road edges) was that it is set at night. You have limited visibility of the twists, turns and obstacles of the road, so it makes for a pulse pounding, exciting experience.

Night Driver's cabinet is produced in all black with standout yellow and pink-purple highlights, depicting the game as a nighttime driving simulator. Its cabinet stands out in a cool and mysterious way with its unique look and is easily recognizable in a crowded arcade; a design feature that Regan Cheng and Gene Lipkin can take credit for. *Night Driver* was already proving itself to be a hit even before it was out on location: During lunch breaks, fully assembled machines would be turned on right on the assembly floor, where engineers and line workers would spend their lunch hour playing the game.

Later on Atari would release *Night Driver* as a sit-down cabinet, using the same fiberglass mold design as the *Hi-Way* arcade released back in April of 1975. The sit-down *Night Driver* would be Atari's second and last all-fiberglass sit-down driving cabinet but not its last driving game. In fact it would seem that driving games dominated Atari's last several months of arcade releases in 1976. Sprint 2 was released in November and bears the co-branding of both Kee Games and Atari on it. What was odd about the name of the game however was that it was not a follow up to Sprint; the '2' indicated this was a 1 to 2 player game. In fact there was then a release of Sprint 4 in December of 1977, and then Sprint 1 arrives in January 1978, two years after Sprint 2.

One of more interesting driving games that Atari would release in November of 1976 was called F-1, a licensed NAMCO game that proved while things were tense with NAMCO they at least still had a working relationship. F-1 is at the end of an aged technology popular in the 1960s, using an electromechanical projection system to give the player the illusion of driving through a course. The massive 60" diameter screen has side blockers that protrude out, with the intent of allowing the player to be more immersed into the first person driving game.

Rounding up the odds and ends for the year, Christmas 1976 is an extra special time for everyone. Betty Dahl is awarded 'Employee of the Month' and then on Sunday, December 12th from 1:00 to 4:00 pm, Atari's Consumer division held a special Christmas "Wing-Ding Party for Tots" (as it was called). Working with the Cupertino Parks and Recreation department and hosting the party in the cafeteria in the Atari consumer building at 1215 Borregas, 30 developmentally handicapped children spent the afternoon enjoying food, playing video games and then receiving gifts from none other than Santa Clause himself, thanks to Lavern Castillo's father dressed as jolly old Saint Nick. Unfortunately not all was jolly, bright and joyful. One Atari employee family met with a turn of bad luck - the Dye's family home burned down and one of their family members was badly burned. Marge Cole over in the F. building coordinated donations and help from fellow Atarians to aid the family, in a strong showing of why Atari was still like a family and a great place to work, even as it had grown into a large corporation.

Somebody Get Me A Mallet!

Warner's purchase of Atari long complete, they were now planning to inject $120 million into Atari in 1977 for the continued development of project Stella and the funding of Atari's ongoing expansion. Again, just like *Home PONG*, getting the chip work done (in this case the "TIA" or Television Interface Adapter) was only one small part of a bigger picture in getting this innovative and important product out the door. Building development systems, hiring game programmers, coding new games to release with the system, board layout work and Industrial Design of the case and accessories would all need to be done next.

The 'case' has the most interesting design factor, later affectionately nicknamed by Atari fans as the 'Sunnyvale Heavy Sixer.' 'Sunnyvale' since these units were manufactured and assembled right in Sunnyvale, California. 'Heavy' because of its thick and quite heavy polystyrene base. In fact, the weight was added on purpose - it was all about buyer perception. If you've ever opened up an Atari Video Computer System and examined its insides, it's almost 50% empty. To give buyers the feeling that they were getting 'their money's worth' from buying this product, it was made heavier. To consumers, 'heavy' meant 'quality' - which meant it was worth the nearly $200 price tag. As for the 'Sixer' part, well, that referred to the six control switches along the front panel. Altogether you have the nickname 'Sunnyvale Heavy Sixer.'

The Polystyrene base may have given Atari a marketing advantage to buyers in its products quality perception; however it was causing nothing but havoc to the assembly line workers trying to put the new VCS systems together. Deadlines were looming and the pressure was on to get the nearly 400,000 launch VCS systems assembled, tested and delivered to retailers for the 1977 Christmas sales season. Atari's future and Warner's massive investment into this risky little Silicon Valley upstart (now major company subsidiary) was all on the line.

Polystyrene is very strong and very heavy when molded in such a fashion as had been done for the bottom casing of the VCS. However there was a problem that no one from Industrial Design or Engineering had factored in, but that became apparent when batches of the bottom cases began to arrive in the assembly building.

Douglas Hardy, one of the designers of the VCS case, recalls: "We had this company up in Oregon doing the bottoms for us. They would ship them down in semi's through the Nevada desert and they were cooking in the back of the trailers. When they got down to us, warping of the bottoms was happening." Doug came up with a solution, going up to the plastics firm and having them cool down the bottoms with cold, 35 degree water when they were released from the molds. He then made arrangements for the manufacturer to ship the bottoms down to California in refrigerated tractor trailers to keep them cool on the hot trip down. While this solved the initial manufacturing and shipping problems, unfortunately the warping was still occurring for some reason in the assembly building.

Russ Farnell, a mechanical engineer at Atari also remembers: "The case bottoms were resting on cool concrete floors in an assembly building with warm air." The two factors caused the material to warp just a tiny fraction, but more than enough to cause the bottom cases to still not allow the top cases to simply and easily fit into place on top of them. Russ continues: "A short period of panic set in on the assembly line until a quick fix was instituted in the form of a rubber mallet. A firm smack of the rubber mallet onto the top case would force it into place onto the bottom polystyrene base and then the pieces could be secured together with screws." The problem was fixed by this decidedly Atarian low tech solution, and away down the assembly line they went. But the lesson learned was still obvious: Atari was still naive when it came to manufacturing consumer products. It's not surprising, given that it was a mirror of the original decision to first manufacture coin-ops; Learning on the job.

Upon further inspection of the insides of the original 1977 production Atari VCS systems, there is yet another interesting anomaly a person may notice, speaker grills and mounting posts for two speakers. What many people even today still don't know is that the Atari VCS was actually intended to have built-in stereo speakers instead of outputting its sound directly through the TV set. Originally, the design was going to take its cue from the previously dedicated consoles like *Home PONG* and the others, which all had built-in speakers. The change from small speakers to television speaker occured when Niles Strohl and Wade Tuma started to examine the design and realized that it was going to cost nearly $10 dollars in parts to add a decent amplifier and speakers into the Atari VCS product design. In no short order, Niles and Wade came up with a solution. "The speakers in TV sets were much better than anything we'd supply in the game console, so we piped the audio channels, remember there were two of them coming out of the TIA chip - we ran them out through an RF modulator design that Wade had come up with to eliminate this $10 dollar cost," recalls Niles. The cost of this solution ended up being a mere $.25 cents in total, and Wade would create the RF modulator that allowed the VCS to send the audio and video to a television. A piece of technology that would be used on many Atari products to come.

When it came time to launch the VCS, instead of the originally suggested four built-in games, the VCS would be packaged with an included game cartridge called *Combat*. *Combat* was actually the culmination of several previous Atari arcade titles put together as one. First and foremost was *Tank*, the original proof of concept and now included as the main game in the cartridge. Joe Decuir had taken that proof of concept and continued to work on the game, which was then given to Larry Wagner to complete. In the process of developing the *Combat* game cartridge, Larry also included the Atari arcade game *Jetfighter*. In all, 27 different variants of games of *Tank* and *Jetfighter* (with bi-plane variations as well) would be included into the cartridge, with the variations becoming a strong selling point for Atari - who marketed them as 27 different games on a single cartridge.

This would be an apropos moment to touch on the programmers of the launch titles for the VCS. After all, with a programmable game system, Atari was going to need game programmers... and a LOT of them if it was going to start creating a large library of new games to introduce and keep the interest level and profit level of the new product line going strong. But before you could have programmers start to program on this new gaming platform, you needed development systems to develop the games on. That's where Jim Luby came in.

Jim would build out five separate breadboard development systems for Stella. The first would be the prototype system Jim himself would build, debug and document. "I then farmed out to Twin Industries to build four additional breadboard systems, I wasn't going to build all of those by myself - they built them based on the circuit drawings and the debugged breadboard prototype," recalls Jim. These would be the first four developer station systems ever built for the VCS. Each of the first four programmers hired by Atari would use these developer breadboard systems to code the first VCS games. Besides the programming hardware system, a programmer's guide would also be needed so that the game coders would know how the system worked and how to access its features and capabilities. Unlike today's books and reams of documentation that developers usually get, the original programmer's guide was actually a stack of Joe Decuir's hand written notes that were photocopied and stapled together.

The power and flexibility of the VCS would be noticed and exploited almost immediately by several of the programmers, most of whom are now well known heroes to 80s home video game fans. Larry Kaplan (hired by Larry Wagner and Bob Brown) can be credited as the first official software designer hired to develop games for the Stella project.

Larry had been working at Singer Business Machines where he developed code for a point of sale system and was also involved in the architecture for an early NMOS based microprocessor chip. After seeing an ad in the local paper, Larry applied for a position as a programmer at Atari and would be hired to begin work on one of the first of the six new VCS games shown at the introduction of the new game console in June 1977, *Air-Sea Battle*. When programming *Air-Sea Battle*, "I discovered early that it was possible to reposition player objects during a screen (which is a frame of the TV picture), though that was not a consideration of the original design specs," recalls Larry. So by designing *Air-Sea Battle*, which had used horizontal bands of player objects, this programming technique was used as a cornerstone extensively within many VCS games. Larry Kaplan continues: "Without that single strobe, H-move, the VCS would have failed as a game platform very quickly." Larry would move on to program *Atari Bowling* as well.

One major advantage of having *Combat* as the pack-in game, and one which would be a hidden marketing gain for the VCS console, was that *Combat* is a two player game cartridge. All 27 variations of the games required two players, which meant that right off the bat a VCS owner would most likely engage a friend or relative to play a few rounds of *Combat*, ensuring the 'word of mouth' would spread to others about this amazing new game console and its enticing games. In fact, all the 400,000 consoles produced for that Christmas completely sold out.

Not to forget our usual sectional odds and ends, as Atari entered 1977, some important events occurred. Specifically in February as Karen Sabo was awarded Employee of the Month. She actually came into work every day a half hour early to go into the game room to practice playing Breakout so she can beat Gil Williams in their next match against one another. Also, an important birthday came up in February for some employee named Nolan. That's right: Nolan as in Bushnell (born on February 5, 1943). Atari's new hires that month also include Paul Kay, the new Cash and Insurance manager and William Parker as Atari's financial planning manager. A company-wide announcement was also made from none other than Chuck E Cheese, to hang on just a bit longer until the new restaurant is opened. It seems the dapper rat is tangling with the San Jose bureaucracy to get some final delays sorted out.

Review In Images

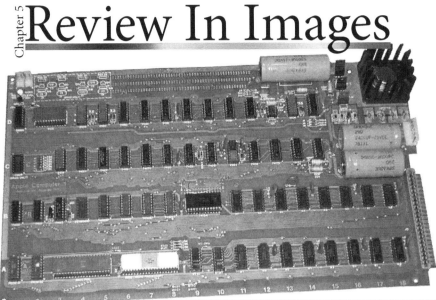

Top: The Apple I computer, designed by Steve Wozniak and sold by former Atari employee Steve Jobs.

Right: A gold-plated PCB of *Breakout* was created in honor of the 10,000th *Break-out* PCB produced.

ATARI STRIKES GOLD!

Yep, Atari struck it rich with our Atari Personnel's favorite Breakout™ Game! Dale Kochenburg of VSM, Inc. arrived at Atari in mid-March to present the Building F employees with a gold-plated circuit board, which we hope to have assembled with gold-plated parts by April 29. This gold printed circuit board symbolizes the completion of 10,000 Breakout boards, just as Atari received a gold board for the completion of 10,000 Tank™ boards. Thank you very much, VSM, and thanks to all of you Breakout lovers and competers too!

Left: Quiz Show, which stores question and answer data on an 8-track casette tape.

Bottom: An example of the 8-track casettes used, in this case for the later multi-game coin-op *Triple Hunt*, the first video game with a soundtrack.

Clockwise from top left: An ad for the Jolt computer recommended by Chuck Peddle. A Jolt CPU card used to help build the above proof of concept. 6502 microprocessor designer Chuck Peddle. The original Cyan built proof of concept prototype for the VCS. This currently resides in the Computer History Museum in Mountain View, CA

The secret location at 471 Division Street set up by Al Alcorn for development of the VCS. Unknown to Al, in Fall of '75 Steve Bristow moved some of Atari's coin operations to the building directly behind 471. Al found out when Owen Rubin poked his head in at 471 one day to see what was going on there, to which Al promptly stated in surprise "What the fuck are you doing here?"

Bottom clockwise from top left: Jay Miner, Joe Decuir, Jay Miner's beloved cockapoo Mitchy who came to work with him every day and had his own Atari id badge.

Top: Joe Decuir's bike Stella, where the project and the custom graphics chip got their codename.

Bottom: The actual VCS prototype, with wirewrap version of the TIA graphics chip. Note the joysticks appropriated from a *Tank* coin-op.

Product Plans and Strategy
Consumer Video Games

Prepared
for
Nolan Bushnell/Joe Keenan
ATARI Inc.

by
Gene R. Landrum
Consultant

May 26, 1976

VII. Conclusion

ATARI, in my opinion, has two definite strengths at this time. One is in the development of electronic games with excellent play value and the opportunity to market test these via the coin-op division. The second strength is a definite head start on all competition which forces them to play catch-up football. This second item is significant when considering the vast repertoire of games immediately available for the cartridge approach with slight modifications.

Based on the above, I recommend a product strategy aimed at the bottom segment of the market and the top or sophisticated sector. I am recommending a product offering in the middle sector vs. the G.I. chip assemblers and National, but do not believe it wise for ATARI to go to the mat with these firms in the crowded and bitterly contested middle segment. There will be many casualties.

The cost advantages due to learning curve, equipment amortization, and personnel experience should allow a toy product to be offered at $19.95 - $24.95 in 1977 and going to $9.95 in 1980. By modifying the existing game library, a cartridge product can be introduced in '77 with 12-15 existing game cartridges ranging in price from $14.95 - $24.95. The console would sell at $79.95 - $99.95 on introduction with some adult games such as gambling or Biofeedback offered immediately.

I believe ATARI should capitalize on its brand recognition as a game innovator and expert, and exploit this brand recognition on Tank, PONG, Stunt Cycle, Trak 10, etc. Also, I feel strongly the name 'ATARI' should be on all products with exception of private label accounts where merchants have a hangup, e.g., Sears/Penneys/ Wards or Quella/Neckerman. Product differentiation would otherwise be made by features, packaging, warranty, price protection, price maintenance, etc.

A strong product commitment by the company at this time can ensure market share, profitability, and long term posture as 'The' electronic game company.

Clockwise from top left: Don Valentine, one of the investors brought in before the Warner purchase and who was also later an early investor in Apple Computer. Steve Ross, CEO of Warner Communications. Disneyland around the time of Steve Ross's visit with his son where they played *Tank*.

NON-EXCLUSIVE CROSS LICENSE FOR VIDEO GAMES

THIS AGREEMENT, having an effective date of
June 8, 1976 and entered into by and between THE MAGNAVOX
COMPANY, a corporation of the State of Delaware, with
executive offices in New York, New York and corporate
offices at 1700 Magnavox Way, Fort Wayne, Indiana (hereinafter referred to as MAGNAVOX) and ATARI, INC., a corporation
of the State of California, with offices at Winchester
Boulevard, Los Gatos, California (hereinafter referred to
as ATARI):

WITNESSETH THAT:

WHEREAS, MAGNAVOX warrants it is the exclusive
licensee under a plurality of patents and patent applications,
the title to which resides in SANDERS ASSOCIATES, INC.,
a corporation of the State of Delaware, having an
office at Daniel Webster Highway South, Nashua, New
Hampshire (hereinafter referred to as SANDERS);

WHEREAS, MAGNAVOX warrants it has the right
under an agreement dated January 27, 1972 (hereinafter
referred to as the OTHER LICENSE AGREEMENT, a copy of
which is attached hereto as Exhibit A) to grant licenses
under such plurality of patents and applications;

This page and the next several pages: Select pages from Atari's licensing agreement with Magnavox. Atari settled before going forward
with the sale to Warner, and it's probably good they did; All the other
co-defendants in the suit lost the following year.

and allowances that are customarily given in the
trade and actually taken, cost of freight, special
packing, insurance, and excise taxes or duty where
separately stated, but before deduction of any other
items including but not limited to agents' commissions.

II LICENSE OF THE MAGNAVOX PATENTS

2.01 MAGNAVOX hereby grants to ATARI, subject to the
reservations and conditions set forth herein, a
fully paid non-exclusive license under MAGNAVOX
PRINCIPAL PATENTS, without the right to sublicense,
to make, have made, use, sell and lease LICENSED
PRODUCTS covered by said MAGNAVOX PRINCIPAL PATENTS
in and for the TERRITORY, and a fully paid non-
exclusive license under MAGNAVOX FOREIGN PATENTS to use,
sell, and lease LICENSED PRODUCTS made or had made
by ATARI hereunder in the TERRITORY.

III   CONSIDERATION FOR THE LICENSE OF
THE MAGNAVOX PATENTS

3.01 In addition to the license under the ATARI PATENTS
as set forth in Article V below and the right
to use the ATARI TECHNOLOGY as set forth in
Article VI below, ATARI agrees to pay as
consideration for the license set forth in
Article II above and for the other covenants

set forth herein, the following amounts on the
dates indicated:

$150,000.00	Within 10 days of execution of this agreement
$150,000.00	January 31, 1977
$200,000.00	January 31, 1978
$200,000.00	January 31, 1979
$200,000.00	January 31, 1980
$200,000.00	January 31, 1981
$200,000.00	January 31, 1982
$200,000.00	January 31, 1983

IV   OTHER COVENANTS

4.01 MAGNAVOX covenants not to sue ATARI or its customers for infringement of any patents presently issued or issued on presently pending applications owned or controlled by MAGNAVOX or SANDERS, in the field of video games, during the term of this license.

4.02 MAGNAVOX agrees to prosecute such suits for infringement of the MAGNAVOX PRINCIPAL PATENTS as may be reasonably necessary to protect against unlicensed competition materially interfering with the business of ATARI hereunder. However, MAGNAVOX shall not be obligated to bring more than one such suit at a time.

V LICENSE OF THE ATARI PATENTS

5.01 ATARI hereby grants to MAGNAVOX and SANDERS, subject to the reservations set forth herein, a fully paid non-exclusive license to make, have made, use, sell

-7-

Unlike what's been claimed in more recent interviews by Atari co-founder Nolan Bushnell, the settlement was hardly a 'junk settlement.' Atari agreed to pay $1.5 million at a time when money was tight enough that they were looking to sell the company.

and lease LICENSED PRODUCTS under the ATARI PATENTS, without the right to sublicense. ATARI further grants to MAGNAVOX and to SANDERS an option to grant non-exclusive sublicenses in foreign countries outside the United States under ATARI PATENTS provided that a payment is made to ATARI of 1% of the Net Selling Price of the sub-licensed products.

5.02 ATARI hereby warrants that it has the right to grant the license herein granted to MAGNAVOX.

VI   RIGHT TO USE ATARI TECHNOLOGY, TRANSFER
      THEREOF AND TECHNICAL ASSISTANCE

6.01 ATARI hereby grants to MAGNAVOX and to SANDERS, subject to the conditions set forth herein, the right to use the ATARI TECHNOLOGY.

6.02 ATARI agrees to disclose to MAGNAVOX and SANDERS from time to time during the period from the effective date of this Agreement through December 31, 1977, for the use of MAGNAVOX and of SANDERS, all the technical know how and information included in ATARI TECHNOLOGY, but only to the extent that such know-how and information is owned by ATARI on the date of this Agreement or acquired by ATARI and its SUBSIDIARIES on or before June 1, 1977, and further only to the extent that ATARI can permit MAGNAVOX and SANDERS to use such know how and information without incurring breach of contract by reason of the transfer thereof.

-8-

It also gave Magnavox rights to all technology owned by Atari for the following year, which they could ask to see up through December '77. They never saw the VCS until after the June 1st 1977 date. Feel free to draw your own conclusion as to why.

inco brate   TARI's kit for the first twenty thousand (20,000) LICENSED PRODUCTS and at three percent (3%) of such NET SELLING PRICE of said complete video game afte the first twenty thousand (20,000) LICENSED PRODUCTS on which royalty has been paid. Royalties paid under this paragraph shall not be subject to any royalty provision paragraphs 3.01 and 8.03.

XX   ROYALTY PAYMENTS AND REPORT

20.01 To the extent that any payments are required to be made by the parties on the basis of NET SELLING PRICE, reports and payments shall be made on a calendar quarter basis with such reports and payments due within sixty (60) days after the end of such quarter. The reports shall include the number of units sold, the NET SELLING PRICE and the royalties payable. The parties shall have the right to have an audit performe of such party by a recognized public accounting firm at reasonable hours and only to the extent to confirm that proper royalties have been paid.

IN WITNESS WHEREOF, the parties hereto cause the corporate names to be affixed by their respective duly authorized officers or representatives.

THE MAGNAVOX COMPANY

By _Thomas A. Bair_
Title _Corporate Patent_
Date _June 8, 1976_

Attest:

_____

ATARI INC.

By _____
Title _Vice President of En_
Date _June 8, 1976_

Attest

-21-

Nolan Bushnell of Los Gatos, inventor of popular electronic table tennis game, Pong, relaxes with friend at $160,000 home. Philosophy is not to worry. He is 33 years of age. — (AP Laserphoto)

Pong inventor rich in year

LOS GATOS (AP) — Not to worry, that's Nolan Bushnell's philosophy. If he fails and loses his shirt, why, he'll just start all over again.

Of course, Nolan Bushnell's shirt is pretty firmly fixed on his back these days, when he's not relaxing

"Does it make sense to work for the good life and not have the good life?"

He started taking weekends off, sailing on the bay, having lunch in fashionable San Francisco

Top left: The July 18th, 1976 article that sent Nolan's ex-wife into a rage, causing Warner Communications to insist Nolan settle with her. *(Courtesy of Bakersfield Californian)*

Bottom Right: The Warner Communications management team of (left to right) Ken Rosen, David Horowitz, Steve Ross, Manny Gerard and Jay Emmett.

Top left: The more common stand-up version of *Night Driver* on the assembly line.

Top Right: Kee Games/Atari *Sprint 2* coin-ops being assembled.

DATE: July 1977

SUBJECT: First Production 2600 on line

ASK YOUR PHOTO RETAILER

The very first Atari Video Computer System to roll off the assembly line.

Top: The launch version of the Video Computer System, known by collectors today as the 'heavy sixer' because of its heavy and thick polystyrene base.

Bottom: Handheld paddles were also included. Both the joystick and paddle include the Atari name and/or logo, which is not present in later models.

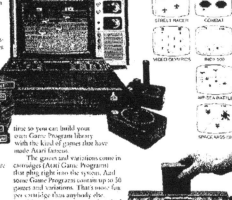

INTRODUCING ATARI'S VIDEO COMPUTER SYSTEM. THE PROGRAMMABLE SYSTEM THAT OFFERS YOU MORE VIDEO GAMES AND VARIATIONS THAN ANYONE ELSE.

Be a flying ace, a race car champion, a tennis star and a space pioneer all in one afternoon with the Video Computer System by Atari; the new computerized programmable video game system for home TVs that is designed to give you the most sophisticated, intricate and fun video games.

The Video Computer System comes with unique joystick and paddle controllers, a difficulty option switch to handicap one or all players, realistic sounds, and Atari's Combat Game Program with 27 thrill-packed action games and variations like Tank, Tank Pong, Jet Fighter and Biplane.

And that's just the beginning. Atari has already developed 160 more games and variations with Game Programs like: Air-Sea Battle, Video Olympics, Starship, Street Racer, Indy 500, Blackjack, Surround, and Basic Math. And there will be more coming out all the time so you can build your own Game Program library with the kind of games that have made Atari famous.

The games and variations come in cartridges (Atari Game Programs) that plug right into the system. And some Game Programs contain up to 50 games and variations. That's more fun per cartridge than anybody else.

More games mean more fun. And more fun means Atari.

VIDEO COMPUTER SYSTEM™ FROM ATARI

More games. More fun

ATARI

ONLY $169.95

The very first newspaper ad for the VCS. It was available through San Francisco area Macy's and Sears on September 11th, 1977.

The VCS was sold along side Atari's last 'dedicated' console, *Video Pinball*. Allowing home play of *Breakout*, *Pinball* and *PONG* style *Basketball*, offering this console at the same time as trying to launch the VCS is confusing. Some at Atari feared it would cut in to VCS sales.

ATARI KNEW TV COULD BE FUN... THEY WERE RIGHT!

ATARI

ATARI VIDEO PINBALL®... 7 big games & no tilt!
Pinball wizards the world over say there's nothing like Video Pinball. The game is so addictive, it's diabolical... with 7 blockbuster games, all in color on color sets, and consisting of 4 pinball games, two rebound basketball and Breakout®. Atari Video Pinball is just about the best thing you could do for your family this Christmas ... only **89.95!**

ATARI VIDEO COMPUTER SYSTEM sure is no toy!
But it sure is as fun as any toy you're likely to find! Grown men have been known to stage marathon Video Computer System matches lasting for days-on-end! There are 27 action-packed game variations ... each more difficult than the last game you played. Shoot down planes ... annihilate tanks ... sink submarines, all at the flick of the controls, all in living color. Computer system, **189.95.** Air-Sea and Black Jack cartridges, **19.95** each.

Besides large multi-player games like *Indy 800* and *Tank 8*, Atari also created unique large "chained machine" efforts as well including the *Gran Trak/PONG/Space Race* multi-machine trailer. Below is the special bank of six *Sprint 2* coin-ops based on Atari's Theatre kiosk, done for the Bay Area Rapid Transit (BART) of San Francisco and installed at the Montgomery Street station. Atari owned and operated the machines and BART collected the money - about $1791 in just the first five weeks of operation. At the top of the bank of games are screens playing continuous slideshows of BART information.

Individual pie-shaped, coin-operated video skill games integrated into an attractive, elegant "Kiosk"

THE ATARI THEATRE

ADAPTABILITY

The Atari Theatre is custom designed to the specifications of the individual location.

The Atari Theatre smoothly blends into the rich sophisticated image of fine hotels, restaurants, stores, etc. because its decor is designed to the specific color scheme, including the logo, of the individual location it's going into.

So, rather than fight each other, The Atari Theatre enhances the location and further identifies the overall image of its surroundings. The end result is a perfect blend between a rich looking entertainment center and the image of the location.

Adapts to any space requirement

The Atari Theatre Kiosk is made up of a number of pie-shaped pieces, and within each piece is a different video game. That means the Kiosk can be put together with two games that fit snugly into a corner. Or three games that fit against the wall. Or five or even six games that can stand freely in the middle of a room, lobby or floor space.

The upper portion is also custom designed.

The upper portion of the Kiosk is available in different sizes and shapes. Or the Kiosk base of video games is available without any top configuration.

The tops provide a unique and interesting space for advertising. It provides clientele with information on special sales or events, or new items, or special hotel packages, or lounge entertainment, or whatever the needs of the specific location. It can be designed with back lighting, front lighting, rear screen projection, or with no lighting at all.

Nolan's original mascott for Chuck E. Cheese, Rick Rat, started making appearances around Atari.

1265 Borregas, Atari's new corporate headquarters after leaving Winchester Blvd. in October of 1976.

Back To Our Grass Roots

What follows is an event-by-event format recount of Grass Valley's Cyan Engineering (Atari's personal "think tank" for new games and gadgets) and several other interrelated short lived groups. Our hope with this format is to convey the feeling of the very project books and scribbled notes much of this information was taken from.

The beginnings of Atari's advanced research group, Cyan Engineering in Grass Valley, California, are just as deeply rooted in AMPEX as Atari's own history was. Steven Mayer and Larry Emmons were both AMPEX employees working in the AMPEX Videofile division in Sunnyvale when they decided it was time to move on and do their own things.

Steve and Larry's contact with post-Ampex Nolan and Ted had occurred early on, while Steve was working on installing a Videofile system at the LA County Sheriff's department. Back in this time period when Nolan was working nights with Ted on the *Computer Space* game project, their shoestring budget found them needing parts, causing him to visit Steve one day asking to borrow any extra he had left over. Not one to turn down an old workmate, Steve actually was able to sneak some parts from the LA County sheriff's department installation and gave them to Nolan and Ted under Ampex's nose, starting a relationship that would soon grow.

Shortly after, despite getting the Videofile system into several key locations, the division was starting to fall on hard times due to this last massive installation for the LA County Sheriff's department. AMPEX did its part for its work on the installation of the largest deployment to date and in fact, including the main office installation and all of the outlying office installations of the Videofile system, the amount of hardware equaled four fully deployed Videofiles.

Everything in the main office location worked perfectly, however there was a problem with all of the other field offices: None could access the main Videofile systems to input scans or retrieve any images or data. The LA County Sheriff's Department had never ordered or installed the microwave communication links to go between all of their offices to network them together, without which there were zero communication capabilities for the Videofile installation.

The finger pointing and blame game commenced but in the end, AMPEX would come out the loser in the argument and the end result was that Larry and Steve had both bailed (with Steve leaving first). The two met up not long afterwards to discuss a company that Steve has joined, and Steve stated that if things didn't work out then the two of them should consider starting a company of their own.

It wouldn't be too long before they would both find themselves working at a company which originally only produced automotive exhaust systems, Arvin Systems. Arvin would in turn acquire Echo Science Corporation and try to leverage its advanced magnetic media recording technology. As Larry Emmons recalls: "Well first there was our work for Arvin Systems, but as far as the Arvin interlude in 1972-73, that is all Steve's fault! But Cyan Engineering emerged out of that goofy (Arvin) enterprise along with several other ex-Arvin guys."

When Steve originally took the job with Arvin, they were attempting to create videodisc technology by the use of floppy drive media and put it into use for military applications. A technology they would produce exactly one product with, called the Arvin Echo, which used the oversized floppy media to produce still-framed video for the military under a government contract.

In the fall of 72' while Syzygy/Atari was starting to manufacture *PONG* en masse, it was clear that Arvin management didn't have clue as to what they were doing. The video disc project they were working on for Arvin simply wasn't panning out as Steve and Larry had hoped, mainly due to Arvin's poor management of the project. They decided to begin working on their own side project, a read/write video disc system they thought they might be able to use to go and start their own company with, and also considered farming themselves out on contracts.

The first people they reached out to look for a contract with were their old acquaintances, Nolan Bushnell and Ted Dabney. So they flew down to meet with Nolan and Ted to see what this new 'Syzygy' and their game *PONG* was all about while hopefully enticing them into contracting them for a new project.

The meeting with Nolan, Ted and Al Alcorn actually went quite well, an Ampex reunion of sorts resulting in a deal being struck to have Steve and Larry work on game circuits for Syzygy/Atari. Steve set up shop in his basement and Larry built a small lab in the corner of his garage, and they both spent a substantial sum to purchase a state-of-the-art Tektronix oscilloscope and other equipment to get things started.

Next Steve and Larry hired a few employees to help out, with Steve hiring a tech named Bob Walker (son of an Arvin employee), and Larry hiring Lanny Netz, (an Arvin electronics technician). Their little side project was finally on its way!

One of the first projects that Steve and Larry would be asked to develop for Syzygy/Atari was a remote controlled version of the *PONG* arcade game. The idea was to transform the TV sets that hung over a typical bar into a *PONG* playing entertainment piece. The catch was that there would be two wireless transmitter controllers to allow the two opponents to be either of the paddles on the screen. Connected to the *PONG* pcb board would be the receiver interface that would be tuned to receive signals from the pair of wireless transmitter controls.

The concept prototype was built by Steve and Larry, with most of the work on this project being done by Larry, as the design required an analog engineer and he was one of the best. In the original *PONG* arcades and the later *Home PONG* consoles, the knobs were connected to electronic components called 'pots' and these would output varying resistance readings to the *PONG* board, with the amount of resistance dictating the position of the *PONG* player paddle on the screen. It would take someone skilled in varying voltages and resistance to be able to build a circuit that would read this in real-time and transmit the data to a receiver that in turn would output the same variation of voltage to the 'pot's' lines on the *PONG* board. Steve delivered the prototype to Nolan and while demonstrating it, they got into a casual discussion as to what other work Steve and Larry were doing. Steve explained to Nolan that they have been working on a read/write videodisc system and wanted to do it for sports instant replay video. Nolan says to Steve: "Why are you doing this hard stuff? If you do it nobody is going to care anyway." Prompting Steve to rethink his and Larry's future direction, it was actually one of the few choice moments where Nolan's crystal ball into the future was a bit cloudy considering the future of mass storage devices.

In February 1973, Steve and Larry were no longer on the brink of being broke (thanks to Nolan and Ted) so they decided to quit 'Starvin Arvin,' as they had nicknamed it. As Larry recalls: "I'm not sure of the connection but I think it was Jim Hebb that introduced us to the Litton brothers, sons of Charlie Litton, the founder of Litton Industries." Charles Litton had actually sold the company in the mid 50s and moved to Grass Valley, purchasing the 'old hospital' which had been built in the late 30's for the gold mining industry. Steve and Larry rented out 1000 sq.ft. on the second floor of the five story building and built a real development lab.

It started with the four of them but soon they needed to hire a few more people, including Jodi, the secretary at Arvin, who helped to keep Steve and Larry honest - almost mirroring the situation between Nolan, Ted and Cynthia the year before. This is the start of what would eventually become Cyan Engineering, which officially didn't have a name yet. Cyan's name wouldn't come for some time into their relationship with Atari, after they had experienced a merger of sorts.

"We were going now, but Cyan Engineering wasn't actually 'Cyan' yet. We didn't have a name and we decided we needed one, and knew enough not to dwell on that subject, so we quickly came up with Cyan, which on the color chart is negative red. We didn't want to be 'In the Red.' Besides, we could now have some fun and call ourselves 'Cyantists!' There were a few times we were referred to as the 'Cyanides' by some, perhaps in jest, or prediction, we just ignored it," recalls Larry.

The 'merger happened when Nolan suggested that Steve and Larry should keep designing circuits for Atari as its official Research and Development arm during one of Steve's trips down to Atari. Steve returns to the Grass Valley group and explains the offer and both he and Larry agree that this will be a better path for them to pursue. Nolan 'invests' into the Grass Valley operation by paying for their drill press, electronic components and other equipment that they had, begining the merging of Cyan into Atari. However, at its core Cyan would still remain as an independent consultancy, and while it would eventually be referred to as Atari Grass Valley, the company always retained its legal name, Cyan Engineering.

This was important for several reasons: One reason was that as Cyan, the engineers could go out and investigate technologies or even the competition without raising the awareness of Atari's involvement. The second and probably more important reason was that many times Atari would be fully extended on its credit with suppliers and needed components to build machines to ship and in turn get paid. By Cyan Engineering being a separate entity it had its own line of credit, so when Atari needed parts and equipment, Cyan would make the purchase. Atari could then build and ship product, get paid and in turn pay off its creditors. With the suppliers and creditors paid, Atari would order more parts and components, ship more product and then pay Cyan back the money owed so they in turn could pay their supplier and creditor bills. This 'creative' financing helped to keep Atari's head above water and survive some very rough times early on.

Cyan's next big project would be to design the prototype for the game called *Gotcha* - the game that came to Al Alcorn while examining defective *PONG* boards. Steve Mayer took the project and designed a circuit to create a random maze generator, control input, coin sensor and other needed features. A wire wrap board and circuit drawings followed – and just like that, Gotcha went from a random glitch, to an idea, to an actual game when it was brought down to Atari to be put into product form.

Everyone was really enjoying working with each other, so with a quick and steady workflow, Steve and Larry then moved to work on some *PONG* arcade variants like *PONG Doubles* and *QuadraPONG*. Nolan gave Steve and Larry the choice of working for a 5% royalty or to be paid $25,000 each in salary. The salary sounded more attractive to them so they opted for that, to not knowing how popular and/or how many units later games would sell (as well as not knowing how profits would drastically increase.) Looking back now, Steve and Larry perhaps made the wrong decision at the time, however Nolan did eventually issue small percentages of ownership in Atari to Steve and Larry. This of course in later years would bear fruit for both of them when Atari would sell itself to Warner Communications in 1976 for $28 million.

The relationship between the two companies continued to grow, and the creative Cyan group was fitting right in. With creative talent (and in some cases, sheer genius), some unique characteristics will often accompany that person. Case in point; the employees of Atari would many times be unkempt hippies with long hair, beards, tie-dyed attire and even exhibit their unique personalities in the cars they drove - or in this instance, what was in one engineer's car. Steve Mayer had what could really only be described as a garden occupying the entire backseat section of his car. "It had all the makings of life, all that was needed was the lightning bolts!" recalls Steve. At one point, Steve had to go renew his driver's license and at the time it required a driver's test. His garden in the back of his car had become so overgrown that the DMV tester refused to get into his car, so Steve had to return another day with a different car, minus the garden.

If you remember, when Atari was originally incorporated Nolan wanted the company to develop a driving game as its first video game product. Set aside for *PONG*, in the Fall of '73 it was finally the right time for that driving game to be revisited and developed. Only the new management situation with Dr. Wakefield and company at Atari would ultimately take a terrible toll on the project.

The across the board management change brought some unexpected negative reactions and feelings by many, including the Grass Valley group. "Things became very divisive and political. We were fortunate to be up here in Grass Valley away from all of that, so we kept our heads down during that period," recalled Steve Mayer. Things had noticeably changed - whenever Steve or Larry came down to Los Gatos with prototypes or design circuit schematics, they now met with everyone behind closed doors having what they described as 'Dueling Cabals.' Essentially communications were not as open anymore, with things more closed and practically secretive to some extent. This early compartmentalizing would cause problems for one of Grass Valley's more notable (or notorious) projects for Atari.

Compounding the issues for Cyan, in September of 1973, Al Alcorn took a leave of absence from the company to take care of his ailing mother, and Lloyd Warman (also from Ampex Videofile) took charge as VP of Engineering during Al's absence. With Steve Bristow also leaving to help start Kee Games, this meant two of the key engineering resources were now gone, leaving the direction of the department fully in Warman's hands.

When the driving game project was put into motion, the new management and engineering structure within the company changed all of the previous flow and methodology. As Alcorn had put it; "they broke the mold." That 'mold' consisted of brainstorming ideas with research and having the circuits and wire wrap designs built based on those ideas. From there, the product development engineers would take on the task of putting the wire wrap boards and circuits into production readiness while the features, controls, cabinet and other areas would be tasked by the industrial design and model shop groups. They would all coordinate together, finalize components, costs and prepare a product for manufacturing. At least this was the original way things had been done prior to the management changes, which now had Manufacturing, Engineering and Research all with their hands into product development

In regards to Lloyd Warman, Al felt that while Lloyd had theories on how to do engineering and he burned the midnight oil to work hard on complex schedules, at some point you had to really understand the product and the people behind it. That seemed to be a big part of the problem Lloyd faced. "Lloyd Warman was a respected engineer and a smart, very organized, good guy. But we were a bunch (of 25-30 year olds) having a lot of fun and developing new things that would be stifled by bureaucracy. Lloyd wanted to organize things, but innovation does not happen that way," recalls Larry Emmons.

Other products that were conceived and started prior to the management change were able to ship out without many problems, but *Gran Trak* was behind schedule; there were problems with the design and it was becoming a costly delayed product - mainly due to the lack of communication channels within Atari.

The mechanical design of Gran Trak had been handled for Cyan by some fellow ex-Arvin friends of Steve and Larry's who had formed 'Eigen Systems.' Jim Hebb, John Sperry and several other former Arvin people had settled into the Litton building on the 3rd floor above Steve and Larry. Jim and John, (also both former Ampex employees prior to going to Arvin) developed the steering wheel encoder, gear shift, accelerator pedal, and other necessary parts to physically replicate driving a car. They went so far as to use actual steering wheels and pedals from automotive suppliers to give the game as real a feel as possible. Not exactly cost effective, and certainly not something that could be put into production. But that should have been communicated via Lloyd, which it wasn't.

Larry created the circuits for the vehicle dynamics, the physics of the car speeding around the track. His circuit designs would create the on-screen illusion of momentum, braking, acceleration and other real world 'feel' to the game play. The design really pushed the game technology at the time and also included a new pioneering feature: the first use of a ROM chip (the 74186 512-Bit '64x8' Read Only Memory (ROM)) to store the track and other objects for the display in the game. No longer needing a custom circuit for each display object, they could now be pre-generated and stored in the character ROM.

However, despite these groundbreaking implementations of game play in the driving dynamics, some real problems started to manifest. These custom circuits designed by Larry Emmons (which he referred to as 'hybrid chips') were being built by and supplied to Atari by National Semiconductor. National was not giving Atari's 'hybrid chip' much fabrication time in their schedule of products to deliver to customers, so they weren't supplying enough of them to Atari to meet the demand. To compound this issue, National Semiconductor many times refused to sell the custom components to Atari. This refusal may have been attributed to the custom components being out of spec when delivered, and Nolan making a public comment that National was the only semiconductor company to "screw up a gear ratio." At this point in early '74, coin-op manufacturing nearly came to a halt waiting on *Gran Trak 10's* sourcing issues. In March, a short test run of *Gran Trak 10's* were done and other design issues become more apparent.

At the imploring of Ron Gordon, in the Spring of 1974 Al Alcorn returned to Atari. Al's first order of business was to redesign the driving game to use different and more easily available components to replace the National Semiconductor components and free up the stranglehold on the product. He would then make other changes and quickly get the design productized.

The game cabinet was altered to a smaller version called *Trak 10* and the game would finally start shipping by the end of July. Kee Games would also release its own copied version of the *Gran Trak 10* design, called *Formula K,* at around the same time. And by late August, a more improved two player design called *Gran Trak 20* would debut along with Kee Games' own version called *Twin Racer* (though both were slightly delayed with the merger of Kee Games into Atari that December.)

When *Gran Trak* finally did ship at long last, there remained one lingering issue carried over that wasn't caught in time. Due to the compartmentalization of the company, the 'Cabal' environment and secrecy, component costs and manufacturing costs of *Gran Trak* had been sorely miscalculated. When the units started selling for $995 each, it was discovered after the fact that the unit cost of the game was $1095. Atari was actually losing $100 for every *Gran Trak* game sold! This issue would be corrected, but only after the damage was done, forcing Atari to report a massive loss for the 1973-1974 fiscal year, much of this directly due to the profit losses from *Gran Trak*. This game would become known as 'the one that nearly put the company out of business.'

One added note: the original *Gran Trak 10* design from the Grass Valley group had a very unique feature: the design had a hardcopy printer that could print out your high score. This feature never made it into production, but it was a very interesting concept to implement.

With Al back in charge of engineering, integration of the groups returned to a positive and healthy structure and as a result, so does production and manufacturing. Atari is righted through this tough time and is back on 'Trak' again!

By early 1975, Steve Bristow would become the VP of Engineering and Al Alcorn was now redirecting his attention to a special 'secret project' he had initiated just a month before which would become *Home PONG* and Atari's new consumer group. A lot of the now legendary (game) brain storming sessions took place during this time as Atari entered the golden years of pre-Warner Atari. These took place regularly at various locations, including Atari's Corporate headquarters in Los Gatos (in the early days), personal homes (up in Grass Valley and down in the Bay Area), later on at retreats at places like Pajaro Dunes, and even at Nolan's home.

These were always open discussions and the sharing of ideas either thought about and jotted down in notebooks to bring to the group… or just off the cuff ideas thought up on the spur of the moment. Overall, Nolan was the visionary in the process and during a lot of these brainstorming sessions, many times Nolan would toss in an idea completely out of left field, the initial reactions from everyone would always be that the ideas were not feasible. However, after further discussions those crazy left field ideas actually started to make a lot of sense and began to grow on everyone. Ultimately, the ideas that everyone first thought were crazy, suddenly became a key feature of the product concept.

There was a new project starting at Grass Valley that involved a game that used mechanical flippers instead of video displays. Grass Valley would not only begin work on a pinball machine, but it would be the very first microprocessor based pinball. A feature that would ultimately draw Atari and the Grass Valley engineers into a heated lawsuit between Williams, Gottlieb and Bally. The Grass Valley engineers would have to give deposition after deposition on how it was, in fact, Atari and Cyan Engineering who actually created the first microprocessor based pinball machine, called *Delta Queen,* and not the companies and their related projects.

The reason for the project was simple: Cyan engineers wanted to computerize a pinball just for the hell of it to prove it could be done, and there was an electromechanical *Delta Queen* by Bally that happened to be available. In reality they had several pinball machines on site that Nolan had sent to them, but the *Delta Queen* pinball had simply been the one that was arbitrarily chosen. They ripped all of the relays, steppers and rotating score wheels out of it and replaced just about everything except the main mechanical components (playfield lights, thumpers, slingshots, etc.) with digital electronics.

An LED score display was installed into the back glass of the machine, and the modified pinball was placed out on location at a local pizza parlor for awhile. Due to this test placement though, they realized the main design flaw was the matrix scanned inputs and outputs; the ball was faster than predicted and the scan rate was not fast enough to sense all switch closures on the playfield. Also, if the light bulb multiplex (a circuit that combines several signals into one) stopped due to a glitch, the lamps would burn out.

The Cyan engineers were frustrated that the first few pinball machines that Atari produced used multiplexes, and not latched input and outputs (logic circuits that directly transfer the current state when switched), but they too had similar problems. This was pointed out by Cyan to Atari, but as Larry Emmons puts it: "No one listened to us!"

While the modifications were installed into the Bally pinball, it was never designed for Bally in any formal business arrangement - this was merely an experiment, and the Bally pinball just happened to be on hand to tinker with. Bally had already had their own subcontractor working on a microprocessor controlled pinball - none other than Dave Nutting of the very same Nutting brothers that had done *Computer Quiz/IQ Computer*. Now with his own engineering contract firm based out of Milwaukee, and called Dave Nutting Associates, his employee Jeff Frederiksen had set about doing the same process Cyan had and converted a Bally *Flicker* pinball machine to be coordinated by an Intel 4004 microprocessor. Gottlieb and Williams had lead similar efforts, and the end result was a lawuit on who's patents were actually valid.

Atari joined Gottlieb and Williams as friends in court in a united offense to Bally's claim to be the inventor, and the Cyan engineers spent quite a bit of time sitting in the hot seat for depositions. "That was actually fun - we were first and proved it. Bally's patent was proven not to be valid," recalls Larry Emmons.

Shortly after their pinball experiment, when Al Alcorn informed Steve and Larry about the consumer project and *Home PONG*, they made the trip down to Division Street in 1975 to see the work that was being done. This was a very important event for the Grass Valley duo. Not only could Atari now design its own custom chips itself, but now Steve and Larry see what is possible with a custom integrated circuit. This little event turned their creativity valves wide open!

Enthralled with the possibilities, they returned to Grass Valley where they began to discuss things further with Ron Milner. When the very early thought of a programmable game system was even considered, it was nothing even remotely close to the VCS that would ship in 1977. The initial model concept was actually based around HP-35 and HP-45 calculators and was a simple one; use a standard microprocessor that would be used in all versions of the platform and in turn use a custom ROM for the game code. "Shortly after the design was conceived, we went to an external ROM connector instead of the ROM being on the board. Other concept ideas were to use a stack of ROM chips and be able to select a game, like a jukebox," recalls Steve Mayer.

In June of 1977 when the Atari VCS was unveiled to the world and the decision was made to start looking at creating the next product in the evolution path for the company to replace the VCS in a few years, a meeting between Steve Mayer, Nolan Bushnell and Joe Keenan takes place. "When the next generation follow-up VCS project first came up, I asked Bushnell and Keenan if they wanted this to be a game player or a computer, their answer was – YES. This contributed to the schizophrenic design criteria of the project. In hindsight, I really should've pushed back harder and nailed down one direction or another from them," recalls Steve Mayer.

During the concept meetings for the Colleen project (as it became named), Steve had wanted to look at the possibility of making the new enhanced VCS replacement compatible if it could be done without much added cost and if the design could use the same components. "I looked at having a system with the ability to have multiple clock speeds, having some of the same registers but enhancing things. It wouldn't be cartridge compatible, but it would allow programming code to move over easily," Steve recalls.

The game playing ability of the computer systems in one view was actually a major positive to the systems. They had custom graphics and I/O systems, the first of their kind in a home computer system on the market. The negative side to this was that because they could play games, the systems were looked down upon as not being serious enough to be considered real computers.

This of course, was the mindset of the times, as serious machines only displayed text on a black screen in white, green or amber colors. To have a computer with the ability to display an entire spectrum of colors on the screen, perform animation and produce 4-channel audio were amazingly impressive feats. Few computers of the time could perform anywhere near this, and this actually placed them into a class of devices viewed as nothing more than just toys and games, even though 'serious' computers could not even come close to doing the things that this system could do. Apple faced that very issue until 1979 when Dan Bricklin and Bob Frankston released VisiCalc, the first spreadsheet program, giving the Apple II inroads into the lucrative business market. The irony is that in today's computer culture, graphics animation and sound are the bars that must be met to consider a computer worthy of being powerful enough to be taken seriously.

Throughout 1977, Cyan conducts research in two areas leading to Atari's first real forays into the toy industry. One involves developing a unique way of building board games with electronic circuit traces painted onto the cardboard itself and connecting electronic components to it. Perceived as a major cost saver, a test project commences to pursue it. Research on the board games continues as July arrives, but now Cyan looks at ways to interface LCD displays to its conductive paint on cardboard designs. The liquid crystal displays are from a company called Robert Parker Research.

The second involves research into ideas for games and aids for the blind which leads to a rather groundbreaking project: Using ultrasonic sensors and mounting them on some custom electronics on top of a pair of headphones. The electronics would in turn simulate sounds from left, right and center based on the range information from the ultrasonic sensors to create what Ron Milner would call a 'Virtual Audio Image.' By the end of June, the initial idea of the ultrasonic system had now moved to some ideas for floor toy navigation, allowing a toy to detect moving objects and provide collision avoidance. Some other ideas come from this including an ultrasonic speedometer for bicycles, joggers, skiers and sailors. The floor toy idea continues to evolve, now with three ultrasonic detectors mounted onto a large gear, with the gear attached to a slow gear motor. When motion was detected, the motor would spin the sensors towards the sound.

Applications for the blind on the ultrasonic system turn out to have already been implemented by a company called Telesensory Systems in Palo Alto, so the focus was now strictly on guidance work for the floor toys. Based on the initial tests, the sensors have about an eight foot range and with some tweaking to the filters, it could be possible to track people in motion. In mid July, some fun sound effects were created including a duck call for the possibility of sound based toys. Other sound ideas included additional animal noises, explosions and gunshot sounds and also airplane sounds.

In July 1977 the board games project continued. Now that the tests on conductive paint have been successful and some other tests have shown good results, it's time to build an actual game. This all starts with working on one of the simplest early games called *The Game of Life*. The game is more popularly known as just *LIFE*. Not to be confused with the board game created in 1860 by Milton Bradley, this is a simulation of actual life invented by Cambridge mathematician John Conway and published in the October 1970 issue of Scientific American.

The game is based off of a concept called cellular automation. Conway created the game in response to a problem posed in the 1940's by the architect of the modern digital computer, John von Neumann. The problem posed was simply this – could a hypothetical machine replicate itself, just as a virus can replicate itself. John Conway would take on the task and solve it, and by doing so, create a highly popular game of the 1970s. Just as *PONG* was a response to building a game based on the ever popular sports game of tennis. An electronic board game designed around the popular game of *LIFE* would be designed. It will be a unique, super low cost implementation using electronics, LED lights, conductive paint and sandwiching it all together between two layers of cardboard with the top layer being separated slightly from the bottom layer. Pushing down on the top layer on designated spots would act as contact points to interact and play the game. Added to the design were the LCD board game's electronics. Finally a prototype was built using a 5x10 LCD grid connected to the 2-player *Game of Life* board game keypads .

With everything running through a 6530 to a 6502 CPU and a ROM containing the game code, the final electrical design hurdle was to implement conductive epoxy to attach the LCD and LED's to the game board. By September, the working prototypes were completed and a 2-player demo would be constructed and tested.

This board game design would spark the creation of an entirely new division within Atari down in its new Sunnyvale offices in Moffett Park: The Atari Board Games Division. After the successful testing of the prototype *Game of Life* board game in September, it appears that doing board games with this construction methodology would actually work very well AND be very cost effective, so on October 20th, Ron Milner wrote up a Company Confidential memo entitled, "Program to Implement Board Game Capability."

In August some circuits are built for the future Colleen enhanced VCS project. One is for a Power Line transmitter/receiver system, with the goal to allow the new system to be able to be used as a Home Automation controller. Home automation was actually a new and exciting prospect in the 1970s: technology gave the consumer the ability to remotely turn lights on and off, control a television with the touch of a button from the other side of the room or, with an intelligent device armed with an internal or light sensitive clock, it could be programmed to perform events at pre-determined times, such as turning on the outside lights at dusk or lawn sprinklers at a certain time of the evening or when no one was home. Previously, a company out of Scotland called Pico Electronics had developed a standardized protocol for devices to communicate through standard home electrical wiring outlets in 1975. Proving it could be done, creating an interface for Colleen to be able to control its surroundings was a very attractive concept to pursue.

Cyan delivered a clucking chicken to Pizza Time Theatre on August, 12th that they had been working on. This project had caused a serious delay in their work on other projects such as the board game concepts that were being tested out for component integration and interfacing before moving to building a prototype board game.

November sees Cyan focusing on a printer for project Colleen. The group examines a Victor print-head and begins seeing what it would take to build a physical carriage for interfacing electronics; the first steps towards what will eventually become Atari's first home computer printer, the Atari 820 had begun.

||||||||||||||||||||||||||||||||||||||||||||||||||||||||||||||||||||||||||||||||||||||||||||||||||||||||||

To wrap up the year, a meeting with Steve Bristow and Fred Thompson is held by the Cyan engineers. They discuss silkscreen vendors and how they could utilize their abilities for spraying on the circuit layouts for the board games onto cardboard for the new electronic board game products. Steve Bristow will set up shop in a small building near all of the other Atari buildings in Sunnyvale, CA in Moffett Park (located at 1364 Bordeaux Drive), and the Atari Board Games Division is officially christened.

The Board Games Division would consist of:

- Steve Bristow
- Dan Corona
- Joel Anderson (who would do the graphics art and design)
- Dave Salmon
- Shamon Kress and his wife Sylvia (who were the chemists and silver conductive paint experts)
- Dennis Koble (who would do the programming work)
- Mark Davis (who designed the hardware)
- Jackie Fowler (responsible for the rework/assembly of the initial run of board games)

Randy Hall did mechanical design and marketing materials along with Joel Anderson. "I actually put together really great marketing materials, but Ray Kassar pushed another marketing firm over my work; the ads they put together we not good," recalls Joel Anderson.

For demonstrations and marketing, as well as showing the new products at the 1979 Winter CES show in Las Vegas, 100 of each of the board games as well as the *Touch Me* handhelds were built. Showcasing the new products at the MGM Grand in Las Vegas could've really been a huge opportunity for exposure and media coverage of Atari's new electronic games division. However, everything was overshadowed by the center of attention at the Atari booth at the show: Atari's new Home Computers would make their debut and Kassar's decision was to focus ALL of the attention and spotlight on Atari's entry into the computer market. But despite the less than stellar coverage the Electronic Games Division received, it still booked over 100,000 units in orders.

The new product line from the Board Game Division shown off consisted of *Pro Darts*, *Pro Coach* (a football game), *Pro Ball* (a baseball game) and *Proteus 4* which was name changed to *Tronic 2* because the Proteus 4 name was not well received. Two other games that made it to concept but never made it to sample run were *Pulsar* and a bowling game concept. Out of all the games, the handheld *Touch Me*'s were very well received and had the bulk of the orders placed. With some solid initial orders in hand, it was now time to go to the next stage and begin manufacturing.

Right off the bat, Atari's now fracturing chain of command started exacting its toll on the Electronics Games Division's efforts. Locally at Atari's Moffett Park manufacturing campus, manufacturing wouldn't give up space to build this new product line. Marketing and sales were also not about to permit any kind of risk to the VCS production volume, since it was tied to their bonus structure. As a result, Atari Taiwan was tapped to look into manufacturing the board games and the *Touch Me*.

On January 16th, 1979, Rick Kreiger (who was in charge of Atari's Taiwan manufacturing plant) recieved the design files for the *Pro Coach* and the *Touch Me* products. During *Pro Coach's* review, there are some concerns about the painting process of its conductive paint and manufacturing of the product overall. Finally, after several weeks, *Pro Coach* was dropped and in a domino like effect all the other board games were dropped with it under the same concerns. The sole surivivng product is now *Touch Me*, whose physical casing is sourced from a calculator firm.

Randy Hall receives word from John Ellis on July, 27th that there is a serious clearance issue with the battery door cover on these reused calculator cases and Randy is sent to Atari Taiwan to address the issue. The depth of the calculator case plastics is not deep enough, causing the batteries to rest too high in their compartment causing the small tab on the battery cover to not lock into place. After two weeks, Randy resolves the issue as best as possible. While not a perfect correction, to make any further changes would would've meant cutting a whole new set of molds, which just can't happen.

By Friday November 23, 1979, Atari Taiwan will manufacture and ship a total of 745,664 *Touch Me* handhelds to the United States market. Shipments to Europe will occur almost a year later in October of 1980, starting with an initial shipment into Italy. Two other electronic games were still in development as well - one would be a handheld *Space Invaders* and the other a handheld *Breakout* game.

On May 25, 1977, the entire entertainment industry and our societal culture are altered in a permanent and monumental way. Nearly every facet of society discovers a whole new world brought to the big screen from a 'galaxy far, far away...' *Star Wars* premieres and takes not just America, but the entire world by storm!

With a storyline that revolves around knights wielding swords made of light, on a secret mission to save the princess from the evil empire, recover stolen plans and destroy the ultimate weapon... a new culture is born and the next generation of technologically advanced cinema lays the groundwork for the complete retooling of the movie theatre environment. All of this is put together with never-before-seen realistic groundbreaking special effects, sounds and a background score written by John Williams and performed by the London Symphony Orchestra.

The movie showcases some of THE most realistic spaceship designs, laser pistols and computer terminals seen to date, along with two 'droid' robots which are not only pivotal to the storyline, but provide an almost comic relief to the movie. One is a bumbling, skittish humanoid looking droid called C3PO who can speak proper English, among its numerous other dialects. The other is a cute small domed top Astromech droid called R2D2.

This particular character cannot speak any verbal words, but communicates by cute and emotionally toned bleeps and chirps, all which convey its demeanor and tone remarkably well to the audience. Unlike the countless sci-fi movies spanning decades prior, *Star Wars* created a used universe instead of shiny, clean and perfect objects and characters. Everything appears used, worn and working just as real world common items look outside of the movie theatre. The technologies shown in this movie seem plausible and reasonable, causing the audience to think and wonder "Why not?" So if there are realistic robots in the movie, why not real robots in today's world?

Star Wars would set imaginations ablaze with the burning desire to see those technologies becoming something everyone could own. With the accomplishments of the space race (landing on the moon, walking on the moon and satellites being lofted into space on a nearly monthly basis), space and technology were a real part of society. Magazine and newspaper articles of the day showed a stream of topics about how computers were improving society and were now within the reach of individuals to own in their own homes.

During the two years prior to the Star Wars premiere, people were already connecting high tech video game devices to their home televisions to turn the usual evening of cards or board games into a futuristic battle of skill on the video playfields. Everywhere within society's gathering places - from bars, restaurants, bowling alleys and more, coin-operated video arcade games were popping up and becoming commonplace. The world was becoming more like the futuristic fantasies of the big screen, so with all of these marvels of technology it was very easy to accept the idea that soon robots would be seeing us to our seats at restaurants and cleaning windows on the sides of tall glass skyscrapers. Who knows - those nights of playing video games on the home TV might soon be played against a personal robot sitting right there holding the controls and battling it out against us in a round of *Home PONG...* that is, AFTER it had just brought out a tray of snacks and a few ice cold drinks.

Just a few weeks shy of the one year anniversary since the premiere of *Star Wars*, Ron Milner and Larry Nicolson of Cyan Engineering draft an Atari Inter-office Memo to Al Alcorn, Steve Bristow, Nolan Bushnell and Joe Keenan. Dated May 1, 1978, the subject is: "Proposal – Kermit the Robot." Kermit is actually meant to be an extension or a compliment to the 'Colleen' computer system. In the memo, it's explained that 'Kermit is an inquisitive little fellow who can get around a bit on his own but whose personality develops fully when working with the Colleen system. He can be operated through Colleen to act as remote eyes and ears for the user's program.' How Kermit would 'talk' to Colleen was a rather unique implementation. Instead of a wireless link, Kermit and Colleen would communicate using audio tones; in fact the tones would actually be a part of the robot's personality and provide a low cost means of communication.

As the R2D2 robot 'talked' through chirps and bleeps to the actors on the screen and to the audiences in the theatres, the Kermit Robot would do very much the same thing to communicate with its intelligent home base – Colleen. On May 26th, the Kermit robot project is approved and work commences. The first order of business is a drive train to allow the robot to move and navigate. Surface measurements for starting and maintaining force are calculated for wood, tile, linoleum, shag rug, pile rug and climbing onto and off of a throw rug. (all that was left to check on would be if Kermit could handle the harsh conditions of the planet Tatooine)

An interesting project was piggybacked off of the robot development called 'Robot Chess.' Since the Cyan engineers were already deep into the development of a robot, these concepts and designs could be further evaluated and implemented into a board game of chess. The design was created on Atari's 6th anniversary (June 27, 1978), however the idea is never worked on past the concept stage.

In December of 1980, a company by the name of Applied Concepts would release nearly the same Chess game design, called BORIS HANDroid. Retailing for a staggering $1,400, the Cyan engineers believed they could have done a product with a retail cost of under $250 back in 1978 - yet another idea that Cyan prototyped goes out the door to be sold as a product, but unfortunately, not by Cyan.

As Kermit is being developed, the team begins to look at fun and playful capabilities and even accessories for the robot. Up and Down servo's are considered so it can 'dance' by bopping up and down - it could have lights, have the top turret turn, floor reflective sensors to follow paths and of course, what robot shouldn't also have its own super-squirt gun for water fights around the house? Yes, a design is drafted for a mechanical squirt gun to shoot water at Kermit's owner and companions. By September, work is proceeding to the point where the team starts to work on its own language for Kermit (called 'ROBOL') to allow simple plain English commands to be entered into the Colleen computer and then translated into Kermit's own language.

Also during September, a second project is spun off from the Kermit design work. Larry Nicholson wants to do a stripped down toy robot based on the early stage design work with a single chip controller onboard and sensors that would include feelers, light and maybe a microphone for detecting sounds. Initially called mini-Kermits, they get their own designations – Varmit, Furmit and Wurmit.

It's finally time for Kermit to stretch his legs, or to be a bit more accurate, spin its wheels. Tethered to a desk control module via a long ribbon cable, Kermit is placed onto a large sheet of engineering drafting paper normally used by Atari engineers to draw out schematics, mechanical drawings and circuit designs. Kermit is fitted with a pen and a test is performed to gauge Kermit's navigational accuracy. Commands are sent to the onboard systems – Run, Turn, Run, Reverse, Turn, Run and Maneuver. Some wheel errors are detected during the turns and the team thinks this can be corrected through the software control. Kermit has taken its first 'baby steps.'

Kermit took a walk with its leash (the ribbon cable attached the desktop control module) in October. Unfortunately, it's quickly discovered that Kermit cannot negotiate carpet! This is a serious failing and several major design changes needed to be made including wider drive wheels and a wider front direction castor wheel. The weight will have to be reduced quite a bit and also, Kermit's center of gravity is too far off because of the weight of the large battery behind the main axle.

Meanwhile the mini-Kermit idea has now moved into its own full blown project and a patent as well. On November 8, 1978, an Atari Invention Disclosure Form is filled out and submitted by Ron Milner and Gene Wise for their invention: Toy Robot. In the electronic toys class, the product is called 'VARMIT.' On December 1st a fully working Varmit is completed and tested using one-wheel drive and two trailing wheels - the design proves to be very agile and maneuverable. Varmit looks like furry mouse; it even speaks by making noises, using a simple 555 timer chip and a small 4-bit DAC to control pitch and a capacitor to do a frequency sweep. The resulting sounds are cute and pleasant and fit the furry little robot.

Ron Milner notes on December 1, 1978 in his engineering logbook that "Varmit is now off to the Warner's Board meeting with Nolan. Some decision can be expected eventually." Unfortunately this board meeting would be the catastrophic showdown between Nolan Bushnell and Manny Gerard that turns into a drop down screaming match and ends with Nolan being removed as Chairman and CEO of Atari. Varmit never gets its chance to become a new Atari product, however, strangely enough, Varmit does not go away quietly.

By the mid 1980s, Varmit will make its return thanks to Nolan Bushnell. Initially called 'Micro Pets,' the new line of robots are officially called 'Petsters' at their release. The Petsters would have all of the same characteristics and features of Varmit, and much more. They will don new personas, coming in all shapes and sizes - from cats, dogs, hamsters… and even a spider which was more of a hardwood floor mop than an entertainment robot.

At Cyan through November and December of 1978, work on Kermit continues and now most of the control and sensor logic are onboard and programming work continues. The team also realizes that the 'Robol' language was becoming difficult to check out and may have been a mistake to create and implement, as it's making debugging the routines hard. Also, teaching Kermit things, like how to self navigate out of a corner and how to choose the longest free path were slow to implement.

Making matters worse, pressure was coming down from the top that Cyan needed to show something that demonstrated and worked properly or the project would be terminated. After two weeks, Kermit was now freely wandering the Cyan labs without bumping into things (most of the time) by using its onboard ultrasonic range sensors. Some housecleaning work on its routines were being done to fine tune its ability to navigate and sense its surroundings, and the team hoped to then start to add in some more interesting behaviors. But before they get to the next phase, on January 21, 1979 word comes to Cyan… Kermit has been canned due to Atari politics. Essentially the project was only being championed by Nolan (whose original mandate to the Cyan guys was 'design a robot that can bring me a beer') as well as Joe Keenan, Al Alcorn and Steve Bristow. However by January 1979, Nolan had been removed from his role in the company, Joe Keenan was now the Chairman and

Steve Bristow was tasked with spinning down the Pinball manufacturing building and retooling it to build the new line of Home Computers which just debuted at the Winter CES in Las Vegas.

Kermit would still continue to be an active member of the Cyan engineering group though, traveling about the office. Chirping, beeping and happily maneuvering around the lab benches. Kermit even had its own Atari ID badge, only the second of two non-humans to ever have the privilege of being officially 'unofficial' Atari employees - the other was Mitchy, Jay Miner's dog.

Brought down to Atari's engineering building in Sunnyvale a few times, finally at one point after the project is no longer being active, Kermit was given to Owen Rubin to become its adopted caretaker. Kermit would sit in Owen's office until Owen began tinkering with its ROM code, trying to add some additional intelligence to its programming. Through some trial and error with this new programming, Kermit is sent off down the hallway to venture around the offices of the engineering building at 1272 Borregas Avenue.

Sadly, Kermit would ultimately meet with disaster. While some basic safety mechanisms were built into Kermit, they were not quite refined enough for long unattended excursions. On the front wheel of Kermit is a drop switch sensor so that if the front wheel of Kermit were to drop down suddenly, it would let out a squealing sound and immediately back up. However the sensor timing and its ability to react were not fast enough to save the little guy from a final deadly spill. One day Kermit took to his usual roaming of the halls of Atari, joyfully chirping and maneuvering about when he happened upon an open door to the stairwell. Kermit moved to the edge of the top stairs… its front wheel dropped as intended, but momentum and gravity would be quicker then Kermit's sensor and programming. Suddenly a blood curdling robot squeal echoes throughout 1272, followed by crashing, bouncing and breaking sounds.

Owen and others in the Engineering department ran to the stairwell - lying at the bottom of the next landing like humpty dumpty was Kermit, its dome cracked slightly and some components jarred out of place. Kermit's days of roaming the halls of Atari sadly came to an end that day and from then on, he would stay in the office, motionless and chirpless. When Owen left Atari, Kermit was taken home to become a part of Owen's collection of Atari memories.

Cyan moved back to working on peripheral ideas and designs now that the home computers had been officially debuted at the January, 1979 Winter CES in a big showing in Las Vegas at the MGM Grand. Everything was examined; from standard peripherals to speech in/out, camera, plotter, burglar alarm and even a remote control system. Now it was time to go back and have some fun designing some unique peripherals and uses for the computers!

In February of 1979, an idea to motorize an Etch A Sketch pad is born. The Etch A Sketch is a wonderful little toy that entrances children with its ability to draw anything from a simple square to complex drawings, dependent upon the skill and dexterity of the child's ability to turn the knobs in just the right ways to move the point around behind the screen, scraping away the silver under coating to draw lines.

Work begins by looking into servo motors and inexpensive DC motors needed to drive the motorization. Ron Milner, Larry Emmons and Lanny Netz start to work on designs for position controls and speed control circuits. As ideas and designs start to be tossed around, it's realized there is a lot more that could be done with the positioning and speed controls than just hooking an Etch A Sketch up to the Colleen to draw images stored in memory. Other ideas like drawing game boards and moving drawn pieces for games such as chess, checkers, tic tac toe, hangman, picture storybooks and other uses are considered.

The modified Etch A Sketch is connected to a development system in March and a pattern of more than a dozen squares are drawn offset over each other. Considered a success, some very noticeable shortcomings are still detailed in an an April, 1979 Interoffice Memo sent by Ron Milner to Al Alcorn.

In the memo, he mentions that the concept can draw decent images, letters and graphics in a closed loop, but that the lack of a way to full screen erase, along with the inability to accurately keep track of the pen and the slow drawing speeds limits the types of games and implementations that could be done. The study was stopped as a result, and while its use short term would not be feasible, a lot of data obtained on motor servo control will be used later for a pen plotter peripheral for the Colleen computer project.

Alexander Graham Bell made the historic statement "Watson, come here. I need you," in 1876. His assistant, Watson would hear the words come through his prototype telephone speaker, causing him to come into the room where Bell had just spoken into his prototype telephone microphone - the birth of the telephone had taken place. Within only two years, the imagination of George du Maurier would evolve the concept with a sketch of a man sitting, having a conversation with a woman seen on a projection screen who was also holding a phone and they are having a visual conversation. By 1910, a French postcard depicting very much the same scene was created stating that this was what the telephone would be in the year 2000.

Bell Laboratories was already researching video telephone technologies in the late 1920's, and the vision is further feuled by the 1927 movie 'Metropolis' in a scene of two men talking on huge wall sized telephone system with a small video screen so they could see each other while talking through standard telephone handsets. Bell Laboratories set up a demonstration of its 'Picture-Phone' between Los Angeles and New York in 1956, finally showing the vision of communicating by live images to be a reailty.

The system actually required three dedicated specialized phone lines; One line each for video to New York, one to Los Angeles and a third line for the audio conversation was then required and all of these dedicate lines had to be synced together across the telephone carrier's network. The really big public awareness of videophones would come at the 1964 World's Faire in New York where demonstrations between New York and Washington DC were shown. Just as the earlier picture-phone prototypes required three special dedicated lines, the 1964 system did as well. Bell Labs attempted several commercial installations of the picture-phone networks into New York, Washington DC and Chicago, however at the cost of up to $27 per minute for a call the product ultimately failed.

Despite the real world commercial failure of the picture-phone due to its specialized infrastructure needs and its overly expensive cost, the public still became captivated by the idea of one day being able to have actual video phone calls. This would reach new heights as the result of the futuristic cartoon show *The Jetson's* when it aired in 1962, making video phone calls a common occurrence in almost every episode. In 1969, Stanley Kubrick's science fiction fantasy '2001: A Space Odyssey' would also show a very realistic scene of a father placing a video phone call to his daughter on what the movie would depict as being an AT&T public payphone in the future.

Only further inspired by all this, AT&T with its research and marketing muscle as well as large coffers of financial resources to tap into, would not give up this uphill battle to take videophones from fantasy to commercial viability. In 1970, AT&T would try it once again with its Picturephone II system and network in Pittsburgh, Pennsylvania. Just as quickly however, it would silently admit defeat and shut it down as the Bell telephone giant would step back and not make another attempt for almost 15 more years.

In the foothills of the California Sierra Mountains in 1976, back in the Grass Valley Research and Development Lab, the Cyan engineering team decided to take up the call. Called 'Phoney,' it's a remarkable design for video transmission technology. "Bear in mind that we did not have DSP chips and a lot of cheap memory available, so it was a challenge to do anything practical," recalls Larry Emmons. The concept design and ideas are shown to Nolan Bushnell and Joe Keenan, at which point Joe came up with the idea that this could be an entertainment-based device, basing the design around a toy instead of something for business or commercial use.

With that in mind, Larry Emmons, Dave Stokes and Michael Cooperhart begin work on building a simulation prototype. While Larry and Dave worked on the engineering side, Michael became the Project Concept Manager - after all, he was hired to do project management and industrial design and to help get projects (specifically the video project) funded and into production. The video project certainly needed a kick start and funding!

When Michael first saw the project in the lab it was just a small 16 x 16 image on a 19-inch open frame monitor, and he immediately knew what was needed was a demonstration prototype and a funding proposal. Moving forward, the team built the demonstration prototype, consisting of two desktop base units that were each wired across the lab into a card cage system holding all of the electronics. Since this was just for the very early stages of product development, its physical size and the need to be able to easily pull out a section to work on, made it a large system requiring a card cage box for all of the major electronic components to reside in.

Unlike AT&T's efforts, the initial prototype didn't actually use a telephone line, but instead used a dedicated wiring system that ran from one office on one side of the lab floor to another office way on the other side of the lab floor. However, to make sure that eventually the product could be compatible with the standard telephone line systems of the day, it was restricted to data rates and capabilities that were possible at the time (modeling capabilities after fax machines which were just out and very were expensive).

Larry Emmons and the Cyan team came up a this theory that telephone conversations had some degree of down time, with pauses between words being spoken where they might be able to insert picture data to transfer. Their test vehicle worked quite well, and the limited resolution photos sent one person's image at a time; first person A's picture was sent from one end of the link, when that completed the process was reversed. With this setup, voice had priority over the picture, and the remote photo would be received line by line during lapses in audio.

One afternoon, Nolan and company traveled to Grass Valley for a demonstration of the picture phone during their regular checking of the status of Cyan's projects. When it came time to demonstrate the phone, they had one part of it set up in the main office, and the second part in a back lab. Everyone played with it for awhile and had a good time testing it out, but as they retired to the main office, Nolan abruptly disappeared. The demo was still active with empty photos being exchanged on the device, when suddenly during their conversation Lanny Netz noticed a troubling and disturbingly recognizable object coming in on the video feed. Trying to divert everyone's attention from the screen, Larry kept everyone talking while he tried to block the incoming image by using up all of the priority data transfer. However, the inevitable occurred: The image fully processed onto the screen for everyone in the front office to discover where Nolan had disappeared to and what he was doing. The site of Nolan's rounded ass cheeks were what greeted the room full of people, a digitized mooning! Not quite the same historic reverence as the famous Bell & Watson 'Come Here!' moment in telephone history, but certainly a memorable, landmark (and classic 'Atari-style') moment for all who were present for this graphic 'full moon' eclipse!!!

After the demonstration, Ron Milner (though not involved in the project) needed a power supply to use for a different project and the demonstration system had a perfect power supply that he could use. Proceeding to disconnect the power supply, he unknowingly let the 110v 'hot' wire which was still live touch the 5v line on the card cage. The result was a room full of fireworks and smoke, as each of the cards proceeded, almost in a queued fireworks sequence to spark, to smoke and burn out. "It was quite a fireworks show. Luckily it didn't burn the lab down or set off the sprinkler system," recalls Ron Milner.

As for courting funding from Atari for a project such as this, Michael became so successful in this process that he gained the nickname Michael "Corporate-Hart" of which he was actually proud to hold the title of. Someone had to help get these great ideas funded and into production and Michael would become the man behind the curtain whose job it was to glorify the great work being done by Cyan.

Although work continued on 'Phoney,' by 1979 it's moved to Cyan's back-burner and then added to a Grass Valley Project Summaries document under the category, 'Disasters.' However in 1981, 'Project P' (as it is now called) makes a come-back when in the engineering summaries for that year it's dryly noted, 'try it again.' This new interest may have been prompted by Steve Bristow's new division called 'Ataritel,' put together to bring Atari into the consumer telephone market with a series of high tech phones with never before seen features. Bristow sees 'Phoney' as a compliment to the new division, and the still separate video phone project becomes known under Ataritel as Eagle or alternately Eagle Eye.

By the end of the 1970s and into the early 1980s, a great many homes were still using rotary dial phones because of the still uneasy process of getting a touch-tone phone. First, you had to order touchtone service for your telephone line and depending on your area, that could cost an extra $2 to $5 per month. Then once you had touch-tone service, you could look to rent a touch-tone phone. That's right, rent - these were the days you couldn't buy your phones, you had to rent them from Bell Telephone. And once you ordered your upgraded phone line and phone, then a Bell telephone technician would come to your home and install it for an additional fee. Hopefully you get the point that there was a market ripe for competition here.

Why were there so few compeitors? Originally, Bell Telephone would not allow any non approved telephones to be plugged into its network or to even allow any modifications to its devices. In 1956, a lawsuit was won against Bell Telephone that would allow the use of non-Bell Telephone devices and the modification of Bell Telephone devices as long as there would be no damage caused to the network or its devices. Unfortunately, save for novelty phones and big business, the stigmatism of only Bell telephones meaning quality still sat in the eyes of the average consumer. It didn't help that during any service calls or installation of new outlets by a Bell serviceman, the service call was accompanied by an installer telling the homeowner that plugging in phones not purchased from the telephone company could cause problems with their service and any service calls could be very expensive. This subtle pressure tactic would be used often in trying to sway people away from going it on their own.

Atari's entry into the telephone market began when Steve Bristow begins to assemble his new consumer research and development team in 1981, one of the technologies that intrigues Steve and his team were wireless intercom systems. So they start to look at the possibility of doing something like that with telephone applications.

They build a prototype line system and bring it out to Warner Communications in New York to demonstrate to Manny Gerard and Steve Ross. Not only is Warner interested in the prototype and the demonstration, Steve's consumer research and development group is also now assigned to be Atari's new telephone division called 'Ataritel.' The idea of developing a line of phone systems that would provide such luxury features to an eager buying public was not to be ignored. Atari engineers could see this need, and Warner Communications fully supported the idea of its high tech subsidiary branching out into this field – a field which would certainly be a strong profit center by delivering much wanted and needed conveniences to homeowners.

Marketing and management at Atari, who had many times shut down numerous game products out of fear they could impact sales of the Atari VCS, also welcomed this new product line. The fact it would not be entertainment-based meant it would not compete in any way with the Atari VCS or its cartridge sales - or more importantly their bonuses.

The planned line of telephones will offer advanced features not commonly seen at the time, such as redial, call waiting switch, mute, hold and a full duplex speakerphone which would allow both parties to talk and hear each other at the same time. Not a problem today, this was a very difficult technological hurdle at the time and would give the product line a huge feature selling advantage.

There is also talk of possibly incorporating home control features, but another very advanced design called 'power line transmission technology' is instead pursued for what will be called the 'Telectra' line of telephones. Many homes were only wired for telephones in specific, high traffic areas - generally in the kitchen as the primary phone and a phone in perhaps a den or living room, and maybe in the main bedroom. This usually posed a problem for the new home telephone market, as you would still be at the mercy of the telephone company to have to come into your home and charge you to run additional telephone outlets in other areas of the home.

Atari knew that in order to get into homes in any volume, they would have to win over the hearts and minds of the consumer by giving them easy to use yet high-tech features far ahead of Bell and everyone else. Most importantly, power line telephone systems would be their solution to get past Bell's control of the phone outlets in the home. A power line telephone system consists of a Master Station which plugs in to the already existing telephone jack and into a standard wall outlet. The catch is, the outlet isn't just for power, but is also used for communication with a set of satellite phones. The master station would essentially be set with its own home telephone network, allowing the homeowner to buy additional extension phones and set them to the same network setting as the master station. All you would have to then do is plug the extension phone-set anywhere in the home into a power outlet, pick up the receiver and you would now have telephone service in that room. Now a homeowner could take a call in the kitchen, place a person on hold, and then go into their office or another room, pick up the extension set and have their conversation. The phones could also act as intercoms between rooms as well.

For the next two years the product engineering and designs would evolve. Porsche Design and Morison Cousins Associates would be contracted to provide design services and give the new products a unique and state of the art look. The designs by Morison Cousins are chosen for their 'Space-tel' look which have very clean, attractive and appealing high tech presence. They're also easy to use and are designed to fit the many different functions that the various models and product lines will need to accommodate. By March 1983, after nearly two years of working in secret, Atari announces its new secret division to the public. To add an additional air of mystery to the whole affair, Marketing, which is handled by Dick Mier, releases that the entire division has been secretly operating under the codename 'Project Falcon.'

In fact, unlike previous Atari products that usually had their codenames after women, the Ataritel product codenames were all after birds - Falcon, Eagle, Pudgy and Parrot. An effective marketing campaign is launched, featuring the Ataritel name covered under a tarp; you could clearly read the name, but it gave the perception to everyone that there would be so much more revealed when the wraps came off. Marketing specialist Kim Soulek would demonstrate the prototype designs at numerous events and tradeshows throughout the year, including the Telephone Show in San Francisco.

Unfortunately, shortly after the showing a number of events occur surrounding the appearance of James Morgan, Atari's new CEO who takes over the reins of the company from Ray Kassar after massive financial losses. After a month long evaluation period, James begins to cut projects and products across the board that he feels are not necessary to Atari's recovery. Ataritel will be one of those projects.

Initially, its staff is cut back in September, but by October most of the division staff has scattered to other projects and departments or they have left the company all together. Internally, Ataritel is shuttered - even Steve Bristow has moved over to the Home Computer Division to work with Dave Stubben on refocusing the division's product strategy and map out new computers and products for the next two years. The phones of the future will not get their chance to be released in the future and Ataritel, treated like an unwanted phone call, is put on permanent hold.

A glimmer of hope for the product line was seen in April, 1984 after a simple announcement that Atari is still considering a release of its line of Ataritel products. But other than this announcement, nothing actually ever comes of it. Word also reaches Cyan that the Ataritel project has been canceled and their work on 'Project P' has been canceled along with it. The video phone too will not get its chance to make it out of Cyan's lab and into the hands of consumers. The Falcon, Eagle and the nest eggs have all been grounded.

During the turmoil of 1984 and the sale of the Consumer Division (which includes the Home Computer Division) to Tramel Technologies, Ltd. on July 2, 1984, the Ataritel division is retained by Warner Communications along with the Coin-op Division and the Atari Adventure Centers division. The former management of Ataritel tried to see if they could purchase the division outright from Warner and spin it off as an independent company separate from Warner. Warner, unfortunately, would not agree to the terms of the offer. Seeing the value in Ataritel's assets and specifically the video phone product, Manny Gerard negotiates to sell the product to a company called Medama, which was a newly formed U.S. subsidiary of Mitsubishi Electric established as a development and marketing company for the U.S. market.

While looking to take Ataritel independent, Roy Elkins approaches Medama for funding and after Warner won't spin off the division he makes the introduction to Manny Gerard about purchasing the rights, IP and assets to the videophone project. During one of the demonstration meetings with Warner, Ataritel and Medama, the Cyan videophone is set up in the Warner conference room in New York. Back in Grass Valley, Michael Cooper-Hart is preparing to send a video transmission to demonstrate the product to the Mitsubishi team from Japan. Cyan's Larry Emmons is also on hand for the meeting, so he initiates a videophone call with Michael Cooper-Hart. Michael is on the speakerphone and tells Larry that a friend dropped by to see him and an image of a Playboy centerfold begins to appear on the screen in the Warner conference room. The room breaks out in laughter, and that pretty much seals the deal to move forward with negotiations to purchase the video phone product.

During negotiations, Manny quickly discovers there is a leak - that Stan Zawadowicz, who is acting on behalf of Medama, knows entirely too much about the product including things not released in documents or prevously discussed. Manny decides to use this leak to his advantage; He begins to discuss internally within Warner and the Ataritel team that Warner has received a far more generous offer for the videophone project and that he is considering negotiating with this other firm instead. Zawadowicz suddenly comes back with a higher offer and Manny jumps on the turnaround of the situation by selling the rights, IP and assets of the video phone project to Medama for a much higher price than he originally planned. The original video phone team, consisting of Larry Emmons, Michael Cooper-Hart, Chris Wright and Roy Elkins will be joined together again over at Mitsubishi's new U.S. subsidiary to take their work on the Atari video phone and refine and complete it under new design guidelines and feature requirements outlined by Mitsubishi. They're joined by an old familiar face from many years ago, Nolan Bushnell's former boss from AMPEX, Kurt Wallace. In 1986 the videophone is finally released as the Mitsubishi Lumaphone.

Grass Valley was one of the Sierra foothill's epicenters during the California Gold Rush of 1848-1849. As legend tells us, while the early prospectors sifted through sand and mud to discover their dreams of gold in rivers and streams, it was by pure accident that the wealth of Grass Valley was discovered. The old story goes that a mining settler, while out looking for one of his missing cows, stumbled over a rock. When he looked to see just what he tripped over, he noticed the rock had lines of gold running through it. At around the very same time, another mining settler, while building a home, went out to gather large stones to build a chimney and discovered a vein of gold quartz. From there, the rest is history. Well, if there was one way to describe the lab at Cyan Engineering, it would be to call it a 'modern day gold mine' and it was a vein not about to run out of wealth.

Now with the Candy and Colleen systems renamed to the Atari 400 and 800 and shipping in 1979, Gene Wise designs something truly remarkable for the home computer division: a dual disk drive. Companies such as Tandem and MPI were charging $50 upward for their single floppy disk drive mechanisms alone. Add in all of the specialized custom circuitry to make these drive mechanisms into intelligent SIO disk drives and the pricing became very expensive, with the result being an Atari disk drive product with a retail price of $500. So the Cyan team decides to design a low cost drive system, but not a single disk mechanism: this will be a dual side-by-side disk drive mechanism. They lay out all of the mechanicals of the drive and build their very own design from scratch so that Atari would no longer be at the mercy of the disk drive manufacturers for its disk drives.

Instead of costly disk drive read/write heads, they use modified cassette drive heads for read/write capabilities. A much simpler and lower part count disk controller was also designed. All these innovations and cost cutting techniques provided a final price of $50 for the dual disk drive system. For the price of just one drive mechanism alone from a third party company, Cyan had developed a fully working, in-house, reliable low cost dual disk drive system with controller. The response from Atari (according to Steve Mayer) was that Atari had gotten too big and didn't want to move away from their 810 disk drive (which was already being made) to take a chance on a new product, even if it would have been a very attractive product design and would have made the home computer division more competitive while bringing in higher profit margins. Cyans far more affordable disk drive solution would spin no more.

The issues of FCC compliance with Atari's consumer products were well behind, now that new regulations had been issued and there were much less stringent compliance rules that had to be met. In 1980, Larry Emmons begins work on proposing a new follow-up home computer system for Atari - essentially going back to the original specifications of Colleen: externally accessible expansion slots, a professional keyboard with cursor keys and separate numeric keypad, built-in power supply and more robust memory and communications partitioning.

The new concept is called the Atari 800B and the idea is proposed to Atari, but again nothing is done with it. The 400 and 800 have just come out and no one wants to discuss a follow-up product at this time.

Also in 1980, Larry begins work on a 'smart' word processor system, a typewriter-styled system in an Atari 800 case with display screen and storage drive all incorporated together. Codenamed 'Nimble Fingers,' several prototypes are built. The design was even shown to Olivetti, who took a strong interest in it - however Atari's corporate management once again shoots down this project, not wanting to get into the business side of word processing and entering a market with the likes of IBM and its very popular 'Displaywriter' line of word processor systes.

Another computer enhancement project that showed a great deal of promise is a prototype modem built into the unused space of the Atari 400's case. Ron Milner worked with sourcing components from Dallas Wireman of Racal-Vadic, building a 300 baud full duplex autodial modem which would featured ring detect and auto-answer capability. John Powers did the software and Steve Davis would build the hardware. With the plan to output audio through a TV-out from the Serial IO (SIO) audio line, Ron's dream was to pursue a telecommunications strategy and present ideas for smart terminals with graphics, supplying telecommunication-aware games and other ideas and approaches. The project died the same death as the word processor, Atari was not going to enter the terminal market.

On January 2, 1979, word comes to Cyan that Atari has licensed the incredibly popular *Space Invaders* title from Taito for home use. Atari's consumer programming group has assigned Rick Maurer to code the Atari VCS version and Rob Fulop would code the version for the Atari 400/800 home computer systems. There is an opportunity to take the license and branch it out into the new avenue now opened thanks to the Atari Board Games Division, which was also being called the Atari Electronic Games division.

One of its new products was a handheld *Touch Me* game being put into manufacturing to ship by the end of the year. So using the LCD prototype technology that the Cyan team had worked on and looking at the current programmable controllers they had been investigating, the team begins work on a LCD handheld game that will use a COP programmable processor chip. Ron Milner will design the electronics around the COP 421 programmable processor; the device will run on a 9-volt battery and use a 32 x 32 LCD display. By July, the 'LCA1' liquid crystal driver chip design is completed by Ron Milner. Deb Meeker will draw up the schematics for the final design.

Development boards using the COP 402 processor are built and shipped down to Steve Bristow who will complete the project in Sunnyvale. Two versions will be developed on the hardware platform – *Space Invaders* and *Breakout*. Design samples are built and packaging is designed. Atari Marketing even runs an ad showcasing the new line of handhelds from Atari Electronic Games which shows the LCD *Space Invaders*, *Touch Me* and the LCD *Breakout*.

Unfortunately, by the end of 1979, only the Touch Me will ever ship. The projects would be completed… and then killed. Again, the Marketing group, seeing any product that could potentially impact its sales of VCS cartridges (and a possible threat to their bonuses) as a threat and ensures that those projects are stopped in their tracks.

Marketing believed that the *Space Invaders* LCD game would compete with the January 1980 release of the same license on the Atari VCS, and the *Breakout* LCD game would compete against the released *Breakout* title already out for the VCS. Two promising products and a strong penetration into the electronic gaming market are shot down to keep a clear path open for the Atari VCS and Marketing's bonuses.

Atari has asked Cyan to initiate a study for a project called 'Super Stella' that will play VCS carts, and has 24 lines by 50 characters. A wish list of possible features are given to Cyan to evaluate the feasibility of implementing are Virtual Memory, 80 characters on screen, ways to interface with the home computers and being able to do home security.

Arcade Accountant is started in 1981, a promising project based around the Atari 800 computer that looks like it could actually be developed into a commercially viable product. Intended to create an accounting system for coin-op operations, using a series of network boxes that connect to one another via phone line cabling, each box will be installed inside every arcade machine on a route or arcade location. The boxes then register how many quarters/plays each machine receives, with the collected data sent back to an Atari 800 computer system through an 850 interface.

Using a custom written software program, it will allow an arcade owner the ability to know which machines are making the arcade the most profit and also to know the total amount of revenue for a specific day or week. The system is also password protected and even records attempts at tampering.

This will prove to be a big coin-op related project for Cyan and prototypes are built, software written and the system manages to make it all the way to be moved into production. The design is shipped down to Dave Windsor in Atari's Coin-op Division in July, 1982 and Atari's coin-op division creates sales sheets as it begins to market the new product, calling it "The Coin Executive." The whole installation package even includes a specialized custom desk with the Atari 800 system, disk drives, printer and 850 interface module all integrated together into it. However, by the time the system is ready for market the arcades industry is in the midst of its own industry crash; the Coin Executive would only see a very limited deployment.

In 1981, Steve Mayer departs Cyan Engineering when he's presented with the opportunity to set up a new engineering company in New York to be called the WCI/NY research lab. As head of the new lab, Steve would report to both Manny Gerard of Warner Communications and as Senior VP of Engineering to Ray Kassar directly. The goal is to develop groundbreaking products and technologies and to also be a New York presence for Atari to directly liaison to Warner Communications. "I had dual citizenship," as Steve Mayer described it. For the WCI/NY Atari Research Lab, Steve puts together just as a diverse and eclectic band of engineers and technical people as Grass Valley and Atari had ever seen. People like Gregg Squires, Steve Ray, Robert Card, Joel Moskowitz, Greg Boles, Phillipe des Rioux and host of others.

One of the first projects for Steve is to reimagine the Atari VCS, and under Gregg Squires it becomes codenamed codenamed 'Val' after Gregg's wife. The NY lab decides to use an entirely different industrial design group, Henry Dreyfuss Associates, as they create a revamped look for the product. The slick new case combines the controllers and console into one unit, providing a dark brown long rectangular wedge shape case and thicker caped 8-position joysticks mounted on each end. Henry Dreyfuss Associates creates the new look after an exhaustive study on joystick shape, size, and distance to each other to try and create the alternative control setup to the original Atari CX40 joysticks.

Steve and company decide to cost reduce the VCS by reducing the number of chips inside the popular system. Codenamed 'JAN,' the reduction process drops the number of chips down to two chips and then eventually to one, putting an entire VCS on a single chip! Designating it with the product number CX-2000, the 'Val' is sent across country to Sunnyvale for evaluation. That's when the problems started - the engineers in Sunnyvale wouldn't accept the NY design because of the integrated joysticks and the non-standard industrial design look and feel that didn't fit in with the other Atari VCS models. Then there were the issues that any changes to the Atari VCS design faced a big uphill battle when it came to manufacturing. Everything at the factories in Taiwan and also Atari-Wong were geared towards cranking out Atari VCS systems by the millions annually, so radically altering the manufacturing process by having to retool the factories and stop current production would again pit management, sales and bonuses against innovation and change.

Regardless, it was still put through market study and further evaluation. The unit was further cost reduced by cheapening the joysticks and the case was changed to a garish 'kid-friendly' blue, causing one to ask how on earth this was any more in line with the previous look and feel. The answer was it wasn't, the engineers in Sunnyvale were setting it up to fail against their own cost reduced VCS they designed in response. And fail it did.

Another project that will come from the NY research lab would be project 'LIZ NY,' based on the concept Steve Mayer had always wanted to pursue since the original Atari home computers were conceived: a hybrid Atari home computer and VCS. Of couse, a computer that could also play VCS games didn't fly with Atari management, which was worried about cutting in to VCS sales. However, the design would be reworked by the Sunnyvale engineers into what would become Atari's new 1200XL computer line. The New York lab also experimented with video animation, lasers, robotics and other technologies during this time.

Unfortunately when things began to look rather dire for Atari in 1984 and Warner began to tighten the purse strings due to the huge losses being incurred on a monthly basis, the WCI lab was slated to be shut down. In a shrewd move, Steve Mayer meets with Manny Gerard and explains what the costs will be to shut down the lab and have everything removed, sold off, etc. So he makes him a proposition; sell the lab to him for the equivalent of the shutdown cost. An agreement is made and Steve Mayer becomes the sole owner of the WCI lab.

The original after-hours project that sparked Cyan, the design a video disc system that could be read/write capable, saw a return in 1981. Larry Nicholson is appointed head the of Video Disc Point-of-Sale system project, as it is now called. Started at the request of Manny Gerard, his concern is the manner in which Atari's home computer systems are being sold. The sales people in the early 80s retail industry at the time had a problem finding a happy medium. With computers being sold everywhere from departments stores, toy stores and more traditional computer stores, the experience for the buyer could be a crap shoot - something that wouldn't be soundly addressed until Steve Jobs' Apple Computer created the Apple Stores in the early 2000's. The problem was the sales people would either be too overly technical in explaining the computer systems to buyers (leaving them confused and intimidated), or they would not be knowledgeable enough to point out the key selling features of the computers or know how to pair up accessories and products to meet a buyer's needs. Atari's new point-of-sale system was their attempt to address these issues in a high-tech early 80s manner. The project would consist of creating an interactive point-of-sale system that would give potential buyers the ability to learn more about Atari home computers that was a step up from the static demo programs usually running on them. Combined with a Pioneer laserdisc system (laserdiscs being the forerunner to DVD's for those not in the know), the actual Atari home computer equipment is to sync its more standard on-screen computer generated demonstrations with the laserdisc's multi-media presentations, further displaying the product's capabilities and features.

Dan Corona is assigned to be the Special Project Manager in charge of the system, which is designated the 'Electronic Retail Information Center' or ERIC for short. Atari's ninth employee who had been with Atari since 1972, Dan coordinates with Cyan, Atari's Home Computer Division and Atari Coin-op (which will design the cabinet to house the ERIC system). The firm target date is to have the ERIC system ready for the January 1982 Consumer Electronics Show.

The system design is very well implemented, which is to be expected, given it's designed designed by the Cyan Engineering team. Just as planned, a Pioneer laserdisc system is used via a custom interface built to connect into the laserdisc player's external controller port. The board then talks with the Atari 800 through a serial connection to the Atari 800 provided by the computer's standard 'Atari 850' peripheral; a communications box that allows an Atari 400 or 800 computer system the ability to communicate with telephone modems, teletype communication terminals and standard printer devices.

With a custom software program written by Harry Brown that loads onto the Atari 800, the ERIC came to life by pleasantly and visually greeting curious onlookers with a group of people of all professions and ages, from a young kid to a grandmother. The host of the demonstration explains commands, and by pressing a key on the Atari 800 keyboard a person would then be given a step-by-step tour of all of the various capabilities of the Atari home computers - from business, to online communications, to programming and of course playing video games. The demonstration would even end with an Atari home computer commercial. ERIC proves to be a success.

Later, Harry Brown writes software code to also allow the laserdisc system to load up and play Dragon's Lair and Space Ace on the Atari 800 computers in the Home Computer division labs. The era of the commercial use of computer controlled laserdisc systems has arrived, and Cyan's point-of-sale laserdisc technology will be adapted the following year for Atari's Coin-op Division who was building a game based on Clint Eastwoods movie *Firefox*. While innovative and remarkable, ultimately laserdisc based coin-op games would be a short lived endeavor. The laserdisc players on the market at the time suffered from a high failure rate from being run continuously for long hours day after day. The issue was further compounded by a single spec of dust being able to cause a locked-up game or a game just not starting up anymore.

In January, 1982, Dr. Alan Kay joins Atari as its Vice President of Research and Chief Scientist - a new title in the company. Alan Kay was previously a Fellow at the famous Xerox Palo Alto Research Center (PARC) where the features of modern computing (graphical user interfaces, Ethernet networking, laser printers, object orientated operating systems, and more) were designed in the 1970s. Having such a noted technologist as Kay on Atari's staff was thought to help improve Atari's standing in the computer and technology circles. Giving Alan the same directive he had at Xerox - research and build what computers will be doing in seven to ten years in the future, Atari will establish several research centers, staffed by teams of engineers and PhD's.

Many viewed the research centers as an Atari $25 million dollar PR stunt - that all Atari was doing was paying R&D 'thinkers' to do plenty of Research, but deliver zero Development - and with a seven to ten year window to deliver, Atari wouldn't see any benefit from this investment for nearly a decade out. However despite the naysayers, Alan Kay does make several efforts to inject his Xerox PARC experience into Atari's computer division personnel.

Giving numerous lectures and tutorials on Smalltalk and the advantages of its use and implementation to Atari engineers, he also works with Cyan Engineering to have them start developing a pointer system for the Atari computers to investigate ways to make the computers more user-friendly and efficient.

As a result of Alan's effort, Ron Milner builds a special interface card that goes into one of the Atari 800 expansion slots. Accessing the keyboard driver of the operating system in memory, the hope is to make a pointer system that on the back-end uses the keyboard's arrow keys. Two pointer systems are designed: one is called 'The Tab Mouse' and looks like a tablet with a joystick attached to it. By moving the joystick around on the pad, the cursor on the screen would move to a location, in the same way as if a user were to have pushed down and held the Control key and any of the arrow keys on the Atari home computer keyboard. Pushing down on the joystick would allow a position to be selected. The entire design had immense potential in the world of word processing and programming.

The second design is a device called an 'Opto-Flea' which is a small mouse design with a tiny light and a phototransistor underneath it. It works by reading how quickly the light reflects off the surface the 'Opto-Flea is rested on it, foreshadowing the development of fully optical mice years later. Unfortunately, it did not perform as well as the Tab Mouse design as it had trouble maintaining a good reading of the light signal. The Tab Mouse design works exactly as Alan Kay wanted it to but doesn't go much further either. Again, the point of the new Research Chief Scientist was about 'research' and not so much about developing an end product that could be used by Atari to create an advantage over the competition.

'Skiometer' is started by Ron Milner in 1982. and draws on some of the earlier motion detection, ultrasonics and range finding work that was researched and developed for Kermit. Quickly renamed the 'Sportsmeter,' the device is designed to record the average speed and distance a person travels to report back speed and distance via a speech synthesized voice. Worn on the waist or chest and listened to with headphones, the group saw the end users of this product being runners, skiers, bicyclists and even horseback riders.

Design work starts at the end of October 1982 by Ron Milner and by February 1983, the prototype is ready for what Ron refers to as its "Maiden Ski Test." Off to the ski slopes to give it a thorough testing! This will actually be a very extensive test for the system design, since it will have to deal with the varying surfaces of the snow; from smooth to broken crust, to large chunks of ice and snow. Ron tries it out and really gets going fast - the box indicates his speed at one point was 23 mph! Flying down the slope, some of the speed reports were erratic at times, so he tries strapping the device to his leg insead. Geting better readings, by the test's end he also finds out the battery life lasts around one hour.

Next was a jogging test. After running for two miles, the system spoke that Ron's speed had been 7.0 miles per hour. Mentally checking the figure, Ron calculates distance and time and finds he was doing closer to 8.8 mph, so the device is registering low. Chuck Meyer further tests the unit out in March by running four laps, and while the the speed is reading fairly accurate now, the distance measurement is off. After a few more adjustments, a few days later it's time to try out a bicycle test - readings for speed and distance are much more accurate now.

Ron begins writing up a product proposal which gives the code name for the new device as 'Jane.' Writing up the various test results from the skiing, running and bicycling test, he writes up the proposed schedule, costing and manpower estimates for the product. The estimates to bring the project from proof of concept to full product are $140,000 for the hardware and a total of eighteen weeks and $150,000 in personnel hours to complete.

Further testing and refinements continue to the design and by August it's time to try the horseback-riding test. The unit is attached to the front chest plate of the horse in a bag, and even though during the ride the bag swayed side to side quite a bit, the results are still very accurate. Testing and adjustments continue until the end of 1983 and by early 1984 Atari's Coin-op Industrial Design group will take the 'Sportsmeter' and build a concept model of what the unit would look like if commercially sold. Their new concept has the 'Sportsmeter' worn around the waist for walking, running and skiing, or attached to a bicycle.

After the splitting of Atari in 1984, Ron Milner is able to purchase the rights to the design from the Tramiel's and take the design with him to his own newly created company, Applied Design. From there he was able to license the 'Sportsmeter' to Nike, who release it as the 'Nike Monitor' in the late 1980s. As a testament to Ron's vision, ultra-marathoner Jim Walker even gives his approval of the device.

The closing of Cyan in 1984 is truly a sad event - so much creativity and fun had been brought to life over the its eleven years, thanks to Cyan's cultivation of spirited forward thinking and the pursuit of people's visions. Larry Emmons remembers very clearly when Cyan was 'dumped.' He and his wife Judy had taken a trip to Europe for the month of May 1984 to visit their daughter Kate, who at that time was a student in Germany. While there, the message about budget cuts and Cyan's planned closing came down. But because there was no way for Atari to contact him during the trip, the residents of Cyan researched on oblivious to their forthcoming demise. The moment Larry returned to the States and arrived back in Grass Valley, the call came in and Larry was faced with relaying the grim message. When he called the crew of eighteen employees together for the inevitable meeting, they were all already in the conference room playing 'Trivial Pursuit.' Informing them about their closing, Larry was not surprised they already had figured it out; he knew he had a very smart crew, even if Atari didn't value them anymore.

Cyan was history by the end of June, 1984 and in early July after the Consumer Division's sale to Jack Tramiel to form Atari Corporation, the Cyan Lab was tying up loose ends and clearing materials for the shut down. Most of the staff had already departed, and Ron Milner was essentially running a skeleton crew to wrap things up before he would move to a smaller space in the same Litton building and open Applied Design.

Showing up one morning, Ron found a group of people in the old Cyan Engineering lab huddled around Cyan's DEC Vax mini-computer, pulling up the floor panels and disconnecting the Vax. When he asked who everyone was and what they thought they were doing, the group introduced themselves: Most of the people were from Digital Research Incorporated, and there was a manager from Atari there as well.

He informed Ron that the Vax was being disconnected and removed, because it had been traded to Digital Research in payment to them to develop a version of their GEM Graphical Environment Manager (a point & click graphical operating system similar to the one operating on the Apple Macintosh and that was currently available on IBM-compatible PC's) for a new series of computers that Jack Tramiel was developing.

Back when Nolan Bushnell started Atari with his partner Ted Dabney, he did so not by being the best or brightest engineer, but by being a visionary. He saw things where others didn't, and envisioned the future - not a future decades away, but what could be done near term with available technologies, or technologies that could be created at the moment. Cyan Engineering was born of that very same spirit; to think outside of the box, but not to daydream about things that could only exist in one's imagination. To research things that could be made into reality with clever thinking and creative engineering.

As a final showing of just how 'visionary' Cyan Engineering was, we offer you this: Larry Emmons and Ron Milner logged a series of notes into an engineering book from September 29th to October 1st, 1982, where they offered an idea for a new product that would be the best way to introduce robots into the home. Summed up here, the consensus was that "A 'vacuum cleaning robot' that Atari could develop and partner with a company like Kenmore to market would be the best way to make home robots a reality." Today, the only commercially successful home robot sold to date has been the product called 'Roomba,' a vacuum-cleaning robot. If Cyan had not been closed, perhaps the technologies we all have today would have arrived a lot sooner... and may have been even better!

Review In Images

Grass Roots

Cyan's office in the Litton Office Building.

Top: The *Trak 10* prototype in 1973 with Larry Emmons' daughter Kate and son Scott 'testing' it. *Bottom right*: The flyer for *Trak 10*. Advertising flyers such as this featured actual Atari employees. That's Carl Lepiane and Karen Bjiorquist

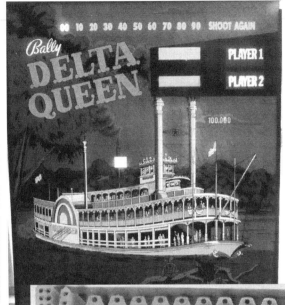

The pinball machine *Delta Queen*'s backglass

The microprocessor driven PCB placed in to the *Delta Queen* to convert it into the first microprocessor based pinball game.

Top: The original proof of concept prototype for the VCS designed and built at Cyan.

Bottom: "Phoney" the video phone.

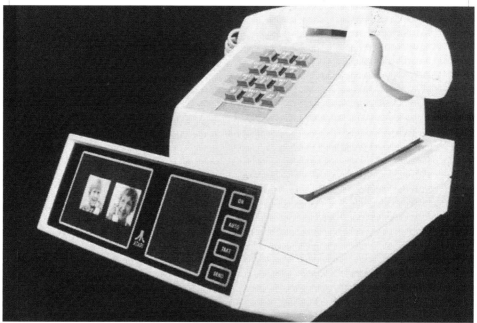

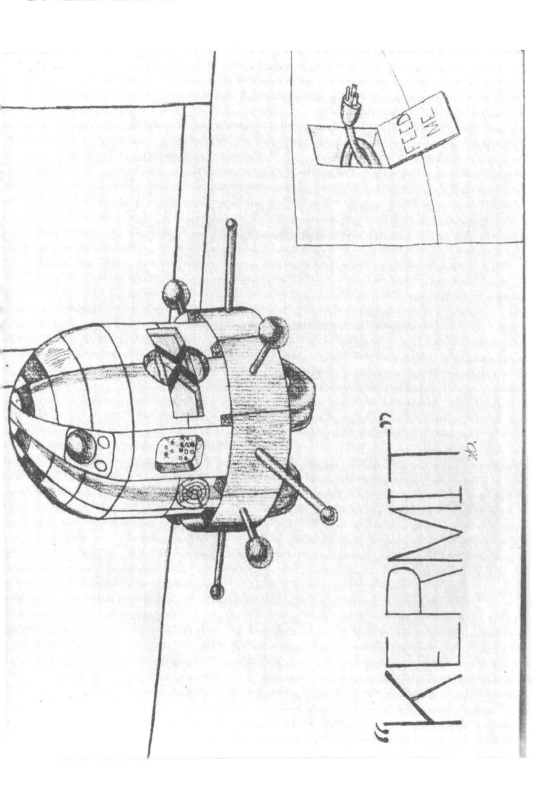

INTER-OFFICE MEMO

ATARI®

TO: Distribution

FROM: Ron Milner *RM*
Larry Nicholson *LN.*   DATE: May 1, 1978

SUBJECT: Proposal - Kermit the Robot

Kermit is an inquisitive little fellow who can get around a bit on his own but whose personality develops fully when working with the Coleen system. He can be operated through Coleen to act as remote eyes and ears for the user's program. A canned demonstration program run on Coleen shows him at his best.

Kermit and Coleen talk to each other through audio tones. This allows the telemetry to be part of the robot's personality besides providing a low cost telemetry system.

This proposal is for design and development of a prototype of Kermit similar in size and behavior to the production version. Mechanical design for production versions could be done either in tandem or subsequent to our prototype development.

Target cost for a production Kermit will be $110 consisting of $40 for electronic subassemblies, $10 for the battery, $10 for the motors and drive, $40 for the body and moving parts, and $10 for miscellaneous.

Physical: 10" diameter x 12" tall
            Two driven wheels - drivable on carpet
              or floor, one idler
            Rotating sensor dome
            2-3 miscellaneous motors for cosmetics
            2-3 flashing lights

Electrical: 6V rechangeable gel cell batteries 5AH
            2 drive motors
            Audio R/C telemetry based on touch tone
              transmitters & receivers
            6500 processor board (1 chip proc in
              production)

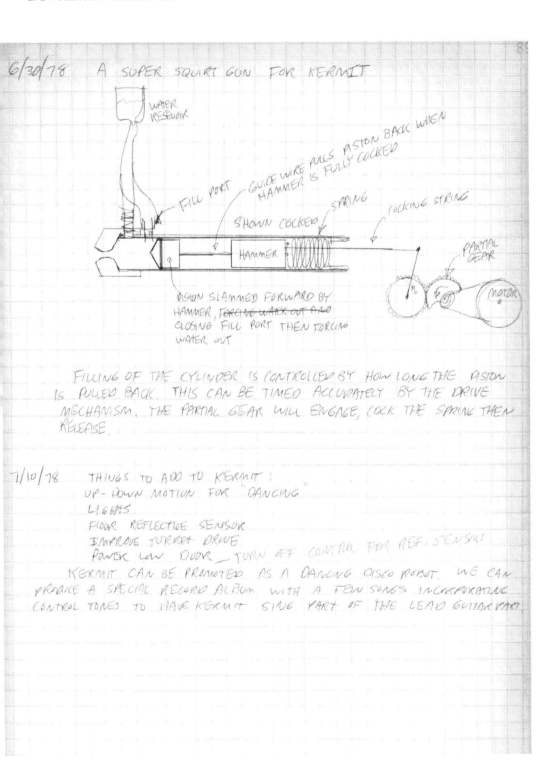

6/30/78   A SUPER SQUIRT GUN FOR KERMIT

WATER RESEVOIR

FILL PORT

GUIDE WIRE PULLS PISTON BACK WHEN HAMMER IS FULLY COCKED

SPRING

COCKING STRING

SHOWN COCKED

HAMMER

PARTIAL GEAR

MOTOR

PISTON SLAMMED FORWARD BY HAMMER, ~~FORCING WATER OUT AND~~ CLOSING FILL PORT THEN FORCING WATER OUT

FILLING OF THE CYLINDER IS CONTROLLED BY HOW LONG THE PISTON IS PULLED BACK. THIS CAN BE TIMED ACCURATELY BY THE DRIVE MECHANISM. THE PARTIAL GEAR WILL ENGAGE, COCK THE SPRING THEN RELEASE.

7/10/78   THINGS TO ADD TO KERMIT:
UP-DOWN MOTION FOR "DANCING"
LIGHTS
FLOOR REFLECTIVE SENSOR
IMPROVE TURRET DRIVE
POWER LOW DOOR — TURN OFF CONTROL FOR REF. SENSOR
KERMIT CAN BE PROMOTED AS A DANCING DISCO ROBOT. WE CAN PRODUCE A SPECIAL RECORD ALBUM WITH A FEW SONGS INCORPORATING CONTROL TONES TO HAVE KERMIT SING PART OF THE LEAD GUITAR AND

Left: Kermit goes for a walk.

Bottom: Kermit's CPU board.

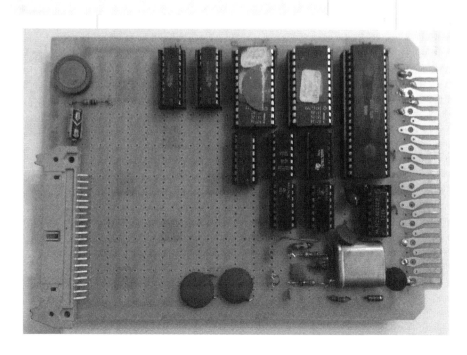

Kermit today with Owen Rubin.
Inset: Kermit's official Atari badge.

VARMITS BEHAVIOR REFLECTED A LIMITED SOFTWARE EFFORT. HE COULD GO STRAIGHT, STOP OR TURN AND WHENEVER HE HIT A WALL HE WOULD TURN AWAY FROM THE WALL.

IMPROVEMENTS THAT CAN BE MADE IF WE PURSUE THE PROJECT INCLU

1) REPLACE FRICTION DRIVE ON TURN AXIS WITH GEAR DRIVE FOR INCREASED TORQUE.

2) PROVIDE SOME SORT OF FEEDBACK OF DOME POSITION TO ALLOW PRECISE TURNING ON VARIOUS SURFACES.

3) INSTALL A SWITCH TO DETECT HE'S BEEN PICKED UP. TH RESPONSE IS TO TURN OFF MOTORS AND MAKE PURRING SOU

4) POSSIBLY INSTALL A SPRAGUE LIGHT MOTION DETECTOR.

5) MAYBE A MICROPHONE INSTEAD?

VARMIT IS NOW OFF TO THE WARNER'S BOARD MEETING WITH N SOME DECISION CAN BE EXPECTED EVENTUALLY.

← THIS SHOWS DRIVE AND TURNING MOTOR AND SUSAN BEARING

12/1/78

Ronald Milner

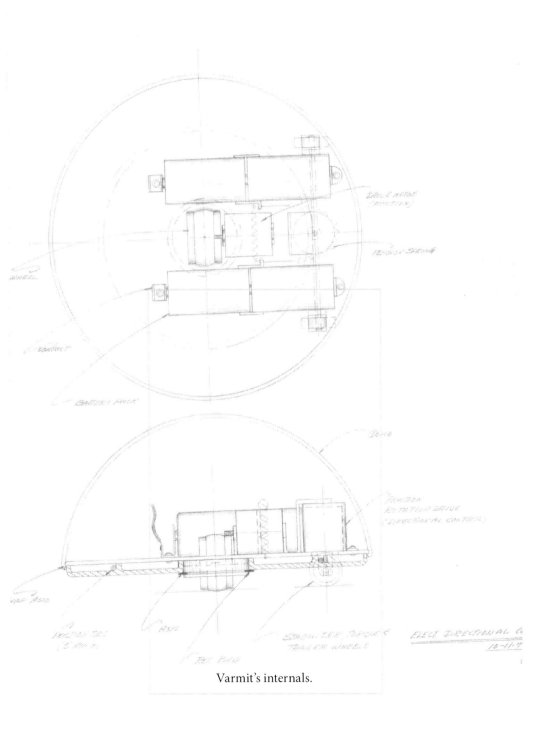

Varmit's internals.

ATARI, INC.

INVENTION DISCLOSURE FORM

No. Of Attachments
Photographs
2 Drawings
Other
I.D. 43

1. INVENTOR(S):

   A. NAME ___Ronald___ ___E.___ ___Milner___
      First   Middle   Last   Social Security #
      ADDRESS P. O. Box 1916, Grass Valley, CA (Nevada)
      County

      Dept. No. 10516
      Division Grass Val
      Citizen Of U.S.A.
      Home Phone 273-7067

   B. NAME ___Gene___ ___H.___ ___Wise___
      First   Middle   Last   Social Security #
      ADDRESS Rt. 2, Box 2015B, Grass Valley, CA (Nevada)
      County

      Dept. No. 10516
      Division Grass Val
      Citizen Of U.S.A.
      Home Phone 272-1798

2. NAME OF IMMEDIATE SUPERVISOR ___Larry Emmons___ MAIL STOP _____

3. TITLE OF INVENTION: ___Toy Robot___

4. SUBJECT CLASS: ___Electronic Toys___

5. TO BE INCORPORATED INTO: (GIVE NAME, MODEL No.) ___Varmit___

6. CONCEPTION OF INVENTION: DATE & DWG. No. OF FIRST DWG.(s) _____

   B. DATE OF FIRST WRITTEN DESCRIPTION ___9/18___
      ENG. NOTEBOOK NO. ___76108-A___ PAGE(S) ___105___
   C. DATE OF FIRST ORAL DISCLOSURE ___9/18/78___ TO: ___Steve Mayer___

7. CONSTRUCTION & TEST OF DEVICE: A. DATE COMPLETED ___11/7/78___
   B. MODEL ___ FULL SIZE _X_ BY WHOM MADE ___Gene Wise___
   C. DATE OF FIRST SUCCESSFUL TEST ___Partially tested 11/7/78___
   D. WHERE CAN MODEL BE FOUND? ___Cyan Engineering___
   E. HAS FIRST SUCCESSFUL MODEL BEEN RETAINED? YES _X_ No

8. PUBLICATION: A. WAS A DESCRIPTION OF INVEN
   B. DATE OF PUBLICATION _____

9. SALE: WAS EMBODIMENT OF INVENTION SOLD?

10. RELATED PRINTED PUBLICATIONS OR PATENT(S) (A

11. OTHER RELATED REFERENCE MATERIAL: _____

12. WAS INVENTION MADE DURING PERFORMANCE OF A
    IF SO - CONCEIVED ___ CONSTRUCTED ___
    A. GIVE FULL CONTRACT NUMBER _____
    B. SECURITY CLASSIFICATION OF CONTRACT ___

13. SIGNATURE(S) OF INVENTOR(S):
    A.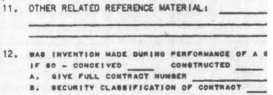
    B. _____
       (GIVE CONCISE DESCRIPTION OR

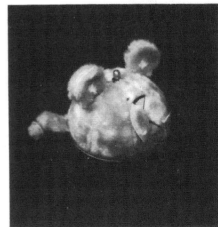

Varmit's patent, and a picture of Varmit himself.

10/30/77
Ron Milner

PROGRAM TO IMPLEMENT BOARD GAME CAPABILITY

I. FORMATION OF CARDBOARD MANUFACTURING GROUP NUCLEUS

>   Packaging Engineer .
>   EE
>   Programmer
>   Artist
>   Technician
>   Production Type
>   Manufacturing Engr

II. STUDY OF MANUFACTURING FEASIBILITY

>   1.) Artwork and tapeups for Game 1
>   2.) Prototype run of game boards at outside vendor (Trend)
>   to tweak printing technology
>   3.) Feasibility study of stuffing electronics on
>   cardboard
>   4.) Develop auto insertion and lead crimping for LED's
>   5.) Extensive environmental testing

III. ELECTRONICS DEVELOPMENT

>   Chip selection, LED's
>   PC layout
>   Programming Game 1
>
>   Game board tester
>   Preproduction run for Game 1
>   Programming for Games 2-5

IV. PREPARATION FOR PRODUCTION OF GAMES 1-5

>   Art and layout
>   Package design, manual
>   Game board test jigs and programs
>   Preproduction run of Games 1-5

V. EARLY PRODUCTION

VI. SET UP IN HOUSE PRODUCTION FACILITY $100K EQUIPMENT
>   2500 sq. ft. Capacity 5000 boards/shift.

Photo courtesy of the Dan Corona Collection

Photo courtesy of the Dan Corona Collection

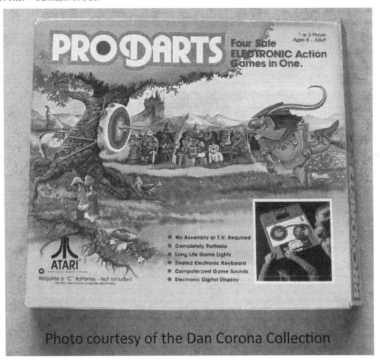

Photo courtesy of the Dan Corona Collection

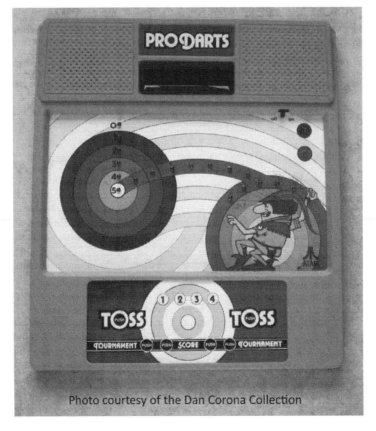

Photo courtesy of the Dan Corona Collection

Right: Game Of Life prototype.
Bottom: Sketch for a Chess game concept.

INTER-OFFICE MEMO

ATARI®

TO   Al Alcorn

FROM   Ron Milner   *RM*

SUBJECT Etch-a-Sketch Study

DATE April 16, 1979

We have studied ways of motorizing an Ohio Art Etch-a-Sketch to provide a high resolution-low cost X-Y display. A standard Etch-a-Sketch was modified to include solenoid driven pen lift and DC motor drive of each axis.

Feedback of pen position proved difficult. A first attempt was made to detect commutation spikes of the motor to count position. This worked in one axis but crosstalk introduced spurious counts into the opposite axis. It is likely that with an extremely careful circuit layout two channels could be made to work. Rather than go to that length, we installed an optical tach on each motor shaft. Problems of count slippage during small pen motions made a reliable position count impossible with a single tach channel. We decided a two channel quadrature detecting tach brought us out of our target price range. Additional problems of cable slippage and tangling when running against the stop were present.

We were able to draw decent quality letters open loop and large graphics closed loop, however, we are not yet able to keep track of pen position while doing letters or small graphics.

Lack of selective or even full screen erase along with low plotting speed severely limits the types of suitable games. "What's It," "Hangman," and computer art were the only games that we came up with. In view of the extensive mechanical and electronic rework that seems to be required to proceed with the prototype and lack of capability of the plotter it was decided to stop the study at this point.

The prototypes for the handheld versions
of *Super Breakout* and *Space Invaders*.

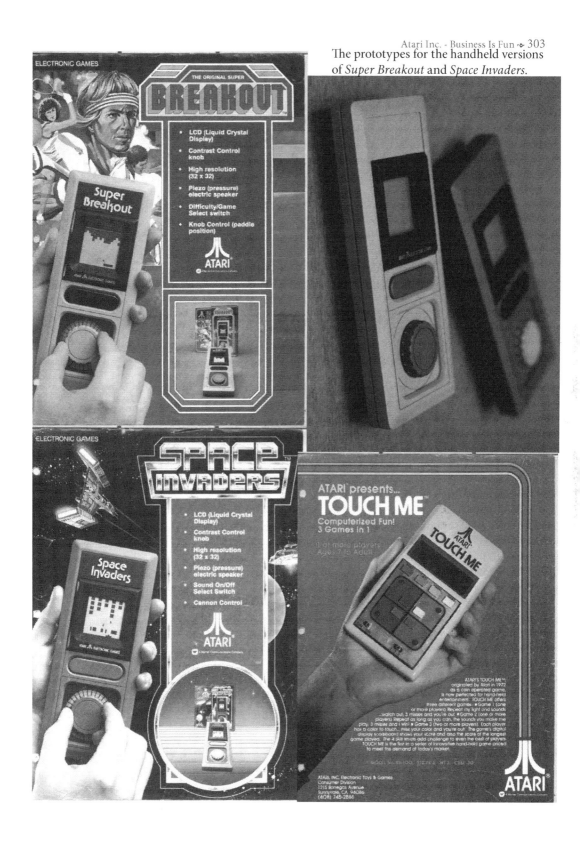

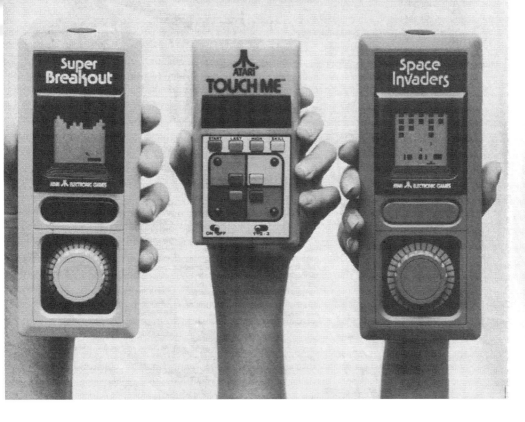

Introducing the golden touch in electronic games.

Atari.

It's really the only name that's synonymous with the fun and excitement of electronic amusement.

After leading the way in arcade and home video games since the very beginning, we're ready to do great things in hand-held games.

With "Touch Me,"™ for example. A new, pocket-size version of an Atari game that's made millions in arcades since 1972.

"Touch Me" is a brain-teasing, computerized test of memory and coordination that captivates players from 7 to 70. The variety and excitement are built in, with three different games for 1-4 players, four levels of skill, plus color and sound.

Now there's no need to take chances with manufacturers who are just getting into electronic toys. Because with Atari, you get the leading name in the field. Built-in consumer acceptance. Quality and reliability to minimize problems with returns. National advertising support. Plus the great, proven games that only Atari can deliver.

Come to the Knickerbocker showroom at the Toy Fair and see for yourself: when it comes to electronics in toys, Atari has the Golden Touch.

ATARI

ATARI INC. Electronic Toys & Games
Consumer Division
1265 Borregas Avenue
Sunnyvale, CA 94086
(408) 745-2896

SEE ATARI
"TOUCH ME" AT THE
KNICKERBOCKER TOY CO.
1107 BROADWAY
ROOM #600.

Bottom: Secret Agent, a prototype in development at the time of handheld *Touch Me*.

Photo Curteousy of Joel Anderson

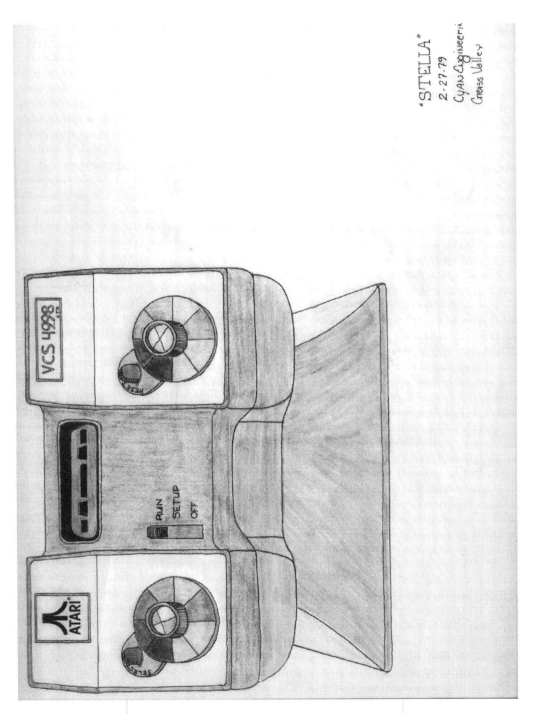

Planning for a prototype of a low cost version of the
VCS that would use *Home PONG's* pedestal case.

Top: Prototype concept for a handheld LCD
Tank game that hooked up to Atari's new
computer.

Bottom: Prototype concept for a smart word-
processor station codnamed 'Nimble Fingers."

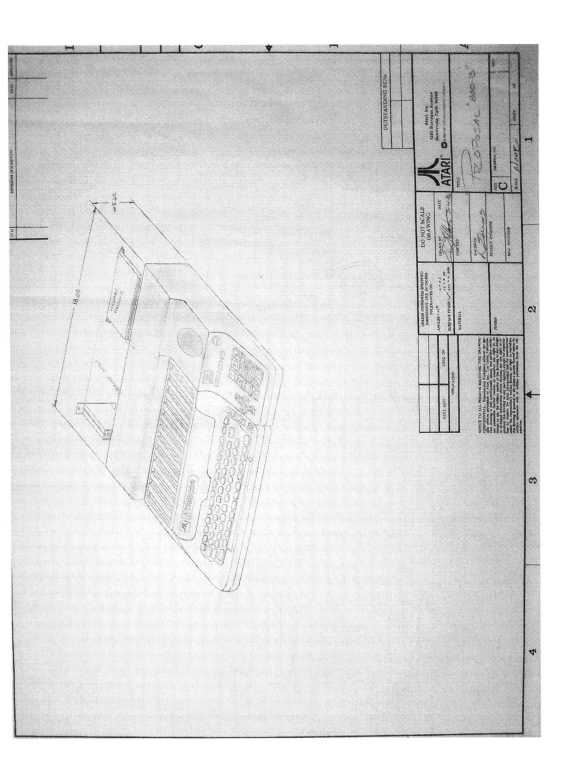

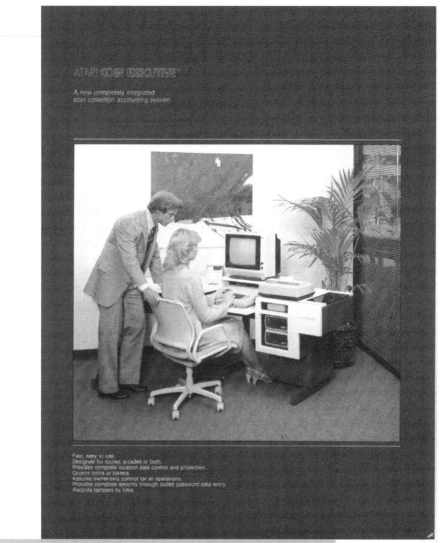

ATARI COIN EXECUTIVE™

A new completely integrated
coin collection accounting system

Fast, easy to use.
Designed for routes, arcades or both.
Provides complete location data control and protection.
Counts coins or tokens.
Assures owner-only control for all operations.
Provides complete security through coded password data entry.
Records tampers by time.

The Sportsmeter, designed at Cyan for Atari and eventually released in the late 1980s as the Nike Sportsmeter.

Project Eagle Eye, the revived video-phone project that would eventually become the Mitsubishi Lumaphone when Ataritel was sold in 1984.

Futuristic Ataritel handsets

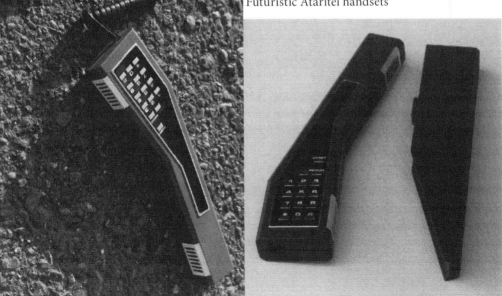

Chapter 6

Rule By The Divine Right Of Kings

1977 thrust several changes on Atari, now that it was owned by Warner Communications. One of the more noticeable of these were the absence of Nolan and Joe Keenan from many day to day meetings, or even being around the new offices much aptly nicknamed 'Mahogany Row.' Built in the executive area of Atari's new corporate building at 1265 Borregas Avenue in Sunnyvale, the lush and gorgeous wood trimmed offices spoke to the heights the company was now rising under Warner.

Manny Gerard had feared a situation like this since first negotiating Warner's purchase of Atari; that by giving these crazy engineering entrepreneur guys cold, hard cash they'd get their money, get distracted and get lost (literally!) all too easily. To force their involvement, he had arranged to give Nolan and Joe the bulk of their buyout earnings in Atari debentures (essentially bonds backed by the full faith and credit of Atari. By doing that instead of Warner debentures, Manny was essentially resting their ultimate value on these guys coming in and working to make Atari successful. Only it wasn't working - they were instead off playing with all of their new found wealth. Atari was no longer being managed the way it had been in the past OR the way it would need to be run to move into the future.

However, despite the lack of leadership from the company's co-founder and its President, the rest of the employees at Atari were still working diligently. They were currently preparing to release several new coin-op machines into the arcades, including Dominos and a very unique arcade game called Triple Hunt, which were also joined by the home market releases of Video Pinball, Super PONG Pro-Am and Pro-Am Ten.

Atari had always been a unique if not different environment to work in. Bushnell had seen to it early on that employees would have good health benefits and that the workday, while not strict or regimented on its work hours, would be observed on a self-policed, flexible basis (at least for those positions like engineering – obviously, those who sat at the front desk in the reception area were compelled to adhere to a more conventional '9 to 5' schedule). What mattered most to him was that the company had a sense of family, with everyone working together towards the ultimate goal of getting the best game products possible out the door. The mantra was always "work hard and play harder."

Often when a fun, exciting new game was being assembled, those games would be played by the workers right there on the assembly floor during break times or after hours. However, on occasion the game play wouldn't always stop at the end of a break hour, much to the annoyance of other workers wanting to get back to their shift, and to Gil Willams who was in charge of manufacturing and had deadlines to meet. The Friday 'after work keg parties' on the loading docks, a mainstay of the Winchester Blvd. and Division Street locations, lived on in the back of 1265 Borregas Ave. and the other new Atari buildings in Sunnyvale. So too did the liberal smoking of pot - though the pot smoking behind the corporate headquarters building was gradually curbed and diminished over time.

Some of the higher paid employees would also head over to places like Khartoum's (which still exists in Campbell, CA) and The Bodega for their after work fun. Referred to in the 1970s as 'Fern Bars,' which was an American slang term for an upscale, or Preppie bar, they were also the 'shark feeding tanks' of the 70s and 80s. Young, rich professionals would come in to hang out, have drinks and grab the attention of young ladies looking to find a rich guy to snatch up.

One such connection would occur with Nolan himself, when he met a waitress named Nancy Nino who was working at Khartoum's as a cocktail waitress. The bar was owned by her family so she most likely wasn't on the prowl like so many of Silicon Valley's gold diggers, but the connection was there between the two of them and it was strong. Interestingly enough, Nancy didn't meet with Nolan first – she had first met Atari's coin-op marketing manager, Frank Ballouz during one of Atari's Khartoum's gatherings. Set to go out on a date, but as fate intervened and cancelled the date, introducing Nancy to Nolan instead. Silicon Valley's most eligible high tech games bachelor and his new cocktail waitress girlfriend soon find their way down the wedding aisle, tying the knot on November 17, 1977. Ever the joker, to this day Nolan still refers to Nancy as his 'child bride,' since at the time Nolan was 34 and Nancy was 25.

Just prior to their marriage, Nolan had purchased a magnificent home in Woodside, CA for them. Although the term 'home' to describe what he'd bought is quite an understatement, because the November 1, 1977 purchase was for the palatial Folgers Estate. Designed by legendary San Francisco architect Arthur Brown Jr. The incredibly impressive mansion is more castle than home - a 13,000 square foot, 37 room, Edwardian-style mansion on 16 acres of land with a pool, tennis courts, horse stable and a groundskeeper house at the entry gate to the estate. Owned by the Folgers family for many years, after Peter Folger's daughter Abigail was one of Charles Manson's victims at the Sharon Tate/Hollywood Hills murders just eight years earlier, Peter had lost interest in the family estate and put it on the market. Exeorcising the ghosts of the past, Nolan and Nancy spent much of their time remodeling the mansion to their liking, further distracting him from Atari and his role as Chairman. While the result was the mansion the married couple always dreamed of living in, it also continued to put his position with Atari in jeopardy.

Just as Nolan was busy with his new abode, Warner was also busy remolding Atari's to their liking. The new 1265 Borregas Avenue corporate headquarters also housed Coin-op Engineering. Split between the first and second floor with Coin-op Engineering on the first, the employees started to refer to the headquarters building as 'The Chocolate Box' for its brown color and box shape.

Next door at 1215 Borregas Ave. in Atari's new Consumer Division building, the brand new company cafeteria opened on May 15, 1977 – a very spacious cafeteria which offered a wide variety of food items to choose from. With everything from freshly made sandwiches to a selection of hot foods and a salad bar, this was a big step up from the previous break rooms of Atari's past. Those old break rooms had been filled with card tables, a foosball table, a pool table was added, and some vending machines for drinks and snacks. But NOW things were different, and 1215's cafeteria was a tangible indicator that things had vastly improved from the old days thanks to Warner's deep pockets. An 'executive cafeteria' and break room were also built in the corporate building, however most of the executives choose to go out to the local restaurants in the area for a more relaxed, civilized lunch, while others would pick up something 'to go' and bring it back to their office desks to eat.

No longer just a coin-op company, the days of having Atari's coin-op offerings out in the corporate lobby for display, sales and playful breaks were over. After the move to 1265, a dedicated game room was built. Behind a closed door off of the lobby, once you entered, the environment was transformed into the actual feel of a video game arcade. Dark and without windows, the strategic lighting insured the room's primary 'glow' came from the arcade games themselves. With the machines set on 'free play,' family and friends were always eager to pay a visit to this wonderland of electronic machines. Over the years, the 'Game Room' was to have its fair share of celebrity visitors, including basketball star Rick Barry from the Golden State Warriors, and perhaps its most famous visitor, Michael Jackson.

Not content to let Coin-op Engineering share space with corporate operations, across the street at 1272 Borregas Ave a new engineering building was in the process of being built. Once completed in June 1978, not only would it hold Coin-op Engineering, but Consumer Engineering as well on the second floor. The new engineering building would be spacious and have its own kind of perks and benefits as well, like a gym, spa and even a hot tub with the Atari Fuji symbol logo on the back wall in orange and blue tile. Quite a few employees shared their 'memories' with us of the infamous Atari co-ed hot tub parties, but we'll just let those tales remain private for those who lived them. After all we don't want to be the cause of anyone's divorce, so let's just move on. But did you know that hot tubs played an important part of many an Atarian's recreational time, and a co-ed hot tub was even built into the future Atari Home Computer group's building at 30 Plumeria?

For those into more traditional break time fare, outside around the back behind 1272 would be an area that many employees would truly enjoy: a horseshoe pit. Besides getting a break from the fluorescent lighting and grabbing some California sunshine, this was a great break from the world of moving virtual balls, bats and paddles on the screen. Joining this area behind 1272 would be a more curious construct - a small windowless building intended for RF testing. We say intended because the unofficial use also as a 'smoke shack,' where employees would indulge in its closed and windowless space to toke up on pot. The 'pot buker' would fill with smoke, creating a 'concentrated' and enjoyable high for everyone in the room. Unfortunately on many inopportune times, the pot breaks would coincide with management or senior engineers giving a facilities tour. During those times, a suddenly opened RF building door resulted in an outward bellowing cloud of pot smoke. While one would expect to find Cheech and Chong lumbering out, the execs were suddenly swarmed by embarrassed (and buzzed!) employees quickly fleeing the scene. The stunned tour guide was left to explain to the guests Atari's rather unorthodox working environment.

As time went by and more of Warner's corporate influence continued to permeate the halls of Atari, the original 'old guard' had to learn creative ways to curb their habits. In the early days of Atari at one of the all-employees meetings behind the loading dock on Winchester Blvd., Gil Williams requested from that point on that anyone who wanted to indulge in smoking pot during their breaks would have to do it off the premises. Only when they were done could they come back onto company property to go back to work. A fast and loose rule over the years, Warner intended to crack down on the unprofessional weed breaks. In a last ditch effort to intervene, at least on the Atari management's behalf, Nolan created a new rule to appease Warner's sensibility: No smoking pot between the hours of 9 to 5. "Nolan came up with a new system - it was called '501.' So at 5:01p.m., he would call over the loudspeaker in the office 'Anyone with a 501, meeting in my office.' We'd all show up and wait for the one with the cannabis to show up and then we'd smoke away," recalls Frank Ballouz.

Honoring the '501 tradition,' during a flight back from New Orleans from a distributor's conference, Gene Lipkin and Frank Ballouz were able to take the Warner corporate jet back to Atari in California. There was a VERY strict policy for the jet by order of Manny Gerard – no drugs on the jet, ever! Silicon Valley renegades that Atarians were, Gene and Frank ignored this, lit up and smoked some pot on the way back. Upon landing, the straight-laced steward on the plane ratted them out to Manny and the next morning Frank is called into Gene's office; on the speakerphone is Manny from New York. "Guys, you were on the plane last night weren't you?" Frank responds, yeah they were on it. Manny then asks them, "Were you doing drugs on the plane?" Frank then proceeds to explain to Manny that the Rolling Stones were on the plane the night before them and don't you think they were doing drugs too? Manny shoots back, "Okay guys, yeah, maybe they were, but let me ask you this - what is their drug of choice? Cocaine! So what is your drug of choice?" Frank and Gene both respond: "Marijuana. It's not as bad as cocaine- it won't hurt anybody." Manny then proceeds to tell them both, "One more question guys. What air does the pilot breathe!?" Suddenly Gene and Frank's eyes go wide and they look at each other. Frank belts out, "Oh fuck Manny! Now we understand." That was the end of the pot smoking on the corporate jet.

All pot smoking aside, one of the other newly added perks of being part of Warner was the expanded Company Store. Routinely stocked with lots of great Atari branded t-shirts, shorts and other apparel, Atari branded desk items, notepads, key chains and more - if an Atari name and logo could be put on it, it was available in the Company Store. Under Warner though, besides being able to buy Atari products with an employee discount (which was very appealing during the Christmas holidays to fulfill family and friends 'Santa lists'), the employees now had access to ALL of the latest albums produced and distributed by Warner's record and music companies. Everything was at a generous discount and many times new music releases were available in the Atari Company Store even before they were available in regular stores. We're told one of the best selling albums in the Company Store during this time was Fleetwood Mac's 'Rumours.'

However, as the months go by in 1977, a trend is occurring. Bushnell and Keenan are becoming less and less involved. Bushnell sporadically shows up from time to time and then disappears. Manny Gerard is having many confrontations with Nolan regarding his absenteeism at the company. As a result, Manny specifically tells him: "Nolan, you need to be involved. You can't show up after not being here for six months and tell people what they are doing is wrong and to do it your way." Manny recalls: "Nolan was an endless string of problems. I told him, you cannot run this company by the Divine Right of Kings. I must've told him that more than 30 separate times." Both Nolan and Keenan are MIA much of the time. Important meetings are missed as well as appointments. "We had a gentleman fly out from the East Coast for a meeting with Joe one day. He shows up, but Joe is nowhere to be found. I called around everywhere but he couldn't be located. I had to apologize to the gentleman that Joe wasn't going to be here for their meeting. That was one of the worst memories I have of my time at Atari" recalls Robert Kendall, Joe Keenan's executive secretary. She later finds out, Joe was at Nolan's house all day in the hot tub and just blew off the meeting. Manny decides it's time to bring in some outside management to fill the void being left by Atari's absentee Co-CEO's.

Adult Supervision Required

What Manyy is really looking for, in his own words, is some 'adult super-vision' for the romper room that he considers Atari's management to be. One afternoon while Ray Kassar is having lunch with Bill Sarnoff (the head of Warner's book division), Bill explains to Ray about this new company that Warner had just purchased called Atari. "Would you like to go out and have a look at it?" asks Bill. The West Coast simply holds no interest for this East Coast native shuttling regularly between a Miami vacation home and his New York textiles industry base of operations.

Ray's reluctance in accepting the consulting project stemmed from his recent success through his own private consulting company. Ray had become a highly successful textile industry executive as President of Burlington House and Executive VP of the Burlington empire. Leaving to start his own textiles firm, he became the first American to import 100% Egyptian cotton into the United States. After thirty six trips to Egypt, his company, Ray E. Kassar Consulting, was doing very well. Ray's textile prodcuts are being carried in major stores like Bloomingdales and Lord & Taylor, so why would Ray really have an interest in doing anything else? And for a video game company of all things?

A few days later, Bill follows up with a phone call to Ray, asking him to 'please' have a meeting with Manny Gerard in New York to discuss Atari. At least this way Bill could say he did all he could to lure Ray in. So Ray agrees to meet with Manny, so long as it's not too long of a meeting. Not too long turned into a four hour meeting, at the end of which Ray agreed to go to California for a brief visit and write a report on the company. Basically what would need to be done to move Atari further into the strong business and source of revenue that Manny knew it could become.

Ray flies out to California in February, 1978 as a Management Consultant. Initially meeting with Nolan and Joe Keenan, he moves on to meet with the key engineering managers and other people during his visit. Returning to New York and writing his report, the list of recommendations are delivered to Manny Gerard. As Ray recalls about it, "I found out that the product (the VCS) was popular, but they had more returns than they projected. The product did not perform. So we had a returns issue - a big issue, they're loosing their shirt. We had no quality control, there's

no fianancial CFO, there's no production manager, there's no infrastructure *at all.*"
It turns out to be just the insight that Manny was looking for, and several days later
Manny gives Ray a call and asks him to come over to Warner for a meeting to discuss
his report. Manny basically tells Ray, "We'd like to have you to do for us all of the
things you're recommending need to be done."

In recently asking Manny why he brought in this textiles consultant to Atari, Manny confirmed again: "Atari needed adult supervision." Ray's impression after arriving at Atari for the evaluation wasn't much different, "The place was disor-
ganized and there was confusion. There was no real management direction, no real
marketing. At that point they were doing about $75 million in sales and losing about
$15-$20 million. It was a loss position."

Ray is certainly not interested in managing the video game products portion of this company nor is he interested in relocating out to California. In his own
sophomoric move, he makes a list of completely unreasonable demands to Manny
that would have to be fullfilled for him to take the job:

- Ray didn't want to live in the Silicon Valley area. Being from New York,
  the closest California substitute would be San Francisco, so he wanted
  an apartment provided for him there.

- He didn't want to have to drive 2 - 2 ½ hours a day, which he felt would
  be wasted time. Instead, Ray wanted a driver to drive to and from work
  because if he was driven he could still do work during that time.

- He also wanted a percentage of Atari's profits.

The demands weren't for the sake of being obnoxious, but rather to kill
Manny's insistence on hiring him. He figured they wouldn't agree to them and that
would be that... but Manny and ultimately Warner agreed to everything.

Surrendering to the situation, Ray agrees to come on board and begin a six
month contract where he's installed as President of the Consumer Products Division at Atari. Given carte blanche to begin organizing and managing the Consumer
Products division of Atari, upon reviewing the sales and returns of the Atari VCS
he found it to be a very popular product. However, defects and returns were a serious problem and that meant Financials and Production management needed to be

bolstered.

One can picture a million different stereotypical ways Ray's new position of authority caused him to clash with the Atari bunch. The notion of a 'suit' walking in to become part of a rag-tag bunch of upstarts has provided fodder for a plethora of cheap 80s and 90s 'B' movies. But the reality is so much more interesting! Here he was reporting to Nolan's office to get orientated with the chairman of the board, only to discover Nolan's personality fit the profile very loosely. Surrounded by a harem of women operating as secretaries, there's Nolan wearing a t-shirt that says, "I love to fuck." Suffice to say, Ray quickly started to realize this was the mentality and cavalier conduct he was up against.

Then not long after that he was invited to join a 3 o'clock management committee meeting with Bushnell, Keenan, Alcorn, Bristow and Lipkin. Agreeing, the prim and proper Ray is aghast when the meeting begins with everyone having a beer. When it comes time to take his beer, Ray turns down the offer and takes a skeptical survey of the room of old guard Atarians. "How could people serious at running a business drink during business hours?" he thought. Then, in his mind, the situation suddenly went from bad to worse when he was then offered some marijuana instead. "What kind of company are you people running here?! I don't have time for this. I have work to do!" exclaimed Ray. At which point he packs up and leaves the meeting.

It's apparent to Ray that he has a lot of work to do to address issues within the company and he can't compete with all these strong egos and personalities. Bushnell and Keenan need to go. "If we all looked back in 20/20 hindsight and were totally honest with ourselves, the Atari-Warner relationship didn't work, not because of Warner, but because of ourselves. Here was this company that wanted to give us several hundred million dollars, and we fought them tooth and nail every step of the way," recalls Gene Lipkin.

"Do not underestimate the value of Warner's money. To grow a business that fast consumed a great deal of capital. Warner supplied it but killed the technical innovation that drove the business. And yes, I drove Manny Gerard crazy because he always knew that he was the smartest man in the room and I was quick to call him an idiot. Ray Kassar was just political," recalls Nolan.

Despite these differences in day-to-day management, meetings and old guard vs. new style, the Consumer Division had a big to-do list ahead of itself for 1978. Ray brings in Dennis Groth to handle finances while he moves on to the next 'to do' of dealing with the quality control issues with the VCS. Software development is also ramped up as a large assortment of fresh games needed to be written in time to be previewed at the next Consumer Electronics Show and readied to ship for the Christmas holiday season.

Cost reduction and redesign of areas of the VCS would also need to be implemented, the first of which would be a complete tear down and redesign of the joystick controllers for the VCS. The original CX-10 joysticks that shipped with the original launch VCS were top shelf all the way: Extremely well designed mechanical internals that only a coin-op engineer could appreciate and love, and lots of bells and whistles to give a high end appearence. But the flip side was they were complex to manufacture, and the numerous parts only added to the cost.

A new design replaces the spring loaded internals with a simple 5-point contact board with metal domed caps, so that when pressure is applied the domes collapse down and make a contact. The resulting plastic driven springiness gives the joysticks and the fire button a much more solid and snappy feedback feel while reducing the cost. The tops of the original joysticks are also changed from the heavy rubber joystick cover with small metal tab that says 'Atari,' to a thinner logo-less version. Another small, but minor change is made to the case design: on the top of the joysticks, the orange ring that dotted around the base of the handle would now have the word 'TOP' in the forward position. Apparently people didn't know how to hold the joysticks to face the right direction, and this little added bit of text would help millions hold the joystick the right way. These new CX-40 joysticks would be the mainstay controller for the VCS and many other products to follow for years to come. In the end, this model of the joystick would become nearly as iconic for Atari as its "Fuji" logo.

Ray also instructs Douglas Hardy, one of the two designers of the VCS case design, to revisit the VCS case once again. The case bottoms were redesigned from the extra thick polystyrene plastic to a standard, more lightweight ABS plastic which eliminated the earlier warping issues of the heavy polystyrene bottoms. Ray left no stone unturned in his attempt to cut down on costs while improving functionality, and even drove other more subtle changes to the game cartridge packaging. Originally, the first batches of games shipped in what were called 'Gate Folded' boxes; a box with a front opening cover and inner slot for the cartridge to rest in, along with another place for the manual. The box design is changed to a much simpler and less expensive top flap 'envelope box' style design pretty much used for the rest of the VCS' life.

As Ray's new management and implementation plans are beginning to come together, the VCS library is also set to grow to nearly 18 titles and a new accessory is ramping up for the Christmas 1978 sales season. The controller, designated the CX-50 keyboard controller, is actually an interesting by-product from the research currently taking place by the VCS hardware design team. Diligently working on adding enhancements to the VCS after its launch, these enhancements eventually morphed into becoming Atari's home computers. The keyboard controllers are really a glorified pair of keypads that are meant to be used with the soon to be released BASIC language cartridge and forthcoming logic games.

I Smell A Rat

The smell of pizza wafted across the wooden rec room styled dining area, mixing with the beeps and boops of arcade video games to create a symphony for the senses. True, the pizza may have tasted like cheap cardboard according to some critics, but the animatronic stage show and fun arcade area were meant to be the real stars. Nolan's vision of "singing barrels and dancing bears" from his days of sharing an office with Ted had become a reality on May 9th, 1977. In 1978, it turns into one of the main reasons why he's not spending as much time at Atari - of course his sail boating and cruising in his Rolls Royce Silver Cloud also contributed to that.

Opened as Chuck E. Cheese's Pizza Time Theatre at 370 South Winchester Blvd. in San Jose, the family pizza and entertainment concept of the resteraunt is formed around a unique mixture of Disney inspired animatronics and Atari's innovative leisure. The center of attention are the animatronic singing characters, including the pizza chef ("Pasqually"), a country western and banjo playing dog "(Jasper T. Jowls"), the voluptuous hippo ("Dolly Dimples") and of course the star of the show, "Chuck E. Cheese." Video games are scattered everywhere, joined by picnic table-styled seating for kids to enjoy the entertainment and the pizza. Making sure not to leave out the adults, wine and beer are included as well.

A portion of the $120 million invested into Atari by Warner since the sale had been steered by Nolan to Chuck E. Cheese's development. The new purse meant that Nolan was able to continue to use Atari as his private playground, diverting its resources to pursue whatever flights of fancy he could dream up. Cyan's technical know-how provides the key to building the animatronics, but he also needed to hire someone with an understanding of business and marketing to help evolve his concept and bring it to fruition. Maybe Nolan was getting smarter now that he was wealthier, tired of rushing in head first to directly spar in industries he had no real experience with. The man tasked with creating what would become Pizza Time Theatre is not from within Atari's ranks, but rather an outside resource brought within Nolan's fold: Gene N. Landrum.

Gene was formerly with National Semiconductor's consumer products group, and had previously done that extensive market study of home video games in May 1976 for Bushnell and Keenan - the one done in preparation for many of the design and feature aspects of the VCS. Appointing Gene as the General Manager of the Atari Restaurant Operating Division and making sure Gene only reported to him, Nolan sat back and let his mouse run the cryptic start-up maze in search of that cheese - Nolan's cheese. Like an updated and far more successful version of the failed Dr. Wakefield experiment, Wakefield 2.0 if you will, Gene understood people, patterns and habits from a marketing and psychology perspective. For example, at one point Gene went to Disneyland several times to observe the audiences at Disney's Country Bear Jamboree attraction. What he noticed was you had kids, parents and grandparents all attentively watching the show completely enthralled by the whirring gears covered in fur and cartoonish clothing. Gene even took his young daughter with him to a repeat visit for gauging her interest and reactions. The end result was the audience and their interaction with the show, if not outright acceptance of the robotic creatures as performers, told him exactly what he needed to know about recreating the experience for Nolan's venture.

Having evaluated what it would take to get an initial prototype restaurant up and running with the interior design, animatronics systems, layout, kitchen design and other details, Gene comes back to Nolan and says the cost for this animatronic pizza joint's journey into reality will be approximately $750,000. A drop in the bucket with Warner's cash, the budget is approved and the project is a go.

Many observations about Nolan have been made throughout this book – some good and some that make you scratch your head, but the overall concept of Pizza Time resonates why Nolan has often been referred to as a visionary. His original push for a family restaurant had everything to do with trying to shed the whole stigma of videogames for the masses - and to remove the dark seedy side of them that was still associated with the old pinball arcade days, the criminal elements, mob ties and just the overall negative perception the public and even some in government had of arcade and coin-operated games.

By creating a wholesome restaurant environment where a family could go to have a pizza while the kids were entertained by video games and singing animals was pure genius. And the fact that he hired someone else to rely on to chiefly bring that vision to fruition shows an increasing level of maturity beyond the 'I like to fuck' t-shirts. Gene notes while he is doing his research on resteraunts that in nearly every location he entered, there were always signs such as "Children must be seated" or "Keep your children quiet." Essentially there were no establishments that allowed kids to be, well, 'kids.' A place where their parents could let their children have some fun and freedom while everyone could enjoy a meal together. There was a niche market waiting to be created and dominated by Nolan and Atari, and the beauty of it was that it was mutually beneficial. Every future location of the planned franchise would provide another opportunity for placement of Atari arcade games, increasing sales and presence in the process. Nolan had tried that before with Atari owned and operated Atari Game Centers several years before, set up in locations like Bayfair Shopping center in San Leandro across the Bay. But these never lived up to the potential that the 'pizza theatre' concept now held.

After all the research and initial studies had been completed, Nolan could tell during Gene's budget proposal that he was very excited about the whole project. Keying into this and understanding his usual motivational tricks wouldn't be needed here, Nolan simply unleashes Gene to go build his restaurant. Gene is in charge of everything - from managing the team to build the animatronics, to getting a costume company to design the characters, to the kitchen and food that will come out of it. Initially reluctant to take on such a massive project, the excitement of the opportunity had him saying a dreamlike 'yes' as if he was one of the animatronic characters he was soon to create.

Instead of having an architect do the floor plan layout, Gene actually does the floor plan layout himself because he wants to ensure that the various areas in the restaurant would have a flow. His reasoning was that when a family walked in the door, the kids would stop, look and say to themselves, "This is my kind of place!"

Next came the need for Gene to focus on the resteraunt's mascot. Nolan had been showing off his rat costume around Atari for quite some time before Gene's involvement. A physical symbol of the vision he wanted to pursue, the 'rat' was presented as the centerpiece mascot long before he had much of anything else. A prominent figure in Nolan's office, he was even there when Manny Gerard first met with Nolan in late spring of 1976 to discuss Atari selling itself to Warner Communications. Nolan gave the big pitch on the rat and the idea of these family entertainment restaurants, but at the time though Manny had no interest whatsoever in the idea. Manny wanted a high tech entertainment company to bolster Warner's continued growth; not to muck around in the restaurant business.

Originally called Rick Rat, the costume was a wider, fatter and furrier creature than the more familiar Chuck E. Cheese, with a floppy, long and more 'rat-like' nose. Disney had Mickey Mouse, and Nolan wanted his Rickey Rat, or just Rick as he was called at the time. Perhaps concerned that someone in Disney's legal department would quickly pick up on the overly familiar sounding name, Rick was a safer bet then Rickey. Regardless of Manny initially shooting the idea down, Nolan would continue to have Rick around him including at the various Atari PR campaigns - even having him present at the Moffet Park construction ground breaking ceremony where he's seen in photographs right in the midst of lined up executives. Rick was in all the publicity photographs of Nolan at the time as well, usually in the background or standing next to Nolan's desk. Championing the rat, he was puting his idea of a family friendly restaurant concept out there for all to see in the hopes that it would eventually 'stick.'

Now that the project had finally taken hold, there was one problem and ironically it was Rick himself. The idea of a rat and food in the same location is perhaps not the most appealing concept for a restaurant. Gene knew that Rick needed a make-over and went to a costume design company to carry it out. In Gene's mind, there was one basic concept that needed to be followed to capture Rick's new look: It should be neither a rat nor a mouse, but a hybrid. Basically he wanted a rat with softer and more appealing mouse lines. Approving their new design, Gene needed to come up with a new name to go with the new look. When it was chosen, you'll be surprised to find out it wasn't Chuck E. Cheese, but rather the 'Big Cheese.' The name only stuck for a short while however, as just a few months before opening the restaurant they discovered that Marriott actually owned that name for their own projected restaurants (but had yet to use it). After discussing still using the name with Atari 's legal department, they came back and advised emphatically "NO" on its use.

The eventual name, Chuck E. Cheese, is chosen in classic Atari style. "Joe Keenan, Nolan and I were drinking beer in the Atari Chairman's office and getting very goofy about Disney being our adversary. It was the days of the Mickey Mouse Club on TV and we started trying to mimic that (characteristic Mickey Mouse) sound, and after many beers it was MICKEY MOUSE ala CHUCK E. CHEESE as it was alliterative. Sounds corny but it's a true story," recalls Gene Landrum. The story seems to differ a bit from Nolan's version though as he recalls that the group did sit around, drink beers and work on a new name, but couldn't come to an agreement and in the end, the ad agency they had hired came up with Chuck E. Cheese. Steve Mayer also remembers the discussions on the naming of the rat and the restaurant. "We had all discussed the names, and it definitely didn't come from the ad agency." Whatever way it happened, in the end Rick Rat was gone, and now Chuck E. Cheese - the derby wearing, Jersey accent sounding character with an attitude - was ready to delight and entertain the kids.

At that point Gene had to start working on the animatronic stage show Nolan had wanted, the festive Disney inspired entertainment for families to enjoy while they ate their pizza. Luckily Atari had their own set of 'Imagineers' in the form of Cyan Engineering in Grass Valley, who would be tapped to do the animatronic mechanisms, controllers and electronics that needed to be developed. Before the project is fully explained to the Cyan engineers, Nolan arranges to have the entire engineering staff flown down to Disneyland. With the airport being fogged in the morning they were to leave, a bus was chartered instead and everyone spent the almost seven hour drive in anticipation of a fun filled day. Little did the engineers know that Nolan was actually making this trip all about business. He wants them to get exposed to the robotics and animatronic systems Disney was using so that he could then present to them his new project for his family restaurant concept. Excited about the project when it was finally explained, when the Cyan engineers got back on their next full work day they dug in to the unfamiliar territory.

Larry Emmons recalls, "We did all of the animatronics for the first Pizza Time at Cyan. A generalized computer board, based on the 6502 processor was used for each 'display.' The audio and computer (instruction for operating the stuff) info was recorded onto a Teac 4 track semi-professional tape recorder (can't remember the exact format for the data, but one of the tape tracks was used for clock info). Playing the tape produced the entertainment in a synchronized way. The mechanical things were all pneumatically actuated using 50 year old (at that time!) mechanical music technology, or by modern air cylinders. It worked great and was reliable. There was no mini-computer, only streaming data from the tape and distributed

6502 controllers. The characters movements, syncing to the music, spotlights turning on/off, etc were programmed by trial and error in a room rented across the hall from Cyan in the Litton building. I can't recall for sure, but we probably had some type of PDP-11/70 mini-computer for the programming that got recorded to a Teac tape. Gary Waters worked a lot on that."

After all of the animatronics were completed, everything was loaded up onto a truck that Gary Waters had picked up from a rental place right near the Litton building in Grass Valley. The animatronics, controller boards, rs-232 cabling systems, the PDP-11/70 mini-computer as well as the Teac 4 track player system were all loaded into it and then Gary drove it all down to the pilot restaurant to begin installation. "The pilot restaurant used to be in an old brokerage building. They still had all these telephone systems and lines running through the whole place. I had to go in and remove everything out of there so that the kitchen, stage and arcade area's could all be setup," recalls Gary. The PDP-11/70 mini-computer was brought down to the pilot restaurant because through trial and error, the whole animated sequence of movements, music and interaction had to be adjusted and reprogrammed to the Teac tape player and run through until everything was synchronized.

As for giving these mechanical creatures from Cyan Engineering their furry personae's, Gene Landrum contracted an artist with great mechanical abilities from Apple Valley, CA - Harold Goldbranson. Harold designed and built all of the animated character skins that would be fitted over the animatronic mechanical assemblies, making these robotic creatures come to life with a visual personality of their own.

When the menu was being put together for Pizza Time Theater, it originally wasn't going consist of just pizza. In fact it was almost going to be a much larger menu of pizza, burgers and fries as well as a salad bar. However, Gene knew they needed to keep the food side of things simple and easy to manage to contrast the upkeep needed for the animatronics and video games. Besides, it might've been a lot harder to market 'Burgers & Fries Time Theater.' And while the idea of kids having their own fun place is what attracted Gene to the project, the idea of subjecting them to unruly teens was certainly not on the menu. Gene puts up signs around the location stating "16 year olds not allowed without a Parent." His concern was about having young children that were 7 to 10 years in age being exposed to wise cracking party minded teenagers of the late 70s that typically hung out in arcades. This was one area though were Gene and Nolan didn't initially see eye to eye. When Nolan came into the restaurant during its successful grand opening, he pushed past the lines out the door to find Gene. Commenting that things were going very well and Gene was doing a great job, he closes with, "But take those damned signs down! I want 15 and 16 year olds in here to play games." Still thinking he's right, Gene ignores Nolan, leaving the signs up. Two weeks later Nolan comes in again and pulls Gene to the side to talk, this time over beers he instead tells Gene to not only keep the signs but to change them from being just for 16 year olds to signs that say "No Teens Allowed Without an Adult." Gene was vindicated.

Another new feature Gene implemented was an elevated crawl maze that looked like a giant wedge of swiss cheese and also incorporate a slide into a ball pit. It's a huge hit with parents, so much so that mothers are showing up from the moment the doors open in the morning just so they can let their younger children loose in the maze and ball pit while they sit and have a drink. However, the kitchen manager was not a fan of the ball pit at all. Going to Gene he tells him, "Get that damned ball thing out of here!" Gene is puzzled and wants to know what the problem is. The kitchen manager responds back: "Don't you know there are little two and three year old kids peeing in the ball pit? We're running a restaurant!" Gene snaps back, "This is not a restaurant - it's a family entertainment business. You have a dishwasher that 's not being used from 11pm to 11am. Wash the damned balls!"

A week before the official opening of the restaurant the doors were opened, and people were invited in to watch the animatronics show to get feedback from them. Allowing the Cyan engineers to make last minute final adjustments to the show sequence and synchronizations before officially opening, even with this pre-opening testing not everything worked according to plan. Part of the show sequence includes a chorus done by a group of three birds who would sing once the curtain to their bird cage rose up and revealed them, inspired by Dinseyland's Enchanted Tiki Room. It's a great visual effect and adds a lot to the whole coordinated animatronic presentation; however during the Grand Opening things didn't quite work out the way everyone wanted. "I wasn't there that night but the way I had designed the curtain around the three animated birds, it pulled up with a cable winding around a drum. I learned not to ever use that kind of arrangement again! The story is that on the big night the curtain started to go up, then down then up then broke kind of spectacularly with the hoop and curtain plummeting onto the diners below," according to Ron Milner. Another more graphic incident happened later on. The Chuck E Cheese restaurant gave a group of disadvantaged children an afternoon of free food and games. In the middle of an animatronic singing show, one of the characters – Helen Henny - had its costume head come loose from the animatronics assembly and fall off onto the floor. rolling under a nearby table. The terrified children, their illusion suddenly shattered like discovering their fun show as full of *Terminator* robots, ran screaming from the area. What was supposed to be an afternoon of fun games and laughs turn into a bit of a mess.

After the opening, it's obvious Chuck E Cheese is certainly a success! Just as video games filled a void for people wanting to play the new 'high tech entertainment' offerings, the void is now also being filled for families to go to where parents could unleash their kids into a wonderland of video games, mazes, slides and animatronics shows, all while scarfing down what would actually become a standard food item at Chuck E Cheese's even 30 years later; really bad pizza.

As Nolan entered 1978, Chuck E. Cheese was taking most of his time if not his complete interest and motivation. In March, with 6% of Atari debentures worth a face value of $12 million, he's in a position to start doing something that he's been kicking around in the back of his mind: negotiating with Warner Communications to buy Chuck E. Cheese from Atari. Still never really wanting Atari to go off in the direction of resteraunts, Manny agrees to negotiate and by June Nolan has purchased the rights, intellectual property and assets to Chuck E. Cheese for $500,000. Moved from an Atari subsidiary to an independent venture, Gene Landrum resigns as General Manager of the Atari Restaurant Operating Division to then become President and Chief Operating Office of Chuck E. Cheese Pizza Time Theater, Inc. Interestingly enough, even with Manny's prejudice against the operation, Warner still maintains a small minority stake in Chuck E. Cheese.

Not long after the purchase, Nolan was lounging around his mansion's pool with his former partner Ted Dabney and their families. The two had remained casual acquaintances since their bitter parting, Ted moving on to a string of different tech jobs including doing some work for Atari competitor Meadows Games in the mid 70s. When Nolan and Nancy's son Brent was born, Ted's now teenage daughter Terri would also often babysit for Nolan and Nancy's newborn son, including accompanying the couple on convention trips to watch over the child. She still raves to this day about Nolan's mansion and what a great place it was for a kid to hang out, including a full arcade and movie theatre, ice cream parlor and the aforementioned pool.

The two had even recently had an encounter with brief third partner Larry Bryan, who had approached each separately about funding a new venture of his own: a porno movie. Feeling bad that he missed out on his chance to be a part of things, they both chipped in a bit to help Larry, and as some have unofficially stated it was even filmed on Atari's premises after hours.

On that particular day of lounging though, Nolan had his staff prepare a big barbecue for the visit, after which Nolan, Nancy, Ted, Ted's wife Joan, and their daughters Terri and Pam along with Terri's friend Erica, have retired to the pool. Nolan was venting some of his frustrations about the pool to his old business partner, having tried to install a solar water heater for it that wasn't working right. Nolan gradually turns the conversation to Chuck E. Cheese and asks Ted if perhaps he'd like to go in on it as a partner? After everything that happened with Atari, Ted said "I'd rather be your friend than your partner in another company." Nolan still asked Ted if he wouldn't mind still going down to his new restaurant and checking it out and telling him what he thought.

When Ted went down to the pilot Chuck E Cheese on Winchester, his first impression is not too favorable. "The place was a bit dirty, it was very noisy. I had no idea when my pizza was ready. I kept going up to the counter and asking the girl until finally my order was up and I took it back to a table and tried it out. The pizza wasn't very good," Ted remembers. The noise, Ted notices is from all of the commotion going on - kids were laughing and screaming and the games even threatening to drown that out with their own noise. Making note of all the serious shortcomings at the restaurant, he contacts Nolan and explains his findings. The dirty conditions, the noise, not knowing when your order was up and that the pizza really wasn't good. Nolan says he can take care of the cleanliness and appearance of the place, but it has to be noisy because of the games and the kids having fun. As for the pizza, Nolan said it didn't matter, "Mediocre pizza is good enough. We're not here to sell pizza - we're here to sell games." Ted knew a bit about the restaurant business, his father having been a hotel auditor where the most common problem was always their restaurants. Ted told Nolan, "Mediocre is not good enough - anything less than good is unacceptable. It's just not right."

Agreeing to disagree (which is really just code for Nolan choosing not to listen to Ted), Nolan was more interested in Ted's input into solving not knowing when your pizza was ready. Just as he had asked many years before when he needed circuits to create Computer Space, Nolan asked Ted to "build me a solution." Ted comes up with a system called the 'NOTALOG' which is a large TV monitor over the pickup counter. A counter person would type the order number onto a keypad on the counter, such as 22. Up on the monitor, the giant-sized number '22' would flash for thirty seconds and then the number would drop down to a list of orders in the queue below in smaller size (with a maximum of sixteen numbers shown at any time.) Once a person picked up their order, the counter person would punch in that number, removing it from the screen.

Some time after Ted designed and built 'NOTALOG,' Nolan again tapped him to build an exclusive quiz game for Chuck E. Cheese. Kind of a nod back to their old Nutting days, it was based around a license Nolan was able to get from Issac Asimov for his Super Quiz brand. On this, Ted is never paid the $40,000 he's owed for all the work done, and the two drift apart again.

Nolan and Ted's complicated 'friendship' can be summed up with a story that happened just after Nolan returned from a trip to France in the late 70s. Nolan had brought brought back a couple of cases of Beaujolais wine to stock his wine cellar. Inviting Ted over, the two proceed to get rather drunk and at one point, Nolan turns to Ted with a stern look and says, "You know what I hate about you Dabney?!" Ted asked him back "What?" Nolan continues to repeat the question several more times in a slightly drunken stupor until finally he gives Ted the answer to his rather blunt question: "Remember how you told me, the only thing that will ever change for us are the number of zero's? You had no right to know that!"

Some Assembly Required

❝ No, not the movie Hatari - it's called Atari." That was the conversation Craig Manning was having with his friend Gil Williams in 1973. Gil had wanted Craig to join him at Atari, and the former had confused the pronunciation with the title of a 1962 movie starring the legendary actor John Wayne. Once the confusion was over, Gil managed to talk Craig into joining and Craig would come on board as a manufacturing engineer. Initially working over in Los Gatos, he still has his first Syzygy/Atari badge. Craig, you see, is just one of the many unsung heroes behind the success of Atari in the 1970s and the focus of this portion of the book. His career at Atari simply provides us with too many interesting characters and stories to pass up.

Craig had an opportunity to see all aspects of manufacturing and assembly, making sure to talk and work with nearly everyone - from those who wired harnesses to even the support technicians. There were two employees who still stand out the most to this day in his mind though. The first was the young and eager technician by the name of Steve Jobs, who Craig got along well, trading a lot of tips and suggestions with each other. The second was Dave Stubben, Atari's unofficial quality control tester.

Dave looked less like someone who should be working in the high tech field and more like a linebacker just off the football field. Dave would often be called over to evaluate a new cabinet design and by 'evaluate,' we mean Dave would try and break it. If it could survive 'The Stubben Test' as it became known, then a game was ready to be put out in the field for testing. Dave would give no mercy to game controls or cabinets, finding their faults and exposing them... literally. Many a game cabinet looked like they just came out the loser of a demolition derby after failing to stand up to 'The Stubben Test.' In one such humorous example of Dave's unique testing style, at one point, a coin-door sales rep came into Atari where the engineers had installed the new 'Tamper Proof' coin-door he was peddling. Designed to keep kids and/or thieves from breaking in and stealing the money from the internal coin boxes, it had been installed onto a cabinet in the shop to show off its new design and features. After the sales rep gave his 'dog and pony show' on how great and tamper-proof his new coin-door was, Dave approached the cabinet. Looking the coin-door over for a few moments, then the sale rep, then back at the cabinet again, he took a step back and proceeded to put his foot right through the coin-door - leaving nothing more than its frame behind as it dangled from the cabinet. So much for it being tamper-proof!

In those early days of Atari there was far less bureaucracy and red tape to muddle through. At one point Craig saw that they were going to need a $50,000 piece of equipment in one of the buildings for manufacturing and went to his boss Gil Williams to make the request. When asked if it was really necessary, Craig explained that it was and would end up paying for itself in a year to a year and a half. Gil slammed his fist on the table and said, "See! THAT'S the kind of innovation I like to see around here! Just go do it!"

Wanting to broaden his horizons and paycheck, Craig began navigating his way out of manufacturing. Working more with Bushnell, Keenan and Bill White to gain a foothold in corporate, he was eventually moved to the head of Facilities, reporting directly to John Anderson. Being responsible for Atari's ever expanding network of buildings was too time consuming for Craig to take on alone, so he needed to hire his first assistant. Turning to a friend of his from the Reserves who was working at HP, Dennis Gregory, the two started focusing their attention on Atari's rapidly growing presence of buildings in Moffett Park in Sunnyvale, CA.

Craig worked diligently to ensure that the Engineering building at 1272 Borregas would be constructed to their needs, Craig was also involved in the design and layout of Consumer Manufacturing at 1195 Borregas, which preceded 1272. And since Craig had a background in manufacturing, he also worked on the layout of the manufacturing lines with Sears on what they wanted for their retail packaging and assembly for the Sears *PONG*. The manufacturing liason between Sears and Atari, the Sears Quality and Assurance team regularly worked with Craig to tweak manufacturing and assembly. He even met with the plastics firm in Morgan Hill, CA and helped to oversee the delivery of plastics to the consumer assembly line for the *Home PONG* consoles. One of the unsung heroes in Atari's expansion - both building wise and into the home market, Craig's position had his hands busy with other areas of responsibility as well.

Theft is a problem with any new and rapidly growing company, and at Atari it was occuring as far back as the early days in Los Gatos. With the company originally hiring secret Pinkerton Security detectives to deal with the losses, by Craig's time he would hire Jack Sheehan, a former Fairchild Semiconductor security officer and ex-Navy seal. Craig knew there were a LOT of problems with thefts, in the consumer products division specifically. and the thefts were only getting worse - to the point where they were affecting retail. There's too many stories of security lunacy to begin to share, but here's three tasty morsels to satiate your curiosity on.

In one stunning example of what Craig and Jack had to deal with, word came down that a very large theft of Atari product was going to occur. Apparently an entire tractor trailer of product was about to be stolen, and Joe Keenan, Jack Sheehan, Craig Manning and Sunnyvale PD all met at a hotel to coordinate the arrest. Sunnyvale PD even had a helicopter on standby if needed. Once it was determined when the theft was actually supposed to occur, the team sat and watched, waiting to pounce. The tractor trailer that was scheduled to go out for delivery was in the back of Consumer as it would normally be, the perfect bait filled with product. "These stupid idiots show up, break into the truck and they couldn't get the truck started," recalls Craig. The whole sting came apart at the seams, because the truck was never actually stolen. The most the guys could get arrested for was was trespassing!

Another time, Craig was driving behind the consumer products manufacturing building one afternoon when he noticed something just didn't look right. A guy closes his trunk, looks right at Craig and looks nervous. Craig pulls right up behind his car, and blocks him in, and proceeds to tell him to open the trunk. In there he had about 10 VCS systems. "Here he is, this low level manufacturing guy - I felt really bad, but the cops came and hauled him away," recalls Craig. With the VCS costing nearly $200 each, that was almost $2,000 in stolen product in his trunk, which in 1970s terms, that was a substantial amount of money.

In 1978, Craig wintessed a total of 23 employee arrests, 77 employee discharges and five security incidents involving non-employees. Incidents varied from felony assault by an employee, to embezzlement, to even several employees being arrested by immigration for having counterfeit ID's. Nothing was safe from theft, when $32,000 in batteries were taken from shipments for Sears' versions of dedicated game consoles. Other incidences were minor if not humorous, such as when three people were removed from the Game Room by the police or when two pinball employees were so intoxicated on the job that their employment was terminated. Then there were other more severe issues, including a big theft conspiracy ring at 1346 Bordeaux that resulted in nine employees being fired… and then, the big $250,000 theft conspiracy at the warehouse at 390 Carribbean, resulting in the theft being thwarted and twenty five employees being fired. Vandalism had also occurred out in the parking lots and the employee responsible was found out and 'dealt with internally.' There were also a string of vandalisms to the sauna room in 1272 Borregas, but management was also able to deal with the matter 'internally.' While everyone turned a blind eye to drug use by employees in the company, security wasn't going to ignore employees stealing and selling parts in trade to pay other employees moonlighting as drug dealers. Over in the Santa Clara buildings, eleven employees were fired for theft and arrest warrants were issued for four employees for drug dealing and accepting stolen merchandise as payment.

In another security incident, this time involving both Craig and Dennis Gregory, during a lunch hour an argument started in a break room that included a pool table. An employee and his supervisor got into an argument, and in a fit of rage the worker came at his supervisor with a pool cue stick. After some rather heated exchanges and threatening swings of the pool stick, the fight is broken up. However word comes back to Craig that this employee is now in his car driving over to Corporate on Borregas to meet with personnel. Dennis and Craig get to the second floor of the lobby at 1265 where the doors were flung open wildly, and in comes the guy -still violently angry. A melee ensues and he ends up with his arm around Dennis's neck as he's trying to throw Dennis over the second floor railing. Luckily, Dennis is able to duck underneath and get around the employee to subdue him. Together with Craig they brought him flat down to the floor; Craig and Dennis held him down and third person had to hold his legs. The receptionist called the police, who showed up very quickly but also had a difficult time subduing the man. After he was placed in the squad car, one of the officers came back in to fill out a report and asked Craig if he felt the police used excessive force, whereby both Craig and Dennis replied, "Oh no, you used just the right amount of force!" Craig actually was so angered by the whole situation with this man, he quite frankly wished the police had pistol whipped the guy. There's no telling if the employee was hopped up on drugs or just pure anger, but the crazyness resulted in a story Craig still likes to tell to this day.

Craig remembers what it was like leading up to Bushnell and Keenan's departure and the time when Ray Kassar took over the company. Having an office on Mahogany Row, he was noticing the same thing everyone else was; that Bushnell was often not around and Keenan, while around far more then Bushnell, was also not as involved as should be expected. By the time Ray took over the company, Craig's immediate boss John Anderson had left and Craig began to report to Dennis Groth for a short while before Craig too decided to leave Atari. Craig met with Manny Gerard numerous times and had a lot of respect for him, however he simply didn't have the same respect for Ray Kassar.

In one final and truly serious incident in 1980, a coin-op employee rode his bicycle over to work. That alone wouldn't merit recounting, except he also brought a loaded rifle with him. Ride his bicycle with the rifle over to Atari Corporate, he assaulted two security personnel while trying to enter 1265 Borregas, resulting in his arrest for assault with a deadly weapon.

When Craig left Atari he decided to try and move over to Apple Computer and become their Director of Facilities. When he applied for the job and was asked for references, he simply said, "Steve Jobs." The next day Craig got a call back - he got the job. Years later, shortly after leaving Apple as well, Craig would have one last encounter with his former Atari compatriots via an approach by Bushnell. Catalyst Technologies, Bushnell's new business incubator was starting up and Craig was briefly hired on to set up telephone systems and facilities to get the company going.

Chapter 6Review In Images

New, expensive corporate offices were built on the second floor of 1265. The offices were nicknamed 'Mahogany Row' for its lush and gorgeous wood trimmed offices.

The cafeteria at Atari's new Consumer Division headquarters at 1215 Borregas.

With the money Nolan received from the Warner Communications
buyout, he purchased the old Folgers estate in Woodside, California.
A 13,000 square foot, 37 room, Edwardian-style mansion on
16 acres of land with a pool, tennis courts, horse stable and a
groundskeeper house at the entry gate to the estate (seen below.)

1272 Borregas, the new building for the Consumer and Coin-Op Engineering departments, under construction (above) and completed (below.)

Top: The ground breaking for the first of the new Atari buildings in Moffett Park in Sunnyvale, California. (Note that Rick Rat is present for the event). Nolan with Rick Rat.

Bottom: A meeting to try and get Atari's top distributors to buy in to what would become Chuck E. Cheese. (left to right) Joe Keenan, Al Alcorn, Rick Rat, Joe Ash (Atari's distributor in Philidelphia), Nolan Bushnell, and Gene Lipkin.

Gene and Nolan going over plans for the first location.

1ST STORE
SAN JOSE

Gene's personal photo of the very first Chuck E. Cheese.

Inside the first Chuck E. Cheese

The following pages show the inside of the first Chuck E. Cheese, including the original animatronic characters.

Detail of the computer-animated installation at Chuck E. Cheese Pizza Time Theater in San Jose, Calif. The concept could become part of a nationwide pizza-parlor franchise chain.

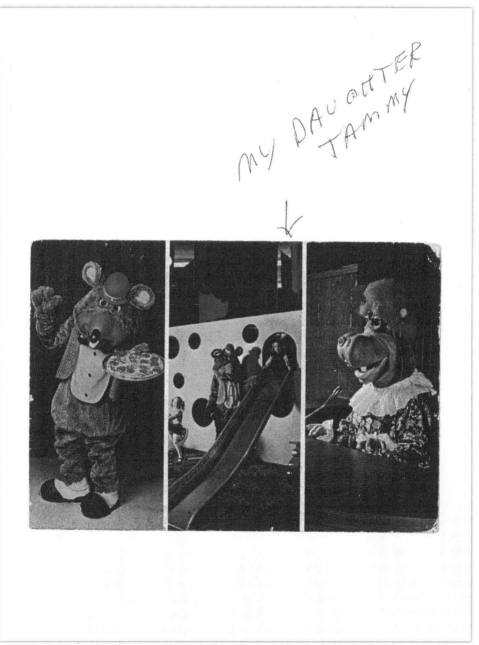

Gene's personal copy of the first promotional postcard, which includes his daughter Tammy sliding down the indoor slide coming out of a fun representation of a piece of cheese.

IN FRONT OF 1ST STORE

By the time the initial building was completed, Gene had Ricky Rat changed over to the much more kid friendly hybrid of a rat and a mouse. Gene, Nolan, Joe Keenan and Steve Mayer sat around during a beer infused meeting and came up with the name Chuck E. Cheese for the new mascot and name of the restaurant.

A special cocktail cabinet video game in the form of a table that could be eaten at, created for Chuck E. Cheese. *Below:* An original game token from the first location.

Announcement for the grand opening.

1ST MENO

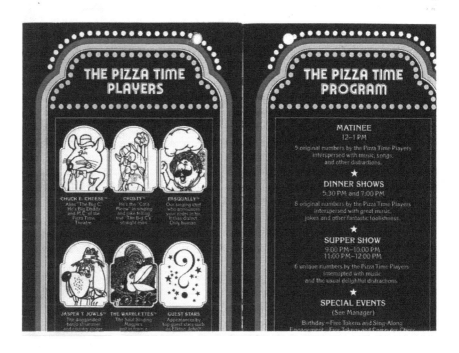

Mayor Janet Gray Hayes and Nolan Bushnell welcome Chuck E. Cheese to San Jose and Atari.

The mayor of San Jose showed up for the opening as did plenty of Atari employees.

More Atari employees and Joe
Keenan shaking the hand of one
of a character.

Nolan's vision and Gene's execution was a hit with patrons. Chuck
E. Cheese was soon turned in to
a successful franchise that spread
throughout the US in the early 80s as
the arcade video game craze reached
its peak. Here, Ateri employee Elaine
Thompson hugs the cuddly mascot.

Purchasing Chuck E. Cheese from Atari in June 1978 for $500,000, Nolan made his new restaurant chain his primary focus when he left Atari in Jaunary 1979.

When Joe Keenan left Atari in September, 1979, he took over Gene's spot as President and COO of Chuck E. Cheese.

NOLAN K. BUSHNELL

NOTES TO STATEMENT OF ASSETS AND LIABILITIES (CONTINUED)

MARCH 31, 1978
(Unaudited)

Atari, Inc. is a wholly-owned subsidiary of Warner Communications, Inc. The debentures are payable over a ten-year period in equal annual installments beginning March 1, 1978. The first and last payments are guaranteed by the parent corporation. The first payment was received on March 1, 1978.

c) Sente Associates, a partnership

Nolan K. Bushnell owns a 48.2% interest as a general partner in this venture formed to develop a parcel containing approximately twenty-one acres of land on Borregas Avenue in Sunnyvale opposite the Atari, Inc. corporate headquarters building. Three other partnerships, Humboldt Associates I, II and III, have been formed to perform the construction phase of this development. Mr. Bushnell is a general partner and owns a 48.2% interest in Humboldt Associates. The amount shown represents Mr. Bushnell's capital contribution, less withdrawals. Market value is considered by the partnership to be substantially greater than book value.

d) Farmers Bank, I.R.A. Rollover account

The predecessor corporation to the present Atari, Inc. was also known as Atari, Inc. Mr. Bushnell was a participant in an Employee Stock Ownership Trust created by that corporation. When the business of old Atari, Inc. was sold to the newly formed wholly-owned subsidiary of Warner Communications, Inc. the E.S.O.T. was terminated and all participants' rights became fully vested. Mr. Bushnell's share in the E.S.O.T. was approximately ███████ which was distributed in cash in 1976. Tax law permits an individual to "roll over" such a distribution into a qualified Individual Retirement Account or to another qualified retirement plan of which he is a member without paying the income tax which would otherwise be due in the year of distribution.

e) Village Green Associates

Nolan Bushnell owns a 4.7% limited partnership interest in this 464 unit apartment complex near Houston, Texas.

f) Burton-Holt Condominiums, Ltd.

Nolan Bushnell owns a 10% limited partnership interest.

g) Deposit on Utah land development

On February 27, 1978, Nolan Bushnell deposited ██████ with Mr. Marlin K. Jensen for the purpose of purchasing and developing a tract of real estate in Huntsville, Utah.

Nolan was already planning his followup move as early as June of 1978 as evidenced by this document (financial figures have been blacked out for privacy.) Sente, a move in the game GO meaning having the 'initiative,' was his way of signaling the next move beyond Atari. When he bought video game company Videa in 1983, he renamed it to Sente Technologies and used it as his return to video games.

Chapter 7

● The world's first video attraction to simulate the actual play action of American football.

● Two players.

How About A Nice Game Of Chess?

While the name of the Atari VCS Model 2600 was the 'Video Computer System,' it still was only a game system. Yes, it did have an on-board 6507 CPU chip; a computer in its own right. However it didn't have a keyboard, disk storage, printers or other more expected 'computer' features. In the mind of the public, computers were viewed as highly sophisticated devices, portrayed on television and in movies as room sized behmoths full of blinking lights, powerful and sometimes even maniacal. In the 1960s and 1970s, computers were depicted as being able to do everything - from launching nuclear missiles at the evil Soviet Empire, to playing a good game of Chess.

It was Chess that was to cause a problem for the VCS not long after it had been released, all because someone in Marketing had decided to add a Chess piece to its packaging. Chess as a game, insofar as what it consists of – a board and some pieces, is fairly simple. Playing Chess, on the other hand, takes a complex understanding of each piece and its abilities, then adding in the strategy. The bottom line – it's a complex and difficult game. A favorite of artificial intelligence and computer researchers since the field's beginnings in the late 1940's, making a computer play an intelligent game of chess usually required programming that took all the system resources to the brink. For a 128 byte console system with 2k to 4k of game program space, the game sounds next to impossible to implement in this medium - even for a system called the 'Video Computer System.'

Well, like it or not, the 'Impossible Mission' would have to be taken on. Seems a VCS owner in Florida sued Atari because of the box showing that pesky Chess piece, and Atari didn't have a Chess program to sell. Atari's programmers were forced to begin developing Chess. Al Alcorn recalls that "The guys were playing around, trying different things," when finally one programmer said he could do it with an algorithm to create the playfield and pieces on the screen. Larry Wagner was that programmer, and it took him close to two years with the help of national chess champion Julio Kaplan to complete the project. Bob Whitehead then did the display in just two days, inventing a programming trick for the VCS to allow it to display eight objects in a row instead of the normal six - a technique later called 'Venetian Blinds'

Chess wasn't just being played on the VCS in 1978, the game of bold moves and strategic thinking was also being played out in Atari's hallways and offices between Nolan and Ray. With his attentions diverted in a million different directions, Bushnell was still not focused on the day to day details of Atari or in being a good business manager. Leaving it to others like Joe Keenan who excelled in this area, the same applied to Bushnell's marketing acumen. That's where Ray Kassar stepped in, and he certainly had the gift of knowing how best to bring in a cadre of marketing people. The result put Atari into the consumer spotlight like never before, boosting the company image to retailers – starting with a $5 million ad budget and a new national ad campaign: "Don't just watch TV tonight, play it!" The ads starred people like Broadway and cinema star, Carol Channing, basketball legend, Kareem Abdul-Jabbar, baseball star Pete Rose, and even comedic actor Don Knotts. Also, after the quality control issues and returns from the 1977 VCS sales were dealt with, Kassar devoted an extensive amount of time toward QA efforts and meetings with distributors to assure them that returns would not be an issue in the coming year as they were the prior year. Confidence in the company and in the product line was boosted thanks to Ray's efforts, which further strengthened Atari's position in the marketplace.

As Ray more firmly asserted his control on Consumer's operation, when Nolan was actually present they began to butt heads more and more. In one instance, Nolan had signed with three major n-channel semiconductor manufacturers to not only get more sources to increase production capacity, but also play one vendor off the other for a better price. Ray would meet with Nolan on this business deal and contend that the agreements were too costly for Atari, with Nolan countering that they were also important in case one vendor had a problem and couldn't deliver. Before the end of 1978, Ray would cancel two of the three factory agreements. A symbol of Nolan's diminishing influence, mainly due to his own fading presence at Atari, this would not be the last confrontation he had with Ray or Warner Communications.

Even with Ray's efforts to strengthen the new Consumer Division, nobody was ready for the outside influence that would wreak havoc that Christmas season: the consumer - or the lack thereof. Nolan had talked Warner into financing the production of 800,000 VCS's in anticipation of strong sales of the VCS, doubling the original launch numbers. Starting at CES that June, orders for about 550,000 units came in and were shipped out, making Nolan and Atari so confident that they held off starting the ad campaign until Halloween. In only three weeks, all the Sears stores in the west coast were sold out, and by the end of the Thanksgiving weekend the major stores across the country had already sold out. Atari wanted to ship more, but the orders just stopped. Even if they had come in the record snows made it hard to deliver more goods that season.

What went wrong? The issue could have been that Atari under Nolan still didn't fully get the consumer electronics industry; retailers were happy with no inventory vs. being flush with stock they'd have to worry about clearing out after the season was over. The problem could have also been the new high tech rising star in the consumer's minds: handheld electronic games. Driven by LED calculator technology, 1978 had become the year consumer purchase of the devices exploded with Mattel's Electronic Football and Coleco's Electronic Quarterback leading the pack. Together with games like Parker Brothers's Merlin and its tabletop hit Simon, these were the items kids were begging about for the upcoming holiday season. With a price tag in the $30 range compared to the VCS's $170 for just the base unit, the smaller electronic games were flying off store shelves and completely sold out at many stored by the time December came around.

With 250,000 of unused stock (not to mention what was still sitting on the retail shelves), that wasn't even the whole problem - there's all the game cartridges as well! When 1978 drew to a close, it was clear the effects of the VCS on the company were just as bad as Gran Trak had been four years earlier. Atari suddenly went from making $40 million in profit for 1977 to just $2.7 million for 1978. To add to that, Atari had also made their first official announcement in the last week of November that they intended to release home computers in 1979. Were the suddenly declining VCS sales now a sign that they were spreading themselves too thin?

Atari needed an answer to the problem quick, and Ray gave them one. First suggested by an executive at Fairchild complaining very publicly about the seasonal driven electronics and toy industry, the executive's answer was to promote and sell consumer video games all year around. Ray decided the best way to move the remaining inventory was to advertise the VCS in print and television all year around now and push retailers to continue selling them non-seasonal as well. As the back stock slowly began moving, it appeared Ray might be on to something.

The Flip Side Of The Coin

tari was being split in half across 1977 an 1978; not just metaphorically, but in every way imaginable. Atari's "old guard" management was at odds with the new Warner owners and their team members being put in place, leading to a possible showdown. The employees (still as free thinking and pot smoking as ever) were becoming more at odds with the rules and regulations being brought on by the new generation of suits at the top. Adding to that was the split of Atari's efforts into two divsions, Coin and Consumer, bringing about a change of focus at the top it seemed to many. Warner's deep pockets and marketing savvy seemed to be primarily aimed at the Consumer Divsion, the "rising star" of the company. Ironic given that with all the problems and losses the VCS caused for Atari in 1978, it was Coin that was keeping the company afloat.

The Coin-op employees are a proud bunch, considering themselves the 'Real Atari.' After all, Consumer is just a recent offshoot; Atari was founded as a coin-op company. Coin is where the bulk of the VCS's games came from and where the next generation of games will continue to come from. It's also where, in light of the VCS's problems, the bulk of the stable growth for the company is coming from.

Wolf Pack is an example of the creativity being put out by Coin. Making its debut at the IAAPA Amusement Park Operators show in December alongside Atari's newest coin-ops and pinball machines, the submarine combat simulator is Atari's high tech answer to Midway's popular 1976 game *Sea Wolf.* Fully fitted with a railing, authentic submarine periscope and deck plating, the game has an authentic look and feel as if the player was right onboard an actual attack sub. It's the technology that really sets it apart though.

Positioned on the periscope is a tiny 6-inch monitor, viewed through the periscope via a clever optical illusion. A 45-degree mirror reflects the inset monitor, whose image also passes through a 'sandwich' of two pieces of glass with liquid halfway up them before it hits the player's eye. The effect being the illusion of a realistic water line on the screen as if you were peering out of the ocean at the enemy. Though some of the enemy ships were crude, even by late 70s standards, the motion of the fairly blocky-looking objects includes advanced scaling effects done with a custom growth-motion circuit designed by Dave Sherman. (Later on, Dave would also develop circuits for a truly revolutionary 3D zoom and pan coin-op game called *I,Robot* but we'll come back to that later.) The graphics also include a new twist to up the ante of video game animation with the appearance of a 'torpedo wake.' One of the three circuits patented for the game, the 'wake-effect' circuit is co-invented by Mike Albaugh and related to the wake-effect for another game in development called *HydroPlane* (referred to as *Sprint* but in the water). Programmed by Dennis Koble with some assistance from Steve Calfee, *Wolf Pack* provides a fun immersive experience allowing the player to hunt down enemy ships through 'expansive' ocean terrain.

What stands out the most in *Wolf Pack though*, and sets it apart from not just *Sea Wolf* and the newly released *Sea Wolf II* but all the new coin-op offerings on the market, is a voice. An eerie robotic voice stating "Danger, danger, enemy close" and confirming the launching of your torpedoes with "Fire one" and "Fire two." Yes, Atari had come a long way since Ted's first inclusion of EM style sound on *Computer Space* or Al's simple hacking of the 'pong' like sound for *PONG*; *Wolf Pack* features voice synthesis - the very first arcade video game to do so!

Besides the unit shown at the show, only three *Wolf Packs* in were built, one of which was also installed for a while at Great America amusement park in Santa Clara, CA. Sadly, this was because Gene Lipkin canned it - basically because he hated boat games. One of the machines would wind up in Jerry Lichac's garage for a while until he had to dismantle it due to its size (and the need to once again be able to park his car in his garage), relegating it to a little heard of technological footnote.

Coin's unleashing of innovation continues when *Sky Raider* is released in March '78. The first game with a fully detailed vertically scrolling background and a very unique zooming effect, the player flys across the terrain in a downward perspective shooting at enemy installations and planes. If it sounds familiar, it's because the game was later copied and expanded by Activision as *River Raid*. It was initially shown at the 1977 ATE show in London, after which Frank Ballouz states "Sky Raider will be a great seller, overall reaction was superb."

Several other games were showcased at the ATE show in London, including *Destroyer* (released in October 1977) - an addictive sea combat game that involves dropping depth charges on enemy submarines. It was originally slated to be called *Depth Charge* - the first 300 units had marquees made with that name on them, but they had to be removed and scrapped when it was discovered that another game with the same name had just been released by Gremlin Industries. Likewise *Tournament Table* is shown, which the company released in March '78. The first example of a consumer product making its way in to the arcades, its innards are a modified VCS with a variant of *Video Olympics* incorporated into it. It also includes *Breakout* among its twelve different games. Built into a sleek rectangular topped cocktail table cabinet that's well recieved, Sue Elliot (Atari's International Marketing Administrator) is on hand to answer questions throughout the show and at a private after show cocktail party at the Hotel Inter-Continental for the Amusement show attendees. In fact it was Sue's continued efforts that was leading to a world wide expansion of Atari coin-ops.

Under Sue's coordianation, German Atari representative Lowen Automaten showcased Atari's coin-ops at the International Coin Machine Exposition from April 26th through the 29th of '78. With Gene Lipkin in attendance, Atari's *Middle Earth* pinball is the featured game at the booth, with daily competitions on the new pinball machines to help promote the fun Atari spin on the old game play. Then in Toronto, Canada at the Canadian Restaurant-Hotel-Motel Show, Atari (represented by Howie Rubin) and New Way Sales exhibited *Middle Earth* and *Skyraider* at the show.

This whirlwind tour of international shows finally culminated with the annual Pebble Beach distributor's conference in May '78, where Atari met with over 100 representatives from Atari distributors worldwide over three days at the luxurious Del Monte Lodge. The conference is intended to educate the distributors, showing Coin's attention to quality control and service at a time when Ray Kassar is struggling to introduce the same to the Consumer Division. In the morning, Atari representatives discuss new programs which would benefit distributors and their customers, moving on to demonstrations on service support that afternoon. During that afternoon session, Atari introduces its new test fixtures, a pinball tester, RAM and ROM chip testers and the new CTF-1 testing system - all custom built service tools meant to show Atari cares about its coin customers even well after a coin-op leaves the docks.

The new service schools Atari is opening are also a topic of discussion. Stemming from the old days when Nolan flew around for Nutting to teach distributors how to service Nutting's machines, distributors are now able to send their technicians directly to Atari schools to be certified. One of Atari's first is the New Jersey office opened in Piscataway - a 10,600 sq ft facility that also gives Atari a sales, service and parts presence on the East Coast. Starting off with just six employees with two more slated for later in the year, it hosts service schools to teach operators and service technicians on how to troubleshoot, upgrade and install new Atari video games and pinball machines. In fact, when the school held its first two day seminar that past March, the limited 50 person slots for each day were quickly sold out. Taught by Fred McCord and Dave Tucker, the attendees were put through the paces in both video arcades and pinball machines, their electronics, troubleshooting, preventative maintenance, microprocessor technology and specific service tips on Atari games.

Also promoted at Pebble Beach is Coin's new toll free Customer Service line for technicians, driven by the technical support group consisting of Bob Salmons, Russ McDonald, Phil Stewart, Bernie Barranger, Bruce Bennett and Jim Alexander. Bill Basset is introduced for the Internaional distributors in attendance, manager of International Field Service. Appointed to manage support for international customers as the rapid growth of Atari video arcade and pinball sales continues, Bill had previously worked in product development in the Atari Pinball Division .

Though the second day focuses on all the marketing, research and future advertising coming up in the future, the real fun begins after the games conference - the perks of coming to the speeches and presentations. Atari is running golf and tennis tournaments and even backgammon for those in the market for something a little less physical (Claus Arrhens (Cherry Group, England) and Masaya Nakamura (NAMCO) would come out the winners of the golf competition, each winning high end golf bags). Tours of the Monterey Peninsula are also offered for anyone wanting to do sightseeing, clearly showing how much Atari appreciated everyone there.

It didn't end there, evenings of the Pebble Beach event consist of hosted parties and fabulous meals. Not missing a trick in continuing to market Atari's games to their customers (and captive audience), the Tuesday evening banquet is also followed with a wonderful cocktail party where distributors see some of the new products Atari would be introducing that year. One of the items on display is a new concept design from Atari called the Wallbox (also called the Consolette), a wall or pedestal mounted arcade cabinet, with the pedestal mounted version looking not unlike an oversized parking meter.

Not one to be outdone with the festivities, Nolan also held court with a private group of distributors from the conference at his mansion in Woodside. Joel Kleiman, Vi and Will Laurie, Nancy McMurdie, Dean McMurdie and Denise Liptman enjoyed a private lunch with Nolan before returning down the coast to Pebble Beach. As the event closed that night, Coin had clearly shown that it was still the backbone of the company. A well established distributor network and keeping a good relationship with the distributors was key to this success, something that Consumer clearly needed to start working on if it hoped to pull itself out of its financial hole. Coin had a reason to crow, and as Don Osborne summed it up in a memo afterwards, "I was extremely pleased that so many of the distributors participated in the recreational activities; it contributed to the overall success of the conference."

International expansion continued throughout the year, with the crescendo being Atari Ireland in September. A year prior, Atari had begun looking at a number of locations in Europe they could use as a base of operations for manufacturing and shipping throughout Europe. In almost perfect timing, a newly built factory located in the town of Tipperary, Ireland had just been completed, and using Atari's main subcontractor in Ardfinnan they were able to aquire it. Subcontracting cabinet manufacturing to a local cabinet manufacturer by the name of Murray Kitchens and using Kromberg & Schubert for wiring harnesses and other components, the first Atari coin-ops soon rolled off the assembly line. From there the games are shipped to Waterford to be exported across Europe by a company named Bell. Once Tipperary Ireland was up and running, Gil Williams, Tommy Martinez and Phillip Stewart managed the new Atari Ireland factory, which soon employs nearly 200 Irish locals. Atari Ireland will also hire as its finance controller Kevin Hayes, who would eventually become the Managing Director of Atari Ireland.

The international efforts in Europe sometimes took on a unique flavor, especially where local coin operators were involved. Such is the case with arcade operator Ray Schweitzer of Stuttgart, West Germany. Started 3 years prior with a $10,000 investment and an Atari *Gran Trak 20* arcade machine, he created one of the most eye catching window displays ever seen at a video arcade! Schweitzer placed the *Gran Trak 20* game into a 36 ft long dragster, with the dragster tilted upward to give the impression of a 'popping a wheelie.' The dragster actually spans both floors of his two story arcade center, with the front of the vehicle protruding up toward the second floor. Originally his sole intent for the unique display was to be an attention grabber to pull onlookers into the arcade. However the game eventually grossed nearly $70,000 in the three years it was on display – a happy and unexpected revenue windfall.

Back in the U.S., Atari was also working hard to keep Coin operations stable enough to handle the demanding new growth. With Atari shipping thousands of games worldwide, it took a concerted effort by a dedicated team to coordinate the sales and get the games shipped to their destinations. That's where Atari's sales order processing staff came in, coordinating logistics between Atari marketing, manufacturing and shipping. Jeanne Angelo, Joyce Kramer, Kim Widmer and Melissa Rudolph expertly oversaw this task and saw to it that Atari's latest and greatest games expediently shipped from the factory... to the distributors... and onto site locations where operators satiated the growing thirst for the lastest video games. As for marketing, the two ladies who were keeping the heart of the department beating strongly were marketing secretaries Ruth Evans and Davia Mountney. They might not get the spotlight or receive the recognition like the marketing managers who attended the shows, but they were the behind the scenes backbone, playing an integral part in Atari Coin-op marketing's success.

Atari's sales efforts are further bolstered when Tom Petit becomes the newest member of the Atari coin-op sales group. Tom was coming to the team with strong, practical experience garnered from working part time in Atari's Development Engineering and Manufacturing departments while attending Santa Clara University. With his education grounded in marketing and his exposure to the engineering side of Atari, Tom had an excellent foundation, making him a vital part of Atari's sales and product support out in the field. Working under Don Osborne, Tom's job is to interface with Atari distributors and operators in the Western Region, further intilling confidence that they made the right choice in going the 'Atari way.'

Marketing Atari coin-ops isn't just limited to distributors and operators though, there has to be a concerted effort to reach out to the players and community as well. You see, Atari was now facing a new front just as the stigma of organized crime and arcades was disappearing; video game violence. The issue was sparked by Atari's friend and sometimes rival up the street Exidy in 1976 with the release of their game *Death Race*. Loosely based on the 1975 film *Death Race 2000* produced by legendary 'B' movie directory Roger Corman, the object is to mow down little stick figures with your car as they try and run away. Tame when compared to modern games like the Grand Theft Auto franchise, in 1976 it simply shocked local communities and drew attention to the growing trend of violence in video games and its possible influence on America's 'impressionable youth.' A plethora of military games alone had been released in the last several years from video coin-op companies, including *Air Combat, Attack, Bazooka, Bombs Away, Cobra Gunship, Destroyer, M-4, Sea Wolf, Sky Raider, Sky War* and many more. There were also 2-player dueling games like *Gun Fight, Knights In Armor, Outlaw, and Warrior*.

Carol Kantor, the editor of Atari's *Coin Connection* newsletter put together a 'Positive Publicity Package' to try and help distributors and operators combat the worries about video games and the youth. Containing positive articles written about games and arcades from newspapers, magazines and other media outlets from across the country, arcade operators were able to use them as mini press kits to show local nay-sayers that the arcade was actually a fun and safe place to be. Atari themselves also began reaching out to local communities to fight the growing stigmatism, and one such event happened in April when Atari coordinated with the De Vargas Elementary School in Cupertino. Bringing in several video game and pinball machines to show to a host of excited 5th and 6th graders as part of a Science Faire, the kids were not just there to play games - they would also be given a basic overview on how these machines worked. This effort was put together by Ted Olsen, a former Atari employee who went on to become the president of Time Zone Family Fun Centers. He brought with him two technicians, (Craig Wheelwright and Steve Coastes) to explain the inner workings of an *Atari Starship 1* video arcade and an *Airborne Avenger* pinball machine. The school principal, Jerd Ferrainolo, was quite pleased that the excitement, science and engineering of the games captured the children's full attention while Ted Olsen was happy to find a new generation of customers.

Atari repeated the exercise in July, at Adams Elementary School in St. Paul, Minnesota. Again coordinating with a local arcade operator (Todd Erickson), three Atari video coin-ops were brought into the school and set up for free play for the school Carnival: *Super Bug, Starship 1* and *Sprint 2*. Atari found these school events successful enough that they'd continue to reach out to the schools and the community in this and other philanthropic ways over the years.

The efforts to expand the public consciousness of the positive influence of video games didn't just end there. Now, Atari coin-op games were even finding their way onto U.S. Navy vessels thanks to Atari participating in the first U.S. Navy Fleet Habitability Symposium in San Diego. The objective of the U.S. Navy was to develop ideas that would strengthen the quality of life aboard U.S. Navy ships. Vice Admiral R.P. Coogan would coordinate the effort through his Navy managers and Fleet personnel to make formal recommendations which included the placement of coin-op games on ships as part of the recreational facilities program. Captain R.P. Perry, Director of Special Services, was very enthusiastic about the concept of working with Atari to place electronic games on ships. Some unique problems had to be overcome however, with space being one of the biggest issues since space on ships is minimal. As a solution, the Navy wanted Atari to look in to cabinets that could be used for more than one purpose, such as using cocktail cabinet designs to serve other functions when not being used for recreation. Wall designed games were also discussed, along with implementing tokens to reduce the use of cash on-board the ships. The outcome of the symposium was very positive, and Don Osborne commented on the experience: "We are looking forward to working with the Navy on this program. We are optimistic that it will provide a new market for Atari products which will bring more enthusiastic players to our games."

The success in marketing to every part of the industry, from distributor to player, means that Atari coin-ops start to become even more popular across 1978. The colorful and unique cabinets are instantly recognizable by fans and in the process become the visual standard in the industry. Due in large part to the tremendous dedication and high level of creative talent within Atari's in-house graphic design group, these artists lead by George Opperman are creating a lasting visual identity for Atari that will last long after the company is gone. Infusing itself in to advertisements, posters, and even manuals, Atari isn't even afraid to go back and make sure some of its more recent releases are up to par for their 'looks.' Such is the case with *Sprint One* getting a visual face-lift after only being on the market for six months. The cabinet is updated from a dull black and white coloring to a vivid, full color graphics of race cars speeding up and across its sides.

Of course, all this success meant they had to keep producing great games. And that's exactly what they continued to do as *Avalanche* is released in April 1978. Designed by Dennis Koble, the game is considered to be the game *Breakout* - only played backwards. Instead of the player paddle hitting a ball UP to the bricks at the top of the screen, the player has several rows of paddles and must catch the falling rocks that drop DOWN from rows at the top of the screen towards the player. Each time a rock is missed, the player loses a row from their stack of paddles and once all of the paddles are gone, the game is over. To make the game more challenging, if the player successfully catches many rocks, the paddles get smaller, making it that much more difficult to obtain a high score. Several years later in 1981, former Atari employee Larry Kaplan would also copy and expand this game for Activision's *Kaboom* for the VCS.

Avalanche was followed in June by the impressive *Firetruck*, demonstrating Atari's commitment to innovation by being the very first video game to feature cooperative game play. *Firetruck* can be played by one player alone, but in two player mode, two people have to control a realistic fire department ladder truck that has to be steered by both the front and rear players. This made for some fun and challenging game play, trying to coordinate the truck to make turns and navigate the streets in this top down view game.

Firetruck is joined that same month by the highly addictive game *Skydiver*. A totally new concept in video games that immediately draws players in. Players are challenged to time their jumps from planes flying overhead, timing the opening of their chute as they fall. Longer falls mean more points, but also a smaller target to land on. For realisim, wind and direction are factored in, impacting the ability to successfully land on the target spots at the bottom of the screen. If the chute isn't opened in time, the player crashes and an ambulance arrives to pick up the pieces - forming an intermission of sorts. The controls for *Skydiver* are designed after the rip-cord handles of actual parachutes, adding to the realistic fun. Designed by Owen Rubin, he incorporates an even more unique twist of innovative uniqueness to it by having the title letters of SKYDIVER on the game's plexiglass light up one at a time, changing every second. A letter is selected when a player jumps, and a successful landing on the target pad awards that letter, which appears above the score on screen. Encouraging players to light up the entire name, players are given double points when they do. Owen's inspiration for the idea came from his love of pinball machines and the way pinballs would light up letters and other playfield areas when players achieve target hits and scoring. The graphic design group comes up with a marketing poster to be released in conjunction *Skydiver*, showing actual skydivers in the air high above the ground below, forming a ring by holding onto each other's arms. Skydiving was a very popular sport in the 1970s, helped in part by the romanticized exploits of the infamous D.B. Cooper and his daring parachute escape with $200,000 from the back of a Boeing 727 he hijacked in 1971. Those game players who might never in their lifetimes muster up the courage to free fall out of an airplane as a skydiver could now, thanks to Owen Rubin and Atari, safely imagine themselves skydiving via a coin-operated video game.

While Owen has been talked about earlier in this book, now is the perfect to fully introduce this colorful character. Owen's career at Atari had been shining bright at since coming on-board several years before, but his love of games began far before that. It actually seems Owen and video games were destined to be together from the beginning, popping up continuously in his early years to inspire him. In Owen's high school they had an old Bendix G15 computer that he had programmed Tic-Tac-Toe on to give himself an introduction to programming. Discovering from the process that he really wanted to get into writing games as a career, he enrolled in UC Berkeley to perfect his programming skills. While there during his freshman year in 1972, he saw an Atari *PONG* coin-op, which convinced him there actually was a possibility for a career making these games. Continuing to follow Atari and its new coin-op releases over the next several years, just as he was ready to graduate in 1976 he made a life altering discovery: Atari was on campus recruiting. Applying and passing the initial on campus screening he was granted an interview at Atari's offices on Division Street. Sadly, he is contacted after the interview by Steve Bristow and told he didn't make the cut, with Steve feeling he wasn't a strong enough candidate for a hardware engineer position. Bewildered, Owen then explains that he wasn't applying for a position in hardware, but rather to program games at Atari. So Owen is instead sent to meet with Tom Hogg and after several more interviews, Owen was hired as Atari's fourth coin-op video game programmer.

First order of business - Owen's boss tells him to come up with a game idea and start working on it. Owen had played Stunt Cycle a lot and thought it would be a good idea to continue along the 'circus theme' idea for a game, so why not write a game based on a human cannonball, and shoot a guy out of a cannon? Voila! *Cannonball* is born. Getting some sheets of graph paper and drawing out the ideas - what the man will look like, the cannon, the wall and the animations, etc., next Owen starts working on programming the game. Being only the fourth programmer at Atari, the problem is there's no real orientation or standards established yet - at least none that Owen was immediately aware of. Seeing an ASR33 teletype terminal connected to a box called a Micbug (which is a Motorola 6800 microprocessor development board with a serial port on it), he assumes this is how game programming is supposed to go here. Hand writing out the code for the game in assembly (the lowest level programming language possible for a computer), he begins typing it into the terminal connected to the Micbug board and saving the resulting code onto paper tape and teletype paper.

After several months of work on the game, Owen's boss wants to review his progress and asks to see his game. Owen runs the game, his glowing animated figure walking across the screen to the cannon. Selecting how much gun powder to add to the cannon and fires the figure towards the digital wall. Apparently close to being finished in his boss's eyes, Owen's boss asks to see the program code listings. Hummm... Owen's not quite sure what he means and explains how he's been developing the game. At which point his boss's eyes bug out in astonishment that he did all the coding directly on the Micbug- it seems Owen was never instructed in the paper trail procedure for programming games at Atari.

It turns out that instead of working directly on Micbug, he was supposed to:

1. write out his code on paper

2. hand it into a program entry operator, who would then

3. enter it into a DEC PDP minicomputer

4. assemble the code

5. have a paper tape with the code punched out

... and a paper listing of the program for more editing and tracking delivered to the game code trackers across the street, which at that time was Cynthia Villanueva and another female employee. The game program source would then remain on the PDP minicomputer for easier editing and updating.

In a slap your forehead moment, Owen now realizes the work he was doing for the last few months may have taken half as long had he known about this procedure. Not in the least bit undeterred from the mixup though, Owen instead sets out to have a bit of fun with sound effects. Thinking that 'human cannonballs' traditionally show up at circuses and carnivals, he thought it'd be appropriate to have some kind of opening circus music in the game. There's one problem though: background music just didn't exist yet. Most sound circuitry was custom at the time, a sign of the times where the most demanding sound that had to be produced were explosions or other sound effects. So improvisation and innovation come together and Owen invented his own way of generating the background music he wanted; by adding a relay into the hardware design and using an 8-track tape with some circus music on it, Voila! The game now has music, making it the very first developed game with background music and Owen the first person to do it.

Owen's next task is to focus on what happens if the figure hits the wall or misses and hits the ground, creating an exercise in giving the main character... some character. Knowing in cartoonish fashion a good 'splat' was needed, Owen again had to rely on his creativity to come up with a way to create it. It could have been a memory from his youth that inspired him - a bunch of raucous kids in the school showers throwing wet paper towels at each other. But that's exactly what he did to create the sound, throwing wet paper towels on a shower floor and measuring the waveform so he could recreate it in the game.

Apparently Owen was too far ahead of his time with the advanced sound work for *Cannonball*. During some location tests the operators made it known that they hated the music, finding the constant repetition annoying. One has to wonder how these operators dealt with it when background music became standard during the 80s. Atari management also found the 'splat' sound effect to be too graphic, especially with the rising tide of anti-video game violence, and want it removed. Despite the game doing fairly well in the field, the issues ensure the game is never mass produced. The lone produced machine stays in Owen's apartment for a time before eventually being sold off to collectors, though a scaled down version is produced for the VCS.

Now when Owen originally developed the effects for *Skydiver*, he remembered the critiques he received about *Cannonball* and instead had the player splashing into water instead of the ground to avoid another incident of the 'splat' sound being rejected. But in a surprising request, Owen is asked if he could incorporate the 'splat' sound effect that he had done for *Cannonball* into *Skydiver*. Management now also wants the player to slam into the ground instead of water AND to create some comical way of displaying this! From *Cannonball* to *Triple hunt*, finding ways of incorporating these expressive sounds into games would become one of Owen's trademarks as he continued to incorporate 8-track audio tape players into his earlier game designs. Later, as sound generation became more advanced, he would write the code used for sound generation for many other games too.

Several months after Owen's *Skydiver* is released, in September it's joined by two new additions to Atari's strong lineup of games. The first is a follow-up to the ever popular *Breakout*, *Super Breakout*. Designed by Ed Logg with a cabinet created by Dan Corona, the game introduces three new ways to test player's skills: Double Breakout, challenging players with two balls in play at once; Progressive Breakout, where the bricks advance downward towards the player paddle and the walls approached faster as the score gets higher; and finally Cavity Breakout, where two balls bounce inside of cavities within the brick walls and once freed each ball adds to the anxiety of game play while doubling the player's score. If the player gets both balls released and has three balls in play simultaneously, the points triple. The game joining *Super Breakout* is *Smokey Joe*, originally slated for release in July. It's a one player version of Firetruck, but with the same great game play in a standard game cabinet.

September also brought forth Atari's most important new addition to date… Brent Nolan Bushnell joined the Atari family on September 5th. Nolan and Nancy were thrilled to announce the arrival of their healthy 8 pounds, 8 ounces and 20" tall son. Nolan's pride was evident as he celebrated with handouts of traditional cigars and candy around the office. "I've got great plans for my son," he proclaimed. Coin also witnessed another wonderful event that month when Elaine Thompson and Steve Shirley were married. Elaine had been at Atari since 1973 and Steve wound up leaving Atari to start his own company around the same time of their wedding.

As October rolls around, another first from Atari is released: *Atari Football*. Codenamed 'Monster Man' during development, it would be Atari's first use of a controller device they call a 'Trakball.' Think of a computer mouse turned upside down - by rolling the ball in any direction, the player's object on the screen will move in that direction as well, in this case x's and o's spread across a side scrolling field. Also, the faster a player spins the ball, the faster the player's onscreen object moves, providing the perfect controller for a football 'game' and a game players couldn't get enough of! In fact with the current football season approaching the fever pitch of the playoffs prior to the Super Bowl, *Atari Football* proves to be immensely popular. Atari winds up leveraging the exposure the Super Bowl can provide the game by strategically placing *Atari Football* games on location at the mega-event as the Cowboys seek to destoy the Steelers. Sports announcers, media broadcasters, journalists and editors from all of the local newspapers, TV and radio stations who are covering the event were given an invitation to come play the game. The Steelers may have won Superbowl XIII, but the reviews were unanimous: the real winner was Atari.

The last game released by Coin is *Orbit* in November. Based on Cinematronics' *Space War*, it's a raster based 2-player video game with more options, selections and features than just about any other space battle game released to date. With gravity effects, fuel, ammunition, ship repair docking and other capabilities, this *Star Wars* inspired game did not disappoint - unfortunately it also has more control panel buttons than the bridge console of the Starship Enterprise. The brainchild of

Owen Rubin, he describes *Orbit* as a sort of *Computer Space 2* meets *Space War*. To meet a demand for product in Europe, he was tasked with designing the game in just eight weeks - though he was still able to put his unique signature on the audio. *Orbit* employs a unique stereo sound design; as the player's ships move from one side of the screen to the other, the sound 'balance' for that object would also move left and right, depending on whether the action was on the left or right side of the screen.

The Beach Clause

E velyn Sumida, Nolan's personal assistant and Loni Reeder, assistant to fa-cilities manager Dennis Gregory were asked to clean out the remaining items from Nolan's old office. He was simply unable to do it himself, to have to walk into the company he co-founded and built up into a house-hold name, struggling through years of barely making it through each month, trying to make sure both the bills were paid AND the employee's were paid. To have sold it, made a great deal of money and then to ignore his company until finally the pow-ers that be were left with no other choice but to remove him from his throne, King PONG had lost his first kingdom.

It had been very quiet in Nolan's old office - even his telephone at exten-sion #2318 has long since stopped ringing. Evelyn and Loni packed up and moved the remaining items from Nolan's office and between the two of them, with Loni's Mercury Comet and Evelyn's Datsun 280z, they filled both cars to the brim and took everything Nolan had remaining from his Atari years over to his new office at Chuck E. Cheese's corporate headquarters to drop off and unpack. Evelyn too had made the move to Chuck E Cheese, continuing as Nolan's personal assistant, at least for a while longer.

Why was this all happening and why was it called the big shakeup of 1978? Let's step back a bit and explain. The poor sales of the VCS for '78 were weighing heavily on the company when one afternoon, Manny is walking down the hall at

Atari's corporate headquarters at 1265 Borregas when someone asked him if he would be attending the board meeting. Manny inquired as to what board meeting, and "who was in attendance?" Apparently the meeting would be 'Atari Only' board members - no one from Warner. "What!? Nolan is calling a fucking Atari board meeting!?" recalls Manny.

Nolan was staging his own form of a coup d'état, however, this was not a game of Chess or Go. Nolan's attempted maneuvering around the Warner Board members would prove to not only put himself into 'Check' but it would set the stage for him to be cornered and face 'Checkmate.' Manny confronts Nolan regarding his stunt, which is so serious that he also gets Warner's corporate lawyers involved and issues Nolan a written notice regarding calling any board meeting that does not include Warner representation. The only thing Nolan had succeeded in was putting Manny into an even more annoyed and irritated frame of mind.

Then the Annual Budget Meeting is held in late 1978 in New York, just two weeks from the huge Christmas sales window. An almost non-event, the planned agenda is discussed, which includes the company product plan and marketing strategies for 1979. This would have been just another typical end of year wrap-up before the holidays - that is until suddenly Nolan gets up, and states "Sell off all of the inventory of the VCS. We've saturated the market. Get rid of it all and cancel the product." As Manny Gerard recalls, at this point the boardroom erupted and starts going crazy because everyone is stunned. Where is this coming from? No one understands Nolan's outburst. Then Manny recalls Nolan going on: "The home computer system is a waste of time. The pinball division needs to be shut down and rethought. Sell off the remaining VCS systems at $150 and cancel the product." This sets off a heated exchange between Manny and Nolan the likes of which had never been seen in a corporate conference room before.

Steve Ross hears about the meeting and immediately calls Manny Gerard into his office the next day, demanding to know, "Why is it over for the VCS?!" Manny at first doesn't know what to say, but since this is a private meeting between just Manny and Steve, this is the only time Manny can just be forthright and skip to the candor. He tells Steve Ross: "Steve, you don't know what you're fucking talking about. Look, we can't do anything until after December 25th. On December 26th, I can guarantee you there won't be an Atari VCS on any store shelf in America - in which case you have a business that is huge! If I'm wrong, I'm wrong. I don't think I'm wrong, but between you and me Steve, there is nothing we can do for the next 15 days, so just relax." Christmas came and went and with it, so did nearly all of the Atari VCS systems on the shelves across America as predicted, and from there thanks to Ray's year around marketing strategy the business went to the moon. "Whatever Nolan thought, thinking that the market was saturated and cancelling the VCS was the answer - history shows that it was the dumbest opinion in the world. That was Nolan at his worst," Manny remembers.

If we are to speculate, Nolan's outburst was probably because he was spooked, if not terrified that there would be an unsold inventory of hundreds of thousands of VCS systems after the Christmas sales season. Atari would take a massive hit and with it, his debentures and their value would be worthless. He wanted to close down the Consumer Division and just go back to being a coin-op only company which he felt more confident in and comfortable with.

The time for change had come, just not in the way Nolan wanted. When Warner Communications purchased Atari, Manny wanted the senior staff from Atari to stay because it would be foolish to buy a company and not have the management team come along with it. However the past two years had proven that it was time for a change - and it would be a big one.

Nolan knew what the ramifications of his outburst and heated exchange with Manny at the annual board meeting would result in. As a result, it appears 1978 will have an unpleasant close, but Nolan at least wanted one last chance to address everyone who had been with him since the beginning. With the holidays fast approaching, he felt a private holiday part would be the best place to do it. Invitations are mailed out for the Christmas party at Nolan's Woodside home, and while there was an annual Christmas party for the entire company, these formal invites to Nolan's home were special - few and far between. Anyone lucky enough to get an invite invariably replied 'YES!'

The night of the party, Nolan's mansion is filled to capacity with employees and friends while a bootleg copy of the recently released movie 'Star Wars' was being shown via a new technology called a 'VHS Tape' on a big screen in Nolan's upstairs viewing room. The viewing room which looks like something out of an Egyptian harem room - you enter through hanging beads and scarves into a windowless room decorated with giant pillows and bean bags. As the Christmas party goes on late into the night, the masses begin to filter out, but Nolan asks several close employees to stick around, with seven or eight people staying until the early morning hours.

Even though Nolan was talking and joking with everyone, there was definitely something else in the air. Loni Reeder, who was one of those asked to stay, remembers: "I can recall the 'after party' at Nolan's that night as vividly as if it happened yesterday. There were just a handful of us left at his house – we were all in the living room, hanging out around the fireplace talking, having coffee, wine, and still nibbling on all of the catered goodies. Nolan didn't want any of us to leave, even though it was way after 2 a.m. Every time someone made a move toward the front door, Nolan was there to direct them back to the living room – he mentioned that this would be the last time that things would be perfect – that 'after tonight, everything was going to be different' – that he didn't want the night to end. The urgency of him not wanting any of us to leave was definitely noticeable." Loni continued: "I didn't know if I would ever get another opportunity just given his demeanor and the undercurrent of sadness – to let Nolan know how much I owed him professionally. Two years prior, I was young, naïve, fresh out of college, just starting my adult life and needed a job. I saw an ad in the San Jose Mercury News to work at Atari Corporate, and Evelyn Sumida was doing the hiring for this position. I know I called and bothered her incessantly for over a week after my interview because I so wanted this job. Evelyn told me at the time I was hired that numerous candidates had interviewed for the position, but sight unseen, Nolan told Evelyn to offer 'me' the job – and to pay me $50 dollars more a month than the position advertised, simply because, as he said to Evelyn, 'If she wants the job this badly, then that means she's going to be a great employee and work really hard for the company.' I recanted this to Nolan that night and thanked him for the leap of faith he took by telling Evelyn to hire me."

On December 28th 1978, Nolan and Joe Keenan were informed in writing that their roles and positions would change in the company. Nolan was removed as Chairman of the Board and re-assigned only as a consultant to Atari. Joe Keenan was moved from President to Chairman and his executive secretary Roberta Kendall would move with him. Ray Kassar was moved from President of Consumer to now being appointed President of Atari, and his secretary Barbara Jenkins would also move with him. Gene Lipkin would continue on as the President of the Coin-Op Division and another change would be implemented: Don Kingsborough, who earlier in the year had been contracted as a consultant, is now hired as Director of Marketing of the Consumer Group.

Via his attorney, on January 26, 1979, Nolan sends a letter to Manny Gerard that begins with, "My authority to continue to conduct and manage the business and affairs of Atari has been continuously and increasingly eroded by Warner until, by virtue of my refusal to endorse Warner's 1979 business plan for Atari (which I consider to be seriously deficient), Warner, by its December 28 letter, now attempts wrongfully to remove me completely from the management of the business and affairs of Atari. My authority has been undermined and my business plans thwarted and rejected by Warner in a manner which has forced me to question the sincerity of the representations made by you and Warner."

Nolan's letter continues, "As you know, I have been in sharp disagreement with your business plans and marketing strategy for some time. I believe many of the decisions that have been made at Warner's insistence and over my protest, have proved to be serious mistakes and are responsible for most, if not all, of the problems Atari is now facing. For example, I have wanted to close the pinball division for some time despite the effect on the amortization of Warner's purchase price of Atari. Warner's failure to follow my suggestions to integrate the pinball division vertically, its failure to concentrate efforts on quality control and customer credibility as opposed to production volume and its failure to concentrate on novelty pinball games have led to serious problems in the division. In addition, the pricing strategy, advertising, and marketing including the decision regarding the video pinball release, have all hurt the Consumer Division."

Nolan further states that he doesn't want to hold onto his Atari debentures if he is not going to be managing Atari and wants Warner to repurchase them, otherwise, as Nolan puts it in his letter: "The purpose of this letter is to state my position regarding Atari and Warner and to offer an alternative to the time, cost and unfavorable publicity inherent in internecine litigation."

Manny and Nolan meet, but in the end Nolan takes the 'Beach Clause.' The 'Beach Clause' is essentially, as part of the original negotiations of the agreement in Atari selling to Warner, the ability of any of the executive management from Atari before the sale to take the option to be permanently sidelined. Warner Communications could also opt to activate this clause as well, and it was more formally called the Reassignment Clause 2.02. Whether an Atari or Warner use of the clause was made, that person would still continue to collect their profits and pay, but no longer have any say or influence in the company. They would be considered consultants only, to be called on if needed and nothing more. Japanese busin5ess have a similar practice, usually used for forced retirement where executives who no longer hold value for the company are moved to meaningless management jobs to live out the rest of their corporate days feeling useless. The Beach Clause would pay Nolan $100,000 per year plus annual incentive cash bonuses and qualified stock options for stock in Warner Communications, Inc.

Being on "The Beach" also meant that Nolan would no longer have access to Atari's resources to continue any projects or ideas he may want to create. He was now more or less an outsider, one without a video game company to tap at his whim. Nolan would also have to abide by a five year non-compete clause as well, whereby he could no longer be involved in the design, manufacture or sale of video games until October 1, 1983.

Not to worry about Nolan however, he is never one to sit still and the gears are already turning in his mind. Nolan's begun working out the details for a new future nest from which to incubate the beginnings of numerous new companies he will fund with just the right "Catalyst" added into the mix. But for now he has his golden parachute - or golden rat. Chuck E. Cheese is doing exceptionally well, so for now Chuck E. Cheese is Nolan's main focus.

At the end of January, Ray calls an all company meeting to formally cover the changes at Atari and his ascension to President. All the departments were there, including the entire engineering teams from both Coin and Consumer. The meeting starts with talking about the obvious changes that have happened with Nolan leaving and Joe moving up to take Nolan's old position while Ray would be taking Joe's. That moves on to structure changes as Ray wanted to continue the management structuring he had done in Consumer in a company wide scale now. Then he goes in to Atari's products and the future he has planned out for Atari's product line. Consumer wise, the VCS is now being advertised all year around and it looks like things are slowly starting to turn around for the Consumer portion of the company. He's also really excited about the upcoming computer line, the 400 and 800 PCS's (Personal Computer Systems), and then begins to talk about his plans for the future of that line.

This is the moment that Ray truly begins to rub Atari's engineers and programmers the wrong way. Reaching back to his Burlington days, when he commanded an industry catering to the needs of home furnishings and fashion, Ray starts talking about how Atari would sell the computers in designer colors so that women would buy them. He then said they would also have home decorating software. To most of the people in the audience, a look of shock or disgust ensued. The men in the room saw him as clueless and out of touch, clearly not getting who the average computer buyer was or who their competition (Apple, Tandy, Commodore) was. The women in the room, most from the San Francisco/Berkeley area - the bastion of women's lib, saw it as completely sexist. Carol Shaw, the first female programmer at Atari, threatened to quit over the whole speech. In hindsight though, Ray clearly was just too far ahead of his time. Looking for a way to apply already established mass consumer marketing techniques to computers and make them acceptable to the average every day person. Steve Jobs did exactly that when re-imagining the Macintosh as the iMac, creating the slogans 'Chic, not geek' and 'iCandy' while producing the iMac's in a rainbow assortment of colors to appeal to younger women. As Joe Decuir, co-designer of Atari's computers stated to us, "Ray was asking good questions: how do we make this PC relevant to the mass of users, particularly women? Also how do we create simplicity? Unfortunately, Ray had no clue as to how to go about it; Jobs did."

Ray didn't know it yet, but this meeting signified the starting of not just a stressful transition period of reorganizing the company to save it from the previous year. Shortly after, a period of employee unrest that would at times seem like a period of all out mutiny, also began.

The first thing to come to a head after the meeting was the issue of bonuses, a topic that had been ongoing since almost the beginning of Ray's tenure in Consumer. In 1977 during the successful launch of the VCS, there were discussions in Consumer engineering about some kind of compensation for the programmers and engineers of the VCS. So the director of Consumer engineering, Kerry Crosson, had made a deal with Joe Keenan and Ray Kassar that they would take a pool of money as an incentive bonus program. Fifty cents for every console and ten cents for every cartridge would be distributed throughout engineering as incentive bonuses. In the Spring, with the great sales of the VCS and its cartridges during that launch season now over, Kerry met with Joe Keenan and the newly joined Ray Kassar to ask what the bonus pool was up to. Joe's response was "What bonus pool? You must have misunderstood."

With this complete denial of the bonus pool or any agreement, Kerry pulled together a meeting with all of Consumer engineering to inform everyone that apparently there is no bonus pool, and that he has been told he was mistaken. The result was a near mutiny, almost forty to fifty people in the commons area are yelling, with many threatening to quit and leave right there on the spot. Word goes up the chain very quickly, and soon the VP of Consumer engineering (John Ellis) is quietly meeting with people that they wanted to retain and making offers of bonus' and salary increases under the table. VCS programmer David Crane would be among those who would see his salary go from $18,000 to $25,000 after just six months or so of being at Atari. Many are still very disgruntled though, even after getting paid under the table. Alan Miller had approached senior management about getting credit in the games and proposed a more formal royalty structure which was rejected. Larry Kaplan and Bob Whitehead also approached management together about a better compensation arrangement and they too wanted some kind of recognition for their work, the answer to them is also 'NO.'

Now, just after Ray's 'pep talk' after taking over as President, the issue was rearing its head again after a marketing memo was circulated to the Consumer programming group listing the 1978 sales figures - among which the top ten best selling cartridges are listed. The context of the cartridge listing is to point out which games sold very well, so they can do more games like that. The games that didn't do well are also pointed out, with an obvious directive of 'don't do any more games like that.' Consumer engineering had already heard that Atari had sold close to $100 million in cartridge sales for 1978, and when Alan Miller, Bob Whitehead, David Crane and Larry Kaplan look more closely at the list they notice all of the top selling games are games that they had coded. Of the four of them, they had accounted for close to $60 million in sales for games they wrote, each of them making around $25,000 a year. This leads them to start talking amongst themselves about this, and thinking if what they are doing is so popular and is selling a lot, then they should be rewarded in some way.

During several off site meetings over pizza in March, the four discuss the whole sales figures issue and what they should do about it. Already disgruntled as it is and having nothing to lose, they decide to ask for a meeting with Ray Kassar. Among the idea's they want to present is that maybe they should all four form their own VCS game development company and then Atari can pay them based on performance. Unforutunately, when they go in to the meeting it never really goes that far; starting to explain how they made all of these games, Ray tells them, "No Atari made these games." He continues to explain that while the four may have written those games, as a total package the games also involve marketing, management, production and much more. So the group counters back that Atari wouldn't have those games if it wasn't for them. Again Ray returns back, this time with the fact that Atari wouldn't have those games without the guys on the assembly line who put them together either, that it's a company and everyone works together. At that point the four are looking for any reason to stay instead of the excuses they thought they were getting. They even would've taken something under the table again, but nothing materialized. So they get up, and as they're walking out of the office, Kassar's senior VP says to them, "Well, it was nice knowing you guys." He knew that they would not stay after that, probably because they weren't the first to meet with Ray to complain about money after his company wide speech.

Jay Miner, the engineer that lead the VCS and Atari's forthcoming computers from concept to reality, also had a meeting with Ray that February. In his case, he wanted to discuss two different topics: expected bonuses and wanting financial approval to move on to a new computer. With regards to the bonsues, after development of the VCS was over, the team had been promised individual bonuses based on the sales of the new console, with Jay expected to get around $.15 cents per unit and Joe Decuir, for example being promised $.10 cents a unit. Although orders were picking up again after the sales problems of the previous year, the team had discovered that Warner's financial people who were filling in at Atari during Ray's restructuring had done what's called 'Hollywood Accounting.' A practice originated in Hollywood for film production, where development costs are padded or shuffled around to show losses at will and reduce the reported profit, thereby getting the company out of paying royalties to investors. In this case it was done with the development costs of the first year, which were written off as a loss thereby eliminating the bulk of any profits that were to come from sales. Ray and management had promised to make it up to the team, but it was the first of two final straws for Jay. The second was Jay's discussion with Ray about wanting to do more advanced projects, including starting development on a next generation 68000 based computer to get a jump over Apple. Ray declined, stating that finances were tight and they really were just getting started with their computer line. With that, the meeting turned in to Jay's exit interview as he left the company.

Ray explains his rationale of not wanting to put more money in advanced computer research as: "With the computers (we were just releasing) I thought we were not planning to do anything big. We were trying to get started, and it was really a learning process. I never thought we really had the tools to do what Apple was doing. And it turned out to be true."

Truthfully, Ray's efforts are focused on rebuilding Atari. Getting manufacturing in place, hiring a financial guy, etc. He had a full plate, and to him moving on to another new computer meant more money and a bigger budget - something they couldn't afford. "We had a lot yet to do just in the Consumer Division. Coin-op was a steady stream money maker though, that's where all the titles were coming from, we had some terrific programmers there. I had great respect for the programmers."

Joe Decuir, Jay Miner's close friend and understudy found out more insight into Ray's position one day when he offered to give Ray a lift after seeing him walking between buildings. As Joe remembers about the conversation, "It had to do with the technical staff exerting technology-push pressure on the market. A good example would be Jay wanting to do something with a 68K processor in it. Kassar wanted to bring in sales & marketing oriented pressure, too. In fact, before Ray I don't think Atari had real marketing beyond Nolan himself. Real marketing is 'Who are the customers? What are they buying? Why are they buying it from you?' What Ray wanted to do was important. In a competent technical product company, these forces (technology and marketing) are balanced."

Joe is actually the next to leave, and has his exit interview with Ray Kassar in June 1979. Joe had wanted to stay on to at least see the computer line through its production and was now looking to leave to start his own company, Standard Technologies. When asked what he would like to still work on if he could be persuaded to stay, besides a 68000 based computer he told Ray that he wanted to work on communications for computers. At which point he described applications like the French Minitel (an early French text only precursor to the World Wide Web where people could do everything from check stock prices to search a telephone directory and check email) as well as what Atari could do with the Arpanet (the precursor to the Internet). According to Joe, Ray got bored, took a call from Manny Gerard at Warner, and that was it.

In August 1979, Larry Kaplan leaves, and in September is joined by David Crane, Alan Miller and Bob Whitehead who all decide to pursue their original option of forming a firm to develop VCS games. The following month, their new company is formed: Activision, the world's first 3rd party game company in the home console industry.

Joe Keenan is the next of the old guard to leave, deciding to resign from Atari and become Chuck E. Cheese's Chief Operating Officer and President during the Fall of 1979; however unlike Nolan, he still arranges to consult for Atari for a short time yet. By becoming another of the original executive member's to utilize his

'Beach Clause' and vacating the top position, the opening is now left for Raymond Kassar to be appointed as both Chairman and CEO of Atari.

As time passed, Gene Lipkin would also resign, 'heading for the beach' in August 1980. Al Acorn too decides to leave Mahogany Row, but instead of leaving the company he instead rolls up his sleeves and returns to the place he felt most at home; in the Atari engineering labs. He began to create a new product line with unique technologies, and then fight hard with no support from management to prove it was a marketable and viable product, only to have his project and lab shut down and dismantled. Disgusted with the lack of foresight and the lack of any forward thinking R&D interest in the company, Al Alcorn finally decided to also pack up and leave and join the others on 'The Beach' at the end of 1981.

Also in 1981, with all the meetings with angry Atari employees and the constant flack from those who just didn't understand what he had to do to restructure Atari almost behind him, Ray was now becoming vindicated. Atari was well on the way to the top of its game in profits, and his company had a string of mega hits under its belt with more on the way. So it's understandable that Ray wanted to crow over his accomplishments and his handling of these challenges a little. Enough so that during an inteview for the Sunday edition of the San Jose Mercury News, Ray referred to Atari's engineers and programmers as 'high-strung prima donnas.' Granted, it was said during what Ray thought was an off-the-record moment, but that mattered little to the Atari employees that read it. The statement had been shared off-the-cuff in repsonse to a question Ray had been asked by the reporter: "You come from a textiles background, how do you get along with the engineers considering you have no experience in engineering?" Ray's response was, "I get along with them just fine, I'm used to working with high-strung prima donnas." Now in a perfect world, Ray's on-the-record response would have been (as he explained to us years later), "I have great respect for them (the engineers and designers). They're very creative, like artists, and I'm used to managing and encouraging creative types." That's actually the context of what he meant by his off-the-record comment, but of course that's not what came off to the Atari employees.

The employees over in Design felt they needed a response to get Ray's attention that they wouldn't stand for that, and proceeded to do so in the best way the knew how: they designed a t-shirt. Well, sort of... what they did is form a committee to design a shirt, and as is the norm with most committees, it went absolutely nowhere. Frustrated, Karlina Ott (a technical illustrator in the Design department) decided to put together a shirt on her own. Using the department's typesetting machine she came up with the stylized text for the front of the shirt that proudly stated "Just Another High-Strung Prima Donna From Atari." She then set about drawing up the back of the shirt: an illustration of a portly female opera singer, belting out notes while holding a trident that features an Atari logo at the tip instead of the normal outward facing three prongs. Putting up her own money and making arrangements for someone to print them up, ironically Karlina was more worried about if she'd make her money back than any repercussions from management. She didn't have to worry though, because when the shirts came in, after only telling a few people the entire first run sold out by the end of the day. The shirts were a hit, and Karlina remembers one incident where her boss Dennis had to quickly get off the phone because he saw someone stripping outside his office. People were literally buying the shirt, ripping off their own on the spot, and proudly wearing the prima donna shirt the rest of the day.

People wearing the shirts soon began being stopped by Ray Kassar himself, asking everyone where they got it. Afraid of the repercussions, of course nobody would tell him. It turns out he had been sent one anonymously from the first batch by Karlina and the group, and thinking the t-shirt was hilarious wanted to thank whoever made it. The smartass display of defiance had actually been well received if not chuckled over. At that point Ray knew it came from Coin, but not where specifically in Coin, so he drafted a general letter of thanks and sent it over. Karlina was pulled in to Lyle Rains' office shortly after, not knowing what it was about, and was surprised when Lyle handed her a letter. Ray's letter of thanks had found her.

It wasn't just coin that had issues however, really though, Ray's image amongst the programmers in Consumer was just as bad. Kassar's personal feelings of respect for the programmers aside, Howard Scott Warshaw felt "Kassar really thought every programmer was like everyone else and didn't understand it took a lot of talent to get the Atari VCS to do more than its basic functionality." Likewise, "Ray never played the games," recalls Franz Lanzinger, which added to viewpoint that he was all about the marketing and sales of what was a generic widget too him. "One day, while I was working on Quadrun, Ray came walking through with an entourage, looked over my shoulder at the screen and his only comment was, 'colorful' and then walked away," recalls Steve Woita. Rob Fulop would find that the management Ray had brought in wasn't much better.

Rob had graduated from UC Berkley with a degree in Electrical Engineering in 1978, and his first job fresh out of college was Atari. Directly hired by Nolan

Bushnell before his departure, he first worked in Atari's pinball division developing the initial work on the sound effects for Atari's last production pinball machine, *Superman*. Moving over to the Consumer Division, on September 30, 1979 had begun coding a version of *Space Invaders* for Atari's home computers, and shortly after that (on February 19, 1980) he programmed *Tennis* for the home computers. That was followed with two very popular VCS games: ports of *Night Driver* released in August 1980 and *Missile Command* in the Spring of 1981. After finishing *Missile Command*, Rob was now getting the chance to work on his own game for release in 1982. "I actually finished another 2600 cart while at Atari, after *Missile Command*. It was an original game... orbiting a rotating landscape sort of thing... a space shooter. We focused tested the game and I recall it not do very well," recalls Rob. Christmas was coming up and Rob was looking forward to seeing what kind of compensation he would receive for developing and delivering such a stellar game as *Missile Command*, which has generated so much in profits for Atari.

When the envelope arrived over in the Consumer programming group addressed to Rob, he was all excited, opening it up and expecting perhaps $10,000-$15,000 or who knows, perhaps even more. After all the company had just made millions from the release of VCS *Missile Command*! So what's in the envelope? Rob received a certificate for one free turkey as well as recognition and thanks for being a good part of the Atari team. Rob in turn realizes it's time to dump this turkey and he quits Atari, and along with Dennis Koble and several others, he forms his own game company... Imagic.

Frank Ballouz would have one of the most interesting tales to tell of his firing and being sent off to 'The Beach' as well. He, Curt Russell and John Anderson were also part of the Warner purchase agreement, placed in a tier under the 'The King and Queen and the five Princes' (which referred to Bushnell, Keenan, Alcorn, Bristow, White, Lipkin, and Williams). Along with Mayer and Emmons from Grass Valley 'The Beach Clause' was avilable to them as well. The tale begins when Ballouz is at an AMOA distributors conference in 1982. Don Osborne had been working for him and he too was looking to leave Atari - in this case for a job over at Midway. Everyone knew that Don was leaving... except for Steve Ross, Manny Gerard and Ray Kassar. However, during the conference word got back to Manny and Ray about Don's imminent departure to Midway. After talking things over, Steve, Manny and Ray's response is to summon Frank during the MOA cocktail party. Upon hearing he's been requested to meet with Manny and Ray immediately, Frank looks around the table to his fellow Atari employees and says, "Guys, I think this might be The Last Supper." He goes up and meets with Manny and Ray and they explain that they have talked with Don and he will be taking Frank's position. Manny and Ray's strategy was to keep Don by getting rid of another one of the old guard and moving Don up. As of that moment, they explain to Frank, he's fired, but if he'd like he can still attend the distributor's conference and meetings. Frank doesn't feel that is fair to Don or everyone at the conference to continue acting as if he's still representing Atari as their International Sales Manager for coin-op. So he accepts his 'surprise' termination. Manny and Ray explain that he will get his full compensation package, and anything else having loose ends will be closed up for him.

Frank returns to his hotel room after the meeting - his girlfriend is in the tub relaxing, and Frank tells her she still has a job at Atari even though he doesn't. Lighting up a joint, he takes a couple of drags and starts thinking. Suddenly, he picks up the hotel room phone and calls up to Ray Kassar. "Ray, my compensation payments; could I get those all in one lump sum paid out to me?" Ray agrees and Frank hangs up. After a few more drags he calls up to Ray's room again: "Ray, my remaining vacation time and expenses pay; I'd like to book my vacation now and use up that time now when I leave the MOA conference," - again Ray agrees to this and Frank again hangs up. Now after awhile and quite a few more drags of pot, Frank says, "Damn what else can I get?" He makes yet a third call up to Ray: "My car, I pay for part of it and Warner was paying for part of it. I'd like Warner to pay it off completely for me." On this Ray pushes back, he's not going to do it. Frank shoots back, "You did it for Al Alcorn for his car, so you should be able to do it for mine." Kassar concedes - if Warner had done it for Alcorn, then yes they'd do it for Ballouz as well.

With that, Frank is fully satisfied with his untimely departure from Atari, hangs up with Ray Kassar and that's it. Frank's been put on "The Beach." Going back down to the cocktail party and saying his goodbye's to everyone, he then heads off to Maui with his girlfriend - who would later on become his wife and then second ex-wife. The sole survivors of the old guard remaining on the Atari payroll would be Steve Bristow, who would stay with Atari until its bitter end and sale in 1984, and Steve Mayer, who moves to NY to run a research lab for Warner Communications until he bought the lab from Warner and ran it himself for several years.

Years later at the New York Toy Faire, Nolan would run into Manny, a meeting of the two ex-business and sparring partners initiated when Manny decided to stop in at Nolan's Axlon room. Seeing Manny walk in, Nolan loudly exclaims, "Look, it's Manny Gerard - the man who fired me at Atari." Manny came back at him: "Yeah, and I'm the guy who made you a millionaire!" After a few moments, Nolan replied back, "Yeah, I guess you're right."

Chapter 7 Review In Images

Above: The original launch box. *Below*: The chess piece image that caused the lawsuit and forced Atari to develop a chess game for the VCS.

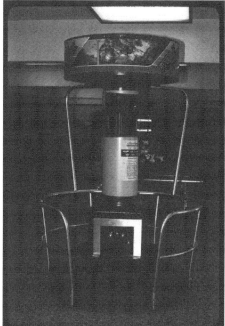

Above: *Airborne Avenger* pinball backglass.

Left: The game *Wolfpack*, only three were built.

Counter clockwise: The marketing and sales wizards Frank Ballouz (top) and Don Osborne (bottom with Gene Lipkin's daughter Ramy). The team responsible for Atari's successful Coin-Op Division expansion and golden years of the late 70s and early 80s.

From left to right - Frank Ballouz, Suzanne Elliott, Lenore Sayers, Tom Petit and Don Osborne having fun while in New Orleans for a convention. *(Photo courtesy of Matt Osborne)*

Don clowing around with Spiderman at a convention in New York. *(Photo courtesy of Matt Osborne)*

Top: Award ceremony at one of the annual Pebble Beach coin-op distributor
meetings. Atari regularly awarded top
distributors, and in this case the Bettle-
man's (a family run distributor company) received an award.

Right: Authorized Atari Distributor
plaque, given to all certified distributors of Atari coin-ops. Distributors who
were authorized had the resources and
training available to service Atari coin-
ops and represent the company in the
field, including providing promotional
materials and contests.

ATARI®
Innovative
Leisure
1265 Borregas Avenue
Sunnyvale, CA 94086
(408) 745-2500

The Corporate building at 1265 Borregas also held a game room that was always well stocked with the latest and greatest releases plus many of the older favorites. That's our editor Loni Reeder in the upper left, this book's editor and former Atari employee, playing Starship 1 in the game room.

Atari built and sold test fixtures to allow distributors and owners to plug PCBs from a multitude of games to help diagnose problems. As seen here, these test fixtures feature a plethora of controllers built in to anticipate the variety of controllers used on Atari's coin-ops. To the left is Atari's CTF-1 Test Fixture released in 1976, and below is an older *PONG/Gran Trak 10* era one.

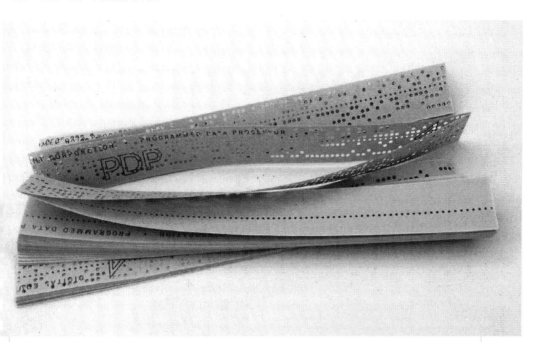

After the transition to microprocessors and the hiring of Atari's first coders in the mid 1970s, the process for game creation involved writing assembly based game code saved on paper tape (above) and read in to paper tape readers (like Atari's home made one below). Both the tape and reader shown here were actually used at Atari during this late 70s period.

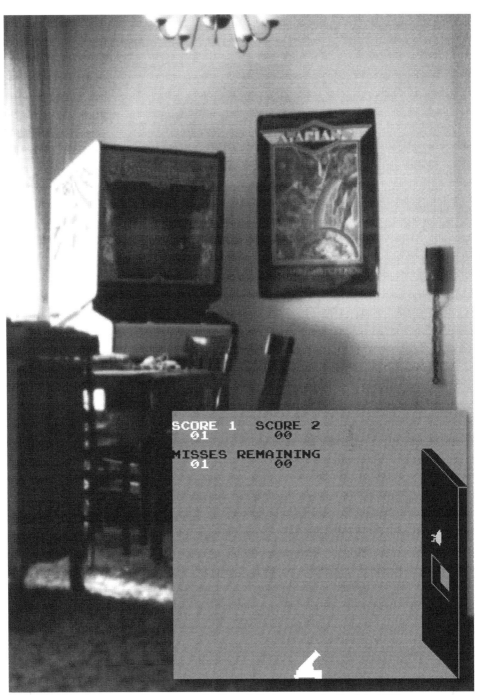

The *Cannonball* prototype in Owen's living room in the late 1970s.
Inset: Screen shot of *Cannonball*.

Owen's three game *Triple Hunt* is the first video game with a soundtrack, using 8-track tapes (inset) for each game's soundtrack since audio hardware technology of the time could not produce the needed sounds.

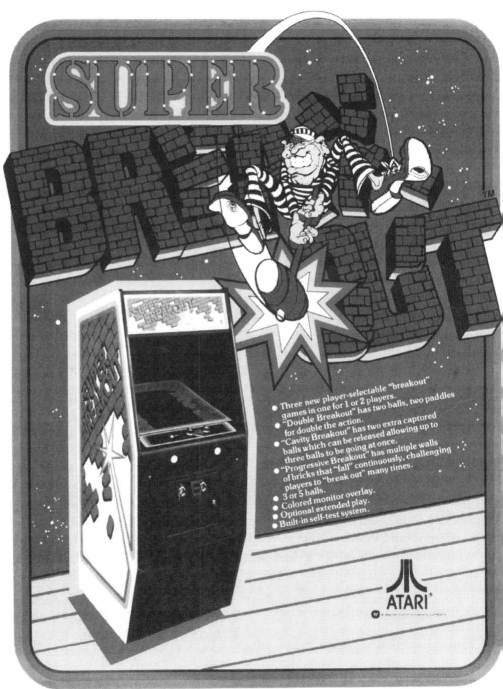

- Three new player-selectable "breakout" games in one for 1 or 2 players.
- "Double Breakout" has two balls, two paddles for double the action.
- "Cavity Breakout" has two extra captured balls which can be released allowing up to three balls to be going at once.
- "Progressive Breakout" has multiple walls of bricks that "fall" continuously, challenging players to "break out" many times.
- 3 or 5 balls.
- Colored monitor overlay.
- Optional extended play.
- Built-in self-test system.

When Atari opened up its European headquarters in Tipperary, Ireland, Atari coin-ops were given their own unique labels to denote their origin. Below is the abandoned factory today *(photo courtesy of Noah Anglin.)* When NAMCO took over the Atari coin-op division (then named Atari Games) in 1984 it went through a succesion of ownership until being sold to Williams (WMS) Industries in 1996. Williams sold the Tipperary plant back to NAMCO later that year and NAMCO closed the plant down in 1999.

Coin Operated Games Division

ATARI®

Atari Incorporated
1265 Borregas Avenue
PO Box 427
Sunnyvale California 94086
408 745 2000

Dear Operator:

Atari is proud to offer its Community Awareness Program to you
as a tool to inform your community about the coin video games
industry.

The program was introduced in March of 1982, when the materials
were supplied to all Atari distributors. The package includes
a 17-minute video tape entitled, "Video Games: A Public
Perspective", a position paper synopsizing the major points
brought out in the film, and a four-page brochure offering
information and tips about presenting the materials to
legislative or community groups.

The "Public Perspective" videotape is a comprehensive,
objective look at the video games industry. In it, parents,
teachers, doctors and community-minded citizens give their
views on the impact video games are having on our lifestyles.

The Community Awareness Program has been used successfully in
a number of communities as an effective educational and
communications tool. The effectiveness is enhanced when an
industry member is present to offer first-hand information
about the role video games play in their communities.

If you are not presently faced with legislation, the program
is an opportunity to educate and possibly prevent problems.
Atari distributors have also been supplied with a one-page
brochure on the program that can be sent to Rotary Clubs,
Parent-Teacher Associations and other civic organizations
before a problem occurs.

We encourage your participation and support, and look forward
to hearing your comments.

Margaret Lasecke
Margaret Lasecke
Public Relations Manager
Coin Video Division

Jamie Pinto
Jamie Pinto
Media Relations Specialist
Coin Video Division

🌐 A Warner Communication Company

A letter sent with a community awareness packet sent to distributors and operators,
filled with articles and other resources to help battle the negative connotation of arcade games and video games in general.

Atari, Inc. 1265 Borregas, Sunnyvale, California 94086

nuary, 1977   Volume 1, Number 2

ATARI THEATRE OFFERS NEW FUN AND GAMES FOR BART USERS

3-D Racing at 190

F-1 is more than a game. It's like a driving simulator.

The new F-1 projects actual three-dimensional images on a giant race course screen while the driver is seated in a realistic race car cockpit.

The constantly twisting track and 3-D racing cars create the excitement of true Formula One racing.

Much of the skill factor involved in the game includes trying to keep from crashing into cars that the player has to pass, or which are trying to pass him, while the driver races towards the highest possible score. Driving off the road also causes a crash.

The biggest attraction F-1 offers comes at the moment of impact with another car . . . when the crash sounds hit the ears and the entire screen is filled with a flame-colored explosion visual.

Scores are digitally displayed on a large, easy-to-read panel above the projection screen. The highest score previously achieved is stored and displayed. A button is provided for score reset. Game time is displayed by a fuel gauge and is operator adjustable. Extended play is awarded after driver scores 3,000 points.

Atari's Theatre Kiosk, a series of six pie-shaped video game units has been installed for the first time at the San Francisco Powell Street Station of the prestigious Bay Area Rapid Transit System.

The six-sided video attraction is located inside the entrance at the station's train level platform.

In addition to the games which offer 90 seconds of play per quarter, a special 35 mm slide projection system along with BART advertising panels is designed into the top structure. Sequential, changing slides present various San Francisco and Bay Area sports, entertainment and information visuals.

"We think the machine, here at this one station on an experimental basis will provide fun for our riders between trains," a BART spokesman said. "And the information and revenue won't hurt, either."

"The BART location is an excellent example of the viability and earning potential of the Theatre concept.

"It is a new entertainment idea that combines extra sophistication and excitement with high profits for any high traffic location," Frank Ballouz, Atari National Sales Manager commented.

Each Theatre provides a complete video package that can be custom designed to integrate into any playing environment.

Two, three or six wedge-shaped units are offered. Operators can fit two units into a corner, three against a wall, or six into a stand-alone island center.

The upper portion can be custom designed, as in the case of BART, providing space for advertising and information.

Video games can be interchanged without loss of time or money. Once the unit is on location, games can be replaced simply by changing the control panel, attraction plex and P.C. Board.

Present Theatre games available include SPACE RACE™, TRAK-10™, TANK™, QUIZ SHOW™, FLY-BALL™, JET FIGHTER™, PONG DOUBLES™, STUNT CYCLE™ and LEMANS™, and soon to be released SPRINT II™, BREAKOUT™ and NIGHT DRIVER™. Current collection figures are available by calling Frank Ballouz at Atari, (408) 745-2500.

* The world's first video attraction to simulate the actual play action of American football.
* Two players.
* New Trak Ball™ allows instant movement and control of key players in any direction.
* Offense can select 1 of 4 different run or pass plays.
* Defense can select 1 of 4 different plays.
* New add-a-coin feature adds continuous time-play.
* Versatile new cabinet is height-adjustable to 40" for standing play, 31" for cocktail table play.
* Built-in self-test system.

The successor to the *St. PONG* newsletter, *Coin Connection* was put out by Carol Kantor. Showing Atari's emphasis was still heavily on coin-operated games, the newletter was also sent to distributors and features articles on the latest games and internal happenings at Atari.

Top: The prototype trak ball controller for *Football*, one of the first appearances of a trackball in an arcade video game. Atari spelled its unique controller Trak Ball to differentiate it from previous efforts, the first of which was invented in 1952 and used a five-pin Canadian bowling ball. Though smaller than an actual bowling ball, this prototype uses a ball made out of the same material.

Bottom: Prototype foot controlled trak ball that uses a full size bowling ball. This was created for an earlier proof of concept of the coin-op Soccer, where the intent was to allow the player to simulate the foot play of the game.

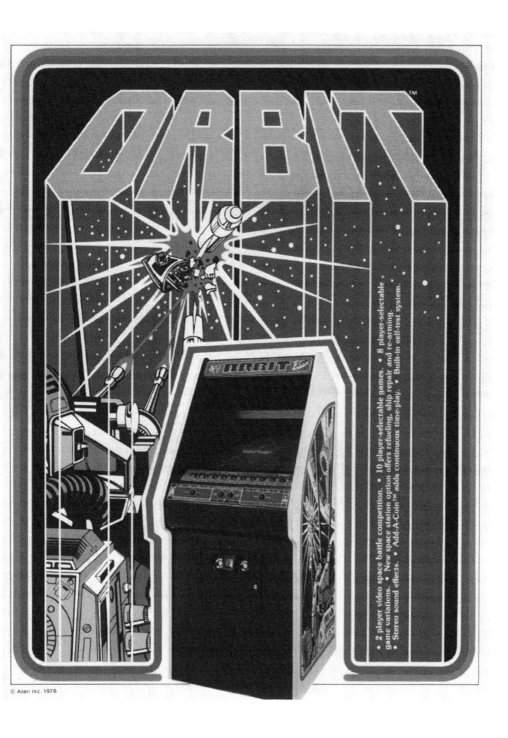

• 2 player video space battle competition. • 10 player-selectable games. • 8 player-selectable game variations. • New space station option offers refueling, ship repair and re-arming. • Stereo sound effects. • Add-A-Coin™ adds continuous time-play. • Built-in self-test system.

The sitdown version of *Night Driver* proved to be so popular that it moved from a limited run to a wider release of 1395 units produced.

A CHRISTMAS PARTY

at the residence of
Mr. Nolan K. Bushnell
3860 Woodside Road
Woodside, California

❋

December 15, 1978
7:30 PM to 10:00 PM

❋

RSVP 408-745-2327

Parking available at Woodside School.
Transportation will be provided to and from the Bushnell residence.

The Christmas party invitation to the private event that would be Nolan's goodbye to many of the Atari employees, as he was 'put out to pasture' at the end of the month.

ATARI°

January 26, 1979

Mr. Emanuel Gerard
Warner Communications Inc.
75 Rockefeller Plaza
New York, New York 11019

Dear Manny:

      I was very disappointed when I received your
December 28, 1978 letter purporting to reassign me to
other duties with Atari. For the reasons hereinafter set
forth, I believe that action violates our oral and written
agreements and has led me (1) to question the bona fides
of the negotiations relating to Warner's acquisition of
Atari and (2) to seek legal advice regarding my rights with
respect to Atari and Warner. The purpose of this letter is
to state my position regarding Atari and Warner and to offer
an alternative to the time, cost and unfavorable publicity
inherent in internecine litigation.

      Manny, as you know, the fundamental principle on
which the acquisition by Warner of Atari was based was that
the then existing key management of Atari, principally Joe
Keenan and me, would continue to manage the company. You
repeatedly emphasized to me and my representatives during
the negotiations that Warner would not acquire Atari unless
it was assured of continuing participation by Joe and me,
among others. That was the reason you stated for using Atari
debentures as part of the purchase price, so that my investment in the debentures would keep me actively engaged in
managing the business and thereby protecting my investment.
From my standpoint I agreed to take Atari debentures rather
than Warner debentures only on the basis that I would continue
to manage the business of Atari and thus be in control of my
own destiny and be able, through my managerial efforts, to
protect my investment. Moreover, an integral part of the
purchase price was represented by the bonus pool arrangement,
which I agreed to only on the basis of your assurances that
I would continue to actively manage the business of Atari.

ATARI INC 1265 BORREGAS AVENUE, P.O. BOX 9027, SUNNYVALE, CALIFORNIA 94086 • TELEPHONE (408) 745-2000 • TELEX 35-74#

Ⓦ A Warner Communications Company

A page from Nolan's last attempt to fight the enactment of the beach clause. The content of the letter is mainly him chastising Warner management and stating if he can't
run Atari he wants his Atari debentures bought out.

Balls Of Steel

What follows is an account of Atari's little known Pinball Division, which included future

legendary Pinball designer Steve Ritchie and video game designer Eugene Jarvis of Robo-

tron:2084 and Defender fame.

I n February 1975, Atari made the move from glowing pixels to shiny steel balls and chopping flippers, finally diving head first into the more traditional area of the coin industry it had been flirting with since 1972: pinball. Going against companies like Bally, Gotlieb and Williams on their own long held turf was a risky move for Atari. Far different than forcing them on to the new turf of video games, these companies all started out in pinball and had long ago perfected the design, manufacturing and marketing of the machines. If Atari was going to compete in their world, it would have to do things that the competition wasn't doing by its established signature of keeping the idea of innovation at the forefront. Microprocessor or 'solid state' pinball machines had already been pioneered at Atari's think tank Cyan, so with that foundation Atari is looking to make every designed pinball machine a solid state pinball machine with the addition of digital scoring and other more advanced design features. The next factor they want to set themselves apart with is to use wide body playfields, pushing the envelope with creative playfield designs. Finally, everything has to be combined with an artistic flare to showcase some of the most gorgeous arcade artwork the company had ever done. In essence, they know they have to create the most unique, challenging and alluring pinball machines the marketplace had ever seen.

When Atari established the Pinball Division, Gil Williams was tasked with getting the division going with the assistance of Don Lange. Initially, Rich Elston, Dan Corona, Bob Jonesi, Eugene Jarvis, Steve Ritchie and Jackie Fowler are brought in to staff the division and begin working on the new generation of pinball games in the building behind the 'secret' VCS project building on Division Street in Campbell, California.

Employing the same sort of brainstorming sessions routinely done for video games at Atari, a lot of ideas are thrown around for pinball designs. Even Nolan and Joe Keenan get in the act, making some suggestions on the playfield design and to relocate the scoring to the lower areas on the back glass. While there were many good ideas during prototype development of their first pinball, the initial feedback from play test on many of the suggested improvements was negative. Going back to the drawing board, the engineering work took place through most of 1976 and by the Fall, the first pinball game was ready… or so the group hoped. Appropriately named *The Atarians*, it's designed by Bob Jonesi and Eugene Jarvis, with Fred Yates doing the programming and George Opperman giving it its artistic flair.

Owen Rubin, by coincidence, was located across the hall from where the pinball engineers were working on *The Atarians* - a great place to be for someone that's such a big fan of pinball. When the game was ready he asked if they wouldn't mind him trying it out. Only Owen didn't just play it; after putting *The Atarians* through its paces, he went back to his office and returned to pinball engineering with a sheet of paper detailing issues and bugs he'd found. Not understanding why this guy is showing up with a list of problems when he's not even in the Pinball Division, Owen is asked if he was assigned to the game as a play tester. Explaining that he wasn't, he goes on to say he was just trying out the new pinball game and noticed some minor to serious issues and took it upon himself to try and help them with this list. (Did we mention Owen really loves pinball?) One major issue Owen found for example, is with the coin credit routine on the game: If you put in funds for ten or more play credits, he discovered it gave the player unlimited lives. Looks like *The Atarians* was not quite ready to make its debut. With that single unplanned list, what they thought was a finished game was now pulled back into prototype stage to begin fixing the bugs.

Atari's first pinball game, *The Atarians,* was introduced in November and with that, Atari had officially entered the cutthroat, extremely competitive world of pinball manufacturing and sales. In an example of some of the early trials and tribulations Atari had making inroads in to the market, when Dan Corona and Steve Ritchie (a board tech) made travel arrangements to go and set up the first *Atarians* for a distributor, they had some rather embarrassing problems pop up. Having to get twelve machines up and running out of the 100 that were shipped for the order, the embarrassment starts immediately after they unpack the twelve and begin testing them. One of the first problems is literally at the very start of the game: the ball isn't kicking up out of the hole to rest in front of the plunger - the balls are repeatedly getting stuck. Steve implements a quick fix by rigging up a wedge, getting the ball to properly kick up in all twelve pinball games. The next big issue: the solenoids in the games, which are failing. For those not familiar, solenoids are a special electromagnetic part used throughout a pinball game to provide motion to parts in the game - from everything like flippers to the bumpers that make the ball magically spring off them when hit. As a result of this problem though, Dan and Steve have to go and unpack countless numbers of the other pinballs to pull enough solenoids to get the twelve Atarian pinballs up and running properly. Looks like *The Atarians* still isn't quite ready for the market yet.

When Dan and Steve return back to Atari, Steve meets with his engineering manager and hands him a ten page list of all of the problems encountered with *The Atarians* at the distributor. Taking the notes, the manager looks them over and instead of just thanking Steve, he gets a serious look on his face and warns Steve not to tell anyone about all of these problems. Steve counters that these are serious problems and they need to be addressed ASAP. While his manager agrees, he also says they will deal with them quietly. Whether it was the manager's need to save face or just not wanting to cause commotion with the higher ups, the move still didn't sit well with Steve when he went home that night. In fact the next day he voices these same issues to Al Alcorn and others, leaving out the fact his boss told him to keep it secret though. The move prompts immediate action, and it takes the determined efforts of Dan Corona, Steve Ritchie, Gary Slater, Eugene Jarvis (and some help from Gene Lipkin) to really get things in working order in Atari's Pinball Division so this never happens again.

The Pinball Division is further rounded out with the addition of several more people that are key to manufacturing and marketing. Eddie Boasberg joined in October 1976 as the division's new Marketing Design Coordinator, also taking on more functions in the division in February 1977 when he becomes the Operations Manager as well as the Marketing Coordinator in February 1977. Bob Russell will join the division as an operations manager in March, with Bob Kolbus becoming the manufacturing building manager in Moffett Park soon after. Furthermore, Jim Uszack comes in to supervise manufacturing engineering around the time 1173 Borregas is officially set up as Atari's pinball manufacturing plant.

With all these reworkings and additions, things began to really ramp up in the pinball division and by June Atari releases its second pinball game: *Time 2000*. Designed by Marty Rosenberg, Eugene Jarvis does the programming and sound for the game. When completed, it's a breathtaking balance of artwork (once again done by George Opperman and featuring a naked butterfly woman strategically covered by her long hair) and playfield design (by Jim Kelly, who also contrubited some sound effects).

Speaking of Eugene Jarvis and sound, if there's anything that can be said about him, it's that his propensity to make awesome sound effects rivaled Owen's signature as Coin's 'sound guy.' Eugene would wind up working on sound effects for five of Atari's pinball machines starting with *The Atarians*, giving them truly unique sound effects that drew players in in the same way the sound in his later video games for Williams (such as *Defender* and *Robotron: 2084*) would. As Eugene put it in an interview he gave to firepowerpinball.com in March 2007, "Its amazing, but I knew nothing about sound when I started at Atari. But by working with the very crude wave table synthesizer we used there, I became enthralled with how sound effects are really the soul of a pinball. The ball is the conductor and the sound program is the symphony. The right sound could magnify the players emotional involvement in the game, and transport the player into a the fantasy world of the game."

Atari's pinball division rounds out 1977 with the release of *Airborne Avenger* in September. Eugene again does the programming and sounds, with George Opperman also providing the futuristic secret angent looking artwork of the game, but the interesting story behind the game is that the designer, Steve Ritchie, was at that time simply a board tech in the pinball division. Steve had started with Atari in the spring of 1974 after walking into Martin Street looking for a job. With a background in electronics from being a US Coast Guard electronics technician and doing electronics work in Vietnam, Atari hired Steve and put him on wiring harnesses with Jackie Fowler. Soon moving to getting involved with special projects and designing the CTS-1 test fixture, during his lunch breaks Steve discovered a love of playing foosball in the break room. The shift in to the field that Steve is now a legend in came one day when Gene Lipkin ran into him and asked if he'd like to be Employee #2 of Atari's new pinball division. Accepting, Steve was given a small raise and became supervisor of the pinball prototype lab. When Steve first started in the position, Atari had already hired Bob Jonesi (a mechanical engineer from Williams) as the divisoin's game designer. A rather gruff individual who had an unflattering view of Atari, Bob kept telling Steve that Atari would never build anything. Steve emphasized to him that they should still try, at which point Bob snapped back at

Steve, telling him, "Don't wise off to me kid!" Gruff or not, Bob did teach Steve how to build a prototype pinball game while Bob designed Atari's first pinball, *Atarians*.

Taking what he had learned from Bob, armed with a t-square Steve started drawing at home, designing his own pinball game. Going to his boss and showing him his work, the response was certainly not expected. Maybe some constructive criticism or a "Nice first try kid." What did this supervisor say to the man who is now described as 'perhaps the greatest pinball designer of our time?' He told him he wasn't a game designer, that he didn't have the background OR the experience and 'No, you cannot design a pinball game for Atari.' Not deterred with that response, Steve didn't just go over the managers head - he went directly to Nolan Bushnell to ask him about doing a pinball. One of Nolan's gifts was having a knack for being able to see into people, down to the core talent within them. Nolan recognized that raw enthusiasm in Steve – the kind of enthusiasm that brings greatness to a company and its products. So he gives Steve a shot, giving Steve his own cubicle and drafting table to work on his game. Eventually meeting and bringing in Eugene Jarvis, together they created the pinball game *Airborne Avenger*.

Atari raised the innovation bar again when it releases *Middle Earth* in February 1978. Designed by Gary Slater, with the artwork once again done by George Opperman. A 'land that time forgot' theme rather than the Tolkien flavor the title may conjur up, the uniqueness of Middle Earth is in the double playfield designed into it. When the ball is put into play, there are two sets of flippers - a set on both the upper and lower levels, with the ball having the ability to travel to both the upper and lower levels throughout the game play. The game also incorporates a TILT sound effect, alerting a location operator to possible machine tampering or abuse. Shown off at the April 26-29 International Coin Amusement Expo by one of Atari's distributors, their booth is filled with plenty of 'oohs and ahhs' by shows end. In June however, *Middle Earth* had to be retooled to address several issues that were identified out on locations after its release. The new design includes things like new linear flippers and replaceable flipper buttons, better match credit and score board circuits, a new snap-lock mounting system to correct vibration problems with the PC boards, upgrading of the drop targets with a much higher reliability and the redesign of the spinning targets to correct a sticking problem. In response to the upgrades, field upgrade packs are also issued to distributors who already have a *Middle Earth* out in the field.

Middle Earth is followed by *Space Riders* in September, envisioned as a futuristic space cycle race-themed game where you compete to score maximum points in BIKE CITY. Designed by Gary Slater with artwork done by both George Opperman and Gjalt Vanderwyk, the artwork is notable as the first appearance of George's 'space warrior' character later used in *Missile Command* and revealed as Commander Champion in *Liberator*.

Atari pinballs were starting to garner a lot of attention and interest throughout 1978 thanks to the great reception and marketing presence. Appearing in the March issue of the Sci-Fi magazine *Starlog* is an article on Atari's innovative solid state pinball games which showcased *Airborne Avenger*, *Atarians*, *Time 2000* and while not a pinball, the article also showcased the video arcade game *Starship-1*, most likely because the ships in the game looked similar to a side profile of the Starship Enterprise from the TV show 'Star Trek.'

As part of its marketing initiative, the Pinball Division followed Coin's lead by sponsoring local tournaments across the country run by distributors or operators. One such tournament happened on January 26, 1978 when a *Time 2000* pinball tournament was held at the Pinball Wizard Game Center in Davenport, Iowa. The Pinball Wizard game centers in Iowa are modern, family amusement arcades located in high traffic shopping areas which have a track record of success with aggressive marketing and promotional campaigns. "Atari pinballs have been top money making games in our centers. The players are attracted to the games by the unique sound effects. They really like the different appearance of the games with the artwork and wide playfields," Dick Galloway, president of Pinball Wizard commented at the time. Sixteen finalists competed for the top score on the *Time 2000* pinball machines. Steve Behrens, 19 of Davenport, was the winner with an outstanding score of 213,630. The top prize is an Atari Home Video Pinball console, a *Time 2000* t-shirt and a game pass from Pinball Wizard. Prizes were also handed out to the top five runner-ups and one for the lowest score. "The *Time 2000* tournament was a success; it brought a lot of people into the game center," further commented Galloway.

At the University of California, Los Angeles on April 15th, five games were selected for a competition and among them was Atari's *Airborne Avenger*. The winner of the competition was Andre Laurencot for his top score of 103,150 points on three balls and he received an *Airborne Avenger* t-shirt, poster and a cash prize. That was follwed in May, with a gathering of eighty pinball enthusiasts at 'The Office' (a bar in Aurora, Illinois). Randy Johnson of Twin Oaks Music and Bob McDade of The

Office organized the event, which is also coordinated in conjunction with Aurora's Budweiser Distributor who provided t-shirts and advertising posters for the event. Seven pinball machines and two video games were set-up for the event, and the top prizes include a home pinball game, hockey table and cash prizes. High scores on individual games would also receive *Airborne Avenger* t-shirts, which seemed to be the hot prize for some players for some odd reason. "One guy kept saying all he cared about was winning an Atari t-shirt," recalled Randy Johnson. Also in May, the 'Fun Factory' in Redondo Beach, California (a massive arcade center almost the size of the football field with nearly every game a player could ever dream of playing) set up a section of the arcade exclusively for pinball, designating the area with a huge sign which says, 'THE BEST.' That area was of course filled with just Atari Pinball machines. Steve Shoemaker, who runs 'Fun Factory' states that the Atari pinballs pulled in the highest earnings, and because he is an artist, he appreciated the beautiful artwork on the games.

In June, Atari helps the handicapped and underprivileged in De Moines, Iowa when the Variety Club holds a pinball themed charity event at the local Pinball Wizard. Seeking to raise $5,000 from the entry fees, over two dozen local businessmen donated hundreds in cash and prizes to be awarded to the competitors according to how long they played. The favorite pinball of the charity event turned out to be Atari's *Time 2000* according to Dick Galloway, President of Pinball Wizard. Not only did the Variety Club raise more than $5,000 for the children, but Tim Woods and Chris Epps, both 17, won top prize for their persistent '100 hour' long efforts. Local news coverage of the event helped to boost public awareness of the event, along with increasing the fan base for Atari's high tech pinball games.

Atari's Pinball Division also recieved great press after a celebrity fan set a world record for pinball play on Atari's *Middle Earth* on July 1st. Mandi Martin (a record producer and songwriter) played *Middle Earth* pinball for 140 hours and 32 minutes, passing the previous world record of 138 hours. Playing the game at the Los Angeles University of Sound Arts, her high score during her marathon game play was 321,400 points. Guinness World Record's strict rules were adhered to the entire time, to ensure that her record could go 'on the record,' which meant witnesses and a notarized log of all of Mandi's hours of game play which would be submitted into the official world record. The most important witness for Atari, however, was the extensive news coverage of the six day marathon that appeared on local television and radio, as well as national newspaper coverage reporting on her achievement. "Middle Earth was superb to play to achieve this record, and it was exciting to play throughout the whole event," recalls Mandi. Frank Ballouz was on hand to witness this record breaking moment as well, and stated "Atari is very pleased that she selected *Middle Earth* as the game for her record breaking achievement."

September would see Atari and celebrity Jerry Lewis team up for the last major media buzz of the year during that classic of American TV programming, the 'Jerry Lewis Labor Day Telethon to fight Muscular Dystrophy.' Atari's 'in' was provided when several fund raising events provided pinball related donations. Herb Francis of Brunswick organized a pinball competition and a special game area for the Telethon in New England. Thirteen Brunswick Recreational Centers and six Dream Machine Centers also held local contests to select 57 qualifiers for the Telethon playoff. The playoff would be a competition on Atari's *Middle Earth* pinball machines, . Atari would donate prizes to all of the players and finalists.

Atari's Pinball Division set up the same advanced Atari brand of service and support that Coin itself had become known in the industry for, providing its own test fixture in August. Released as the PBS-1: the Pinball Test System, it's a complete pinball simulator consisting of two small bench-top units, a display cabinet and a selector switch cabinet. An operator simply attaches all of the boards from inside the troubled pinball game to the units, where each function of a pinball game could be tested through the select switch unit. The PBS-1 can also check all switches, solenoids and lamp outputs for proper scoring on each target. During October and November of 1978, several inter-office memos were issued from Rich Adams, Norman Avellar and Steve Calfee with the constantly reiterated topic revolving around the age old issues with the solenoids; both for their mechanical issues, but also that programming interrupt routines in the games needed to be adjusted to stop solenoids from missing firing when they are supposed to. However, even with all the marketing and press, service and support, and just plain old advanced technology, Pinball was doomed at Atari. The Pinball Division just hadn't been able to make the market penetration that was hoped, and Nolan wanted to shut the entire thing down. Warner looked in to the possibility of cost reducing the machines to make them more competitive, but ultimately no significant savings are found. Since its inception, Atari's Pinball Division had always faced an uphill battle. Atari was a video game company and pinball was a completely different 'animal' of coin-operated games. "What we would do in months, Bally and others could do in weeks," recalls Dan Corona.

When January of 1979 comes around, Atari quietly stops all future pinball game development. Its final two products, *Superman* and *Middle Earth,* will go into production, and with that, Atari's short lived entry into the world of pinball machine design and manufacturing will come to a close.

Superman, released in March, is a game made possible by Atari negotiating a license with fellow Warner subsidiary DC Comics to make a Superman pinball game and VCS video game. *Superman*'s origins go back to when Gene Lipkin ventured over to the pinball engineering group and met with Steve Ritchie, telling Steve that he decided to make the assignment of the next project into a contest between Steve's team and Gary Slater's. Whomever designed the best playing and best sounding game would have their game become *Superman,* the other team would get the consolation prize of having their game made in to a different branding. Of course, Steve and Eugene's design won, but the eventual closing of Atari's Pinball Division would make sure that Gary's team would never see its promised consolation prize. On an interesting note, Superman's sound hardware was initially started by future VCS programmer extraordinaire Rob Fulop (*Night Driver, Space Invaders, Missile Command, Demon Attack*), but was completed by Eugene Jarvis. *Superman,* then and now, is considered by many to be Atari's best pinball machine for its game play, and especially for its sound effects.

Atari releases its final pinball, *Hercules,* in April, appropriately named after the mythical son of Zeus who was known for his size and strength. The largest pinball machine ever made, its eye popping dimensions of 93" long, 39" wide and 83" high make sure it lives up to its inspired name. It's so large in fact that a pool table cue ball has to be used for the game's ball, since normal sized steel pinballs would have been lost within its monster sized playfield. When the game was previewed in November 1978, it was met with unbelievable enthusiasm from both distributors and operators. Ironically, Atari's last released pinball game is a licensed game. Designed by Steve Bicker with artist Jim Kelly, the two are employees of the company Arcade Engineering, which was founded by Gene Lipkin's old boss from Allied Leisure: Allied co-founder Ron Haliburton. Gene had been trying (unsuccessfully) for some time to get Ron to come over to Atari. While Gene couldn't get Ron, he did manage to get Atari this pinball. Originally done in 1976 as a prototype for Bally called *Bigfoot,* when Bally declined to manufacture it the prototype instead makes its way to Atari thanks to Gene's connection to Ron. From there it was further developed in to *Hercules.*

After the last of the pinball orders were built and shipped out, Steve Bristow began the shutdown of Atari's pinball manufacturing plant, as the 1173 Borregas address is scheduled to be converted into the new Atari home computer manufacturing and assembly building. Prior to closing the building though, engineers built a small run of one of the most interesting and unique pinball game machines that not only Atari, but any other manufacturer had made to date. While Atari's pinballs had focused on being 'wide bodies' and would finish up with the monstrous sized *Hercules* pinball machine, this pinball is on the other end of the spectrum. Called *Monsa* and it was a cocktail table pinball game, cramming the electro mechanical fun of pinball into a table that players can sit down at.

Two of the three other pinball designs that never made it out were the proposed but never built *Secret Agent* and the built (but with no completed graphics or backglass) *Neutron Star*. *Neutron Star* was designed by Gary Slater and Milt Loper, using a very promising whitewood cabinet. Sitting as an unknown relic of Atari's forgotten division, it would eventually find its way to a new home after Atari is split in July, 1984: Consumer Division engineer Dan Kramer, who is famous for his design of the 'Trakball' controller for the Atari 5200 Supersystem. *Road Runner* is the last prototype that was built (designed by Marty Rosenthal), resulting in two fully finished units.

Looking to the future, in February 1979, another unique pinball game was released - but not from Atari's Pinball Division of course. With a huge plunger to pull back and launch the ball onto the playfield, it also has buttons on either side to activate the flippers to shoot a ball back up onto the playfield and keep the game play going. Sounds pretty standard for a pinball game, right? However, this new pinball game also has no coils, no electro-mechanical devices, no physical targets - in fact, its entire playfield and even the ball were all video. Appropriately called *Video Pinball,* it's designed by Ed Logg, and while not a mechanical game like all of Atari's other pinball machines, it was a fun, challenging new twist to an old format. Unfortunately, Nolan Bushnell did not have a very favorable opinion about the *Video Pinball* arcade game introduction. In his January 1979 final letter to Manny Gerard where he expressed his belief that the Pinball Division should be shut down, he also voiced his discontent about *Video Pinball's* introduction.

Over the years, hope would continue to surface from time to time that the Pinball Division might be resurrected. In 1983, there was indeed one last attempt at a pinball machine when a 3rd generation pinball prototype is built and fully decked out with graphics, back glass and playfield. The pinball game is called *4x4* and was designed by Milt Loper, with the back glass graphics done by the same artist that did the graphics for the *Super Bug* arcade cabinet. It has a clever artwork element on the sides of the cabinet; knobby, off-road tires are brought into Atari's art department, where they are rolled through paint poured onto a tarp. The tires are then carefully picked up and rolled across the sides of the pinball cabinet, leaving a pattern of tire tracks across them. The tracks end here though, as this is as far as the resurrection of pinball would go at Atari.

Review In Images

Balls of Steel

The next several pages consist of a gallery of some of the absolutely gorgeous back glasses on Atari pinball machines and their playfields. Back glasses being the colorful area directly across from the player's face that usually includes scoring and ball number info, and playfields being the area the ball actually moves around in. Below is the standard back glass used on all Atari pinballs to hide their true identity while they were out in local arcades for field testing.

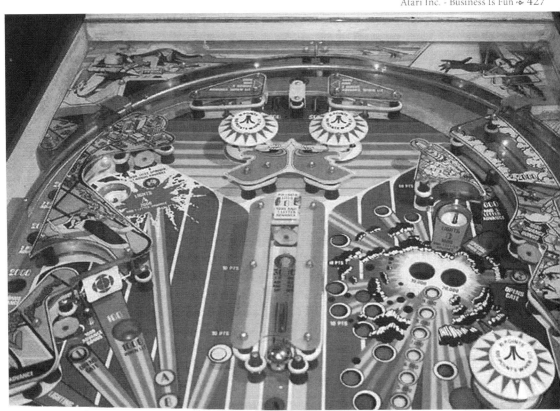

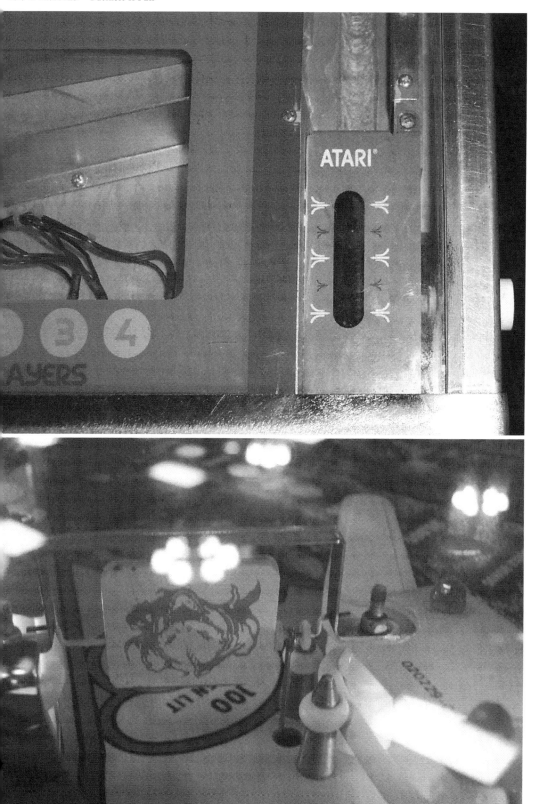

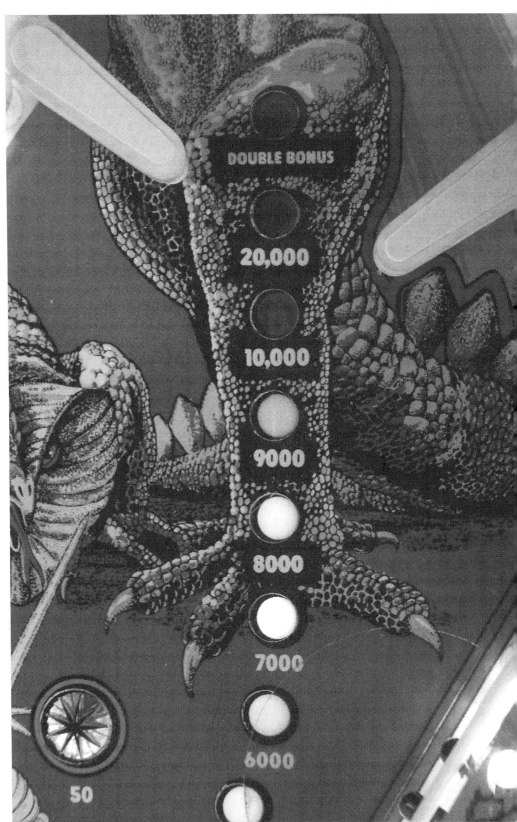

PINBALL
INTRODUCTION

A seminar on the theory of operation, including special test features of Atari's new solid state pinball games

JANUARY 17 AND 18, 1977

8:30am–4:30pm

SANTA CLARA MARRIOTT HOTEL

GREAT AMERICA PARKWAY · SANTA CLARA, CA

- Accommodations will be available for seminar attendees at the Santa Clara Marriott Hotel at $25.00 single, $32.00 double occupancy.

- Lunch on both session days will be provided by Atari.

- Limousine service from the San Jose Airport is provided by the Marriott Hotel.

- Your reservations must be made no later than January 12, 1977. For fastest action call our toll-free number: **800 538-6892**.

- The seminar will be open to distributors only.

CLIP & MAIL

RESERVATION FORM

Please complete and return no later than January 12, 1977 to:
Mr. Don Smith, Manager Customer Service
Atari Inc., 2175 Martin Avenue, Santa Clara, CA 95050

Name_____   Company_____

Address_____

City_____   State_____   Zip_____

Telephone_____

☐ How many persons will be attending.

ATARI®
Innovative
leisure

77 Atari Inc.

An invitation to introduce dealers to Atari's new pinball *Atarians* (released only two months before) and the new solid state technology behind it.

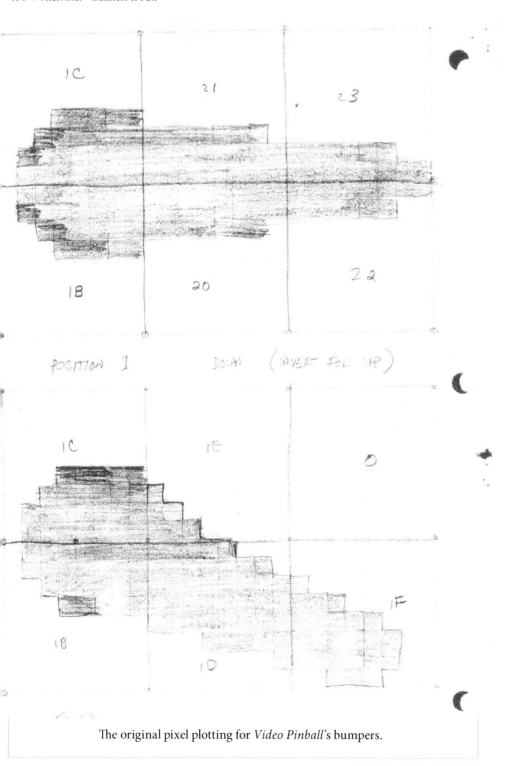

The original pixel plotting for *Video Pinball*'s bumpers.

- World's first video attraction to simulate an actual pinball game.
- 1 to 4 players
- Compact cabinet size
- 3-D blacklight "Disco" playfield combined with video scoring objects and features
- Pinball rules and scoring
- "Nudge" feature
- "Extra Ball", "Specials", via replay levels
- 3 or 5 ball
- Extended play
- 4 languages
- Famous Atari pinball sound effects

ATARI®
A Warner Communications Company

©Atari Inc., 1979

The unreleased prototype for the followup to *Video Pinball*, *Solar War*. Originally to be called *Superman*. It was re-themed after the license fell through.

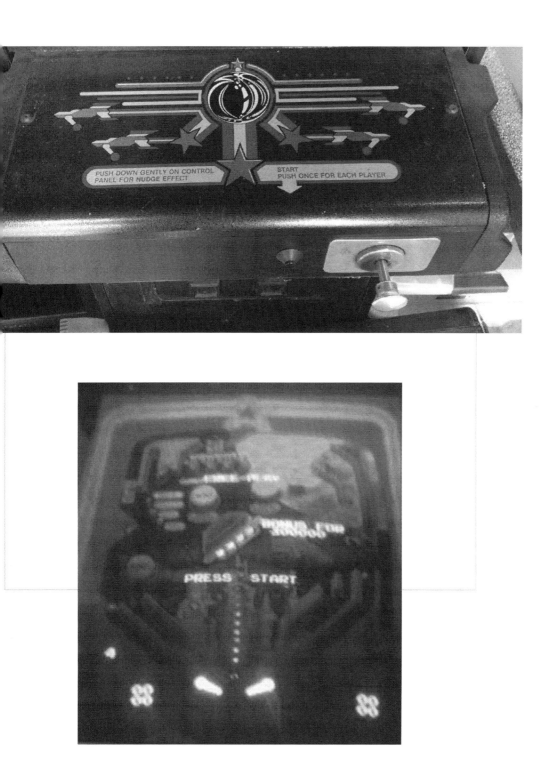

The *Neutron Star* pinball prototype.

Technical Report:

ATARI'S ENTRY INTO

HOME COMPUTERS

Giving Stella Some Character

Author's note: This 'technical report' describes the genesis of Atari's home computers - a story that has never been told fully or in great detail until now. Written with a mix of timeline, event listings and storytelling where appropriate, this chapter may come off to some as just dry and boring facts, figures and dates. However, to truly detail how Atari's home computers came to fruition, we believe everything needs to be recounted - including all the gory technical details. Fair warning for those who aren't technically inclined!

W hile the history surrounding the creation of 'Stella' (the Atari VCS game console) is fairly well known, the genesis of Atari's home computers is not. Rumors and stories have sprung up over the years in leiu of the truth, including a colorful story about Atari wanting to build an 'Apple Killer.' Other stories, such as starting from the building of a next generation game machine ala the 5200 only to be 'frozen' and have its chipset taken for use in a newly designated computer division, are equally false.

It all started right after the VCS had been wrapped up and completed. Joe Decuir and Jay Miner had taken what was initially a proof-of-concept design built by Ron Milner from Atari Grass Valley and turned it into a fully realized programmable microprocessor-based game system. Not one's to rest on their laurels, the two lost no time moving to their next project, beginning an initial engineering discussion on February 17, 1977 for a project called 'New Machines.' Jay and Joe are looking at adding a character chip to TIA, the VCS's graphics chip. The feasibility of ideas like including 3-level screen mapping, displaying numbers and characters and scanning a keyboard are also all discussed. Larry Kaplan also contributed ideas, such as turning off objects and having a 2-level screen map. What this all means is the Stella engineering team is attempting to add character set capabilities to Stella, and at the same time, lay the groundwork for a more advanced gaming system.

While the VCS is being introduced at the Summer CES, meanwhile back in Sunnyvale inside of 155 Moffett Park, another product is being put onto a drawing board. The concept is called 'Stella A/N' or Stella Alpha Numeric. It's an initial design concept that would give the Stella 'TIA' Television Interface Adapter its first attempt at character generation. Using a new chip spec in the design called ANTIC ('Alpha Numeric Television Interface Chip'), this concept would be the benchmark in attempting to design a more capable system, and it's followed shortly after with another effort simply called "Home Computer." With this direction, Joe and Jay are taking their original Stella design and morphing it into a home computer. More comprehensive than Stella, it contains a 6502, 6532, the TIA and a 6820 PIA for keyboard interfacing. Additional logic is added for video output, character addressing and keyboard strobes.

So, why the sudden interest and work on new designs and looking to expand the capabilities of the TIA chip in the Stella design? It was believed by the Stella team that the VCS would have a lifespan of about three years, and while the VCS was being unveiled to the public, they felt they needed to begin work on a follow-up system immediately. Of the features decided from the onset for this new system, it would have a character set as mentioned and would also have a keyboard and use of peripherals such as disk drives and printers.

Meanwhile Steve Jobs is causing a little 'employee-related' problem at Atari, which needs an immediate resolution. Atari's Consumer Division is literally staffed with engineers and manufacturing people from other tech companies in the area, including National Semiconductor, thanks to Al Alcorn. Potential employees wanted to know exactly what was in it for them 'over and above the salary' if they came to work for you. At this point in time, Atari's 'perks' (as they are called) are head and shoulders above everyone else's. As a result, Atari was able to acquire a bench of incredible engineers, including one guy by the name of Ron Holt. However, this growing stable also made Atari a poaching target for other firms as well. They noticed small numbers at first, but as time passed, Al and Ron were literally watching week-by-week as people left Atari. As it turns out, they discover that Steve Jobs has been luring them over to Apple (who at this time was only blocks away). This prompts a furious phone call from Al to Steve, telling him to stop. Steve of course tells him, "Yes, no problem, won't happen again," but it wasn't long before Steve would go and steal another employee from Al's group. Infuriated even more, Al calls over to Steve again, only this time Steve is no longer picking up or returning Al's calls. Most likely thinking there's not a darn thing Al can really do about it and besides, Apple needs this talent more than Atari does, he's employing the old 'busy executive' tactic. Most in the situation would run away or risk exposing themselves to the famous Steve Jobs wrath. Only this is Al Alcorn we're talking about here, one of Steve's ex-bosses and an ex-Football player size individual that could squash the mouthy Steve like an accordian (if it were in his nature). Employing an even more imposing sharp mind, Al calls Jobs at Apple and tells his secretary, "This is Al from the FCC and I need to speak with Mr. Jobs immediately." Steve picks up, and then realizes it's Al from Atari. Once again, Steve is given a stern warning about pilfering Atari engineers, and once again, he swears he won't do it... but once again, within days Steve has stolen yet another Atari employee.

That's it! Al Alcorn is livid and has had it! Steve Jobs needs to be put in his place, and he's not going to get the best of him Al decides. In response, he comes up with a brilliant idea to send Steve a severely pointed and very personal warning via an indirect but clever route. He knows Apple is still quite small and that Atari can outsource them and out manufacture them, essentially putting Apple out of business if they wanted to. Al makes a call over to coin-op and tells them to start working on building a clone of the Apple II computer, stating "We're going to be taking over Apple's market share of personal computers." Coin-op has absolutely no interest in doing this, and Al had no real desire to do it either, but still pushes them to proceed. Why? The goal isn't the computer: "If there is one secret we had at Atari, it is this – we can't keep a secret," recalls Al Alcorn. This was just what Al was betting on; that the secret project would be leaked and that word would quickly spread to Apple that Atari is about to go into business making clones of Apple's computer systems.

Two weeks after Al put Coin-op on the project, he gets a call from Steve, who simply states "Message received." Steve finally understood that Al was dead serious about this, thus ending once and for all Steve Jobs's pilfering of Atari's engineering and manufacturing staff. With the fake Apple clone project quickly cancelled, all focus of computer development at Atari now goes back to producing their own original design.

Throughout the next several months, ideas are drafted to attempt to interface keypad and keyboard matrixes into the Stella, resulting in an unintended product for the VCS: the Atari CX-50 keypad controllers. Released in June 1978, you may be asking yourself "What does a game console made to play *Tank* and *Breakout* need keypad controllers for?" Well, the pads open up the system for games that traditionally require more keypad type input - games like *Concentration* and *Memory Match*. Then there's the curious release of BASIC Programming for the VCS that also uses the keypad. A 'stopgap' of sorts for those wanting to learn programming but not ready to by a full computer, it features a scaled down custom version of the BASIC programming language. The only problem is, it's so different than actual BASIC that any programming skills learned are superficial at best. Not to mention you can't actually save your programs, they're lost once the VCS is shut off!

Focusing back on the task of building a more capable system, other CPU chips are evaluated to interface with the Stella 'TIA' chip, including the 6510 and the MOS 'VIC' chip. July briefly sees the dawn of Project 'ADDA' which utilizes a 6502, PIA, 512 bytes of memory, and a 'VIC' chip to produce a system that could display 36 characters wide by 14 lines down of character display on a screen.

Texas Instruments salesman Tom Addie visits Atari's Consumer Engineering group in July as well, to deliver some datasheets on the TI9900 series microprocessors for review. Upon examining TI's 9940 microprocessor, while it appears to be a good controller, it has poor memory expansion. Additionally, the 'design goal' of the computer project is to have a processor cost of approximately $10 dollars, which the TI9940 can't meet.

The computer project get's its official name, 'Colleen,' on August 9th and sees what is termed as the 'Major Concept Consensus' for the basic box with CPU. The specifications for the Colleen project are outlined as follows: 4K of RAM memory, tape drive, ANTIC chip, a revision of the TIA called 'STELLA X', RS488 and/or RS323 interfacing and game controller ports. The planned basic system would be expandable, and have plug-in sockets for RAM, BASIC language, 'super games,' phone controller/modem and an educational package.

The chip concepts for Colleen have the following assignments planned out:

- POKEY has Pots, Keys and Serial Bus.
- PIA handles tape recorder, game controllers and panel switches
- ANTIC handles TV non-moving video display
- TIA2 handles Object Generation and Audio

Joe Decuir and Steve Mayer also spec out another component to the computer design which will be in two parts, with a second box that the basic system will connect to - an expansion box. The expansion box will have a bus expander, large power supply, one or two floppy disk drives, a RS488 communications bus, a resident Disk Operating System ROM and 8K of RAM. On August 22nd, the computer concept base line of Tape device, ANTIC and TIA, PIA and POKEY, CPU chip, 4 to 8K of OS ROM and 4K of RAM is accepted by all of the major engineers and marketing including Jay Miner, John Ellis, Al Alcorn, Bob Brown and John Vurich.

While the project is a follow-up to the Stella console, it's noted during an August 22nd meeting that, "STELLA compatibility is not required." However, for the new system, Steve Mayer wants to do compatibility if it's cheap and if the total number of different components can be kept to a minimum. So the question begs to be asked: At what point is the decision made not to build a game system but to build a computer instead? Well, it turns out that from the very beginning of 'Project Colleen' that there would be two versions of 'Colleen' - one being the basic computer and the other for 'serious work.'

The basic computer is described as an 'entertainment machine,' able to play video games, use Dorsett educational tapes, communicate over the phone, have house control, play music, do simple programming and be used as a smart terminal. The 'serious work' machine, in turn, will have all of expansion box features from the August 9th spec; however it will take those features and incorporate them into a single package. The plan is for it to support 'serious' programming, sophisticated peripherals, compilers, small business word processing and scientific number crunching.

This decision to lay out two paths forward leads to the eventual creation of the Atari 400 (the entertainment machine, codenamed 'Project Candy') and the Atari 800 (the seious work machine, codenamed 'Colleen'). Both designs are planned to be able to use the same cartridges and peripheral devices. However, because it's mainly for playing games, 'Candy' is to be a simpler design with more limited capabilities, while 'Colleen' is the more evolved system with outputs for adding a computer monitor and full keyboard. Likewise Colleen has the ability to utilize larger and more complex cartridges, as well as having an expansion bay for memory and operating system modules.

Joe Decuir flies up to Grass Valley R&D August 12th to work on the ANTIC breadboard design. He is able to get it to display 40 characters per line in black and white on the screen and creates a test pattern through an RF modulator to a Sears color television set. By August 16th he's able to add color output to the ANTIC breadboard, and soon after that ANTIC now has three communication lines between it and what it being termed 'TIA2.' Meanwhile, Joe also examines a borrowed Radio Shack computer - the newly released TRS-80 Model 1 - to see what physical port designs it has as well as its features and capabilities.

Jay Miner receives a report in September on the latest specifications for 'Colleen,' which have now been revised to be 4K of RAM and a ROM cartridge port that can be 8K or larger. The CPU is currently 6502 but the 6509 is also being considered. The design also includes POKEY and keyboard, VIA and serial expansion, a 64K resident ROM, no built-in cassette drive, ANTIC and TIA, two cassette drive jacks with motor start/stop and automatic rewind, light pen capability, audio and digital tape loading. The specifications are becoming more and more familiar to what will later become the final design of the Atari 410 tape cassette drive and SIO interface.

With regards to most of the ANTIC address generation, by the end of October 1977 the ANTIC-TIA2 object collision and priority displays have been defined as well as the pinouts for the TIA2. Also during this month, the concept for a Development System for Colleen is being fleshed out. That's followed up by more work on the expansion bus on October 25th, and defining the pinouts for the ANTIC and POKEY on the 26th.

Shortly thereafter, the interfacing of POKEY to a keyboard begins, and the decision is made to use two 4051 MUXes to interface a keyboard matrix into POKEY. The layout for the keyboard calls for several side keys – HALT, SS, TRACE, GO, RESET, and Joe Decuir makes a simple but very descriptive note for John Ellis regarding the keyboard: "Keyboard must be sexy."

At some point the decision is made to put the 'smarts' of the the casesette drive directly into the device itself instead of in the computer, creating a template for the computer using 'smart devices,' an important step towards making the computers and their peripherals very easy to use. For compatibility with Atari's various controllers for the VCS, the controller ports on the computer system are planned to be the "same as Stella."

On November 29th, a meeting on the Collen project is held at Pajaro Dunes, a beachfront vacation resort area on the Pacific Coast. With condos, resorts and a Conference Center for meetings, Pajaro Dunes (not far from Silicon Valley), as well as the retreat in Pebble Beach, would be two of the places where Atari is holding design and idea sessions with engineers from across its divisions. Many of the sessions were strict, all business meetings and design sessions, while others could only be best described as Atari's version of 'Engineers gone wild.'

Coin-op seemed to be exceptionally mischievous in its pranks. After one particular concept and design meeting at Pajaro Dunes, Coin-op's national sales manager Frank Ballouz return to his hotel room, only to find it completely empty - all of the furniture, TV, everything had been stacked outside on the balcony. Another time, a large ice sculpture had been created for an Atari employee dinner and thanks to the devilish antics of some Atari pranksters, the ice sculpture became a 'backseat passenger' in Frank's sports car. A fact Frank discovered when the parking attendant brought the car around to the front of the resort for him.

But pranks and mischief aside, the specification of the home computer system is finalized at this Pajaro Dunes meeting, and they come away with two proposed final designs. Well actually there are three, but while the third will be designed, it will not be introduced with the other systems. This is when the basic 'game computer' design gets its official name – 'Candy,' with its defined functionality as a "game player, non expandable." It's not even going to have a keyboard or peripheral interface - only a cartridge port that's compatible with Colleen. Engineering log notes also state: "Will use all same IC chips." The 'Colleen' will have two cartridge ports, a peripheral interface, a keyboard and expansion capabilities. The third design, called 'Elizabeth,' will be the Colleen design but with a built-in 13 inch color monitor. Discussions on the VCS come up and the team expects that Atari will continue to build VCS's into 1979.

There are two things that concern the team at this point though with the three proposed designs: First, there will be FCC problems with the Colleen due to its expansion box. Second, there will be Underwriter Labs (UL) problems with the Elizabeth as well because of the integration of the monitor. To avoid the complications at launch, John Vurich suggests the addition of a serial peripheral port to 'Candy,' and that 'Colleen' should be removed from the product line-up, being replaced altogether with Elizabeth.

Later that same day, the discussion moves to Synertec and CPUs - specifically the 6502, M6502 and S6509 - and t heir their compatibility. That's further followed by the question of "What is really in the 'Candy' for I/O?" Al Alcorn, Steve Mayer and John Vurich see two answers: one is to make Candy's cartridge I/O compatible with Stella if it doesn't cost extra. The second, an optional keyboard and cassette interface accessed through the front four controller ports could be implemented.

By the time December 9th comes along, the LSI (Large Scale Integrated) parts designations and pinouts have been formally named and refined, although the CPU is still a toss-up between the 6509 and M6502. ANTIC is finalized and TIA2 is now formally called CTIA, while POKEY and the PIA have also been finalized and it's been decided all these chips will be 40-pin IC chips. Mike Albaugh also discusses the ANTIC with Jay Miner and convinces him that the Display List Counter design (part of the system's advanced graphics method where Display List code runs and Antic and tells the computer how to display various graphical info) should be loaded by the CPU. Mike also discusses the Serial I/O port with Joe Decuir, centering on various "Baud Rates" of the Serial I/O and clock synchronizing issues that may occur.

ANTIC chip design continues into January of 1978 and the DMA (Dynamic Memory Access, a way of sharing the computer's memory with various peripherals) timing is worked out. Things are really begining to move into high gear now as a more formal team is defined and the home computers begin to go from specifications and designs to physical reality.

Jay Miner is now appointed the Chief Engineer of the home computer project, while Joe Decuir continues work on ANTIC and brings in Francois Michel to do the logic design. George McLeod is working on the CTIA and the new spec calls for supporting eight moving objects on screen, handling collisions and video generation. Doug Neubauer focuses on the POKEY chip, which is being used for potentiometer scanning, keyboard scanning, the Serial I/O functions and audio. Scott Shiffman is focusing on how the whole system works together, which includes the CPU, the custom IC chips, PIA, RAM and ROM, buffers, decoding interconnects and other areas. Applications programmer Alan Miller also joins the team to work on RAM selection, serial protocol, as well as software/hardware communications. The final member on the project is Howard Bornstein who works on the System Monitor/Resident Firmware for the design.

Yet another 'Definition Meeting' is held for Candy/Colleen in January 1978 and Al Alcorn, John Ellis, Jay Miner, John Vurich, Joe Decuir, Wade Tuma, Niles Strohl and several others join in. Memory is still being defined as 4K RAM for both Candy and Colleen, and a decision needs to be made on the type of memory as upper management is putting pressure on a decision so that pricing can be hammered out. An Audio track and interfacing system also needs to be incorporated into the design that is 'cheap' and must include motor on/off control. Current design differences between Candy and Colleen are now as follows:

COLLEEN	CANDY
Chipset	Chipset
4K RAM	4K RAM
2 Cartridges	1 Cartridge
3 Panel Switches	3 Panel Switches
Built-in Keyboard	Plug-in keyboard on ports 3 & 4
4 Joystick ports	4 Joystick ports
Audio Cassette Interface	Audio Cassette Interface
Serial Interface	No Serial Interface
Bus Expansion	No Bus Expansion

Another meeting is held up in Grass Valley R&D later that month to discuss the main storage methods available to home computers at the time: cassette tape and floppy drives. Larry Emmons, Steve Mayer, Gene Wise, Ron Milner, John Ellis, Jay Miner, Joe Decuir, Niles Strohl, Wade Tuma and Dave Estes are all in attendance. John Ellis is looking at low cost audio cassette drive systems with pause control, stereo and compatibility with Dorsett tapes. Larry Emmons conunters with the common problems with cassette tapes and various issues with the 2-track and 4-track heads used in them. Niles wants to discuss using the cassette system as a transmitter/receiver type system, possibly for a simple MODEM device. The discussion also includes the separating of digital and analog signals, questions about software protection, and whether Atari should design and build its own disk drive and printer mechanisms. John Vurich recommends using OEM parts from other companies for the short term and to do in-house designs at some point down the line.

A further meeting on Candy/Colleen is conducted on January 31 to tighten the design specifications, with the result that Candy is to be an 'all-game playing machine' and its cartridges are to be compatible with Colleen. Discussion centers around the still needed keyboard at this point, with the questions "Does Candy have a keyboard on a separate connector or a built-in keyboard?" If it's the former, should Candy's peripherals then include a low cost keyboard, cassette drive and a modem with possibly an acoustic coupler type design? Another discussion focuses on whether Candy and Colleen cartridges might be different sizes. Some old designs and specifications make a return visit in the meeting as well, one of which is the "Elizabeth" design and whether it should continue with its planned built-in color monitor or possibly moving the color monitor into a separate cabinet. In summation of the further points of discussion:

- The Expansion bus for Colleen is also discussed and whether it should be behind a knock-out panel that a user would remove.

- Disk drives are reviewed and the idea is to add slow versions to work only over the Serial I/O Port.

- The B&W/Color switch is to be removed from all designs.

- There is talk of one connection port with all connections put together.

- Connectors for controllers are still specified as four controller ports.

- Audio is being considered to come out as its own separate port.

- Power connection is also discussed.

- The video connector is discussed ("should the systems have monitor and TV output?").

- A light pen peripheral and an X/Y potentiometer controller are being reviewed.

- "Slow" peripherals have been listed as cassette drive, slow floppy, printer, modem, acoustic coupler modem and possible AC Controller for home control.

- The Serial I/O (SIO) and Printer Ports are also discussed.

The keyboard design is also becoming a problem it seems. Having separate cursor control, combined with the rising cost of parts (now up to $19 dollars), is posing a serious problem in the design that needs to be solved.

The new 6500 series processor is a talking point in February, and for the next two days the focus is on the possibility of an Atari designed version of the 6509. By February 4th though, the work turns back to the ANTIC and revisions to the address tables, registers and vertical control logic. ANTIC/CTIA codes are also revised by the 8th, and Francois suggests some ideas for missiles and objects (Atari's name for different types of sprites) as well as instruction sets.

March 1978 fast approaches and a sidebar conversation ensues with Bob Brown about an idea of using a 6502/6509 as well as the POKEY and PIA chips from the Colleen specs to design a "Music Synthesizer." A simple layout and block diagram is put together of a design.

Later that month it's now time to head back up to Grass Valley and have a meeting on the development system for Colleen. Grass Valley will use a Cromemco Z-2 S-100 bus computer fitted with a yet to be supplied 6502 board, Memory, traceboard and interfacing from Jay Miner's group. (*Writer's note*: Cromemco was a computer manufacturing company founded by Stanford University grads Harry Garland and Roger Melen. Launched in 1974 and located in Mountain View, California, Cromemco specialized in Z-80 CPU based S-100 Bus computer systems). The Atari engineers choose the new Z-2 model because it no longer needed the complicated switchboard panel similar to the IMSAI 8080 computers. The Z-2's also include a parallel port added to the serial port already built in.

By the end of the month, finally the physical testing of breadboards for the computer system, chips and overall design are coming together. The computer team is now also examining the MC6809 chip from Motorola for the computer's main microprocessor. Peripheral designs also continue to be worked on, as well as 6502 sourcing from Synertek.

April 1978 arrives and the Colleen development systems based around the Cromemco Z-2 boxes (with special development boards built by Grass Valley) are now moving to become Chip development systems with microprocessor cards, ANTIC cards, CTIA cards, PIA cards and POKEY cards. Once the chips are working, the next stage is to connect the Z-2 boxes through the test connector or microprocessor connector of a real Colleen motherboard, at which point the microprocessor to breadboard interconnects can now be defined.

In the meantime, Joe Decuir meets with Mel Snyder from Zilog regarding a new microprocessor coming out called the Z8, as well as another chip called the Z8000. During this meeting, Joe also finds out that a hard disk system is in development. Possible future plans and products are considered, but for right now, Colleen needed to become physically functional - taken off of the design sheets and breadboards and moved to its next stage. A meeting occurs with the circuit designers regarding the electrical specifications, as well as discussion of loads, data bus and channel lengths, as are the output levels.

In May 1978, Liza Loop (a consultant specializing on the various uses of computers in education) is brought in to present talking points on topics such as 'Learning in Western Culture,' 'Home and Family,' 'School Curriculum,' 'Vocational Training' and 'Recreation.' It's obvious to Liza that there is a huge opportunity in the educational arena with Atari, and by using Atari technology, she sees a way to reform the existing educational system. She sees the Atari home computers as a viable tool which could bypass the school and the traditional education process and bring real learning directly into the home. Up to and including this point in time, the only computer delivery systems for education had consisted of MITS Logo, Xerox's Smalltalk, Mitre's two-way cable learning system, Control Data Corporations 'PLATO' learning network, the National Library of Medicines CAI demo lab and the PILOT learning language.

It quickly becomes obvious that education is going to be a strong focus for these new computer systems, so much so that one of the very first application cartridges designed and sold for use on Atari's computers will be the 'Educational Master Cartridge.' Used together with the specially designed cassette drive system peripheral being proposed, it will allow the use of a vast library of educational and vocational training courses through the new Atari computers. Atari would continue to follow this path with its Conversation Languages series, making available Italian,

German, French and Spanish courses through its 'Type & Talk' educational series. Touch Typing, Jugglers Rainbow as well as States & Capitals would all be available through Atari's educational series of software offerings. Liza will also write the user manuals for the completed computers, which is a rather challenging task considering these computers hadn't even been built yet, nor was there an operating system specification or a user interface for the computers.

Back in the LSI design lab, changes are needed to ANTIC, including altering the "vblank" non-maskable interrupt to being maskable and the csync pin being deleted and making the NMI external for the reset button. The Address Map for Candy/Colleen has also been updated. Another follow-up computer design for 1979 is also being examined, based the Motorola 6800 demo design. However, focus is quickly redirected back to the more pressing matters at hand; specifically, the bus interface on the Colleen development system designs.

After spending most of June 1978 debugging the first development system, the schematics for Colleen, the CPU board and RAM board are done, and the following status for the project is reported:

- Missing are the schematics for Candy, the cartridge boards and other boards.

- Timing diagrams for RAM, clocks and system timing are complete.

- Specifications of all chip pinouts, I/O ports and Colleen manual are complete.

- Drawings for the keyboard layout are also completed.

- Mechanical drawings for Colleen's case design have been underway for over two months and refinements and revisions are being made.

- Some additional changes have been added including a System Reset button, test connectors on both Colleen and on Candy.

- Colleen's overall design and look is nearly completed by the end of April

1978. Candy's ability for RAM expansion and Serial Port are still being debated.

Colleen's aluminum shielding, integrated housing and the final designs to the case are completed by May 1978. From June through August, the finishing touches to the function keys, keyboard assembly and the side ports panels are then completed. At this point, Colleen's physical design is finished, with only minor revisions still needed. Candy, on the other hand, still does not have a final case design. The issue of interfacing and a decision on whether to include a keyboard or offer it as a plug-in option are still being reviewed and debated, causing the delay. The November 30 schematic drawing of Candy still shows the Pokey chip interfacing its keyboard lines out through the front controller ports 3 and 4.

Candy and Colleen get their product name designations in November of 1978, and are now officially named the Atari 400 and Atari 800 PCS (Personal Computer System). On December 6th, The New York Times runs an article on Home Computers and includes the announcement that Atari will be entering the home computer market very soon.

Waiting to the last minute, in early 1979 the decision on just what Candy is going to be is finally made: Candy will not be a 'game player only' machine, but will be a low-end computer system with a built-in keyboard. However, since it is intended to be more of an introduction computer for younger children, it will include a unique keyboard design with a spill proof membrane. Candy will also have an SIO port after all. The eleventh hour decision means that when Atari introduces the 400 and 800 'Personal Computer Systems' at the January 1979 Consumer Electronics show in Las Vegas, a mock-up of the Atari 400 (model C-7000) has to be shown in comparison to the finished 800. Complimenting the unveiling are the Atari 410 cassette drive, the Atari 810 disk drive and the Atari 820 40-column printer. Atari also showcases a large assortment of educational software. Both systems are now to come with 8K of memory, with the Atari 800 capable of being expandable with far more RAM (sold separately) when it was available for release.

The prototype case design releases are completed in March, but the decision to include a built-in keyboard on Candy versus offering a keyboard add-on had serious ramifications for Atari's position in the console marketplace. The whole original point and concept of the 'Colleen' project was to provide a more capable game player system, which meant this system was supposed to be the eventual replacement for the VCS. However, now that the game player system design had been moved to a personal computer, it was no longer in contention to replace the VCS and keep Atari's consumer gaming products well ahead of the competition. With that, the first step towards the demise of Atari's domination in the console market had been taken.

Computers For People

T
he Atari 400 had one of the most uniquely shaped computer case designs ever done, never replicated in its functional artistry by any other competitor. Clean, attractive, space age, and non-intimidating in its appearance, it's also easily understood by even the most novice of users. VCS case co-designer Doug Hardy recalls, "I designed the case for Candy. I think I have the patent for it too. The design was started right after the VCS went into full production. Candy was meant as the eventual replacement for the VCS." Discussing the unique, small-wedged shape design of the Atari 400, and its keyboard, Doug continues: "Candy was meant to be a laptop computer. This is before LCD displays and such. What I mean is, it was designed to be able to sit in your lap, but connected to a TV. It was a game console, but could use the same cartridges as the other system and it had a keyboard - I also designed the spill proof membrane keyboard." While the membrane keyboard was perhaps best viewed as a touch typist's nightmare, it's quite capable and functional for entering key commands and doing basic, simple typing - an important aspect. "We wanted the systems to be able to play complex games, for example - *Star Raiders*, so having some kind of a keyboard was always a feature in the Colleen and Candy designs," explains Joe Decuir.

Most of the major mechanical design work for the two new computer systems was completed in March and April of 1979. Kevin McKinsey was the Industrial Designer of the Atari 800 and Hugh Lee turned Kevin's design into a functional product case. Kevin McKinsey explains the whole background behind the look of the Atari 800: "I wanted something that would look like a futuristic typewriter. A design that was easily recognizable and approachable by ordinary people who already knew what typewriters were."

The Atari 400 and 800 home computers truly lived up to the marketing slogans "Computers for People" as well as "Computers Designed for the Home." No easy task, it was accomplished because Atari's engineers and designers implemented several subtle, yet key features into the designs of their two new computers which would separate them from anything else offered by any other product line or company at the time. First and foremost is the "SIO" or Serial I/O port, a trapezoidal 'Peripheral' port that's Atari's answer to easily hooking in peripherals. An amazing accomplishment for Atari in conquering its entry into computers, the ports are large and so are the device plugs for the 'SIO Cables;' they can only plug in one way so there's no mistakes or confusion. Many people were nervous enough and even fearful of technology, and for many consumers the bottom line was computers scared a LOT them That wasn't an issue for younger children though, who were instantly drawn to computers - they simply had no preconceived notions or fears. No linking of computers to doomsday movies or the Vietnam war machine like the older generations. To kids, and specifically this first generation of kids growing up with personal computers, technology was exciting and fun! But for the adults, this 'SIO' port stripped away the huge hurdle of the fear of plugging something in the wrong way. Visions of exploding electronics and being electrocuted were put at ease. Furthermore, the SIO is a universal device port, allowing all external devices to daisy-chain one into the other until they reached the computer. Everything from cassette drives, to disk drives, to other peripherals that were slowly coming on to the market. Some printers plugged directly in as well while others would plug into a later device called the Atari 850, allowing more industry-standard printers and modems to interface through the SIO.

It was in sharp contrast to competitors and their never ending power consuming messy expansion, most eloquently summed up by Al Alcorn after he returned from a computer conference and stated "I have seen the future, and it is strangled in extension cords!" With Atari's SIO, disk drives, modems, printers, serial devices and parallel devices: all of these devices plugged into a single universal port, the concept of which may sound very familiar. In fact, the SIO port acts a lot like today's USB (Universal Serial Bus) ports. Well, it even turns out, the USB and SIO ports have a lot more in common than anyone might imagine: Joe Decuir helped with some of the work on the SIO design and today Joe holds several Patents in the design of the USB port as well. Essentially, the SIO port is the Great Grandfather to today's USB ports. Seems Atari was way ahead of its time back with the 1979 introduction of the Atari 400 and 800 home computers.

However, the SIO port is also a major drawback to the Atari computer design for one specific reason: most devices that connect to the computers through their SIO ports require that they be intelligent devices. This meant that most had to have their own CPU chip onboard, firmware code to run the device and support the communication protocol across the SIO bus. For Atari and third party manufacturers, this meant the line of peripherals had to be far more expensive than offered by competing computer companies. When Atari released the 810 disk drive for the home computers, they cost $599 each. Meanwhile an Apple disk drive II with a controller cost nearly as much, however purchasing a second disk drive II would cost $100 less because the buyer didn't need another controller card. Each Atari disk drive has its controller built into it, so whether you bought one or four, they still cost the same. This pricing issue wasn't so much a problem in the beginning as most competitors' products were initially expensive. However, when their pricing quickly dropped, Atari's pricing couldn't follow.

As mentioned, the SIO wasn't the only advanced and innovative feature of the Atari home computers though. Looking at the Atari 800 specifically and its overall design, what truly set's it apart from the competition is the way it separates the owner from the electronics - creating a true 'computer appliance.' Other computers, such as the Apple II, the TRS-80 Model 1 and the S-100 bus computers all expose their owner operators directly in contact with their electronic innards to expand and upgrade. Sensitive IC chips prone to damage from static electricity, exposed edge connectors and the even more dangerous exposed power supplies (some with lethal levels of voltage) are common hazards at the time to those wishing to brave in to the new frontier of home computing.

But the Atari 800 completely separates the owner from such exposure by the convenience of clean, simple upgrades and add-ons that are so easy to implement. The first safety and electronics separation feature of the Atari 800 is its cartridge access door. Built into the door is an interlock switch so that when the cover is lifted, power to the computer is shut off. Protecting the computer from damage caused by someone ripping out a cartridge while still powered on, the user is also protected from accidental shock in the process. The cartridge ports themselves are also covered with a uniquely keyed cartridge guide so that the game or application cartridges could only be inserted one way. The Atari 800 expansion bay is so well crafted and designed, that even the most timid and technologically fearful computer owner would have no problem accessing and installing expansion modules. With the cartridge door open, there are two latches on either side of the inside of the cartridge door, the turning of which unlocks them and allows the top cover of the Atari

800 to be removed. On the Apple II computer, if you remove its top cover, you're greeted by the computer's power supply and motherboard. Not so on the Atari 800! In comparison, the Atari 800 presents the owner a safe, orderly and easyily accessible expansion bay. The Atari 800 has four expansion slots in total, with the front slot, closest to the keyboard, containing the Operating System module. The other slots are for Memory Modules, and each module is a fully encased unit with only the contact fingers at the bottom of each module partially exposed. Every module, whether it was the Operating System or Memory Module, has a visual overview on the side of all of the possible combinations of installed modules into the expansion bay. Purposefully or accidentally installing the wrong modules into the wrong slots would not damage them or the system – but doing so would simply cause the computer to not function until the modules were installed properly as visually shown. The entire design provides for an upgrade process not much different than plugging in RAM to today's desktop computers.

Not too long after the release of the Atari 800 computers, Service Bulletins were issued to service centers informing them that later releases of the Atari 800 would eliminate the expansion module enclosures for the Operating System and Memory modules (wrapping the PC boards within these cases caused overheating problems, computer lockups and component failures). Atari would also later offer the Atari 800 computers fully maxed out with 48K of memory, and the top cover latches of these were replaced with two screws and washers locking down the top cover from access. While the Operating System was an 'easy to swap out' module, other than the CX801 and CX801P Operating Systems, Atari never released any further Operating System modules, even though it did internally block out model #'s CX801 to CX809 for Operating System or 'Personality' modules as they were called (attempting to attribute a sense of personal interaction with the owner's computer, as if it had its own unique personality).

Though easy to use, the expansion area is limited to potential future Operating System upgrades and adding more memory, but not much else and the reason was due to several factors. Joe Decuir explains: "We wanted slots badly, just like the Apple, but Atari was very concerned about Radio Frequency issues and not passing FCC testing." One solution to keeping the Radio Frequency, or "RF" noise down is to encase both the Atari 400 and Atari 800 computers in a 2-millimeter thick aluminum chassis, reminiscent of the original launch VCS, which actually became integral parts of the computers case designs. Joe Decuir continues: "We had no external slot access. That and everything else went through the SIO bus port for devices. Apple got around all of these issues by not having an RF modulator built into their computers. If you wanted to use a television set, you had to buy an RF modulator from a third party company - they got around the FCC issue. We depended on staying on good terms with the FCC due to all of our consumer products needing FCC approval to connect to TV's, so were weren't about to try the same thing."

At one point, a possible solution came to Atari's doorstep in July 1977 in the form of a Texas Instruments components salesman. Joe Decuir recalls the story: "He walked in to try and sell us a cheap fiber optic cable with a transmitter molded on one end and a receiver molded on the other. The idea that I had was, if we build a computer which is optically isolated from the TV, then we can just put the bundled fiber receiver and RF transmitter into the FCC for approval, make a really quiet fiber-to-RF converter. We could then do whatever we want in our Atari computers, including having slots. I told this application to the TI sales guy whose eyes almost popped out." Joe Decuir explained the idea to his engineering manager Wade Tuma and Wade said, "No way. The FCC would never let us get away with that stunt." Meanwhile the salesman went back to Texas Instruments and told their engineering staff about the proposed Atari idea. Joe Decuir continues: "So the TI guy goes back and tells them my idea, and this included the team we didn't know about who were designing the new TI 99/4 Home PC." So TI goes to the FCC in 1979 with their new TI computer bundled with the fiber cabling, using the same idea Joe Decuir had proposed in thinking out loud to the TI salesman. Well, just as Wade Tuma had predicted, the FCC said "NO WAY" and failed them on their FCC testing. Now this was a bigger problem than just a computer company trying to get a new FCC product test passed.

The whole event turned into a big stink, because Texas Instrument's home Congressional District was represented by the then Speaker of the House, Jim Wright, a powerful man. Despite attempted pressure by him to get TI's fiber-to-RF design passed for its home computer, the FCC would not cave in. Upon hearing the news of the TI FCC fallout and now a major delay in their PC release, Wade Tuma was jubilant. He said, "Joe, you could not have sabotaged TI better if you had tried." As a positive result of this mess though, the FCC Class A and Class B specifications were born.

On May 9, 1979, Wade Tuma submitted the Atari 800 computer system for FCC testing and approval and on June 15th, John T. Robinson of the FCC sent Wade back an approval for a Class 1 TV Device (game), FCC Approval No. TV-639. The

Atari 800 is clear for manufacturing and sale.

Not content to stop with the creation of the 'Colleen' project, on June 8, 1979, Joe Decuir lays out a simple block diagram proposal for the 'Stops Out High Power Entertainment Computer.' A Z8000/68000-Class CPU powered system with two port memory segments, serial DMA channel, a disk channel for floppy and hard drives, audio channel and a video subsystem marked 'TIA3.' Unfortunately as we detailed, work on the next evolutionary stage in Atari's computers would not come to pass at this time. However, the spirit of this design did not die on the vine, and what 'appears' to be this very design would eventually find its way into reality through a project codenamed 'Lorraine' several years later. The project's chief designer is none other than Jay Miner, now at a company called Hi-Torro and joined not too long after that, by his old apprentice Joe Decuir. Their company, and their computer, would be better known as Amiga.

The Whole Kit, And Caboodle

I n June 1980, Atari is showcasing the Atari 400 and Atari 800 computers at the summer Consumer Electronics Show along with the Atari 410, 810 and 820 peripherals again and the new Atari 16K RAM module for the Atari 800. Atari is also showcasing a large assortment of 'Talk n Teach' educational and vocational learning series programs that work with the 'Educational Master System' ROM cartridge. Several games are also shown, as well as coding programs such as the BASIC and Assembly Language ROM programs.

The big question always looming over personal computers and people buying them is, "What can I do with a computer?" The general answer was always a standard response: "You can balance your checkbook, and it can play games too." At the time, the problem with computer systems was that they weren't considered what is referred to as, 'Turn Key;' That is to say they weren't just turn it on and start going. Today when you buy a computer, everything is pre-installed - from the needed hardware such as memory, storage and video, to the operating system and even applications. In these early days of the marketing and sale of computers, most are sold alone and in bare bones configurations of just installed memory, video and sound. The buyer would have to go out and then purchase a disk drive to read and store programs, and even then had to load a separate disk operating system to even use the disk drive. The same would go for printers: a printer would be purchased, then a printer interface was needed to connect the device to the computer, and then the buyer would need to buy software to use the printers for their applications, like word processing or for printing graphics.

For Atari, a solution to that problem came by way of its October 1980 hire, Roger H. Badertscher. Brought in as the president of the newly formed Home Computer Division (removing it from under the Consumer Electronics Division), he's someone from the outside with experience in the semiconductor industry. Roger came to Atari from Signetics Semiconductor where he was the vice president of their microprocessor manufacturing division, and one of his first initiatives is to implement a better way for people to buy useful, ready packaged kits for their home computers.

These innovative ready-to-go 'kits' allow buyers to choose the one that best meets their interests or needs. For example, if a buyer wants to be able to connect their computer to a telephone line and dial into an online service, such as the then popular CompuServe, or check their investment holdings through Dow Jones or The Source, they could purchase 'The Communicator' kit. This kit includes everything needed to allow the buyer to connect their Atari home computer to online services. All of the needed hardware, software and introduction account packets for online services are all right there in the box. Again, Atari had designed its products to be so simple that anyone could easily plug in the devices and be ready to go. No jumpers or board settings, cables or other scary items needed to be put inside of the computer to make it work. Just follow the easy directions that are included for getting online. How easy? Plugging the modem into the 850 interface and a cartridge aptly called 'Telelink I' into the cartridge slot, putting your phone's handset in the modem and hopping on to one of the free introductory accounts for CompuServe and other on-line services that were available at the time were included for consumers to try.

The 'The Communicator' kit also has an interesting tale to it. Before being incorporated into a 'kit,' Atari was preparing to show the new 850 Interface at the Summer CES (Consumer Electronics Show), however, marketing realized they had nothing written to demonstrate the 850's capabilities. So Scott Scheiman receives a panicked phone call from his manager explaining that Atari has this new hardware but nothing to actually demonstrate it. Scott Scheiman recalls: "So in four days I wrote a terminal program to talk to the Atari 850 interface and allow it to be able to command a modem connected to it. We demo'd it at the CES and I found out later that my terminal program would become 'Telelink 1' and would be packaged with the 850 Interface module in their Communicator kit and to also be sold separately."

Atari had now successfully tackled three separate fronts in the war for electronic dollars: the arcade arena, home gaming consoles and now, home computer systems. Utilizing top tier engineering, attractive and enticing casing designs, presentation and packaging, and combining it altogether into friendly, easy-to-use machines, Atari had created a triple threat - a diverse line of high tech products covering all areas of major entertainment and technology.

The Atari home computers caught the attention of yet another computer company, who was no stranger to building 'computing devices' and had been doing it since the company was first formed in the late 1880s. A result of three companies merging together, 'Tabulating Machine Company,' the 'International Time Recording Company' and finally, the 'Computing Scale Corporation,' together they incorporated in 1911 becoming the 'Computing Tabulating Recording (CTR) Corporation.' By 1914, CTR would hire Thomas J. Watson, Sr. from National Cash Register. Watson would become the founding inspiration for the corporation and instill the principles of the company. He would also create the company's slogan "Think." CTR, with its headquarters in New York, would see huge growth over the next ten years, including the establishment of manufacturing plants in Europe. Given that the company was growing into an international entity, Watson decided it needed a name to reflect that growth and in 1924 CTR was renamed the International Business Machines Corporation, or as it is better known by its abbreviation: 'IBM.'

IBM had become a leader in mainframe computing systems, thanks to the introduction of its most famous workhorse mainframes; the IBM System/360 in the 1960s. With that product IBM is now the biggest of the eight mainframe companies in existence, jokingly called 'Snow White' to the other smaller companies callled 'the seven dwarfs.' Looking to make an important expansion outside its comfort zone of mainframe computing systems, IBM is completely unsure of how to take advantage of this new and rapidly growing industry for personal computers. It simply went against everything IBM had ever done before, as all of its products were meant for small businesses, corporations and government offices, never to individual consumers. It was unheard of in IBM culture to have a computing system that was standalone, independent and for just one person. IBM had capitulated to its curiosity and attempted wading a few steps in to the consumer pool (sort of) with such efforts as the IBM System/23 minicomputer, but these larger systems still weren't targeted towards the regular consumer market.

William Lowe would be the one to break from IBM's standard business methodologies and models. He knew if IBM was going to have a new class of product, then it couldn't be done through the normal bureaucracy channels of 'Big Blue.'

So he looked at two avenues. One would be to set up an island, a totally separate team outside of IBM to build an entirely new system design. The other would be to evaluate existing computer companies and look to acquire them or their technologies, and it was in this avenue that he took particular note of some intriguing new designs from a company out in California called Atari.

William Lowe contacted Atari in 1979 and requested a meeting to discuss their home computer systems. "We had two meetings actually, one in my office and another at my apartment in San Francisco with IBM," recalls Ray Kassar. "I was asked to come down from the Cyan offices up in Grass Valley down to the Sunnyvale offices to meet with IBM. We discussed our computer systems with them. I think the two problems were, we had a closed proprietary design and also, because our systems had to work on televisions, we only had 40-column displays, and those factors just wouldn't work for IBM," recalls Steve Mayer. For one brief shining moment, IBM had actually considered acquiring the Atari home computers to use as IBM's new personal computer systems. If that had happened, the open architecture personal computer landscape that made Bill Gates a multi-billionaire might have looked far different.

Review In Images

Top: 155 Moffett Park, where Atari's initial computer line was designed. *Bottom:* Part of the original schematics for the Alpha Numeric STELLA, an attempt at combining the VCS's TIA chip with a character generation chip called ANTIC.

Opposite: Schematics for one of the TIA based designs.

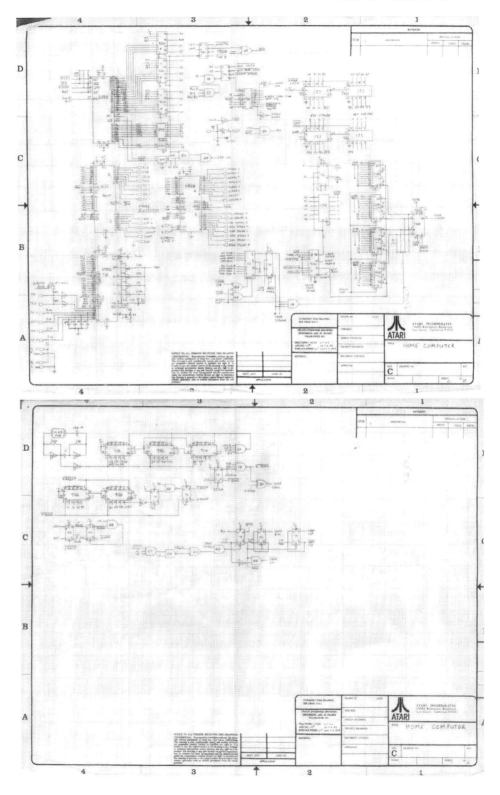

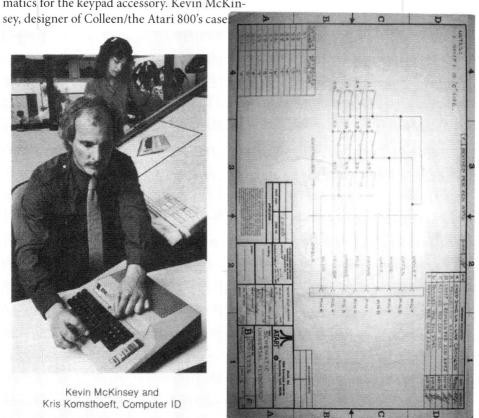

Clockwise starting above: Joe Decuir on the
Cromemco development system. A test cartridge
used during development of Colleen. The schematics for the keypad accessory. Kevin McKinsey, designer of Colleen/the Atari 800's case.

Kevin McKinsey and
Kris Komsthoeft, Computer ID

WARNER COMMUNICATIONS INC.

This year the Consumer Electronics Show in January in
Las Vegas will be very exciting. For Atari it will
be triply so. Not only will we have our Video Computer
System^{TM} with 10 new cartridges bringing our total up
to 30; and we will have on display the Atari-400^{TM} and
the Atari-800^{TM} personal-home computers, but we will
also be introducing and have on display several Electronic
Strategy and Action Games from our new Electronic Toy and
Game Division. The following people will represent Atari
and Warner Communications Inc.:

> Emanuel Gerard
> Office of the President
> Warner Communications Inc.
>
> Jonas Halperin
> Assistant Vice President
> Warner Communications Inc.
>
> Ray Kassar
> President
> Atari, Inc.
>
> John Ellis
> Vice President of Consumer Engineering
> Atari, Inc.
>
> Alan Alcorn
> Vice President of Consumer Engineering
> Atari, Inc.
>
> Wade Tuma
> Director of Consumer Engineering
> Atari, Inc.
>
> Peter Rosenthal
> Manager of Software Planning
> Atari, Inc.
>
> John Vurich
> Manager of Product Planning
> Atari, Inc.

We look forward to seeing you there. We will be staying at
the MGM Grand Hotel.

75 Rockefeller Plaza New York, New York 10019 212 484 8000

ATARI 820 Printer. High resolution, dot-matrix printer keeps a permanent record of your programs and their results.

Joystick, paddle and driving controllers. Let you direct the action in some of the most challenging computer games you have ever played.

ATARI 810 Disk Drive. Dramatically increases your memory storage capabilities.

Atari pre-recorded cassette tape programs. In a wide range of subjects, from computerized study to small business management.

ATARI 410 Program Recorder. Lets you write and store your own programs on standard audio cassette tapes.

Diskettes (not shown). Standard 5¼ inch size. Store a full 88K bytes per diskette.

Atari plug-in cartridge programs. A complete library of education, practical applications and dynamic entertainment.

ATARI 800 Personal Computer. Easy to operate. Easier to own. This is where the age of the personal computer begins.

Computer control keyboard. Full 57 key. Operates like an electronic typewriter to give you full upper and lower case alphanumeric and graphic display control.

Expandable memory. An 8K or 16K Memory Module™ gives you the ability to instantly expand your computer's memory up to 48K.

The 800 System.

MONITOR   PERIPHERAL   2—CHAN.—3   POWER ON OFF   POWER IN

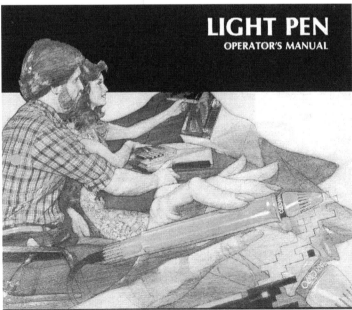

Above: A co-workers doodle expressing the same frustration as Al Alcorn's statement "I've seen the future and it's strangled in extension cords!"

Left: The 800 also had a light pen available, a throwback to mainframe lightpen interfaces of the 1960s.

Opposite: The 815 dual disk drive, Atari's short lived double density disk drive. Only 60 units were produced and sold for $1,500 before production was cancelled.

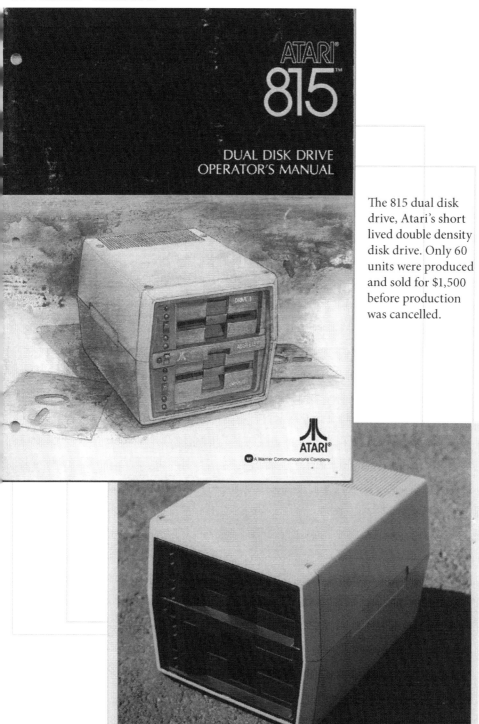

The 815 dual disk drive, Atari's short lived double density disk drive. Only 60 units were produced and sold for $1,500 before production was cancelled.

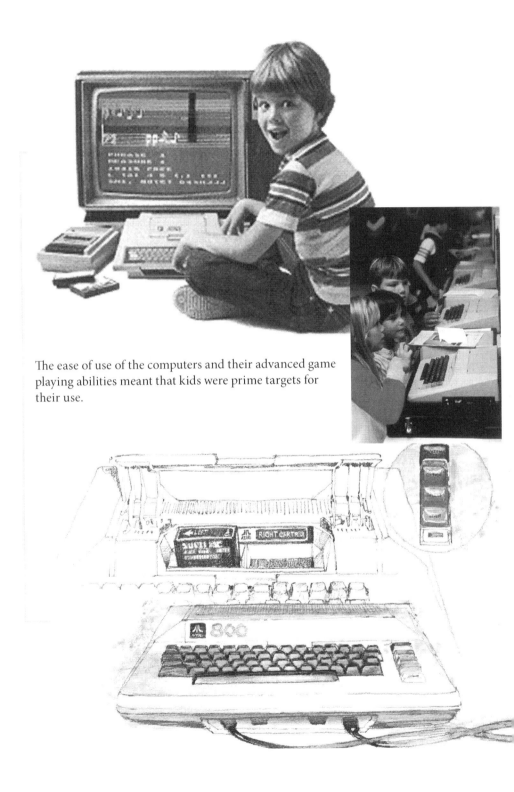

The ease of use of the computers and their advanced game playing abilities meant that kids were prime targets for their use.

ATARI PERIPHERALS & SOFTWARE

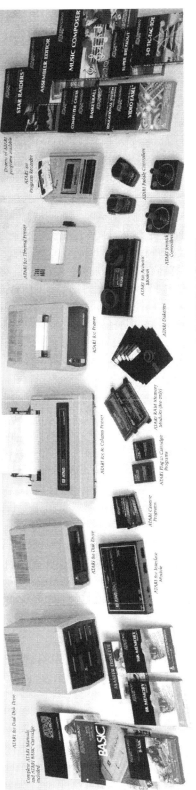

ATARI 800 Manuals and ATARI BASIC Cartridge included.

ATARI 810 Dual Disk Drive

ATARI 810 Disk Drive

ATARI 850 Interface Module

ATARI Cassette Programs

ATARI 825 80 Column Printer

ATARI Diskettes

ATARI RAM Memory Modules (800 only)

ATARI Plug-in Cartridge Programs

ATARI 820 Printer

ATARI 822 Thermal Printer

ATARI 830 Acoustic Modem

ATARI joystick Controllers

ATARI Paddle Controllers

ATARI 410 Program Recorder

Dozens of ATARI programs available

ATARI SOFTWARE

ATARI's growing library of software includes programs such as bond and mortgage analysis, stock charting and a TeleLink™ which allows your ATARI to communicate with other terminals or access data services. The ATARI Accountant™ provides computerized general ledger, accounts receivable & parable, inventory control and order entry. Dozens of useful, educational and entertaining programs are now available for ATARI Systems™.

ATARI SPECIFICATIONS

CONSOLES: FCC approved, with built-in RF modulator. Connect to any TV.

CPU: 6502 Microprocessor. 0.56 microsecond cycle. 1.8 MHz.

COLOR: 16 colors, each with 8 intensities.

SOUND: Four independent sound synthesizers for musical tones or game sounds. Four octaves. Variable volume. Internal speaker (in addition to audio through TV).

MEMORY: ATARI 400™ 8K bytes of RAM. ATARI 800™ includes 16K of RAM. The ATARI 800 Memory Module™ system allows memory expansion to 48K with 8K or 16K user-installable RAM modules. The ATARI 400 may be expanded to 16K RAM at an ATARI Service Center. Both systems include a 10K ROM Operating System. ROM may be expanded by up to 10K with user-installed solid-state cartridge programs.

KEYBOARD: Full 57 alphanumeric keys plus 4 function keys. Upper and lower case. Inverse video. Full screen editing. Four-way cursor control. 29 keystroke graphics. ATARI 800—full stroke keyboard. ATARI 400—mono-panel keyboard.

I/O: Serial input output port for simple connection to peripherals. Four controller jacks for light pen, joystick or paddle controllers.

LANGUAGES: ATARI 8K BASIC ROM cartridge included. Assembly language cartridge optional.

DISPLAY: Television screen (or monitor for the ATARI 800). Resolution 320 x 192. 24 lines of 40 characters.

POWER: AC transformer. UL approved.

DIMENSIONS: ATARI 800— 16"x12½"x4½"; 9¾ lbs. ATARI 400— 13½"x11½"x4½"; 5¾ lbs. **WARRANTY:** 90 days parts and labor.

ADDITIONAL ATARI 800 FEATURES:

RAM MEMORY: Expandable to 48K bytes with user-installed RAM Memory Modules.

MONITOR JACK: Composite video output for connection to a monitor.

ATARI SYSTEMS PERIPHERALS

ATARI 410™ PROGRAM RECORDER. The Recorder provides synchronized audio and data tracks for use with ATARI Talk & Teach™ courseware and other program cassettes. Up to 100K bytes of data may be stored on a 60 minute cassette.

ATARI 810™ DISK DRIVE. Up to 88K of high speed data access per 5¼" diskette. ATARI systems can individually access up to four disk drives (16K RAM required).

ATARI 815™ DUAL DISK DRIVE. For higher volume data handling, each twin drive provides over 320K of data access and storage. Access times are as low as 236 millisecs. ATARI systems can individually access up to 4 disk drives (16K RAM required).

ATARI 820™ PRINTER. 40-column dot matrix impact printer for hard copy printout of computer data and program material. Prints upper and lower case at 240C characters per minute.

ATARI 822™ THERMAL PRINTER. Quiet, affordable lightweight unit. Prints 40 characters per inch and 37 characters per second (c.p.s.) in 5 x 7 dot matrix form. Bi-directional printing.

ATARI 825™ 80-COLUMN PRINTER. Full 80-column 7 x 8 dot matrix printer. Selection of three type styles. Single sheet, fanfold or roll paper. High speed operation: 50 c.p.s. at 10 characters per inch. 83 c.p.s. at 16.7 characters per inch. 79 c.p.s. (avg.) with proportional spacing. Paper not included.

ATARI 830™ ACOUSTIC MODEM.* Through the modem. ATARI owners are able to transmit and receive data from other computers and terminals via telephone. Allows access to newswires, stock quotations and other useful data bases.

ATARI 850™ INTERFACE MODULE. A system expansion module that allows connection of RS232C compatible peripherals and the ATARI 825 Printer.

ATARI ACCESSORIES

ATARI CONTROLLERS. Attach a light pen, up to four joystick controllers or up to 8 paddle controllers through the controller ports.

ATARI CK 852™ AND CX 853™ MEMORY MODULES. 8K and 16K user-installable RAM memory modules (ATARI 800 only).

ATARI Systems, software and peripherals are available at your ATARI dealer.

ATARI reserves the right to make changes in materials and specifications without notice.

*Requires ATARI 810 Interface Module

*Some programs require more than 8K RAM

*A Warner Communications Company

Discover the Four Secrets of ATARI Home Computer

Secret #1 Modular Design.

You don't have to be an electrician to custom tailor your home computer system. The secret? Atari's modular design. Start with an ATARI Home Computer and an ATARI Program Recorder or ATARI Disk Drive. Then add programs and accessories. Atari specifically designed these computers in a modular fashion for easy expandability.

ATARI Program Cartridges are ready-to-use packages. Get the system you need today. Then expand it as your needs increase. Your ATARI Computer retailer is an expert who can help you make the right decisions in choosing the system that fits your needs.

Secret #2 Creative Space.

Expand your ATARI 800 Home Computer to let it do bigger jobs. The secret? ATARI Memory Modules allow you to add hard-working memory in 16K steps. Lift the console cover and push the ATARI Memory Modules into the slots provided. Many Atari programs require no more than 8K or 16K of Random Access Memory (RAM) to run, but more complex programs like The Bookkeeper require fully expanded 48K systems. Added memory lets you sort more names and addresses with Mailing List, analyze more facts and figures with Statistics 1, or write longer programs with ATARI programming languages. Whether it's that novel you've been thinking of writing with the ATARI Word Processor, or the musical score you'd love to record with the Music Composer. ATARI Memory Modules give your creativity enough space to flourish.

Systems

Secret #3 Easy-To-Use Programs

Whether you're after entertainment, education, or home office programs, your ATARI Home Computer is ready. The secret? ATARI programs are friendly. ATARI'S solid state cartridges are particularly easy to use. Open the console cover and pop one in. Snap the cover shut and the program appears on the screen. Or use the ATARI 810 Disk Drive. Slip in a program diskette, close the disk drive door, and turn on the computer. The computer is ready to go. With the ATARI Progam Recorder, you simply insert a program cassette, type "CLOAD" and press RETURN to load the program. At the READY sign, type "RUN" and press RETURN. Away you go! All ATARI Home Computer programs are friendly. In fact, many programs are designed for children to operate by themselves. There's also the ATARI Program Exchange (APX) which makes available a wide variety of exciting and interesting user-written programs and useful accessories.

Secret #4 Convenient Peripherals.

ATARI Home Computer peripherals are designed for convenience. The secret? They simply plug in. Link them in daisychains. Connect your ATARI 810 Disk Drive to your ATARI 800 Computer. Then connect the ATARI 822 Thermal Printer to the disk drive . . . and so on. For even more expandability, plug in the ATARI 850 Interface Module. Connect the ATARI 830 Acoustic Modem and use the TeleLink I cartridge to turn your ATARI Home Computer into a window to the world, bringing networks of news and information into your home over your standard telephone. You can connect with the program libraries of large computers and greatly increase the number of applications available to you. Also, a variety of other accessories like graphics tablets, plotters, even daisy-wheel and graphics printers are available from other companies.

A Message to All Employees

First Quarter 1979 sales for both the Consumer Division and the Coin-Op Division were the best Atari has experienced in its history and significantly better than for the same quarter of last year. This exceptional performance is a credit to the outstanding job being done by Atari employees throughout the Company.

1979 will be a year of new product introductions. The most ambitious of these new products is our line of personal computers, the Atari 400 and Atari 800. The entry into this marketplace is a significant challenge to all of us. The market is very competitive and the quality and product performance standards very high. I am confident that Atari people are equal to the challenge. Additional new product introductions will occur in Consumer and Coin-Op. The new line of hand-held games, specifically "Touch Me", was enthusiastically received at the Toy Fair. In Coin-Op, Superman™ and Hercules™ pinball machines were well received. In addition, Coin-Op previewed Subs™, Basketball™, Baseball™, Lunar Lander™, and Sebring™.

The greater challenge lies ahead. We anticipate continued sales improvement throughout the course of the year and significant performance over last year. Achievement of this objective depends on you. Additional units of all product lines will be required for the balance of the year. We must continue to reduce costs and improve productivity to overcome burdens remaining from last year. To ensure success and minimize product returns we must deliver quality products to our customers. One of our objectives for 1979 is "Quality Products from a Quality Company". We want Atari to be a Company of which we all can be proud. Your continued outstanding performance will help to ensure that.

Thank you for giving me the opportunity to convey this message on such a positive subject.

Thanks for a job well done!

Raymond E Kassar

Raymond Kassar
President

MORE COLOR. MORE SOUND. MORE GRAPHICS CAPABILITIES.

ATARI 400

ATARI 800

Compare the built-in features of leading microcomputers with the Atari personal computers. And go ahead, compare apples and oranges. Their most expensive against our least expensive: the ATARI® 400.®

Start with graphics capabilities. The ATARI 400 offers 128 color variations. 16 colors in 8 luminance levels. Plus 29 keystroke graphics symbols and 8 graphics modes. All controlled from a full 57 key ASCII keyboard. With upper and lower case. And the system is FCC approved with a built-in RF modulator. That's just for openers.

Now, compare sound capabilities. Four separate sound channels and a built-in speaker. With the optional audio/digital recorder, you can add Atari's unique Talk & Teach® Educational System cassettes.

Here's the clincher: Solid state (ROM) software. For home management, business and entertainment. Or just plug in an Atari 10K BASIC or Assembler language cartridge and the full power of the computer is in your hands.

Memory? 8K expandable to 16K. And that's just for the ATARI 400 at a suggested retail of only $549.99.

The ATARI® 800® gives you all that and much more.

User-installable memory to 48K. A full-stroke keyboard.

With a high-speed serial I/O port that allows you to add a whole family of smart peripherals. Including up to four individually accessible disk drives. And a high speed dot-matrix impact printer. And, the Atari Program Recorder is included with the 800 system. Suggested retail price for the ATARI 800 (including recorder) is $999.99.

Make your own comparison wherever personal computers are sold. Or, send for a free chart that compares the built-in features of the ATARI 400 and 800 to other leading personal computers.

ATARI

PERSONAL COMPUTER SYSTEMS

1265 Borregas Ave. Dept. C, Sunnyvale, California 94086. Call toll-free 800-538-8547 (in Calif. 800-672-1404) for the name of your nearest Atari retailer.

CIRCLE 2

Computers for people

Jerry Willis
Merl Miller

This Advanced Personal Computer is a Great Educational Gift—
Audio/Digital Cassettes Talk and Teach Through Your TV

1 ATARI 800 PERSONAL COMPUTER.' Provides the services of a teacher, a secretary, a financial advisor, or a companion right in your home. All the programming of this powerful computer is stored on cartridges which can be operated simply and easily. Connect the Atari 800 to a TV and it's ready for use. Data may be entered into the system by a variety of media including cassette tape (not included, see [2]), disk memory (not included—see [4], pre-programmed cassettes (see [5]) or the system's keyboard. Once entered the data may be recalled and displayed on the TV screen or printed for hard copy (order printer [3]). Complete manual included. Unit includes basic language cartridge. Typewriter-style operating keyboard. 2 cartridge ports. Modular construction for easy memory expansion. Includes 16K Ram (random access memory) expandable to 48K memory. Measures 12⅜x16x4½ in.
X 641-0393 A—Delivery weight 24 lbs 1080.00

2 CASSETTE RECORDER.' Push-button controls for rewind, fast-forward, stop, record, play, and eject. 2 channels (1 Digital, 1 Audio). 3 digit tape counter.
X 641-0427 A—Del. wt. 4 lbs 89.95
SAVE $150 When You Buy Atari [1] and Printer [3]
X 641-2886 A—Wt. 38 lbs .... Both for 1,529.95
SAVE $150 When You Buy Atari [1] and Disk [4].
X 641-2951 A—Wt. 35.50 lbs ...... Both for 1,629.95

SAVE $300 When You Buy All Three [1], [3] [4]
X 641-2969 A—Wt. 49.50 lbs ...... All 3 for 2,079.90

3 PRINTER FOR ATARI 800' uses standard roll paper and ribbon. Dot matrix impact type print-out. Prints 40 characters per second, one line per second. Constructed with a power switch and indicator. paper advance button, and a built-in microprocessor.
X 641-0443 A—Del. wt. 14 lbs $599.95

4 FLOPPY DISK DRIVE FOR ATARI 800' stores over 92K bytes of information on one disk. One disk incl. Up to four disks can operate with a system. Constructed with an automatic standby (built-in microprocessor). crystal controlled for accuracy
X 641-0435 A—Del. wt. 11.50 lbs 699.95
Blank Disks. Package of 5
X 641-2884 A Del. wt. 1.20 lbs 25.00

5 PRE-PROGRAMMED SOFTWARE FOR ATARI 800. In color, used with color TVs
Educational Cassettes: Require Dorsett Cartridge (below) 01 spelling. 02 U.S. history; 03 U.S. government; 04 great classics of the western world; 05 basic psychology. 06 economics. State subject number-and-name.
X 641-2068 B—Del. wt. 0.50 lb 24.95

Dorsett Educational System Cartridge. Required for use of educational cassettes (above).
X 641-2035 A—Del. wt. 0.50 lb 24.95
Game Cartridges: 01 superbreakout. 02 basketball. 03 video easel; 04 chess. State subject number-and-name when ordering.
X 641-2076 B—Del. wt. 0.50 lb 39.95
Entertainment Cartridges: 01 music; 03 star raiders. State subject number-and-name.
X 641-2084 B—Del. wt. 0.50 lb 59.95
Game Stick for use with game cartridges above. Adds maneuverability to games
X 641-2027 A—Del. wt. 0.50 lb 19.95
Paddle Control for Superbreakout Game Cartridge (sold above). Del. wt. 1.70 lbs.
X 641-3330 A—2 paddles 19.95

'110-120V. AC. UL listed.
Warranted by manuf.—write for copy, see p. 363.

6 ATARI BASIC MANUAL. How to read, write, and understand the programming language used in the Atari 800 computer system. incl. with the Atari 800.
X 640-2713 A—Delivery weight 1.20 lbs. 5.95

7 SAVE $70
Only Till
December 27, 1980
On Craig M-100
Language Translator
NOW ONLY **99⁹⁵**
After Dec. 27, Order at Reg. Price

Perfect Gift for the Traveler

7 CRAIG M-100 LANGUAGE TRANSLATOR. Uses self-contained, interchangeable memory capsules. Enter foreign words or phrases on the keyboard, and they appear in English. Translates from English. Accepts up to 3 language capsules at a time—order capsules below (English module is included). It's also a metric system converter and 8-digit calculator. Portable. Operates on 4 "AA" batteries (not incl.)—UL listed. Adapter/recharger incl. Warranted by manuf.—write for copy, see page 363. 6½x3⅜x1¹¹/₁₆ in. Reduced from our big Fall '80 Catalog, see page 759. Delivery weight 1 lb.
X 641-0500 A ...... Reg. $169.95; NOW 99.95
Language Capsules for Craig M-100 above. Languages: 01 French; 02 Spanish; 03 German; 04 Italian; 05 Japanese. State language number- and-name when ordering. Delivery weight 0.50 lb.
X 641-0419 B ...... Each 24.95

Of Course You Can Charge It—see page 363.

354 JCPenney

The Atari 800 (top) and 400 (bottom) in action. *Photos courtesy of the Tribune Photo Archives.*

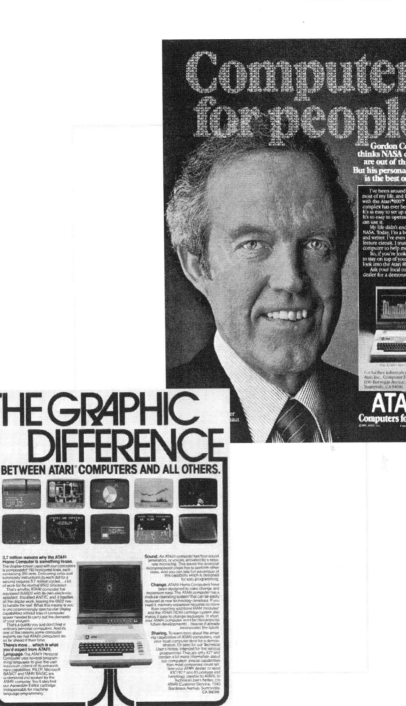

Some of the ready made kits Atari sold separately for users to expand their basic computer system depending on their needs.

SPRING 1981

VOLUME 1, NUMBER 1

THE ATARI CONNECTION™

$3.00

EDUCATIONAL SYSTEM

BASIC

PREMIERE ISSUE

Innovative Oddities

A Look in to some of the innovative, yet uncommon projects that were started at Atari

tari's history and popularity is admired, respected and revered, not just for its successfully released products, but also for the myriad of various rumored, talked about and briefly glimpsed at unreleased prototype products. While some of these unreleased prototypes were simply products that were canceled due to technical issues or marketing conflicts, there were also several 'scratch your head' Atari products that defied understanding and have become infamous in Atari lore.

One such product was created when Atari's dedicated *PONG* consoles were still going strong, despite the strong shifting focus on to the VCS. In what was to be the final run of this console format, the slated release for early 1978 included *Video Pinball, Stunt Cycle, Ultra Pong* and *Ultra Pong Doubles* and a dedicated console shown at the 1977 Summer CES called *Tank II*.

Based on the exceptionally popular Kee/Atari *Tank* arcade game, the console contains some rather unique controllers: a pair of joysticks, which were in fact, the earlier designs of what would eventually become the VCS joysticks. The controllers sit inside openings on the top of the *Tank* console and by moving them both forward or back, or alternating the controls to turn left or right, a player could control the tank just like in the arcade game. For two player games, the joysticks lifted out of their compartments and with attached cables, two players could each hold a joystick and play head-to-head competition against the other. A strange aspect of the product though is its model number. While all of the other dedicated consoles had model numbers such as C100 for *PONG* up to C450 for Stunt Cycle, *Tank II* has a rather odd model number – C4600. Regardless, even though the product was shown off and set to be sold through Sears, it was never released. Quietly canceled in August '77, *Tank II* had just been created to hedge Atari's bets. Had the VCS not been received well, it would have been the one quietly canceled instead, and *Tank II* would have been the one to move forward.

Another interesting console blip that appears on the radar briefly appeared at the 1978 Summer CES. Called the 'Game Brain' Model C-700, it's a cartridge based console system, but it's not microprocessor based like the VCS. Instead of game code, each cartridge actually contains a dedicated IC chip from one of Atari's various dedicated home consoles, such as *Super PONG*, and *Video Pinball*. The 'Game Brain' console itself is more of a docking station-type box; the 'Brains' (which are in the cartridges) are be placed into the top cartridge opening by lifting up the lid and placing the cartridge down inside. On each cartridge is a slider switch, and by sliding the switch forward, it actually slides the entire PCB contained within the plastic case forward, 'docking' it. As for the insides of the console, it had nothing inside except connections to the built-in controls, power input and a TV signal output. It was essentially another alternative to the VCS and a way for game buyers to own one system and still be able to buy all of the various dedicated console games to play on it. That of course may have been the 'market sell' side for the product but the 'insider view' within Atari was that perhaps it was a way to sell off their remaining dedicated IC chip inventory and clear the warehouses of these 'quick to become obsolete' components. Either way, the 'Game Brain' makes its one and only brief appearance and is never seen again.

Our next little known prototype device that'll really throw you for a curve is the VIDCOM. It's actually a system of devices including the Vidcom I and Vidcom II, which are a combination of a visual communication display device and an acoustic coupler modem device which plugs into the visual communicator, thus turning it into a TTY device (TTY stands for Text Telephone). These devices are also sometimes referred to as TDD devices, or Telecommunication Device for the Deaf. TTY is the more widely accepted term, since TTY's are also used by persons who aren't necessarily deaf.

TTY devices let people who are deaf, hard of hearing, or speech-impaired use the telephone to communicate and allows two people to 'talk' to each other by transmitting messages back and forth via this assistance device instead of actually having to speak and listen. A TTY device is required at both ends of the conversation in order to communicate in this matter, but not everyone that would need to receive a TTY message had such a device, so TTY dial-in services are available. A TTY user can dial into this service and request that a telephone number be called. The service then has an operator receive the messages from the TTY user and then speak the messages to a person at the number called. This gave deaf persons, individuals with speech impairments and those hard of hearing, the ability to place calls to non-TTY persons. For example, if they wanted to order a pizza from a local pizza shop, this device would make that possible.

So in 1978, Atari would develop the VIDCOM system. The brainchild of David Salmon (with input from Nolan Bushnell), Cary Crosson was the project manager, Alfie Gilbert, the electronics engineer, Dan Kutsenda the mechanical design engineer, Tom Westberg would program the microprocessor for the project and Sally Wengrover would be the electronics tech on the project. Howie Delman was also involved and developed the Vidcom II modem. The handheld Vidcom I device utilizes a very unique and innovative technology inside of the product; a flexible, plastic component 'board' called a 'flex-circuit.' Due to the space constraints and the size of the handheld unit and all of the technology that needed to be crammed into such a small device, the IC components would be adhered to this flexible plastic material and carefully folded into the inside of the device. It would also use rechargeable batteries that would be charged when the device was plugged in using the supplied wall outlet plug (still referred to in the documentation as a Battery Eliminator).

"Vidcom had an acoustically-coupled modem for it in a bag that could carry the modem and the communicator. The modem worked with baudot (the older style used by most communicators in use by the deaf at the time) as well as the new-fangled Bell-103 at 300 baud! Who could need more?" jokes Tom Westberg. Approximately 1,000 units were built and sold and/or donated to various hospitals and other healthcare providers. "We wanted to show the public that Atari could do something good, something philanthropic, so we designed a device for the deaf," recalls Steve Bristow.

In 1980, Atari's Coin-Op division developed another unique prototype product - this one for McDonald's and called the 'Kids Counter.' Owen Rubin developed the software for the device and Frank Ballouz became the marketing force behind it. McDonald's had wanted a device that hung over the counter, at child eye level, using McDonald's big yellow, red and white trademarked colors to show the menu items on the front with buttons under each choice. If the child wanted fries, a burger, etc, they would press the corresponding button for their selection. Each button pressed would make a sound and highlight the fries, burgers and so forth as they were selected by the child and then on the back of the unit facing the counterperson it would show what they ordered. Now the Kids Counter wasn't actually directly connected in any way to a register, so upon an approving nod from the parent the counterperson would then have to enter the selections shown on the Kids Counter into the register. Then after placing the order, the counterperson would press a button on their side of the Kids Counter which would cause it to play the tune, "You deserve a break today!" and then dispense a coin to the child to take and select their kid's meal prize by dropping the coin into the unit and pressing the prize button.

When the first design was presented to McDonald's, there was a problem with the coin size Atari had come up with; it was too small and was a potential choking hazard, so the coins and the coin dispensing system were redesigned with a more oversized coin to avoid that. McDonald's also gave a long list of specifications to Atari for paint colors and the type of paint that was food safe. The units also had to be liquid proof, have no sharp edges or corners, no openings that a child could get a finger or hand stuck in and the units would have to be UL approved.

A number of the Atari Kids Counters were built and tested at various locations for McDonald's in Chicago, but the project stalled and never went anywhere after that. Frank Ballouz tried to revive it and he and Owen took Owen Rubin's test unit back to McDonald's to try to get the company to reconsider its deployment, but it still never went any farther.

Finally there's ProVision, which is a project started in one of Atari's research and development groups - Atari Advanced Products (AP), run by Al Alcorn. AP had an open charter and was responsible for the creation of numerous game and toy prototypes. They ranged from Indy Turbo (a full scale coin op race car with a water-cooled video projector and large 1st person projection screen), to a voice-altering helmet (making you look and sound like Darth Vader when wearing it), various hand-held electronic toys including Pro Coach (a 2 player LED game programmed by Dennis Koble), and several other projects. Roger Hector, who had been with Atari since 1976 was working in AP by the late 70s/early 80s recalls, "I was a lead creator and managed the group along with Harry Jenkins. There were around a dozen designers and engineers and a small prototype fabrication shop. About 20 or so people as best as I can remember."

ProVision was created by AP in 1980, a fully tested and working 'high-end' home VCS prototype. ProVision included all of the then current VCS games at the time (built into a single PCB based on Atari's VCS Point of Purchase story display), completely selectable via capacitive touch switches done in a clean Bang & Olufson style. The entire system, complete with all the various controllers, was packaged in a rolling cart-like side table that looked similar to a piece of office furniture. "It was easy to build the board into this special prototype. It looked pretty cool, and the R&D group built an actual 'living room' in the Advanced Products office to convey the idea," recalls Roger. It would never go into production or be sold, but it showed that Atari could potentially offer a point of purchase system for high-end video game retail centers. Also, in an interesting side note, one of the a tech and programmer working on the ProVision is Tom Westberg. Tom will later work for a company called GCC or General Computer Corporation, that will soon do some major work for Atari Inc., including building their last game console.

Review In Images

Innovative Oddities

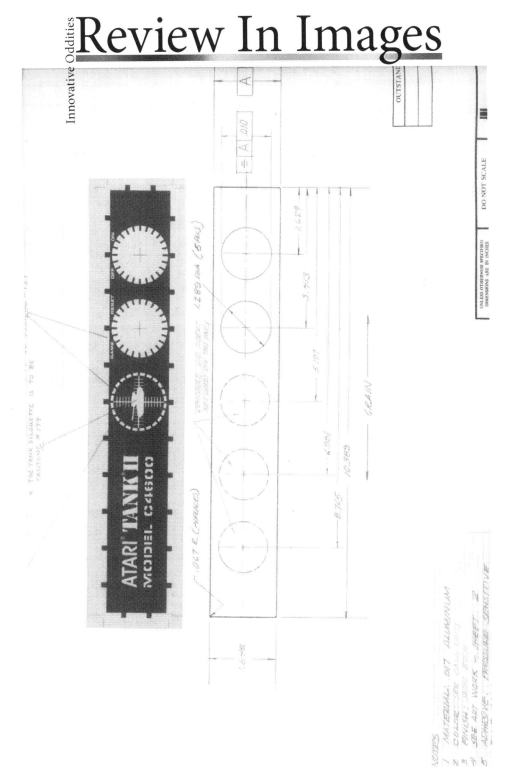

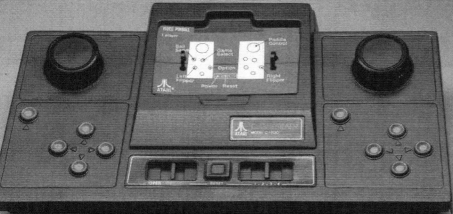

THE GAME BRAIN™
BY ATARI

America's Favorite Video Games In A Moderate Price Programmable System

ATARI®
MORE GAMES.
MORE FUN.

Ⓦ A Warner Communications Company

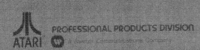

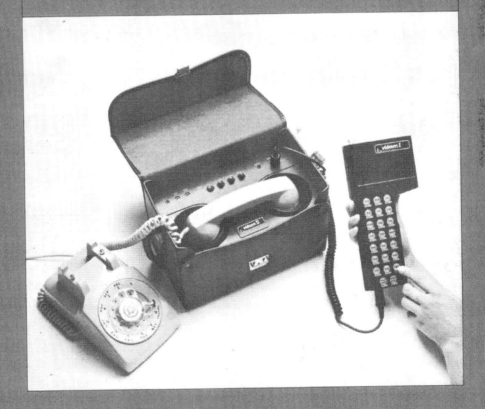

vidcom
communications
system

The Portable Communications System for the Non-Verbal

vidcom I

 ATARI PROFESSIONAL PRODUCTS DIVISION

VIDCOM I—actual size 9½" x 4¾" x 1¾"

VIDCOM I—A PORTABLE VISUAL COMMUNICATIONS DEVICE FOR THE NON-VERBAL

Introducing the VIDCOM I, a portable visual communications device for the non-verbal. Whether communicating face-to-face or by telephone,* the VIDCOM I provides a medium for non-verbal individuals, which can be used and understood by the speaking and non-speaking world.

VIDCOM I is manufactured by the Professional Products Division of Atari. A leader in applied solid state technology, Atari has taken its expertise in the manufacture of interactive video electronic devices and incorporated it in the VIDCOM I.

Three years in development, the VIDCOM I has undergone extensive evaluation by speech and hearing professionals, as well as field testing by non-verbal individuals. The desire to gain total insight into all the many and varied needs of the disabled has guided the development of the VIDCOM I. Attention to detail has resulted in a product which can be operated by people with a wide range of motor and language skill levels. Thus the VIDCOM I owner can utilize the physical and intellectual abilities he possesses to overcome the barriers to his communication problems.

Universal communications compatibility,* battery power or AC operation and rugged solid state design, make the VIDCOM I a versatile, portable and reliable product.

Economies derived from advanced micro-electronic technology allow the VIDCOM I to be priced within reach of private individuals, and provides features and capability not found in other communication devices.

*Optional acoustic coupler/modem for telecommunications available. Consult the VIDCOM II product information sheet for full details.

Actual Size

LIGHTWEIGHT, COMPLETELY PORTABLE

Weighing less than 2 lbs., constructed of hi-impact plastic casing and equipped with its own self-contained battery pack, VIDCOM I can be taken anywhere.

LED DISPLAY

FRONT FACING—Display positioned at the leading edge of the VIDCOM I to duplicate normal face-to-face communications.

SHIELDED—A protruding rim shields the display to reduce character washout from bright sunlight.

HI-LO ILLUMINATOR—Display has two levels of illumination intensity, allowing user to adjust display brightness according to environment.

AUTO SHUTOFF—Built-in timer automatically turns display off after one minute interval of non-use. This avoids draining the battery pack should the VIDCOM I be inadvertently left on.

6/10" CHARACTERS—Display is composed of 8 LED characters, approximately THREE TIMES the size of a hand-held calculator display.

ERROR STRIKEOVER—If an error is made user can correct misspelling immediately by back spacing and striking the correct letter over it.

POWER SUPPLY

RECHARGEABLE BATTERY PACK—Built-in battery pack provides 4 hours of continuous operation. Can be recharged up to 1200 times. Has a life expectancy of more than three years, under normal use.

AC WALL PLUG ADAPTOR—Recharges battery pack and allows the VIDCOM I to be run off any 110 volt AC (ordinary house current) electrical outlet.

DUAL TONE AUDIO PAGE

This signaling device can sound two distinct tone patterns from a miniature speaker built into the VIDCOM I. The NORMAL TONE allows the non-verbal user to announce his desire to communicate, attracting the attention of his audience. The persistent beeping of the EMERGENCY TONE forcefully calls for immediate assistance.

VIDCOM MEMORY

PREPROGRAMMED VOCABULARY—Fixed sets of commonly used words or their symbolic representations are permanently stored in memory. Allows

user to signal desire for such things as "phone" or "bathroom" by depressing a single key, versus spelling out the word letter-by-letter.

THE KEYBOARD

LARGE, LOW ACTIVATION FORCE KEYS—Each short stroke key pad is approximately twice the size of a touch tone telephone key and requires considerably less pressure to activate. The domed key caps have a TACTILE FEEDBACK mechanism that assures the user contact has been made.

RECESSED KEY WELLS—The walls of the key wells are beveled to act as an aid in capturing and guiding a finger, stylus or whatever is being used to depress a key.

21-KEY ALPHANUMERIC/SYMBOLIC FORMAT—Keys are clearly marked with letters, numbers 0 through 9 and fixed sets of commonly used words or their symbolic representations.

WORD SHIFT KEY—Allows user to combine letters with preprogrammed words as he spells out his message to speed communications.

IN-USE INDICATOR

A miniature lamp, located above the keyboard, flashes each time a key is depressed. This gives the user visual feedback that key contact has been made and that the character is being displayed.

UNIVERSAL COMMUNICATIONS COMPATIBILITY"

TELEPHONE COMMUNICATIONS—The VIDCOM I can transmit and receive communications via normal telephone lines, by means of its acoustic coupler/modem.

OTHER COMMUNICATIONS DEVICES—VIDCOM I is universally compatible with all standard TTY devices including Deaf Network Communications and other telecommunication systems.

THE KEYBOARD

Actual Size

Telecommunications capability achieved via optional acoustic coupler/modem. Consult the VIDCOM II product information sheet for complete details.

Due to ongoing research and development, features and specifications subject to change.

---

vidcom I **Professional Products Division** • 1183 Bordeaux Drive, Suite 32, Sunnyvale, CA 94086 (408) 745-2846

Atari Advanced Products   ProVision Prototype   Roger Hector

Atari Advanced Products   ProVision Prototype   Roger Hector

Chapter   8

PERPETUAL MONEY MACHINES

We've Been Invaded And Need A Bigger Bank

In 1978, the U.S. was still knee deep in an ongoing economic and energy crisis. The energy crisis itself caused America's appetite for fuel efficient cars to grow, and leading the charge to satiate that hunger was Japan. Japanese car imports now counted for half of the U.S. import market and a resulting growing influence for Japan into the U.S. economy that would last in to the next decade. However, it was now in the field of high-tech entertainment that Japan would see its next great contribution, when in 1978 video games started making a significant change thanks to a coin-op company by the name of Taito.

The vast majority of games at the time were racing, sports, skill and general action games. Taito's new game would invent a whole new game genre called shoot 'em up (or shmup for short). It was a genre that gave the player the thrill of flying their ship in to battle against immeasurable odds, relying solely on their ability to continue tapping their fire button to cut down wave after wave. This particular game from Taito involves rows of aliens that move left to right and then back, progressing their way down the screen to the an ever increasing frantic heartbeat sound. Protecting the player are bunkers that shield their laser cannon as it moved along the bottom of the screen back and forth. As you may have guessed, the game being described is *Space Invaders*.

When *Space Invaders* was released in Japan in early 1978 the game was a massive success, with over 100,000 machines installed throughout Japan alone.

Earning $600 million that year alone, it became so popular that in Japan it actually caused a shortage of 100 Yen coins as they flew from the pockets of kids into Space Invaders arcade machines.

Space Invaders was designed by Tomohiro Nishikado, who claimed Atari's game *Breakout* and the film *War of the Worlds* as the inspiration. But truth be told; Taito's older EM game based on the same concept, *Space Monsters*, was also a big influence behind the scenes. In fact, some of the characters were actually used as test screen objects on some of Taito's early video arcade development efforts as well.

Using an 8080 CPU that could barely keep up with the game's demands, the microprocessor had first been used by Taito's partner in the West, Bally subsidiary Midway, when they converted Taito's game *Western Gun* from its original discrete design to a microprocessor driven one. The result was Bally's *Gun Fight*, the first microprocessor driven video arcade game, and a continued lasting partnership between the two companies. A partnership that involved Midway beginning work on a US version of the coin-op that August of '78 and would ultimately lead to a huge success for Midway and a worldwide phenomenon for *Space Invaders* itself.

The emptying of change from pockets was successfully transferred to the US, with quarters taking the place of 100-yen coins, though the results were the same though: lines of kids waiting to play the game. In order to 'get in line' to play an arcade game, a player would walk up to *Space Invaders* and if someone was already playing the game, they would take their quarter and place it onto one of two places that claimed their position in the queue: the metal ledge under the game title graphic (called the 'marquee') or on the front of the game where the monitor bezel glass met the control panel. This culture of the coin, so prevalent by the early 1980s, even had its own self developed etiquette; If you distracted the person playing, bumped them or otherwise blocked them from playing, you could end up owing the player a quarter. In fact any disturbance of the player, including crowding them during an intense button smashing session, would result in generally dirty looks from the player and the on-lookers. Besides disappearing in the coin-slots to feed the 'perpetual money machine,' coins would also often disappear for other reasons: if a coin-op was serviced and the clamps or screws holding down the control panel were not fully secured, many times a hard tapping of the button or a pull of the joystick on other games could shift the control panel back away from the monitor bezel. The result being the entire row of quarters would simply vanish into the machine, and generally the arcade staff would not be inclined to credit you back a replacement quarter or token for such a mistake.

Waiting in line for a popular game was always the norm in the arcades thanks to *Space Invaders* and the shooter titles that followed. You couldn't play the games anywhere else - even when games did eventually make it to the home, the home conversions were only a pale rendition of a game that would be done as best as the game console hardware and programmer's finesse could produce. The arcades were always the place to go for the hot new titles and the latest game innovations. When such a game appeared in a local arcade, roller rink, pizza parlor or other location, word of mouth always spread like wildfire, sending droves of eager player's with quarters in hand to get a chance at a taste of playing it. Whether you were an instant 'pro' at a game and picked up the rhythm and patterns or a total video gaming dweeb, it didn't matter. Just to be able to step up to the control panel, look at the screen, take a deep breath and feel the excitement of finally playing this new source of excitement and wonderment while a dozen or more eye's watched over your shoulder. It made it all the more worth it as you'd take your quarter, slide it into the coin slot, hear it bang its way into the coin mechanism and see your credit appear on the screen. It was time to play.

Space Invaders popularity became quite evident within the halls of Atari in late 1978, when over at the Engineering building at 1272 Borregas Ave, on the first floor in coin-op engineering several installed *Space Invaders* coin-ops were quietly leading an 'invasion' of their own. Wanting to size up the competition (and to just get their hands on the latest games out there for inspiration), Atari would always purchase their competitors new releases through distributor channels; *Space Invaders* would be no exception to that rule. On this particular day, Manny Gerard made his usual walk from Corporate across the street to Engineering to look at the progress of the various projects. Upon walking into coin-op engineering however, he was greeted with a large crowd of employee's excitedly talking and cheering each other on. Walking over to see what the fuss is about, he notices the employees are all huddled around several *Space Invaders* machines they had shipped in from Japan and installed in the coin-op area. To see Atari people so overly excited about a competitor's product definitely catches Manny's attention, especially since everyone in the industry knew about *Space Invaders* and how it was changing the entire dynamic of the arcades. Moving on in his rounds like a doctor inspecting his patients at the hospital, he continues walking around engineering and heads upstairs to the consumer engineering floor to observe the VCS game designers and coders working. Suddenly an idea comes to mind, and Manny quickly exits the engineering building and makes a beeline back across the street to corporate.

Heading right upstairs to the executive offices and going directly into Ray Kassar's office, he barks "Get us a license for *Space Invaders* and have the game developers make that game on the VCS. If you can't get a license, steal the game play and make the game under a different name." Following orders, Ray Kassar immediately contacts Taito and begins negotiations for the rights to the home license for *Space Invaders*. This simple eureka moment of Manny's would be a monumental move for Atari and due to some shrewd negotiating from Kassar, the rights are secured for all of Atari's home product lines including their computers and some other products that are in the works.

When it was eventually started, *Space Invaders* for the VCS would be programmed by Rick Maurer - his first project at Atari after leaving Fairchild Semiconductor at the closing of their Channel F game console group. Rick had programmed #17 *Pinball Challenge*, #18 *Hangman* and #24 *Pro-Football* for the Channel F, and was now being asked to code the intensive *Space Invaders* for his first game on a new hardware platform. Coming from the rather primitive Channel F console to the more powerful but even more challenging to code on VCS console, the contrasts between programming for the two are immediately evident to Rick. It was a rather risky gamble by Atari management though... to place such a key game translation in the hands of a fresh newly hired programmer, but it paid off in spades.

While the arcade version of *Space Invaders* was black and white and used color gel overlays to show the rows of aliens in different colors, the home VCS version was able to be in color. Likewise, Rick's version would also have something that the arcade version didn't have – variations. The game would actually have a record breaking 112 different variations in game play, making the it a constant source of new challenges for VCS game players. Even though it was long before the term was ever coined, *Space Invaders* can truly be labeled as the VCS's 'killer app.' When released in 1980, not only were sales through the roof for this home version, but it would pull in over $6 million dollars in net profits. To add to this, a new phenomenon occurred, one which would catch the attention of Atari's sales and marketing: People were going out and buying a VCS just so they could play *Space Invaders*! The license was a win-win for Atari, and would ignite a licensing craze by them that would see the company becoming the leader in bringing arcade titles home.

After programming *Space Invaders*, Rick would also do another highly popular game for the VCS called *Maze Craze*, a VCS version of the 1973 Atari coin-op game *Gotcha!* Unlike the coin-op version, the VCS version would include a staggering 256 different variations of the game, and the large number of game variations started to become a sort of calling card for Rick's games. This would be the most variations ever for a VCS game title however.

Over in coin-op in 1979, Atari was about to release its own 'killer app' for the arcades. *Space Invaders* could truly be seen as the game that broke the mold on the traditional fare of arcade offerings, but Atari would counter in 1979 with a game who's popularity would see the coin-op division revenues double and profits nearly go up 10-fold. The game is called *Asteroids* and at the time it was set to make arcade game history for Atari. While it wouldn't sell the same physical number of cabinets as *Space Invaders*, its popularity and quarter gobbling addictive game play would set new records in player earnings.

Ed Logg would be selected as the project leader, programmer and game designer, although the game idea was originally by Lyle Rains. Paul Mancuso would be assigned as the technician, and the hardware would be done by Howie Delman, who had previously designed the vector game *Red Baron*. In fact, Howie used same board design and simply altered the sound hardware.

Ed's journey with *Asteroids* started while he was working on something earlier and of course un-related: the alpha-numeric's and self-test routines on the vector *Red Baron* coin-op. Lyle called in Ed to discuss a game project and reminded him of his old game idea called *Cosmos*, "I said, I remember that old game, I said yeah it's a really stupid game," recalls Ed. *Cosmos* was a two player space dueling game with the concept of a big asteroid on the screen - only you'd shoot it and nothing would happen. So Lyle then said "Let's be able to shoot the asteroids and blow them up." Lyle also originally wanted to do the game in raster, however Ed knew the game would work better in a higher resolution that at the time only a vector display game could deliver. Of course Ed already having exposure to the *Red Baron* vector hardware would make designing *Asteroids* down that route more logical. "I had played *Spacewar!* on the old PDP screens which were vector screens. From this experience I got many of my ideas like the pointed ship to indicate where you were aiming, wraparound, etc" recalls Ed Logg.

According to internal memo's discussing wrap-around shooting and other changes to the game over time, the flying saucers that appear during game play to cause deadly distractions for the player were nicknamed 'Mr. Bill' and 'Sluggo,' both of which were characters in the *Saturday Night Live* clay figure comedy skit *The Mr. Bill Show*. Their usage actually caused Ed Logg to receive a letter in 1981 from a lawyer representing the Mr. Bill Trademark, after an article on *Asteroids* done for the February issue of *Esquire* mentioned the saucer's nicknames.

Just as *Space Invaders* contained a simple, repeating and increasing background thumping sound effect, *Asteroids* too would have an eerily haunting background heartbeat sound effect as well. As the game play progressed, the beat would continually increase in speed, driving the anxiety and pace of the game play to maddening heights. The background beat was inspired from the same music as the movie *JAWS*, where the eerily primal thump-thump beat would start out slowly and speed up to a nail biting finish. Unlike the blood red churning ocean water in *JAWS* though, the further anxiety is driven by smaller pieces of broken up asteroids flying in all directions. Players would desperately shoot at the oncoming objects, which are all moving towards the player's ship to crush and destroy it in an attempt to steal another player life. Each lost life bringing them closer to 'Game Over' and another quarter to put into the perpetual money making machines.

The sharp, clean simplicity of the game screen allows players to really focus on the oncoming barrage of asteroids coming at them, while also watching out for the annoying flying saucers that will appear and fire at the player, adding more to the already tense on-screen chaos. When *Asteroids* makes its debut in the summer of 1979 for its play testing and focus groups, it scores higher with younger players, but many of the older players are confused as to the object of the game - thinking it's to avoid the asteroids and then destroy the flying saucers. Even during these generation gap driven results though, Asteroids was showing that it was going to be a very popular game. And once the game was officially released in November 1979, the numbers truly spoke for themselves: The quarters began pouring into the Asteroids machines and distributors couldn't get enough of them to sell. In fact the story goes that the game was so popular that *Lunar Lander* cabinets were being used to build many of the initial runs of *Asteroids* to meet demand, and this is in fact quite true.

On Thursday October 29, 1981 at the Chicago Expo Center, Atari helped put on the World Championships tournament with TGI, which included *Centipede* and *Asteroids*. *Asteroids* mania was still in full swing, at least in the United States, having now surpassed *Space Invaders*, selling over 70,000 units at $2,700 each in the U.S. but only selling 100,000 worldwide so far. There had been hope of attracting nearly 10,000 video game and table game 'Olympians' battling it out at the championship,

with many competitors already having won local Atari supported *Asteroids* quali-
fier competitions. When they arrive though, most competitors are surpised to find
that the main competition is for *Centipede* ($50,000 in cash and prizes) and that
Asteroids was instead a side challenge ($25,000 in cash and prizes). Regardless, once
the dust settled many a gamer would walk away with strained eyes and sore thumbs.
They were just happy to have given their all in battle against Atari's latest and greatest coin-ops. There would be just one small snag: It seems that while the entire 4-day
long event was a major success and Atari's $100,000 investment into the whole
$400,000 spectacular had paid off in great press, exposure and excitement… some-
body back in accounting for TGI hadn't accounted for a lower turnout. The event or-
ganizers had hoped for a higher number of participants and in turn a higher amount
of incoming revenue to cover costs, and checks started bouncing accordingly when
that didn't happen. Atari had to step in and add an additional $25,000 to cover prize
awards that it paid out directly to those players who's checks had bounced, which it
had no obligation to do since it had already fully funded $100,000 toward cash and
prize awards. They simply did it to save face and not to be dragged down by the nega-
tivity of the situation, though it also ensured there wouldn't be another such event
the following year.

With a popular game generating massive revenue, of course the rip-offs follow. Sidam's *Asterock* would be one of them, along with *Meteors* which was another
blatant rip-off of *Asteroids* but in raster video. *Meteors* would use the same code but
with a different board and sound circuit and the company even used the same operator's manual.

Sales revenue for Atari in 1980 through 1981 were as explosive as the on-
screen battles in its most popular games. So popular are the next batches of home,
computer and coin-op titles that revenue is flowing from Atari and into Warner
Communications coffers at an unbelievable rate. In consumer sales alone, Atari saw
revenues of $178 million in 1978, $238 million in 1979, $512 million by 1980 and
a staggering $1.2 billion by 1981. A trifecta of ground breaking new and addictive
Atari coin-op games, combined with home releases of those games as well as home
releases of licensed titles, were all channeled through Atari's aggressive advertising
and marketing efforts. And the efforts of the marketing machine were paying off in
substantial leaps in revenues.

Now here is an interesting albeit unrelated side story with Ed Logg: After Ed
had finished working on the *Super Breakout* arcade, the company offered to allow

Ed to purchase the prototype of his game for $50. Ed took Atari up on the offer and purchased his game and kept it in his office in coin-op engineering. He soon loaned it to Consumer Engineering so that Nick Turner, a VCS programmer, could adapt the game to the VCS for release in 1981. About a year or so after loaning his *Super Breakout* arcade to consumer programming, Ed went and retrieved his arcade game to take it home. Shortly after though, Ed then finds out someone called the police to report the game was stolen, causing him he to get into a tit-for-tat argument with Consumer management: "It's our game, no its my game, no its ours." Finally it's explained, it was with Consumer only because Ed loaned the game to them. Regardless, the argument wasn't going any farther anyway, the game was already in Ed's home and he wasn't about to bring it back, it was his.

As for *Centipede*, Ed Logg was the project supervisor and programmer on *Shoot the Centipede* as the game was originally titled internally. Among others on the project, Ed also hired Dona Bailey, Coin's first female programmer, to do the graphics and some of the programming with him. There was a bonus pool at end of the project, and details surrounding it would cause some bad blood between Ed Logg and Dona Bailey after Ed wound up getting a bigger chunk than Dona. Ed actually raised a stink about it, getting himself in trouble for it and in turn Ed's manager and so on up the chain. Though Ed did do a large chunk of the work, including the self-test feature, because while Dona was a good programmer, she was slower than Ed and the project deadlines were looming. He also got involved in more of the programming because he was none too thrilled with being a project supervisor; in Ed's mind he was a programmer and that was what he preferred doing. Ed's complaining did work out though and the bonus figures were reworked and changed to be more fair for all in the team. Dona also got an added 'bonus' when Atari's marketing latched on to her involvement, promoting Centipede as the first coin-op video game programmed by a female even though it was Ed who did most of the actual coding.

Unlike *Asteroids* with its stark and simple visuals, *Centipede* is a colorful, playful and enticing game. It's kind of difficult to imagine designing a hit game around the premise of bugs, or even coming up with this odd concept of a centipede moving through mushrooms while being fired at by a 'shooter,' but that was how the game came to be. The creatures weren't repulsive or even disgusting; in a sense they were almost 'cute' as far as bugs go. The constantly rotating pastel colors, along with the marching sounds and the triumphant bonus life music made *Centipede* a fun and addictive game playing experience that also appealed to women. As with many other popular games, the formula of increasing speed, more opponents and a quickening background sound effect would draw players into the anxiety inducing thirst for a higher score than previously played. This addiction would need to be fed over and over, until the player reached into their pocket and opened up their velcro latched wallet to find it at long last emptied. The machine would quietly stand there, waiting for the next challenger to step up, slide a quarter into the slot and see the player 1 button light up and blink, indicating it was time to feed the next 'addict.'

After *Centipede* was released in June 1981, it seemed again (just like *Asteroids*) that when you have a very popular game and its making a lot of money, the cockroaches crawl out of the cracks to try and feed off of the crumbs, or in this case, they'd steal the whole loaf of bread. Games like *Magic Worm* to *Mill Pac* to *Centicrab* started to show up and sure enough, upon inspection and some high tech detective work, the evidence that these were direct copies started to reveal itself. In *Centipede's* case a hidden secret was placed into the code of the game by Ed, that unless a person was familiar with it, they'd have never known it was starring them right in the face.

In the 90s movie *Independence Day*, after aliens have invaded the Earth in a plan to strip it of all its resources, a final and desperate counter-attack plan is made. Coordinated by the U.S. military, the message needs to reach all of the other surviving allied military units around the world without alien interception. The answer comes in a nearly forgotten art form of communication called Morse Code. Before the age of the internet, before television, before telephones or even radio, a method of communications was created to send an electrical signal over wires (and then later when radio was invented, over radio waves) to a small device that when power was applied to it, would 'tap' down. So a code was created for this then new communications medium where a certain amount of long and short taps would mean a letter or number in the alphabet. For example if a ship out at sea needed to send a distress signal it would transmit over its radio a message 'short short short… long long long… short short short' which would mean S-O-S or Save Our Ship. In the *Independence Day* movie, the battle plan is transmitted by morse code to all of the countries around the world, who are now able to coordinate an attack against the aliens with the United States. In the end, Will Smith and Jeff Goldblum light up some stogies, fireworks go off and the world is free from the alien scum. It seems that 15 years earlier, Ed Logg had taken a similar tactic to defeat Atari's own inavders out to strip its earnings.

All of the pirate games were using nearly the same hardware, but altering in one way or another, the code of the game stored in ROM. Ed would of course be able to examine the pirate code and find certain security checks were bypassed or altered and that Atari's name and copyright date were removed or altered. However what none of illegal pirate coders caught onto was some 'garbage code' that Ed had embedded. When we say garbage code, that would be how most programmers might've viewed it; just some spare bits hanging around and not doing anything. It just looked like some leftover crumbs, crumbs that the cockroaches ignored while going for the whole loaf of bread. Well, this garbage code wasn't garbage at all - it was in fact Morse Code. If one had been familiar with it, they would've quickly realized that it spelled out:

.BYTE 2,0BB,5A,30 (where 0 is dot and 1 is dash and nothing for a space)
.BYTE 5F,0EE,7D,0A8   ;MORSE CODE FOR "COPYRIGHT 1980 ATARI"

When the meaning of this code was revealed in court, and shown to be in all the pirate versions of the game, the crooks were easily foiled and shut down.

After his project supervisor experience with *Centipede* however, Ed told his supervisor Dave Stubben that he didn't want to be a project supervisor and especially didn't want to do any more hiring or firing. Instead, Ed took a break from coin-op programming for a short bit, working on a side project during late 1981 where he jumped over to Consumer programming to create *Othello* for the VCS. He created the game based on Carol Shaw's (Atari's first female programmer) VCS *Checkers* game kernel, since the game was also based on pattern matching. Now there was a small catch in Ed's jump to Consumer though: Ed wasn't really authorized to work on this side project, after all he was really employed in Coin-op and not in Consumer programming. So Ed actually worked on the project after hours at night in his home. The clandestine programming was let out of the bag during the development of the game when there was a bug in the game code and Ed was using a black box in his office to work out the issue. Just as he was finishing the ROM's in his office, Dave Stubben walked past Ed's office, stopped and noticed the game... and that would be the last VCS game Ed did. Ed received a rather stern look from Dave – which would probably frighten most men!

Insert Quarter
for New Game...

Two more games came out of Atari Coin during this period that represent vastly different stories of success, but no less innovative than one would expect from the designers creating hit after hit in the arcades. The first is started and released between *Asteroids* and *Centiepde*, and would be the 'hit' of the two. Its ending explosion scene complete with the words 'The End' is most iconically shown at the end of the 80s high school romp *Fast Times At Ridgemont High*, but its origins are anything but fun filled.

In the 1960s through the 1970s the Soviet Union and the United States had been engaged in a massive nuclear arms build up to the point where the two Super Powers could annihilate the entire planet ten times over with their stockpiles of thermonuclear weapons. During the 1960s the Super Powers had begun to deploy a series of 'ABM' systems. These Anti Ballistic Missile systems were capable of intercepting and shooting down incoming nuclear missiles as a deterrent, but instead of their desired effect they ended up causing an escalation between the two nuclear Super Powers. This in turn lead both to create even deadlier systems called 'MIRV' or Multiple Impact Re-entry Vehicles. With MIRV, now a nuclear missile could loft a payload of 3 or more independently targeted nuclear warheads that would return into the atmosphere and would now give the ABM systems not one, but several targets that would need to be shot down. The result would be the overwhelming of the technology in the then current ABM defense systems ensuring that at least some of the nuclear warheads would reach their intended targets.

Consequently, the United States would build a massive defensive monitoring and interceptor system called 'Safeguard' in North Dakota, and the Soviets built their counterpart called the A-35 located around Moscow. In 1972, the Super Powers signed an ABM Treaty to help reduce the build-up of nuclear weapons in response to these defensive installations. By 1974 the Safeguard ABM system was deactivated and used primarily by NORAD (North American Aerospace Defense) to monitor attempted Soviet and China launched nuclear attacks against the United States and Canada.

Simultaneous to all of this was yet another system; an older system put in to place during the 1950s and 60s designed to counter an attack by Soviet Bombers. Called NIKE AJAX, it was a ring of defensive missiles that were placed around Los Angeles and other vulnerable major cities along the coast of California, creating what was called 'The Ring of Fire.' These defensive batteries stood watch over the skies of the California coast awaiting the sign of a sneak attack by the Soviet Union using its nuclear bombers. They were also armed with NIKE HERCULES missiles, which were nuclear tipped defensive missiles that could be launched into the middle of a large group of incoming attack bombers, detonating a massive aerial nuclear blast and destroying all of the incoming threats. These NIKE AJAX installations were also shut down in 1974.

If this all sounds like a crazy Cold War arms race story, it really is a prime example of the military arms race lunacy of the time. This story, better than anything Hollywood could script up, also provided Atari with the backdrop for one of its most popular arcade and home console games. With the Cold War as frigid as ever in the collective thoughts of the world and in the culture of the 1970s and 1980s, it was in fact fitting to see Atari release a game based around the theme of nuclear war. It all begins in the late Winter of 1979 when Dave Theurer's manager, Steve Calfee, told Dave to create a missile defense game with a radar display. Running with the idea and tossing the radar screen idea, on May 30, 1979 Dave Theuer and Rich Adam send their full game proposal to Steve Calfee. With example names such as *War World III, Armegeddon* and *Edge of Blight*, the game concept is now to defend a coastline of cities from incoming nuclear warhead bearing missiles using a trackball controller and three fire buttons.

Initially the concept details both defensive and offensive missile systems, a radar display of incoming missiles, status of cities, populations, missile stockpiles, etc... It also discusses the use of MIRV missiles to split apart and target multiple cities. Different coastline possibilities detailed (suggesting to perhaps use display overlays) are for California, East Coast, Europe and the Mediterranean, but for the initial design however, California was chosen and along with six cities – San Diego, Los Angeles, Santa Barbara, Monterey, San Francisco and Eureka. All six cities are to be covered by three ABM missile batteries. There had also been discussions of a version of the game that would have the U.S. launch against the Soviet Union, though this is nixed pretty quickly when Dave Theurer would only agree to doing a game where the U.S. would defend against a nuclear attack by the Soviet Union. "I didn't want people to glorify war. A purely defensive position wouldn't, because defending millions of people from annihilation is more noble," says Dave.

As the game design progresses, the cabinet proposals are sketched out for *ARMEGEDDON* and a prototype cabinet design is also built. Though it would later be fitted with the final production name chosen by Gene Lipkin, *Missile Command*, the top of the cabinet over the player in this prototype version has various status lights turning on and off to interact with the game and add more of an in-depth 'command center' experience for players. The status lights proved to be distracting for players during field testing though, and were removed from the final production design, causing a more scaled down appearance to the final cabinet. Other elements tried and removed from the game itself include a railway intermission to restock the missile silos in between waves, missile launching submarines, and the ability for operators to enter in custom names for the cities.

In June 1980, *Missile Command* makes it debut and, appealing to the Cold War nuclear threat ever lurking in backs of people's minds, while providing a chaotic and fast paced shooting game to defend cities from nuclear annihilation from incoming ICBM's (Inter-Continental Ballistic Missiles), bombers, killer satellites and 'smart bombs' all trying to destroy the six cities in the game. One part of the game that is considered very controversial after the release is the game over screen, something Dave put in on purpose. "The final lesson has to be that there are no winners in nuclear war," recalls Dave. To reinforce this, when the player loses all of their cities, the entire screen flashes in big letters with an explosion sound in the background - THE END. It creates a chilling and final warning to the game based on nuclear holocaust, and might be the first game with a defined ending. Hollywood would pick up on Dave's lesson three years later with the Matthew Broderick driven hacker film *Wargames*, where nuclear war is nearly averted in a scene that mimics one of the original *Missile Command* concepts. As the runaway computer Joshua seeks codes to unlock nuclear warheads to launch at the Soviet Union for real, against a flickingering background of mock U.S. vs U.S.S.R. nuclear attacks a young hacker tries to teach Joshua the futility of what it's trying to do by making it play itself in games of tac-tac-toe. Finally realizing there can be no winner in tac-tac-toe or nuclear war, Joshua simply states "A strange game. The only winning move is not to play."

But playing *Missile Command* is exactly what people did, and the game becomes a major success. Enough so that the VCS programmers soon chose to start their own version by the end of the year (programmed by VCS *Night Driver* programmer Rob Fulop) which also became wildly successful after its Spring '81 release.

Nuclear war was of great concern to most people in the 1970s and 1980s and many people felt that any day it would start, with one mushroom cloud followed by another, and then our missiles would launch signaling the beginning of World War III. *Missile Command* affected Dave Theurer personally for over a year after he completed it, resulting in month after month of nightmares of nuclear war. It didn't help that Dave lived near the NASA AMES Research Center where supersonic jets were constantly taking off and hitting the sound barrier, letting off the double sonic-boom sound causing Dave to believe that a nuclear bomb had just been dropped on a nearby city and within seconds his home would be destroyed by the nuclear blast. Today, nuclear war is not something most people are as concerned about, but with the ever changing political climate and the continued cold shoulder that Russia (the former Soviet Union) is giving to its short lived peacetime ally, the United States, signs of a new Cold War are beginning to appear not to mention new nuclear threats from the Middle East and North Korea. The days of full scale nuclear conflict could one day become more real than the fun and harmless enjoyment of defending those cities on a video game screen.

The second game not only represents a triumph of technology and game play, but a frustrating series of starts and stops during development that finally allowed the game to be released in February 1982 long after its planned window. We're talking about the game *Space Duel*, designed by the notable Owen Rubin. Though the first interesting part of the story is that the game was actually started by Rick Maurer, who envisioned and began programming a game where each ship has weight and vector on the other ship, causing a unique motion of the conjoined ships about the screen. It's planned to be a color vector version of Asteroids, using Atari's in development Color Quadrascan technology. An unfortunate thing happened to Rick on his way to completing this fun demonstration of physiscs though - he had a mental breakdown. Working on games and creating fun is certainly a fun profession, and at Atari it's an institution. However, working on fun, having fun and not letting the pressures of the challenges of life and work get to you are not always an easy balance. Not only stopping work on *Space Duel*, Rick also resigned and left Atari entirely. The game is left in limbo for a short while before Owen steps in and takes over the game taking it further than originally imagined, but it's soon put on hold in favor of *Asteroids Deluxe* being the followup to *Asteroids*.

Like a yo-yo, *Space Duel* was started up again after *Asteroids Deluxe*, but in the interim a lot of Owen's code wound up in other people's work that he never received a nickel for, causing some resentment. Owen did all the graphic work for *Space Duel* himself before the game was put on hold, and in the interim his color vector generator code was used by Dave Theurer in *Tempest*. Owen never received a nickel from *Tempest*, though the money was a less important issue to him than the credit or lack thereof. To this day, many people think *Tempest* was the first multi-color vector game because it came out before *Space Duel*, but *Space Duel* was actually the first. To top it off, Owens sound routine coding also found its way onto *Tempest*.

Now, this type of resentment over using other's hard work isn't just going on amongst Coin, most in Coin also resented what was going on over in Consumer. While many a person has heard of Ray Kassar and his cadre of MBA's all living the high life, the consumer programmers were living pretty darn well themselves too. During this time, over in the Consumer programming group there had been a lot more competition due to the royalty bonus program and all those big checks being cut and issued out. On bonus check day, the consumer programmers would line up for their $10,000 to up to $300,000 bonus checks, and everyone would quickly dash off to the nearby bank. The curious lot of banking customers would step up to the teller window and right away the teller would look down the line at the glowing and smiling line of eager customers, all with their check in hand and realize the Atari people were there. Then in the days to weeks that would follow the programmers start showing up in brand new cars, dabbling in a little more upscale pharmaceuti-cals usage and just spending money like there would be no tomorrow. One consumer programmer actually bought two of the same car and if one broke down, he'd leave it and just drive the other. Over in Coin there is a lot of resentment towards Con-sumer, after all why were they making all that money off of game's designed in Coin? Coin-op felt it was the REAL Atari - after all they would invent the games and the Consumer Division was just making watered down low resolution shadows of their work. And to add insult to injuries, the original game designers weren't even getting credit in these versions let alone being consulted.

After the delay, Owen wanted to make sure the game was a Tour de force of his graphical prowess. Becoming so much more than 'color *Asteroids*,' using pre-drawn 2d animation to create a plethora of spinning '3d' objects. As Owen stated, "Had it not been delayed because of *Asteroids Deluxe*, it might not have been so fun, because it would not have needed to be so different from *Asteroids*." When it's released in February 1982, *Space Duel* is a really beautiful and vivid multi-color vector display game, a feast for game player's eyes to devour. Rick's surviving two-ship physics coding adds a very real feel to the game play, where the player can almost feel the drag of one ship over the other when the thrusters are fired. A talented player could quickly learn how to use these physics to their advantage by performing a slingshot type of effect, literally tossing the two tethered ships around the screen to avoid the barrage of odd objects put into the game from the menagerie of Owens creative mind. The two player cooperative mode stands out as well, where while flying across the screen, two players can work together blasting away at these enemy objects in this multi-colored madhouse of a space shooter.

Poking Stars...

W hile *Asteroids* is Atari's own 'killer app' in the arcades during 1979 and the in development *Space Invaders* will provide the same function for the VCS, what could very well be considered Atari's 'killer app' for its home computer line, *Star Raiders,* is also developed and released in 1979. *Star Raiders*, written by Doug Neubauer, actually starts out in 1978 as a program written to test the systems capabilities while Doug is waiting for the other chips that make up the Atari home computers to be finished. Doug was the POKEY chip logic designer, and had been joined by his other ex-National Semiconductor co-workers, Mark Shieu on the chip design, Steve Stone laying out the chip design and Delwin Pearson as the technician to assist the team on the POKEY chip. Doug wanted to design a game to have a 3D view looking out a cockpit giving the same feeling as what had already been seen on the *Star Trek* television series or in the radically popular *Star Wars* movie still in theatres.

Though later immortalized as a standard screensaver in Windows computers, at this time it was going to be a challenging task since no one had done this kind of graphic implementation before. Nor had such a personal computer with as much graphics power as the Atari computers ever been built or sold before. Add to this that Doug wasn't sure what a 3D computer algorithm for this effect should be. "Anyway, after stupidly wasting a few weeks trying to guess the algorithm, I finally sat down and worked out the trigonometry on paper and ten minutes later I had the formula," recalls Doug. *Star Raiders* developed in to a combination action and strategy game. During the fights, the player engages targets in real time by using a joystick controller they can pan left and right and up and down creating a space fight not unlike Exidy's late 70s coin-op *Star Fire*. Certainly a step above that game, *Star Raiders* also has options to see behind the ship or to select Short Range Scan and see an over view of the ship and space around it, including the enemy ships. Not just some flat top-down or side view scan, the player is treated to a full 3D representation of the space around the ship, and by using the joystick the player can move the point of view to see the space in a full 360 degree angle from all 3 axis.

The other innovative part of the game is the strategy side. Using a Galac-tic Map (which was a direct carry over from the early Star Trek board games and computer text games), the player is able to see the various Quadrants, where their own Starbases are located, how many enemies were located within each quadrant, and then deduce if any Starbases needed to be defended. To add more depth and realism to the game, the player also has to monitor fuel status, systems and damage. Everything is controlled by the player, from turning on the shields to the computer and other systems. Also adding to the sense of realism, during combat if the ship is hit, systems can be slightly damaged. Repeated hits also result in other systems being damaged or a system to fully fail, and if the ship becomes too damaged to engage in further combat or fuel was running low, the player cam actually warp to a quadrant with a Starbase. There they can perform a docking sequence where a small refueling robot flies out to the ship, repairing all damage and refueling the ship. Truly innova-tive gameplay and features at a time when anything close to it on personal computers were text only games, leaving the entirety of these visuals up to the imagination.

The enemies in the game are called Zylons, with their ships looking like a combination of *Battlestar Galactica's* Cylon fighters and base-stars as well as the tie fighters from *Star Wars*. The combination of realism, action, strategy and a trade-mark "shot sound" from firing the ships cannons made *Star Raiders* a strong hit, placing it as a must own game for the Atari home computers and the perfect demo for showing off the gaming capabilities of Atari's new computers on their launch. In later years *Star Raiders* would see versions on the Atari VCS (for which special keypad controllers are released for), and the Atari 5200 Super System. When Atari is split up and sold in 1984, two games in development based on the movie *The Last Starfighter* are retooled to become *Star Raiders II* and *Solaris* respectively. *Star Raid-ers* will also find its way on a new computer system and many years later on a 64-bit game console... but all of those stories will have to wait for the next book.

Around the time *Star Raiders* was in development, back again in the coin-op division, our faithful Owen Rubin was also developing a game he planned on breaking new ground with. Originally called *Tube Chase* and later renamed *Tunnel Hunt*, Owen's inspiration for the game design came from a sequence of the movie *Alien* in where the smaller ship heads towards the planet to land. Thinking it might be a fun concept for a game, he starts out using the vector hardware from the soon to be released *Asteroids,* and some code from the *Night Driver* game. Owen created an early version where a player could fly down tunnels, but during this process discovered a major drawback in the vector system - it couldn't handle hidden line removal, so the tunnels really didn't look like tunnels. Owen soon finds out that another engineer has designed some hardware that could draw multiple ellipses, but the catch is it's based around a raster display. So in 1979, Owen proceeds to re-write his game to use that hardware instead, with the end result of a really great looking and playable game that has multiple tunnels with split tubes and rotations.

Sadly, the one big negative to this design is the ellipse drawing hardware is just way too expensive to make it cost effective for production. Management decides to rework the hardware to save costs, morphing the tubes from ellipses to circles, but even after that the hardware was still too expensive. After another reworking it's changed again, this time to display rectangles as well as loosing the ability to split tunnels. Feedback from marketing on the game suggested that just flying was not going to be fun enough, so Owen added *Star Wars* like ships to fly down the tube toward the player, who would have to shoot them or die. The *Tunnel Hunt* prototype cabinet also incorporates some unique designs at Owens request, including a unique vacuum form part that literally wraps around the player's head to help pull the player into the game, feeling more like a sit in cabinet than a stand-up arcade machine. It also includes a unique joystick, allowing the player to fly and shoot with one hand. The wrap around effect of the cabinet helps further induce the closed in, vertigo effect on players as the game play intensified.

Once field testing started the game was playing very well, and although it remained a strong number two in the arcades it was being tested in for over ten weeks, it never hit the coveted number one spot. In response, marketing kept requesting more and more changes, and the game would be placed out on field tests again and again where it did well in the number two and three spots over and over. Apparently, never making number one, it was considered not strong enough for Atari to go into production and ship it. Described by Owen as "the game that would not die, " it was instead licensed to Centuri as *Tunnel Hunt* in 1981 (after being originally licensed to Exidy as *Vertigo*). It will be the only arcade game that Atari would license out to another company. Interestingly, Sega releases their own game in 1982 that produces Owen's original vision for running through through vectorized 'elliptical tunnels,' but during its transition between waves: *Tac/Scan*.

An interesting note regarding the game play of *Tunnel Hunt*: as the game gets more difficult and the speed of traveling through the tunnels increases, the game actually started to make players a bit dizzy in an almost vertigo induced effect from the constant movement of the patterns of graphics zooming in towards the player. Additionally regarding sound in the game, Owen had helped Doug Neubauer to create the shot sound in *Star Raiders*. After Doug had left Atari, Owen was working adding sound to *Tunnel Hunt* and wanted to recreate that same shot sound, but without access to the routine he used a logic analyzer to analyze the sounds in an effort to recreate it. In the end it allowed Owen to create a routine to input values into the POKEY audio chip that was used in not just the Atari home computers, but in many of Atari's coin-op games as well. Rusty Dawe would also rewrite the routine into a system he called 'RPM' for Rusty's POKEY Music, causing many people to credit him for creating the routine even though it was originally created by Owen Rubin (bringing up that pesky issue of credit again).

Chapter 8 Review In Images

Consumer Division programmer Brad Stewart looking over
some source code with unknown woman.

Atari ran VCS *Space Invaders* competitions all over the world across 1980 and 1981. Here are photos from a few.

VIDEO GAME PLAN FORM

NAME OF GAME: __Asteroids__   Number of Players: __1 or 2__

ENGINEERING TEAM: __Ed Logg / Howie Delman / Paul Mancuso__

BRIEF DESCRIPTION OF GAME PLAY: __The object of the game is to destroy the asteroids and saucers. Shooting a large asteroid breaks that asteroid into 2 medium sized asteroids. Shooting one of those pieces breaks it into 2 small asteroids. Shooting [over]__

PLAY FEATURES TO EMPHASIZE: __Scoring: Small rock = 100, medium rock = 50, large = 20 large saucer = 200, small saucer = 1000. Every 10,000 points you will get an extra ship. Using hyperspace is risky because there is a probability of destruction upon reentry.__

PLAYER OPTIONS (if any): __Controls: 2 (left + right) rotate buttons, hyperspace buttons, thrust button and fire button__

OPERATOR OPTIONS:

   Game Times: __None__

   Extended Play (describe score levels, amount of time, etc.):

   __None__

   Coinage: __Free play, 1 coin 2 plays, 1 coin 1 play, 2 coins 1 play; Middle coin mech = 1 or 2 coins; right coin mech = 1, 4, 5, 6 coin__

   Language(s): __English, German, French, Spanish__

   Other Play Options: __Start each player with 3 or 4 ships__

OVERALL DIMENSIONS: Height_____ Width_____ Depth_____

MONITOR SIZE: __X-Y monitor (standard size)__

OTHER FACTORS: __If the players score is one of the ten best, he/she can enter his/her initials. The ten best scores, and the players initials are displayed in attract mode.__

Left: Ed Logg during a brainstorming session.

Bottom: *Asteroids* hardware engineer Howard Delman proclaims just how smart he is. Pete Takaichi from the Industrial Design group is on the far left.

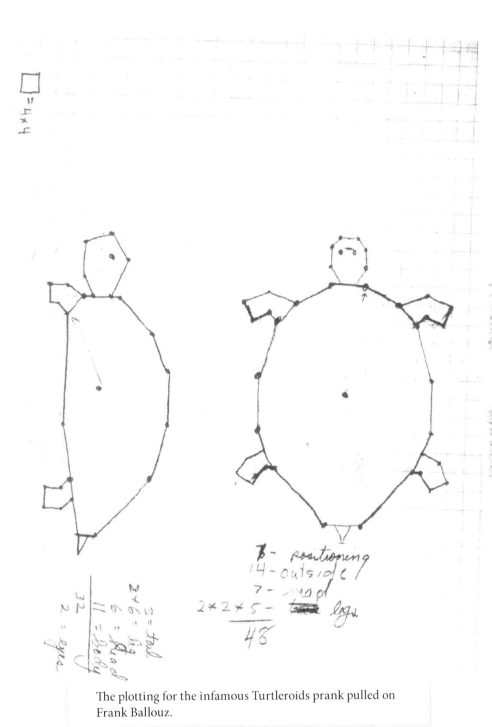

The plotting for the infamous Turtleroids prank pulled on
Frank Ballouz.

Top: Award given ou[t] at the 1981 Pebble Beach distributors conference to trumpet *Asteroids* being number one in sales. That's an actual RO[M] chip containing the *Asteroids* game code encased in solid luci[te.]

Left: Ed Logg (in 199[?]) with the special gold *Asteroids* that was made to commemor[ate] the 50,000 *Asteroids* machine produced.

Right: Warner's Manny Gerard playing *Asteroids*.

Bottom: Don Osborne posing with *Asteroids* for a promotional flyer.

Opposite Page: The cease and desist letter regarding the saucers in *Asteroids* being nicknamed after characters from *Mr. Bill*.

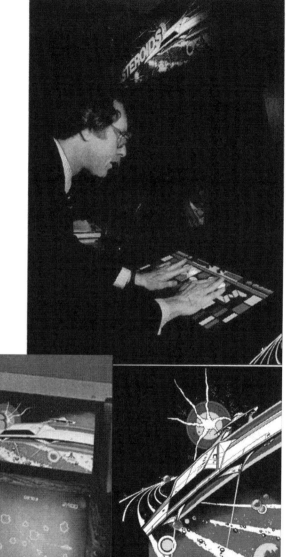

THOMAS M. SAUNDERS
ATTORNEY AT LAW
645 FIFTH AVENUE
NEW YORK, NEW YORK 10022
212.688.6445

January 19, 1981

Mr. Edward Logg
Atari, Inc.
200 Fifth Avenue
New York, N.Y. 10010

Dear Mr. Logg:

I was quite interested in reading the article entitled
"How to Win at Asteroids" in the February 1981 Esquire.

As the attorney for Walter Williams and Real Good Productions,
Inc., proprietors in all rights in the "Mr. Bill Show" and
related characters, I am always interested in public mention
of our names.

However, please be aware that the names "Mr. Bill" and
"Sluggo" are protected by United States trademark and copyright laws and various state and local laws.

I am sure the personalities associated with these names are
helpful in conceptualizing the behavior of elements of the
Asteroids game. Kindly refrain, however, from utilizing
these names in any phase of the manufacture, use or sale
of Asteroids.

Yours truly,

Thomas M. Saunders

TMS:jv

A copy was given to Skip Paul for a future statement.

Atari, in partnership with Coke, held *Asteroids* competitions across the world durin 1981-1982. *Clockwise from top:* Competition poster, Asteroids patch, two competition buttons, an official score card, and an official competition shirt.

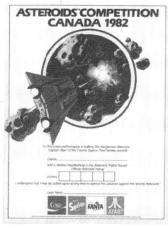

INTER-OFFICE MEMO

COMPANY PRIVATE

TO: Dan Van Elderen

FROM: Ed Logg

DATE: July 17, 1980

SUBJECT: GAME DESCRIPTION: SHOOT THE CENTIPEDE

This game would be a one or two player game on a black and white, or color raster monitor. The game would be a modified SOCCER hardware. The controls consist of a joystick and a fire button.

The player controls a gun which moves back and forth, and up and down within the bottom four rows. The player always shoots upward on the screen. One or more multiple segment centipedes would appear across the top of the screen and move back and forth descending toward the player. If the centipede hits the player then the player dies. The player will start off with a given number of lives and will be able to earn an extra life at a certain score. He must shoot and destroy the centipede to earn a bonus score. The player's shots can split the centipede if it hits between the segments, or if a segment is destroyed. As each centipede gets destroyed the next one can become faster, longer and smarter. We could also send down two or more smaller but faster centipedes. The centipede segments have legs and the motion of the segments will correspond to the movement of the legs. We also could add obstacles in the upper portion of the screen which would absorb any of the player's shots and would deflect the path of the centipede. These spots could randomly change with each wave. We could also add bugs that would either traverse the screen or advance towards the player.

EL/cp

cc: L. Rains
    D. Stubben
    D. Bailey

Top: The original game description for Centipede, at that time called Shoot The Centipede.

Following Pages: Ed Logg's design notes and field test results showing how well Centipede tested against other popular games of the time.

CENTIPEDE INSTRUCTIONS

Ed Logg
2/4/81

CONTROL PANEL

"FIRE" _above_ Asteroid style push button

"1 PLAYER START" or pictogram of one player (ala Japanese game
to the right of the CHERRY switch

"2 PLAYER START" or "   " 2 players

FRONT PLEX

⬙ 1 point

◯ 10 points

◔ 100 points

🦐 200 points

} see Ogna or myself for a better drawing of these pictures.

🕷 ? points

〰 1000 points

• Shoot to destroy advancing creatures for points.

• Collisions with any creature will destroy you.

• An extra life is given every ⑩000 points.   →20

In a two player game, players alternate until his supply of lives is exhausted.

Hold the fire button down for repetitive fire.

• S̶u̶p̶e̶r̶ "ones" mushrooms

• It requires two hits for the flea/ant

LOCATION: MOUNTAIN VIEW TIME ZONE - CENTIPEDE UR 2/27 TO 4/16/81

Overall, CENTIPEDE performed very well during its initial field test at the Mountain View Time Zone. CENTIPEDE was the number one game in the location during the entire testing period.

As a result of player survey findings, a large trak-ball was installed during the fifth week of collections for testing. After two weeks of relatively stable earnings, the small trak-ball was reinstalled. The conclusion was that there is no significant improvement in CENTIPEDE's earnings with the large trak-ball. Because of this and other factors, it was decided to produce CENTIPEDE with the small trak-ball.

During the testing period the high scores on CENTIPEDE were 54,852, 48,171, and 46,284. This test piece is similar in game play to the "hard" setting on production games.

Game	Rank	Time Period	Average Collection	Best Week	Worst Week	Average % of gross
CENTIPEDE UR	1	2/28-4/16/81	$449	$548	$366	5.6%
Gorf	2	2/28-4/16/81	359	407	280	4.5
Berzerk	3	2/28-4/16/81	310	361	237	3.9
Pac-Man	4	3/7 -4/16/81	291	320	243	3.7
BattleZone	5	2/28-4/16/81	285	314	264	3.6
Asteroids	6	2/28-3/27/81	300	342	247	3.5
Moon Eagle	7	2/28-4/16/81	240	258	196	3.0

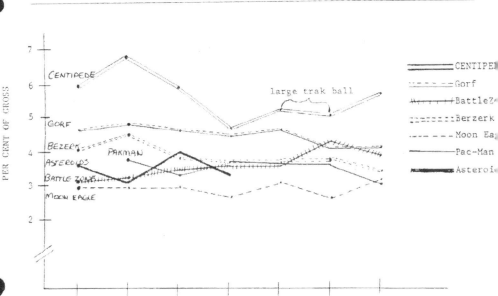

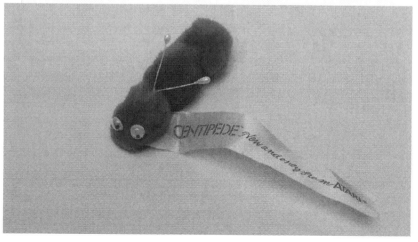

er Office Memo

ATARI
Coin Operated Gam

Ed Logg

Frank Ballouz

ct: Atari $50,000 World Championships   Date: 9/1/81

Ed, as you know, Centipede is going to be the game used
at the World Championships in Chicago--utilizing the
special program you are developing with an automatic
shut-off at three minutes.

What I need to know is, if you were a player in the
tournament, and knowing the game as well as you do,
what would your strategy be to achieve the high score
within the three minutes?

FAB/rd

cc: D. Vanelderen
     M. Layne

INTER-OF

TO: Frank Ballouz

FROM: Ed Logg

SUBJECT: ATARI $50,000 World Championship

DATE: Sept. 3, 1981

There are several strategies which can be used on Centipede at
the World Championships. The most obvious strategy is to shoot everything that moves as fast as you can. This is the strategy which I
feel will be used.

Another possible strategy would be to try for the high point
objects such as the spider and scorpion. This strategy has a high
element of risk and it may backfire if no scorpions appear.

There is another strategy used in arcades to achieve long game
times and high scores which will be at a disadvantage in a timed
event. This strategy requires the player to eliminate all the mushrooms in the upper middle portion of the screen and leave mushrooms
at the bottom of the screen. This means the flea does not appear
and the centipedes take their longest path to the bottom.

There is one point you should be aware of; when a player dies
if he has lots of poisoned or partially destroyed mushrooms, the time
needed to restore these mushrooms will reduce his actual playing time.
Hence the player should avoid dying or shooting too many mushrooms
(i.e. don't miss the centipede, spider, etc.).

I am setting up the program to allow a one player start only.
This makes programming easier and a one player game should suit the
preference of the contestants. If this is not acceptable please
let me know as soon as possible.

EL/clm

cc: M. Layne
     D. Stubben
     D. Van Elderen

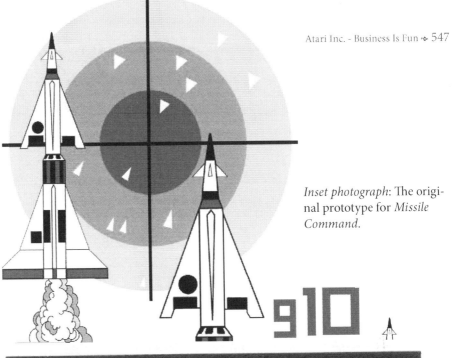

Inset photograph: The original prototype for *Missile Command*.

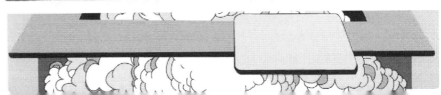

Avid video game fan Steven Spielberg with his own
personal *Missile Command* in the early 1980s.

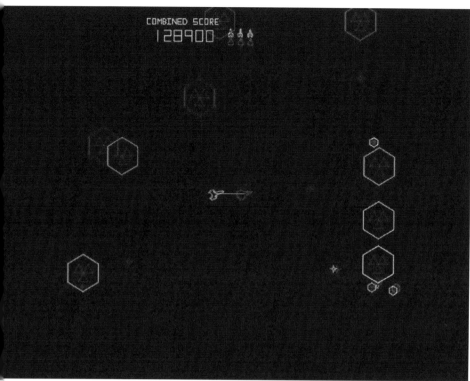

Opposite Page: Flyer promoting the QuadraScan display technology used in *Space Duel*. That's *Space Duel* creator Owen Rubin in the background.

Top: Screen from *Space Duel*. *Bottom left*: *Space Duel* is featured on The Who's 1982 album *It's Hard*. *Bottom Right*: *Space Duel* on the assembly line.

The Atari® Era. A New Vision.

The Atari Era is a new age of video entertainment. It's Atari "Visioneering" combining tomorrow's technology with creative game ideas. Enter the Atari Era. Discover the pacesetting profit performance of CENTIPEDE™, TEMPEST™ and the fantastic 4-games-in-one SPACE DUEL™. Talk to your ATARI distributor now or contact us for referral at Atari, Inc., 790 Sycamore Drive, P.O. Box 906, Milpitas, CA 95035. (408) 942-3100.

ATARI
A Warner Communications Company

COMPUTER ADVENTURE

STAR RAIDERS™

ATARI® A Warner Communications Company

Model CXL4011
Use with
ATARI® 400™ or ATARI 800™
PERSONAL COMPUTER SYSTEMS

By 1981, Atari was geared towards a trifecta of high tech industries: coin, home console and home computer.

Chapter 9

Atari At The Speed Of Light

A l Alcorn, Atari's first hired engineer is now a denizen of 'Mahogany Row,' but things had changed rapidly since the ouster of Nolan in December of 1978 and the departure of Joe Keenan the following year. In the early days of Atari, if Al needed to speak with anyone in management, it was as simple as walking down to someone's office, knocking on the door and going in to discuss an engineering issue or anything else on his mind. In those early days of the company, things were more open; everyone contributed together and worked together. Company bureaucracy, hierarchical management structure and titles were never a hindrance or a roadblock to getting work done.

However, with Ray Kassar taking the helm as Chairman and CEO in 1979, Al felt things had become too compartmentalized - and with a revolving door of marketing and management guys coming and going, there was no longer cohesion or continuity within the company. To make matters worse, the company was no longer a balance of marketing and engineering working together to solve problems and create products. Marketing felt it was in charge and would dictate products and the path of the company, making what engineering had to say less influential on such matters in the Consumer and Home Computer divisions.

This all became crystal clear to Al one day when he stepped in to run Consumer Engineering for two weeks while Steve Bristow was on vacation. There was a discussion of moving from the 2K to the larger 4K sized ROM cartridges for the VCS gaming system, and Al was against this kind of move because it would spell the end to ever doing any games in the older sized ROM's. However, he was willing to go into a meeting with the marketing guys to discuss the situation.

So he brings in some of the guys from engineering to attend the meeting with the marketing guys. The first question Al puts out on the table is "What is the cost of goods? What's the delta between price of goods sold and cost?" Marketing's response: "That's confidential. We can't give you that information." Al, slightly stunned, comes back and says, "Excuse me?" Once again, the marketing director states that the information is confidential and they can't share that information with engineering. Al comes to find out that the engineers knew this was happening quite often and had been keeping silent about it. So Al decides that marketing needs to understand the mechanism for them even getting this 'confidential information' in the first place.

Al asks, "Where do you think the cost of goods comes from?" The response: "Accounting - it's the bill of materials." Now Al shoots back, "Yes! Who do you think selects the bill of materials? Engineering!" Al is 100 percent correct; without engineering, this 'confidential information' would have never even reached marketing. Yet after clearly explaining the mechanism for this information, marketing still wins the argument by again saying that the information is 'confidential' and they will not give him the information. "Well, that's it then - I guess this meeting is fucking over!" and Al gets up and leaves the meeting. Al knows flat out, without question, this is crazy time. The company is brain dead and he has no reservations in telling Ray Kassar this bluntly. However, even with Al explaining this, the company had become so compartmentalized and closed off that Al felt Kassar was the last to realize this.

Al simply had enough of Mahogany Row after that experience, and enough of the conga line of well-perfumed executives marching to and from the corporate offices who knew absolutely nothing about video gaming or technology. It was time to go back and do what he loved best; being in the Atari research labs, designing something new and exciting. Al enlisted Roger Hector to join him on this new product engineering adventure, which was to be based on the field of Holoptics or holograms.

Roger had come to Atari by way of the Huffy Company, where he had taken a job in Ohio in 1975 designing bicycles. Originally from California, it only took one

Ohio ice storm that Winter to make him want to return to California. Educated in Industrial Design at San Jose State along with current Atari employee Pete Takaichi, he called Pete to inquire as to whether there were any industrial design job openings in the area. As luck would have it, Pete was working in the design group at a company called Atari, and although Roger had played *PONG* in various bars he really knew nothing about the company. Nonetheless, when Pete suggested working at Atari, Roger of course said yes - anything that would get him out of Ohio. Pete was able to hire Roger in June of 1976, basically because they knew each other. Roger started work in the old roller rink, placed in the offices around the rink area where the manufacturing was going on. Roger figured he'd work there for a while, and then find a real job; he didn't consider working on games as a serious profession at the time.

"When I got there, it was unlike anything I'd ever experienced. It was exciting and an unconventional kind of business," recalls Roger. "Nolan would kind of bounce in and out of the design shop, always interested in what was going on. Because I was a designer and an artist, I would do these sketches and drawings in a coin-op world. I would come into work some days and I'd find out that Nolan was raiding my desk and taking my drawings to show around to people. So I got this reputation of being a good concept designer. When I started my work on some coin-op games, my first project was *Super Breakout*. So I designed the cabinet, artwork and control panel," recalls Roger.

Another project that Roger would work on was the Two Game Module, a high tech cabinet that could house two games in one, using mirrors to position two monitors on opposite sides and allowing locations to double their profit intake by having two separate games in the same footprint of one cabinet. Roger would also work on another famous Atari coin-op game, called *Battlezone*. Designing the 3D tanks, missiles and other objects in the game, Roger tapped into his old engineering background to create 3D wire frame visuals so the lines would connect and give the perception of the objects having depth and dimension.

Atari was very free-wheeling, especially compared to the strict business structure that Roger came out of from Huffy. "I remember the cool lobby in the (Winchester) building, all wood, really nice and Nolan had hired this receptionist. She was an exotic dancer at night and the company receptionist during the day," recalls Roger. The hippie culture permeated all areas of the company and it was beneficial to the creativity and free flow of ideas. "We even had this break area kind of cafeteria in the back and the games out in the lobby set on free play and the games working in the manufacturing area to play, that was pretty amazing for the time. For hours after working we would be playing these games. I remember playing this driving game, going as fast as possible and then having to come back to reality when actually driving home for the night," recalls Roger.

As the company grew to well over 1,000 employees, the layers of bureaucracy grew as well. However, before the company grew too big, there was still a feeling of everyone wanting to work together to see it succeed - and there couldn't be a better example of this than during the 1977 production of the VCS that Roger was involved with. Nolan and the senior management were concerned that production numbers were going to fall short, so that year everyone pitched in, whether they were a line worker or a senior staff member - everyone rolled up their sleeves and got to work to make sure that the VCS (as well as the other consumer products heading out for the Christmas sales season) would make the sales order numbers. Roger was right there in the thick of it pitching in as well, installing the round rubber washers onto the six pole switches for the VCS consoles. This was a case of a square peg going into a round hole - the washers had to be stretched to be fitted over the switches. By the end of the week, Roger's fingers were a mess and he noticed the line workers all had bandages on their hands. This led to a change in the design, thanks to Roger bringing this to manufacturing's attention, and would be one of many changes that had to be made along the way to the numerous consumer products being designed and built by Atari. Roger would later work on prototyping many of those products before winding up with Al on his Holoptics project.

Atari's previous foray in to hand held and board games provided the impetus for Al's new project, with the COP programmable microcontroller technology developed from the LCD hand held games opening the first doorway toward Al's Holoptic game system. What Al wanted to do now was leapfrog everything done before and take on the hand held/tabletop electronic gaming market in a new and unique way, utilizing holographic technology for a home video game system.

Holography can trace its roots back to the 1920's through the 1930's when, in an effort to improve the electron microscope, researchers at the Thomson Houston Company in England stumbled upon the effect that created electron holography. However, it wouldn't be until the 1960s that holography would be able to generate 3D images thanks to the advent of lasers. Initial holograms were only visible by passing laser light through them, called 'transmission holograms.' The method was further improved to allow regular white light to pass through the back of the holo-gram to reveal an image, known as 'rainbow transmission holograms' because of the rainbow effect the image would give off as the light passed through the holographic image. Finally the 'Denisyuk' method of hologram generation was created, allowing the holographic image to be displayed by shining white light on the same side of the surface as the hologram, allowing for multi-colored images as well.

Now as we said prior, if you remember, Al Alcorn stated Atari's biggest se-cret was, "We could never keep a secret." This was still quite true and he wanted to ensure that the competition would not find out that Atari was about to embark on developing a holographic home gaming console. So during the initial designs and schematics for the project, the project was presented as a Coin Division project whose title was 'Arcade Holographic Game System.' "We figured if we threw some bullshit out like holography in the coin-op market, we knew the traditional coin-op industry was so far behind us, and they so desperately wanted to catch up - we knew if we threw something like this out there, they would waste their time trying to compete," recalls Al Alcorn. So Al sets off to assemble his team and begin work on designing this new system.

One edict that comes down from marketing and specifically from Ray Kas-sar; this is going to be a low-end game system so its cartridge price point needs to be set at least at half of what the VCS cartridges were. The VCS needs to stand out as the high-end gaming system.

Al looked at the VCS cartridges and realized the most expensive part in the cartridge was the ROM chip, so he would eliminate this from the his holographic system and put all of the programming into the game system itself, completely cut-ting out the major portion of the cost out of cartridges. This in turn would allow Atari to sell the holographic system and generate a strong revenue stream from the cartridge sales. The system is to be based around the COP Series programmable processor, thanks to the fact that two development stations were already down in Sunnyvale from the canceled LCD hand held games project. Specifically the COP 441 chip with more I/O lines and memory to handle the eight games that it would contain.

Roger Hector would have a fun and creative task on this project: Build the models for the games that would be photographed using a special set of equipment in the Holoptics lab. The models were to be used as the backdrops for the LED games (although 'backdrops' isn't really the proper description of the holographic displays that would be used in the console).

The idea behind the Holoptics game system is to change the way people play electronic games. Companies such as Mattel and Coleco had previously produced LED based games, which by the time of Al's system were already starting to get long in the tooth. These were usually games with LED's sticking out from a playfield, which would light up in succession to show a ball or player movement - the players imagining the little light was either a ball or player. Others would have LED's behind a dark tinted piece of plastic with playfield lines on them with the LED's lighting up in patterns to show ball and player movement. And still newer ones had started to use LCD watch technology, showing more detailed pre-rendered liquid crystal patterns for game objects

The Holoptics game would be much different, though its basic operational concept was very similar to Magnavox's original Odyssey home console; each game would consist of a 'cartridge' that would slide into the top of the unit, with 'keys' on the back that would press buttons on the inside electronics board to instruct the microcontroller as to which game to play. The system had two light bulbs inside; each one would light up to show one of two separate scenes on the affixed holographic image.

Games such as *Asteroids, Space Invaders, Superman* and others would start by showing their 'Scene A' and you would play the game on that playfield. If you lost a player life, then the system would light up the second light bulb which would show a different holographic display, which would be 'Scene B' and this would add more depth to the game. Other games like *Football* and *Basketball* would show one half of the playfield, and as you moved your player across to the edge of the screen it would shift scenes to show the other half of the playfield, giving the game player the sense of a much larger playfield and more intense interaction. Sound effects would vary from all sorts of different missiles, shots, explosions and other sounds to further enhance game play.

Besides Roger, Al would bring in a new hire by the name of Harry Jenkins, a mechanical engineer. Harry would work for Al not just on this project (which officially became known as Cosmos when it was revealed), but on other possible implementations of the use of Holography including a drum cylinder design which was codenamed Specter. Specter would quickly spin a holographic drum to produce a 3D image. "I loved working with Roger and Harry. We had a really great time doing this project," recalls Al.

The holographic plates were done by Steve McGrew and Steve Provence, who mastered the process of the two scene-transparent holograms that made the Cosmos possible. Steve Provence had actually studied holography in 1975 at the New York School of Holography and again in 1976 at the San Francisco School of Holography, so his qualifications in this newer field and understanding of its demanding needs were impeccable. He and McGrew frequently came into the Atari Holoptics lab to test the latest holographic plate samples to see if the angles of the lighting and the player field of view were optimum… and tossing them if they weren't.

The holographic plate design process for this consumer class holographic device was truly breaking new ground for Al, Atari, and even the entire entertainment industry. Creating 3D holographic images isn't like taking a snapshot of an object with a camera. It's a complex process of exposing objects to a laser to achieve an image, and even then that image would have to be exposed at numerous angles, with each of those angles of exposure being processed onto a holographic plate. The exposure time for the laser would last for more than minute, and the objects couldn't move within a quarter of a wave length of light. Foam board, paper and other material would have to be utilized to marginalize the possibly of motion, as even the slightest bit of movement and the object would disappear from the image being exposed. So the process for making the models required a lot of invention as it had never been done before.

The model for *Asteroids* was one of the easier ones, because the ship model that Roger built was plastic and the asteroids were lava rocks, though the bulk of the planned games were difficult to produce. *Road Runner's* 3D objects had to be carved out of plastic. *Superman's* cages in the model had to be aligned and scaled so that the game playfield would have to match up with the LED's behind the game field screen. *Basketball* had to have the basket exactly line up with the LED. These were all very difficult challenges to face when designing, building and laser imaging the models to create the holograms.

The Cosmos case design is done by Roy Nishi, who was head of the Consumer Electronics Industrial Design group, and Linda Whitten would build the first model sample of the Cosmos. Compared to other desktop and handheld electronic games, the Cosmos was rather large because of the angles needed to display each of the two separate holographic scenes that would be shown during game play. The holograms themselves were also large, measuring close to 6" x 6"in size, so the display window that the player would view the game through had to be wide enough to see all of the game play.

The product boxes for the Cosmos were created and sales flyers made up, which were sent out to Atari's distributors in sales packs. Everything appeared to look as if the Atari Cosmos was ready to go. However, Al Alcorn was receiving very little support from Atari's marketing. In fact, Al had to go to the January 1981 CES in Vegas to demonstrate the system and take orders without any real company support, just his team members Roger Hector and Harry Jenkins in attendance.

While reviewing the unit in the Atari booth, Many retailers commented that the game wasn't truly a 3D holographic game. Al, Roger and Harry had to continually explain that this was the first of its kind implementation of this type of technology in a game system - a pioneering effort. And despite some of the naysayers, the Cosmos pulled in a very respectable 8,000 units in sales orders from those first showing, which proved that with proper marketing muscle behind it and a stronger sales presence, the Cosmos would definitely be a strong selling product for Atari.

The Cosmos would even receive a CES Award for the 1981 show, though that probably only helped put it even more in the cross-hairs of the marketing department, now looking to eliminate it. Even with Ray Kassar's guidelines, Cosmos was considered a possible threat to sales of the VCS and its cartridges. The plug was pulled on the project and Al's Holoptic lab was ordered to close down. On that day, Steve Providence showed up to see that the lab was closing without warning. "I suspect there were probably 1,000 shells tossed away from our lab storage," recalls Provence. From production line notes and engineering logs, the Atari EG500 (as the notes refer to Cosmos as) had a pilot run of up to 250 units. Whether that many units were ever made is not known. "I worked for Steve McGrew for about three more months after the Atari deal fell apart. Steve McGrew then threatened to sue me and tried to block me from working in the holographic field for darn near ten years. Paul Jakab, Atari's attorney, said it was all BS (as far as 'non-compete's go)," Steve recalls.

"When things went to hell in a handbag, I grabbed five working production Cosmos units before everything went into the dumpster. I put them out in my home garage for safekeeping and one day I went out to the garage to look for them and my wife told me – 'yeah I threw those out,'" recalls Roger Hector. OUCH!

After the closure of the Atari Holoptics lab, in 1983 Steve would found Steve Provence Holography to produce holograms for advertising and for security applications as well as large format holograms. Ken Haynes, another holographer involved in the Cosmos project would move on and begin producing security holograms for credit and debit cards for American Bank Note.

The only other use Atari made of its advanced hologram technologies was in the use of hologram stickers on its cartridges and hardware to cut back on counterfeit products being sold. Al Alcorn, who headed the Cosmos project noted: "Ray Kassar was too scared to take a chance on the hand held/tabletop market. The VCS was the only thing he had faith in."

This would be the final straw for Al Alcorn; as the years had passed, research and development he was interested in Atari pursuing had continued to be cut and curtailed, and finally crippled to the point where the company was no longer about innovating and producing future technologies. Atari was now almost all about marketing and cost cutting. Atari's first hired engineer resigns at the end of 1981, being put on the 'beach' and leaving Atari behind him.

Chapter 9 Review In Images

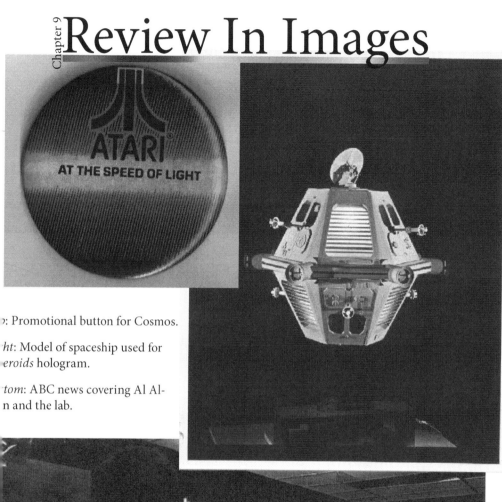

p: Promotional button for Cosmos.

ht: Model of spaceship used for *eroids* hologram.

tom: ABC news covering Al Al-
n and the lab.

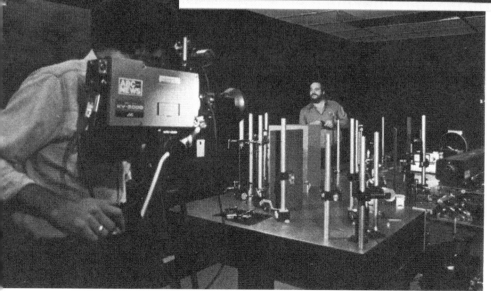

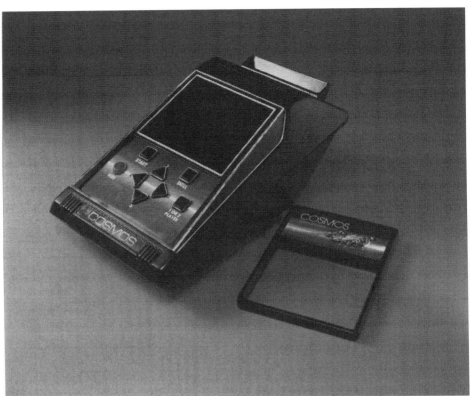

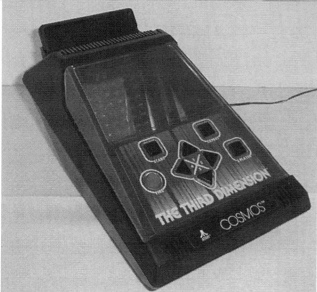

Top: The hologram from *Superman*.

Left: Closeup of Cosmos showing the LED matrix that's used to light up the different views of the inserted hologram.

The Specter tabletop system, which used holographic drums spinning rapidly to produce a hologram during gameplay.

Chapter 10

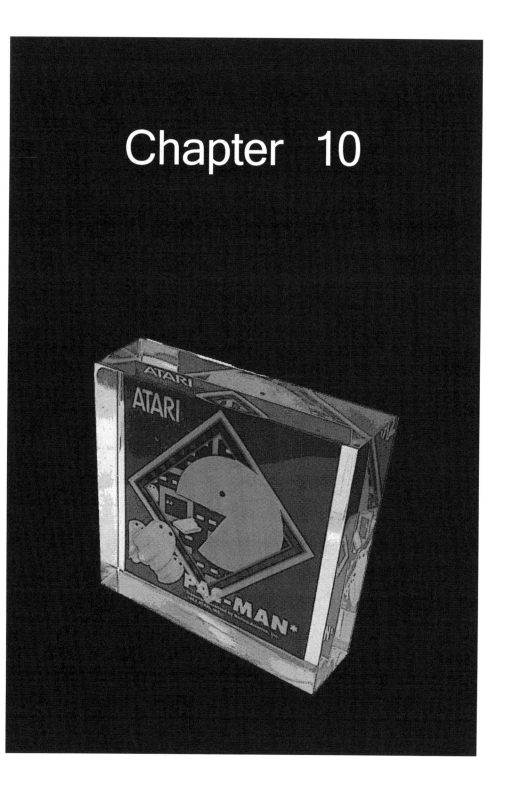

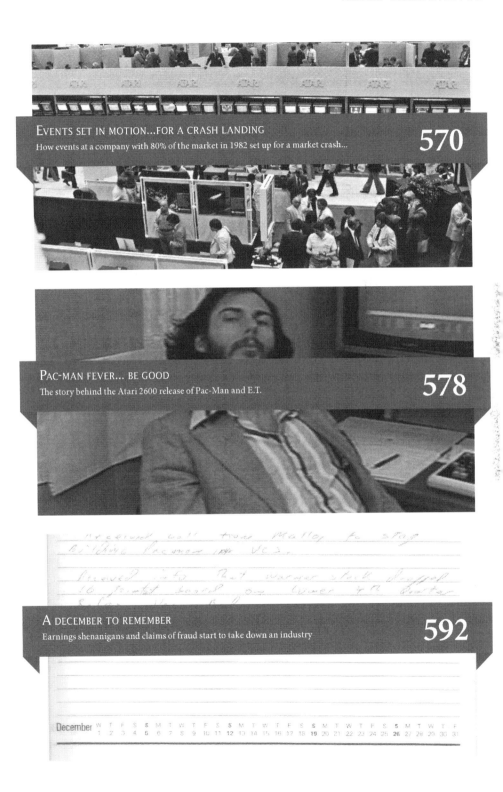

EVENTS SET IN MOTION...FOR A CRASH LANDING
How events at a company with 80% of the market in 1982 set up for a market crash...
570

PAC-MAN FEVER... BE GOOD
The story behind the Atari 2600 release of Pac-Man and E.T.
578

A DECEMBER TO REMEMBER
Earnings shenanigans and claims of fraud start to take down an industry
592

Events Set
In Motion

Many people attribute the great video game crash to simplistic reasons such as bad versions of Pac Man and ET games, while still others will argue that computer prices dropped so drastically they overlapped the video game prices causing a drop in video game sales. Then there were the dozens of companies that sprang up overnight to sell video games based on anything just to put a game out, which caused a glut of bad games on the market. While these may all sound plausible, no single event can directly assign blame for the great video game crash. A series of other factors, many originating directly from Atari, were put into motion that set the stage for the great video game crash, more succinctly described as the U.S. consumer industry crash. These events start to unfold and snowball starting in 1981.

When Ray Kassar first came to Atari as a consultant in early 1978, he noted that it was apparent to him he had a lot of work to do to address issues within the company, but to effectively address these issues, he couldn't compete with all the strong egos and personalities. Specifically, Bushnell and Keenan were viewed by Kassar as key 'problem children.' However, as time went by, Ray too (according to Manny) fell into the spiraling trap of his own ego.

"When Ray Kassar first came onboard, he was great and did a great job, but as time went by he became as big a problem as Bushnell and Keenan," recalls Manny Gerard. While some fault Ray's lavishness with such things as the helipad at Corporate Headquarters and the grandiose, 'pomp and circumstance' entrances made on occasions to impress the local television networks, these demonstrations were many times per Warner's direction. They were meant to instill how impressive and power-ful Atari had become, and its tremendous influence over the industry it helped to create and grow. Ray took one such helicopter ride from Moffett Field to land near Atari headquarters in a Warner Corporate helicopter which had been affixed with a 'temporary' Atari name and logo. The ride unnerved Kassar a bit and he felt the whole event was a complete waste of time and money, even if it was for the company's image.

The fact that Kassar never drove himself anywhere, and that his daily co-mute from his apartment in San Francisco to Atari headquarters in Sunnyvale each day was via his own chauffeured town car, added to the negative perception. Among the laid back Atari employees, this established a bad image for him because most thought that this luxury chauffeuring was pretentious and unnecessary. Especially in the counter-culture, polar opposite of the New York City business environment, Silicon Valley. This was the perception of those not understanding the bigger picture – in reality, Kassar used this time during the one hour each way commute to and from his San Francisco apartment to his advantage to prepare for the day to come… and to review the events of the day on his way home.

Ray's image of excess was only enforced when under Ray's direction a five star equivalent corporate dining hall is built out in the back corner of the second floor of 1265 Borregas in 1981. Meant to entertain and impress potential business partners, customers and special guests, the dining hall includes a private chef and wait staff, providing a dining experience that rivals anything California's culinary crème de la crème could possibly offer.

One idea that Kassar wanted to pursue that had less to do with image was the elimination of the scattered and disconnected existence of Atari as a company. While a fair number of Atari's buildings were situated within Moffett Park in Sunny-vale, they were still separate buildings that were walking and sometimes driving dis-tance away from others. Other buildings were located miles away, including Coin-op which was completely an island of its own over in Milpitas. Kassar approached Ge-rard and Ross with the idea of the construction of a single large structure or a group of multiple large buildings all connected into a campus to bring the entire company together and eliminate much of the disconnect in communications and curb the fiefdoms of management in the individual buildings. The project would cost a staggering $300 million and by the time Kassar presented the idea to Gerard and Ross, there was already a great deal of concern about the future of Atari. In November of 1981, Warner's vice president of corporate affairs Roger Smith wrote a detailed assessment of Atari and what he strongly cautioned were signs of volatility in its far too rapidly increasing earnings. He urged that this rate of earnings could suddenly subside or collapse. Ross agreed with his assessment.

However, one thing that Kassar would not be able to escape was the continued nurturing of his direct decision management style - that everything had to go through him and the growing cutthroat management environment within Atari Corporate itself. Midlevel management quickly learned that if they couldn't get their presented ideas or products approved by the managers they directly reported to, they could go around them by going directly to Kassar. Ray also encouraged and rewarded the monarchial style of management that he had fostered. Perks and lavish rewards are offered to sales and marketing staff that could further increase sales and performance of Atari's profits, specifically if it related to its favored product, the VCS. When Atari broke the $1 Billion sales mark, instead of the annual sales meeting taking place in California as it had in the past, it became an over-the-top celebration in, of all places, Monte Carlo, where Kassar would stay at the ultra upscale Hotel de Paris. The continued impressive sales figures would further bolster Kassar's own compensation as well, so it was in his own best financial interest to ensure the company continued its monumental climb from hundreds of millions in sales to a staggering figure of nearly $2 Billion in sales.

The rewards, perks and bonuses that would be offered, from a corporate perspective, could be viewed as a wise and beneficial way of motivating staff to further the health and well-being of the company as a whole. However, this attempted motivation had the opposite effect on the version of the company that Kassar created. The first major effect seen is in the development of new products, as potentially vital and needed updated products and technologies started either being canceled or crippled to always ensure that the VCS had a width berth. Favoring the bonuses generated from the VCS sales, the objective by many now was that nothing would impact its sales or the sales of its software cartridges. "Ray Kassar would always say, why should he take a chance on an untested product when he can just build another factory to make more Atari VCS systems?" recalls Steve Bristow. Even though Ray's intentions were good from the onset, the implementation of his vision had taken a bad turn and was beginning to severely impact the company and its future. Even Al Alcorn, who would resign from Atari at the end of 1981, commented that Kassar had become so compartmentalized that he would be the last to know just how bad things were getting.

There was a strong reason why the VCS was the focus however: since 1980 its popularity with the public had only increased. When released in January 1980 on the Atari VCS, *Space Invaders* not only sold beyond anyone's wildest dreams, but actually causes a new phenomenon to take place: People were actually going out to buy a VCS just so they can play that game. Word would spread quite fast and before long, many households across the nation were buzzing with the inquisitive interest in this hot new game for the home available only on the 'Video Computer System.' In today's vernacular people will ask, "Do you play video games?" but in the early 1980s people would ask you, "Do you play Atari?" and the company itself would jump onto this cultural term with its commercials that would end with the jingle, "Have you played Atari today?" Atari (and the guys in Marketing) also hoped to repeat the runaway success with its exclusive home use license of the insanely popular *Pac-Man* arcade game. *Pac-Man* was such an important license to Atari that the company was not only looking to put out games based on *Pac Man,* but marketing also wanted to position the *Pac-Man* character to become Atari's official 'spokes-character.' Marketing was even having costumes made up for a series of *Pac-Man* World Tour events.

Atari also continued to promote its public presence by supporting charities like the United Way, where during the month of August Atari employees all help out by making generous donations to the Santa Clara County United Way. Within Silicon Valley, Atari was truly becoming the benchmark and hub of major employment and many budding future business owners and entrepreneurs were eager to cut their teeth in the business environment. So Atari offers a College Certificate Program for college students and then sponsored projects in the Junior Achievement Program for High School students. With the college program, Program developer and Corporate Training director Brad Fregger assists the De Anza, Foothill and Mission community colleges in helping students receive experience in Business Finance, Management, Communications, Secretarial Skills, Information Services and other courses. In the Junior Achievement Program, Atari sponsors two different groups that would compete against each other by functioning as small companies. Run through the Employee Activities manager, Laurie Chistensen, the kids are expected to manufacture products, sell them and manage all aspects of the business. Group One is IRATA and Group Two is RAINBOW, and under both, a total of 53 high school students are given the opportunity to come into Atari's offices to meet, plan and run their companies. The students are also required to learn good work habits, decision making skills and fundamental leadership and motivational skills all in an effort to learn the workings of both the management and labor sides of the fence.

Atari and Warner also offer some very creative and fun scholarships to the sons and daughters of permanent Atari employees making $40,000 or less, all co-ordinated by Nanci Mahenski. Sukhbir Sandhu, Allan Saadus and Christine Radar are among ten recipients of the WCI scholarships in 1982, along with Kimra Fer-guson, Mark Matthiessen and Anne Naylor. Trying to also keep up the image that video games aren't promoting couch potatoes, Atari also sponsored the "I Shaped Up at Atari" weight loss and fitness contest for employees, the Atari Karate Club and Atari's Jazzercise classes which are held on Monday and Wednesday nights at the Sunnyvale High School cafeteria. Even with all these employee perks, it was still clear the old Atari 'family' had changed to those who had been there pre-Warner.

When Atari first started, everyone worked together and worked hard be-cause employees wanted to see great products go out the door and to feel a sense of pride and accomplishment of being part of such a great company that provided revo-lutionary video game products for the masses. Fast forward into 1981-1982: as sales and marketing had taken the reins of the company with the goal of profit and bonus-es for specific individuals, the company's health and future was no longer the focus. Neither was seeing great products go out the door. This isn't to say there weren't any great products making it out, because there were some truly amazing things that At-ari was producing despite itself. However, the detrimental effect was eating its way at the very foundation of the company; specifically the Consumer Electronics Divi-sion and the Home Computer Division. And truly it was the Consumer Division that continually tested Ray's skills as an effective leader of the company. For example, their was the continual drama with the newly set up Atari Taiwan.

Just prior to the big Monte Carlo annual sales meeting, Ray Kassar and Skip Paul arrived in Atari Taiwan for its official opening and clearance by the Ministry of Economics. During the cocktail party, Ray Kassar hands Rick Krieger (the factory manager) a letter he's received from Ron Budsworth accusing Rick and David Chiu of taking money. Atari's security does a check, and it's discovered by Peter Howard that David Chiu's family owns four factories where Atari ATMC sources cabling, and their prices vary wildly and without explanation. On May 8th Rick informs Skip Paul of the situation, which results in Rick firing David on May 13th. Then on May 25th, Ray Kumavich is suddenly assaulted by someone with a lead pipe and is seriously injured. Rick informs Ray Kassar of the situation and Ray wants Rick to return to the U.S. for a personal meeting. Then the next day, Ray Kassar calls back Rick again, very concerned about the situation and the reprisal resulting from Da-vid Chiu's firing. Rick is instructed not to fire any other vendors so they don't risk any further problems, and then to have guards posted at the factory and at man-agement's homes. Yet when Rick returns to the factory on June 14th from his U.S. trip, he is informed that now James Fu had been attacked and stabbed seven times.

Suspecting the Chiu family again, Rick meets with them to discuss their involvement in the attack and visits James at the hospital afterwards. Rick has some serious decisions to make, and that afternoon gathers all of the managers together for a meeting regarding the attacks and security issues. This grave, life threatening situation escalates, with Paul Malloy, Skip Paul and Consumer Division head Perry Odak arriving to meet with Taiwan's government officials about what has been happening. Maybe the Chiu family were triad members, or this simply could have been chalked up to the same emotional craziness one sees regularly during the fights that break out at Taiwanese governmental meetings. But after this final meeting, things 'seem' to return back to normal and on Monday, July 5th, the first 5,000 units of VCS *Star Raiders* are finally shipped to Sunnyvale.

That is until September 15th, when the problem rears its head again after a local mob gang visits one of Rick's managers (Lawrence), and he's informed that they are the ones who attacked James Fu. Claiming that they can no longer guarantee anyone's safety without a settlement, the 'bad guys' as Rick Krieger notes, are paid off 100,000 NT to settle for protection on September 18th. By November 6th, things were back to normal as Atari Taiwan built and shipped 900,000 Atari 5200 systems. Then they're instructed on November 29th to start packaging Atari *Pac Man* with all VCS models - it appears *Combat* will no longer be packaged with it, and they're to use the existing inventory of *Pac Man* cartridges as pack-in's from now on. On November 30th, the factory also receives two of the secret Atari 1200XL computers from Andy Pracheck, however they won't be publicly announced until December. Either way, the initial assembly of the 1200XL's will occur in Sunnyvale, with plans to eventually produce them overseas later in 1983.

Atari's Coin-op Division wasn't seeing the same issues on product development as Consumer was. Being located in Milpitas, it was more isolated from the other divisions and there wasn't a focus on placing one single product category as priority above all others. Coin-op was also the true innovative division where the original, new and fresh game concepts were emerging from, and then would eventually find their way over into the Consumer and Home Computer divisions as ports to be sold to home game console buyers and home computer buyers. That's not to say Coin didn't have its own problems starting, though they were completely out of its control. The coin market, which had rapidly expanded to non-traditional locations like convenience stores and gas stations during the late 70s, was starting to see a bit of saturaton in late 1981 that would snowball in to a full coin industry crash by the following year when these non-traditional locations started drying up. There were only so many places a new arcade machine could be placed and by this point video arcade machines were literally in every possible location - from small candy shops, supermarket checkout areas, movie theatre lobbies, barber shops, pizza parlors, malls, and of course, video arcades. Unlike game consoles or cartridges that only cost a small amount, arcade machines ran into the thousands and being able to continually purchase newer machines while still finding placement for older and sometimes no longer wanted machines was becoming a problem.

As 1982 rolled by though, the tone was different at Warner and they were beginning to worry about their cash cow and the consumer video game industry as a whole. At the end of 1981, Steve Ross was concerned that Atari may be nearing its peak, given Roger Smith's dire warnings from his November 1981 assessment of Atari. Several ideas are put on the table as solution to buffer Warner should they have already reached the peak; one is to take Atari public in a 20% stock sale worth $600 million with a plan to eventually make as much as 50% of the company stock available publicly. This way Atari would be taken out from under Warner's wing and if it were to falter for any reason, as an independent entity, it wouldn't directly harm Warner Communications. For some unknown reason, this option was never acted on and Atari would eventually cause severe damage to Warner Communications when it did in fact falter in late 1982. Steve Ross even considered looking to find a buyer to sell Atari to; however, Atari had become such a massive entity, finding a potential buyer was going to be a very tough challenge as only a small handful of companies would possibly have the financial resources to buy the ever-growing juggernaut called Atari. So Steve Ross takes a different route to hedge his bets; for the first time since he had brought Kinney Service public in 1962, he sold 360,000 shares of his personal stock in the company in December 1981. The ever vigilant ears of Wall Street caught wind of Ross' selling of his personal shares from his April 30, 1982 public disclosure. Immediately rumors and whispers quickly circulate about Ross wanting to sell Atari, which cause Wall Street speculators to begin building the notion that the 'Video Game Fad' was coming to a close. In the May 1982 issue of the Wall Street Journal, an article further cements this notion that the video game market is close to saturation, which ignites a fire under many stock traders to begin short-selling Warner stock in expectation that the stock price would drop. One surprisingly aggressive short seller is none other than Gordon Crawford, the very man who had originally called Manny Gerard about buying a certain California-based high tech entertainment company back in 1976 called Atari. In fact, Gordon Crawford would sell his entire investment position in Warner Communications by August 1982.

The timing of the April stock disclosure, combined with the May Wall Street

Journal article created the beginnings of the eventual avalanche that Atari would be swept away by. But this was just the beginning… there were other growing issues which would weaken the company further in the interim…

Pac-Man Fever...
Be Good

R ay Kassar had pulled off a major licensing deal for Atari and acquired the exclusive worldwide video game rights (but not the electronic games rights) for *Pac-Man*. With everything riding on this game, Ray made sure it was assigned to one of Atari's most experienced programmers, right? Nope. This monumentally important game for Atari is thrown up on the bulletin board (in an area called 'The Zoo') for any programmer to take, and it would be Tod Frye who would anwer the call of the big yellow mouth... as his very first game project at Atari.

Tod Frye got heavily into programming at US Forest Service Computer Center – a place where Berkeley High School students were given access to computers for programming. Another Berkely High School student by the name of Ian Sheppard had graduated from there several years before Tod, and after going through college was hired by Larry Kaplan at Atari. Ian in turn helped Tod get an interview at Atari, and with his experience programming on a Kim-1 developer board and Apple II he owned, the interview goes well and Tod is hired. Two games came up for availability around the time Tod was hired, and since Tod and fellow programmer Bob Polaro were not assigned to any projects at that time, it was their time to choose the next two games slotted for development of the list on the bulletin board. *Defender* and *Pac-Man* were the two newest titles and in fact *Pac-Man* and the *Defender* coin-ops were in the back arcade room in the consumer programming building getting plenty of play. Now Tod had really loved *Defender*, and would have preferred to have programmed that instead of *Pac-Man*, but because Bob didn't feel *Pac-Man* could be done in the limited ROM size for cartridges they were allowed, he chose *Defender*, leaving *Pac-Man* for Tod by default. At the time in 1981, 4K had become the standard ROM size for games, and Carl Nielson from engineering had just developed a new cartridge design that would utilize 8K. Unfortunately, the first game that is slated to utilize this new design is VCS Asteroids; the majority of games planned for development, including *Pac-Man*, were still only given the 4K ROM size.

Unfortunately for Tod, around the time he was taking *Pac-Man*, he had just received his annual review from his boss Dennis Koble, who had already put Tod on probation - leading Tod to believe that Dennis really didn't like him much. So, despite the very open and lax work environment of consumer programming, Tod put in a LOT of hours and effort into *Pac-Man*. Now this wasn't to say that Tod was all work; as a programmer there were times you just had to let off some steam, but booze or drugs were not always the answer; Sometimes you just needed to go take a nice walk. However, Tod's idea of a 'walk' would become infamous within the Consumer programming building at 275 Gibraltar. If Spiderman was known as the 'wall crawler,' he had nothing on Tod. Being a very tall man, through his powers of deduction Todd was able to figure out that he could put one foot on one wall in the hallway, his other foot on the other wall, and by using a hopping motion he could bounce his way UP the wall. Eventually, with practice and a little effort, Tod could make his way down the entire hallway walking on the sides of the wall. This was all quite entertaining to both Tod and all of his fellow programmer friends until one day while strolling down the hallway (of course, on the walls!), Tod wasn't fully paying attention and ended up slamming his head against a sprinkler head on the ceiling, whereby he came crashing down and ended up with a deep gash on his forehead. After being rushed to the hospital to treat the profusely bleeding gash, it's explained to a triage nurse how he got his injury. After a short laugh, she asked, "Seriously - how did he really cut his head?"

For *Pac-Man*, one of Tod's many goals was to implement what he considered to be the important features of the game, focusing in on these so that game play would be accurately transferred over going after the looks because of the limited space he had. For example, *Pac-Man* is a two player game. Tod used a great deal of memory just tracking where each player had left off with eaten dots, power pellets and score. (When he looked at the code for the arguably better looking VCS *Ms. Pac-Man* in later years after its release, he noticed the programmers were able to use much more memory for graphics because it's only a one player game). *Pac-Man* also implements ghost patterns as well, which takes up more memory and leaves even less room for graphical accuracy in the limite space. As for other differences: "We were still new at doing advanced arcade ports to the VCS - there was *Space Invaders* and *Asteroids* - both of those used their own color schemes, and *Asteroids* looked and played different from the arcade. I wanted to add more color to the maze instead of black and blue, so I chose the colors. The maze was also very difficult to implement, so the exits were placed on the tops and bottoms instead of the sides. My primary focus was on the game play and making sure the game mechanics of the arcade were in the VCS title as close as could be done," recalls Tod.

Interestingly enough, Tod had also developed a flicker reduction kernel and had found ways to reposition sprites arbitrarily. Brad Stewart (Tod's manager) came by his office one day and took a look over Tod's shoulder to see what he had on the screen. Hummm... he discovers that Tod has developed a very clever technique to reduce the on-screen flicker of objects. Brad thought the technique was impressive and had never seen it done before, and wound up borrowing it for his coding of *Asteroids*.

The problem really was that in the early 80s arcade games themselves had become more powerful and sophisticated, making the early attempts at coding ports of such games on the VCS's limited hardware and storage more difficult and challenging. Prior to this, many of the VCS arcade ports were of arcade games that had graphics and game play not much more complex then the mid 70s titles the VCS had been designed for, so those versions were much closer to the originals. Coding for VCS *Pac-Man* was started in the last week of May and wasn't finished until the second week of September 1981. Labels for the cartridge were then completed in late November, and the game was sent for ROM masking, manuals and packaging to start production and prepare it to ship before the Spring of 1982.

Just before Spring however, more good news arrives to Atari and its *Pac-Man* license: On March 18, 1982, Federal Judge George N. Leighton ruled in favor of Atari versus Magnavox when Atari accused Magnavox of creating a game too similar to its licensed *Pac-Man*, *K.C. Munchkin!* Atari had purchased the exclusive rights to *Pac-Man* prior to the *K.C. Munchin!* release. The earlier ruling in the Federal Court had ruled that the game by Magnavox was not in violation of any copyright laws because the source codes of the two games were different. That while there were similarities, there were also differences in the game play of the two games. However, Atari appealed the decision and the new ruling went in Atari's favor. Magnavox was ordered to stop selling *K.C. Munchkin!* and to pull the game off store shelves immediately, making it a collectors item for fans of the Mangavox's Odyssey2 system.

Pac-Man for the VCS starts to appear on store shelves on March 16, 1982, thanks to many stores jumping the gun before 'National Pac-Man Day' because of the incredible pre-release buzz the game had been getting. Atari spokesman Jeff Hoff says Atari is scheduled to launch a $1.5 million ad campaign for *Pac-Man* alone. Sears and Roebuck stores nationwide begin to receive shipments and were sold out in three days. Up until this point, sales have all been through word of mouth and local ads - Atari hadn't even started its ad campaign, which was set to begin at the end of March. Atari will produce a total of 12 million cartridges of the game by the end of the year, even though market analysts point out that Atari has only sold approximately 6 million consoles to date. Why more *Pac-Man's* than Atari has consoles out in the public? *Pac-Man* fever had been gripping the U.S. throughout 1981, and was accurately summed up in late 1981 when BGO records took a chance and released a record by Buckner & Garcia called *Pac-Man Fever!* Selling nearly 10,000 copies almost overnight, in early 1982 it was already ranking among Billboard's Top 100.' Atari's Marketing department is hoping to tap in to a bit of that fever while scoring another *Space Invaders* moment with their home version of *Pac-Man,* driving buyers to go out and purchase a new console so they could play the ever popular and addictive *Pac-Man* game at home. To that end, Atari prepares a marketing campaign to bolster console sales for Mid-April in connection to *Pac-Man* purchasing, hoping the extra push does the trick.

As the April 3, 1982, official Atari National *Pac-Man* Day approaches, Atari begins ramping up for the excitement by running national ads counting down the date five days before. And when it finally arrives, Atari officially introduces *Pac-Man* for the VCS by holding events in 25 cities across the U.S. where costumed *Pac-Man* characters and ghosts are on hand to greet gamers and fans. There's also customized Volkswagen vans called "Pac Vans" on hand. In New York City, Atari's *Pac-Man* Day promotion includes taking over the ever trendy Doubles Restaurant, where a costumed *Pac-Man* hob-knobbed with the celebrities, including Cher, Liza Minnelli and Cliff Robertson. *Pac-Man* will even become a roving reporter within Atari for its internal newspaper, along with fellow Atari reporter Patti Crovicz.

Pac-Man is being manufactured in all three of Atari's North American factories located in Sunnyvale, California, Puerto Rico and in El Paso, Texas, and by the end of the year will also be manufactured at ATMC, (Atari's Taiwan Manufacturing Company) under the direction of Paul Malloy and plant manager Rick Krieger. In mid April, Atari also starts a nationwide promotion; if you buy a *Pac-Man* cartridge and a VCS, you receive a free *Pac-Man* t-shirt. In May, the snack maker 'Corn Nuts' announces that they are holding the trademark to *Pac-Man* hostage, and in an effort to garner some playful attention, they warn Atari not to let its electronic *Pac-Man* take any bites out of any stalks of corn. As people become worried over this faux-announcement, Atari Spokesman Peter Nelson comments, "Atari is not concerned about its license in regards to Corn Nuts, they are just having some fun."

When it comes down to it, Tod Frye had done an admirable job on Atari's *Pac-Man* as a game, impressing his co-workers with all that he was able to squeeze in to the limited resources. While it differs in colors, maze layout and sounds, it's a solid game based on the difficulty of coding such a game at the time. Even the VCS version of *Asteroids,* released in the Summer of 1981 and written by Brad Stewart, doesn't look or sound just like the arcade version. Nor is the game play exactly the same, but it's still a solid game which also sold very well. Atari *Asteroids* for the VCS sells nearly 3.8 million copies while VCS *Pac-Man* would sell over 7.7 million copies, though sales significantly slowed by Summer time. Because of the initial rush and flurry of purchases by people to buy a home version of *Pac-Man*, the game would earn nearly $200 million in gross profit sales for Atari. Even being this very strong seller, some felt the game slightly tarnished Atari's image by releasing what was considered a poor looking port of the arcade game. The result backfires on Atari by causing consumers to behave differently when purchasing games. There was already a growing mass of new low quality third party 'spam' titles on the market, and now with the experience from rushing to buy *Pac-Man* for a premium and getting disapointed at its look, the tipping point for a new buyer environment is created. An environment where people will no longer blindly rush out to buy a newly released game, but will cautiously wait for reviews or feedback from others who've bought a game. As a result, game purchases appear to be more curtailed than in the past in the second half of 1982, causing another new complication that sales and marketing will have to grasp and account for.

For Tod's effort in coding his first game, when he received his first bonus check for $320,000 for *Pac-Man,* the result was a screaming, yelling, and cheering Tod - all while walking the walls. Tod even makes a photocopy of his first check and tapes it to the door of his office. At the end of its selling run, he would receive a total of nearly $1.3 million in royalties from *Pac-Man,* his very first game at Atari. Internally amongst his fellow coders though, there was some obvious bitterness and resentment that Tod made so much money on his first game. A *Pac-Man* poster in the back arcade area was hung up not long after, and someone had written on the poster 'Why Frye?' When Tod saw the poster, he drew a straight line over the 'Why' which in engineering speak meant NOT, so now the poster said, 'Why NOT Frye?'

Slowing *Pac-Man* sales wasn't the only problem plaguing Atari in 1982. Steve Ross and Warner force Atari to produce a game based on the movie *E.T.* - a title Atari had already turned down. Steve Ross had met Spielberg in 1981 after seeing the string of cinematic accomplishments under his belt – ranging from Spielberg's perseverance through the nearly disastrous *JAWS* filming, to his monumental success with *Close Encounters of the Third Kind* and R*aiders of the Lost Ark.* Spielberg was tightly bound to Universal Studios and Ross was very determined to see about breaking that bond to bring him over to Warner. Courting Steven Spielberg to produce movies under the Warner Studios moniker, the two began meeting for a long 4-day weekend at the Villa Eden in Acapulco in the Spring of 1982. Ross managed to get his foot in the door with Spielberg by getting a license for Atari to produce a game based on *Raiders of the Lost Ark* for the Christmas season, programmed by Howard Scott Warshaw. Liking the results so much, in the Summer of 1982 after his movie *E.T.* had been released, Spielberg informed Sidney Sheinberg at MCA/Universal that Steve Ross would be given first rights to acquire the video game license.

Sheinberg instead tells Spielberg that Coleco Industries and MCA were already in talks on a license. Coleco had become a very aggressive licensor as of late, with Atari directly in its cross-hairs, looking to de-thrown the mighty video game company. When Speilberg informs Atari of the competition, they knew they did NOT want to lose this deal! Skip Paul, legal counsel from Atari's Coin-op division, presents Sheinberg with what he believes to be a very generous offer, one that Atari had never extended to any company before: $1 million and 7 percent of royalties from sales. Sheinberg then informs a shocked Skip Paul that a deal had already been struck between Spielberg and Ross for $21 million. The $1 million made sense to Skip, but a guarantee of another $20 million on top of it as well? WHY? It turns out, Spielberg took advantage of the opportunity of Steve Ross' desire to do just about anything to get Spielberg over to Warner Studios.

E.T. The Extra-Terrestrial opens in movie theatres on June 11, 1982, and for Atari's 10th Anniversary coming up on the 27th, Ray Kassar arranges for the more than 5,000 Atari employees and their family members to go to free screenings of the movie at De Anza College's Flint Center. Everything is coordinated for the event by Atari Employee Activities Manager Laurie Christensen who makes all of the arrangements for the movie to be shown. Corporate Security Manager Michael John and his team managed the automobile traffic flow in and out of the parking lots and made sure that only employees and their families were permitted in for the showings. After the event, a big 'thank you' went out in the internal Atari newspaper thanking Ray Kassar for making Atari's 10th Anniversary even more enjoyable. But soon after Ray has even more pressing concerns caused by the little alien visitor.

Ross's deal goes through, and it's going to be literally one of the major undoing's of Atari itself. Then Ross personally contacts Ray Kassar and informs him that he's secured the rights to the *E.T.* movie for home video games, agreeing to pay Spielberg $21 million for the home rights to *E.T.* Now for the bombshell (if those insane numbers weren't enough): Ross informs Ray that the game must be out for Christmas! Ray pushes back - it can't be done - it's already late July and there wouldn't be enough development and debugging time to have a game ready to go into production. Instead of supporting Ray's opinion, Ross instead gets annoyed at Kassar's lack of excitement over the amazing license deal he just landed, not wanting to hear about any issues. He informs Ray that this is a done deal and to make the game happen - period.

Meeting with Skip Paul and Universal's legal team in Monterey, CA to finalize the deal, Ray makes a call over to George Kiss over in the Consumer programming group at Gibraltar Ave. to let him know about the insane specifics of the project coming his way. George is the manager of the Consumer programming group, known as 'The Zoo' where George would become the 'zookeeper.' "These guys didn't like management or respond well to it. They got things done, but it had to be their way. I really didn't know what to make of them," recalls George Kiss. Perhaps a 'Menagerie' was a more appropriate term for this building, because contained within it were a group of people who, if it not for their unbelievable talent at coding games, they all most certainly would have been locked away in an insane asylum (that is, after spending a few months in a detox and rehab center for their drug and alcohol abuse). "My day would always start with walking around the building and checking to see if there were any dead bodies around. Did anyone work themselves into total exhaustion? Anyone overdo it with drugs or booze? Is anyone in trouble, arrested or in jail? That would be the start of a typical day," recalls George Kiss.

"Fridays, someone would be handed a corporate credit card and were told to go pick up lots of booze for the Friday parties. I remember hearing someone yell out 'the Friday party has started' and everyone would cheer and head to the break room. It was a free environment. I could've gotten up at anytime and partied and these were good parties I can tell you, but sometimes I'd be so deep into my work that I really wanted to get it done. That was the kind of devotion we had working there," recalls Rob Zdybel. "We were making games for a living. We were surrounded by games. We would play and test each other's games. The lines would get so blurred you didn't know what work was anymore and what was play. It really came down to self-discipline and managing your own time to get the job done," recalls Rob Fulop.

Many in the company, by 1981 and 1982, viewed Atari as a 9 to 5 job, going home or out to dinner or to a bar after work and put the day behind them. Some in Engineering or Manufacturing worked later hours and got paid time and a half - there was more intense devotion involved to the company from them. Then there were the programmers - on the weekends and sometimes deep into the night, many parking spaces were often filled with their cars. They would show up on these odd hours because they wanted to, not because of any overtime pay - there wasn't any. In fact, there was no pay on the weekends. "I remember when I first started, they handed me some manuals to study, assigned me a game and told me if I needed help to ask some of the other programmers. That was it, the game assignment was due in six months and only when my game was ready did anyone want to hear from me. Getting help from the other programmers was not so easy, you had to prove yourself first or they wouldn't want to waste their time with you or even accept you into the fold. You needed to be able to show something - you'd have to write your own kernel for your game. Every game started like that. If you could show that you had a basic grasp of the VCS and could actually code, then and only then would any of the other programmers even talk with you," recalls Jim Huether.

On a late July day, George Kiss receives the news from Ray Kassar that Atari has to code a game for the VCS based on the movie *E.T.: The Extraterrestrial* and it must be ready to ship in time to get in stores for the Christmas holiday sales season. George realizes in a 'what the fuck' moment that from a game development standpoint this poses two immediate problems: one, what if the movie isn't something that is adaptable for a good game? The second, it's late July! That means the game will have to be coded in just a few weeks to make it to the factory and have ROM chips with the game code on them fabricated, so they can then be manufactured into game cartridges, then packaged and shipped in time to reach the distributors and finally onto the retailer store shelves. Bottom line - this is INSANITY! So who best to handle this than one of the head insane residents of The Zoo, Howard Scott Warshaw? Of course it helped that Spielberg had specifically requested Howard after his previous experiences with him on *Raiders of the Lost Ark*. Howard himself is also well known within the halls of Gibraltar, having started making his mark almost immediately after arriving about a year and a half before.

Howard had joined Atari on January 11, 1981, although he almost wasn't hired. Told he was too stuffy and straight, apparently it was believed he lacked the creative talent to be able to be a game programmer. Mind you this couldn't have been further from the truth. Before Atari however, Howard had been working at Hewlett Packard and was deathly bored. "I felt like this was the place where programmers went to die," recalls Howard. To relieve his boredom at Hewlett Packard, Howard had been doing lots of goofy stuff and just trying to have some fun. Then one day, one of his fellow HP employees came over to him and told Howard that his wife worked at this place where people did that goofy stuff all the time: Atari. Howard knew about arcade games, but really wasn't very familiar with Atari. The co-worker could have just been trying to get rid of Howard and his pranks to let everyone go back to their regularly scheduled death march, but when Howard is told that Atari was doing their games on microprocessors, that was all Howard needed to hear. Not the games part, but that they worked on microprocessors. Howard goes in for an interview and meets with Dennis Koble, Rob Fulop, Carla Meninsky, Bob Smith and several others from the Consumer group. When Dennis calls Howard on the phone to tell him how the interviews went, instead of the results he hope for Dennis tells him that they can't make him an offer. First, Howard's current salary at HP is too high, and Atari can't match it. Howard told him he's willing to take a pay cut to please make him an offer, but none is made. Not wanting to let it go, Howard remains persistent and keeps calling Dennis, finally wearing him down. Howard is offered a position and a salary of $22,000 at the beginning of 1981, but he won't be starting for four weeks. In the interim, Dennis reluctantly trusts Howard with a copy of a programming manual.

On Howard's first day at work, he showed up and made sure to bring the essentials; his programming manual and a joint. During his interviews, he had learned that the place is pretty wild, so not wanting to make a bad first impression and have to ask for a smoke off of someone else, he brought his own. Put in an office with Rob Zdybel and Tod Frye, Howard received his first compliment while talking with Rob. At no point did Rob say he didn't like Howard - which is something Rob has no problem with doing if he doesn't like you (apparently he did to about half the people Howard had just met). With Howard spending much of that first day reading through manuals, at one point, Tod came into the office, slams the door and tells Howard, "I'm gonna get high - if you don't like it, get out." Howard reached into his pocket and offers Tod his joint, at which point Tod states firmly, "No thanks, I only smoke really good stuff." Tod lit up, Howard tried Tod's joint and he's right - it's some really good stuff (and the bonus was his joint got to remain in his pocket for later). That was Howard's first day.

Dennis Koble gave Howard a choice when he was ready – prorgram on either the VCS (now renamed the 2600) or the new 5200. Asking which is the harder system to work on, Dennis told him it was the 2600, which he of course chose right away. His first assignment for it is a port of *Star Castle*. While looking at the arcade version however, Howard came to an important realization when comparing it to the resources he had available for the 2600: it's going to suck as a conversion because of the size constraints. Considering what had been done in Space Invaders and was being done in Asteroids at the time, Dennis understood and allowed Howard to redo the game in a different way. Called *Time Freeze* during development (because Howard originally wanted a freezing of time leading in to a dramatic explosion), unexpectedly the game evolves in to an incredibly unique game. Probably the first completely original game to come out of Consumer, since it wasn't based on a port of an already existing arcade game or a concept originally done elsewhere; That game is *Yars' Revenge*.

For his first time out he pulled out all the stops, not just wanting to create something brand new but to also be creative. Rather than catering to what the consumers might find most appealing so it would perform well on the market, Howard wrote *Yars'* with the idea of pleasing himself. "I felt that I was a gamer, and I thought that if I do a game that I enjoy, that I really like playing, then a lot of gamers would enjoy it," recalls Howard. Likewise, Howard was an experienced and formally trained programmer, giving him what he considered more experience than most of the programmers that are programming for the 2600. Consequently, Howard was able to be very creative in pursuing features he wanted and added in some new 'firsts' for home video games in *Yars'*: A pause between game levels (where a player can simply not hit the fire button to start the next level, allowing them to take a break), an immersive playing experience via a black borderless playfield (with his idea that kids would be playing it in a dark room anyways, hence the black screen and dark room would all blend together), and a full screen death sequence explosion (fullfilling his original wish to program the first game with a full screen explosion). Howard also got to pick the name of his game, though only after tricking the people over in Marketing. When marketing sent over some names they were considering for the still in development game, Howard thought they were all terrible. Asking if he could submit a name, he came up with Yars' Revenge (with Yar being Ray for Ray Kassar, spelled backwards. Including a self-written storyline (placing the game in the Razak solar system - also similar to Ray's last name) to support it, he didn't get much of a response from Marketing. That is until he "leaked" the secret correlation of the names to a friend of his in Marketing and Product Management, creatively adding that Ray had already found out about the name and liked it! Not checking with Ray, the name was approved and *Time Freeze* became *Yars' Revenge*.

Yars' Revenge almost didn't make it out of Atari though, as Steve Wright (Director of Game Development and also programmer of *Chapionship Soccer/Pele's Soccer*, the first video game to license a sports personality) hated it, insisting there was something wrong with it. By the early 80s, Marketing insisted all games had to be play-tested by groups of people who would play head to head with another in development game, and then judge them on a score from 1 to 5 (low to high), so Steve tried to kill off *Yars'* by pitting it against the forthcoming home version of *Missile Command*. The plan backfired, and *Yars'* ended up testing with an average of 4.5, rating it as one of the highest play-tests Atari ever did and ensuring its release.

At the time, Atari was also breaking new ground by pairing with fellow Warner subsidiary D.C. Comics, by having D.C. create pack-in comics for a number of its games in development, the first of which would be *Yars' Revenge*, followed by *Defender* in 1982. *Yars'* once again became unique in this aspect, because besides being the first to have a comic, Howard's backstory was also used (with an expanded storyline called 'The Qotile Ultimatum'). The rest of the pack-in comics for those in development games (*Defender, Berzerk, Star Raiders, Phoenix, and Galaxian*) were instead based around a joint D.C. and Atari creation called 'Atari Force,' a futuristic team led by Commander Champion and further tied in to an arcade followup to *Missile Command* to be released in 1982, *Liberator*. (The pack-in comics would spawn a full D.C. comic series of the same name, and together with Atari's ongoing movie placements in films like *Blade Runner* and *E.T.* the following year, pioneered cross-marketing and promotion for the video games industry). Howard's comic also had one other feature the others didn't, and that the other programmers had yet to achieve: official recognition and credit as an Atari VCS game programmer. Though he didn't get credit for the storyline, his name does appear in the credit page in the comic as Cartridge Programmer.

The game would be a major success - its original game play and unique concept turns it into a very successful release. So much so, at one point the idea is floated within Atari of Dave Theurer making it into an arcade game. Unfortunately that never came to fruition and the competitor to Atari's 5200, GCE's Vectrex, would hold that honor when GCE's game *Cosmic Chasm* was licensed by Cinematronics for the arcades. But *Yars'* popularity solidified Howard's arrival at Atari as an in demand game programmer, so he was allowed to volunteer to do a very important game for his follow-up: Atari's first licensed movie title, Spielberg's *Raiders of the Lost Ark*.

Flown to Warner Studios to meet with Steven Spielberg himself about a game adaptation of the movie, as an interview of sorts Howard had to show him his previous work (*Yars'*) and present his concept for the game. Howard wanted to base his concept around the earlier 2600 game *Adventure*, creating a big step up from that game to what he wanted to be the best ever adventure game on the 2600. Spielberg approved of Howard enthusiastically, looking forward to partnering with this programmer and the largest brand in this new medium to create history - the first (official) video game based on a movie. This is where the rest of the programmers at Atari got to see Howard's true nature, and how the people he originally interviewed with got to see just how wrong they were when they had called him 'too stuffy and straight.' To get into character and the proper frame of mind for the game, Howard began roaming the hallways in a fedora and cracking a bullwhip; in his mind he had to be Indiana Jones to properly pull this game off. During one hallway walking whip cracking session, new hire Steve Woita was greeted by the wild eyed madman cracking a whip while walking into the front lobby of Gibraltar on this, his first day of work. Asking one of the other programmers what that was all about, Steve was told that Howard is conducting R&D - 'Research & Discipline.'

When it came time to code the game though, Howard was all business and he once again uses a lot of new techniques in the game design. Employing low resolution graphics so he can free up more of the 2600's very limited memory, he is able to use some new techniques for graphics and animation on the 2600 that really push the envelope for the game, such as using the 2600's hardware based missile sprite (previously only used for balls and shots) to help draw graphics like a realistic slithering snake. The graphics tricks and expanded availability of memory allowed Howard to concentrate on being very creative in the game play part of the game, creating an expanded unique sounding colorful world full of puzzles based on the movie. Indy has to collect items and solve various puzzles on his way to discovering the lost Ark, at which point the player is treated to another first in video games: an actual ending to the game. To make it even more interesting, Howard also included short cuts so that the game could be solved a number of different ways, as well as a tribute to *Adventure* with the hidden placement of his own initials that could also be unlocked.

Spielberg met with Howard several times for lunch to discuss the progress on the game, but never pushed or pressured Howard on any of the ways the game would be done. It was all in Howard's lap as to how the game would come together, look, and play. How did Howard responded to the awesome responsibility laid on him by Spielberg? By making a movie for the 'A' class movie maker. For the upcoming June CES, Howard made a video of *Raiders* to demo for Spielberg at the show. Stepping in to the studio, Howard played through the game while narrating it, playing the game perfectly (which he proudly remembers he's done only a few times in his life). After showing the video to Spielberg at the show, the first words out of his mouth were "It's just like a movie." Howard has once again hit the mark. After the game is released that Fall of '82. almost immediately Atari's customer support is flooded with calls and letters asking how to solve the game. In response, another first is created when Atari released an official 'hint nook' to help players navigate the game and solve its puzzles. *Raiders* is a big success for Atari and for Howard.

In the end of July 1982, just after George Kiss received his call from Ray Kassar, Howard's phone begins ringing as well. George has Ray on the line direct from his hotel room in Montery, and Ray asks Howard if he's up for doing a game based on the *E.T.* movie, stating that Spielberg personally asked for him again. Howard says, 'Sure,' but that's when Ray informs him he only has until September 1st to complete the game. *Yars' Revenge* had taken almost seven months to complete, and *Raiders* took almost nine months; now he was being given 5 1/2 weeks. Howard agreed to do it if the money was good, and once his terms were set he spent the next two days trying to come up with a basic game concept that he knew could be coded in the limited time. Immediately after the two days, he hopped on a plane with Lyle Rains (who was going to do the coin-op version) and the two flew down to meet with Ray, Skip Paul, and Spielberg to go over their planned games. The game would be about saving E.T., avoiding the evil government agents, finding candy and assembling the pieces of the phone so E.T.'s spaceship could land and take him home. It's meant to be a more good-natured, warmhearted kids friendly game. Howard asks his good friend and co-worker Jerome Domurat to do the *E.T.* graphics design for the game, and between the wall of empty pizza boxes towering in Howard's office to the development system he had installed at his house, Howard will eat, sleep and breathe the coding of *E.T.* for one month straight. When finished, he had developed a unique six sided environment that the player would float around, with navigational indicators on the screen to help the game player.

The game (amazingly!) is completed on time, but by no fault of Howard, it just isn't a game that will have the needed mass appeal to make it the all out hot seller it would need to be to allow Atari to recoup the $21 million licensing AND the additional expedited manufacturing and production costs of the game. While the game design is excellent and the game overall is fun, it's just not the intense action-packed type of game people were more used to. "Kids like to shoot and destroy aliens, not save them," recalls Ray Kassar. Even the brief run of focus group tests done on the game showed that it would be a popular game, but it was not going to be a strong enough selling game to make it profitable for the company. The major complaint is the constant falling into the pits, which Howard realized later was an issue, but was so tight for time to get the game completed that it wasn't addressed at the onset. However, he knew once you've played the game a few times, you know where the pits are and then they became more easily avoided.

In total, five million copies of *E.T.* are produced. Why that many? Four million games was the amount that would be needed just to recoup costs and the guaranteed royalty. As it stood, from the focus groups feedback and the estimates from the sales and marketing team, they didn't expect to sell any more than 1.5 million games. Initially only 500,000 games are sold, with another million eventualy joining the sales. Out of the five million *E.T.* carts that would ship out to the distributors, a staggering three and a half million games would be returned in total, many still in the distributor boxes; the retailers hadn't even sold enough to break open additional distributor shipping boxes to require a restock. Even with all this it's still considered a very strong selling game overall at Atari, and in fact, it ranks a very worthy place as #8 among the top twenty games of that time in sales. However there were three and a half million unsold games and in the end, the *E.T.* licensing deal is a complete loss for Atari. It was the underlying royalty deal, and the need to produce and sell an astounding four million games just to break even.

Even the coin-op version of *E.T.* is a loss and winds up cancelled. During development, the game play became too involved and lengthy, which is not something that fits within the framework of immediate gratification required in coin-op games. Coin-op games are normally designed to be over quickly, so that another player and another quarter can be spent on the game. Atari also developes a home computer version of *E.T.* called *E.T. Phone Home*, using some new development tools that the Home Computer Division created for sound, graphics and animation. While the development tools (called 'SWEAT' for SoftWare Editors And Tools) are a success, the home computer version of *E.T.* is not, proving the entire experience Atari had with the little glowing fingered alien was nowhere near as enjoyable as Elliot's.

A December To Remember

December 7, 1941, was "a day that will live on in infamy" for Americans. A sneak attack air strike by the Japanese on the U.S. naval base of Pearl Harbor in Hawaii would deal a significant and deadly blow to the military personnel stationed there, leaving in its wake a death toll of 2,402 and 1,282 wounded. Of the U.S. fleet, nine ships were destroyed and 21 others were severely damaged.

Exactly 41 years later, that same date would now live in video game infamy. Also viewed by some as a sneak attack, even to some of those within Warner and many within Atari itself, it would threaten to not only take down Warner and Atari, but the entire U.S. video game industry as well. On Tuesday, December 7, 1982, Warner Communications was expected to make its earnings announcement, but it was far from being what anyone had expected. Internally, sales and earnings forecasts just weren't adding up, and there were the issues with inventory and sales cancellations. Something was just wrong.

In 1981, manufacturing just couldn't keep up with demand. Distributors would order 1,000 units of a game and many times there would only be enough to ship them half of their orders. This was happening so often that the distributors started to order twice as many units. So now, they'd order 2,000 units with the expectation that they'd only get 1,000, which was what they had originally wanted - and therefore would have the needed quantities to sell out to retailers. Manufacturing had finally caught up with demand, so when distributors ordered 2,000 units they would get 2,000 units. This was further compounded by the fact that in October 1981, during a meeting with its distributors, Atari had asked them to commit to ordering product for almost all of 1982. Because the demand for home video games had been so high that year among consumers, but there had been nowhere near enough product production to fill it (even from competitors), it had made sense at the time to do that size of an order. But what nobody saw coming was that when the second half of 1982 eventually arrived, the competition from third party game manufacturers and other game consoles had heated up to such a degree that the battle for shelf space was causing distributors to cancel half or more of their orders. As Geoffrey Wheeler, editorial director of *Game Merchandising* magazine would tell the *New York Times* on December 9th, "In June 1982, there were about 100 different game cartridges on the market; now there are about 400, and more every week. We'll be glutted by next year." Richard Simon, an analyst with Goldman, Sachs & Co. would also state in that same New York Times interview, "1981 was a wonderful window to enter the business; you could build up a power base immediately; Yet if those same companies tried to enter the market in 1982, with the same talents, they would find it much more difficult. It's a tough business now."

Atari was now suddenly faced with mounting inventories and sales projections dropping by half or more. "Any sales manager who knew the industry should've saw these signs and dealt with this ahead of time," recalled Manny Gerard. However, on December 20th, 1982, Manny would also admit "We were just dumb and blindsided, because Atari had never experienced such competition and massive order cancellations before."

Another problem adding to the projected losses was rampant theft on a scale never before seen at Atari, and this was despite Atari hiring Dick Keiser as Atari's new security director in 1982. Dick had a 20 year history with the Secret Service, having served under Presidents Kennedy, Nixon, Ford, Carter and then President Reagan before accepting the position at Atari. His focus was on employee security and access, insuring everyone clearly wore their badges and that magnetic access readers would be placed throughout the company to lock and secure buildings, departments and sensitive areas. And it also included guard coverage at the warehouses, engineering building, and corporate headquarters. Dick had even ordered an increase in roving patrols, janitorial escorts were engaged to reduce petty theft, a full time investigator was on staff and also an undercover investigator.

However from March through May of 1982 on the loading docks, a bit of a shell game was being played directly under Dick's nose. Distributors were showing up to pick up orders and were claiming that they were there to pick up far more then what they had ordered or paid for. "Distributors came up to the loading docks and were supposed to pick up half a truckload of product. They'd tell the dock loaders they were picking up a full truckload. They were stealing other people's orders. They got away with this for a few months in Spring of 1982," recalls Michael Moone. Sales and inventory just weren't adding up and trying to get a handle on it was proving even more difficult. Even more so when the returns started and some of these distributors began returning these stolen goods looking for credit on product they had never initially paid for.

Atari had never faced any real returns before because its products and games were so popular that it had always been a one-way street. Now with both order cancellations and returns pouring ins, the issue was sending Atari into a dizzied tailspin behind the scenes. Jac Holzman, who had sold his company Elektra Records to Warner Communications, could see an all too familiar pattern of Atari's mounting excessive inventory as the Summer started. He easily recognized it from his time in the record industry, and decided to write a memo directly to Steve Ross on the matter to advise him. Holzman also clearly pointed out the new problem Atari was facing with product returns yet having no real mechanisms to deal with it.

Issues overseas were starting to mount as well as Rick Krieger notes on Tuesday, March 9th, when Atari Taiwan starts issuing cutbacks to all subcontractors for the next three months due to a build-up of 2600 inventories. Warner sends Peter Howard out to Atari Taiwan in early April to conduct a full audit, and after analyzing the results, on Tuesday March 23rd, Atari Taiwan is ordered to change production of the new 2600 *Star Raiders* down to 700,000 in August for the September release. Cancellations for all vendors on the 2600 joysticks also start in June, and during that same month Warner's stock slides down into the $40's range. When the second quarter earnings are announced in July, Warner's finance executives understate earnings by several cents to make sure the lower than expected earnings would only be off by a tiny amount. Bert Wasserman had perfected the process of under-reporting for Warner Communications. Everyone knew that the record profits weren't going to last, but at the same time, anything even mildly negative was poison to Wall Street, so they were trying to ease things down in a controlled fashion. So instead of going nose down and colliding, they were trying to negotiate a crash landing that they could survive. The charade would still make the second quarter of 1982 just barely come in higher than the same quarter of 1981, and while this helped ease out of the downward slide, it was nothing more than a way to forestall the mounting events that would culminate in the December 1982 event.

When August 11th came around, even Manny and Steve Ross could no longer turn a blind eye to the negative numbers that were coming in. Excess inventory was accounting for up to a $65 million loss, and while the warehouse managers at Atari were confirming substantial inventories, nothing was still being solidly confirmed. Finally, Warner sends out Bert Wasserman and Warner's new CFO, Fred Tepperman, to meet with Ray Kassar and Dennis Groth. Numbers are refined down even further, and an August 24th revision to the previous report is issued with earnings now projected at nearly 25% lower than the May numbers.

At Atari, Ray Kassar, Dennis Groth and Perry Odak all point to the new competition in the marketplace that Atari is facing as the culprit. Noting that Mattel is now aggressively marking down and issuing rebates on its own systems and cartridges, all the new factors in this newly agressive marketplace and the impact they'll have is still not fully known. Warner Exec's themselves start to sell off their stocks after the August 24th revisions - which includes everyone from Steve Ross to Manny and even Bert Wasserman. Damage control for the third quarter will be instituted in the form of early retailer shipments. Atari pressures major retailers to take full receipt of their orders so that sales and profits would reflect high for the third quarter. Also, some creative calendar work is done in the form of adding a week to the third quarter, which means one additional week of sales and revenue to report. While this is a common practice, it is usually only done during the fourth quarter, not on a mid-year quarter, later raising further alarms for some analysts.

The forced full deliveries on retailers, as well as the addition of the extra week in the third quarter are a feat of financial magic, causing Warner to issue its best quarterly earnings in its history on October 18th. Wall Street responds jubilantly and the stock price soars back up into the $50's range. Steve Ross however continues to still sell his shares of stock, and the day after the earnings report he sells another 190,000 shares of his stock, bringing his total shares sold to more than 550,000 shares. When it was time to head into the fourth quarter, which was always the most profitable because of all of the Christmas sales, hopes were a little higher that the stuck inventory problem would be resolved. However, on November 17th, Atari reports back to Warner that projections have been revised again and that they are now down by over $80 million in earnings. This puts Atari's estimated fourth quarter profits at half of the August projections. Manny orders another fourth quarter earnings forecast in response.

The Atari 5200 Super System is released in the interim, slightly delayed from its planned October release. Positioned as a higher end offering to the 2600 and designed to compete against Mattel's Intellivision, it suddenly found itself going head to head against a newer competitor when Coleco unveiled its Colecovision console that past June at the Summer CES. Nearly equivalent to the 5200 in graphics and sound, the Colecovision also gained a window of advantage over the 5200 with its August 1982 release, giving it several months of sales without any competition from Atari. To make matters worse for Atari, the 5200 Super System's pack-in was no match for the Colecovisions. Atari had chosen the lackluster pack in *Super Breakout* for the 5200; hardly a game worthy of showcasing the new console's abilities, nor a game that would excite buyers to go out and purchase the new console with the same eagerness as they were buying the new Colecovision for the sole intent of playing its own pack-in game: *Donkey Kong*. A home version very close to the original arcade version that had been a runaway hit for Nintendo.

As Dec. 7th arrives, securities analyst Lee S. Isgur had just come from a meeting with senior executives of Warner Communications, and assured his investment clients at Paine Webber Inc. that Warner's earnings for 1982 would be less than 25 percent higher than in 1981. Manny is still not comfortable with the reports and figures and that evening he again demands the figures be run and rechecked - something just isn't adding up correctly. Manny finally gets precise accounting - the figures all add up now. Projections are more than $50 million less than the $80 million downward figures. "Things were in a whole new world," recalls Manny. The response to all this, instead of building the needed inventory control over the past several months, was to now fire Perry Odak. Back over at Atari Taiwan, Rick Krieger receives a call from Paul Malloy informing him that Perry Odak has been fired and that production of the Atari 5200 needs to be increased.

Suddenly on December 8th, the entire financial charade begins to crumble. With the problems mounting instead of being solved, and knowing they can't hold out any longer, Warner Communications issues a press release that earnings for 1982 are well below all of the previous stated projections due to significantly lower earnings in Warner's Consumer Division of its Atari Subsidiary. Profits would only be a little more than 10 percent, not much more than half of the fourth quarter for 1981. Warner's streak of seven years of profitable quarters comes to an end, and their stock becomes the most heavily traded on the stock exchange, falling 17 points. Atari Taiwan gets another call from Paul Malloy to Rick Krieger two days later, where he is informed to stop producing *Pac-Man* for the 2600. Rick is also informed about the huge stock drop and the lower fourth quarter sales, and how very bad things really are.

The report sends shockwaves through the rest of the consumer video game industry, as stock prices for Mattel, Coleco, Tandy, and more fell drastically. Mattel was also now reporting an expected loss for its fourth quarter due, to the same intense competition and industry slump that hit Atari. In fact most of the companies started reporting the same sobering news. But it was Atari that had set the dominoes in motion. As Michele Preston, an analyst for the Wall Street firm Cyrus J. Lawrence Inc. stated in the December 10th New York Times, "We've been looking for a shake-out in cartridges all along. The surprise was we didn't expect Atari to be the one shaken out."

Before the dust even settles from this disaster, rumors and accusations of insider trading immediately follow the announcement, causing a further drop in Warner's stock value. It turns out the accusations were set off because Ray Kassar had sold 5,000 shares of stock just prior to the stock announcement. "This was a planned sale already arranged with my broker, as planned for the end of the year. This barely represented 1% of my total portfolio. No one would risk insider trading for such a small amount," recalls Ray Kassar. Dennis Groth, Atari's CFO would also come under scrutiny for his December 1st stock sales, and several other Atari executives executed trades as well. The primary focus of the Securities and Exchange Commission will be on the trades made by Ray Kassar and Dennis Groth though, and a settlement for the two would finally be reached August 20, 1985 when Warner Communications agrees on SEC violations totalling $17,250,000 plus accrued interest from January 1, 1985. Of that settlement amount, $290,000 plus interest would be paid by Ray Kassar and Dennis Groth, both of whom are able to admit no guilt or wrongdoing in the selling of their stock prior to the Warner earnings announcement. They would pay back the profits earned from the selling of their stock, plus interest, and with that, the matter is officially closed.

While December of 1982 certainly was a hard month on Atari, it was not all doom and gloom as Atari protected its patents and and released some new products as well. Atari is awarded a temporary injunction against Commodore Business Machines for patent infringement on Atari's joystick controller design when Commodore released its own white version of Atari's stylized joystick. Michael Sheppard, one of Atari's patent attorneys, filed suit against Commodore on October 11th stating that the VIC-20 joystick controllers that Commodore was selling were an exact duplicate of the Atari design, but molded in white instead of black plastic. Irving Gould, Chairman of Commodore tells the Wall Street Journal that Commodore has sold very small quantities of the joysticks, and then heavily discounted them because they weren't selling well. With this comment having zero impact on the ruling, Commodore filed an appeal.

Elsewhere in the court system on December 10th, Atari files a $350 million lawsuit against Coleco Industries for patent infringement for its Coleco Expansion Module #1, which allowed the Colecovision game console to play Atari VCS cartridges. Firing back, Coleco files an anti-trust countersuit against Atari for $500 million.

On December 14, 1982, in New York City, a large media event is held to unveil Atari's newest computer, the Atari 1200XL Home Computer System. Packaged into a new, low profile sleek high tech case design and sporting a fully installed 64K of memory, built-in self-test diagnostics, international character set, special function keys, a new Help button and placement of ports and connections in more convenient locations, this machine is a worthy replacement for the 1979 Atari 800 computer system. But a dark cloud was looming over Atari given the events of the prior week. Over time, the hovering clouds would grow darker still when more was made known about the 1200XL.

Chapter 11 Review In Images

Ray hosted Atari's International Sales Meeting for 1982 at the extravagant Hôtel de Paris Monte-Carlo in Monte Carlo, Monaco.

Site seeing cruise in Monte Carlo. Mr. Keith Schaefer (President of Atari Computer Division), Mrs. Karen Breuhl (wife of Anton Breuhl, President of Atari International Division).

Right to Left: Claude Nobs (Warner Bros. Swizterland & founder of Montreaux Jazz Festival), Greta and Klaus Ollman (MD - Atari Germany), Perry Odak (in yellow shirt, President of Consumer Products Group), Guy Millant (MD - Atari France).

Right to Left: Mr. and Mrs. Harry Alexandrer (sales rep. for Baltimore), Donald Kingsborough Director of Marketing. Don was giving Harry a hard time for being seasick.

Top: The Atari Taiwan group during a dinner meeting at the conference.

Bottom: At the opening of Taiwan Manufacturing Company (ATMC) the week before.

Top: Atari's gigantic booth at the June '82 Consumer Electronics Show. Completely oblivious to the growing problems, it was business as usual as evidenced by the meetings on the top level. *(Photo courtesy of Alan Light)*

Left Top: John Constantine (far left), Managing Director of Atari Far East Ltd., with (l to r) Ray Kassar, Manny Gerard and Paul Molloy (VP of Manufacturing).

Left Bottom: Manny discovers John's bar.

Opposite: John oversaw Atari's attempted expansion in to East Asia's consumer market. Standing next to him is Hong Kong's national VCS *Asteroids* champion.

PLAY BALL
OR SPACE INVADERS*
OR MISSILE COMMAND™
OR SUPER BREAKOUT®
OR NIGHTDRIVER®
OR ASTEROIDS™
OR PAC-MAN†

SPACE INVADERS	GOLF	VIDEO OLYMPICS	OUTLAW
VIDEO CHESS	CASINO	BREAKOUT	NIGHT DRIVER
CIRCUS ATARI	OTHELLO	PAC-MAN	SLOT RACERS
DODGE 'EM	FOOTBALL	MISSILE COMMAND	HAUNTED HOUSE
MAZE CRAZE	SKY DIVER	ADVENTURE	ASTEROIDS
BASIC PROGRAMMING	3-D TIC-TAC-TOE	STREET RACER	BACKGAMMON
VIDEO CHECKERS	HANGMAN	HOME RUN	HUMAN CANNONBALL
COMBAT	BRAIN GAMES	INDY 500	WARLORDS
AIR-SEA BATTLE	VIDEO PIN	PELE'S SOCCER	CANYON BOMBER
	BOWLIN		SUPER BREAKOUT
SPACE WAR			BASKETBALL

ATARI MAKES MORE HOME VIDEO GAMES THAN ANYONE.
HAVE YOU PLAYED ATARI TODAY?

ATARI
A Warner Communications Company
©1982 ATARI, INC.

* Space Invaders is a trademark of Taito America Corp. †PAC-MAN is a trademark of Midway Manufacturing Co. licensed by Namco America, Inc.

This page: In the early 80s Atari's slogan and jingle "Have you played Atari today?" became a pop culture fixture.

Following pages: Thanks to media giant Warner's marketing muscle, Atari pioneered video game brand and product awareness, reaching to new heights across '82-'83.

Keys to Success. Carry your keys with class — choose your favorite video game emblem in a scratchproof crystalite dome on a suede/velour backing.

Atari	Item Code A33	$2.50
Pac-Man	Item Code A34	$2.50
Berzerk	Item Code A35	$2.50

Long-Playing Disc. You'll have hours of summer fun with this official Atari Frisbee.* It's a genuine Wham-O Frisbee — the farthest flying, fasest flying disc there is!

Item Code A23 $3.50

Available only from The Atari Club!

No Sweat! Bjorn Borg, ex... cial Atari headbands and... Club members only! Perfe... cling, basketball — you ne... ner with this attention-ge... headband and a pair of wri... and logo.

Available only fro...

ATARI

ASK ABOUT THE NEW CARTRIDGE OF THE MONTH

ATARI YARS' REVENGE

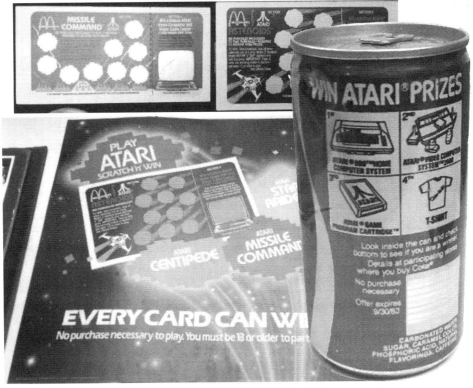

Top: 275 Gibraltar, home of the Consumer Division's game console programmers.
Bottom: Game programmer Steve Woita (*Quadrun, Taz, Asterix* and *Garfield*) at the front of Gibraltar. *Following Pages*: Photos of Steve during game development.

W e've got a bumper crop
of new games coming
out this year; games that
are more sophisticated and more
exciting than ever before. And to
keep the excitement growing all
year long, we're planning to introduce new games all year long.
*Inside: A calendar of new game
introductions planned for the first
half of 1982.*

```
1981-1982          CONTENTS ON E.C.N. ROM FILE #2           Jan Boehm X2285

  2-1  C012539A    Othello............(Rev A).........(PAL)..........01/13/81

  2-2  C011239A    Othello............(Rev A)........................01/13/81

  2-3  C012010     War Lords...........................................02/24/81

  2-4  C012619     Stellar Track.....................(PAL)..........02/24/81

  2-5. C012037A    Dodge'Em...........(Rev A)..........................02/27/81

  2-6. C012637A    Dodge'Em...........(Rev A).........(PAL)..........02/27/81

  2-7. C012008     Super Breakout......................................03/03/81

  2-8. C016449     Asteroids...........................................03/06/81

  2-9  C017449     Asteroids.........................(PAL)..........03/20/81

 2-10. C012610     Warlords..........................(PAL)..........03-24-81

 2-11. C016449A    Asteroids...........(REV A).........................03-20-81

 2-12. C012632A    Space Invaders......(REV A).........(PAL)..........03-24-81

 2-13. C012608     Super Breakout....................(PAL)..........04-01-81

 2-14  C011214     Steeple Chase.....................(PAL)..........05-19-81

 2-15  C016449B    Asteroids...........(REV B).........................05-20-81

 2-16  C017449A    Asteroids...........(REV A).......(PAL)..........07-06-81

 2-17  C012008A    Super Breakout......(REV A).........................08-24-81

 2-18  C012054     Nightmare Manor.(Haunted House)....................10-16-81

 2-19  C012046     Pac Man.............................................11-10-81

 2-20  C012055     Yar's Revenge.......................................11-20-81

 2-21  C012009     Defender............................................11-23-81

 2-22  C012654     Haunted House....................(PAL)..........11-23-81

 2-23  C012610A    War Lords...........(REV A).......(PAL)..........11-23-81

 2-25  C012032B    Space Invaders......(REV B)........(PAL)..........01-12-82   1982

 2-26  C012608A    Super Breakout......(REV A).......(PAL)..........01-12-82

 2-27  C012038A    Missle Command......(REV A).........................01-12-82

 2-28  C012655     Yar's Revenge....................(PAL)..........01-20-82

 2-29  C012646     Pac Man..........................(PAL)..........01-20-82
```

A schedule of expected dates for the supplying of finished games to Manufacturing for production.

San Francisco Mayor
Diane Feinstein on
National Pac-Man day.
*(Courtesty Steve Ringman /
The Chronicle)*

ATARI®
"PAC-MAN"* :25/:30

CLIENT: WARNER COMMUNICATIONS   COMM'L. NO.: QACX 2133

(MUSIC UNDER)
CHORUS: First the PAC-MAN eats through a maze of dots.

GIRL: (LAUGHTER)

CHORUS: Then the PAC-MAN heads for the corner spots.

Then he eats his fill

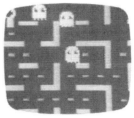

of a power pill

and then

all those ghosts turn blue.

Boo!

And PAC-MAN eats them all too.

(SFX)

Have you played Atari® today?

(MUSIC OUT)

*PAC-MAN is a trademark of Midway Mfg. Co., licensed by Namco-America, Inc.

Lifelong Atari fan Clay Cowgill visited Atari during this time. A wide eyed kid during the heyday of the "age of Atari," he's said that visiting Disneyland shortly after was kind of anti-climatic in comparison. These photos were taken in Atari's 1196 building.

Yars' Revenge, Raiders of the Lost Ark, and *E.T.* designer Howard Scott Warshaw above, graphics specialist Jerome Domurat (responsible for E.T.'s startup screen) below. (Opposite upper right) Howard with Steven Spielberg.

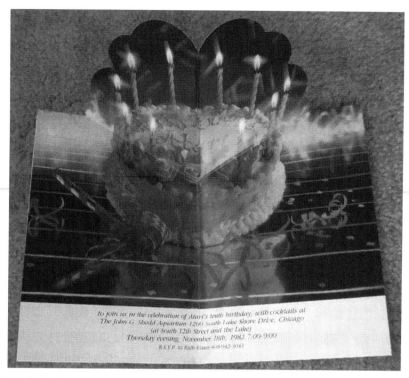

to join us in the celebration of Atari's tenth birthday, with cocktails at
The John G. Shedd Aquarium 1200 South Lake Shore Drive, Chicago
(at South 12th Street and the Lake)
Thursday evening, November 18th, 1982 7:00-9:00
R.S.V.P. to Ruth Evans 408-942-3043

Several weeks before the announcement that would change Atari's and the U.S. consumer video game industry's history, Atari celebrated its 10th anniversary. Below is the 10th anniversary logo designed by George Opperman. *(courtesy of Matt Osborne).*

December

1982

9 Thursday

Bob Hartley - traffic manager resigns

10 Friday

Received call from Mattel to stop
building Pac-man into VCS.

Received info that Warner stock dropped
16 points based on lower 4th quarter
Sales. Very Bad

Charlie Gee & Joe Player leave - good boys

December W T F S S M T W T F S S M T W T F S S M T W T F S S M T W T F
         1 2 3 4 5 6 7 8 9 10 11 12 13 14 15 16 17 18 19 20 21 22 23 24 25 26 27 28 29 30 31

A page from Rick Krieger's (factory manager for Atari Taiwan) personal 1982 calendar. The same day he received news of Atari's continued stock drop due to its December 7 announcement, he was also oredered to stop making *Pac-Man* for use as the VCS's pack-in.

Chapter 11

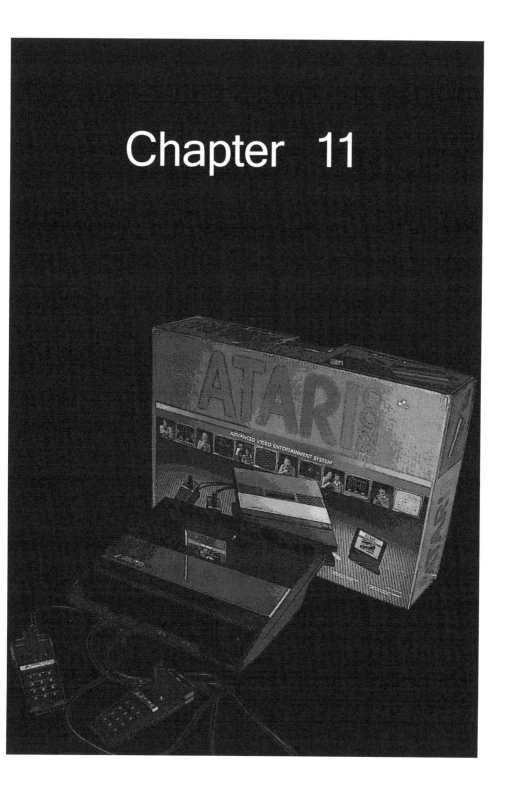

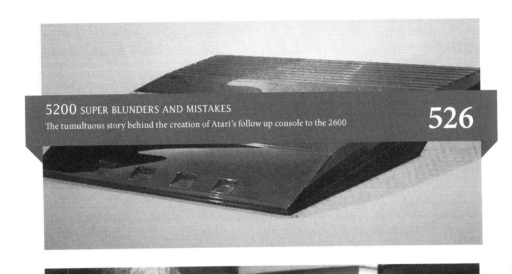

5200 Super Blunders And Mistakes

Pink slips, or the Atari equivalent of them, is the first news that greets Atari employees in the first days of 1983. The company has survived layoffs and financial problems before, but this time is different... this time Atari's problems seemed to be affecting the whole industry as well. Imagic for example, which was set to go public in December, now had to the cancel their plans. (Though humorously, both executives from Imagic and rival Data Age felt the announced 56% profit drop at Warner and Atari own losses were done just to derail Imagic's plans). Many of the other consumer video game companies, with the exception of Coleco, were also reporting huge 4th quarter losses further compounding the effects.

It's not that the market is dying - the demand and sales are still there. To that note, Coleco and Activision talked up a great game on their profits and the industry being up, such as when Activision president Jim Levy stated to Mark Andrews of the Free Lance-Star "Things really are booming, and with the continued support of our customers, we'll keep them booming." Sounding more like a plea to consumers for help, the problems the consumer industry is facing aren't from the consumers. Really what it comes down to is the fact the market was changing so rapidly that the companies involved with the explosive growth were now having problems adjusting to its natural contraction and maturing. With so much competition on the market, the rules for producing a successful game had been rewritten. Billboard magazine notes it now takes around $2 million in television advertising alone to launch a new video game, which is 10 times the cost of putting out a new modestly promoted album. Add to that a projected 500 new game cartridges to be released on the market in 1983 (which doesn't even include computer games), and you have room for maybe a handful of titles to become a success and make it worth the cost of development. It's resulting in a "release as many as you can and hope for one that really sticks" attitude that's mimicking the music industry - only without the advantage of that industry's established financial methods or inventory control.

Atari was paying for its problems of 1982 by now announcing a planned elimination of 1,700 employees from its domestic manufacturing and production facilities to drastically cut costs. That's 1,700 employees out of 7,800 in the U.S. (there are currently 11,000 employees worldwide), or almost 22% of Atari's U.S. workforce eliminated at the flick of the wrist! The first 600 were to take place almost immediately, with their layoff notices sent out on February 23rd, and the remaining 1,100 are planned to be eliminated over the next 4 months. The reason given for the layoffs is the moving of manufacturing operations to Taiwan and Hong Kong in an effort to cut costs in this extremely competitive market. Looking at the move for some time, its timing made it a thinly veiled subterfuge to Wall Street. Atari's manufacturing plants in El Paso, Texas and Fajardo, Puerto Rico, which just opened the year before, will remain unaffected... for a little while longer. These layoffs and manufacturing moves were only directly related to the Consumer Electronics and Home Computer divisions of the company, and luckily the Coin-op division was not affected; however layoffs in Coin-op would unfortunately be coming down the pipeline soon as well.

Unlike many companies that simply would hand employees a cardboard box and escort them out the door with a security officer like they were doing a 'perp-walk,' leaving a loyal and valued employee feeling humiliated, Atari was holding 'employment connection' workshops and also assisting former employees in trying to locate and secure employment elsewhere. Atari's early days of 'family' and working together as a tight knit group may have been long gone; however Atari's Human Resources Department was filled with individuals who are human, and tried to do what they could to put a little salve on the wounds of those laid off - many even being close friends with the departing. Atari may have become a large corporate entity, but still in many ways, the benevolence never left the company - and the feeling of family endured during these times.

Adding to the intensity of the first half of 1983 is that Atari's new console, the 5200, is facing an uphill battle on the market. Selling well, the problem for it was simply timing; it had the unfortunate situation of being introduced in a now seriously overcrowded market and going head to head with an unplanned serious competitor in Coleco with its Colecovision. Atari had finally jumped into unchartered waters with its long overdue 'high end' companion to the 2600, but perhaps some would think it was a dive 'head first' into the shallow end considering the current situation. Perhaps if it could have been released in 1981 it would have been better situated, but the convoluted path from project to final product of the console formerly known as System X didn't allow it. It all began back in 1977 when a project was launched to create a follow-up to the 2600, but instead of it being a follow-up, a whole new product line... in fact, a whole new DIVISION would be created, dedicated to home computers. Then in 1981 a second effort at a follow-up to the 2600 would come into being, however, once again what was supposed to start as a follow-up quickly became to Atari, a new product category and a new product line. It was originally conceived as one of three products that Atari would introduce; one would be Stella - as a newly renamed version of the 2600, but with zero changes from the original. Then there is Sylvia - a higher end console, also called Super-Stella - which was meant to be an Intellivision competitor based around an enhanced version of the original TIA chip. Finally there was 'PAM' or Personal Arcade Machine, which would eventually become the Atari 5200.

Sylvia would have a new updated TIA version called the STIA or Super-TIA with more enhanced graphics, and a full 6502 microprocessor instead of the 6507 in the original 2600. It's also to include a new chip called FRANTIC, that would be a variation of the ANTIC chip used in Atari's home computer systems. Along with a generous 8K of memory versus the 128 bytes of the original Atari VCS, it's also intended to have an onboard Speech Synthesizer. Sylvia's case design was based on a low profile, sleek, modern 80s look, similar to the earlier Atari 2700 prototype wireless console design. You see, the age of 1970s wood grain era was coming to an end, and the kid's rooms covered in Farrah Fawcett and wood paneling were very much over. The 1980s is 'the decade of high tech' and Atari's products needed to reflect that futuristic look.

None of these latter two consoles were intended to replace the Atari VCS when they came out. Oh no... Marketing was not about to sacrifice its sacred cash-cow. There was still entirely too much left in 'Old Bessie' to 'milk.' During the development of PAM it was already being positioned as a higher end product, completely in its own category and different target audience. Atari was wringing its hands and with a devilish look in its corporate eyes, the focus was on putting nails into the coffin of its arch-enemy, the Mattel Intellivision, by sandwiching it out of the market. And who knows - perhaps throwing the pompous-sounding George Plimpton featured in the Intellivision's commercials, into the coffin too!

PAM was not a console designed in a vacuum; it was in fact the product of an exhaustive marketing research project that started at the beginning of 1981 whose findings were reported November 11, 1981, in a report delivered to Roy Nishi of Atari's Consumer Electronics Division. The question put to gamers in 1981 was "What do you want in a new console?" Some of the feedback received on the 2600 stated that graphics and definition were not as good as Mattel's Intellivision and other computer games ('Classic games are not as good as Mattel's; there is no computer keyboard or future programming potential'). The use of the name 'Video Computer System' also confuses some consumers, so the new system should not be called the 'Atari advanced computer system' and also, the initial idea of 'Atari Video System X' was too ambiguous and meaningless. The study also concluded that three products and three price points would be rejected by both retailers and customers, leading to the dropping of Project Sylvia. The two planned systems were then moved to just Stella (Atari Game System 16), and PAM (Atari Game System 64). The plan for PAM would be targeted at primarily 'game buffs, heavy coin-op players and those who always buy top price,' according to the report findings.

Internally, input was also received from Ron Appin (consumer research), John Hayashi (industrial design), Conrad Justson (VP of Corporate Planning), Alice Locke (sales promotion), Evelyn Lim (senior graphics designer), Michael Moone (President of Atari CED), Roy Nishi (Industrial Design Manager), Steve Wright (Director of Advanced Software Projects), Riley Rowe (market research), Jewel Savadelis (software engineering), Alan De Schweinitz (Director of Engineering), Ron Stringari (VP of Marketing), Nancy Theobald (Packaging Director) and Colette Weil (Director of Market Research). Input from major retailers was also received: Art Ross (Almo Electronics), Warren Zorack (Bloomingdales), Bob Oliveri (Childworld), Bernie Scharf (Straight Line Distributors), Charlie Sampson (Lechmere), Neil Freedman and Marvin Katz (Lionel Leisure), Barry Firman (R&S Distributors), Dick Lahrberg (Sears Roebuck & Company), Sy Ziv and Hal Sidel (Toys R Us) and Irve Mosier (Woolworths) were all consulted on what retailers wanted in the new console design and features.

Now, to support two different game systems in the retail marketplace, there would need to be 'an elimination of visual clutter at point of sale.' This meant a new design language for the packaging of the 2600, as well as a separate one for PAM's packaging. For game cartridges, the name 'ATARI' must show prominently on all sides of packaging - the packaging must be uniform in appearance, with the product name and number clearly shown to distinguish what console the game is for use with. The products and games must also promote a perceived 'sophistication' and look 'State of the Art,' so their boxes would be silver (since silver says "Ooh, futuristic!) with different additional colors to denote the relationship with a specific system. The packaging and cartridge labels also now had to depict a controller line drawing to clearly show what controller is to be used with each game. 'New cartridge designs should have grooves so that cartridges can stack and have grips onto sides for easier handling.' Further guideline notes indicated 'Labels should designate 'NEW' and announce on packaging that game is home version of successful coin-op game.'

The overview of the Atari Video Game System 64 (PAM) at the time listed:

• 'An internal hardware system identical to that of the ATARI 400 computer combined with "state of the art" game programs that provide you with the ultimate home video game system!'

• 360 Control with rate Omni-directional controller with 12-character key board and two triggers.

• 64K of memory address space

Rob Zdybel details the controller inputs in October of 1981. Departing from the 2600's digital joysticks, these would be analog controllers with 15 keys in total, three of which are planned for special functions. The initial operating system was also defined as well for such things as interrupts and vertical blank handling, RAM allocation and other features. Realizing it's all just preliminary and things could change on the hardware at a moment's notice thanks to Marketing, Rob humourously notes in his October 1981 O.S. description memo: "Hell, it's an interim O.S. and subject to frivolous change at any time."

In December, Rob defined 'PAM Controllers II' and went into detail on the self-centering of the controller positions in the system's software. By February of 1982, 'PAM Standards' had been outlined the and three special keys are now assigned as RESET, START and PAUSE. The standards also describe across the board game requirements, such as that all games are also to required to have an arcade style 'attract mode and they must have a Select Mode to select options and players. Power Up sequencing and housecleaning and End Game protocols were also defined, and though a PAL version of the 5200 was never released, details for handling PAL were also incorporated into the PAM Standards.

Also on February 26th, Rob issued a notice to all PAM Programmers of the arrival of the PAM Trakball and all development systems have been modified to accept it. The Trakball controller had been designed by Dan 'The Trakball Man' Kramer, and was a masterpiece of engineering. Dan is wonderful, lighthearted, but also a creative and determined engineer – his trakball design truly was his passion, so much so he would go toe-to-toe with Atari's design group over how his creation should look. Dan's issue and argument with the mechanical design team had been over the design of the case for the 5200 Trakball. While it made sense to have both left and right handed player fire buttons on either side of the trakball, as he wanted to, what Dan had an issue with was the inclusion of two separate keypads on the case. There was no reason to have two keypads except for aesthetics and he would argue insistently that the design only needed one, that what they were proposing was adding cost to the product and made no sense. Well in the end, just like the old game of 'rock, paper, scissors,' in this case it would be paper covers trakball; mechanical design would win over 'engineering common sense,' and the 5200 Trakball controller would be released with two keypads built into the design instead of just one. Also unique in the design, the trakball controller uses actual pool cue balls, which gives rise to another great story. It's really one of those times where you just had to be there to truly enjoy the humor... Rich Pasco from the Advanced Engineering group just happened to be walking by the assembly building the day the first delivery of cue balls arrived at Atari for assembly into the trakball controllers. "The manufacturer Atari contracted with was not very astute at packing a semi-trailer load of pool balls. When the truck doors were opened, balls went everywhere that day." Pool balls flying off a pool table are dangerous enough. Imagine a truckload of them flying and bouncing everywhwere!

Rob Zdybel had released the final revision of the 'PAM OS' on March 18, 1982, at which point all programmers were notified to download the latest release and debug their game code against it. The case design for PAM was in full swing at this point as well, lead by Roy Nishi, the head of the Consumer Electronics Division industrial design group. Roy, besides being the manager of the group, was also the buffer between his designers and management. "Management would come down, tell us to change things or reject certain things. I would simply agree and when they left, I'd tell everyone to keep things the way they were," recalls Roy. The group were all big fans of the aesthetics of the high end audiophile equipment by Bang & Olufsen, a Denmark based company started in 1925 that creates unique, cutting edge styled audio/visual equipment for homes. It is this futuristic, state of the art styling that the group would draw its inspiration from, and the cancelled Atari 2700 wireless game console was one of the first examples of their homage to the company; The 2700's wedged shaped style had been reminiscent of an early wood cabinet tube radio that Bang & Olufsen produced. Sylvia's design from 1981 also based its appearance on this same high tech wedged look. Regan Cheng, formerly in Coin-Op's Industrial Design group, was now reporting to Roy and playing a major part in PAM's case design. Going to task crafting a product of behemoth beauty, he would take the new PAM system design a step further though by creating a device that looked like it was right out of the future. PAM's casing features a smooth, sleek black styling, a mini-malistic 'power only' button and a brushed metal product label. Just as the 2600 was designed to look at home in a '70s era home entertainment center, the PAM system's look was intended to mesh perfectly next to the look of 80s era stereo components.

As entertainment centers grew in to the 80s to include more devices, including cable boxes, so did the rats nest of wires and cables behind the scene. According to the 1981 research, it was also revealed that buyers didn't want this clutter - or at least a way for the video game console to cut down on its own contribution to it. The PAM system would address this on multiple fronts, such as having a controller storage area in the top of the unit with openings to allow the cables to come out from the storage compartment and stay plugged into the front of the console if the owner wanted. The mess of cords coming from the back of the console to the TV and electrical outlet would also be reduced, thanks to another issue addressed by the research of a common complaint from retailers and consumers: always having to reach around behind the TV to manually switch the connection box from TV to Game and then back each time. Atari engineers tackled this by expanding a previous competitor's solution to include a new Automatic Power/Switchbox. In the 70s, when RCA had released its Studio II to compete with Atari and Fairchild's offeriings, they had released a unique combination power/tv connector box that allowed the Studio II to have a single cable coming from it for both power and the signal sent to the TV. The problem was (besides the sparks that came from people plugging the console's cable in while already having the electrical outlet hooked up as well), was that it wasn't auto-switching. You still had to reach around and slide the TV/Console selector which also functions as the Studio II's power switch. Atari upgraded the solution to include an auto-switch. When PAM's power button on the console is pressed, the switchbox automatically turns the game console on while switching to 'Game' mode on the switchbox to allow PAM control of the TV display. No other console would offer features such as these at the time of PAM's release, presenting a futuristic looking advantage for the console.

PAM's case design drawings were completed in November 1981, and hard tooling began in December of 1981. Hugh Lee, Sharon Cassella (Ashton), Ken Ashton, Dave Estes and Russell Farnell were charged with taking Regan Cheng's industrial design drawings and turning his vision into a physical product. That included all the parts most consumers take for granted: the mechanical design aspects of the case, power button, cord, storage and other physical aspects of the case design. By December 1981, the engineering drawings were noting both 'PAM' and '5200' in the project box, and on June 14, 1982, like a fine artist putting the last strokes onto a masterpiece, Sharon Cassella (Ashton) would complete the final designation to the brushed aluminum nameplate drawing, adding 'Atari 5200 as per marketing's instructions.' The model number of the console, 5200, had become its product name, no longer being the PAM or Personal Arcade Machine. This is when the VCS or Video Computer System was officially renamed the 2600 after its model number as well, in keeping with the well laid out division of the two consoles as separate efforts.

As for the controllers for the 5200 Super System, this is where innovation unfortunately met overkill. In its snooty George Plimpton ads, Mattel had always touted that its controllers have 16 ways of direction and Atari's are only eight. Tackling a solution to this for the 5200, Ron Milner of Atari Grass Valley had developed an entirely new controller design called, "The Trakplate" controller. A flat plate controller, just like the Intellivision design, it boasted 16 ways of direction which can plug into and work in a standard 9-pin controller port already in use in Atari's other cosumer devices. Craig Asher was tapped to do the controller casing, and had been working on controller designs for Atari going back to the *PONG* console days when he had developed the detachable paddle controllers that plugged into the early dedicated *PONG* consoles, and then later designed the cartridge casing for the 2600 game cartridges as well. The new controller would go beyond anything Atari had ever achieved in a handheld controller device.

However, Craig saw an opportuninty to do a different set of internals as well. Taking advantage of the fact that the 2600 and the home computers all could use analog inputs from paddle controls, Craig saw an opportunity to design a controller that could use 2 potentiometers normally used in the paddles to instead measure precisely left to right and up to down to form a player position. Working just like a trackball controller, when merged together it would give a game player a full 360 degrees of movement - totally blowing the doors off of the Intellivision's capabilities. Also, through some clever software coding, the farther you pushed the stick, the faster a player's movement could be made to go; the controller would be speed sensitive too! Nothing like this was ever developed for a home game controller; even

Atari's soon to be toe-to-toe competitor, the Colecovision would only have an 8-way directional joystick.

One issue not addressed in the design however was centering the joystick back when no pressure is applied. Making the stick slap back to its center position would be important for games that only need 4 directions, like Atari's forthcoming Pac-Man for the system. Likewise, the first revision of the joysticks would had a very thin boot around the joystick base that unfortunately would wear and tear within several days of use. Focus group tests came back with complaints about the difficulty in using the controllers and the lack of self centering. Even Atari's own consumer electronics engineers wrote a memo to the head of engineering and over two dozen engineers signed the memo pleading to hold back on the release of the 5200 system with the current controller designs. Marketing wouldn't listen, and the controllers were still shipped, figuring they could always release a fix or upgrade. Atari would address this with much thicker boots in a future revision, that were more durable and which also caused the joystick to go back to almost center, but not completely.

The controller also employs a full 12-button keyboard to control game functions, having the player insert overlays into slots over the keys on the joystick to show what function each button controlled. The original prototyped joystick/keyboard controllers actually started as a marriage between the 2600's joystick and keypad controllers, and in their final wedge shaped controller design represent a vision of not only one-upping Mattel, but of showcasing high end design. To this end, subtle design touches and really innovative thinking abound in nearly every part of the 5200, even in its cartridge designs. The overlays for each game are easily stored directly on each game cartridge; on the back of each 5200 Super System cartridge is a place to insert and store the game's overlays so they wouldn't be lost. The controllers Start, Pause and Reset on the buttons also add an advanced arcade style touch; there would never be a need to reach over to the console except to remove and install a new game - everything would be available via the joysticks. To squeeze all of these features and capabilities into the controller, it used a new technology internally, called 'conductive contacts.' The controller's circuits are actually printed on a sheet of plastic called a 'flex-circuit,' flexibile in nature. Besides being more economical than using traditional switches and contacts, it also provides more opportunities in casing placement and shaping over traditional hard PCBs. These were all cutting edge technologies for their time being put to use in a consumer product that had never been done before.

What turned out to be another unfortunate initial design decision however, was the use of soft rubber buttons for the fire buttons on the controllers. Taking a page from Mattel and trying to appeal to both left and right handed game players, the controllers were designed with 'A' and 'B' buttons on both sides. Unfortunately this made the controllers even more complex than they needed to be, and combined with the soft rubber buttons having a very poor tactile feel causing further complaints from the public.

When the 5200 Supersystem was released in 1982, it was truly a masterpiece, a work of art its own right. With sleek clean and sharp lines, its simplicity is its allure; this is Atari innovation and design at its best insofar as appearance is concerned. The 5200 controllers though, would suffer through lots of complaints, scorn and ridicule from consumers due to all these reasons mentioned. Given the groundbreaking technology implemented into the controllers and the use of untried technologies, Atari made some very bold moves with the 5200 controllers; they were certainly innovation overkill, but they were also ahead of their time. But sadly, the gaming public simply wasn't ready for such an advanced controller. (Editors note: In the decades that followed, analog controllers made a reappearance in the industry via thumb controlled sticks. Solving the self-centering dilemma that Atari faced with the 5200 controllers, they simply showed Atari was just too far ahead of its time in their implementation, which is the risk with those who introduce new formats and technologies.)

The last item that plagued the 5200, and only added to its 1983 market problems, was the collective wonderment by consumers as to Atari's choice of the pack-in game: *Super Breakout*. "Why the hell was that chosen as the pack-in game?" was a common utterance among teens. Some even wondered if Atari was just being cheap, and hadn't wanted to include a hot title like *Pac-Man* with the console because Atari would rather sell it separately to make more money. However, the answer is once again a result of the Marketing department and their 'wisdom.' Their marketing research report directly recommended to "Include a 'Family' cartridge with the hardware package. A more general cartridge than 'Combat' should be included – one which could be enjoyed by the entire family (perhaps in the 'Skill Gallery' or 'Adventure Territory' categories)." But somewhere in the short-sighted research, no one had realized that things were quickly changing in the consumer's appetite during the early 80s, mainly thanks to the quick appearance of recently hot arcade arcade titles on home game consoles. Only whetting people's appetites for the arcade experience at home, it was a complete irony that a system designed around 'heavy coin-op players' wasn't coming with a title they were most likely currently playing.

Pac-Man would eventually be packaged with the 5200 Super System after the release of its smaller cost reduced version in 1983, but by then Coleco had already done its damage including a pack-in title gamers were actually playing in the arcades: *Donkey Kong*. The initial launch line-up of the 5200 also included *Centipede, Defender, Galaxian, Missile Command, Pac Man, Qix, Realsports Baseball, Realsports Football, Realsports Soccer, Space Invaders, and Star Raiders*. A decent linup with fairly recent games, the problem was they were all updated releases and/or releases carried over from Atari's Home Computer line. Atari had spent nearly two years prepping to go toe-to-toe with Mattel, and while it did outshine the Mattel Intellivision console with the Atari *Realsports* titles, the real threat now was directly from Colecovision. Atari had been completely blindsided, and that initial game offering was not enough to truly set the system above its new rival.

At the same time, another complaint about the 5200 Super System was that it could not play the massive library of 2600 games. When a 2600 adapter for the 5200 was finally released, initially the perception was that it was done in response to companies such as Coleco and Mattel that were quick to release 2600 adapters for their systems. However, the 2600 adapter had already well underway by late 1982 in its design, and planned to be released at the same time as the 5200 launch. The problem was it wound up being delayed because of a technical problem; not with the adapter, but with the way the new 36-pin cartridge slot was designed in the initial release of the 5200. The adapter and the console were not electrically compatible and plugging an adapter in would actually damage the 5200! On May 4th, Atari consumer engineer Gary Rubio came to the rescue with a procedure to upgrade the existing inventory of 5200 system boards to make them compatible with the new 2600 cartridge adapter, which in turn would save Atari nearly $1 million in 5200 system boards inventory. Atari then issued this procedure out to its Field Service Centers to perform free upgrades to existing owners, and also made sure to redesign the cartridge port in the forthcoming cost reduced version of the 5200 (that featured only two front controller ports instead of the four on the launch version) to accept the new adapters.

Spring Is In The Air

While the 5200 was battling it out with Colecovision in the consumer marketplace of the new version of this industry, the ever weakening one, unbeknownst to most at Atari its replacement was also underway. A replacement that came by way of one of the strangest new relationships and business agreements in Atari's history. The relationship had first started in 1981 after an unlicensed upgrade to Atari's *Missile Command* coin-op was released by a small company out on the East Coast. The company and the upgrade were started in much the same fashion as the garage startups of the Valley. Back in late 1978, three electrical engineering students at the Massachusetts Institute of Technology (MIT), were looking to make some money on the side by taking advantage of the video game craze. The idea was simple enough: Doug Macrae, Kevin Curran and Steve Golson set up Doug's brother's pinball machine in one of the campus dorms and became instant coin-op operators. As money started to come in, they brought in more games and eventually would have multiple games set up in three different dorms. While the revenue was coming in good in the beginning, the three started to notice that after awhile, their games were not pulling in as much. Watching the games, they see they're constantly being played, so it's not an issue of people getting bored no longer playing them. Instead, what they did notice is that players were getting better and better at playing the games, which meant longer playtimes and fewer quarters were going into the machines.

The three were aware of the various 'speed-up' kits that were beginning to show up in local arcades, which would enhance game play by speeding up the action.

One of the first types, for example, was a speed-up kit for Atari's *Asteroids* machines. Then came the *Galaxian* kits that wouldn't just speed up the game, but added more aliens and turned the game into *Super Galaxians*. Doug, Kevin, and Steve had three *Missile Commands* at the MIT dorms at the time, which were extremely popular and constantly being played, but their revenues dropped drastically because the players were getting better and better at playing, with the games lasting long periods of time.

The guys decide to call around and see if there are speed-up kits for *Missile Command*, and a lot of places said they were working on a kit, but there were none currently available. Faced with what most would consider a dead end, they did what any young entrepeneurs would do: they built one of their own. Doug and Kevin borrowed money from Doug's mother, and they purchased a 6502 CPU General Radio (GenRad) development system to begin hacking together their upgrade from. Setting up the development system in the living room of the campus house they were living in, they wheeled in one of their *Missile Command* machines, setting it up right next to the development system. They worked on their new speed-up kit from March through May of 1981, calling themselves General Computer Corporation (GCC).

Instead of modifying existing game code, they designed a small 'daughter-board' to plug onto the existing *Missile Command* board that works much like the aliens in the film *The Puppet Masters* or the harness creatures in TV's *Falling Skies*; hijacking the game and overlaying their own code over certain parts of Atari's *Missile Command* ROM code to make it a 'new' game. They only planned to change about 10% of the code with their overlay code, and they designed some circuitry in their daughter board so that people couldn't rip-off their code by just copying ROM chips and burning new ones. This had been a huge problem faced by those selling speed-up kits - they weren't making money from their work because people were just making copies of their modified ROM code. Likewise, none of the three thought that their boards would pose any kind of legal problems for them with Atari, but just to cover their bases, Kevin made a call to Atari and explained the details about their kit, and whomever he spoke with said it wouldn't be a problem.

Once ready, they put together a full color flyer and started running ads in the coin-op industry magazines *Replay* and *Playmeter* for their upgrade kit, called *Super Missile Attack*. Now, their boards only cost them about $30 to build and they were selling them for $295, which meant they turned quite the profit per each kit sold. Their new *Super Missile Attack* kits sold very well, enough so that United Parcel Service was showing up daily to pick up boxes of shipments going out.

Given the success of thir first kit, the guys decide to start working on a speed up kit for *Pac-Man* next. Then came the knock on the door from Atari on August 3, 1981 via a notice that Atari's legal department was suing GCC for a total of $15 million. Filed in Boston in U.S. District Court, Atari was seeking to stop GCC from manufacturing and selling their add-on board and receive punitive damages: $5 million against GCC, another $5 million each from a suit against Doug Macrae and Kevin Curran, and all profits from the sales of their add-on board kits.

A big company with high priced lawyers, Atari had thought they could take the traditional route and intimidate this tiny little Massachusetts startup company, causing them to crawl into some hole and just go away. Well little did Atari know that Kevin and Doug thought the whole lawsuit was great, and that it'd be even more fun than building kits! They would get to go to the Federal District Court and this was going to be a blast! The reason for this cavalier enjoyment over the turn of events? They had absolutely nothing to lose – only the corporate entity of GCC could be sued and they were protected under that. A fellow friend of theirs (Jerry Hoser) agreed to be their lawyer for a staggering fee of... three meals a day for his work; he too thought the whole thing would be fun.

Well, the first court appearance on a Friday didn't quite turn out to be as much fun as they thought. Atari's first order of business against GCC was to file a restraining order to bar them from selling their kits, causing an immediate dent in their sales. Well the disappointment caused by that action was very short lived, because by that evening it all turned in to a game to the three boys again. The court had instructed them to stop selling their current kit... okay, fine, they'd come up with a new kit to address problems they'd found in their original design anyway, so no problem! By Monday they had a whole new version of their kit and started selling the new one!

Meanwhile, during the whole court battle, people kept calling up GCC to order their *Super Missile Attack* kits; the guys tell the callers that they can't sell them, and that they should call Atari and complain to them about it. Atari is now getting blowback, and Warner doesn't want a negative grass roots movement springing up against its golden goose. Seeing that these MIT guys are smart... AND talented... Warner's thought is why continue suing them? If they are all so smart and talented, then it would be a much better idea to have them work for Atari. Warner forces Atari to drop the suit against GCC (which Atari does with prejudice), and not too long after that, they have GCC sign a developer's agreement to do engineering development work for their Atari subsidiary.

As part of GCC's engineering contract deal with Warner and Atari, they could develop and sell other kits, but only if they received permission from other manufacturers of the original games. At that point, no one knew publicly about the contract between GCC and Atari; all anyone knew publicly was that Atari dropped its suit against GCC. The *Pac-Man* kit had continued to progress and had moved from being a speed up into basically a whole new game which they call *Crazy Otto*. Following the agreement, Kevin Curran contacted Midway and spoke with Midway's president David Marofske, explaining that GCC won against Atari and he doesn't want to go to court. So why not work out an agreement? Midway at the time was dealing with a huge wave of illegal *Pac-Man* games, t-shirts and other materials. Not wanting to add another suit on to their plate, Dave asked the GCC guys to come out to Midway to demonstrate their kit and discuss a possible license agreement. Steve Golson, Doug Macrae and Kevin Curran flew out to Midway's offices and installed the kit onto one of the *Pac-Man* arcades right off the assembly line. When Dave Marofske and his engineers play *Crazy Otto*, they unexpectedly turn around and suggest that Midway just buys the rights to the kit outright from them instead of a license. GCC has its second major development deal!

Some time later, the guys were continuing their development and engineering work for Atari when Mike Horowitz came into the office and showed Chris Rodes a recent copy of *Time Magazine*. They're running a feature article on video games, and in one of the photos in the article there is a picture of *Missile Command*. That's not what catches their attention though, it's what's in the background that raises eyebrows. Labeled as a *Pac-Man* machine, upon careful examination of the screen it could be clearly seen it was in fact, one of the three *Crazy Otto* machines Midway had put out for field testing. Out of the thousands of *Pac-Man's* out in arcades, *Time Magazine* just happened to snap a photo of one of the *Crazy Otto* prototypes in the Chicago area. Midway's field tests are going so much better than expected, that Midway asks for changes from the GCC guys to the game to move it to production. It would seem they wanted to get in to the "illegal game" business by releasing their own follow-up to *Pac-Man* without talking it over with *Pac-Man* creator NAMCO. By the time the changes are applied, *Crazy Otto* became Midway's *Ms. Pac-Man*.

With what was rapidly to become a hit original game under their belt, in a year's time the college dropouts had come a long way from selling kits out of their campus house in 1981. GCC's next several coin-op games they developed for Atari were to follow, the first of which was released in November of 1982: *Quantum*. It's an interesting game that is, in a way, something only a group of MIT geeks could truly love. Just as the title suggested, the game is based in a very general way around quantum physics, with the player having to surround small atom particles to eliminate them and gain high point scores. While it's certainly a very interesting game, it's not a solid action skill type of game most players were interested in. However it did show a lot of originality, and it used Atari's new color vector display and a trakball controller.

Bringing us up to date, GCC's involvement in Atari's consumer operations began in early 1983, thanks to Steve Ross now being more involved in his Atari subsidiary (unbeknownst to Ray Kassar). Well aware of these MIT engineers and their involvement with Atari as an engineering development contractor, he decides to see about having them do more for Atari. So he sets about having them work on developing games for the 2600 and 5200 game systems. What Steve Ross finds, is that unlike the programming groups in Atari's Sunnyvale offices, these Massachusetts engineers are turning around game requests and delivering games so fast that Ross will nickname them 'The Toaster.' He would tell people that Warner would pop in a game development request and they'd pop out a finished game in no time. As Sunnyvale's programmers would contend though, this was because GCC would put several programmers on a single game whereas Atari would have just one. Ross's meddling with hiring outside contractors who operated separate from Atari's own group would cause some conflicts with the programming group in Sunnyvale though. At one point the Sunnyvale group were set to begin work on an 2600 version of *Battlezone* when a completed *Battlezone* is shown to them - all done without their knowledge. Apparently the game was done by someone named Mike Feinstein, a programmer working at GCC out on the East Coast. Then it happened again with *Millipede* for the 2600. Unknown to the Consumer programming group already working on *Millipede*, the GCC coders were working on a version at the same time. They found out when they submitted their version for review and found it going up against the GCC version. Management would pick the Sunnyvale version of *Millipede* over the GCC version, but the damage was done. What's the point of having two teams work on the same game? It's a complete waste of money and resources, let alone the communication breakdown it represents.

While the Consumer game coding shennanigans are going on, GCC also completed another game that in turn is released by Atari in July 1983, called *Charley-Chucks Food Fight* and its a smash hit. In the same vein of Williams' *Robotron: 2084*, Charlie has to run around an open playfield avoiding four annoyed chefs named Oscar, Angelo, Jacques and Zorba, with the goal of making his way to a melting ice cream cone before it completely melts away. All the while food is being thrown in all directions, including by Charile who has to run over the food to be able to pick it up and throw it at his pursuers. *Food Fight* offers a really enjoyable and less violent alternative to *Robotron* (watermelon, tomatoes and pies being thrown at others is generally not a leading cause of death…), all in a uniquely colorful experience similar to *Centipede* and *Crystal Castles*. The game becomes a good draw for younger players and female players, and proves again that GCC can design unique new games.

GCC's biggest contribution for Atari though had begun shortly before doing all these consumer and coin-op games for Atari. In the fall of 1982, there were proposals at GCC to do a super RAM cartridge for the 2600, which in turn would allow it to be able to display higher-res games and possibly even do more advanced games. Then shorly after, this cocky group of engineers decided they can do just about anything when they had the idea to build their own game console, codenamed 'Spring.' It would be an Intel 80186 microprocessor based game console/home computer 'System.'

Steve Golson remembers putting a big whiteboard into the back of the company car - a Volvo wagon - and driving up to Kevin's Curran's house in New Hampshire to pitch the idea. Art Ng, Tom Westberg, and Chris Berg also attended the meeting. As the proposition is written: "It's called SPRING and it's a home game machine/computer – fully architected and planned out. It will be a high resolution game system with upward expandability, and would be a shared design for a more powerful computer that would also be expandable. The system would have high resolution graphics, sophisticated controls, keyboard add-ons and more."

A very bold proposition indeed, but again, this cocky group of engineers was on top of the world, nothing is impossible for them. In November 1982, Atari's 5200 was officially released and GCC received a 5200 for evaluation. Mortified, they feel the overall design is a failure, and among their top concerns is the fact it appears to be a repackaged Atari 400 computer without any computer functionality for the user. Adding to that the fact that it's not 2600 compatible right out of the box, and the entire console comes off as a travesty to them. They responded in very early 1983, with the idea to do an upgraded 2600. "Make a TIA with more players" is what Steve seems to remember was the initial concept they based their idea on. The GCC group joked that the project should be called 'Pre-Spring Fling,' which was the name of a late winter dance held at MIT.

Then it morphed in to the idea of a 2600 compatible console, but with better graphics and sound, because by early 1983 GCC sees that Colecovision has a 2600 adapter and the 5200's own 2600 adapter isn't due out for several more months. Their first idea to accomplish this is to take the 2600's TIA chip and add better graphics to it, but upon further thinking they hit on a better move of combining projects. The GCC engineers decide they would take what they planned for 'Spring' and implement it into their new design, simply building the TIA into their chip. The entire idea quickly grew into a totally new graphics/sound chip named TIA-MARIA, then later to just MARIA.

Their new game console concept proposal is shown to Warner, who introduced the new project idea to Atari to begin the joint development of this product. Why show it to Warner and not Atari? You have to remember, when GCC signed their engineering development contract, it was with Warner Communications and not with Atari. GCC's direct business relationship with Warner in turn afforded them an exceptional leveraging position. Atari never would've allowed GCC to propose and build a game console directly, especially the Marketing department. However with Steve Ross' loss of confidence in Ray Kassar and his increased involvement with Atari, he would essentially force-feed GCC's new product design down Atari's throat. Fortunately, politics and egos aside, several of Atari's managers such as Don Teiser and engineering managers like Michael Coppack saw beyond the view of them being an outside firm, and instead saw the direct potential this new product design was offering. The project was welcomed by the majority of engineering within Atari. This isn't to say everyone would agree to allow these East Coast upstarts to hawk their wares within the hallowed halls of Atari engineering though; some just couldn't get past their own pride in Atari and their own egos and believed that they could do better. It's a problem that plagues many engineering firms called 'Not Invented Here' or NIH, where anything not done at that company somehow is automatically inferior. Some product prototypes are quickly put together by these engineers, pairing Atari TIA's to home computer GTIA chips, or using two GTIA chips together and trying to come up with a quick and dirty solution using what was already done at Atari. However, management saw the true potential in the MARIA design and everyone had grown tired of reusing old late 70s Atari technology over and over again. The MARIA would be the first time in years that fresh, new and advanced technology would be used in an Atari game console project, and this was the way everyone in charge wanted to head towards.

GCC begins to talk in with the chip fabrication company called VTI in April, the same firm who had done Coleco's engineering design work for their 2600 cartridge adapter for the Colecovision. This was the perfect company to approach for their new enhanced 2600 compatible game console, since VTI had already done the dirty work developing an Atari TIA clone (though GCC wanted to know nothing about that).

By now GCC had begun to call their console the '3600' - the next step up from the 2600. What GCC didn't know however, was that the 3600 had more competition at Atari than just the quickly patched together counters of a few engineers. Atari had already been in talks with Nintendo since April about handling the world wide release of their own soon to launch Japanese console, the Family Computer or Famicom. Don Teiser reports back that during a trip out to Japan, Nintendo has demonstrated to him a very crude game of *Donkey Kong* supposedly being played on what would become the production Famicom hardware. The proposed deal from Nintendo could best be viewed as one of the most one-sided licensing deals any company would ever engage into. Essentially, in typical Japanese pride and style, Nintendo's generous terms would include them engineering all the electronics and PC board design, with Atari simply allowed to design the plastic case and packaging. To add to that, Nintendo would be the sole source for programing the cartridges (charging Atari for the programming), and only Nintendo would be allowed to manufacture the consoles and the cartridges (selling them to Atari, and Atari would also pay Nintendo for the license). Plus it would all have to be agreed to very quick so Atari could meet Nintendo's demand of having it out by Christmas. If the thought of this type of deal leaves you clutching your bottom side feeling violated, many at Atari felt the same way about it. Atari would basically just be selling Nintendo's product for them in the U.S. and the rest of the world under the Atari brand name, but it'd be Nintendo's product and Nintendo making all the real money.

Atari is internally comparing both the Famicom and the 3600 system by June, and they surmise that the 3600 would be a far superior system. However the 3600 system isn't done, and the system's MARIA chip is still in development. With Nintendo pushing on wanting an answer, Atari was planning to lock Nintendo into a licensing deal just to buy time. However in early June Ray Kassar was fired (though publicly in July it was announced he resigned), and without his direct involvement in the Nintendo deal (and the resulting shuffle of management with John Ferrand temporarily trying to manage things along with assistance from Manny Gerrard), the Nintendo negotiations will lag and become severely delayed. A squable between Coleco and Atari over Nintendo's licensing for the home computer version of *Donkey Kong* didn't help either. Then with Jim Morgan taking his time coming on board, finally handling the Coleco issue but then freezing all development for a month, Nintendo has grown frustrated with all of the delays. Realizing that there was no way the product could meet the Christmas deadline and that Atari had enough of its own problems, they walk away from the deal with Atari.

Back during the first week of April, the GCC team was full speed ahead on the MARIA chip right after the first meeting with Gary Boone. Fairly quickly, the 'Spring' game system/computer was dropped as all hands started working on MARIA/3600, with the MARIA/3600 taking much of the expansion and future proofing ideas behind the original 'Spring' game console/computer proposal. Ideas such as being expandable into a computer, having the ability to add more memory and using more advanced controllers, producing a design that's more broadly expanded than the original planned to combination of the Atari TIA chip and the new GCC Maria chip (an effort also called TIA-MARIA). However after some stops and starts, MARIA is developed as a separate chip design that will work side by side with the Atari TIA, making the system 2600 compatible and using the TIA as its sound processor when in '3600-mode. The first 'tapeout' (a layout of the actual chip that would be transferred to a large magnet media reel to reel tape with the data on how to have a chip company fabricate samples) of the MARIA chip was done by early July 1983. The GCC guys are all huge *Star Trek* fans, and hey who isn't in the tech field? Well, the Starship Enterprise was NCC-1701 and General Computer Corp was GCC, so they designated their first MARIA as the GCC-1701. Unfortunately, when problems with the first chip samples appeared, they didn't have Scotty to handle it. The first samples of the chip prove to be faulty; its running too slow and the engineers have to make changes to the design. While they didn't have a 'Scotty' to fix their warp drive, they did have Atari's chip engineers. Working with Atari's ASG (Advanced Semiconductor Group), in October the GCC-1702 is ready and it's working much better. That was until late January 1984, when some additional errors are found in the chip design. Working again to fix it, in April '84 the GCC-1702B is ready for production as the now renamed Atari 7800 sets off to boldly go where no Atari game console since the Atari VCS in 1977 has gone before… to become a success.

A few subtle things done on the 7800 are also intended to correct some of the previous mistakes of the Atari 5200. Dan Schwinn will design a new controller for the 7800 console called the Precision Proline controller. Nope, it won't have a gazillion buttons on it, only two side mounted ones. Its redesigned wedge shape also fits in the player's palm much more comfortably than the 5200's (but it will still eventually be tagged with the nickname 'the Painline Controller.' (*Author note:* Dan will also have some fun during the 7800 game console design, when as the PC board layout engineer working at GCC Dan hides his initials in the circuit trace lines on the 7800 PC boards. If anyone has every opened an Atari 7800, taken the aluminum shielding off of the PC board and then turned it over, with a careful eye you will notice the initials DJS as part of the circuit line traces on the PC boards for Dan J. Schwinn.)

Marketing of course will put their stamp onto the 7800 console, and fortunately this time around they weren't allowed to dictate the console features or functionality; this is why the 7800 became a console that consumers wanted versus what marketing 'thought' consumers wanted like with the 5200. In this case, their contribution was limited to coming up with the 7800 product number. Their reasoning for the number was simple: since the console was going to be 2600 compatible with 5200 level graphics, the numbers would be combined. To take that one step further with the product color designation, since packaging would need to look different from the both the 2600 and 5200, marketing would come up the same formula – Atari 2600 which was RED and Atari 5200 which was BLUE, mix them together and you get PURPLE, the Atari 7800 color designation. "That must've taken Atari marketing months to come up with!" said Steve Golson jokingly.

By the time the 7800 ProSystem is readied for the 1984 Summer CES in June, Atari will announce the console, along with 14 game cartridges: *Pole Position, Ms. Pac Man, Galaga, Dig Dug, Desert Falcon, Centipede, Asteroids, Joust, Robotron 2084, Joust, Food Fight, Ball Blazer, Track and Field, and Rescue on Fractalus*. Also shown is a computer keyboard add-on; an Atarilab module, and as Steve Golson recalls, "We designed a 5200 adapter so that all those poor souls who bought a 5200 could play the new 7800 cartridges." Also announced is a 'high score keeping' add-on. Projections from the El Paso plant where the new 7800 consoles will be built are that Atari could produce one million systems in the first year and up to three million systems per year the following year.

Where There's Smoke, There's Philip Morris

R ay Kassar had entered 1983 with a massive restructuring plan for the company. Part of that plan, as mentioned, was the 1982 proposal to consolidate Atari's many spread out buildings into a single campus. But the high cost of approximately $300 million and the concerns over Roger Smith's detailed assessment that Atari's all too rapidly rising profits could suddenly collapse made such an endeavor too risky to pursue to Steve Ross. That assessment now a firm reality given the events of December, the other part of Ray's plan was now solely invested in moving most of Atari's manufacturing overseas. Ray had been actively meeting and discussing overseas manufacturing with Paul Malloy, John Constantine and Rick Krieger during late 1982, so in January, Ray made the final plans to begin the shutdown of domestic manufacturing and move operations to ATMC (the Atari Taiwan Manufacturing Company) and the new Atari WONG plant which is still being brought up to speed by Brad Saville. That had resulted in the February announcement of 1,700 layoffs and the immediate release of 600 of those workers.

As the weeks continued into 1983, Ray notices that Steve Ross has gotten more involved with Atari. During a high level meeting with all of the top managers from the various divisions and groups within Atari, Ray finds that during the course of the meeting, Steve Ross literally takes it over and is running the show. Directing the course of not just the meeting, also specifically giving his own details, not discussed with Ray, on the company and its future direction and changes. The signal Steve Ross was giving couldn't have been any more obvious than if he had literally stepped in front of Ray while Ray was in mid-sentence. After the meeting, Ray and

Steve have a private sit down and Ray says to Steve point blank that if he has he lost confidence in him, he will resign. However, Steve tells Ray he's doing a fine job. "Steve could never fire someone, it just wasn't in his nature - it wasn't him," recalls Manny Gerard. What Steve had told Ray was in fact a lie, and Ray quickly discovers that Steve and Manny are countermanding many of Ray's decisions and are redirecting certain decisions around Ray's own direct input and management.

Ray got a call from Manny in early June '83, just after most of the major manufacturing restructuring had been completed and domestic manufacturing in Sunnyvale had been completely closed down. Wanting Ray to come out to New York for a meeting, Ray flies out to New York and meets with Manny at Warner Corporate headquarters at 75 Rockefeller Center. Ray recalls it was a rather awkward meeting, as Manny appeared to be having a difficult time trying to explain the situation with Ray. Finally the bombshell is dropped: Ray has been fired. Ray asks Manny why Steve just didn't tell him this several months ago, as it would've saved a lot of time and trouble. Knowing he wasn't going to get a solid answer though, and realizing it would do little to delay the inevitable, Ray quietly accepts his termination. Without discussing the situation with anyone back at Atari, he heads back to San Francisco and packs for a planned vacation trip out to London. Surprisingly, Ray gets a call from Manny while in London, and Manny explains to Ray that he has just spoken with Steve Ross and would Ray consider coming back to run Atari until September while a replacement is hired. Ray is flabbergasted, first they fire him and now they want him to come back to run the company while they work on finding Ray's replacement?!? Ray tells Manny, "Are you crazy? You just fired me from the company; I'm not going to do it." Manny explains to Ray that Steve would appreciate it, and Ray tells him that if Steve appreciated him more than he did, we wouldn't have this disaster. Manny asked Ray again if he would agree to come back, and for the sake of the company and for Ray's own public image, Warner would agree to release a statement that Ray was resigning and not being forced out. Ray agrees to come back and on July 8, 1983, it is officially announced that Raymond Kassar will resign his position as Chairman and CEO of Atari. No reason is given for his resignation though.

Lee Isgur, an analyst from Paine Webber Inc. (who back in December of 1982 was originally assured by Warner that its earnings would be higher than the 1981 earnings of that previous year), publicly surmised that Warner Communications wanted to remove Ray Kassar to help repair both Warner's and Atari's image. He, like many on Wallstreet, believed that much of the problems of the earnings being in error leading up to the December 1982 report were due to Kassar's overly autocratic leadership of the consumer electronics subsidiary of Warner.

Atari's announced replacement for Kassar is James J Morgan, who has served as Executive Vice President, Marketing at Philip Morris since 1978, working for the company for 20 years in a series of marketing positions. Apparently the now-known reason Steve Ross and Manny Gerard were requesting that Ray Kassar return and continue to run Atari until September, was because James Morgan, while accepting the position as Chairman and CEO of Atari, would not begin his new appointment at the company until September 6th. You see, James wanted to take a lengthy vacation before starting at Atari. While publicly it was announced that Ray Kassar would be a consultant to the company, internally Manny Gerard would run Atari until James Morgan begins work at Atari in September.

The question again becomes obvious. Warner hired a management and marketing executive out of the textile industry to run Atari back in 1978. Now they hire an executive out of the tobacco industry. Why? Manny Gerard had several corporate headhunting firms out looking for a suitable new CEO for their Atari subsidiary and James Morgan was highly recommended. True, he is not from the technology field; however, he has a very strong history of working closely with those in a company all the way down to those in the trenches. He is a very talented marketing expert as well. These are strengths that Steve Ross and Manny Gerard see as absolutely essential in trying to put Atari back on course, so James Morgan is hired to hopefully stabilize things.

Not that the problems in Consumer were the sum total of Atari as a company of course, as Coin was now doing well having survived the coin-op industry shakeout. With many of the competing coin companies either going away or being bought out by one another, the coin industry was now seen as starting an upswing cycle, and Atari aimed to take full advantage of it. Before Ray had left, Atari released a coin-op based on a major movie license deal with George Lucas. Atari's *Star Wars* was released in May 1983, however it was a game that at one point might not have been released at all.

Jed Margolin had just put in a really long day working on *Star Wars*, heading home at 3:30 a.m. to get some sleep. He'd planned to come back in to continue working all weekend on the prototype game in the coin-op lab. When returning just before 2:00 p.m. on Saturday, April 16th, he walked into the lab, only to find a heart-stopping sight: It seemed that the building facilities crew had decided to wax and polish the floors in the labs that weekend. One would think that's a good thing, right? After all, you want to keep the labs clean and at their best. Well, not quite…

To accomplish this task, they disconnected and moved all the various equipment in the lab to different areas throughout the building. As another engineer's radio was blasting at full volume in the background, Jed was treated to the sight of his *Star Wars* prototype... in pieces. It had been moved, and all of the circuits and cabling had been carelessly strewn about. The game was no longer working! Jed contacted security and tried to get someone from facilities on the phone to find out who the hell had disrupted and moved the equipment in the lab. This was not the first time this had happened, nor was it the first time that delicate equipment and work in progress games, boards and cabling had been moved about with little to no regard to their importance. But this was the final time this was going to happen as far as Jed was concerned. Jed had been gone for less than twelve hours, leaving the lab very early that morning at around 3:30 a.m. and everything was exactly where it belonged. Now he came in to this mess, which would make Jed have to wind up spending the entire weekend undoing all the (what he deemed as) 'sabotage' to his work. Eventually getting the *Star Wars* machine back up and running again, he would contact his boss (Rick Moncrief), as well as John Ferrand, Mike Hally and Dan Van Elderen and request that they demand facilities under no circumstances move any equipment in any of the labs without prior approval. Fortunately 'The Force' was with Jed and the team on that particular game; despite the uphill battles and the near calamity of the floor waxing incident, *Star Wars* would be released on time for May and become a huge hit with game players everywhere.

Atari seemed to have a lot of hits and misses when it came to trying to adapt movies to its video games. *Raiders of the Lost Ark* did exceptionally well on the Atari 2600, and even though *E.T.* for the 2600 didn't sell enough to recoup its licensing and manufacturing costs, it also sold very well... at least initially. The *E.T. Phone Home* game for the Atari home computers didn't fare very well at all however. But now *Star Wars* in the arcades was doing spectacularly well.

Atari decided the timing was right to adapt another movie; this time it would be *Superman III*, and the project was started in the Home Computer group. Due to the time constraints and pressure to have a game ready around the time that the movie would be released in June, three programmers worked on the game: project lead/code integrator Tan Duong, Dave Comstock as lead programmer, and a junior programmer. The Atari 'SWEAT' SoftWare Editors and Tools would also be used to develop the game. Because of needing to work on the game before the movie had even been released, the decision was made to try something different and design the *Superman III* game from the script alone! That's right, no private pre-screening or backstage access, just a script. After they had a chance to read the script, they brainstormed ideas for what the game should be about and look like. One of the key elements in the film was Superman trying to prevent an incredibly powerful computer from draining cities of power to make itself even more powerful. The first game concept that came to mind was a variant based on the game play ideas from *Missile Command*. Brad Fuller would create the sound and a short piece of music for the game, which was actually a very close variation of the *Star Trek - the Motion Picture* theme music. The graphics for the game are created by Gary Winnick, who also did the artwork for several of the Atari home computer games that came right after *Superman III*. Gary is probably best known for the artwork he did for Lucasfilm's later Atari games, such as *Rescue On Fractalus* and *Ballblazer*.

On June 17th, the day the *Superman III* movie came out, Atari treated the entire Home Computer Division to the movie screening. That's when the first doubt about their game began to set in. The movie may not have been a total flop, but it was definitely wasn't a strong movie, leading many to wonder if game sales would suffer blowback. As the game was already close to being ready to ship, it would be put in front of focus group's to play and give the final answer. The focus group's feedback wasn't as strong or positive as marketing had wanted, so with the *Superman III* movie was very quickly fading in popularity in the theatres, Atari decided not to release the game.

During the filming of the *Superman III* movie, Warner Studios looked to Atari to generate a high resolution computer fight sequence for the movie. Taking up the task, Steve Wright lead a group of programmers on the porject, headquartered across the street from Atari's consumer programming group on Gibraltar in the Special Projects building. It took Atari's two Symbolics 3600 LISP based machines over fourteen weeks to generate the less than thirty seconds of computer animation for the computer fight sequence against Superman in the movie. The background sound effects for the sequence were a different story; they were simply lifted from the 2600's *Pac-Man* game.

Coin followed the success of *Star Wars* with another great game as *Crystal Castles* is shown at the October AMOA show in New Orleans, and begins shipping in November. A fun, unique 3D world of game play starring a furry little hero named Bentley Bear, the game is designed by Franz Lanzinger. With some help from graphics artist Barbara Singh, 'Bentley' will go from looking less like a robot to more like a cute little bear with lots of charisma. Susan McBride, a talented graphics animator who will work on several other famous Atari coin-ops such as *Return of the Jedi*,

Gauntlet and some short work on the never-released *E.T.* coin-op game, will also create the animation of Bentley bear being attacked by the swarm of bees that appears several times during each level of the game. Barbara Singh and Dave Ralston did the other graphics designs in the game, and John Ray was assigned as the Team Leader. Scott Fuller was the Project Leader, and the hardware was designed by Sam Ly.

Crystal Castles, interestingly enough, was never supposed to be the children's story like game filled with bears, witches or castles when it was first created. It originally started as a 3D version of Asteroids that might have looked like something along the lines of the vector game *Red Baron*, where the player was supposed to fly over a 3D landscape of mountain ranges shooting at alien encampments while avoiding falling asteroids from the sky. It was also intended to be given a surefire name that probably would've tanked it right from the start: *TOPOROIDS*, an amalgamation of TOPO standing for topography of the landscape and ROIDS came from *Asteroids*. Franz Lanzinger hated the idea of the game right from the start, but liked the 3D aspect, so he began programming mazes. Instead of the planned mountainous terrain, castles started to appear instead, each with doorways and later with elevators. The game then saw the addition of gems (originally asteroid rocks) that the robot (now bear) had to retrieve while avoiding the swarm of constantly attacking killer bees.

Initially the castles and mazes attracted players in field tests, but then players stopped returning because the game seemed too hard. Franz's response was to tone down the bees, and then adding other creatures to the game. Franz's storyline is now built around the castles being guarded by Berthilda the Witch and her evil creatures. The changes make the game suddenly become more colorful, and cute, with an assortment of evil foes that were added right out of a storybook forest; evil trees, skeletons, and odd bug like creatures called Gem Eaters. A honey pot and the swarm of bees stay in the game, but are nowhere near as aggressive as in the original design since there's plenty of danger for Bentley to spread around now. During another round of play tests after the redesign, not only did players respond more favorably, but they kept coming back and word spread until the game began to build an ardent following of fans. With its unique game play, glowing red trak-ball, and custom cabinet look, *Crystal Castles* would become the end result equivalent of *Asteroids* meeting *Centipede*, creating a wide appeal for all who played it.

Some time later, Franz found out that a version of his game had been written for the 2600. Not only is he surprised, but when he sees the game and how much it differs from his arcade version, he's even rather annoyed. It had little to do with whether or not he would receive any royalties, as many who created games that originated out of coin-op had; it was that no one from Consumer had bothered to contact Franz to ask for his input on porting the game to the mighty little 2600. He felt that had he at least been made aware about the porting, maybe he could've offered some ideas and insight to make that version a little more playable and fun than the poorly received version that it was.

Also released in November 1983 is *Major Havoc,* whose development story is again an odyssey unto itself and marks the return of Owen Rubin to the arcades. In August, Owen had started work on a vector-based game he called *Tholian Web,* a game influenced by an old 1960s *Star Trek* episode of the same name where alien ships would build a web around an enemy and capture them. Owen's game would start by having web spinners come out onto the screen which would first draw a web around the outsides of the playfield until the player was caught. The player was expected to shoot the spinners to stop them, loosing their life if they failed. The game wasn't working by itself and what Owen really wanted was a character in a game. So during some brainstorming sessions he thought about another game that itself would feature more games within it; a space level, a maze level and so forth.

Tholian wound up being put aside, and Owen instead worked on pictures of his character named REX, who would eventually become Major Rex Havoc and then just *Major Havoc*. The storyline of *Major Havoc* that Owen creates centers around a great space hero and a group of scientists who clone him, using him to create a great clone army so he can attack and destroy the space stations of the Vaxxian empire. Lyle Rains drew out the vector graphics of the *Major Havoc* character for Owen's game, and a patent was actually filed for the animation method for the character but was never pursued.

The game wound up having many different names during development, such as *Tholian Web,* then *Alpha-1* and then *The Adventures of Rex Havoc*. Owen programmed the game based around his character running around four mazes he'd already designed; there wasn't enough time or space to do more mazes, so he added fireballs, tea pot robots, suddenly appearing walls and transporters to add more variety. Owen also added a lot of fun, subtle aspects into the game for the observant gamer to find. For instance, if the player stops moving *Major Havoc* for several seconds, the figure on the screen will cross its arms and tap its toe as if waiting impatiently for the player to continue the game. This is in fact a representation of Owen himself, as he would often stand near the artists (Lyle Rains), arms folded and his foot tapping the floor. Additionally, when the character falls, it gets up and shakes its head and gets its composure back in a humorous way. If the character is too close to an edge, it will do a sort of tightrope walking balancing act. Owen and Lyle had a great deal of fun adding in the comic relief animations to the game play, which resulted in the main character having... character.

Owen also wanted scrolling credits for the entire team in the game, and management said 'no.' So while everyone was at the AMOA in October, Owen had written the whole back story behind *Major Havoc* and the Vaxxian Empire in response, which displayed in the attract mode of the game. His managers didn't want people to stand in front of a game reading an attract mode screen; they wanted people to put in a quarter and play a game. So Owen was told to rewrite the story and keep it short this time. In truth, the storyline and many of the game elements were influenced by the world around Owen. The Vaxxian Empire is in fact a play on the DEC VAX minicomputers made by Digital Equipment Corporation that Atari's programmers used to assemble code for their games. He was also a big *Battlestar Galactica* fan, and accordingly the enemy fighters in the space wave look like the Cylon ships, while *Major Havoc's* 'Catastrofighter' ship looks like a viper fighter ship.

As the game play progressed, Mark Cerney was looking for some work and joined the project. Mark would be responsible for the surreal flying fish space wave, and he also designed the last four mazes (Author's note: these are known as being insanely difficult!) In the early game design, the fourth space wave actually had a *Star Castle* type of wave, however the wave would last about three and a half minutes. Judged being just too long, it was replaced with a wave featuring ships and your ship's shield pieces dropping off.

Upping the 'game within a game' concept to more of an infinity mirror, as a player stars each wave, by pressing the fire button they can play a round of *Breakout* on the right side of the tactical display. By completing the round, they are able to win an extra life for use in the main part of the game. What was Breakout doing smack in the middle of this futuristic space platform game? Owen's answer is simple: because he could. *Breakout* was added because the alloted ROM space for *Major Havoc* still had some programming space left. With just 89 bytes left, Owen suggested that he could add *Breakout* into that space. His manager said "No way!" and Owen responded in kind with "You wanna bet?" taking up the challenge and adding it. This mini-game is also where a player can secretly enter codes to warp to jump to higher levels. (*Author's note:* The warp codes are: Red-23, Yellow-46, Green-824 (which is Mark Cerny's Birthday), and Aqua-315 (which is Owen Rubin's Birthday)).

The game play only requires the player to move the ship or the character from left to right. In the maze levels, the character has to drop down through openings in the maze and then using the jump button, the character can jump back up and out of the maze. This allowed for a totally new controller design to be made, a roller control device. Think of a trackball controller that can only move from left to right and back, so not only does *Major Havoc* introduce a whole new world of game play in a color vector game, it also introduces a whole new controller design as well. During the field testing, the game was called Alpha-1 and by the time it made its debut its final name is *The Adventures of Major Havoc*.

Major Havoc would have the honor of being playtested by a celebrity before its release when Steven Spielberg was visiting Atari and Owen offered to let him try the game out. Spielberg blasted through all four levels on his first attempt, causing Owen to become a bit depressed seeing how easy his game was bested by someone who'd never seen it before. Spielberg really liked the game though! Owen's only regret on *Major Havoc* is that he felt it would be have been more widely accepted if the game had been done as a color raster game instead of a color vector game. Distributors by 1983 had really had it with vector games due to the enormous problems with their special displays. Other recently released vector games such as *Star Wars*, were accepted because... well it was *Star Wars*. However there was some reluctance from distributors on carrying an unknown vector game like *Major Havoc*.

After Owen had left Atari, he heard there was a legal issue that arose over *Major Havoc* stemming from several messages Owen had inserted into the game code during development and never removed. One such message was "Keep playing, the home world is near," which was left over from an earlier game design idea that eventually the player would reach a home world. What had Owen originally envisioned for the 'home world' was that it would be the planet of Vax, where the factories were that the robots would be assembled. Having trap floors, it was also to have an invincible robot called Maximilian based on the robot from the Disney movie *The Black Hole*, that would roam the maze on the home world.

A game player saw the message appear and took it to mean that the game had an ending. The story has it that he spent thousands of dollars playing *Major*

Havoc trying to reach the non-existent home world. Apparently irate that he could never reach this home world, he would send a picture of a screen shot of level 56 to Atari's legal department, threatening to sue Atari for the thousands he had invested in playing the game trying to reach a 'home world' ending that didn't exist. That high a level meant the last four waves of the game were being played over and over, getting harder and harder. Dan Van Elderen contacted Owen and explained the situation, asking him what should Atari's legal department tell this guy threatening to sue. Owen suggested to Dan: "Tell him he forgot to make a left turn." Needless to say, that was not what Atari would tell the game player, settling with him for cash and giving him his own *Major Havoc* arcade machine.

Time for the El Paso, Texas plant unfortunately ran out... at least the time that had left it untouched and pristine. Just as James was coming in at the beginning of September, the plans Manny had come up with to try and move Atari's recovery along during August were announced. Publicly Bruce Entin, VP of Press Releations, announced that Atari would be retooling the El Paso plant from manufacturing video games and home computers to repairng the same. The move would result in a laying off 380 of its 650 employees effective September 15th, but the fact was it wasn't the full story. El Paso wasn't being turned in a service center, instead it was having money pumped in to it to make it more automated. Maybe the subterfuge was because in a time of major losses, when most people are tightening their belts, Atari was moving forward with modernizing the plant. Manufacturing game cartridges had been a large part of the El Paso plant, but the new retooling left no room for them in this time of overstock and the movement of such operations to Asia. El Paso's automation was for the manufacturing of hardware - consoles and computers.

The resulting clearance of truckloads of faulty and unused stock starting on September 22nd resulted in anything but positive press for the company though, as it seemed Atari just couldn't catch a break from the media. Under cover of the night, several semi-trailers convoyed out of the plant to drive about an hour and a half south west. They were bound for a city dump in Alamogordo, New Mexico, chosen because New Mexico has a state law forbidding scavenging of landfills. The landfill is run by Browning Ferris Industries, who contracts with the city and is making $300-$500 a truckload from Atari, all to cover their dumped contents with garbage and dirt and then steamroll them.

As Sunday came around, Atari had already dumped eight truckloads when promising BFI only three a week, and still more were on the way. But that wasn't the worst of it; the public had found out. First it was the locals, who when word got out that Atari was dumping lots of cartridges, consoles and computers in their backyard, started sneaking in to the dump to pilfer what they could. Like a law was going to keep them away from free games. The hardware may have been crushed beyond use, but many of the games were still salvagable. It was when those games started showing up around town, titles like *E.T., Pac-Man, Ms. Pac-Man, and Raiders of the Lost Ark,* that the local media picked up on the story. Kids running around boasting of their free games and enterprising youths looking to sell them to video game stores are what tipped them off, and the Sunday the 25th article in the *Alamogordo Daily News* entitled "Dump here utilized" only garnered the operation more attention.

Atari had brought in a security guard, Capt. Javier Barrera, to watch over the site to stop the pilfering, but it did little stop the prying eyes of the media, and by Monday the national press was all over the story. This innocent dumping, a miniscule amount when compared to the entire size of Atari's actual overstock across the country, was done as an afterthought. However, thanks to article titles like UPI's "City dump gobbles Pacman," the dumping was fast becoming a symbol of the industry's problems. Bruce Enten only made matters worse, claiming it was all inoperable scrap and that Atari had different procedures for disposal. "For instance, if the grocery has bad vegetables on a Sunday you might see cartons of the stuff out back. We've got to dispose of the stuff," he told Marian E. McQuiddy of the Alamogordo Daily News. Except you don't pour concrete over bad groceries or unusable scrap, and that's exactly what Atari did on September 29th, which only further fueled the interest over the dumping. Around 14 truckloads had been dumped before the PR nightmare was over. Not even a month on the job, James Morgan was in for a tough road ahead to try and get Atari's reputation back.

(*Author's note:* Yes, this is the very happening that gave rise to the myth of the supposed dumping of almost 3.5 million *E.T.* cartridges in the Alamogordo dump. We hope this cleared all that up for everyone. Most of the overstock of game cartridges languishing in warehouses around the U.S., comprised of a wide breadth of Atari's home titles, were indeed disposed of - that's where myth meets reality. But this occured in a dump in Sunnyvale. And no, we're not telling where - we made a promise and the last thing local businesses now there need is an onslaught of fans looking to dig things up!)

While Owen was working on the *Major Havoc* storyline during the October 1983 AMOA show, Atari planned to publicly demonstrate its first laserdisc arcade game based on the Clint Eastwood movie *Firefox,* which had been released in June of last year. A special sit-down cockpit version of the game with a fighter seat fitted into it was shipped down to the AMOA show in New Orleans. After being set up for testing, the engineers discovered it wasn't working! To make matters worse, Clint Eastwood was scheduled to stand with the game during the show.

Owen Rubin was one of about only three people to skip the show and stay behind at Atari, so he was lucky enough to get the frantic phone call asking him if he can start up the development system to see why *Firefox* is not booting. Running up to the lab, he starts up the *Firefox* development system, but he couldn't get it to boot either. They frantically ask if Owen can debug the code and find out what's wrong. The Firefox project was developed by Roy Machamer's research department, and not only would it be Atari's first laserdisc game, but it was also the research department's first project. Mike Hally was Project Leader on the game; Greg Rivera and Norm Avellar were the programmers, only they're not there - just Owen is. Digging in and examining the unfamiliar code trying to find out why the game isn't working down in New Orleans, he finally finds a few errors in the code. After coming up with fixes, he finally gets the game code to boot on the development system. It turned out that the culprit had been some last minute changes that were made to the code, and due to the rush to get the game out for the AMOA show, the code wasn't fully tested. So Owen calls back and reaches the Atari engineers at the AMOA, telling them that he's got the game booting on the development system.

They tell Owen to get a set of ROM's burned and put them onto a spare board set in the lab, but Owen's big concern is - he can't FedEx the board set down to the show; it just won't make it to the show in time. So how can he get it out to the show? Someone from Atari (Owen believes it may have been Al Alcorn) called Nolan Bushnell, whose private jet was at the San Jose Airport. Nolan had planned to go out to AMOA on the second day, conveniently allowing Owen to catch a ride on Nolan's jet down to the show. By the time they arrive, he's exhausted from just having worked 28 hours straight, so Owen hands the board set off and it's rushed to the AMOA show. Unfortunately, despite all of Owen's efforts, as well as the onsite efforts of Minh Nguyen and Dave Wiebenson (the two technicians assigned to the project), Don Osborne has to announce at the AMOA show that the *Firefox* game is not working and will not be demonstrated. Well, at least it was a pretty cabinet to stare at, even if no one could play the game. While the game worked on the development system, it simply wasn't working properly on the board sets at the show. By December, the three board stack of hardware and the game code have been fully debugged by Jed Margolin, and in January of 1984, *Firefox* is shipped to distributors. A fun game, unfortunately it would become part of the short wave of laserdisc based arcade games, notorious with operators for their poor upkeep due to the laserdisc machines breaking down so often.

Not too long after the whole *Firefox* debacle, Atari lost one of its own in a tragic event when the beloved Don Osborne suffered a severe heart attack and passed away. Don was truly one of the most well liked and respected members of the Atari family, and losing him left a noticeable void in the company and in the lives of so many who were lucky enough to call him 'friend.' As a lasting tribute, a dedication screen with Don's name appears in *Firefox* game.

In December 1983, upgrade kits were made available to turn rival Williams' *Robotron:2084, Defender, Stargate,* and *Joust* cabinets into a new Atari game called *Cloak & Dagger.* John Ray was the team leader on the game project, which was programmed by Rusty Dawe. *Cloak & Dagger* was originally called *Agent X* and was designed to plug directly into the existing power supply in these games, reusing the Williams sound board (without the CPU and ROM) for audio amplification. For anyone who's ever played the game, if the game play of *Cloak & Dagger* looks somewhat familiar, that is because it uses two joystick controllers. One is for controlling the movement of 'Agent X' on the screen and the other joystick is to control the direction of firing at the enemy robots in the game. It was Rusty Dawe's own salute to *Robotron.*

Atari's *Agent X* development and the fact that Universal Studios was filming a movie called *Cloak and Dagger* couldn't have been timed any better. Universal approached Atari looking to see if they could develop a video game based on 'spies' and fortunately, Atari already had the coin-op game *Agent X* well along in its development. Atari sent Universal an *Agent X* arcade, one of twenty five prototypes that had been built for field tests. Rusty Dawe then went down to Universal and worked closely with the editor of the movie. During the movie, a character named Morris, who owns a video game store, is trying to crack the code in a video game to unlock the secret stealth plane plans by reaching the score of 1329542. The game play on the screen is from the real *Agent X* game (by now renamed *Cloak & Dagger* for the film) and after the score is displayed, 'Hollywood Movie Magic' takes over, showing graphics and animation that the coin-op (and certainly not the Atari 5200 game console shown in the scene) were in no way capable of producing. To make the filming of a game play sequence in the movie go more smoothly, Rusty actually played the game that's displayed during the entire scene.

The whole concept of *Cloak & Dagger* as a game, and especially as a movie, was very appealing at the time of its release in the summer of 1984. The United States and the communist regime of the Soviet Empire were, in real time, locked in a global conflict of good versus evil. The fate of the entire free world rested on the United States winning the Cold War. During the decades of tension between the two Super Powers, both sides would go to extraordinary lengths to learn the secrets of each other's tactics, defenses, technologies and weapon systems. For decades, the U.S. and the Soviet Union would employ thousands of covert agents and spies to infiltrate each other's countries and play a game of spy craft to gain access to sensitive data on missile systems, nuclear arsenals, troop deployments and fighter technologies.

With art imitating life, in the movie, enemy agents attempt to steal plans to the United States most advanced stealth planes at the time; the SR-71 Blackbird. The plans are cleverly embedded into an Atari 5200 video game cartridge that becomes one of the focal points of the movie. The movie itself is almost like a free publicity showcase for Atari. Besides the main character running around with an Atari 5200 game cartridge that says *Cloak & Dagger* on it, various scenes throughout the movie show the character playing Atari games. The store where the characters meet is also a veritable showcase of Atari games and products, many of which are for products that Atari had planned to release, and others, for games which are never released. (*Author's note*: all of this fueled a fire of speculation and rumors for years to come amongst game players and collectors looking for clues and traces to find these elusive treasures.)

Coin did end 1983 on a confusing note though. For two years, the Glaziers, Architectural, Metal and Glass workers local 1671 had been trying unionize the Coin workers in Milpitas. On December 1st though, the National Labor Relations Board receives a slap in the face from Atari's Milpitas workers after a vote on whether or not to unionize is held. 143 employees rejected and only 29 favored union representation. A strange decision, considering the massive layoffs in Consumer manufacturing going on at the time, however outside of the Atari Coin-op building, employees wearing anti-union t-shirts and buttons cheered the decision. "The employees have spoken and… given a message to all unions as loud as it is clear: we don't need a union at Atari," said Bruce Entin. Would the decision come back to haunt them?

Review In Images

The Atari 3200, codenamed Sylvia. *Opposite Page*: The Super TIA chip layout.

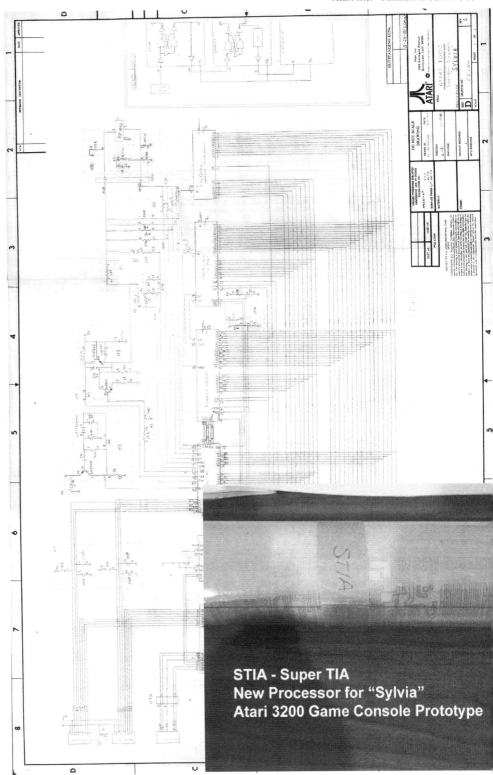

STIA - Super TIA
New Processor for "Sylvia"
Atari 3200 Game Console Prototype

This page and next: Concept sketches for PAM.

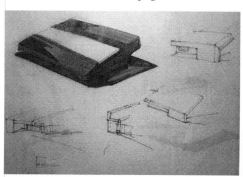

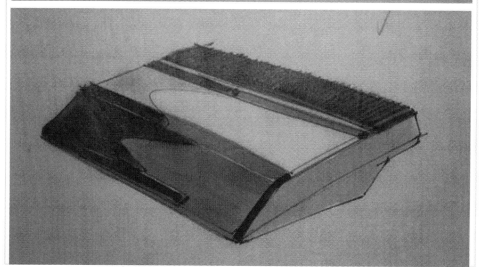

ATARI®
INTRODUCES
A *NEW* GAME!

This *new* ATARI® game is the future for home video games. It gives you a leading edge product to build sales excitement, with features like:

☐ Realistic game play, to challenge your mind as well as your reflexes.

☐ Life-like sound effects, and graphics in vivid colors.

☐ Super Controllers that combine Joystick, Paddle and Keyboard capabilities, to put *all* the action at your fingertips.

☐ A pause feature on the controllers that lets you interrupt game play whenever you want.

☐ A deluxe switchbox (combining two cords in one), plus built-in cord and controller areas, for a sleek and attractive appearance.

☐ Game Program™ cartridges that open up new worlds of game play and graphics.

THE *NEW GAME* WILL BE MATCHED WITH *NEW* GAME PROGRAM CARTRIDGES.

A new generation of Game Program cartridges that make full use of the powers of this new system will be introduced in 1982.

There will be updated versions of some proven winners:

☐ SUPER BREAKOUT™
☐ SPACE INVADERS¹
☐ MISSILE COMMAND™
☐ ASTEROIDS™

And a series of sports games, including:

☐ BASEBALL
☐ FOOTBALL
☐ SOCCER
☐ SKIING

Along with some intriguing combat games, like:

☐ STAR RAIDERS™

Of course, we'll include arcade favorites, starting with:

☐ PAC-MAN²
☐ GALAXIANS¹

And that's just the beginning!

1 Trademark of Taito America Corporation
2 Licensed by Namco-America Inc
©1982 ATARI Inc.   Printed in USA

PAM was temporarily renamed System X several months before its official introduction as the 5200.

Product Release

ATARI
A Warner Communications Company

Atari Incorporated 1265 Borregas Avenue PO Box 427 Sunnyvale California 94086

Contact: Ginny Juhnke
         (408) 745-2883

         Jeff Hoff
         (408) 745-4436

         Karen Esler
         (408) 745-2129

June 6, 1982

   Welcome to the new age of inter-active video entertainment. Atari, Inc.,
the leading designer and manufacturer of video games -- the company, in fact,
that started it all -- is pleased to announce the new generation of Atari
home video computer games: the ATARI 5200^{TM} Home Entertainment System.

   The ATARI 5200 is the state of the art by which all other game systems must
be measured. Detailed graphics painted in spectacular colors are combined with
dramatic sounds of incredible realism to provide the most sophisticated and
challenging games ever produced for home play.

   The ATARI 5200 has far more power and memory potential than the ATARI
Video Computer System^{TM} (VCS^{TM}). This new power gives the games an audio and
visual quality comparable to arcade video games. Yet the ATARI 5200's
suggested retail price is $299.95.

   The new 5200 is not a replacement of the ever-popular Video Computer System.
It is a new generation of video games. "We have created two home game systems
in the same spirit in which an automobile manufacturer builds different models
to suit different tastes," explains Michael Moone, president of Atari's Consumer
Electronics Division.

   "The ATARI 5200 was created for those players who demand state-of-the-art
video game technology," Moone continues. "We will continue to support the VCS

---more---

Top: The 5200 on display at Toys "R" Us. *Bottom:* Steven Spielberg being shown the 5200 by Ray Kassar and company,

5200 TRAK BALL CONTROLLER CX53

SUGGESTED RETAIL PRICE: $64.95
FEATURES:
• Precise 360° control
• Includes left- and right-handed keypads and fire button controls
• Delivers arcade-action at home
ADVERTISING: TV (included in the 5200 campaign) Game Enthusiast Magazines Full co-op support

VCS CARTRIDGE ADAPTOR CX55

SUGGESTED RETAIL PRICE: $74.95
FEATURES: Five year peripheral device expanded sales for you.
• Makes the 5200 game compatible with all 2600 software and controllers
• Easy to use (1) snaps into the 5200 cartridge slot
• 2600 value—customers can play all ATARI cartridges on one system!
• Ideal for customers who have traded up from the 2600 system
ADVERTISING: TV (included in the 5200 campaign) Direct mail (to 5200 owners) Full co-op support

5200 SUPERSYSTEM
CX5200

SUGGESTED RETAIL PRICE: $199.00

TARGET MARKET:
• Older teens and families
• Arcade players

FEATURES:
• Extraordinary arcade graphics
• All-in-one controllers (with precision joystick, keypad, and pause, start and reset buttons)
• Optional accessory allows use of 2600 cartridges
• Advanced line of software - includes many arcade hits
• Free PAC-MAN* cartridge with purchase

PROMOTIONS:
• $30.00 rebate

MERCHANDISING:
• 5200 Counter Demonstrator (Display holds 5200 system, controllers and 13" TV)
• 5200 Floor Demonstrator (Built-in TV monitor and rolling drum with software descriptions)

ADVERTISING:
• Television
• Game enthusiast Magazines

A promotional catalog introducing the 5200 for 1982.

ATARI IN
THE 5200 SU

No one knows better than Atari what arcade players want. And that's just what we've given them: The new Atari 5200 SuperSystem.

Everything Atari has learned since we invented video arcade games has gone into the 5200 SuperSystem. Arcade graphics, arcade action, arcade sound. All so real, it's unreal.

The 5200 has its own special arcade-quality cartridges. Like Centipede,™ PAC-MAN,® and Galaxian.® Plus the most lifelike sports games anywhere.

Its controller is the most advanced in the world. With an incredibly precise 360° analog joystick. A

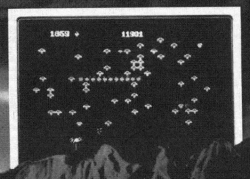

TRODUCES PERSYSTEM.

12-digit keypad. Plus start, reset, and fire, all in your hand. Even a pause button for stopping the action without ending the game.

And that's just the beginning. Defender,[3] Dig Dug,[4] Vanguard,[5] and other arcade hits, are coming in 1983. Along with an optional TRAK-BALL™ controller. And an adapter that accepts all the ATARI 2600™ cartridges.

The ATARI 5200 SuperSystem.

No other home system looks like it, feels like it, or plays like it. Because nobody beats Atari at its own game. Except Atari.

ATARI
A Warner Communications Company

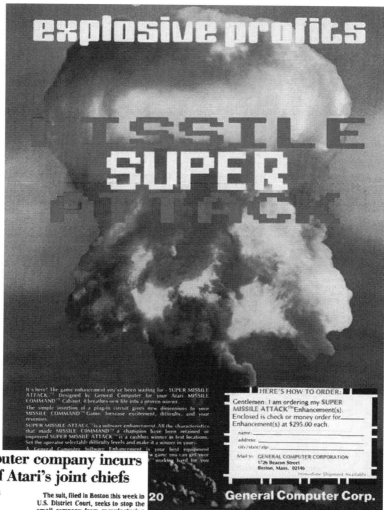

explosive profits

MISSILE SUPER ATTACK

It's here! The game enhancement you've been waiting for - SUPER MISSILE ATTACK.™ Designed by General Computer for your Atari MISSILE COMMAND™ Cabinet, it breathes new life into a proven winner.

The simple insertion of a plug-in circuit gives new dimensions to your MISSILE COMMAND™ Game. Increase excitement, difficulty, and your revenues.

SUPER MISSILE ATTACK™ is a software enhancement. All the characteristics that made MISSILE COMMAND™ a champion have been retained or improved. SUPER MISSILE ATTACK™ is a cashbox winner at test locations. Set the operator selectable difficulty levels and make it a winner in yours.

A General Computer Software Enhancement is your best equipment investment. Simply plug it in and turn a game you can get your working hard for you.

HERE'S HOW TO ORDER:

Gentlemen: I am ordering my SUPER MISSILE ATTACK™ Enhancement(s). Enclosed is check or money order for_____ Enhancement(s) at $295.00 each.

name: _____
address: _____
city/state/zip: _____

Mail to: GENERAL COMPUTER CORPORATION
1726 Beacon Street
Boston, Mass. 02146

Immediate Shipment Available

General Computer Corp.

Small computer company incurs the wrath of Atari's joint chiefs

By RONALD ROSENBERG
Boston Globe

WAYLAND, Mass. — When Atari's coin-operated video game Missile Command gets dull, arcade operators can breathe new life into it just by sliding in a printed circuit board.

Instead of scrapping the game and buying a different machine, which costs $2,500, General Computer Corp. of Wayland will retrofit it for $295 with a board that contains the software for a new game that provides more play objects and a greater degree of difficulty to challenge customers anew.

But, inexpensively tweaking Missile Command (there are more than 10,000 already installed) for greater play value does not sit well with the joint chiefs at Atari, a wholly owned subsidiary of Warner Communications Corp.

So they have fired off a $10 million lawsuit against Kevin Curran and Douglas Macrae, who last month founded General Computer, claiming they have violated Atari's copyrights and trademarks.

The suit, filed in Boston this week in U.S. District Court, seeks to stop the small company from manufacturing and selling the single board. The Sunnyvale, Mass., game firm also wants $5 million each in punitive damages from Macrae and Curran along with all profits from the add-in board.

"They (the General Computer game enhancements) appear to our customers and to the public as Atari products, creating confusion and siphoning off legitimate returns from our investment in research and development," said Frank A. Ballouz, Atari's vice-president of marketing for the coin-operated video-game division in a prepared statement.

Curran claims the enhancement, the company's first product, has been originally engineered. It went on sale in early June.

"We have tried to avoid all legal difficulties," he said. "We have not copied or infringed on their software and we will respond to their suit."

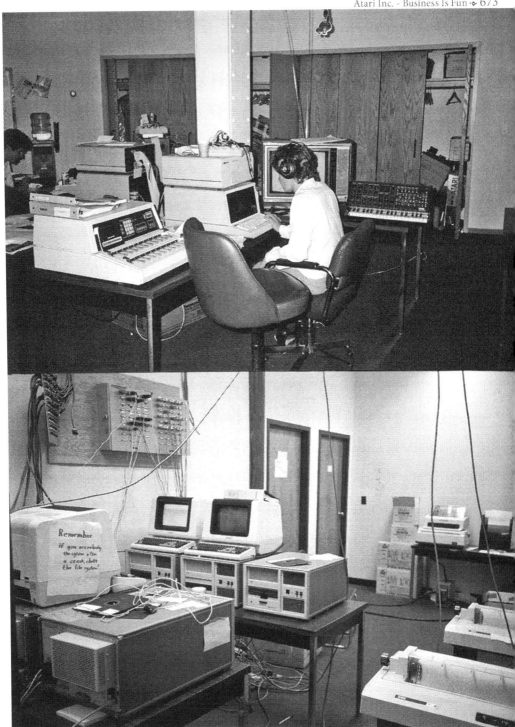

GCC's GenRad development system used to develop arcade games.

Top: Some of the arcade games GCC developed. *Bottom*: GCC's 'research lab' for home conversions. Most of the home games they coded were created solely by extensively playing the originals

Programming and testing more arcade games. On the bottom is one called *Nigh-mare*, which was never released.

CONFIDENTIAL

SPRING

Prepared by

Kevin G. Curran
Steve Golson
Scott Griffith
Art Ng
Chris Rode
Tom Westberg

January 12, 1983

This and the next two pages: Part of GCC's specs for the Spring game console.

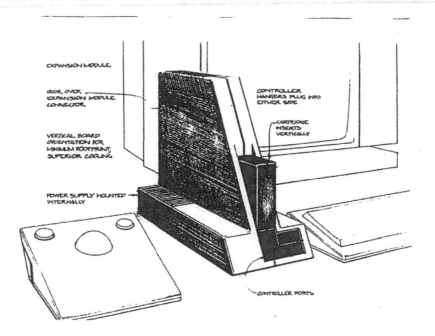

EXPANSION MODULE

DOOR OVER
EXPANSION MODULE
CONNECTOR

VERTICAL BOARD
ORIENTATION FOR
MINIMUM FOOTPRINT,
SUPERIOR COOLING

POWER SUPPLY MOUNTED
INTERNALLY

CONTROLLER
HANGERS PLUG INTO
EITHER SIDE

CARTRIDGE
INSERTS
VERTICALLY

CONTROLLER PORTS

ILLUSTRATION   1

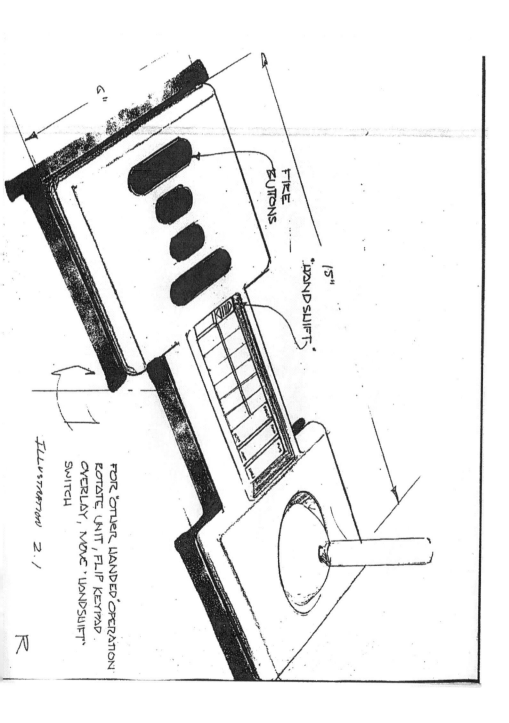

FIRE BUTTONS

6"

15"

HANDSHIFT

FOR 'OTHER' HANDED OPERATION
ROTATE UNIT, FLIP KEYPAD
OVERLAY, MOVE 'HANDSHIFT'
SWITCH

ILLUSTRATION 2.1

RICH,

------> NEEDED THIS A.M.

PLEASE CREATE AN OUTLINE FOR ME, COMPARING THE FEATURES OF THE
NINTENDO UNIT, THE COLECOVISION, THE 2600, THE 5200, THE
INTELLIVISION, THE VIC20, AND THE TI99/4. PLEASE LEAVE COLUMNS
FOR THE TIA-MARIA, THE TIA SQUARED, AND THE TIA-GTIA SYSTEMS.

PLEASE DO WHAT YOU CAN, RICH. I NEED TO TAKE IT WITH ME THIS
WEEKEND TO CHICAGO. ADD, CHANGE, DELETE, REORGANIZE, ETC. THE
ABOVE AS YOU SEE FIT. PLEASE DO THIS TABLE ON THE 11/23 SO THAT
I CAN MAKE MY ADDITIONS QUICKLY USING FASTEXT. LET ME KNOW WHICH
DIRECTORY IT IS IN SO THAT I CAN MOVE IT TO MY ACCOUNT SPACE.

THANKS. I THINK THIS WILL HAVE A MAJOR IMPACT ON THE COMPANY'S
DECISION MAKING IN THE NEXT FEW WEEKS.

This page and the following pages: Internal emails discussing the pending negotiations with Nintendo, who had approached Atari wanting them to release its forthcoming Famicom game console world wide.

INTEROFFICE MEMO

TO: John De Santis   cc. Dave Stubben, Jeff Heimbuck,
                 and John Cavalier

FROM: Don Teiser

DATE: 6/14/83

SUBJECT: Nintendo

As we discussed with Dave Stubben yesterday, I am to remove myself from any further involvement with the Nintendo project..... and Dave has indicated that you are the one to take it over.

I have provided you with a copy of my file containing my previous memos on the subject (with corrections); the approach letter from Nintendo; all of the schematics and mechanical drawings of the Nintendo machine which we have received to date; and Ed Levy's mechanical drawings which attempt to fit the Nintendo machine into the 2100 plastic.

We spent the latter part of the afternoon yesterday discussing the history of this deal and what needs to be done next by both sides. Let me review those points here and expand upon them for your reference.

Mr. Henricks received a letter from Mr. Arakawa and Mr. Lincoln of Nintendo America on April 4, 1983. In that letter, Nintendo provided us with some preliminary specifications on their new home video game machine. A couple of days later they came to meet with Mr. Kassar to explore whether Atari had any interest in this product. In addition to Messers Arakawa, Lincoln, Henricks, and Kassar; Messers Groth, Malloy, Moone, Bruehl, Ruckert, and myself were invited to attend. Mr. Malloy and I framed some of the initial questions which needed to be answered about the capabilities of the machine; and Mr. Lincoln promised to get the answers to me within a few days. Those answers were sufficiently intriguing to Mr. Groth that Alan Henricks, Dave Remson, and I were asked to travel to Kyoto immediately to see their TTL emulator in action and get more details about the final product.

On the 11th of April, 1983, we met with Nintendo at their headquarters in Kyoto. By happenstance (fortunate or unfortunate), a large contingent of Atari executives were in the Far East for other reasons .... and they all decided to come to Kyoto to have a look, too. In attendance from Atari were Messers. Bruehl, Moone, Malloy, Lynch, Hennick, Mitoh, Henricks, Remson, and myself. Attending on Nintendo's behalf were Messers. Yamauchi (President), Takeda (Manager of R&D, Coin-Op), Arakawa (Pres. Nintendo America), Lincoln (internal attorney for Nintendo America), Uemura (Manager of R&D, Consumer Products), Todori (Export Manager), and two of their electrical engineers.

We were shown working (but not complete) versions of Donkey Kong Junior and Popeye running with only minor display glitches on their TTL emulator. A VHS video tape (without sound) of that demo is attached to this memo. Please keep in mind that the actual TV image is significantly better than could be captured on tape. In fact, there is a noticable difference when viewing the composite video output on a monitor as opposed to the RF output on a standard TV receiver.

At that time, Nintendo had only just received their 1st pass silicon (with some bugs) and were not able to show us a fully assembled and working prototype. My memo of 4/16/83 (with corrections) describes what we saw and were told in that meeting.

On 4/15/83, Messers Kassar, Groth, Moone, Bruehl, Paul, Henricks, Remson, and myself met in Mr. Groth's office to view the videotape and discuss what we had learned from the meeting on the 11th and what we knew to-date on the MARIA chip being developed by General Computer. As both systems were seen as being in the same price range with graphics capabilities superior to the 2600 and comparable (and in some features, superior) to the 5200, it was felt that we needed to see what could be done with both machines for an intermediate priced game machine .... the 3600.

I was asked to become as completely informed about the MARIA chip as possible so that a reasoned choice could be made between the two machines. To that end, I have spoken with the folks at General Computer several times by telephone and have made two trips to their offices in Cambridge, Mass. It appears to be a superior machine, but the MARIA chip is not yet finished. First silicon is not expected until mid-July (if there are no further schedule delays). Also, since this chip is a VTI device there is some question as to the manufacturability/testability/cost of the chip. In other words, it will not be until mid-July (mid-August if the first silicon is faulty) that we will be able to make a fully informed choice between the Nintendo and the MARIA machines. Therefore, it was decided by Executive Management that in any negotiations with Nintendo we would need to string out the signing until at least mid-July.

We were committed to respond quickly to Nintendo, however, as to whether we were interested or not. So, Alan Henricks did contact Nintendo with the word that we were interesting in continuing the discussions; and the next negotiating meeting was arranged for May 17th in Kyoto. Skip Paul and Alan Henricks were to represent Atari. Two or three days before that meeting, Nintendo informed Mr. Henricks that they would be having their senior engineering managers present in the negotiations, and Nintendo requested my attendance as well.

That negotiating session began with a statement from Mr. Yamauchi as to the terms and conditions which he demanded, namely:

1. that Atari would purchase the assembled and tested main pc board for the FCS from Nintendo, for sale outside of Japan. Nintendo would sell the FCS on its own in Japan.

2. after some minimum purchase of assembled and tested pc boards, we would be able to buy the 2 custom chips from Nintendo without having to have Nintendo assemble them into the final unit.

3. that Nintendo would only disclose the electrical specs for the PPU and CPU, the circuit diagram of the FCS system, the test programs, and the "cassette" specs (meaning the ROM cartridge and cartridge edge connector specs).

4. that there would be no disclosure to Atari of the programming specs for the PPU and the CPU.

5. that Nintendo would program titles of our choice for the FCS system and would sell us the assembled and tested, unlabeled ROM carts at 1,500 Yen each FOB Japan for retail sale by Atari. The minimum quantity required by Nintendo per title would be 100,000 units and at that level there would be no fee for non-recurring engineering/programming expenses.

6. that Atari would hereby obtain a "right of 1st refusal" on future Nintendo coin-op titles for use worldwide (outside of Japan) only for the Nintendo FCS system .... again, by programming and manufacturing those carts themselves for sale to us.

7. that the cost of the assembled and tested main pc board would be higher than the 5,300 Yen quoted earlier to cover the cost of FCC compatibility. Also,that the resulting new pc board would not fit into the plastic being used by Nintendo for this unit in Japan.

By the time we finished the negotiations on that trip (5/17 - 5/20), the deal was changed to be as follows:

A. Nintendo would disclose all items called for in my memo of 5/13/83 (to Henricks and Paul) except for item 13., namely, the LSI tapes for chip fabrication. This disclosure would take place upon signing of the deal. All items which are originally in Japanese are to be furnished to us both in Japanese and in English.

B. Upon signing the deal, Nintendo would reassure Atari about the source of supply of the 2 custom chips.

C. Any increases in the cost of the main pc board due to FCC compliance will be a straight cost pass through (no additional profit to Nintendo).

D. Atari and Nintendo would work together to attempt to legal protect the CPU and PPU designs.

E. Nintendo would receive $5. Mil upon signing as an advance against future payments.

F. Atari would have to commit to a minimum purchase of 2 million hardware units (some mixture of assembled and tested pc boards and CPU/PPU chip sets) over the term of the contract.

G. The term of the contract would be 4 years with a 4 year option to renew.

H. Nintendo would receive an additional $3.5 Mil in a line of credit as an advance upon future payments upon delivery of the 1st production-ready prototype of the PAL West Germany version of the FCS (no later than 1/1/84). Similarly, an additional advance of $1.5 Mil for SECAM.

I. The 2 million unit commitment would be broken-up into 1 million NTSC, 700,000 PAL, and 300,000 SECAM. If Atari goes over in one catagory, it would directly reduce our requirement in any other catagory of our choice. As Skip Paul likes to put it, "cross-collateralization is the key!"

J. Nintendo would commit to produce 100,000 units of the assembled and tested pc board by August 31st if the new pc design (to include FCC and to fit whatever plastic we choose) can be completed by Nintendo and approved by Atari by July 20th. In essence, unlimited quanities (in excess of 1 million/month) thereafter .... upon 3 months notice from Atari.

K. Atari will have the right to program for this system with the full assistance of Nintendo.

L. Nintendo will, in the interests of expediency for this Christmas season, program 4 Atari titles of our choice. Source and object code which meets our satisfaction (with respect to basic design, tuning, and bug-free) to be delivered to us no later than Sept. 1, 1983. The fee would be $100,000./title or no non-recurring engineering fees would be charged as long as we buy a minimum of 100,000 carts.

M. Carts would cost us 1,500 Yen/cart if in plastic but unlabeled or 1,350 Yen if not in plastic (F.O.B. Japan). Rate of production would be max. 5,000 units/week/title

This page: Programming the 7800 version of *Centipede*.

Opposite: A mockup of the 7800 and planned keyboard, and the 1984 test marketed version of the console on the bottom.

Opposite:: A prototype of the keyboard.

Left and below: The unreleased 7800 adaptor for the 5200.

Far bottom: press photo of a family using the full 7800 setup including the light lab scientific module.

This page and next: Atari's booth at CES during the debut of the 7800, and a press kit photo. Inset: The test market version of the 7800 released during the Summer of '84.

James Morgan from Philip Morris, recruited by Steve Ross to replace Ray Kassar to try and turn around Atari.

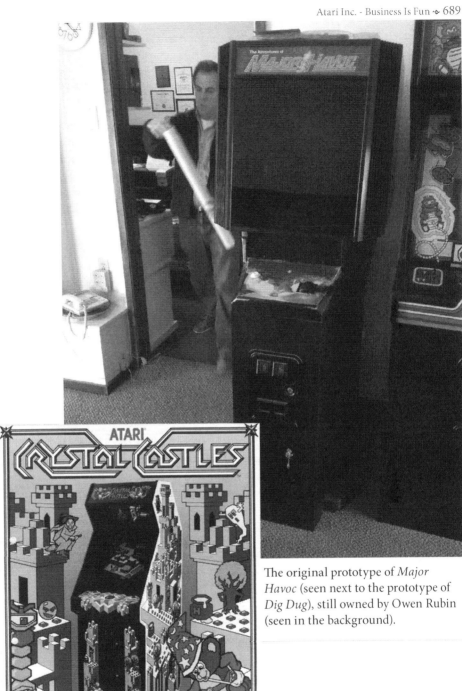

The original prototype of *Major Havoc* (seen next to the prototype of *Dig Dug*), still owned by Owen Rubin (seen in the background).

Workers at the El Paso, Texas assembly plant, which was primarily used for game cartridge manufacturing. It was switched over to become chiefly a hardware factory and automated, prompting a dumping of unusued stock in nearby Alamogordo, New Mexico.

Top: A concrete mixer leaving after pouring concrete on top of crushed games, consoles, and computers. *(Courtesy of the El Paso Times)*.

Right: A closeup of some of those crushed games and systems.

Years later, this event would lead to a myth that Atari had dumped 3.5 million *E.T.* cartridges there. A pop-culture fixture of 80s video games trivia and a symbol of the home video game market crash, unfortunately it's simply untrue.

Scenes from the Universal Pictures 1984 film, *Cloak & Dagger*. Although it was a remake of the 1949 film *The Widow*, the entire movie was really one giant commercial for Atari - years before Nintendo did the same thing with *The Wizard*.

Atari R&D:
Lots Of R, But Not Much D

What follows is an account of Atari's attempts across '82-'83 at following up their original

8-bit computers with a new generation. Fair warning again for the non-technical types, this

chapter goes out to all the computer geeks!

During the development of the replacement for the 2600, the home computer project would see not just two, but three design specifications called Colleen. And while the low cost computer was called Candy, there was also a third computer proposed. Called Elizabeth, it never progressed any farther than a concept description on paper... that is until another new computer is announced in December 1982. Also codenamed early on in 1981 as Elizabeth, with a product model designation Z800, it would then be renamed project Sweet-16.

Sweet-16's original product number was the Atari 1000 Home Computer, which eventually became the Atari 1200XL. "Roger Baderscher wanted a more modern update to the 800," recalls Mark Lutvak, project leader on the 1200 project. During the development of the peripherals for the new computer line, they were given designations to match the computer model number, just as the peripherals matched the Atari 400 and Atari 800 computers. Unfortunately, the peripheral designations were assigned while marketing was still referring to the product as the Atari 1000 computer, so all of the peripherals received product model designations such as 1010, 1020, 1025 and so forth instead of designations such as 1210, 1220 and 1225 to match the Atari 1200XL eventual product model number .

The Atari 800 computer had an expansion bay with slots for its operating system module and up to three memory modules, but due to fears of failing FCC compliance, Atari severely restricted the systems expansion and kept everything tightly wrapped behind an aluminum encasement. With the loosening of FCC restrictions and the redefining of FCC classes, Atari now had an opportunity to go back and revisit the Atari 800 design and to design a system much more expandable and capable. Larry Emmons of the Atari Grass Valley R&D office had already begun preliminary design work on a project called the Atari 800B Proposal but it never went any farther than a design sketch and some notes submitted down to Atari in Sunnyvale. Mike Albaugh, at one point, designed a new Operating System module with a Real-time clock and other features that would improve the Atari 800; however, new home computer marketing and management hired into the company from Control Data Corporation not only shot down the upgrade, but actually issued a stern warning to the home computer engineers on designing upgrades to the Atari 800 (essentially stating that anyone continuing to pursue such upgrades would be fired). At one point a cost reduction project for the Atari 800 is also initiated, with a design that would consolidate the main, CPU, operating system and memory boards together into one single board. Codenamed Colette, it would fit inside an existing Atari 800 case and use the existing Atari 800 power I/O board.

In New York, Steve Mayer's research lab had been working on project (LIZ-NY) to make a new cost reduced home computer system that would be also be able to play 2600 game code with some alterations. "The 1200 was mainly developed in NYC, but ideas from marketing came from Sunnyvale/San Jose," recalls Mark Lutvak. Atari NY and Sunnyvale begin to collaborate on taking this design idea and designing a new cost-reduced home computer system to replace the Atari 800. The project, now codenamed Z800, began moving forward when on August 25, 1981, the product specifications were defined. That was followed shortly after with the firmware specifications on October 7.

The initial case designs are drawn based on concept sketches created by Atari Industrial Designer Regan Cheng on November 2, 1981. Regan's new case would take Atari's computers out of the 1970s look and thrust them into the sleek high tech look characteristic of the 1980s. "Designs are based around venting, allowing air to flow out of the case to keep the electronics from overheating. I designed the styling of the vents and the concept sketches for the shape of what the computers could look like," recalls Regan. In New York, Steve Mayer's lab uses Henry Dryfuss Associates to create an industrial design look for the LIZ-NY and the early Elizabeth case designs. All brown on the top with long vent lines across the top of the units, Atari Sunnyvale's industrial designs are chosen instead, and work progresses by late 1981 to begin the mechanical designs of the new computer case. Hugh Lee would do much of the initial mechanical designs of the new computer, still codenamed Z800.

The Modem Inerface Module for the Z800 is being worked on in parallel startin on September 17. This simple little device would end up causing a major design change to Atari's new computer and will be the root cause for the upcoming woes that Atari's newest computer will also face. By February 10, 1982, the Z800 begins to change, as does the project name: it was now S-16 or Sweet-16. Game controller Ports 3 & 4 had been eliminated as has cartridge Port B. The operating system would now also have a NTSC/PAL video timing option to allow the system to easily work worldwide. Even though cost reduction is a goal, so is upgrading the ease of use of the computer to enhance the computer experience. A Help key for programmers to provide easily accessed help in their programs is defined, as well as 'function keys' F1 through F4. Also included is an onboard self test that runs each time it's powered up, but will not display on the user screen unless an issue is detected. The user can force the system into self test though, and display an options menu on the screen by pressing and holding the HELP button during power up of the computer. Mike Colburn programmed the self test routines. (Of interesting note: in the initial version of the self test, Mike hid his name in the test. By selecting to run all tests, during the keyboard self test, if you watch carefully, it cleverly spells out M-i-c-h-a-e-l-C-o-l-b-u-r-n on the keyboard keys) Changes to the Operating System are included as well; and it's already noted that software will only be "Atari Supported, in general be limited to software using published and supported entry points and database variables in the operating system." However it's also explained that Visicalc and Atari's own Bookkeeper product, as well as Atari Program Exchange (APX) cassettes with protections might be rendered incompatible with the new proposed Operating System, possibly cutting down on Atari's rapidly growing softare library. In another hardware change, no built-in speaker is to be included, as all key click audio and bells would be directed out through the audio lines and RF modulator to video or TV monitors.

The initial design of the A1200 or Sweet-16 project has two unique new features; one is the elimination of the proprietary 13-pin oversized SIO connector port, which will be replaced with two 15-pin standard DB-15 type connectors. These new port connectors provide all of the signals of the SIO ports from the Atari 400/800 systems, but also include new 'Peripheral Wake' lines. When the computer is turned on, so will be the new line of peripherals being designed for the computer. This way the peripherals would load their specialized drivers into the computer automatically and be ready to use. The second feature: a 50-pin high-speed system bus connector from the LIZ-NY design, placed on the back of the computer. It's intended to support future expansion via an expansion box that Dave Stubben is proposing to allow for even greater flexibility, however the connector never made it past February 10 in the designs.

Mike Klimowicz shipped the first sample 1200 to Electro-Service Corporation to perform RF emissions testing on January 6, 1982, and on March 22, 1982 he noted: "Changes Requested by Marketing. Engineering changes found to be needed during development." One of those changes is the elimination of the 'Peripheral Wake" so that the system does not require a delay in loading up device drivers from the enhanced I/O ports, which apparently Marketing found was ruining the startup experience. Accordingly, the operating system receives fixes to omit the system power-up delay, and the expansion bus portions of the operating system are cancelled all together. By March 26th the electrical designs of Elizabeth begin to be implemented and an 8th revision (Rev X8A) will be the last revision of the A1200 design to include the enhanced 15-pin ports and the 50-pin expansion bus. In July, revision X10A is released and now has one Atari 13-pin SIO port on it and the entire expansion bus removed from the design. Revision X10A would also be the last revision to say both Elizabeth and Sweet-16 on the system board, with Revision 11 becoming the revision to go in to production, so it no longer needed to bear the designation on the system board.

Meetings are held august 25th and 31st with the Sweet-16 team, now consisting of a large roster of engineers including Michel Howard, Bill Lapham, Chris Berg, John DeSantis, Fred Lawrence, Bob Honeycutt, Bill Lewis, Andy Prachick, Dave Sovey, and Paul Laughton. The discussion centers on the FCC submission of the A1200 and the single board 800 prototype called Colette, as well as the production timetable with product inventory expected to be ready by January 15, 1983.

Two systems are shipped by Mike Klimowicz to Charles Slease at Electro Service Corporation on August 26th for FCC Part 15, subpart J class B qualification testing. One system is the Revision X10A Atari 1200XL computer, the other is a cost reduced model 800 computer - that 800 being the Colette prototype design that seals the computer and eliminates all of the boards plugged into the main board. A 250 piece pilot run of the 1200XL's for Marketing's product engineer Harish Shah is also scheduled to be completed shortly, and a UK version of the project is also discussed.

While the overall project had been codenamed Sweet-16 for the 16k memory of what was going to be one of two product models, a 16k and a 64k version, the actual working designation of the product is called Sweet 64 since the final computer is to be shipped with 64k of memory. "Initially there was talk of using that version of the 1200 for the PBI prototype, but it was not done in that manner for production.

The marketing guys for the 1200 thought of it as a 'Toaster' product. The idea was to make it completely closed so consumers couldn't get themselves into trouble messing with it. The customer service burden involved in trying to deploy a consumer computer was enormous. The hardware and OS were really far too primitive to make such a machine useful. The later 14xx series was envisioned as a 'powerful' computer with built-in drives to address serious computer users such as business people. The 14xx computers were pretty good for 8-bit machines," recalls Earl Rice.

Marketing had also reviewed the new modem module being developed for the A1200 that past Spring, which would load not just its driver, but a new feature allowing it to actually load its own built-in software right into the computer. The modem's design was conceived from the earlier Atari 850 interface module that gave the Atari computers their 'eyes and ears' to the outside world of communications and printers. What's re-used specifically is the 850's ability to 'install' itself, that is to say it's like a 'Plug and Play' device - a feature that will become very popular in the decade to follow thanks to a then tiny little upstart company called... Microsoft. What this means for Atari is as planned, the modem can actually install its own device driver software onto an Atari home computer, allowing the computer to know just how it worked, how to use it and how programs can access it. Marketing feltt the design fit well in to their vision of a totally enclosed system, and sparked marketing's drive to do all future expansion directly through the lone SIO port of the computer. "The expansion connector and expansion box never made it into production, plus all of the layoffs," recalls Dave Stubben. The Modem Module specification calls for it to also have an onboard communications program, so not only would it load itself into the computer operating system, but it would also load up its own communication software too.

Atari receives its Class B certification for its 1200 computer, revision 10 By November 2, 1982, however Bill Lapham is informed bia an inter-office memo that the production version still needed to be tested and certified. Initially, the Atari 1200XL will be built domestically in Atari's Sunnyvale manufacturing plant with plans to move production to Atari's ATMC Taiwan Manufacturing plant. However the 1200XL, Atari's next generation computer and replacement for the Atari 800 computer will have a very short ride. Complaints come from across the board due to the Operating System incompatibility issues and the negative feedback from Atari user groups, press and publications on the system's lack of expansion (as well as its high cost). Released in early 1983, it will only remain in production until June of 1983. At the time of the cancelling, already in the works is its new sibling and the replacement for the Atari 400, the Atari 600XL - a 16K version of the 1200XL in a smaller case. Initial schematics and case design drawings had been completed around the time of the 1200XL's cancelling with plans to produce the new computer at the Atari WONG manufacturing plant in Hong Kong. Two other higher end systems were already in design as well (one is codenamed the A1201), along with a third: the direct replacement for the 1200XL

After the mishaps of 1982, Atari had a sobering wake-up call in the form of bad press, poor sales and bruised egos. No longer the darling of the industry, the cracks in this crystal castle had begun showing in a very public way. 1983 would have to be the year to change course and set about correcting many of its shortcomings across the board. Not that the 1200XL was a great start to 1983, but several projects commenced in both the Consumer Electronics and Home Computer groups that would hopefully put things back on track. Two new computer designs had been in the works since March 1983, which are smaller, more cost effective and have the expansion capabilities which were lacking in the 1200XL. Based on the original LIZ-NY design, they have an expansion bus edge connector allowing a future expansion box to plug into these new systems and expand their capabilities.

The first, the 600XL, has its formal product specifications released on May 20, 1983. Starting as LIZ-NY and then became known a Crazy 8, S-8 and SURELY (NY lab memos referred to it as Shirley), the 600XL (just as the other three systems) is specified to use a new custom IC chip called FREDDIE. However the FREDDIE chip was not scheduled to be ready in time for integration into the production versions of the 600XL and the replacement to the 1200XL, so its omitted from their schematics and designs. (*Author's note: The schematics also provide a 'Fact' versus 'Myth' situation – many a story will circulate over the years that the Atari 600XL was to originally have composite monitor output on it, but it will be removed to cut costs by Atari's new CEO James Morgan. This is in fact false; the original design of the 600XL specifications and its electrical layout from March 1983 forward never had a composite video-out circuit in the design.*)

The 600XL's case design wasn't the only case design completed that June, as the 1200XL's direct replacement is also revealed after its case completion: The Atari 800XL, a 64K system. The 1200XL had been assembled in Sunnyvale, CA. However by June, Atari's U.S. product manufacturing facilities had been shut down and all equipment dismantled and shipped to Atari's facility in Hong Kong (called Atari WONG) as all Domestic production of Atari's consumer and home computer products are moved to Taiwan and Hong Kong. The Atari Taiwan Manufacturing Company (ATMC) at that time was only geared for production of Atari's consumer consoles and accessories as well as cartridge games, while Atari's El Paso, Texas facility as well as Atari's Fajardo, Puerto Rico plants are geared for cartridge production. The Atari WONG plant had been gearing up for quite some time, based on a partnership between Atari and the WONG family. Rick Krieger, John Constantine, Paul Malloy and Brad Saville would see that WONG is brought up to speed to handle the manufacturing of Atari products. With all procedures in order, Atari's new home computers, the 600XL and 800XL, are slated to be manufactured initially at WONG's.

For the first four or so months of development, the two higher end computers did a dueling dance of product numbering until their respective June 6th and 7th formal specifications (Rev 1A) are released. The first went from A1201, 1200XLD, 1200XLT and the Atari 1250 Home Computer before settling on the 1450XL, and the latter went from A1201, the Atari 1200XLD and the Atari 1200XLT Home computer before settling on the 1400XL. The use of the same numbers caused great confusion from engineering management, and they had finally made HCD come up with their final model names. Though the formal specifications were first released in June, that doesn't mean that work on both of these computers hasn't already started; in fact, electrical designs of the systems had been in progress since March 18, 1983. Greg Roberts laid out the address allocation block diagram for the 1400XL and completes the final address allocations on June 30, 1983. On July 12, 1983, H.Y. Shih prepares a sample 1400XL for FCC approval, though he finds out the sample currently doesn't have an RF shield and has so far at Atari ATMC has only passed self-test, paddle tests and RAM tests. After notifying Bob Green, H.Y. requests further information and testing before shipping the FCC sample back to the U.S. for submission for official FCC testing. The 1400XL fails its FCC July 16th testing, and will then go back for X3A revisions, scheduled to be retested on September 23, 1983... or so everyone thought. Work also continued in parallel on the 1450XL, and the 1450XL will be nearly identical to the 1400XL board, except it will have an onboard power connector and a ribbon header connection for a disk drive controller board that is being worked on by another engineering team.

Going back to the 600XL and 800XL's – the UK/PAL versions of the 600XL and 800XL schematics are completed on June 29th and by August 23, 1983, the SECAM version of the 600XL schematic design (codenamed Pauline) is completed.

The first engineering sample of the 800XL is submitted to Tom Cokenias of Electro-Services on September 27, 1983, by William Lapham (with Dave Stubben's approval) for FCC compliance testing, and its specifications are for manufacture by Chase Electronics of Hong Kong, also known as Chelco.

Rumors soon begin to circulate throughout computer magazines and trade journals; word around the Valley is that Atari was working on of all things a computer that was {gasp} IBM PC Compatible. It turns out the rumors are in fact quite true. Ajay Chopra, a brilliant engineer in Atari's Advanced Engineering group was working initially on his own with the assistance of a young but very talented engineer named Jim Tittsler on the project. However they quickly realize this is going to be outside of the norm for Atari's engineering groups, and by the Summer of 1983, they began talks with Toshiba about a joint project to build not just a PC Compatible system, but a dual processor system that in one mode would run as an Atari 8bit XL computer and in another mode, would run as an IBM PC compatible (well – a semi-compatible). It would have both 6502 and 80816 CPU's on the motherboard and would also have all of the Atari custom IC chips, but the design would share memory, I/O and video.

The system is publicly called the Atari 1600XL (internally the project is codenamed "Shatki" and was also called the Atari 25601). By Fall, the project has progressed remarkably far in such a small amount of time: Jim has written a BIOS to allow the system to boot and access the PC side of the devices, a full system board is built by Toshiba as per Ajay's specifications and Tom Palecki from the Industrial Design group has just finished the case design and a mock-up is built. Now the interesting thing about the mock-up - it's not in plastic. Atari has spent entirely too much money and resources over the years on investing large amounts of development funds to projects that many times were canceled. So in a cost cutting move, new concept designs are built out of cardboard. That's right, cardboard and foam board - like a high school science fair presentation, but on a far more professional level. Though made out of cardboard and foam board, the model mock-up looks like the real deal and it is a gorgeous looking design! Though two designs are actually made when Tom is instructed to make one for the 1600XL (that will have a standard flat face design with disk drives), and a slanted front design for another project (which Tom believes was Sierra). He'll actually build two of the slanted designs; one is all white and another in XL brown and crème color styling. In both renderings, the cases are just the right look for such a bold, new product that will soon be going on the market.

The 1600XL means that Atari is about to get serious and play with the big boys in the IBM-PC compatible market... or so everything thought until James Morgan stepped through the doors of Atari on September 6th. After that, the Atari PC computer team would find themselves feeling rather 'Blue.'

||||||||||||||||||||||||||||||||||||||||||||||||||||||||||||||||||||||||||||||||||||||||||||||||||

June through July 1983, the advanced product group have several meetings attended by Dave Stubben, Don Teiser and Don Lang to discuss the meetings that Roy Snyder has had out in New York with a small company called Lecht Sciences. Lecht Sciences is headed headed by Charles Lecht, a well-known computer expert, lecturer, regular contributing editor to "Computerworld" magazine and the author of *The Waves of Change*... The meetings center around hiring Lecht to consult for Atari on designing and building a super user-friendly 'Apple Lisa-type machine.' Seeing him as sincere and highly intelligent, the group also finds the meetings with Lecht are very insightful. While there is a great deal of interest in things discussed, such as a foot-mouse and user interfaces, Atari is also faced with concerns over Lecht Sciences' small size and limited resources. Plus with Atari going through its own re-structuring, there's now limited allocations to Atari and non-Atari projects. Consequently, after a detailed report on staffing, tasks, scope and development, the project doesn't go any further.

In the same note, during that time an engineer named Rich Pasco came over from Xerox PARC to Atari's Home Computer Division (HCD). While working at Atari he noticed something missing which he had become quite used to over at Xerox: a "Mouse." Xerox, you see, was the developer of the first GUI (Graphics User Interface) and the Altos systems were among the first computers to utilize mice extensively. The Xerox Altos and Star 8010 utilizes desktop metaphors, point & click and all the other features we have come to know and use, and were well in use at Xerox for years now.

Wanting to work in a more familiar and friendly user interface environment on the Atari home computers, Rich Pasco went to Hawley Systems, a maker of computer mice. Purchasing a version of their mouse that would interface with the Atari 800 front controller ports, he then wrote a screen driver. Soon after, he was able to move his mouse pointer all over the screen to work in almost any programming language to do point and click functions. After working with the mouse and proving its effectiveness, Rich Pasco approached the marketing department with the mouse and his driver in hopes of persuading them to include a mouse with every Atari 800 sold (Rich's compact driver could've easily have been integrated into the Atari OS ROM board or loaded via disk or cassette). Marketing tried to work with the mouse, but it was like watching your grandparents or parents the first time they fumbled with one. Used to playing with joysticks, this strange foreign device was too difficult for them to understand or effectively use, so they wielded their now god like power and ignorance won over innovation; the mouse was rejected.

This wasn't an isolated incident, as many talented and ingenious Atari engineers such as Rich created internal devices or interfaced existing components to Atari systems and approached Marketing with these ideas. Each were rejected - a true shame in hindsight... but it has to be remembered that at companies such as Atari, they were venturing into unknown and uncharted territory in both design and marketing. Marketing felt each idea was a gamble and many times the luck of the dice rolled a craps.

Speaking of Xerox PARC, another more famous name comes over to join Atari during this time as well: Dr. Alan Kay, a founder of Xerox Parc and leader of one of the several groups that together developed modern workstations, the Small-talk object orientated langauge, the overlapping window interface, Desktop Publishing, the Ethernet, Laser printing, and network 'client-servers.' In 1983, a prototype of a local area network (LAN) system is developed in the Atari LA Lab for use with the Atari 800 computers. Called the 'ALAN-K,' only one installation of these is done outside of Atari - at a Club Med of all places! The name ALAN-K was a play on both the fact that it was A LAN and of course ALAN and K as in Alan Kay. The Club Med installation of the ALAN-K network is a really bold project, but one that would be sabotaged by a mix of salt water, humidity, obnoxious Club Med staff, an impossible time table and deadline for a dog and pony show press conference. The LAN would work for the Press conference, but a tired and highly irritated engineering team from Atari would head home to leave it in the hands of an uncaring resort staff. Done in within a short period of time, the LAN would never work again.

After it is publicly announced in July that Ray Kassar has resigned (even though internally Steven Ross has fired him), James J. Morgan is hired as Atari's new

Chairman and CEO. Steven Ross publicly states, "We were fortunate to find an executive of the most exceptional leadership skills and proven achievements in administration and marketing to succeed Mr. Kassar." Taking sabbatical for the Summer. James Morgan finally arrives on September 6th to begin work in his new position as Chairman and CEO. Looking to further cut costs, one of the first things announced after James takes over are plans on consolidating Atari's spread out buildings, and a press release is issued on September 7th; 'Steven J. Ross (Chairman of and CEO of Warner Communications) and James J. Morgan (Chairman and CEO of Atari) announce plans for the development of a major office and research complex on 65 acres.' Talk about a slap in the face to Ray Kassar! While his idea of a consolidated campus for Atari was shot down, the company fully embraced the idea 'after' Kassar's departure. The timing of this announcement was also impeccable, breaking this news the day AFTER Morgan started at the company. But unlike Kassar's plan (which would have cost $300 million), the expected cost for this newly announced complex would be approximately $60 million.

Futhermore, after reviewing the company structure and the dispersed buildings that make up the company, Morgan decides he needs to institute a plan to create a cohesive management structure. Having daily face-to-face meetings with all of the top managers in the company to review the state of products and projects, he also announces a thirty day halt to all projects while he reviews the current overall condition of the company and its products. This will wind up being one of Morgan's 'growing pain' mistakes as he settles into his position at Atari. Not the reviewing of projects, that was a given and needed to be done. But his thirty day review made very costly delays on products that were already a go for manufacturing. For example, this delays a decision that has to be made on production of the new Atari 600XL and 800XL computer models, which are expected to complete FCC testing this month and begin production. However, the production is currently slated to begin in the Atari WONG plant. The Chase Electronics Company plant is still getting set-up and simply isn't ready to take this on, and even if approved, it will still need at least 30 days from approval to be ready to begin production. The 'up' side of this is that using the Chase manufacturing plant will be more cost effective than manufacturing the units at the Atari WONG plant. James' immediate decision was NO decision on which plant would handle the manufacturing, since he refuses to make one until his own 30 day review of the situation is completed.

Atari has a lot of pokers in the fire at this point within its various R&D and project development groups, but James thinks there's just too many for Atari's current financial state and begins chopping projects after the 30 days are up. The casualties will be within the consumer electronics and home computer divisions, and amongst them are several ambitious projects and products:

- The Graduate Computer and its peripherals and software products

- The voice module for the Atari 2600 and 5200 systems

- The Atari 1400XL and Atari 1450XLD computers

- The joint project between Toshiba and Atari to develop the Atari 1600XL IBM compatible

- The Atari 1060 CP/M add-on module

- The Ataritel division

They're all cancelled because Morgan wants the company to be more singularly focused on using its resources and abilities to ensure that other existing products and projects are completed and shipped. Pure irony considering Morgan's 30-day delay to decide on which manufacturing plant would produce the Atari 600XL and 800XL computers - a decision that would greatly impact Atari's computer sales for the 1983 Christmas holiday season. When the decision is finally made to go with Atari WONG, it will actually cost more to produce the XL computers in this plant. The tradeoff is needed though - the days remaining to meet Christmas season shipments are rapidly disappearing, and moving to the CHELCO plant is not possible without losing the entire Christmas sales window.

Atari announces a price increase on both its 600XL and 800XL home computer systems on November 9. Both the 600XL and 800XL will see their prices raised by $40 each; also, the 2600 will increase in price by $5 dollars. The price increases will go into effect on January 1, 1984. To do some P.R. damage control over the sting of the increases and to also ease the manufacturing of its computers over to Chase Electronics (CHELCO), Atari also announces that its new XL home computer inventory is sold out and that Atari will not be accepting any additional orders on those products in 1983. Atari 'claims' that it is trying to elevate computer prices to undo the severe price gouging in the marketplace that had brought home computer prices down severely.

You see, just a month earlier in October, Texas Instruments announced that it would exit the home computer market and stop all production and sales of its

TI99/4A computer system after the company had lost nearly $223 million in 1983 alone. They were leaving as a direct result of Jack Tramiel and his company Commodore's agressive undercutting of prices. Jack's war had caused complete havoc in the personal computer industry, and it seemed as if the shakeup was finally coming towards end. As Everett Purdy, senior vice president of merchandising for computer retailer Service Merchandise at the time said back in the June 19 *New York Times*, stated: "I've been in retailing 30 years and I have never seen any category of goods get on a self-destruct pattern like this."

Commodore comes out the winner during this whole period; with reduced inventories of Atari computers on store shelves, the announcement of TI exiting the home computer market and with delays by Coleco on its home computer, Commodore has a wide berth of sales for 1983 with its Commodore 64, boosting its growing elevation for dominance in the home computer marketplace.

While the Home Computer Division is certainly not too pleased with Morgan's attention to it and the their results, the Consumer Electronics Division was receiving many visits from Morgan as well. "James Morgan used to come into the consumer programming building at 275 Gibraltar, he'd put one leg up on a chair and he'd take a drag from his cigarette and he'd strike this great pose and tell everyone that we were important assets and an important part of the company - he really supported us and gave us a good morale boost. I wish I could pose the way he did, we used to call him the Marlboro Man," recalls Steve Woita.

Another group not at all happy with one of the product cancellations is a group out on the East Coast running a tiny engineering firm called Peripheral Visions Incorporated (PVI). Their product was the by now-canceled Atari Graduate, also known as the Atari My First Computer. Back in late September of 1982, fresh from finishing the Commodore 64 computers, three former Commodore engineers began brainstorming a new idea to sell in large volume. Looking to Atari with its installed base of close to 12 million 2600 video game consoles, they decided to create a computer keyboard add-on for the console and Peripheral Visions Incorporated (PVI) was born. Finding that Atari has an office right on the East Coast in New York, they contact the NY/Atari Lab and present their project idea to them. Steve Mayer is intrigued by the idea of this product, so he discusses it with the Sunnyvale engineers who countered that such a product couldn't be done with the system's limited ability to display text. PVI wasn't going to back down, and took up the challenge to create a proof of concept.

Now mind you, Bob Russell, Bob Yannes and David A. Ziembicki had never programmed on the 2600 before, yet in two days they were able to create a text screen demo to show Atari. To make their presentation at Atari offices more mysterious, they placed their ROM chip into a large black box that they weighed down with a power supply and other items to make it seem like there was much more to their project than just some fancy programming. With ribbon cabling coming out of their mystery box soldered to a modified 2600 cartridge board, they plugged it into a 2600 and powered it up. The demo was convincing enough to the Sunnyvale boys that Atari decided to pursue the project. Designated the CX-3000, Marketing would outline the requirements for the device and PVI was on its way! Their design would turn into a remarkable little device that loads a looping program into the 128 byte memory of the 2600, simply turning the 2600 into the Graduates video support hardware. All the real magic takes place under the Graduate's hood.

The Graduate has 8K RAM with specifications to allow it to add another 24K through an external buss connector. While Atari called it The Graduate, PVI called their device the FRODOTYPE after the character Frodo from *The Lor of The Rings*. The schematics are done by November 23rd and the first prototypes that the PVI team would deliver are cast in resin for the shape of the keyboard case, having a membrane keyboard. Yes, PVI actually went to the same keyboard supplier that Atari used for Atari 400 keyboard. One noticeable difference was apparent on the prototype; a PVI logo was in place of the Atari "Fuji" logo on one of the keys. Regan Cheng would design Atari's production design case for The Graduate.

Things start to get out of control for the Graduate in a very short period of time though. Like everything else, Marketing decided to jump into the driver seat and began to demand features that simply push the limits of the product design. Their first requirement: the system needs to be able to talk to an external set of peripherals. Originally it was just supposed to be upgradeable with a plug-in memory module, but now Atari wanted a modem module, printer and a wafer tape drive. This was of course going to raise the cost of the product, and would require a lot more engineering time and a higher development cost. Then Atari came back and required that the system enhance the 2600's graphics. Internally, Atari's engineers had been working on a graphics upgrade design for the 2600 called 'BUBBLES,' and now they want PVI to incorporate it into their keyboard add-on. Keep in mind, these are the same guys who designed the VIC-20 and then the C64 computers for Commodore, so what was being asked might've scared others off... but for the PVI guys, this is just another challenge looking for a solution. They begin to architect an entirely new system, well beyond the original idea of a simple computer, 8K and onboard BASIC programming language. Their new prototype, the Frodotype Rev 2, is laid out by May 9, 1983, and now the Bubbles chip is incorporated into the design along with another new chip. The two chips are codenamed Fred and Wilma, and keeping with the cute *Flintstones* reference, the Frodotype is now being referred to as Pebbles.

The Graduate is first shown off along with a very ambitious line of peripherals and cartridge titles at the June 1983 CES, with the Graduate's release date given as October. It would seem that Frodo would not survive his adventure in Mordor, better known as Sunnyvale… and the product is canceled in September thanks to product cancellations under James. Not deterred by this unfortunate turn of events and the evaporation of the dreams of their royalties, the PVI team sets off on their next adventure.

In early November 1983, Atari took notice of a small Silicon Valley startup, previously called Hi-Toro, and now renamed Amiga. Their new chip designs were architected by some former Atari engineers who were now working there - Jay Miner and Joe Decuir. The chips were planned for a new game system/computer capable system called 'Lorraine,' and Atari was curious as to the very close similarities of its design to previous work done by both engineers just a few years ago while working for Atari on its home computer chipset. On November 21, 1983, Atari and Amiga signed an agreement to discuss possible further business between the two companies and Amiga delivers to Atari specifications of its "Lorraine" system and its early business plan. Apparently the talks and exchange of information go very well during the initial November meeting. During a later high level budget status and brainstorming meeting at Atari on December 20, 1983, Steve Bristow notes in his engineering log details of future product plans for the Atari Home Computer Division, among them is the mention of a new system called the "Atari 1850XL: 68000 based clones of Amiga game player system." Had the original architects of Atari's computers managed to get their vision for a 68000 based followup into Atari afterall?

R&D Not Much D Review In Images

Concept sketch of the 1200XL case by Regan Cheng, the characteristic vents on the XL line, and 1200XL assembly inspection.

Don Jones (left) and Kip Todd (right) send a bin of 1200XL components to assembly.

Bill O'Hallaren (left) and Bob Knapp (right) review one of several tests performed by Melinda Tzer (center) on the 1200XL.

This page: The 1200XL debuting at the 1983 Winter Consumer Electronics Show.
Next page: The 800 XL and 600 XL with their respective peripherals.

ALDA
FOR ATARI

Alan Alda, then at the height of his fame during the winding down of the TV show *M*A*S*H*, was hired by Atari as their computer spokesperson.

Atari is putting America's best known, best liked computer enthusiast to work for you.

Alan Alda believes in the computer revolution. And in Atari's new XL Computer System. That's why Alan Alda is featured in the most important advertising campaign Atari has ever run for any of its products.

Alan Alda Knows Computers.

It's hard to imagine a better person to tell people about ATARI Computers. Atari bought his first computer in 1980. He programs in two languages. His new ATARI Computer is kept busy helping edit scripts, speeches and correspondence, collecting and storing background information for future projects, even helping sort out academic research. Alan's ATARI Computer is "going all the time!"

America knows Alan Alda.

The prestigious TV Q national survey rates Alan as the best known, best liked television personality in America. America trusts Alan Alda because it's obvious that he doesn't get involved with anything he doesn't really believe in.

Demonstrating how America can do more with Atari's new XL Home Computers.

Atari will be telling your customers about the most exciting new home computers of the year, the ATARI XL Systems three beautifully designed computers and thirteen versatile peripherals. But just as important, Alan will be demonstrating some of the more than 2,000 software programs people can run on the new ATARI XL Computers.

Alda, only for Atari.

Atari's XL Computer advertising program is the most important television and print effort in the industry. It will deliver over 3.6 billion network TV impressions. And that doesn't count additional spot support in key markets. The print advertising schedule will include attention-getting spreads in newsweeklies, and core-oriented magazines and computer buff publications.

In short, Atari and Alan Alda are both totally committed to getting America into computers. And we know the first step is to get America into your store.

You'll do more with Atari Home Computers.

ATARI 600XL™

ATARI 800XL™

The Camp Experience That Lasts a Lifetime.

ATARI COMPUTER CAMPS

Beautiful Locations All Across The Country

Welcome! Blue sky, fresh air, grassy playing fields, tennis courts, computer classrooms, crystal clear swimming pools. Along with these features, another advantage of Atari Computer Camps is the choice of camp locations offered throughout the country—from the majestic Pacific to the charm of the New England countryside.

Each site is on a school campus, chosen for its beautiful setting, comfortable housing, range of facilities, and accessibility. Each Atari Computer Camp features extensive computer equipment and peripherals, plus a library with over 100 Atari software titles. A book library, ranging from science fiction and fantasy to manuals and workbooks, is also available at each camp site.

The Housing The housing is comfortable, uncrowded, and meets Atari's high standards of quality. In a dormitory setting, boys and girls are housed separately under the supervision of a mature and dedicated counseling staff.

The Food Nutritious and well-balanced, all meals are prepared by chefs and bakers in modern facilities. Delicious multi-course meals are served buffet style, and campers can eat as much as they want. Mealtime is one of the special times when campers and staff can get together and talk about the day's activities.

The Staff Each camp is headed by a Director who is an educator with many years of camping experience. An Assistant Director shares the administrative responsibilities. Overseeing the computer program is the Director of Computer Instruction, who has years of experience in computer programming and teaching.

Each computer class is headed by a professional Computer Science Teacher, aided by one or two Teaching Assistants. Teaching Assistants are college students majoring in computer science. In addition, each site has an on-site computer expert to instruct advanced campers and assist other campers with technical questions.

General Counselors are chosen for their camping experience and most importantly, their concern and affection for young people. Counselors live with campers on a 24-hour basis.

Atari Computer Camps also have Specialty Counselors who are all experts in their fields. The swimming specialists are certified by the American Red Cross as Water Safety Instructors. Other specialists include a Sports Director, Tennis Pro, Drama and Arts & Crafts Instructors.*

*For a complete list of all the special activities offered at each camp, please see the Location Brochure.

"I loved it. You learn a lot and have lots of fun while doing it. I made lots of friends. The friends I made, I still keep in touch with. It was a great experience."

Sarah Cohen, age 13

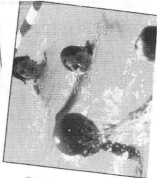

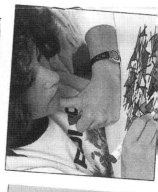

Everything A Summer Camp Should Be

The computer curriculum is an important part of Atari Computer Camps, but it is by no means the only part. The following scheduled activities are also offered to provide every camper with a well-rounded summer camp experience.

Daytime

Team Sports Participation and fun are the goals of Atari Computer Camps' team sports program. Basketball, touch football, softball, volleyball and soccer are just a few of the activities planned.

Tennis Campers will learn from qualified tennis instructors on regulation courts. Classes are small to allow more personalized instruction.

Swimming Atari Computer Camps have selected sites with excellent facilities for swimming and other water sports. Swimming instruction, Red Cross Life Saving programs and free swim are all available for campers of every skill level.

Aerobics By popular demand, an aerobic dance exercise program is offered at Atari Computer Camps. Qualified instructors have choreographed easy-to-learn routines intended to improve coordination and build stamina.

Arts & Crafts Creativity is the theme for Atari Computer Camps' arts & crafts program. Sculpture, ceramics, painting, sketching and weaving are only a sampling of the program's offerings.

Evening

Barbecues, campfires, drama, lectures, movies, rap sessions, scavenger hunts, indoor games, moonlight swims and sing-alongs are just some of the evening activities in store for campers.

Singing around the campfire, having fun with new friends...that's what summer camp is all about. At Atari Computer Camps, the evenings are as exciting and fun-filled as the days.

Camp Equipment: Computers, Peripherals, Software

At Atari Computer Camps, campers will learn to use a full range of the very latest in Atari equipment including the new Atari 1200·XE™ Atari-compatible equipment and software will also be available. Computers, peripherals, software...Atari equipment gives campers a new world to explore.

ATARI 1200-XL—Home Computer with 64K RAM capacity.

ATARI 800™—Home Computer with 48K RAM capacity.

ATARI 400™—Home Computer with 16K RAM capacity.

ATARI 810™ DISK DRIVE—A storage mechanism for storing programs on disks.

ATARI 1025, 1020™, 825™ and 822™ PRINTERS—Campers will use the printers to print out listings of their programs to take home. Printers are also used at camp to print pictures, graphics, and documents composed on the word processor.

ATARI 830™ MODEM—Telephone communications device between computers. Modems are used at Atari Computer Camps to connect electronic bulletin boards so campers can send and receive messages between Atari camps.

ATARI PADDLES AND JOYSTICKS—Controllers used to move images around on the screen.

SPEECH SYNTHESIZER—Produces sound of human speech.

GRAPHICS TABLET—A tool to make graphics easier. Graphics tablet places graphic images on the video monitor.

TERRAPIN TURTLE—A small robot that looks like a turtle which campers will learn to control with the Atari Home Computer.

LIBRARY—An extensive collection of books and magazines relating to Atari Home Computers, as well as science fiction, puzzle and game books and magazines.

SOFTWARE—A large library of Atari and APX favorites and many other programs. Pictured and listed below are some of the more than one hundred titles available at each site:

Atari Writer™
Atari Pascal
Player Maker
Advanced Music System
Starware
Defender
Galahad and the Holy Grail

Atari Computer Camps Are Just The Beginning

The fun and learning don't have to end when the camp session does. Campers can remain involved with computers and Atari through APX, the Atari Program Exchange. Atari created APX to distribute user-written software for Atari.

Campers can submit programs they create to the Exchange and compete for prizes. Programs submitted which meet APX standards are listed in a quarterly catalog.

On-going involvement with each camper's progress will be maintained with a special toll-free number campers can call for help with their programs.

Trademark of William of Electronics, Inc.

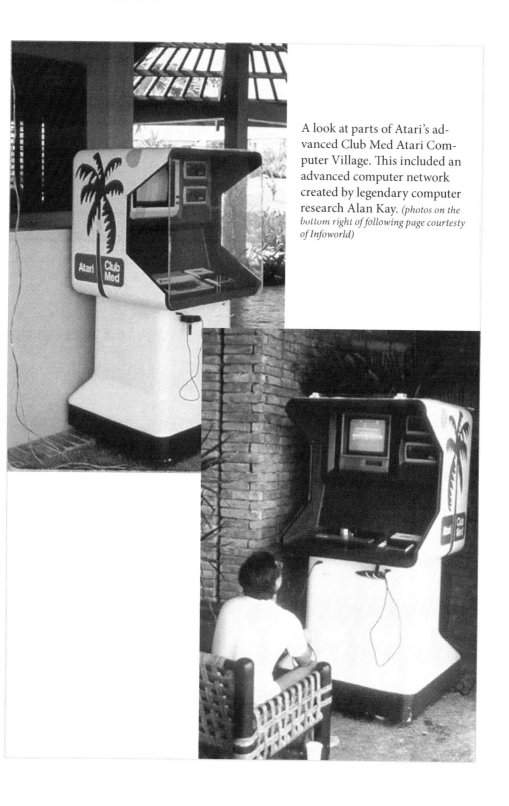

A look at parts of Atari's advanced Club Med Atari Computer Village. This included an advanced computer network created by legendary computer research Alan Kay. *(photos on the bottom right of following page courtesty of Infoworld)*

The Club Med-Atari Computer Village welcomes family vacationers.

Keeping a carefree vacation spirit, members compute outdoors.

ATARI ENGINEERING LOG SHEET

9

GAME OR PROJECT

12/20/83

Budget meeting

Ferrand, Kay Wick, Paul Mallox, Lyzze,
Fred Simon, Tom Kennedy, John Hey,
Dave Stebben, Sek?, Joe Santos

+ 1650 XLD spec

1650 XLD – do cost +
schedule – probable
1985

800XLD – 800XL + disk
in 1950 plastic
cost + schedule
probable late 84

1850 XC – 68000 based
clones o= Amiga
game player system

WRITER | DATE | WITNESS | DATE

This page: Steve Bristow's engineering log detailing some of the planned advanced computer research projects.

Following page: The 1600XL prototype.

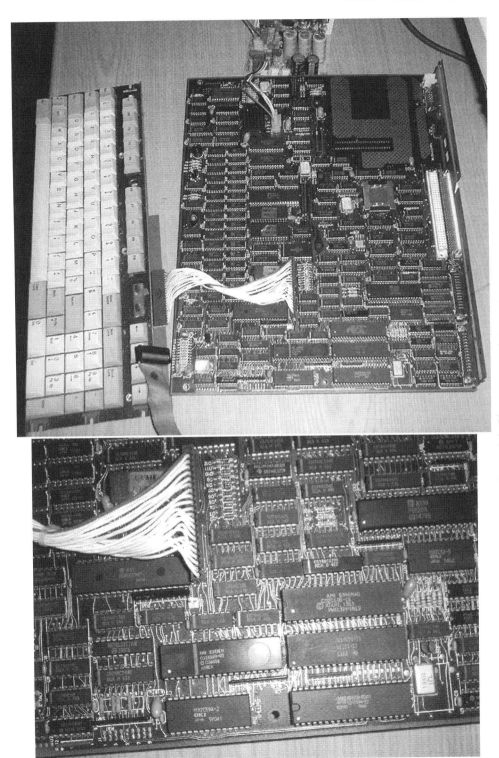

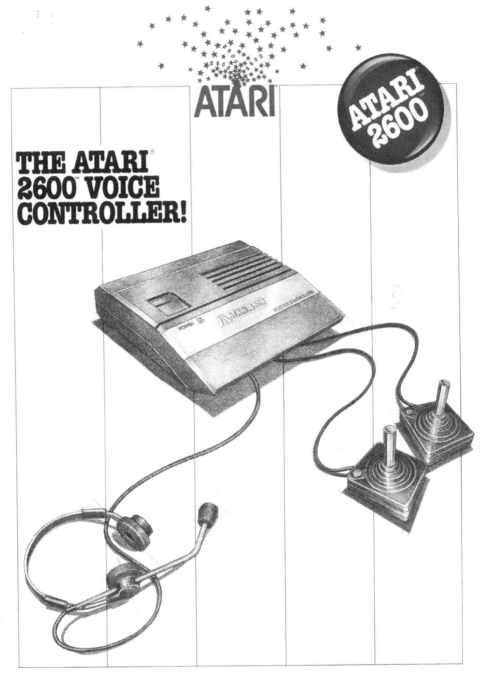

THE ATARI® 2600™ VOICE CONTROLLER!

Previous page: The Atari Graduate Computer, an attempt at expanding the 2600 into a full fledged computer.

This page: Long before Xbox-live made headsets with built in microphones popular, Atari planned its own advanced voice control.

Chapter 12

Warner to Sell
Most Assets
Of Atari Unit

Commodore International's
Former President to Pay
$240 Million of Notes

By Dennis Kneale
And John Marcom Jr
Staff Reporters of The Wall Street Journal

NEW YORK — Warner Communications Inc. agreed to sell most of the assets of its loss-ridden Atari Inc. unit to Jack Tramiel for $240 million in notes and said it expects to post a second quarter loss of $425 million before tax adjustments as a result of the transaction.

Warner valued the Atari assets involved in the sale at more than $60 million. The transaction ends months of uncertainty and shopping for an Atari sale by Warner. The unit had a book value of $134 million as of year

Atari reorganizes management
Executives shuffle titles, duties in shake-up without firings

By Mary A.C. Fallon

Charles "Skip" Paul, former

pany in financial difficulty.

Key executives have new titles, some have more responsibilities and there is also a new reporting hierarchy. However, no executives lost their jobs in the realignment.

John Farrand, 39, formerly president of Atari's coin-operated games unit and engineering, was named president of Atari. He was also named president and chief operating officer of Atari Products Co., a newly created operations division. Farrand has been with Atari

tive vice president of resea development and product deve Paul Malloy was named execu president of operations and engineering

Steve Calfee was named se president of entertainment soft

They will all report to Farra Alan Kay, who has done e work on making computers eas was named "Atari Fellow," the ranking technical position in t

Strangers In the Night...

There's a phrase in prison lingo that's used to refer prisoners on death row as they make that final walk to the location of their demise: "Dead man walking." You may be living right now, but you're already marked for death in the near future. Some take the walk stoically, others do it sneering in the face of death and still more cry hysterically, not wanting to die. They all have one thing in common though: they know they're making that walk. Atari, on the other hand, did not. As the company entered 1984, James Morgan kept doing right what he was supposed to do - looking for ways to cut the mounting losses by making Atari a leaner and more profitable company.

As CEO, James moved up John Ferrand, the president of the still somewhat profitable Coin Division, to be President of Atari itself and of the Atari Products Company (APC), while Skip Paul was moved to replace John as head of Coin. APC was originally initiated by Ray Kassar that past June as a way to cut down on overhead by consolidating all of the Consumer and Home Computer divisions and their duplicated efforts into three main divisions. APC is in charge of all consumer product development and marketing in to a single division, Atari Sales and Distribution Company (ASDC) is in charge of all sales and distribution, and Atari Manufacturing Company (AMC) oversees the now international manufacturing efforts. Atari Coin Division and Ataritel remained separate.

The divisions went through several lineup changes by the time James appointed John Ferrand, and most were holdovers from the Kassar days. Wallstreet analysts kept assuming James would clear house at some point, but it never happened. John Cavalier, an appointment from Kassar, headed APC until October, when he was poached by Steve Jobs and John Sculley to become General Manager of Apple's Personal Computer Division. He was replaced by David Ruckert and then by John Ferrand in January. ASDC is headed by Donald Kingsborough, on his second tour of duty at Atari, analysts speculate he wasn't cut by Morgan because he knew whre all the skeletons were in Atari's and Warner's respective closets. Paul Malloy, also a Kassar appointment, continues to run AMC.

James also shutdown Atari's Fajardo, Puerto Rico plant and laid off 250 employees at Atari's Coin-op division in Milpitas, totaling 550 more employees that were given pink slips. Then he moved to shut down Atari's WONG plant, as production work on home computers and video games moved to Atari's expanded El Paso, Texas factory. While this will see about 1,500 employees in their overseas operations eliminated, it will creates a yet unknown number of new positions in Atari's El Paso location. Finally, with the 7800 on its way, he also quietly shut down all 5200 manufacturing in February. Atari's 'Super System' was now just a blip on the game industry's radar, having been on the market for not even a year and a half.

The problem was that it was doing little to boost Warner's confidence in light of their own problems. You see, Warner had been battling the possibility of a hostile takeover effort by the infamous Rupert Murdoch since the Fall. Starting innocently that past August (if anything with Rupert Murdoch can be considered innocent) when Murdoch asked Steve Ross if Ross minded if he bought some stock in the company, by the Fall he owned 6.7% of Warner and was looking to take advantage of Warner's compounding losses to take control. Of course, that was done by making Steve Ross and his management look completely inept, with subsidiary Atari as the shining example. Both sides began posturing, with Warner engaging in a deal in December to buy almost half of Chris-Craft Industries (an odd mixture of boat manufacturer and tv station owner) in return for Chris-Craft getting 19% of Warner to make it harder for Murdoch to take over. Murdoch, in turn, filed fraud and racketeering charges as well asking the Delaware court to stop the Chris-Craft/Warner deal. Murdoch further retaliated by sicking reporters on Ross to dig up dirt and publish scandalous material in one of his newspapers, the New York Post.

Murdoch wasn't getting anywhere with any of his suits, but the sum total of his efforts was screwing with Ross's mind, causing him to want to buy Murdoch out against the advice of other Warner executives. Warner announced on March 10th, it was buying back Murdoch's shares in the company at $31 a share at a time when it was trading for about $10 below that. Costing Warner $172.6 million plus another $8 million in legal expense reimbursements to News International PLC, Murdoch's subsidiary that had actually purchased the stock. The event was done, but not for Warner's subsidiaries. Warner was still vulnerable because of the continued losses it was taking, and Steve Ross knew he had to do everything he could to put a stop to it so a takeover attempt couldn't happen again. A number of subsidiaries were under the gun, but first and foremost was Atari.

Manny and Rob Newman were cruising around Atari in April, going from building to building and location to location. They weren't cruising for any of the hot chicks that continued to work at Atari, though they did pick up the much more mundane status reports from the top reporting managers. Their trip had another purpose though, one that was designed to specifically fly under the radar of Jim Morgan and Atari's management: They were there to take a visual inventory of the company, and all physical assets. After a week of this charade, Manny headed back to New York with nobody the wiser of the true purpose of his visit; or that it had been done at the request of Steve Ross.

Steve and Manny discussed the findings on their almost eight hour plane trip from New York to Amsterdam. Why were they heading there? Steve was looking to sell Atari to Philips Electronics N.V., ironically the parent company of competitor Magnavox. The rumors that Steve was going to sell Atari had been persisting amongst the halls of Warner Communications since the previous Spring, but the truth was that Steve had been talking to Philips CEO Wisse Dekker since last August on topics from investing in each other's companies, to becoming an investor in Atari or purchasing it outright. Now Steve was here to actually make one of those things happen.

Their series of face-to-face meetings commence and are cordial, with Steve's pitch on Philips purchasing Atari going as well as one could hope. However by the end of several days of meetings, Steve is unable to sway Wisse Dekker that the purchase would be in any way beneficial to Philips. You see, their subsidiary Magnavox had just left video games after shutting down its Odyssey2 operations and canceling its planned Odyssey3 followup. True, the market crash had just been limited to

North America and Philips was doing well throughout Europe with its Videopac series. But the European market itself had been rapidly changing to be dominated by the home computer thanks to the increasing popularity there of the Commodore 64 computer, Sinclair's Spectrum line and the recent MSX standard for 8-bit computers that Kay Nishi of Microsoft Japan had been championing. Thinking quickly, Steve floated the idea of Philips just investing for a 50% ownership in Atari, but Wisse doesn't have any confidence that even that would be in his company's best interest and no further negotiations would change his mind. Steve was going to have to look somewhere else if he was hoping to unload Atari.

Mind you, all of this is going on without James Morgan's knowledge. As far as he knows, he still has Warner's and Steve's confidence, and is continuing to work on steering Atari towards what he thinks will be a much more profitable direction.

Hard Habit To Break

James' forced evaluation of Atari and the re-startup period that followed had been successful for the most part, trimming a lot of the fat and allowing APC to focus on projects that James felt would be more profitable for the company. One of the efforts that was now at the forefront was the internal fight for the new support chips to power Atari's next generation of computers. They just couldn't be content to rely on the same rehash of the the original chips designed by Jay Miner's team, while other companies such as Mindset and Amiga Corp. were now touting the development of their own impressive graphics and sound chips.

Among the projects underway at Atari is a project lead by Chris Jeffers called 'RAINBOW,' which had been borne out of the Corporate Research group, headed by Alan Kay. 'Rainbow' is the specification for a group of chips to supply high-end graphics and sound capabilities. The graphics portion is a pair of chips called 'Silver and Gold' and they're joined by the audio portion called 'Amy.' Though Amy was still under development, the chipset samples of Silver and Gold are ready to begin integration into a test system design around March, to be joined by Amy later. The project, lead by Doug Crockford and Rob Alkire, is named 'the GUMP.' Named several years before the more famous Forrest was introduced in Winston Groom's cherished novel, the name actual drew on another previous novel according to Doug Crockford: the follow-up to The Wizard of Oz, The Marvelous Land of Oz. The GUMP was a character from this 1904 sequel, a member of a species of elk-like creatures that live throughout OZ, with this specific 'Gump' being an elk head on a plaque attached to a sofa. Of course trying to explain to management just where the heck this odd project name came from was going to be a bit awkward, so Doug also came up with a quick and dirty acronym: GUMP - Graphics Und Music 'Puter.

"GUMP was a reference design for Rainbow, one of several, in fact. Gold was the VDAC and HSYNC/VSYNC generator - Silver was the SPRITE generator. We were trying to keep costs low and at the time 40-pin chips were about the max we could go without getting pricey. This meant splitting the graphics into two chips," recalls Robert Alkire.

As AMY was getting far enough along, it was shown off to stunned visitors - many who felt it easily rivaled Commodore's own popular SID sound chip. Built around a bank of 64 oscillators with onboard ramp generators, it results in a hardware based sound method quite similar to the much later software based MP3 format. In fact, during Michael Jackson's visit to Atari during Amy's development, he recorded himself singing Hello Dolly and was treated to an almost perfect digitized playback.

The GUMP team held no illusions about the importance of their work though. With they way things were running at Atari now, it could be cancelled any day. For instance before GUMP, Robert Alkire worked on another project called 'Sierra,' which was also planned as a next generation Atari computer. Trying to get it off the ground had been a challenge... well actually, so was trying to get off of paper. Robert Alkire explains the 'Sierra Disaster' in a bit more detail: "Sierra... It had a different processor weekly and was designed by committee - suffice to say - it was a mess. It was nearly impossible to make any headway, so I opted to drop out of the Sierra project and left to work with Steven Saunders on Rainbow and the idea of a clean API for a graphics chip. It was the two of us who designed the chips to RTL level. We worked with the chip guys for the actual layout."

John Palevich wrote up the specifications for the GUMP's Operating System, an advanced UNIX based system with a windowing based Graphical User Interface (GUI). "We looked to use BSD Unix with a GUI on it - codenamed 'Snowcap.' I wanted to use sprites to implement the window system," recalls Douglas Crawford. The project never made it into wire wrap and unfortunately time was against both the project and Atari. Big things were going to happen on the second day in July, and things would never be the same.

Atari's Home Computer group in APC was also busy, but in this case reviving a project that had been axed by James Morgan in 1983, the Atari 1450XLD (just as the 1400XL is being cancelled). The 1450XLD was brought back on deck as a product to complete and release for the Summer of 1984, and though it was getting a second chance, it was no longer based off the original 1450XL design - codenamed 'Dynasty.' This new version, codenamed 'TONG,' implements many changes to the original 1450XL design from 1983, including incorporating several new gate chips for handling device selections within the system (Modem, Voice Synthesizer and Disk Drive(s)) and would potentially be able to handle more memory directly. The new prototype motherboard design is huge by any standard of the day, in fact, close to the size of an IBM PC/AT motherboard, assuring this computer will easily trump the 1200XL in size.

The 1450XLD is also going to be joined by an expansion box for the XL computers, which at this time consist of the 600XL, the 800XL and the soon-to-be completed 1450XLD. The expansion box, which had been specified back in May of 1983, is the Atari 1090XL Expansion System and surprise, it's being worked on by the recently returned Joe Decuir! Finishing his stint at Amiga as badge #2, Joe was now under contract to design the plug-in cards for the expansion box.

Then there's the project Mark Filipak had been working on as well from January through March, called OMNI. A very sophisticated high end computer and gaming system design based around a whole new set of graphics and audio chips – Penny, Vivian and Heather. Capable of 648 x 488 resolution and built-in 3D scrolling, smoothing and other very advanced graphics features, it began its journey to chip design under Atari ASG directed by Gary Summers. Time and events would be against Mark and his creation however. Other than a comprehensive set of design, theory and user guides, along with some initial chip layout work and a lot of potential, sadly OMNI would never see the light of day.

GAZA is another promising computer from this period, that unfortunately wold never make it out of Atari either. Lead by Tom Hogg, the team including Bruce Merritt, Bill Galcher and Paul Resch were originally formed to develop 68000 microprocessor based systems. Yes, the same microprocessor both Jay Miner and Joe Decuir had wanted to build a computer around back in 1979. In 1983, after meeting directly with Warner management, Tom's team (part of the Advanced Engineering Group) was given permission to pursue these new high end computer systems. GAZA was their first attempt - an advanced hi-res color graphics workstation, something like an Apollo graphics computer of that time, which had three Motorola 68000 microprocessors and two massive one-megabyte video buffers (all wire-wrapped!!). Working on a two microprocessor prototype, after Apple released the Macintosh in January, the team decided it needed a comparable OS and user interface. That's when GAZA started running an alpha-release copy of CPM-68k that the team obtained from Gary Kildall and his company Digital Research Inc. in early March '84. After some work with the new operating system, they got the system up and working smoothly enough that they felt it was time for the dog and pony show with Warner brass (since Warner now had to give corporate approval on projects for anything to continue). "We run the demo to Warner and they look at us in puzzlement. At first we thought something had gone wrong. Something did go wrong - the team showed up with an actual working product. The normal process for R&D at Atari had been lots of 'R' but usually never much 'D' and we kind of broke the cardinal rule - we actually showed up with something that worked," recalls Bruce Merritt. When they asked for approval to continue the project and move it into a marketing evaluation phase, the response they got was far from expected. "Well now, that's not really for playing games, is it?" said one of the Warner executives. Their advanced computer, which could have entered Atari into the lucrative emerging computer workstation market, was officially canceled around April 17, 1984. "Once it became clear that manufacturing computers for business wasn't consistent with the Warner/Atari business model, Gaza was killed," Bruce further elaborated.

Elsewhere in the computer industry though, another machine was getting a lot of attention as whispers of its capabilities began to spread. The computer was being designed at the little known Amiga Corporation, under the expert direction of none other than Jay Miner (along with his protégé Joe Decuir). His prototype, named Lorraine, had made its public debut at the January 1984 CES. Well technically a private debut, as Amiga was showing their new technology behind closed doors at the show to a select few; though these same doors had already been open some time for Atari and Warner. During the January CES, John Ferrand, Ken Nussbacher and other Atari management were meeting with Amiga President Dave Morse, lead designer Jay Miner and other Amiga personnel to continue the discussions previously started back in November 1983 on Atari financing the completion of Lorraine. There was still plenty of further development to do on this amazing chipset, and with several investors already on board Dave Morse and Jay Miner were hoping to get Warner and Atari as well. Mind you, Jay's former company wasn't considering it out of love or some sense of loyalty to the man who had designed Atari's original 8-bit computer, nor was Jay's offering which was done as a last resort. No, Atari's goal was to obtain usage of the chipset for possible use in its arcade, console, and home computer divisions as part of its ongoing efforts to invest in new technology companies.

Amiga is a company abundant in talent, however what Amiga was continually lacking in was money; with the company in dire straits financially and Atari looking to get itself back on top in the market with some killer technology, both companies simply had something that the other desperately needed. After several weeks of legal back and forth, in February 1984, David Morse of Amiga and John Ferrand of Atari come to basic terms on a Letter of Intent between the two companies: Atari would advance $500,000 on signing of the LOI so that Amiga could continue funding the development of the 'Lorraine' chipset while Atari and Amiga worked on creating and getting signed a full Licensing Agreement. The $500,000 bought Atari access to Amiga's engineers so Atari could begin working on its own reference board to plug the chips into when they were finished. In the meantime, all the chip layout documents and other materials related to the chipset would stay in escrow, released to Atari once the LA was signed. The planned framework of that agreement would then have Atari pay Amiga another $1 million upon the signing of the license, purchase 1 million preferred shares of Amiga at $3 a piece, and then pay $500,000 for delivery of each chip. Then there were the royalties that the LA was to agree to as well: $2 per chip in consumer devices, and a $100,000 a year minimum guarantee from coin-op at $15 a unit. The initial terms of a license between Amiga and Atari would grant Atari exclusive usage of the Amiga chipset for its video game business only. Atari would receive non-exclusive usage of the chipset in the home computer business; however, Atari could not do anything in the computer field until 1985 and only as a keyboard upgrade to a video game system using the chipset. In 1986, Atari could then sell a dedicated computer system based on the chipset. This would allow Amiga the ability to market and sell its own system without competition in the computer field from its licensor, Atari.

Likewise, it was all carefully crafted not to interfere with David Morse's end game: selling off Amiga. David was very clear up front that any buy in that Warner and Atari did could never interfere with this ambition, it was purely a technology exchange for cash. Warner and Atari agreed, but they needed some sort of assurance as well. After all, Amiga was continually at deaths door and could still go under before the LA was signed, and if that happened there was the line of previous investors there to split up the assets before Warner and Atari. The stipulation then was that companies would have to come to terms on a final LA by June 30th, otherwise to recoup its advance of $500,000, Atari would be given all the assets in escrow license and royalty free.

On March 7th 1984, Atari delivered check #068935 to Amiga Corporation for the $500,000, and shortly after the signing, on April 3, 1984 the Amiga technical doc's are delivered to the Advanced Engineering Group. Carl Goy sent out an email on the Home Computer Division MV8000 Data General Minicomputer system to alert the engineering group that he had received the Amiga chipset technical documentation; it was about a ream thick and if anyone needs copies, just contact him.

Then April 5, 1984, the team lead by Tom Hogg that had just come off GAZA were then re-assigned to the new Amiga project after a short detour on another 68000 based project called Minnie. It was an obvious fit, and Warner wanted the team to use all of the experience from the GAZA project to develop a consumer 68000-based product. The team was informed that Atari had just invested into Amiga Corporation to fund the completion of their chipset, and that Atari now had an agreement to work on a game console system and a computer upgrade using the chipset. Tom Hogg's team talked with the Amiga engineers and met with them at their offices, reviewing their wire-wrapped prototype system and receiving technical documents on the chipset. Tom codenamed the project 'Mickey,' nicknamed after his wife, and it seemed that Project Mickey was certainly in the right hands. The team went straight to work on creating the system that would accept the 'expected to arrive' chipset from Amiga. The specifications and functionality were being outlined. System schematics, bus architecture and wire wraps were even built as well. Everything was ready; the team would take a long July 4th holiday weekend and upon returning, the chipset from Amiga would be delivered and they would begin integration testing… or so they thought.

It seemed Atari under James Morgan was tinkering in nearly every possible avenue trying to get a new line of computers out, and if you listen to what James was stating publicly you begin to understand why. As he told the Antic, the magazine dedicated to Atari computers, for their March, 1984 issue: "In my judgment, the home computer companies have not treated the consumers with the respect and consideration they deserve. The real issue is this: Which company will be the first to go to the American consumer with microprocessor technology that makes the consumer say, 'Gee, I didn't know a computer could do that,' and second, 'I have to have one.' So far (other than word processing), the computers currently offered to the public really do not do anything much easier than you can do by hand." It's no surprise then that there's one more computer project in the wings, and this one is meant to make the computing experience just a little easier by making it portable. Don't ask what the actual name of this project is though, because it had more names than James Bond's Aston Martin had license plates. They seemed to mostly center around the idea of a trip to the North Pole with names like 'Eskimo,' 'Dogsled,' and 'Explorer.'

Initially the work on this new laptop is carried out by Rich Pasco, formerly of Xerox, who had come over to Atari at the same time Alan Kay did. He's joined by Tom Palecki from Atari's Industrial Design group, who's tasked with creating numerous product designs and physical packaging concepts, from a thin lightweight fold-up laptop to a bulky luggage styled design with a built-in printer. Laptops were pretty new to the industry, so it's not like there was an established mold they had to fit in to. All that freedom available to the designers on the project tends to be a double edge sword, because there's no focus or finish line yet. The many hurdles faced by engineers in these stages can actually set you down a lot of wrong paths. Questions like, "Who's the target audience and how would it fit into the product line?" "Would it be compatible with the existing computers?" "What processor type should it run on?" "What about the display?" These were not easy questions to answer when you're trying to design a device with little to reference against at the time.

Jim Tittsler, who back in 1983 had worked on the ill fated Atari 1600XL IBM compatible joint project between Atari and Toshiba, wrote up the third specification for the portable computer - the one called Explorer. The problem is, even in this third iteration it's still a mix of both suggesting specifications and asking the same questions as before: which processor, display, etc. to choose from, what would be the benefits... what would this device be targeted for... and how would it fit into Atari's family of products? Explorer goes through one final attempt at a specification, before it was time to decide "Ok, now let's just build the damn thing." The problem was, there just wasn't enough time... time was something that Atari's engineers and their projects were running out of. In a matter of weeks, everything was about to change.

In the meantime, as Atari is preparing for its showing at the Summer CES in June, the news that time ran out for one of its products was finally announced to the public. While internally the Atari 5200 was already canceled, the public is made aware of this fact for the first time on May 21st in one of two press releases distributed that day. The second press release is announcing the 5200's replacement, Atari's new 7800 Pro-system console. Confusing market analysts enough with this announcement of replacing this relatively new console with yet another console and 10 planned launch titles considered 'more of the same,' it was the May 31st announcement that provided a real bombshell to those same analysts; another 1,000 employees are to be laid off. Since January of 1983, Atari's ranks have shriveled from 7,800 down to only 2,500, and now with this latest round Atari is brought to only 1,500 employees globally. In this case though, the layoffs are all part of James Morgan's restructuring and cost savings plan which he called NATCO or 'New Atari Company.'

James is looking to pare the company down even further, his actualization of his previously stated philosophy of purging the excesses of the past from Atari. NATCO is based around a Noah's Ark concept: gather up good divisions and personnel in a new company focused on putting up a smaller amount of well defined products that are more apt to make money. The rest of the company and people left outside the Ark? They'll be put in another company and phased out like the unicorn, not part of the new creator's plan. The layoffs begin on July 1st, after which Morgan's NATCO is expected to be fully activated.

This all lead to the press trying to start things off on a sour note for the re-vamped Atari's Summer CES showing, and it was only further fueled when James Morgan wasn't there on the opening day at CES, May 31st. The reason was simple: James Morgan's daughter was graduating on the same day and like any parent, he chose to go to his daughters graduation instead. After all, it was a one day once in a lifetime family event. CES, on the other hand, would run for several days and James would be able to attend on those remaining days. The press being the press, specula-tion and rumors immediately spread like wildfire that James Morgan had been fired. Knowing the magnifying glass he was under though, James had prewritten a memo to the press to immediately put those rumors to rest when they sprung up. Clearly explaining why Morgan would not be in attendance that first day, it didn't quell the real reason they were all ready to pounce on the slightest irregularity; they were all waiting for the other shoe to drop announcing major changes for Atari, possibly even the implosion of the company.

At the show, Atari showcased its crowning achievement: the Atari 7800 Prosystem - Atari's all new home video game system. An affordable game system, priced under $150, it includes a lineup of fourteen titles. And this time, unlike the 5200 Super System with its 'yawn inducing' *Super Breakout* pack-in, the Atari 7800 would come with a home version of *Pole Position II*, the hot arcade game released just last year. The title showed off the graphics potential of the new console perfectly, as did the other games, showing off games that looked and played just as well as their arcade counterparts. Other items announced at CES for the 7800 are a computer add-on keyboard, Atarilab learning modules, a high score cartridge for storing high scores from compatible games, and for those curious enough to notice a small open-ing on the side of the Atari 7800 marked 'Expansion,' they would be thrilled that a future laserdisc interface is planned to be released for use with the console. *Dragon's Layer* and *Space Ace* anyone? So not only had Atari designed a new game system, but it's also affordable, it looks good... plays good, is expandable and oh... did they also mention, it also plays all the Atari 2600 game cartridges - just plug them right in - that's right - no add-on expansion adapter, nothing extra to buy...

The console certainly looked like a winner and in the days that followed, the press gives the console very favorable reviews, though some continued to complain about the launch title offerings being "more of the same." There were still more that questioned why Atari was releasing a new home console with the market in the state it was. Unknown to most CES show goers and the press though, a group of proud fathers were watching from the sidelines. The engineers, chip designers and programmers from GCC were standing there at Atari's booth, proudly watching the excitement and smiles of those having a look at GCC's new baby. If GCC's team could've run around the show passing out cigars and thanking everyone for coming to see their newborn, they probably would have... From a cocky idea for a revolutionary game/computer concept drawn a whiteboard presentation up in New Hampshire back in late 1982... to the layout and design of an entirely new graphics processor... to an expandable game console system - the GCC engineers had really outdone themselves. Now thanks to Atari, they were standing there seeing their dreams become reality at the Summer CES.

Another Atari product that received skeptical, questioning looks at is a device called Mindlink - a headband controller that actually controlled game play on a TV by a person just looking at the screen and 'thinking' about moving an object. It's demonstrated with a modified *Breakout* game, called *Bionic Breakout*, though the device doesn't really read your thoughts or mind. What it does do is read the resistance of the muscles in a person's forehead and interprets them, sending the appropriate joystick or fire button signals to the game console or home computer it's hooked up to. When it worked, it worked quite well - but a marketing rep goof-up at the show sort of overshadowed Atari's attempted seriousness of presenting this product. While explaining the features of Mindlink, the marketing rep's Mindlink suddenly loosens up and ends up drooping down over his eyes, resting on the bridge of his nose and nullifying the 'psychic experience.' It's a nice comic relief moment from the hustle and bustle of the CES show and a welcomed bit of lighthearted humor, even if it was at the marketing rep's expense.

The Atari XL computers are on display as well, along with their assortment of peripherals such as the 1050 disk drive, 1025 printer and 1030 modem. Also in attendance for all to see.... Several Atari 1450XLD computer systems which were met with very eager enthusiasm from show attendees and press.

Coin is there as well, with what will be the final arcade game under the Atari, Inc. moniker called *I, Robot*. Created by Dave Theurer and Rusty Dawe, it's the first arcade video game with polygonal 3D graphics - simply way ahead of its time. Too far ahead of its time actually, and only 750 were produced with even less sold.

There was a myth, still a rumor now years later, that approximately 500 *I, Robot* arcades were 'accidentally' knocked overboard in the Pacific Ocean during shipping – this is totally false. Though during its development and testing, Rusty Dawe would have LIKED to have dumped about 500 *I, Robot* controllers into the Pacific Ocean. "The controls were a nightmare - we were using the Hall Effect controllers," recalls Rusty. What was happening can only be best described as the popular phrase, a 'ghost in the machine' effect. The games were being tested in an arcade location up in Seattle, WA. But what no one had realized was that the arcade was located right next door to a metal scrap yard, which in turn had one of those massive cranes with an electromagnet on it to pick up large metal pieces and move them around. In order to be able to pick up hundreds to sometimes thousands of pounds of metal, these electromagnets are extremely powerful and have a very strong radius. The *I, Robot* arcades were situated only about 100 yards from where this crane and magnet were operating, so due to the magnetic pull, the arcades were mysteriously playing by themselves at times. If you're asking how, it makes more sense when you understand that Hall Effect joysticks are contactless controllers that actually use their own electromagnetic effect to create precision control of the characters on screen. So needless to say, a massive magnet swinging anywhere near these games were actually impacting the controllers and causing the games to play by themselves against a player's input during game play. After spending months changing out controls and engineers becoming frustrated at not being able to isolate why this was happening, finally someone noticed the 800 lb. gorilla in the room... or should we say the 100 ft. tall 80 ton electromagnetic crane next door. The answer was simple of course; ground and shield the controllers separately from the main PCBs and add yet more shielding. Exorcising the ghosts from the machine was about as close to an overboard moment the game came to.

Take the Money and Run...

On the return flight from the Netherlands in April, Steve Ross and Manny Gerard discussed what their options and next moves will be for Atari. If Philips wasn't even interested in investing in Atari, what hope did they have of finding another sizable company to offload Atari on to? They needed to do something quick, because Atari was still sinking and dragging down Warner. The consumer video game market, the source of Atari's troubles, wasn't showing any signs of an upward cycle any time soon. If anything, it was getting worse as they noticed more and more companies dropping out of every month. What Manny didn't know at the time though was that Steve had already made up his mind on a solution. Upon their return to New York, Steve made a call to the least likely person anyone would have thought someone associated with Atari would call on...

The phone call went to Jack Tramiel, founder and former CEO of Commodore, who had left the company back in January (for more on this and Commodore itself, check out Brian Bagnall's Commodore: A Company on the Edge). Rumors had been abounding that Jack was shopping up and down the West Coast for a potential companies and/or technologies to purchase and help in the production and manufacturing of a new computer he aimed to create. Apparently, Jack had cut his 'world retirement tour' short as news of his old company Commodore begane appearing . Portraying it as being in trouble, the news was followed by further predictions that Japanese computer manufacturers would most likely make a strong entrance in to the U.S. computer market. As Michael Tomczyk, Jack's former assistant at Commodore, put it in his November 1984 book The Home Computer Wars, "He told me he didn't plan to get back in the industry unless he felt he was really needed, for example, unless he thought the Japanese were coming into the market in a big way and Commodore couldn't beat them. I interpreted this to mean he wasn't getting back into the business, but I should have caught the cryptic message, because the Japanese were planning to invade the U.S., with a secret weapon called MSX."

Not seeing any other current U.S. computer manufacturer that he felt would be strong enough to answer the pending Japanese invasion, he had come out of retirement and set up Tramel Technology Ltd. (misspelled on purpose so people pronounced his last name right) that March. You see, Jack's oldest competitive enemy had been the Japanese, who had severely undercut him in both the typewriter and calculator markets while he was still at Commodore. It was an enemy that Jack also respected greatly, enough so to study and employ some of their methods in his effort to beat them ("Gentlemen, the Japanese are coming, so we will become the Japanese" is one famous quote of his). He had even gone so far as to even establish Commodore Japan and engage Japanese companies like video game designers HAL Laboratory (now more famous as a subsidiary of Nintendo) to write games for the Commodore Vic-20. With the Japanese knocking on the door of the U.S. market, Jack saw this as a personal calling to defend the very market he had so decidedly triumphed over with the one two punch of the Commodore Vic-20 and Commodore 64.

Before the phone call, Jack had already begun talking to some of his ex-employees at Commodore about becoming involved in the new venture, such as engineer Shiraz Shivji who he engaged to design the new computer. Jack had also already visited with new tech companies like Mindset Corporation and even Amiga Corporation, though the meeting between Jack and Amiga left Amiga's engineering team with a very bad taste in their mouths. Jack, being honest and upfront, was very interested in the Amiga technology, but not in the company's engineers; essentially this cash-starved company was only offered an opportunity to pay their bills – the deal would have them turning over all their work to Tramiel and company, and be left with nothing afterwards (except perhaps a trip to the unemployment line). Looking far ahead as well, Jack also made a trip to the Far East to discuss part supply deals with component suppliers in Japan.

Jack was actually out traveling on vacation with his wife at the time when he received the call from Steve Ross in April, causing him to cut that vacation short as well. Steve Ross explains he's looking for a buyer for Atari, in part or whole, and that he's ready to make Jack the deal of a lifetime. The potential deal is a windfall for Jack; not only would he gain access to the world's most recognized brand in home technology, but there was an entire campus of engineering, manufacturing and management buildings in the Moffett Park complex in Sunnyvale, California. Plus Atari has substantial overseas manufacturing plants and offices... What more could Jack possibly ask for to build an entirely new company with? Well, he knew what he didn't want: Jack was interested solely in the Consumer Division operations, including everything under APC - the home video games and a computers groups. Which was fine with Warner, because Coin was doing well enough that they could still work with that division, and the rest they could continue to just shut down and sell off certain valuable Intellectual Property (IP) assets.

So, why did Steve Ross approach Jack Tramiel to buy Atari from Warner? Well, Manny Gerard gave us the answer: "I wasn't involved in the negotiations, it was all Steve Ross, but I can say this – Steve wanted out of Atari and Jack would make a deal very quickly to make it happen." By early May, Jack would have his lawyers begin discussions with Martyn Payson, who will handle the negotiations for Warner in New York on the terms of the sale of Atari's Consumer Division. Since Atari had such a major presence in Moffett Park area, shortly after Jack arranged to rent office space right down the street at 455 South Mathilda Avenue in Sunnyvale, literally a five minute drive from Atari's corporate headquarters over on Borregas Ave. It would give Jack a staging site to work from while negotiations were going on, and also serve as an office for Shiraz to begin laying out his ideas and designs for the computer project (now called 'RBP' or 'Rock Bottom Price'), since Shiraz and two other engineers were now planning to leave Commodore and join up with Jack later that month. Then Jack had one of his lawyers do a formal Nevada incorporation of 'Tramel Technologies Ltd.' (TTL) on May 17th - the very same day several former Commodore personnel, trusted and loyal associates of Jack resigned their positions and immediately join Jack on his new endeavor. It was beautifully timed, like the end of a Godfather movie, and among them are the engineers of Jack's next generation computer: Shiraz, Arthur Morgan, John Hoenig and Douglas Renn. They were followed by Lloyd Taylor, president of technology; Bernie Witter, vice president of finance; Sam Chin, who ran finances for Commodore's Asian operations; Joe Spiteri and his assistant David Carlone, who ran manufacturing; John Feagans of Commodore PET fame; and Gregg Pratt, operations vice president. For the incorporation of the new company, Jack also brought in his son Sam as President, Secretary and Treasurer. The alarms were set off at Commodore; Jack is back and he's pilfering our people.

This brings us back to the June CES, where at the time John Ferrand of Atari is having last minute talks with a company that was about to unknowingly insert itself smack in between these two colliding giants of Jack and Commodore: Amiga Corporation. Amiga was at the show as well, now showing off their Lorraine to the general attendees amid "Wow's" and questions of "Where the real computer driving the display was hiding?" Behind the scenes, Amiga President David Morse was meeting with John to discuss some issues he had with final version of the License Agreement (LA) they were planning to sign at the end of the month. Lorraine had been progressing nicely thanks to Atari's money and they were planning on having a full printed circuit board and work chips by the signing. The issue at hand is a stipulation Warner and Atari had insisted on being in the LA, that when David did sell Amiga, he couldn't sell it to a listing of computer companies that Atari had provided. The reason? Atari specifically viewed those companies as direct competitors to Atari in the computer market, giving Amiga an unfair advantage in the marketplace and making the licensing agreement Warner and Atari were agreeing to unfair. On his end, David's main concern was that the license was restricting his ability to manage Amiga the way he wanted. That the list was too severely hampering Amiga's ability to merge, sell or do business with whomever they wanted. Still both wanting the deal to proceed, over the course of two meetings at CES, the two agreed to five companies that Amiga should not merge into/be bought out by: IBM, Apple, Commodore, General Electric and Philips. At the top of the list of course were Apple and Commodore. Hammering out that and any other remaining issues, the two counterparts shook on it and parted ways, both happy and looking forward to signing the full LA at the end of the month.

A funny little thing happened just after CES though when Steve Greenberg called up David on June 14th. Steve is an advisor to Commodore and Jack's former consigliere on all things financial. As chairman of Anametrics Inc., a New York management-advisory company, he'd been handling financial public relations for Commodore since 1978. He was calling David now because this man who was responsible for bringing roller disco to the public with his club The Roxy, was looking to bring Amiga to the world - via Commodore. Over several phone calls, Steve Greenberg continued to woo David about licensing the Amiga technology to Commodore, forcing David to make a serious decision about the future of his company and the contract with Atari. The irony here is that the only reason Commodore (a company used to inventing from within) was calling was because they had been turned on to Amiga by Lloyd Taylor, who was now with Jack. And even then Lloyd himself had been given the lead by Red Taylor, the same man who pointed Jack towards Amiga back in April.

David's decision soon turned in to going for the gold and going through with licensing Amiga's chips to Commodore, going against the agreement he was supposed to sign with Atari at the end of the month when Amiga delivered their chips. He could have felt the opportunity to eventually sell out completely to Commodore was also just around the corner. An opportunity that would most likely never come again, having already been turned away by Hewlett-Packard, Silicon Graphics, Sony, and even Philips and Apple. They had all passed, with Steve Jobs even deriding the sheer amount of hardware in the Lorraine prototype. David decided the risk of a lawsuit was worth getting one step closer to meeting his endgame, and flew out to Commodore on the 19th to meet with Marshall Smith and try to come together on an unrestricted licensing deal. Interested, Commodore would need to evaluate their technology first of course, but then he fed them a story based on a partial truth and designed to convey a sense of urgency: that they wouldn't be ready to honor Atari's contract by the end of the month, and if they couldn't deliver the chips to Atari then, they'd take possession of Amiga's technology, so they needed to pay back Atari's loan quick. So Amiga needed this deal very soon if it was going to happen, because there was a clause where they could pay the money back from the original loan.

Of course Commodore had no way of knowing David was twisting the truth, that there was no escape clause and the late June date was only a tentative period easily negotiable. Likewise that (as David would later testify in court), they would indeed have the chipset and main PCB done by the end of June, right on schedule. But they sent out their reluctant group of engineers lead by Robert Russell; reluctant because they were already working on their own next generation Commodore computer, the Z8000. Convinced that Amiga was heading in the wrong direction with their overall computer design, Robert still reported back to headquarters that the chipset was exactly what Commodore needed and a "step up" from what Commodore was already doing.

All this time, David was still in contact with John Ferrand and his other counterparts at Atari, still smoothing out details for the final LA. On Atari's end, they thought everything was a go and right on schedule. Then suddenly all communication stopped. When Dave's June 28th, 1:30pm meeting with Atari Intellectual Properties lawyer Ken Nussbacher arrived, they finally hear from him again - exactly at 1:30pm to cancel. What could be the reason for David's cancellation of the meeting? Unbeknownst to Ken, David can't make the meeting because he's on his way to a different meeting... with Commodore. Commodore's Marshall Smith had Adam Choweniac and Nick Lefevre go out California on June 27th with a draft agreement. When it's signed by both parties in California on the 28th, David's stipulation to Marshall that the agreed upon payment must be wired immediately into Amiga's account is enacted. A total advance of $750,000 is wired over to cover the cost of trying to pay Atari back the initial $500,000 plus calculated interest. The following day he took the amount and was driven to Atari's Corporate Headquarters, where he walked into the lobby, and asked for John Ferrand to come down and meet him in there. When John came down he approached David with an open hand to shake, looking to greet him and say "Hello." Instead of John's hand gripping David's hand though, it was instead met with a check. David hands him a check saying they can't get the computer chipset to work properly, and that here's the money back with interest. John tells David that he's not even sure if he's authorized to take the check, and if it's more time that Amiga needs then it's no problem - Atari's not interested in the money, more time is not a deal breaker. David simply tells him again that they can't get the chipset working, the deal is off, and then quickly steps outside to his waiting car to drive off. John Ferrand is left standing there, check in hand, not quite sure what just happened. He wouldn't have much time to worry though anyways.

Now selling a massive company such as Atari is not something you do over lunch in an afternoon, or a weekend retreat down at Pajaro Dunes. It's a multi-hundred million dollar company with dozens of buildings, tens of millions in inventory, thousands of employees, a complicated spider's web of hundreds of licenses and countless other elements too long to list in detail. The problem was, everyone at Warner and TTL wanted a deal AND they wanted it fast. Selling the corporation and its holdings in about six weeks time is actually very fast in business terms; much too fast to even put together a proper transition. In comparison, when Atari was just a tiny $39 million company in 1976 took six long, painful and at times, irritating MONTHS to sell to Warner. And in this case, one of the parties didn't even know half of it was about to be ripped out and sold. Well, at least nobody at Atari had known until Thursday, when James Morgan was finally informed of the coming final agreement sessions and ordered to keep it under wraps. So on the evening of June 29th, while John Ferrand was still puzzling over the check from Dave Morse, James Morgan went home for the weekend seeking solace and looking to plan his response to the announcement. And in New York, TTL's General Manager Greg Pratt, along with TTL's lawyers, are heading over to 75 Rockefeller Center at Warner Communications on the final leg of negotiations. Starting Saturday, Several leaks are issued to the press that Tramiel's people were currently in negotiations in New York with Warner, but the news won't find its way to most Atarian's, many of whom had taken an extra long July 4th vacation starting that weekend.

Jack's lawyers lead by Leonard Schreiber, along with Warner's lawyers lead by Martyn Payson, spend the weekend in a non-stop final negotiation session that concludes literally just before midnight on July 1, 1984. TTL is now the owner of certain consumer assets from Atari, Inc., retroactive from Saturday. Taking the Atari's main Consumer Division assets, which basically consist of APC, ASDC and AMC, Jack would also have shared ownership of the Atari name and logo. Warner Communications will retain ownership of the other half of the company: Atari Coin-op division, Ataritel division and Atari Adventure Centers arcade locations chains, though the Coin IP will be shared between Jack and Warner. They'll also have to append the word "Games" to anything they do with this half, to differentiate it from Jack's new company. In total, Jack Tramiel agrees to purchase Atari Inc. for $75 million in cash, $140 million in senior debentures at 13% and $100 million in subordinate debentures at 9%. Warner would take a $425 million pre-tax loss on the sale... and Steve Ross would breathe a huge sigh of relief. The deal was done - Steve Ross' $538.6 million pool of quicksand was gone.

As the sun starts to rise early that cool Monday morning in Manhattan just before 6am, the lawyers all sign off on the sale. By the time Jack walks in to Atari Inc.'s now shared corporate headquarters in California at 8:30AM California time, It will be a warm, clear sunny day in New York and a perfect day for all involved in the somewhat clandestine transaction. However, back in California, James Morgan, (who's still CEO of the part of Atari Inc. that Jack didn't take) now finds his company renamed to Atari Games Inc. as part of the deal. James helped several days to try and bring some assemblance of a transition to the chaos, he also announces he's going to be taking a leave of absence for several months; he'll never return. Jack immediately releases a statement of his plans to the press, saying, "Our aim is to be number one. There's much work to be done but we already are moving swiftly... to restore Atari to prominence and profitability. Both the home computer and video game market places continue, in my view, to offer great opportunities. At Atari I believe there is the capability and the foundation which will enable us to fulfill this tremendous potential." The rest of the Atari management is in limbo as Jack starts combing over them to see who he wants to offer to bring over to his new company - at least where he didn't already have positions filled by his son's Sam and Gary (also joined by Leonard a week later), and the Commodore management that had jumped ship and were continuing to. Nobody knew what to call Jack's new company, and the press started simply referring to it as "Atari" and that Jack had taken over "Atari." The name becomes public on July 11th when TTL, and all the Atari assets it absorbed, is then merged with the Nevada created Atari Corporation. For most of the people at the still operating together Atari's however, for at least the next several weeks it was still business as usual...

To be continued in:

Atari Corporation - Business Is War

and

Atari Games - Last In Fun

Chapter 12

Review In Images

News Release

ATARI
A Warner Communications Company

Atari Incorporated   1265 Borregas Avenue   PO Box 427   Sunnyvale California 94086

Contact: Bruce Entin
          (408) 745-4691, 4692   FOR IMMEDIATE RELEASE

WARNER COMMUNICATIONS INC., ATARI INC., ANNOUNCE PLAN FOR

NEW ATARI HEADQUARTERS

SAN JOSE, CA., September 7, 1983 -- Steven J. Ross, chairman and chief
executive officer of Warner Communications Inc., and James J. Morgan, chairman
and chief executive officer of Atari Inc., today announced plans for the development of a major office and research complex on 65 acres of land in San Jose,
California.

Mr. Morgan said Atari plans to establish its worldwide headquarters at
River Oaks Park, a site owned by its corporate parent, WCI. River Oaks Park
is bounded by River Oaks Parkway, Zanker Road, Montague Expressway and Research
Place. Atari currently has its headquarters in Sunnyvale, California.

WCI has named Wolff-Comstock as joint venture partner and lead developer
of the property. Development and construction costs are expected to total
approximately $60 million.

Mr. Morgan said Atari will occupy approximately 400,000 square feet of
office space for research and development, marketing and administration purposes.

In commenting on the plan, Mr. Morgan said, "The new headquarters represents a long-range commitment to Atari's dedicated employees and also to the
local community.

"For Atari's employees, the new headquarters will improve communications
among colleagues and also speed decision making." In addition, Mr. Morgan
said, "an enlarged headquarters is more economical to operate than several
dozen buildings in Silicon Valley."

-more-

Ray's plan to condense Atari into single campus reappeared under James Morgan.

Atari reorganizes management

Executives shuffle titles, duties in shake-up without firings

By Mary A.C. Fallon
Business Writer

Atari Inc., the Sunnyvale video game and home computer manufacturer, reorganized its management Monday and named a president. But it wasn't the usual shake-up expected at a company in financial difficulty.

Key executives have new titles, some have more responsibilities and there is also a new reporting hierarchy. However, no executives lost their jobs in the realignment.

John Farrand, 39, formerly president of Atari's coin-operated games unit and engineering, was named president of Atari. He was also named president and chief operating officer of Atari Products Co., a newly created operations division. Farrand has been with Atari since 1981.

Both positions are new at Atari.

Atari has combined its sales and marketing, research and development, software development, product engineering and manufacturing into the division headed by Farrand.

"The operating division will speed communications and product development," said Bruce Entin, a company spokesman.

James J. Morgan, who took over as Atari's chairman and chief executive officer five months ago, is putting his stamp on the company, said John Reidy, an analyst with Drexel Burnham.

"Morgan is expected to make a series

Charles "Skip" Paul, formerly senior counsel, replaced Farrand as president of the coin-operated games unit.

A senior counsel will be named later, Entin said.

Marcian E. "Ted" Hoff, inventor of the microprocessor, was named executive vice president of research and development and product development. Paul Malloy was named executive vice president of operations and product engineering.

Steve Calfee was named senior vice president of entertainment software.

They will all report to Farrand.

Alan Kay, who has done extensive work on making computers easy to use, was named "Atari Fellow," the highest ranking technical position in the company.

Dennis Groth, executive vice president of Atari Inc., will take on the

James re-organized the top level management, but layoffs continued as well.

Cover stories like this were commonplace. While the media was wondering if James could really save Atari, Steve Ross had already lost confidence.
(Courtesy of InfoWorld)

Programs Cash In on Fitness

InfoWorld

The Newsweekly for Microcomputer Users

February 27, 1984   Volume 6, Issue 9   K 46908 $1.50

IS ATARI GOING DOWN THE TUBES?

During 1983, Atari suffered astounding losses and bruising company politics. Can a new chairman — James Morgan (right) — and a new president — John Farrand (above) — recapture the magic of former times? How much of a pounding can one company take?

Right: James Morgan in early '84, proudly showing off Atari's consumer products. The 5200 console, shown in the bottom right of the photo, was quietly cancelled as production stopped shortly after this photo. *(Courtesy of InfoWorld)*

Bottom: Media magnate Rupert Murdoch attempted a takeover of Warner Communications. Although he failed, it was enough to resign Steve Ross to the fact that Atari couldn't continue to make Warner weak. He moved quickly to find a buyer.

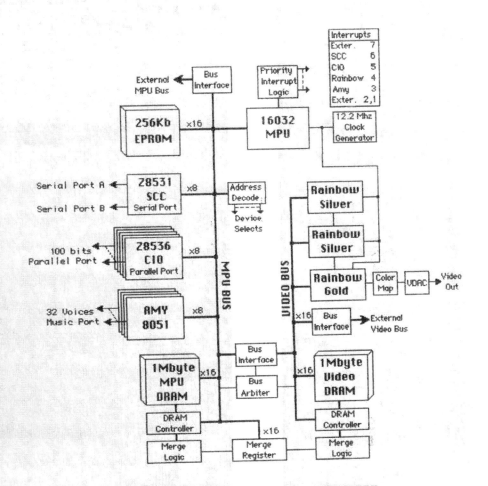

Interrupts
Exter. 7
SCC 6
CIO 5
Rainbow 4
Amy 3
Exter. 2,1

ATARI SUNNYVALE RESEARCH LABORATORY

GUMP

Experimental Computer

by

Robert Aikire

April 24, 1984

Note : x8 & x16 are data bus widths

Top: Block diagram for GUMP.

Opposite: Concept drawings and a case mockup for Sierra.

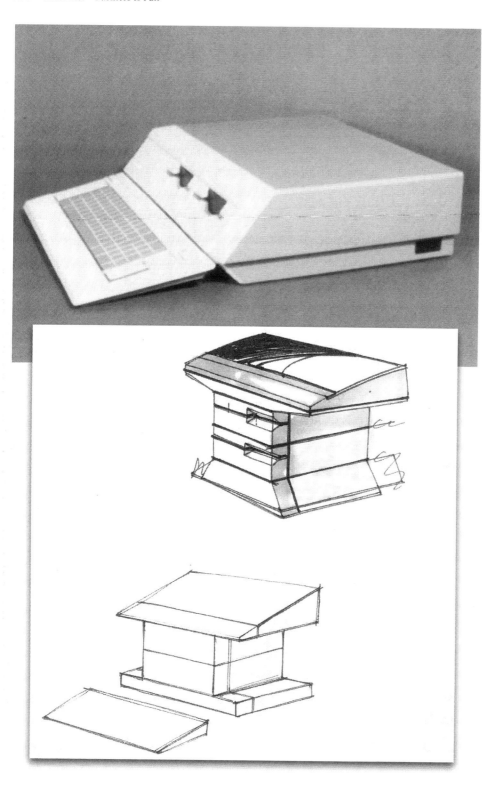

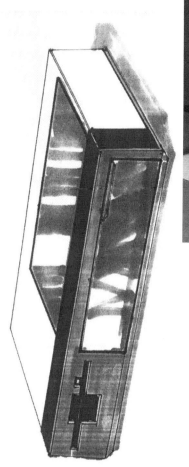

Previous page: Legendary research Alan Kay, holding a mockup of his late 60s invention of the Dynabook (the ancestor of the laptop computer), and during his days at Xerox in the inset. Instrumental in helping to create much of modern computing, he continued his work at Atari. That is until May 1984 when he left for Apple.

This page: Drawings of the Atari Explorer, Atari's own planned portable laptop and the Atari Mindlink.

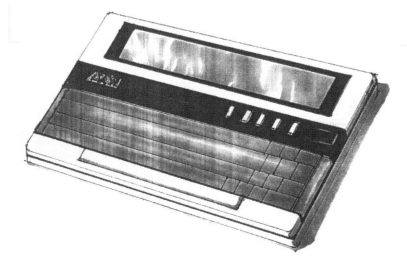

News Release

ATARI®

A Warner Communications Company

Atari Incorporated 1265 Borregas Avenue PO Box 427 Sunnyvale California 94086

CONTACT: Jamie Williams
(408) 743-4289

FOR RELEASE NOVEMBER 18, 1983

Margaret Lasecke
(408) 743-4810

ATARI ADVENTURE LAUNCHED

MILPITAS, CA (Nov 19) -- Atari Adventure, a revolutionary concept in family entertainment centers, was announced today by the Coin Video Games Division of Atari Inc. The first of several Atari Adventure centers is scheduled to be open by mid-November at Northwest Plaza Shopping Center in St. Louis, MO.

Atari Adventure, a unique alternative to the conventional entertainment center concept combines a "high tech" video game room, a hands-on computer learning center area and a special display area of the latest video game technology.

The learning center section will feature the Atari XL computer line in a classroom setting. It has been specially designed to appeal to all levels of computer users, from beginners to experienced programmers. Patrons can purchase time segments at the computer work stations, whether it be to balance a checkbook, do homework, use a word processor, play games or for any number of other applications. The computer learning center will be staffed by a full-time instructor, and will also provide regular classes for those wanting to learn "computerese", or become computer literate.

- more -

This page and next: Photos inside the St. Louis Atari Adventure Center. A primordial Apple Store, they were meant to promote Atari's trifecta of arcade, console and computing entertainment to the masses. Besides playing the latest games, classes in computing were also held on location.

Atari was everywhere leading up to the Summer of '84 as they sponsored the Summer Olympics, including the U.S. Women's Volleyball Team.

March 6, 1984

Mr. David S. Morse
President
Amiga Corporation
3350 Scott Boulevard, Building 7
Santa Clara, California 95051

Dear Dave:

This letter will outline the terms we have discussed with regard to the proposed purchase by Atari Incorporated ("Atari") of (i) 1,000,000 shares of Series B Preferred Stock (the "Shares") of Amiga Corporaton ("Amiga") and (ii) a license for three 68000 based integrated circuits as described in Schedule 1 (the "Chips") being developed by Amiga. Our objective is to enter into, as soon as feasible, a formal stock purchase agreement (the "Stock Purchase Agreement") and a license agreement (the "License Agreement") between Atari and Amiga.

The Stock Purchase Agreement will include among other things, the following provisions:

1.   Upon completion of development of all three of the Chips by September 1, 1984, Atari will purchase the Shares at a price of $3.00 per Share. The consideration for the Shares shall be cash and/or cancellation of indebtedness of Amiga to Atari. (See below for description of advances to be made to Amiga by Atari for the development of the Chips.)

2.   You have informed us that the current capital structure of Amiga consists of 3,500,000 shares of common stock, all of which is owned by the company's employees; 500,000 shares of common stock reserved for issuance to employees under stock option plans adopted by the company's board; 2,000,000 shares of common stock reserved for issuance to InterMedics Corporation upon exercise of warrants having a total face amount of $5,800,000. Except as set forth in the preceding sentence, there are no equity securities, or debt or other instruments convertible into or exchangeable for equity securities, or rights, options or warrants to purchase or subscribe for any such securities outstanding. All outstanding securities are fully paid. We understand that Amiga proposes to sell up to 2,000,000 shares of Series A Preferred Stock having rights, preferences and privileges no more favorable to their holders than those of the

Top: The first page of a letter outlining the 'Intent Agreement' that resulted in Atari giving Amiga Corp. $500,000, locking the two into the License Agreement to be signed later. Inset is the cashed check.

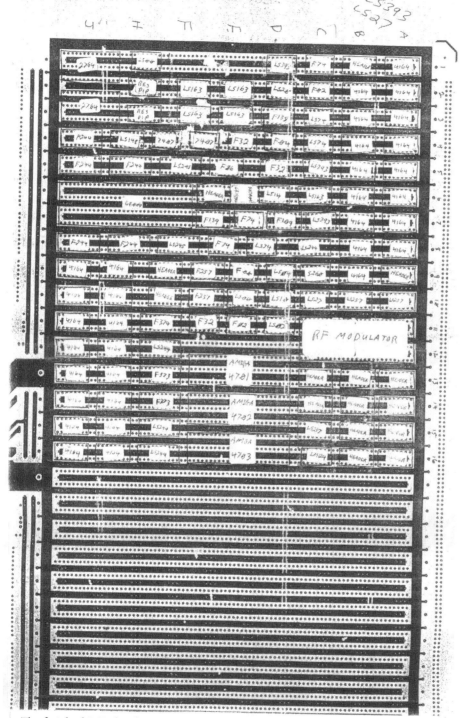

The finished PCB for the Mickey prototype, all ready to drop in Amiga's custom chips upon delivery (as denoted with the Amiga 4701-4703 blocks).

81

MR. BERMAN: Q.   Fifteen minutes.

THE WITNESS: A.   Dave came into my office and said that he wanted to give us a check for $500,000 as repayment to the advances.   And I said, "Why?" And remember being annoyed.   I also remember being upset, because it appeared --

Q.   Well --

A.   -- some kind of game was being played.

Q.   Right now my question, Mr. Farrand, is the discussion.

A.   That's what I'm giving you.

Q.   Oh, you mean you said, "I appear upset"; that is what you said?

A.   Oh, no, I think I said I was upset.

Q.   What else did you say?

A.   Why were -- they wanted to get the money back and Dave said that he was -- he had to do because under the -- the terms of the letter of intent, they had to deliver the chip sets by the end of June or Atari could go into escrow and obtain the schematics for the chips.

I said, "Well, Atari has no intention of doing that.   If that's your reason, there's no need to give the money back."

Q.   Go ahead.

A.   "Why are we going through this process?"

And so they persisted in wanting to give the money back.   And I said, "Well, I'm sorry, I don't even know whether I'm in a legal position to accept the money.   I will go and speak to my attorney," meaning Ken Nussbacher.

DEPOSITION OF JOHN S. FARRAND

A page from John Farrand's testimony, describing David Morse's returning of Atari's advance to Amiga.

I, Robot, the last arcade game released under Atari Inc. A fitting swan song, Atari had just created the first fully polygonal 3D arcade game, a technology that wouldn't catch on in the rest of the industry until the early 90s.

VT634C

ASSETS PURCHASE AGREEMENT

between

TRAMEL TECHNOLOGY, LTD.

and

ATARI, INC. and
Certain of its Subsidiaries and Affiliates

July 1, 1984

Above: Jack Tramiel and sons. While the media and public saw Jack as taking over 'Atari,' in truth he had taken over the consumer portion of the brand. Truth be told, the people in Coin felt they were the original Atari - which was still going strong.

Left: The cover page of Jack Tramiel's purchase agreement. As part of the agreement, Jack purchased the Consumer Division from Atari Inc. This included the Atari brand name, consumer intellectual properties and ownership of the copyrights and trademarks of Coin's titles. Jack took all this and folded it into his Tramel Technology Ltd., which in turn was renamed Atari Corporation. Atari Inc., in turn, was forced to rename itself to Atari Games Inc., while Warner Communications and Steve Ross looked to whittle it down further.

There were many at Atari who felt Jim did much to turn the company around during his short time at the helm. This 'goodbye poster' was put together by members of Atari's art department.

A Gallery Of the Winchester Blvd. Days

Assorted Atari Events

Atari Blood Drive

Picnic 1975

Jim Luby Going Away Party 1978

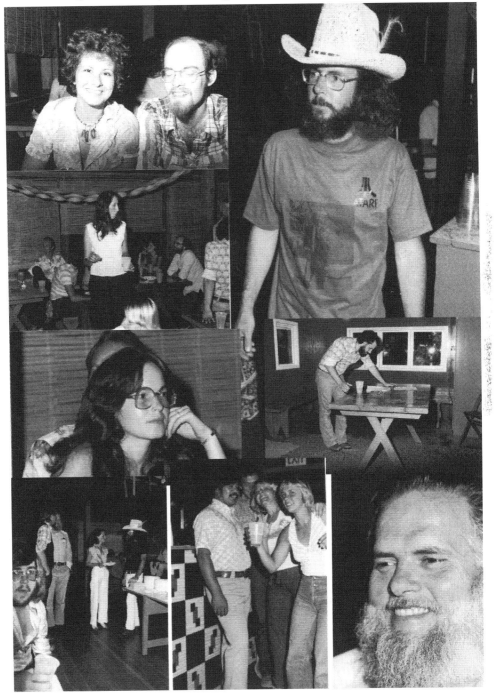

Atari Softball League

Atari Company Store

A Gallery of
Badges and
Business Cards

Corporate Division

James E Cutting
Research Scientist
Corporate Research

Atari Incorporated
1196 Borregas Avenue
PO Box 3427
Sunnyvale California 94088 3427
408 745 4905

A Warner Communications Company

Corporate Division

Ed Schleeter
Associate Design
Engineer

Atari Incorporated
Shaw's Hill
PO Box 1875
Grass Valley California 95945
916 273 6194

A Warner Communications Company

Home Computer Division

Paul C Laughton
Manager
Systems Software

Atari Incorporated
30 E Plumeria
PO Box 50047
San Jose California 95150
408 942 6711

A Warner Communications Company

Atari Products Company

David R Stubben
Atari Fellow

Atari Incorporated
30 East Plumeria Drive
PO Box 50047
San Jose California 95150
408 942 6501   Telex 17 1610

A Warner Communications Company

TOM HOGG
Senior Flunky

ATARI INC
1265 BORREGAS AVENUE
SUNNYVALE, CALIFORNIA 94086
TELEPHONE (408) 745-2000 2774
TELEX 35-7488

A Warner Communications Company

JOSEPH DECUIR
Microcomputer Systems Engineer

ATARI INC
1272 BORREGAS AVENUE
SUNNYVALE, CALIFORNIA 94086
TELEPHONE (408) 745-2650
TELEX 35-7488

A Warner Communications Company

BANKATARICARD
VIVA
GOOD THRU
408 745 250 0   013030

Coin 40th Anniversary
Reunion - August 2012

"Yes, those are bottles of Ensure on the bar menu!"

Loni Reeder and
Nolan Bushnell

Cynthia Villanueva Russell and Jeff Bell
The very first employee and the last one out
respectively.

Mike Albaugh and Owen Rubin

Steve Hendricks (graphic artists responsible for much of the 2600 box artist), Roger Hector, Bob Flemate (coin artist responsible for cabinet art on such games as *Tempest*)

Rich "Lunar Lander" Moore

Dave Shepperd, Bob Weiss, Thomas Smith, Chuck Eyler

Dennis Harper and Dave "Missile Command" Theurer

Dave Stubben

Atari Audio Group

Elaine Shirley, Andrea Bettelman and
Mary Fujihara

Elaine Shirley, Jackie Fowler McCoombs
and Holly LaMontagne

Farrokh Khodadadi, Mike "Gravitar & Star
Wars" Hally and Karen Graham

Jeff Bell, Rod Peterson and
Tim McCullough

About the Authors

Martin Goldberg - A Milwaukee, Wisconsin based writer and programmer in the video game industry, Goldberg has had a lifelong fascination with all things electronic entertainment since first playing *PONG* and *Tank* as a child at his local arcadesin the 70s. As the former site director of IGN/GameSpy's 'Classic-Gaming.Com' and a current freelancer for *Retro Gamer* magazine from the U,K,, Goldberg has been writing about video games for 13 years. Along with Dan Loosen and Gary Heil, Goldberg is also a co-founder of the Midwest Gaming Classic, one of the largest electronic entertainment expos in the United States open to the general public. In 2004, Goldberg also founded the Electronic Entertainment Museum (E2M), a non-profit archive whose mission is to help preserve the history and artifacts of the video game and home computer industries. In line with this goal, he's also a member of the International Game Development Association's (IGDA) Game Preservation SIG, a hub and community for those interested in digital game preservation and history.

Curt Vendel - A former IT Systems Engineer, Vendel is also a self-taught Electrical Engineer with a Bachelor's in Computer Science. In the 1980s, Vendel had begun collecting Atari products, engineering logs, schematics, drawings, and technical materials from former Atari employees - even making trips to Atari's buildings in California to salvage Atari's valuable history from its dumpsters. Founding the Atari History Museum in 1998, the Atari History Museum archives have amassed over 15,000 files, folders and documents, two archival rooms of schematics, mechanical drawings, artwork and PC board films. Vendel is frequently tapped as a valued resource for Atari insight and archival information by Atari, SA., Atari Interactive, numerous research institutions, trade publications and entertainment magazines, television networks and movie studios.

Made in the USA
San Bernardino, CA
01 April 2018